Richard K. Lenz

Post-LBO Development

GABLER RESEARCH

Entrepreneurial and Financial Studies

Herausgeber:

Professor Dr. Dr. Ann-Kristin Achleitner
und Professor Dr. Christoph Kaserer

Die Schriftenreihe präsentiert aktuelle Forschungsergebnisse aus dem Gebiet der Entrepreneurial und Corporate Finance. Sie greift an der Schnittstelle von Wissenschaft und Praxis innovative Fragestellungen der Unternehmensfinanzierung auf.

This series presents research results from the fields of entrepreneurial and corporate finance. Its focus lies on innovative research topics at the interface of science and practice.

Richard K. Lenz

Post-LBO Development

Analysis of Changes in Strategy, Operations, and Performance after the Exit from Leveraged Buyouts in Germany

With a foreword by Prof. Dr. Christoph Kaserer

GABLER

RESEARCH

Bibliographic information published by the Deutsche Nationalbibliothek
The Deutsche Nationalbibliothek lists this publication in the Deutsche Nationalbibliografie; detailed bibliographic data are available in the Internet at http://dnb.d-nb.de.

Dissertation Technische Universität München, 2009

Die Reihe erschien von 2003 bis 2007 im Verlag Wissenschaft & Praxis Dr. Brauner.

1st Edition 2010

Editorial Office: Ute Wrasmann | Britta Göhrisch-Radmacher

Gabler is part of the specialist publishing group Springer Science+Business Media.
www.gabler.de

Cover design: KünkelLopka Medienentwicklung, Heidelberg
Printed on acid-free paper
Printed in Germany

ISBN 978-3-8349-2163-5

Foreword

Private Equity and leveraged buyouts have become common in Europe, including in particular Germany. They are a catalyst for corporate restructuring and growth. Over time, financial investors have started to exit their investments. The development of some former LBOs raises the question whether the financial investors traded long-term growth against short-term cash flow and expropriated value. Financial investors are further accused of reducing employment, cutting salaries, offshoring production, and leaving companies financially instable.

Researchers have questioned the sustainability of performance improvement and tested changes in performance indicators. The findings confirm that the financial performance of former LBOs declines. The decline occurs with a time lag, but research fails to explain in detail its determinants of this decline. In particular, the decline seems to be caused by increase strategy diversification, the recurrence of inefficiencies and reduced management focus on efficiency. These observations are limited to companies that exit through a public offering, not through a trade sale.

This study seeks to enhance completeness and precision of research into the post-exit period. Given the secrecy of the industry, no empirical data has been gathered that in detail analyses how the way the LBOs are supervised and managed changes at the exit. Research on the subsequent changes in strategy and operations is sparse and limited to those companies pursuing a public offering. A greater understanding of the source of performance development requires further plowing through major corporate activities.

In an unprecedented breadth and depth, this thesis sheds light on LBOs and their post-exit development and overcomes the limitations of former studies. The author provides an unforeseen review of causal relationships between changes and inter-dependencies of corporate governance, management objectives, strategy, operational setup and resulting financial performance. The empirical research is based on three case studies consolidating external and internal information as well as interviews with both managers, former financial investors and post-exit investors. The author makes several important contributions to theory development and tests hypotheses from both agency theory, strategic management, corporate entrepreneurship, operations and last but not least financial performance.

In summary, the presented thesis provides an excellent insight into the buyout and general corporate governance research. In spite of the limitations of a case study and the holistic research approach, the thesis remains highly relevant to researchers and practitioners, and should be seen as a highly valuable contribution to the ongoing discussion and research in the field.

Prof. Dr. Christoph Kaserer

Acknowledgements

When I started to consider wirting a doctoral thesis about private equity and former LBOs, I was rightly warned of the thorny territory I was intending to enter. At the end, it was to the support and encouragement of various people to whom I express my sincerest gratitude that made me finalize this academic journey as an enjoyable and fruitful experience.

Firstly, I would like to thank my academic supervisors Professor Christoph Kaserer and Professor Ann-Kristin Achleitner of the Technical University Munich, Germany, for their academic guidance and encouraging support. Professor Kaserer was very supportive throughout the development of my dissertation and provided me with the necessary theoretical groundwork, motivation and patience with respect to my parallel professional obligations. Professor Achleitner encouraged with the case studies and her genuine insights into the Private Equity industry.

Secondly, I am indebted to my former colleagues Dr. Jürgen Meffert, Dr. Holger Klein and Fabienne Serfaty at McKinsey & Company with whom I enjoyed a highly inspiring time. The questionnaire of the growth initiative for German medium-sized companies was, so to say, the initiating spark for starting my thesis. Jürgen Meffert was an invaluable support as thought leader throughout my thesis and provided my with the freedom to invest sufficient time and resources. Holger Klein relentlessly pushed me with writing while sharing his thoughts and experiences. I am further heavily indebted to Fabienne Serfaty. Without her support in finding the right case studies and her permanent encouragements in the office I would have not been able to finalize this thesis. I also owe greatest thanks to Professor Herbert Henzler for his unrivalled support in providing access to various interview partners. Finally, thanks must go to Dr. Berthold Fürst at Deutsche Bank, M&A, Germany, for his support in providing me with the freedom to finalize my thesis.

The thesis would have not taken place without the time commitments of the interviewees at the case study companies that provided me with various information and insightful comments to the data gathering. I would in particular want to thank Sven Kassner and Heinz-Georg Stiller (Wincor Nixdorf), Curd-Hasso von Flemming and Horst Einzelmüller(Techem), Steffi Brobowski, Egon Kircher and Albert Beer (Trevira). I am further indebted to several Limtied Partners and supervisory board members who provided with invaluable insights on the way they managed the companies and who commented on my research findings. Special thanks go to Silke Scheiber (KKR), Dr. Alexander Dibelius (Goldman Sachs), Stefan Zuschke (BC Partners) and Dr. Axel Wieandt (Deutsche Bank).

Furthermore, I owe thanks to various colleagues from the CEFS and McKinsey that supported me with invaluable insights. Dr. Annabell Geidner and Dr. Oliver Klöckner shared with me their knowledge and experience for the theoretical groundwork and reseach approach. Dr. Achim Berg shared his collected material on Private Equity and LBO, and was a stimulus from his own theoretical groundwork. I also owe thanks to Dr. Nils Hoffmann for continued discussions.

Finally, I carry inexpressible gratitude for the support and help of my family and friends. My father was my biggest inspiration, being surprised but grateful by my late desire to write a doctoral thesis. In the last months, he remembered me continuously of finalizing the thesis and thereby set me the final spurs. I especially would like to thank Josef Arweck, Dr. Andreas Franz, Dr. Daniel Hildebrand, Matthias Hommer and Dr. Marc Tenbücken, not only for their great friendship but in particular for their inspiration and contribution to make the intense research very social and enjoyable. Last but not least, I want to thank Miss Sarah Wild, that entered half-way of the thesis my life and walked along all the ups and downs of this path, patient, never urging, cheering and making the time working worth living.

Dipl. Ing. (Univ.) Dipl. Kfm. Richard Lenz

Table of Contents

Index of Figures

Index of Tables

Index of Abbreviations

AG	Aktiengesellschaft
AktG	Aktiengesetz
ATM	Automated teller systems
BCG	Boston Consulting Group
BVCA	British venture capital association
BVK	Bundesverband deutscher Kapitalbeteiligungsgesellschaften (German association of private equity firms)
CAGR	Compound annual growth rate
CAPM	Capital asset pricing model
CAR	Cumulative abnormal return
CEO	Chief executive officer
CFO	Chief financial officer
CMBOR	Centre for management buyout research
DAX	Deutscher Aktienindex
DB	Deutsche Bank
DBI	Deutsche Bank Investor
DCF	Discounted cash flow
EBIT	Earning before interest and taxes
EBITDA	Earning before interest, taxes, depreciation and amortization
EBO	Employee buyout
EPOS	Electronic point of sale system
et al.	Et alii, et aliae, et alia (Latin), and others
etc.	et cetera (Latin): and other things, and so forth
et seqq.	Et sequentia (Latin): and the others following
EUR	Euro
EVA	Economic value added
EVCA	European venture capital and private equity association
e.g.	Exemplum gratii (Latin): for instance, to exemplify
FAZ	Frankfurter Allgemeine Zeitung
FTD	Financial Times Deutschland
GEX	German Entrepreneurial Index
GDP	Gross domestic product
GmbH	Gesellschaft mit beschränkter Haftung
HLT	Highly leveraged transaction
IAS	International accounting standard
IBO	Institutional buyout

IPO	Initial going-public
IRR	Internal rate of return
KGaA	Kommanditgesellchaft auf Aktien
KKR	Kohlberg, Kravis & Roberts
KonTraG	Gesetz zur Kontrolle und Transparenz im Unternehmensbereich
LBO	Leveraged buyout
LMBO	Leveraged management buyout
MBI	Management buyin
MBO	Management buyout
MDAX	Mid cap DAX
M&A	Mergers and acquisitions
NOPBT	Net operating profit before taxes
NOPLAT	Net operating profit less adjusted taxes
NPV	Net present value
PE	Private equity
R&D	Research and development
RBV	Resource-based view
ROE	Return on equity
ROIC	Return on invested capital
S&P	Standard and Poors
SEC	Securities and exchange committee
SIC	Standard industry code
SG&A	Selling, general and administrative expenses
SDAX	Small cap DAX
SME	Small and medium-sized enterprises
TFP	Total factor productivity
UK	United Kingdom
USA	United States of America
USD	United States Dollar
US-GAAP	United States generally accepted accounting principles
VC	Venture capital
WACC	Weighted average cost of capital

A Introduction and Founding Theory

1 Introduction and Overview

1.1 Relevance of Thesis

Leveraged buyouts (LBOs) have become common in Europe, including in particular Germany. They are a catalyst for corporate restructuring and growth, and typically involve equity from professional managed partnerships. Some EUR 21.6 billion was invested in German LBOs by 2006[1], thereof the five largest transactions accounted for EUR 12.5 billion.

The LBOs involve significant changes in the way a company is managed. Interest alignment of management with the investors is increased by granting co-ownership. The company's capital structure is optimized by raising debt and ownership itself is concentrated in the hands of investors who actively monitor company performance. Research into a significant number of LBOs in various regions and sectors, also in Germany[2], shows that these changes lead to a significantly enhanced performance of LBOs.

Once companies have repaid a considerable part of the acquisition debt, which typically is imposed on the company, investors consider exiting their investment. Investors' preferred exit strategy is the return of the company to public trading, depending on circumstance, through an initial or secondary public offering. Investors opt for a trade sale to a strategic buyer if equity markets suffer illiquidity and investor sentiment is low. The exit volume in Germany has increased from EUR 0.7 Billion in 1998 to EUR 10.3 Billion in 2006[3].

Exits from LBOs again prompt changes in the governance of the company. Managers usually cash out on their investment and reduce their stake, primary offerings decrease debt leverage, and the buyout investor's remaining equity is distributed to either institutional investors or a strategic buyer.

A few former German LBOs raise the question whether the buyout investors traded to their advantage long-term growth against short-term cash flow and expropriated

---

1 See CMBOR 2006

2 A detailed overview of the existing research on LBO performance is provided in chapter B5.2. The most known surveys are Kaplan 1989a, Smith 1990b, and Muscarella and Vetsuypens 1990 (all US) and Luippold 1991, Wegner 2003, and Kitzmann 2005 (all Germany).

3 See the discussion on the development of LBO exit volume in chapter B5.3.1 and in CMBOR 2006.

value[4]. German politicians who likened private equity and hedge funds investors to "locusts who feasted on German firms for profit before spitting them out"[5] fuelled this discussion. They accused the buyout investors of reducing employment, cutting salaries, offshoring production, and leaving companies financially instable[6].

Existing research confirms that the accounting performance of former LBOs declines. The research shows that the decline occurs with a time lag of three to four years when these companies underperform against their industry average. The time lapse indicates that the inefficiencies are not the manager's intent, but the result of various small decisions not taken that would have been in the best interest of the company. Slack resources are re-introduced and sub-optimal investments made. Change in how the company is managed is largely a function of changes in governance at the exit. Bruton et al. in a survey on the very changes note that:

> "Nonetheless, agency theory predicts that there would be a reintroduction of inefficiencies and a loss of previously experienced performance gains. [...]. As manager ownership declines, growth goals once again become important because they are more consistent with the manager/agent's personal utility. Increased diversification and firm size lead to greater compensation for the manager. "[7]

German companies include a large number of attractive LBO candidates given their strong market position and stable cash flows that result of operations in mature markets and proven products. They offer considerable growth potential from increasing internationalization and entry into new market related to their core business. Given their low capital base, given the fact that they are often family-owned and their lack of management focus, these companies benefit from takeovers by large corporations that serve as catalysts for growth and restructuring[8]. The locust analogy nonetheless fueled resistance of German companies to buyout investors. Family-owned companies were already standoffish towards private equity investors because of lack of experience and different cultural backgrounds[9].

LBO research until now has not looked at former German LBOs. It is primarily based on a relatively small sample of US and UK-originated and floated LBOs, most of

---

4 See the case of the secondary LBO of Friedrich Grohe AG, "Investoren - schmeißen Sie die raus", Der Spiegel, November 28 2005, "Grohe dreht auf ", Sueddeutsche Zeitung, May 25 2007

5 See "Locusts in Lederhosen - business in Germany", Economist October 20 2007

6 See „Die Zeche zahlt der Wirt", Der Spiegel May 2 2005, „Die deutsche Lektion", Financial Times Deutschland, May 13 2005

7 See Bruton, Keels et al. 2002, pp. 713 and 714

8 See Achleitner 2008,p.88

9 See Achleitner and Poech 2005

which were studied in the 1980s and 1990s[10]. Researchers have also not reviewed performance development of trade sales in the post-exit phase because little data is publicly available. Most importantly, researchers admit to not having attributed a cause-and-effect relationship to post-exit performance decline.

1.2 Research Objectives

This thesis seeks to achieve the following objectives and furnish answers for subsequent questions:

Objective 1:

How does corporate governance of a former LBO change after the exit?

As part of detailed empirical work on the new 'leveraged buyout' phenomenon, researchers have won a detailed understanding of how corporate governance changes at the entry into a buyout. Several studies collected detailed analysis of changes in the debt[11] and equity structure[12]. The studies also reviewed changes in management compensation schemes as well as the constituents of German LBOs[13].

Studies on exits from buyouts focused on companies with a public offering. Analysis therefore depended on those aspects of corporate governance that could be measured with publicly available data such as changes in debt leverage[14] and ownership structure[15]. Understandably, the activity level of governance in terms of intensity and quality of monitoring fell beyond the scope of empirical studies and constitutes a research gap. The public unavailability of information on exits through trade sales means that the database is limited to exits through public offerings. Commenting on the financial performance of reverse LBOs, Holthausen and Larcker said:

> "While the accounting performance and valuation implications of leveraged buyouts have been studied in numerous academic articles, the performance of reverse leveraged buyouts [...] is a largely unanswered question. Examination of reverse LBOS can provide additional

---

10 A detailed overview of studies on the performance of LBOs can be found in chapter B5.3.

11 See DeAngelo, DeAngelo et al. 1984, DeAngelo 1986, Marais, Schipper et al. 1989, Kaplan 1989a, Muscarella and Vetsuypens 1990, Kaplan and Stein 1990, Kaplan 1991, Cotter and Peck 2001, Wu 1997

12 See Maupin, Bidwell et al. 1984, DeAngelo and DeAngelo 1987, Kaplan 1989a, Kaplan and Stein 1990, Singh 1990, Kaplan 1991, Phan and Hill 1995, Wu 1997, Cotter and Peck 2001, Bruton, Keels et al. 2002, Peck 2004

13 See Luippold 1991, Forst 1992, Gräper 1993, Vest 1995, Jakoby 2000, Wegner 2003

14 See Muscarella and Vetsuypens 1990, Mian and Rosenfeld 1993, Holthausen and Larcker 1996, Jalilvand and Switzer 2002

15 See Muscarella and Vetsuypens 1990,Mian and Rosenfeld 1993, Holthausen and Larcker 1996, Bruton, Keels et al. 2002, Peck 2004

> evidence about the extent to which leverage and concentration of ownership provide desirable incentives within organizations"16.

Because observation of public offerings is to some degree incomplete and for trade sale non-existent, analysis will have to start with understanding changes in the constituents of the governance. How will debt leverage change? Will the company benefit from any sale proceeds? Will the ownership structure remain concentrated? What effort will new shareholders put in monitoring management? To what degree, will management get equity stakes? How is the LBO governance in Germany different to other countries?

Objective 2:

How do changes in corporate governance affect management objectives?

Adjustments in the company's governance structure will most likely lead to changes in management's goals and objectives. These changes will lead to modifications in the company's strategy and operations. Management objectives, even though they only offer limited insight into actual changes in strategy and operations, summarize the overall re-direction and serve as a proxy indicator.

High debt may focus management on maximizing productivity of operations and increasing available cash flow. It may also diminish focus on growth as long as current operations do not produce sufficient profit. Research into LBOs has tracked management objectives and measured considerable change at the entry into a buyout[17].

Laxer governance after the exit may involve a change of objectives, with little focus on efficiency and entrepreneurship. An open shareholder structure with reduced monitoring and low management stakes may re-motivate managers to build up slack resources and pursue non-value-creating growth. Initial first empirical evidence of an LBO exit indicates the recurrence of inefficiencies and reduced management focus on efficiency[18].

Again, these observations are limited to companies that exit through a public offering, not through a trade sale. This study seeks to enhance completeness and precision of research into the post-exit period. How will management view the importance of continuing operational improvement activities? Will it take unpopular measures even if they lack power as owners after selling their shares in the exit? Will

---

16 See Holthausen and Larcker 1996, p. 294

17 See Easterwood 1989, Phan and Hill 1995, Zahra 1995, Bruining and Wright 2005

18 See Bruton, Keels et al. 2002

management maintain the same level of entrepreneurship and put personal effort into achieving comfort in new business fields and unfamiliar technologies? How does control exerted by new shareholders facilitate management focus on, for example, relying exclusively on financial controls as opposed to an intense strategic dialogue?

Objective 3:

How do changes of corporate governance affect the company's strategy and operations?

A number of empirical studies have examined how changes in corporate governance influence the strategy and operations of a company under a buyout regime. These studies range from corporate restructuring in general, manufacturing, working capital, and administration to R&D, market development, and human resources[19]. They establish a relationship between the LBO regime and the way a company is managed[20].

After the exit, research on the subsequent changes in strategy and operations is sparse and limited to those companies pursuing a public offering. A greater understanding of the source of performance development requires plowing through major corporate activities. How intense will management continue to review the progress of improvement activities? Will close monitoring of working capital be maintained? Will management advance with growth projects with lower relative returns? How do R&D expenses change after an increase of free cash flow generation? To what degree can the company benefit from detailed expertise provided by supervisory board members and their industry network?

Objective 4:

How do these changes influence the corporate performance development of the company?

Since the emergence of buyouts as a new form of organization with enhanced incentives and monitoring, researchers have questioned the sustainability of

---

19 The studies are reviewed in detail in chapters B3 and B4. To name some prominent examples: for corporate restructuring see Phan and Hill 1995, for manufacturing see Lichtenberg and Siegel 1990, for working capital see Smith 1990b, for administration see Muscarella and Vetsuypens 1990, for R&D see Long and Ravenscraft 1993a, for market development see Vest 1995, and for human resources see Bacon, Wright et al. 2004.

20 Singh, in his attempt to explain management's willingness for drastic changes, concluded: "The need to service high debt payment forces them [the management] to slash unsound investment programs, reduce overhead, dispose of assets [...], and restructure an organization to increase accountability and control" (Phan and Hill 1995, p. 706).

performance improvement and whether an increased performance constitutes a wealth transfer to the disadvantage of other parties involved. As a result, research has extensively tested changes in performance indicators, particularly operating income and cash flow, during the buyout restructuring.

Empirical data of buyouts exiting through a stock market flotation has been revised in a number of studies of former LBOs because of newly available public data[21]. This data, however, has until now not included former LBOs originated in Germany. In addition, researchers have not reviewed performance development of trade sales in the post-exit.

Post-exit performance depends on the new governance structure of the former buyout. Motivation and efforts of parties involved - managers, employees, and owners - further depends on their share of benefits related to the company and the individual utility function. After a review of the financial performance of reversed buyouts, Holthausen and Larcker summarized:

> "Our tests at least provide some evidence that there is a decline in performance subsequent to the reverse LBO and that this is related to the change in the ownership structure after the reverse LBO. [...] Our analysis indicates that [...] they (buyouts) retain some of the ownership structure of a typical U.S. corporation, as opposed to moving back toward an LBO-like structure."

The interesting question, therefore, will be whether changes at the exit constitute a return to pre-buyout structures or the emergence of a significantly different governance structure that allows a post-buyout superior performance. Will management allow re-introduction of slack resources? Will less alignment because of lack of shareholdings, lead to less optimal investment decisions that only serve individual interests?

In this context, one will have to understand whether changes in strategy and operations are profound enough to prevent a return to pre-buyout habits. A company may have overcome a potential misalignment of interests and established a governance with optimized agency costs for the shareholders (and debt holders), while transferring the beneficial effects of the LBO to the post-exit governance structure.

---

21 See Mohan 1990, DeGeorge and Zeckhauser 1993, Mian and Rosenfeld 1993, Holthausen and Larcker 1996, Jalilvand and Switzer 2002, Bruton, Keels et al. 2002, Jelic, Saadouni et al. 2005

1.3 Research Approach

The answer to research objective 1 lies in constructing a conceptual framework that accounts for changes in corporate governance. Research of post-exit performance development and changes in strategy and operations presumes that the changes in the governance structure, particularly debt leverage, concentration of ownership, activity level of the investors, and extent of management stakes, are exogenous. Predictions for the post-exit period should therefore be founded on changes in ownership (property) rights and their delegation to agents. They then have to consider how assets and resources developed under different governance structures. This leads one to refer briefly to neoclassical financing theory and to the basics of property rights and transaction costs theory. The author will then discuss in more detail potential implications of the agency theory and resource-based view for the post-LBO development of a company. To incorporate more complex interactions of a buyout, the author will in detail discuss implications for corporate governance-theory based on agency theory.

A different challenge lies in the answers to objectives 2, 3 and 4. The complexity of interactions requires developing a comprehensive and unbiased insight into the progression of a company over the buyout cycle. No theory development has systematically covered this research area. Analysis requires therefore an iterative, theory-building approach.

A number of limitations preclude analysis based on a survey by questionnaire. These limitations include the fact that private equity companies are hesitant to share information such as details of financial performance and ownership structure. Sharing of confidential information requires mutual trust between the company and the buyout investors. Beyond the reluctance to share information, various data that would significantly exceed the scope and ability of a questionnaire would be needed to answer the three objectives. The conceptual framework requires four levels of analysis within a single study[22]. Finally, the research objective is to develop a suitable conceptual framework in terms of an explanatory research (theory building) as opposed to a confirmatory research (theory testing).

---

22 The four levels are: (1) post-exit changes in governance structure; (2) the effect of a new governance structure on management objectives; (3) the effect of a new governance structure on managerial activities and applied levers of value, both strategic and operational; and finally, (4) the effect of a new governance (post-exit) structure on corporate performance. A detailed illustration of the basis model is provided in the introductory chapter B1.

A case study approach therefore appears most appropriate for the formulated research objectives and the explanatory approach. Eisenhardt said on the suitability of a case study approach:

> "The case study is a research strategy which focused on understanding the dynamics present within single setting. [...] Case studies can involve either single or multiple cases, and numerous levels of analysis [...] Case studies can be used to accomplish various aims: to provide description, test theory, or generate theory."23

The author will undertake an a priori specification of constructs and substantiate these into hypotheses to establish a firm understanding of the research approach. Even if the hypotheses are confirmed, the basic conceptual framework and related theory may evolve with data interpretation[24]. While a hypothesis may be confirmed, omitted, or revised, the difference of the case study approach to a statistical sampling is that each hypothesis is examined for each case individually. The researchers seeks to understand why or why not emerging relationships are maintained In particular, the multi-level analysis requires establishing internal validity as an apparent relationship may reflect an independent variable leading to a spurious correlation. The following discourse will be judgmental since no statistical tests can be applied. The author will then present all implications with the evidence to allow independent assessment of the findings.

Clearly, case study research has the shortcoming of a limited population. Multiple case studies enhance the reliability and validity of findings[25]. A cross case-study comparison allows for identifying similarities and differences when using the same constructs and hypotheses[26]. However, usage of multiple cases is for theoretical sampling as opposed to statistical reasons. As demanded by leading researchers of case studies[27], the authors has chosen three case studies to mirror different theoretical categories.

The author relied on multiple data sources that were congregated in a cumulative, iterative manner. Besides all publicly available information, data was supplemented by multiple in-depth interviews with the company's management and former LBO

---

23 See Eisenhardt 1989b, p. 534

24 Eisenhardt noted on the shaping of hypotheses: "One step in shaping hypotheses is the sharpening of constructs. This is a two part process involving (1) refining the definition of the construct, and (2) building evidence which measures the construct in each case.[...] Researchers use multiple sources of evidence to build construct measures [...] The difference is that the construct, its definition, and measurement often emerge from the analysis process itself, rather than being specified a priori." See Eisenhardt 1989b, p. 541 and 542.

25 See Roll 2003, p. 315

26 See Eisenhardt 1989b

27 See Roll 2003, p. 315, Eisenhardt 1989b, p. 537

investors. The author then shared his observations with company representatives and discussed their interpretations. The triangulation of multiple data source enabled refining the substantiation of the constructs and hypotheses.

1.4 Structure of Analysis

Part A establishes the theoretical and notional foundation of post-exit analysis of leveraged buyouts. Terminologies are introduced, in particular the research objective 'leveraged buyout'. Basic cause-and-effects relationships are presented, thereby discussing between different principals over the buyout cycle, e.g., buyout investors, stock market, and corporates. The author further elaborates a conceptual framework to analyze changes in the post-exit period from the perspective of change in the governance structure. Agency theory, resource-based view, and corporate governance-related theory (as a derivative of the agency theory) furnish complementary aspects of finding the right framework for analysis.

Part B involves model building and hypothesis formulation to analyze how companies develop over the buyout cycle and particularly in the post-exit period. Changes in the constituents of the governance structure - debt leverage, ownership concentration, activity level of governance, and management stakes - over the buyout cycle are discussed in detail. Considerations from the theories presented in part A are broken down into the underlying cause-and-effect chain and discussed in light of observations from empirical research. The most conclusive conjectures are subsumed and codified in hypotheses. Further hypotheses are formulated around how changes in governance affect management activity. Firstly, the author outlines changes in terms of efficiency-focused management activities by the major categories operations and administration. Secondly, the changes in terms of entrepreneurial, growth-focused management activities are discussed. Activities are broken down into activities related to strategy, innovation, market development, and human resources. Changes in governance are thereby broken down into their constituents and discussed as they affect the individual lever. Finally, changes in the governance structure and its respective constituents are discussed in light of their implications for performance development.

Part C outlines the findings of the case studies of Wincor Nixdorf, Techem and Trevira. The relevant sample of former LBOs in Germany is derived and chosen research methodology presnted. In the following, the author presents three cases according to the analytical approach of the research model. Each case includes a descriptive part where the development of the company before and after the exit is outlined. In the second chapter, the analytical part, changes of governance are explored and studied in relationship to the research model. The subchapter corresponds to the structure of the research model and breaks down the analysis in terms of changes in the sequence of (i) management objectives, (ii) efficiency- and entrepreneurial growth-focused management activities, and (iii) performance development. Each hypothesis is tested and discussed in detail. The chapter closes with the case analysis, evaluating the hypotheses by comparing the observations and conclusions from the three case studies.

Part D draws the conclusion of the research and summarizes the findings with regards to the initial research objectives. The author reviews the findings in view of their contribution to research, including lessons from and refinements for agency theory and theory related to corporate governance, for operations management, strategy and entrepreneurship research, as well as for finance research. The findings are discussed in terms of their contribution for practitioners, particularly post-exit investors and shareholders. Finally, this part closes with the limitations of the study and outlines the most promising areas for further research.

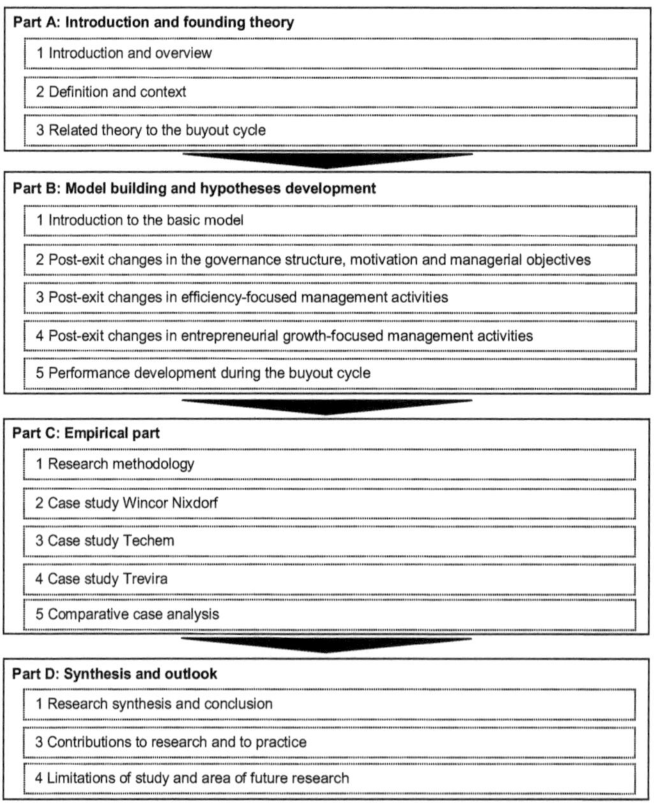

Figure 1: Structure of analysis

2 Definition and Context

2.1 Buyouts: a Definition

The subsequent analysis requires an unambiguous delineation of the term 'leveraged buyout', since the term has not commonly been defined[28]. The term 'buyout' is the superordinate genus and can be differentiated by the criteria (i) type of financing and (ii) type of investor. For the research objective of this thesis, the author will narrow the nature of the buyout to be examined in terms of identical characteristics of corporate governance.

A 'buyout' may be financed with equity and debt as well as alternative, hybrid forms of capital. As to be outlined in the following chapters, a buyout may thereby be equipped with a considerable share of debt - or debt-like instruments. In such case, a buyout is classified as 'leveraged' and, in the corollary, benefits from the leverage effect of tax-minimizing debt interests enhancing the equity return. A standard threshold from which on the capital structure can be classified as 'leveraged' has not been established[29]. At the start of the LBO phenomenon, one of the key success factors was the ability to receive financing for companies below investment grade rating, commonly referred as junk bonds. Similar considerations were subject to the definition of 'highly leveraged transactions' (HLT) by the US authorities under the auspices of the Federal Reserve Board to mitigate the advancing default risk. One of the guidelines related to the capital structure demands that the financing (i) either doubles the borrower's liabilities and results in a leverage ratio greater than 50%, or (ii) increases the leverage ratio higher than 75%[30]. Comparing this definition to the observations from changes in the capital structure of German buyouts, a substantial number of buyouts do not fall into this category, as opposed to the higher leveraged US buyout transactions[31].

---

28 For an overview of the various definitions of 'buyouts', see the discussions in Hite and Vetsuypens 1989, p.955, Wegner 2003, pp. 11 and Kitzmann 2005, p.12

29 See Schmid 1994, p. 41 and 42, Drukarczyk 1990, p.545, Wegner 2003, pp. 11 et seqq., Kitzmann 2005, p.8

30 The term HLT is related in general to a bank loan for a highly levered company. The HLTs are considered to resemble junk bonds as they both face default risks. A loan to be classified must meet the following guidelines: (1) used for buyouts, acquisitions or recapitalizations; (2) designated as an HLT by the syndication agent. The guidelines were issued by the US Office of the Comptroller of Currency, the Federal Reserve Board, and the Federal Deposit Insurance Corporation.

31 As outlined in chapter B2.1.1, the share of debt to total capital in German buyouts ranges from 63.7% to 79.7%, resembling an average of approx. 75%. The leverage for US-based buyouts ranges between 60.7% to 91.0%, with an average of around 85%. The author will further detail the structure of debt, e.g., the different debt instruments used and maturity levels in the aforementioned chapter.

Furthermore, researchers and practioneers may differentiate a 'buyout' by the investor who is willing to provide the risk-bearing equity. Firstly, professional intermediaries may provide private equity for the investment[32]. Such buyout investors will typically lead the transaction and acquire the majority of shareholdings in the buyout company. Secondly, the management group may acquire a significant share in the company. Hereby, the management group may receive a minority stake as incentive and alignment instrument[33]. In those cases where the incumbent management team acquires a controlling stake and takes the lead, the buyout may be referred to as management buyout (MBO), irrespective of the underlying capital structure. There is no clear indication from what threshold onwards a buyout may be considered as management-led. Most researchers classify a MBO starting at 50% shareholding, arguing that any lower shareholdings can only be classified as incentive[34]. One can observe that shareholdings between 10% and 20% are typical for US-based buyouts, as indicated by one of the leading buyout investors, Kohlberg, Kravis and Roberts[35]. Germany-based studies esteem a shareholding between 15% and 25% as representative[36]. In the corollary, the author classifies only a small part as MBO in the narrower sense. The leading researchers have defined leveraged buyouts in the broader sense is considered as a combination of leveraged capital structure with a minority management participation[37]. Other leading investors groups may be

---

32 The role and institutional background to buyout investors will be discussed in chapter A2.3.1. Further, the motives and change of motives over the buyout cycle of buyout investors will be analyzed in detail in chapter B2.2.

33 See DeAngelo, DeAngelo et al. 1984, p.370, Singh 1990, p. 111, Liebeskind 1992, p. 73,

34 See Schwenkedel 1991, p. 5

35 See Roberts 1989, p. 65. One should consider the notable higher average size of US buyouts as upwards bias to the management shareholding.

36 As elucidated in chapter B2.1.2, the level of managerial shareholdings in buyouts in the US varies between 16.0% and 57.2%, with an average of around 35%. For Germany, the share of management varies between 25.4% and 74.4%, respectively. The average lies around 45%. See also Kropp 1992, p. 19.

37 DeAngelo, DeAngelo and Rice note that "Going private proposals can classified into (1) pure going private transactions, [...], and (2) leveraged buyouts, in which management proposes to share equity ownership [...] with third party investors [...] The term 'leveraged buyout' is also used to describe the purchase of an operating division by divisional managers [...] with outside investors" (See DeAngelo, DeAngelo et al. 1984, p. 370). Singh also considers to incorporate both management shareholdings and leveraged as quoted "Management buyouts [alternatively used as leveraged buyouts] are transaction in which managers, with the aid of investors, replace public shareholdings in the firm with relatively closed held equity and high levels of debt. The level of debt may be as high as 90 percent" (See Singh 1990, p. 111). Achleitner and Fingerle assign the similar attributes to a MBO: "[...](1) das Management ist wesentlich am Eigenkapital des Unternehmens beteiligt; (2) die operative Geschäftsführung liegt weiterhin beim Managementteam; (3) die Transaktion wird häufig mit einem hohen Fremdkapitalanteil finanziert" (see Achleitner and Fingerle 2003, p.3). In a German analysis of buyouts, Loos defines an leveraged buyout "as a transaction in which a group of private investors, typically including management, purchases a significant and controlling equity stake in a public or non-public corporation or a corporate division, using significant debt financing, which it raises by borrowing against the assets and/or cash flows of the target firm taken private" (See Loos 2006, p. 12).

found in outside managers seeking to replace or strengthen the existing management and provide own personal funds[38]. The observations for such buyins indicate considerable differences to buyouts given the enhanced information asymmetry of the new management team, their necessity to adapt to the unfamiliar business environment, and their acceptance problems within the company[39]. Alternatively, the employees may acquire a leading share in the company both in terms of shareholdings and in terms of voting rights[40]. Such cases are in particular found for companies facing severe restructuring and corporate transformation[41]. Often, the investor offer the employees ownership through an employee share ownership plan (ESOP) to facilitate a participation in the value creation and to extend the positive alignment effect beyond the management team[42]. Such programs are to be delineated from an EBO, as the employees may receive considerable cash flow rights, though hold restricted voting rights to ensure that the lead investors maintains far-reaching control[43].

Some researchers introduce the origination of the transaction as further criteria to classify a buyout[44]. A buyout may be originated from (1) the succession of a company, from (2) the divestment of a parent company, from (3) a turnaround situation, from (4) a privatization, or from (5) a going-private (delisting). Since the forthcoming analysis will analyze in particular the post-exit period, the origination is of minor interest in comparison to the traditional research for the buyout period[45].

As outlined, the sample to be studied will consider buyouts that correspond to an identical setup of constituents of corporate governance. Thereby, the leveraged

38 In so called 'management buyins' (MBIs) outside managers become the major non-institutional shareholders (See (See Robbie 1992, p. 446, Wright 1994, pp. 21 et seqq., Achleitner and Fingerle 2003, p.8, Bacon, Wright et al. 2004, p. 328). Thereby, the new management team in most cases establish a newly created entity to effect the purchase rather than to use a group which already exists (See Robbie 1992, p. 446).

39 See Gräper 1993, pp. 10 and 11, Robbie and Wright 1995, pp. 544 et seqq.,

40 Such a buyout is called an 'employee buyout' (EBO) and typically exhibits 50% or more shareholdings by the employees of the company, including all hierarchies and management (See Wright 1989, p. 405 et seqq., Vest 1995, p.17, Achleitner and Fingerle 2003, p.8, Bacon, Wright et al. 2004, p. 326 et seqq.)

41 See Vest 1995, pp. 17and 18, Then Bergh 1998, p.13,

42 See Wagner 1993, pp. 46 et seqq.. In addition, the instrument to both align and motivate employees during (and after) a buyout are discussed in detail in chapter B4.5.

43 See Gros 1998, pp. 79 et seqq. , Then Bergh 1998, p.14

44 See Luippold 1991, pp. 18et seqq., Vest 1995, pp. 19 et seqq., Hoffmann and Ranke 1990, pp. 18 et seqq., Kitzmann 2005, pp.15 et seqq..

45 The pre-buyout period and origination, respectively, will be discussed as part of the descriptive introductory into the case study. Relevant considerations in term of corporate governance will be presented if required.

management buyout forms the basis for the delineation. Henceforth, the buyouts[46] to be analyzed in the post-exit period have to comply with the following criteria:

- (1) Leveraged capital structure: a debt leverage of at least 75% at the transaction to ensure a sufficient leverage;
- (2) Financial investor in the lead: a financial investor that leads (with at least 50% majority) both in terms of cash flow and voting rights the buyout;
- (3) Management continuity: a considerable continuity in the management team to avoid any interference of information asymmetry and adjustment behavior by a new management team;
- (4) Managerial shareholdings: to ensure that the management is aligned (to some degree) with the owner's interest.

2.2 Characteristics of Buyouts

Having established a common definition of the term 'leveraged management buyout', the question arises to what degree the buyouts share common characteristics besides their corporate governance and capital structure, respectively. In particular, how do these characteristics alter along the buyout cycle? Is the likelihood of buyouts related to the industry the company is operating? What are the considerations to exit an LBO structure?

A set of criteria, covering both company and industry related attributes characterizes the ideal buyout candidate. Researchers and practitioners have provided varying lists of criteria. The leading buyout investors, Kohlberg, Kravis and Roberts, formulated a brief list of criteria with an emphasis on predictable cash flows and a strong market position[47]. Some investors may require even tighter requirements, e.g., limited requirement for working capital, low future capital expenditure and a strong asset base for collateralization. Inasmuch as the requirements differ, they all demand

---

46 In the subsequent chapters the term 'buyout' will be used as abbreviation for the definition of the 'leveraged management buyout' presented above.

47 KKR name the following criteria for selecting companies for acquisition as buyout: (1) Financial characteristics including (1.1) a history of demonstrated profitability and the ability to maintain above average profit margins. [...]; (1.2) Strong, predictable cash flows to service the financing costs related to the acquisition; (1.3) Readily seperable assets of businesses which could be available for sale, if necessary; further (2) busines characteristics including (2.1) a strong management team; (2.2) products with well-known brand names and a strong market position; (2.3) status as a low-cost producer within an industry, thereby creating a competitive advantage; (2.4) potential for real growth in the future; (2.5) not subject to prolonged cyclical swings; and (2.6) products which are not subject to rapid technological changes (See Kohlberg, Kravis et al. 1989 p. 66). Vest consolidated a the buyout criteria on basis of a series of papers on the buyout-suitability with emphasis on German situations (See Vest 1995, p. 118)). See further Ballwieser and Schmid 1990a

both industry and company-specific characteristics. In the corollary, one may assume that the occurrence of buyouts is driven not only by the company-specific attributes, but also by the suitability of an industry for buyouts in general.

Supposing a company fulfills the LBO criteria and is acquired by a private equity firm, the costs of a buyout may outweigh at some point the benefits. Alternatively, the buyout regime may be a long-term form of organization with superior properties and most attractive to the shareholders.

(A) Industry-specific	(B) Company specific
(1) Limited competition intensity	(1) Defendable market position
(1.a) Low bargaining power of customers	(1) Well-differentiated market position
(1.a) Low bargaining power of suppliers	(2) Considerable market share
(1.c) High market entry barriers	(2) Experienced management
(1.d) Low substitutability of products	(3) Stable, predictable cash flows
(1.e) Low rivalry amongst the competitors	(3.a) Fairly efficient operations
(2) Mature markets and life cycle position	(3.b) Technical mature products
(3) Low to medium technology intensity	(3.c) Diversified, broad product program
(4) Limited demand cyclicality	(3.d) Proven technology, no expected leaps
	(4) Low debt leverage
	(5) Asset base suitable for collateralization

Table 1: Criteria for the LBO suitability (author)

2.2.1 Industry-Specific Characteristics

Research has directed its interest in measuring how strongly the industry contributes to the buyout activity level. Evidence has been found support for the 'industry-effect' hypothesis. It indicates a significant higher occurrence of buyouts in industries with lower R&D expenditure and slower growth prospects[48]. The identified industries though only demonstrated a weak correlation with the expected characteristics, e.g., low growth rates, high free cash flow, cash flow stability, and under-exploited debt capacity. The researchers conclude that company-specific factors are the primary motivating forces for buyouts[49]. Some observations contradict the correlation of

48 Lehn; Netter and Poulsen confirm the industry-effect hypothesis (See Lehn 1990). Ambrose and Winters reject the null hypothesis of an equal distribution of buyouts across all industries. From the 62 industries studied, 10 showed significant buyout activity. The latter industries were typically labor intense (e.g., textile and apparel products) and heavily dependent on natural resources (e.g. paper products, food stores) (See Ambrose and Winters 1992, pp. 90 et seqq.). Wegner notes a lower average level of R&D and a lower likelihood of revolutionary innovation in comparison to industry average (See Wegner 2003, p. 175).

49 See Ambrose and Winters 1992, p. 100

industry sector and buyout activity level[50]. Te strong economic growth and massive upswing in buyouts in the first half of the 1980s has diluted the correlation proposed, instilling a sense of optimism and impairing the decision makers' rationale[51]. In the period after 1985, the explanatory power of the industry determining buyout activity falls significantly[52]. Research that is more recent alleviates the occurrence of buyouts in mature industries, and observes an advancing share of buyouts in industries with a higher growth profile, referred to as 'growth' buyouts[53]. Thereby, one has to delineate activities related to entrepreneurial growth that can occur also in a leveraged buyouts setting[54]. Such LBOs continue to occur in mature industry. The majority of aforementioned growth buyouts relies, however, on a higher equity share, and, therefore, cannot be considered as leveraged[55].

The profit potential of an industry is, according to Porter, determined by competitive forces[56]. The weaker the forces are, the lower the intensity of competition is, the higher the profit potential of the industry will be, and the higher the interest of buyout investors is. Some industries have successfully managed to build entry barriers and defense mechanisms to weaken the forces. They may have reached a high level of scale, deterring the entry of any aspirants by forcing either large scales or a cost disadvantage. Further, high investments into assets, especially in R&D and automated production facilities serve as a major hurdle for likely entrants[57]. Toward suppliers, the industry may ensure a diversity of companies with standardized and undifferentiated products that allow a switching at low costs. Further, the companies have built a credible threat against any forward integration. Against substitute products, the industry has to ensure that the price-performance tradeoff stays

---

50 Epplin and Pourjalali compare the premiums paid at going-private buyouts to the level of cyclicality. The industry-level cash flow cyclicality was not found to be significant in relation to the premiums paid in buyout transactions. See Epplin and Pourjalali 1997, pp. 20 et seqq.

51 Similar results to Epplin and Pourjalali are found by Blair and Schary. They divide the buyouts into a pre- and post-period to 1985. Prior to 1985, they find evidence for a model determining buyout activity with significance for low technology intensity, for high free cash flow, for debt capacity, and for the tax rate. See Blair 1993, pp. 173 et seqq.

52 Before 1985, the model explains 18% of variances in buyout activity, after 1985 only 5%. The strongest decline in significance in found in the technological intensity, approximated by the level of R&D to sales. See Blair 1993, pp. 178 et seqq.

53 See Wright 2001, pp.12 et seqq., EVCA 2001, p.9

54 Wright et al., to name the leading research paper, refers to an 'entrepreneurial mindset' that can be observed in various LBOs (see Wright 2001). See in particular the details on entrepreneurial growth-focused activities as major lever to advance a companies growth prospects in the setting of an leveraged buyout in chapter B4.

55 Wegner analyzes the profile of so called 'growth buyouts' in Germany. He measures an average debt leverage of 57.8% (see Wegner 2003, p. 190)

56 See Porter 1980, p. 36

57 See Porter 1980, pp. 37 et seqq.

superior. Finally, the intensity of rivalry within the industry determines the profit potential. High fixed costs, overcapacity, low product differentiation, and high exit barriers, while facing low growth, will only reap modest profits. However, the company may have some opportunities to improve its individual profit potential by a specific strategic position. In Germany, buyouts benefit from high market entry barriers, from low bargaining power from suppliers and from a minor threat from substitute products[58].

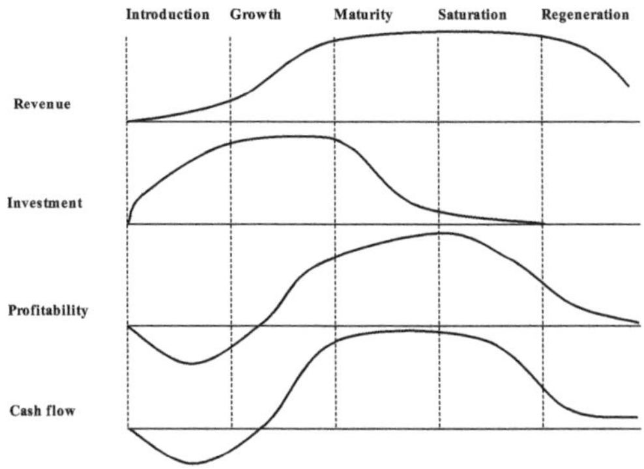

Figure 2: Product life cycle with investment need and cash flow generation (illustrative)[59]

Further, industries with high cyclicality are less appropriate for a buyout. Researchers have observed the cyclicality on the level of the industry and on the level of the individual product along its life cycle. An idealistic life cycle supposes different stages - starting from introduction, over growth and maturity to saturation - and allows some simplified assumptions to investment need and cash flow generation (see Figure 2). During the end of the growth phase and throughout the maturity phase, the investment need is modest, likewise profitability and cash flow generation the highest. A company will have several products with different positions over the product life cycle and will strive to balance cash-consuming and cash-generating positions. For a buyout, the investor will select a company will a good share of mature products and growth prospects, however, he will have to balance paying debt versus investing in new products[60].

58 Vest reports that the buyouts face a considerably high level of competition nurtured by the bargaining power of customers. The bargaining power is related to the fact that the majority of observed buyouts are spin-offs and are dependent on their former parent company as major customer (See Vest 1995, p.138 et seqq.). Wegner thereby measures no differences in competition intensity for the entire sample of examined buyouts (See Wegner 2003, p. 173).

59 See James 1974

60 See Gräper 1993, p. 46

From a financing perspective, companies with a high share of intangible assets are less suitable as they cannot be collateralized and are subject to technology changes. Similar arguments are found for industries with high levels of asset specificity, with high R&D expenditure and capital investments[61].

2.2.2 Company-Specific Characteristics

The non-industry, company-specific characteristics can be found in the area of strategic and market position, management, and financial performance.

A defendable strategic position allows achieving stable profits and generating cash flow. In best case, the buyout candidate offers well-differentiated product-market solutions and carries the ability to lead its markets. In worst case, the company is subsumed in a commodity-based business with uncontrollable factors, e.g., strong suppliers, varying input prices, and threatening new entrants. Indicators of a sustainable strategic position are the competitive position, reflected in the market share and growth prospects in the company is positioned in[62], and the brand position, reflected in customer loyalty[63], to name but a few. However, niche positions with a close market focus may offer a much higher profit potential. Further, the aforementioned list of buyout characteristics foresees the ability of disposable assets, which often refer to business field not regarded as core business anymore[64]. The studies for buyouts have partly confirmed a strategic distinctiveness of the buyout candidates, though have also partly rejected any specific advantage to the strategic position of buyout. For Germany, the studies do not report any superior positioning in terms of market growth and market share[65]. Inasmuch a defendable strategic position is required to ensure stable cash flows, a buyout will serve as catalyst for improvements to alleviate a strategic misfit or pursue a strategic turnaround[66].

---

61 Industries found with high buyout activity may be utilities (e.g., water, electricity, gas), retailers, producers of short- and medium-term consumer goods (e.g., tobacco firms, food producers, super market chains, publishing houses), and industrial companies with limited specific assets (See Graebner 1991, p. 19, Achleitner 1998, pp. 194 et seqq.). The relationship between debt propensity, maturity structure, and the related industrial setup will be discussed in detail in chapter B2.1.1.

62 Gräper and Vest recommend an analysis along the BCG matrix analyzing relative market share vs market growth (see See Gräper 1993, pp. 46 et seqq., Vest 1995, pp. 149 et seqq.).

63 See Gräper 1993, p. 43

64 The reduction of diversification during the buyout holding period are elucidated in detail in chapter B4.2.2.

65 Vest examines for a series of spin-off buyouts the positioning of the core business in the BCG market growth to market share-matrix. He reports a considerable high share of 'dogs' (low market share, low market growth) as opposed to the promising 'stars' (high market share, high market growth) (See Vest 1995, pp. 149 et seqq.). See also Lütjen 1992, p.114 and 115

66 The adjustments in strategic position a buyout runs through are presented in detail in chapter B4.2.1

Surveys confirm that buyouts indeed are highly more likely to happen if case of a high strategic misfit between owner and company[67].

The quality and competence of the management is one of the most important precedents for the success of a buyout[68]. The challenges for a buyout are multi-faceted, and require an experienced management. For the buyout investor, the management team has to prove its experience in taking the operational responsibility for the company, either as the executives responsible for the buyout company before the transaction or in a comparable position in terms of enterprise size, growth rates and international exposure. Beyond operational management, the executives have to be willing to take increased responsibility for strategic decision-making and the entrepreneurial development of the company[69]. Managerial resources will be much tighter, since the support from senior management on the corporate board in a large corporation will no longer exist. Hence, a close review of the existing functional skills on a stand-alone basis is crucial[70]. In addition, the management has to be willing to follow the strategic plans of the buyout investors. For many management roles, this will mean a significant change in their objectives[71]. Therefore, an alignment of the objectives, beyond the implications of increased shareholding of management[72], is essential for the buyout investor's willingness to engage. Inasmuch as the incumbent management caliber is crucial, the buyout investor may also opt to bring new managerial expertise from experience senior managers to the board[73]. The empirical evidence underpins the importance of the incumbent management for the buyout success[74]. Further, the evidence confirms the challenge to ensure sufficient management resources, in particular in the course of a spin off[75].

---

67 A survey by the EVCA reveals that 44.6% of participants mention as reason for the sale of the business the lack of strategic fit with the vendor (See EVCA 2001, p.8). Wegner measures a high discomfort of managers with the former strategic positioning and the motivation to realize their own strategy in an buyout environment (See Wegner 2003, p. 179). The (strategic) motives of the pre-buyout owners will are briefly discussed in chapter B2.2.

68 See Gräper 1993, p. 55, Sharp 2003, p. 19

69 See Kessel 1991, p. 19

70 Many resources and know-how will have been provided by the corporate head. For instance, procurement and sourcing is often concentrated in a group function to improve the bargaining power. The buyout investors will, therefore, assess to what degree the stand-alone buyout company has the necessary functional skills at its disposal See Sharp 2003, p. 22

71 For example, the chief financial officer or finance director will have to act as a devil's advocate for the business lines, translating the buyout investors' debt payments plans in monthly cash flows from operations. He will, in agreement with the CEO, daily decide on important tradeoffs, which is totally different from the former governance in a multi-divisional business.

72 A detailed discussion on the implications of increased management shareholding is provided in light of reduced agency costs in a buyout governance structure in chapter B2.1.4.

73 Refer to chapter B4.5.2 for the changes in management during the buyout period.

74 Kuemmerle measures the highest priority of the quality of the management team for the due diligence of a

Finally, the suitability of a buyout has to materialize in convincing financials and in particular in a solid cash flow generation to service the high debt payments that will occur after the leveraged financing on the company. The investor will review the cash flow from operations on basis of historic performance and of anticipated revenue growth and margin development. Further, investments have to be considered for working capital, for tangible and intangible assets, e.g. for new production facilities, and even for necessary acquisitions with respect to an industry consolidation not uncommon the mature markets the buyouts typically operate in. Debt propensity is the second financial criteria for the suitability for an LBO. The investors will calculate in what time the debt can be paid off. Gearing and interest coverage should be at or below the industry-average, otherwise the propensity for new debt is highly limited[76]. To ensure an approval by the lending banks, the company should allow a sufficient collateralization on basis of the asset base. The proceeds of the disposal of underperforming assets will further facilitate the leveraged financing. Even though researchers and practioneers on the one hand demand such criteria[77], the evidence from surveys on the other hand does not confirm the rigidity in the selection of buyouts[78].

2.2.3 Longevity of Buyouts and their Exit

Having reviewed the criteria for a company to be acquired by a buyout investor, one should now discuss the considerations and arguments are under which a investor will decide to exit the buyout and under what circumstances the costs of being in a buyout regime may outweigh the benefits.

The longevity of buyouts can be debated from two angles. One stream of researchers argue that companies benefit from the reduced agency costs from high leverage, high managerial equity ownership and close monitoring from an active investor over a longer period. Empirical results indicate that not all buyouts will reverse, i.e.,

---

buyout candidate in Germany (see Kümmerle 1998, p. 11). Vest and Gräper confirm the importance of the incumbent management, outlining in particular the qualification and motivation as crucial. ((See Gräper 1993, p. 55 et seqq., Vest 1995, p.195). For non-German buyouts, evidence is provided by Sharp (Sharp 2003, p. 19).

75 Nadig reports that the incumbent management has often not acted as a leadership group of a stand-alone entity. Numerous managers choose to move to the parent company (See Nadig 1992,p. 98).

76 See DeAngelo and DeAngelo 1987, p. 40

77 Greaper outlines the importance of the free cash flow as adequate indicator to both predict the cash flow for repaying debt and to assess the default risk. (See Gräper 1993, p. 50 and 51).

78 Vest measures a low level of saison and business cycle-dependent cash flow profile for German LBOs (See Vest 1995, p.173). Further, he observes that the minority of surveyed spin-off LBOs offer significant non-core business, disposable assets. He reasons that the spin-offs only unhinge the necessary core assets to the business (See Vest 1995, p.175 and 176). Vest does not confirm the collaterializability of assets for the German LBOs. He argues that the financing is directed to an cash flow-based financing (See Vest 1995, p.179 and 180).

arguing that the net benefits of private ownership with high leverage and ownership concentration seem to be permanent[79]. Jensen concludes that a buyout is a new long-term form of organization with superior efficiency properties. Even after the buyout, the company can apply multiple instruments to imitate the beneficial characteristics of a buyout and remain attractive to equity shareholders[80]. He outlines that companies should encourage large investors to act as active investors, enhance pay-for-performance systems based on cash flow, decentralize management and dramatically reduce their staff. On the other hand, researchers disencourage the expectations to a buyout and restrict the beneficial nature of a LBO as to being a mere vehicle for a transitory form for the organization[81]. So long as public companies are managed and governed by best practice, they will return superior profits. Further, the buyout regime displays significant costs of inflexibility to competition and change. These costs will outweigh after some time the benefits from the buyout structure[82].

The empirical evidence undoubtfully shows that a majority of LBOs stays in private ownership for a very long time. For instance, Kaplan, examining the post-buyout organizational form of buyouts, observes that 62% of buyouts remain in private ownership, 14% stay publicly owned, and 24% are delisted mostly due to the acquisition from another company[83]. Wright, Thompson, Robbie and Wong report that after seven years, 71 % of the buyouts are still in private ownership, as opposed to the 56% reported by Kaplan[84]. Thereby, there is no unambiguous evidence that the holding period differs between a trade sale and a going-public[85]. Kaplan elucidates that the likelihood of the return to public ownership is largest in the second to fifth year of the buyout, and then significantly declines[86]. Van de Guchts and Moore

---

79 See Gucht van de and Moore 1998, p. 299

80 See Jensen 1989a

81 See Rappaport 1990

82 See Kaplan 1991, pp. 288 - 289

83 Kaplan measures the status of ownership in 1990 for a sample of firms entering into the buyout structure between 1979 and 1986. For those firms that return to public at some point in their life cycle, there average median time private is 2.6 years. For the total sample, the median life of remaining in the buyout structure is 6.8 yerars. (See Kaplan 1991, pp. 291 et seqq.)

84 Wright et al. argue that their sample consists out of significantly smaller buyouts (See Wright 1995, p. 472).

85 A further survey by Wright, Thompson and Robbie measures an average holding period of 3.3 to 4.5 years for going-publics and 2.7 to 3.8 for trade sales (See Wright 1993, p. 317). Van de Guchts and Moore compute an average holding period of 3.5 years for reversal and 3.8 years for trade sales (See Gucht van de and Moore 1998, p. 303). The authors relate their longer holding period to the extended observation period. Muscarella and Vetsuypens measure for the subsample of reverse buyouts an average (mean) time unter private ownership of 34.7 months or 2.9 years, repectively. The mean for divisional buyouts was slightly lower (33.9 months) than for full buyout (29.0 months) (See Muscarella and Vetsuypens 1990, p. 1392).

86 See Kaplan 1991, p. 300

measure the peak in reversal probability for the year seven and eight[87]. The scientists do not find other factors beyond the corporate governance constituents that determine the buyout longevity[88].

In terms of the governance structure though, several reasons may exist why a company decides to return to public. A reverse leveraged buyout might be appropriate after having resolved severe agency and operational inefficiencies. One may distinguish the reasons into four groups: (i) investor's desire for divestment; (ii) management's and employees' desire for diversification and divestment, (iii) desire for growth, and (iv) overcoming one-time restructuring.

Naturally, a buyout investor will aim to cash out as soon as he has surpassed his target return rate and does not foresee do earn additional value creation. Closed-end funds have fixed requirements to provide returns to their investors. In most cases, the investors plan a potential exit already at the entry, but changing market environments and varying progress make a deterministic planning of the exit challenging. The investors regularly review their portfolio and assess potential exit options[89]. Mian and Rosenfeld find a higher likelihood of takeovers with the participation of an active investor (26 of 33) than without (only 33 of 85)[90]. This may be an indicator that the return to public is at least partially motivated by the investor's desire to liquidate. However, the time horizon and the investment approach may differ significantly between the buyout firms[91]. Manager-owners significantly invest their personal wealth into the buyout. It is therefore understandable that will be anxious to reduce their risk after some time, and diversify their risk by selling some share[92]. In addition, managers may wish to continue their career as managerial employees again, or retire. Van de Gucht and Moore, however, measure that for those LBOs that decide to reverse to public ownership, management participation delays that decision[93]. The empirical research

---

87 See Gucht van de and Moore 1998, p. 312

88 Analyses by Kaplan and Van de Gucht with Moore reveal further insights. First, the size does not significantly affect the likelihood of returning the public. Second, the support of a prestiguous buyout firm does also not not affect the likelihood of being private. Third, former divisions of corporates have also no difference in the public to private status than former public companies. (See Gucht van de and Moore 1998, Kaplan 1991). Wright, Wilson, Robbie and Wong report that for larger buyouts, in terms of firm size, short-term performance improvements are greater. They have a shorter lifetime as buyout as opposed to than medium-sized and small firmsSee Wright 1995, pp. 472 et seqq.

89 See Wall 1997, pp. 11-12

90 See Mian and Rosenfeld 1993, p. 57

91 See Wright 1994, p. 218

92 See Wright and Robbie 1991, p. 55

93 See Gucht van de and Moore 1998, p. 313

indicates a higher probability of exiting in the early years[94] and a faster return to public markets[95] for buyouts with smaller managerial shareholdings. Similar considerations to diversification and cash-out can be found for employee shareholdings[96]. For the broader shareholder base, intensified competition and the need for capital may accelerate the need to exit. Financial distress might arise from insecure market developments. High debt levels with concentrated ownership can lead to inflexibility towards environment change and competition[97]. Furthermore, the buyout company might redefine its strategy during the buyout restructuring, for instance as reaction to industry consolidation, requiring a large critical mass to survive[98]. In general, the aforementioned costs of inflexibility towards significant changes in the competitive environment, as proposed by Rappaport, will outweigh the benefits from the LBO[99]. Increased equity financing will compensate and allow securing future growth opportunities[100]. In addition, the necessity for an LBO may cease after a series of one-time restructuring measures have been taken. Kaplan classifies a significant number of buyouts as a "shock therapy" for the company. The benefits from the buyout regime are one-time events, in particular the divestment of unproductive assets. Further, the company may have suffered from pre-buyout constraints on investment policies, new product development and others[101]. The LBO will benefit from releasing the constraints, however, the positive effect will not be permanent. Empirical research confirms such constraints, as pre-buyout public sector firms with arguably higher constraints exit much faster than average private firms do[102].

In some cases, manager-owners and investors may be prejudiced by an overconfidence bias. In this case, the managers systematically overesteem their prognosis and success rates[103]. In the context of an LBO investor seeking to exit, they may time the exit too early. Further, the sunk costs during the preparation period may have investors hold on to an investment, instead of turning the company over to receivership. An indicator may be found in the similar longevity of buyouts heading

---

94 See Wright 1994, p. 220
95 See Halpern, Kieschnick et al. 1999, pp. 302-303
96 See Wright, Robbie et al. 1994, p. 93
97 See Rappaport 1990
98 See Wright and Robbie 1991, p. 56
99 See Kaplan 1991, pp. 288 - 289
100 See Kaplan 1991
101 See Wright 1994, p. 219
102 See Wright 1994, p. 221
103 See Paffenholz 2004, pp. 104 et seqq.

for going-public as opposed to receivership[104]. Finally, not all companies actually leave a buyout structure in an abrupt, discrete manner. Some firms just repay slowly the debt to a normal level and stepwise divest managerial shareholdings. Others continue to be in a buyout form by continuous capital withdrawal and releveraging. Some buyouts that return to public are characterized by their ownership structure as "hybrid" between a buyout and a typical corporation[105]. A substantial fraction of the LBOs that remain above average in private ownership are thereby described as remaining highly leveraged[106].

For the buyout life cycle in Germany, researchers have not consolidated detailed data on the duration of the buyout period and factors influencing the likelihood of returning to public. Not surprisingly, the longevity of buyouts is dependent on country-specific factors. For instance, the parties involved in a buyout are reported to have different importance across different countries, in particular for the role of management[107]. Capital markets and the market for corporate control are differently developed. In principal, the characteristics for the German market imply a higher longevity for buyouts. The entry into an LBO in Germany is for a company, in comparison to other countries, often initiated to realign interests of managers and owners. In many cases, the founding family possesses the majority of the company, at the disadvantage of a low equity participation of the active management, if at all. A sale of the family stakes to the active management will motivate management and enhance performance. The repayment of debt will presumably hold up for a substantial amount of time. Further, the control benefits in Germany lead to organizational slack. The rigid LBO regime will discipline management and release efficiency improvement potential. However, since the slack has been part of the company for a longer time, the investors will not be able to exit too fast. Since the management shareholdings are comparatively high for German buyouts[108], they possess less urgency to divest and may choose to stay a longer period as an LBO.

---

104 A study by Venture Economics measures a nearly identical life time (See Thomsen, Venture et al. 2003)

105 See Holthausen and Larcker 1996

106 Privately owned LBOs are measured to maintain debt levels similar to the levels when the buyout was completed (See Kaplan 1991, p. 300).

107 See Wright, Robbie et al. 1994, pp. 105 et seqq.

108 See for empirical evidence in chapter B2.1.4.

2.3 Institutional Governance Framework

Before entering into the analysis of the changes in the relationship between shareholders (investors) and the buyout company, a clear understanding of framework of governance of the company has to be established.

Shareholders (investors) rely on performance incentives that influence the behavior and the level of effort of management. The investors may directly interfere with corporate policy-making through formal and informal means of control related to their equity shareholding rights. Further, they will provide their advice in strategic and operational issues in the manner of counseling to the management board. The different episodes of governance to be detailed are the LBO holding period, the post-exit governance by the public equity market after a going-public, and the post-exit governance by a strategic buyer after a trade sale (see Figure 3). In the case of a trade sale, the corporate level senior management substitutes and internalizes the role of supervising shareholders.

Phase	**Before the exit**	**After the exit**	
Route	**A. Leveraged buyout**	**B1. Going public**	**B2. Trade sale**
Shareholder structure *(illustrative)*	Buyout investor, management	Public equity markets, institutional investors, management	Strategic investor
Shareholder representatives	Buyout professionals, advisors to the buyout investor, industry experts, senior managers	Industry experts, senior managers, shareholder representative's	Senior management from parent company
Relevant entity	Portfolio company	Listed company	Business unit, division
Instruments of governance			
I. Performance incentives	Managerial ownership Mgmt. employment contract Type of equity	Managerial ownership Mgmt. employment contract	(Managerial ownership) Mgmt. employment contract
II. Means of control	Board representation Access to capital (Majority) voting rights Covenants	Board representation Access to capital Simple voting rights Change of control Daily stock price	Corporate board Access to capital Resource distribution Functional integration

Figure 3: Institutional governance framework (illustrative, author)

At this point, the objective is to outline the conceptual framework in which the shareholders operate. The author will later elaborate on the change in the way the shareholders engage in the context of founding theories[109] and during the

109 Agency theory, the resource-based view and the more specific theory of corporate governance are discussed on the basis of (i) the performance incentives and (ii) the formal means of control of the three stati. See the following chapter A3.

hypotheses formulation[110]. The author will also discuss the individual motives of the parties involved, encompassing shareholders and other stakeholders[111].

2.3.1 Buyout Investors

The market of private equity consists of managed investments in private and public companies by professional intermediaries. These intermediaries are partnerships that raise money from institutional investors, such as corporate and public pension funds, endowments, insurance companies, bank holding companies and wealthy families. The intermediaries around private equity should be differentiated by (i) the managing company (general partner) and (ii) the investing fund (limited partner). Latter part is responsible for the holding of the portfolio companies, the former part for the actual selection, control and management of the portfolio companies[112].

In the following thesis, the author will refer to those private equity companies that provide the equity for leveraged buyouts as 'buyout investors'. They provide funds for acquiring companies operating in mature markets and seeking for capital required for corporate succession, turnaround, or expansion, to name a few[113]. The emergence of both general and limited partnerships is an outcome of the increasing information asymmetry between ownership and management[114]. The buyout investors have developed a set of unique mechanisms to align the interests of both investors and management in an efficient way[115]. In Germany, around 47% of the public equity companies are leveraged buyout investors[116]. In most cases, the professionals structure the independent funds in the form of a limited partnership[117].

The buyout investors rely on three basic instruments to steer the company they have acquired in their interest: (a) by performance incentives, (b) by means of control, and (c) by advice.

The core instruments in terms performance incentives is the provision of management with a significant share of ownership. As a former corporate division,

110 The hypotheses are based on the changes in performance incentives and formal means of control and extended by secondary effects, e.g., the change in debt structure, activity level of investors and in particular in managerial objectives in part

111 See chapter B2.2

112 See Zemke 1995, p.114. For an overview of the generic structure of the private equity industry see Fenn 1995,p. 4 and Prowse 1998, p. 23, and for the private equity entity in detail Achleitner and Müller 2004,p. 10.

113 For a detailed listing of the characteristic of a leveraged buyout portfolio company refer to chapter A2.2.

114 See Prowse 1998, p.22. For the closing of the information asymmetry, see the discussion related to the governed corporation as a result of active ownership by buyout investors in chapter A3.5.

115 See Fenn 1995, p.33, Prowse 1998, pp. 29 et seqq.

116 See Feinendegen, Hommel et al. 2001,p. 572

117 See Kraft 2001,p. 39

the managers only partly participated in their efforts with no or limited equity ownership[118]. Similar, the participation in a former family-controlled company for non-family management was sparse. At the entry into the buyout, managers receive a significant share of ownership[119]. In addition, the employment contracts with management are finetuned to avoid moral hazard[120]. The contracts may include equity ratchet attached to performance development to offset low work effort. Excessive risk taking and other moral hazard may be penalized by cut-backs in the equity share and by replacement. Further, the shareholdings of management are often at risk by convertible preferred stocks from the buyout investors. In the case of a liquidation, management will prefer convertibles over common stock. In the consequence, management will seek maximizing performance to increase the value of their stock. They will also closely manage their risk position to avoid financial distress.

Further, the buyout investors hold a number of mechanisms allowing direct control of the company in hand. Above all, they dominate the supervisory board as, in most cases, largest investors[121]. They decide over the appointment of top-managers, including the CEO, and continuously assess company's performance. Further, the investors will control the access to (additional) capital. Management may opt for an acquisition and require additional financing. Without the support or direct financing by the buyout investors, it is unlikely that management will be able to arrange the financing. In contrary to the US one board-system, the management is not represented on the supervisory board and has no voting right. The equity shareholdings allow the buyout investors to exert voting rights, in most cases as majority shareholder. Detailed covenants that are tied to the purchase contract complement the voting rights[122]. The buyout investors will typically require frequent and detailed reporting directed to overlook the debt repayment and progress in performance[123]. It may also cover company visits or the installment of outside experts to accelerate the restructuring if needed[124].

118 See Hite and Vetsuypens 1989, pp. 955-956, DeAngelo and DeAngelo 1987, p.40

119 In a forthcoming chapter, the change of managerial shareholdings over the buyout cycle will be discussed in detail, in particular in respect to the change of joined ownership and risk preference. See chapter B2.1.4.

120 The composition of employment contracts as opposed to the post-exit period are discussed in chapter 0. See for instance Hatherly, Innes et al. 1994, p. 29

121 Buyout investors take more representation on the board than other type of investors. Cotter and Peck 2001 compute a shareof 37.4% (372%) as opposed to .4.0% (20.7%) who are buyout investors (equity investors with control) (See Cotter and Peck 2001, pp.137-139.

122 See Hatherly, Innes et al. 1994, pp. 22-23, Achleitner and Müller 2004,p. 17

123 See Prowse 1998, p. 31, Baker and Smith 1998, p. 106. The changes in the reporting system at both entry and exit from the buyout are elucidated in chapter B3.3.3.

124 For instance, the buyout specialist may insist on the engagement of a management or operations

Beside the performance incentives and control rights, the buyout investors provide advice on strategic and operational issues[125]. Firstly, a representative of the buyout investor typically joins the supervisory board and provides his advice on both long-term decision and day-to-day operations[126]. Thereby, the investor may add new expertise in terms of industry and market environment not present on the management board. Secondly, the buyout investors bring valuable insights and resources out of their industry contacts and their advisor network that typically consists of experienced senior managers to the company[127]. Typically, the buyout investors formulate at the transaction a business plan, or, more adequately, a value creation-plan that consolidates the objectives of the investment in concrete performance targets for the management and reflects the industry understanding of the buyout investors and their advisor network[128]. Such a plan is the basis for the monitoring during the holding period.

2.3.2 Stock Market

Even though the governance framework as a company listed on public stock market is to some degree similar to the one observed under the ownership of a buyout investor, there are some considerable differences.

The shareholder base may consist of institutional investors, hedge funds, and owner-managers, to name but a few. Thereby, a shareholder may hold a significant equity portion with a minority voting rights position. The supervisory board will reflect the composition of the shareholder base and include both shareholder representatives and independent industry experts, e.g., senior managers engaged in adjacent industries. A high level of ownership concentration characterizes the German stock market. More than half of the listed German companies have a dominant owner with 50% equity stake or more[129]. The concentration is further reinforced when taking into account the controlling power throughout chains of direct stakes, typical for the high

---

consultant to anchor the value cration-plan in the organization and to accelerate required strategic and operational changes.

125 The advice is substantiated in the appoirntment of representatives not only from the investing private equity firm, but also from associated industry ecperts. See more details on the resoures during the buyout cycle in chapter A3.3.1.

126 See Baker and Wruck 1989,p. 183, Kester and Luehrman 1995, p. 123, Bruining and Wright 2002, p. 165

127 See Baker and Smith 1998, p. 174, Bruining and Wright 2002, p. 165

128 See Hatherly, Innes et al. 1994, p. 22, Heel and Kehoe 2005b. The monitoring level of active investors is discussed in detail in chapter A3.5

129 For instance, Franks and Mayer report that in 1990, 85% of 171 large listed companies in Germany had a dominant shareholder with an ownership shareholdings of more than 25% of the capital and 57% had a single shareholder owning more than 25% (see Franks and Mayer 2001). The ownership structure in Germany is discussed in detail in chapter B2.1.2.

level of crossholdings in Germany. A small number of large, complementary shareholders balance this concentration of ownership[130].

In terms of performance incentives, it is unlikely that management will be provided with the same amount of ownership as in an LBO setting. In the contrary to a buyout, the equity base is much larger given the higher leverage, making (significant) shareholdings for management much more expensive[131]. As compensation for the lack of equity shareholdings, many listed companies introduce alternative participation programs[132].

Board representation, access and provision with capital as well as voting rights can be exerted in the identical way as in an LBO. In a dispersed shareholder structure, however, the individual shareholder will be much less incentivized to invest in monitoring because any benefits from monitoring are shared, known as 'free-rider' problem [133]. Minority shareholders particularly benefit from the monitoring[134].

> Excurse: German two board system in the AG
>
> The German Aktiengesellschaft is the legal form of the entity that is entitled to list shares on the stock exchange135. The AG consists of three governing bodies: (1) the Annual General Meeting, (2) the supervisory board, and (3) the managing board136. In general, the shareholders at the AGM decide by simple majority, with specific laws and status requiring different voting rules. They elect the members of the supervisory board137. The supervisory board must at last have three members and include worker representatives for all but the smallest AGs138. The supervisory board again appoints the managing board that must have at least one member139. No supervisory board member may be on the managing board or in a position of similar executive power140.

A large ownership stake will incorporate the same rights and influence as a majority buyout investors bears. A highly dispersed ownership, however, incurs a loss of control. The dispersion of ownership leads to a wider distribution of formal control rights and a dilution of power of shareholders to company's management. Voting

---

130 Becht and Boehmer report an average size of 7.4% of shareholding for other large owners, whereas only a second shareholder is found for only 20% of the companies with a concentrated owner. See Becht and Boehmer 2003.

131 See details on changes in management shareholdings at the exit in chapter B2.1.4.

132 The changes in the compensation scheme of managers over the buyout cycle is outlined in chapter 0.

133 For the free-ridership problem, see chapter A3.4.2.

134 See Alchian and Demsetz 1972, p. 778

135 The two case studies that exit through a going-public, Techem and Wincor Nixdorf, are correspondingly a German AG.

136 See §33 AktG.

137 See §101 AktG.

138 See §51 AktG and §6 AktG.

139 See §6 II AktG

140 See §104 AktG.

rights will be downscaled to a minority shareholder or even a general shareholder position, if the shareholders do not in act in a concerted manner. The shareholder can submit proxy proposals and actively use their voting rights.

Institutional investors have started to communicate directly with the management. They have informal discussions with corporate representatives to address directly their issues. The increased activism by shareholders in the past two decades can most likely be associated to the substantially enhanced average shareholdings[141]. In some cases, the management board has to provide communication to two layers of stakeholders: the direct representatives of the board, which may exclusively encompass independent industry experts, and the representatives of the institutional investors. Even though the latter group may not currently hold the rights as supervisory board, they actively engage in corporate policy-making. Researchers have referred to the active cooperation of managers in the monitoring process as 'relationship investing'[142]. Evidence underpins that managers actively invest time to reduce information asymmetries with the shareholders[143].

Nevertheless, stock market listing offers various advantages for control. The threat of a takeover (change of control) is a powerful mechanism for disciplining management. An offer of a potential acquirer seeking to obtain the value gain will force management to undertake significant restructuring efforts and improve performance[144]. Management may quickly sell unprofitable businesses and increase debt to underline its commitment to performance improvement. Still, agency problems will prevail[145]. In Germany, the likelihood of a hostile takeover is still minute, since the share of pubic equity is low and hostile takeovers infrequent[146]. A

---

141 See Gillan and Starks 1998

142 The institutional investor has, in contrast to the model where the large shareholder is interested in taking over the entire firm or in obtaining control benefits (see Shleifer and Vishny 1986), no interest in gaining control of the firm, simply by the investment requirements for both non-controlling amount and yet a diversified portfolio. Also, this model does not resemble the aforementioned 'governed corporation by Pound (see Pound 1995. Much more, the institutional investors serve as an intermediate passing on the private information of the managers to other shareholders. See Chidambaran and John 1998, p. 1

143 When analyzing costs related to monitoring, and, in more general terms, governing activities, theoretical research has focused on the costs related to the investor (principal). By extending the research to the costs of monitoring related to the manager (agent), the analysis indicates that the monitoring of managers reduce investor's costs. In an equilibrium, the manager's costs are passed on to the entire shareholder base, leading to a reduction of the free-rider problem of monitoring activities from large shareholders.

144 See Hart 1995, p. 684, Short, Keasey et al. 1999, p. 345

145 See Short, Keasey et al. 1999, p. 345

146 The German governance system is in general is still classified as bank-centered (See also Franks and Mayer 1990. Such a hostile bid will typically arise from a listed company. In some cases however, the resident management group may approach the corporate management with a proposal of a management buyout, backed by a buyout investor and arguing to improve governance and increase management attention after the change in ownership

further beneficial aspect of being listed is the daily stock price as direct measure of the shareholders' appreciation of corporate policy, imperfect as it may be[147]. Any activities from management that are transparent to the stock market and do not find the approval of the shareholders will lead to a relative valuation discount.

2.3.3 Strategic Owner

Under the ownership of a strategic buyer, the former LBO company will be integrated into the corporation as a business unit. The governance by a supervisory board as in the previous two cases will be substituted by the control of the corporate managing board and delegated senior managers from the new owner.

Concerning the performance incentives, the interest alignment of management on basis of shareholdings is in most cases significantly reduced, if not even entirely omitted. After the acquisition, the new owners seek to obtain the 100% control of the company. The corporate will introduce appropriate employment contracts to ensure the interest alignment with performance targets tied to the development of the business unit (former LBO) and to the financials on corporate level.

In terms of direct means of control, the right over resource allocation and functional integration enhance the direct means above the access to capital. A number of researchers have developed prototype models to describe the organization and related internal governance, acknowledging the emergence of companies operating in multiple businesses. The U-formed corporation by Berle and Means is characterized by a high level of centralization and functionally integrated units[148]. The individual managers are responsible for the performance and excellence in the separate functions. Such companies operate in business with a high level of economies of scale and scope, and hold participation of business units along the value stream. The managers in each of the business units contribute to the operational targets on business level, typically without direct linkage to the corporate level goals. Therefore, the responsibility for the financial performance materializes not until the level of senior management. The coordination of functional integration and resource distribution will challenge the senior management, may neglect their role to provide strategic advice to the business units, e.g., in terms of entrepreneurial activities[149]. As an antipode, the H-form structure is a holding with loose ties to the operating units. The business units are established and managed as fully independent units, being responsible for their financing and with no significant

---

147 See Rappaport 1990,p.3
148 See Berle and Means 1932
149 See Williamson 1985, p. 280

synergies between the individual business units. Such a holding company is little more than a corporate shell[150]. The governance is similar to a stock market in terms of members of the supervisory board being placed by the holding company. The core decisions of the parent company towards the portfolio companies circle around divestment, acquisition, and appointment of managers. The M-form structure overcomes the high level of management discretion of the U-formed firms by a more direct orientation towards profit maximization[151]. The business units receive operating responsibilities and are held fully accountable for their results in form of profit centers. However, it adds to the H-form (i) a distinct strategic planning, (ii) a joint resource allocation and (iii) a monitoring and control tasks. Hence, an internal capital market is established that allows the corporate office to monitor the efficiency of the single business divisions. The business units receive capital from the internal market according to the yields they achieve. Still, the M-form governance structure may not prevent managers from using their discretion at the corporate level[152]. Further, the capacity for good governance in the internal market is limited. The high level of information asymmetry between internal and external markets dampens the threat of a takeover. Some researchers further report a failure of the internal capital market due to either strong retention of the surpluses by the operating units or centralized direction[153].

To summarize, the relationship between investors (holding unit) and portfolio (business unit) company varies by the organizational setup chosen. The M-Form implies a high level of monitoring, while the U-Form monitoring seems more directed to coordination inasmuch as senior management has both a coordinative and supervisionary function. In an H-Form, the level of monitoring is the lowest[154].

3 Related Theory to the Buyout Cycle

The research of the post-exit value creation and changes in strategy and operations presumes that the changes in the governance structure are exogenous. Predictions for the post-exit period should be founded on changes in ownership (property) rights and their respective delegation to agents. The changes itself in the firm have then to consider how assets and resources develop under different governance structures.

150 See Williamson 1985, p. 281
151 See Williamson 1985, pp. 283 et seqq.
152 See Hoskisson and Turk 1990
153 See Thompson 1988
154 See the details of organizational forms in chapter A2.3.3.

The author briefly refers to the neoclassical financing theory and to the basics of the property rights and transaction costs theory. He then discusses in more detail potential implications from the agency theory and resource-based view for the post-exit development of the company. To incorporate the more complex interactions of a buyout, the author will further discuss implications from a corporate governance perspective.

3.1 Introduction

According to the neoclassical financing theory, there is no theoretical legitimation for an LBO and for the existence of professional buyout investors. Modigliani and Miller propose that the 'market value of any company is independent of its capital structure and is given by capitalizing its expected returns'[155]. Considerations of dividend policy and of debt to equity ratio are irrelevant. In the corollary, the market value is independent of its capital structure and leverage, respectively. Therefore, private equity partnerships cannot provide any benefit beyond bond and stock markets.

Fama bases his model on the nature of a perfect capital market[156] encompassing no transaction costs for bondholders and issuers, no insolvency costs, no taxes, and no costs for information and control rights. The financing decision does not affect the characteristics of the portfolio opportunities available to investors. Further, information is assumed costless to all market agents, leading to homogeneous expectations. Research has doubted such functionality of capital markets. Fama defined different levels of efficiency based on the speed and completeness by which markets incorporate the information into their prices[157]. Evidence suggests the existence of the weak form of information efficiency and the partial existence of the semi-strong form of information efficiency. Further arguments also contradict the neoclassical financing theory. First, the deductibility of interest, not dividends, favors debt as financing instrument. Second, the risk for insolvency increases with a higher debt/equity ratio. Investments in highly specific assets, e.g., in R&D-intensive industries, will have higher depreciation in the case of insolvency. Hence, companies tend to use equity instead of debt to finance such investments.

---

155 Further, any 'yield of a share of stock is equal to the appropriate capitalization rate pk for a pure equity stream in the class, plus a premium related to financial risk equal to the debt-to-equity ratio times the spread between pk and r', where r is defined as the rate of interest.See Modigliani and Miller 1958, p. 268

156 See Fama 1978, p. 273

157 Fama differs between (a) strong form of information efficiency (current prices reflect all available information, both from public and private sources), (b) semi-strong form of information efficiency (current prices reflect all available information from public sources, e.g., accounting data and analyst reports) and (c) weak form of information efficiency (current prices reflect all available historical information, e.g., technical analyses). See Fama 1978, p. 276 et seqq.

The theory of property rights comprises different analytical concepts that seek to explain the creation, features and assignment of ownership rights. Property rights are attributed to any goods and define the right of any individual to deal with it[158]. Furubotn and Pejovich define the economic actors, the humans, as individuals that are rational in the sense that they maximize their utility. Further, the researchers regard the individuals as being self-interested. Some basic tenets of the neoclassical financing theory are applied and further developed. Capital market efficiency and complete information are substituted by the premise that the definition, the exchange, policing, and enforcement of property rights and their contracts incur costs. The theory allows some insightful, comparative assessments of the optimal design of property rights. If the rights are distributed among several individuals, inefficiencies are expected since (a) economic consequences stemming from the behavior of an individual only partially affect them and (b) difficulties arise in enforcing the property rights. The behavior of others leads to potentially positive or negative externalities. These costs may not be compensated for and may not be accumulated as costs for the single individual. The optimal distribution of property rights to various institutions should internalize any prevailing consequences. The criteria for alternative property rights constructions are the transaction costs incurred, the residual loss, and potential agency costs. The key question for property rights are therefore: (1) What is the structure and distribution of property rights at a given time? (2) What are consequences of the structure of property rights for the interaction of individuals? And (3) what was the process of definition and distribution that led to the prevailing structure?

Implications can be derived for managerial freedom, entrepreneurial orientation and the relationship between owners and managers of LBOs, especially for divisional buyouts. As a business unit within a conglomerate, the responsibility for decision-making between corporate headquarters and the management of the business unit is often complex and multi-level. The LBO allows strategic decision-making to be concentrated in the actual management board and reduces potentially residual losses[159]. Further, the concentration of property rights in small and flexible organizational units have been proven to enhance innovativeness. Both the control and assignment of success seems to increase entrepreneurship and motivation while reducing monitoring costs. As a subsidiary, decision-making will though often be

158 The property rights connected with any goods are: (1) the right to use the good (ius usus), (2) the right to obtain the income from a good (ius usus fructus), (3) the right to change the form or substance of a good (ius abusus) and (4) the right to sell a good (ius succesionis). Property rights can be held by a single individual or can be shared among a group of individuals. See Demsetz 1964; Demsetz 1966; Demsetz 1967

159 See the advantages of external venture management analyzed by Nathusius 1979, pp. 189 et seqq.

supervised by cross-functional units. Although the implications are highly dependent on the specific context of a LBO and partly cannot be generalized, the property rights theory provides a strong basis for developing further theories for the new institutional economy. Agency theory and transaction cost theory, which will be discussed in the following, are based on the theory of property rights and contracts.

Transaction cost theory refers to the costs attributed with the definition, exchange, policing and enforcement of property rights. Any kind of financial transactions incurs substantial costs to find appropriate investors and debtors, to retrieve and consolidate information, as well as to negotiate and finalize contracts. Therefore, transaction costs increase the price of any financial relationships. Potentially interested parties may be deterred when faced with the costs related to market based transaction. The theory of transaction costs is, therefore, in direct contrast with the neoclassical financing theory.[160]. A transaction will only be incorporated within company if its costs internal lower than in the market place. The costs are driven by the frequency with which a transaction occurs, the uncertainty related to the transaction, potential opportunistic behavior, and the specificity of the assets. Hence, the theory facilitates the understanding of existence and scope of a company's boundaries. The specificity of assets can lead to opportunistic behavior. For an industry in which assets are highly specific and extensive investments are necessary, the transaction partner may force a lower price since the assets are of less value than they would be for a different transaction. Transactions with high asset specificity will tend to be incorporated within companies. Williamson details how asset specificity in particular contradicts the irrelevance of capital structure[161]. Transaction cost theory differentiates debt and equity more by governance structure than as financial instruments. Debt holders require regular interest payment and, in the case of default, will exercise preemptive claims against the assets in question. These claims decline as the degree of asset specificity increases. However, the cost of financing will increase and management will favor, therefore, assets of greater redeployability, which might not incur the cheapest production costs or highest quality. Management may also consider using equity. Its governance properties include a residual claim on company earnings, lifetime duration and a board of directors, to name but a few. The board of directors will control management and seek to reduce the cost of capital for

---

160 Williamson details the assumptions about human behavior. First, individuals continue to be rational in the sense that they maximize their utility. Second, human actors behave opportunistically in the sense of showing self-interest. Third, individuals are subject to bounded rationality, implying that the rationality has limits in both storing and processing information as well as in articulating their knowledge comprehensively. See Williamson 1985, pp. 47 et seqq.

161 See Williamson 1988, pp. 579 et seqq.

projects that involve limited redeployability. Equity is 'more forgiving than debt'[162] and will seek to preserve the values of a going-concern.

The asset specificity and governance structure raises some intriguing perspectives for financing LBOs[163]. On the one hand, the specificity and the intangibleness of assets come along, from a transaction cost perspective, at lower cost with an increased equity to debt ratio. Indicators for asset specificity are industries with sophisticated technology and industries with a high level of automation. On the other hand, a focus on growth under uncertainty will be financed at lower cost with increased equity. Indicators for entrepreneurship are growth and innovation leadership strategies, partially independent of the industry sector. The increase of equity after the exit may lower prospective transaction costs related to the investment in long-term projects under uncertainty. Investments with a higher level of specificity may also benefit.

3.2 Agency Theory

The agency theory relies on the delegation of property rights between a principal and an agent and analyzes the related transaction costs, in particular for financial relationships[164]. Corporate managers are typically the agents of shareholders, the principals, described as a 'relationship fraught with conflicting interest'[165]. The theory shares the rejection of a perfect capital market with complete information efficiency with the transaction cost and property rights theory. The delegation of property rights incurs costs of monitoring and control for the principal. The specification of individual rights determines the allocation of rewards and costs among different participants in an organization. Both explicit as well as implicit contracts are the basis for such specifications and determine behavior in organizations, especially that of managers. Contractual agreements and co-ownership by agents influence the related agency costs.

An agency relationship is a 'contract under which one or more persons (the principal(s)) engage another person (the agent) to perform some service on their behalf which involves delegating some decision-making authority to the agent'[166]. The behavioral and risk-related assumptions are: (1) both parties act rationally and are utility maximizers in the relationship and, (2) in most cases, the principal is risk-

---

162 See Williamson 1988, p. 580
163 See Philips, Chang et al. 1983
164 See Jensen and Meckling 1976, Arrow 1985, Ross 1973
165 See Jensen 1986, p. 323
166 See Jensen and Meckling 1976, p. 310

neutral and the agent is risk-averse[167]. The agent is unable to diversify their risk, whereas the principal can undertake various investments. To limit potential divergences due to (1), the principal will include appropriate incentives for the agent.

Three potential conflicts between the principal and the agent can arise. The first conflict lies in the adverse selection of the agent where the latter may claim to have certain skills at the point in time at which they are hired. Since the principal is unable or, only at high cost, to verify completely the skills mentioned, agents with only average or below average skill level may well accept the principal's offer. Adverse selection is referred to as the 'misrepresentation of ability of the agent'[168]. In worst case, the principal will not enter into a contractual agreement with an agent, leading to a failure of markets for employing corporate managers. The second conflict arises when the agent does not engage at the agreed level of effort. You might say the agent is shirking. The agent's intentional underperformance is called moral hazard. The third conflict is due to the different risk preference as mentioned before. The risk-averse agent may not undertake those projects the principal would want to pursue.

In practice, many instruments are used to counter potential conflicts. For adverse selection, agents will strive to reveal upfront any useful private information on their skills and abilities. References from former employers and academic degrees might be relevant indicators. To reveal the underlying hidden information of the agent, a self-selection scheme is introduced whereby managers choose between different contractual agreements. The assumptions and expectations underlying the chosen contracts indicate the hidden information of the agent. In addition, the principal may actively screen the market for information on the individual agent. For unobservable behavior in terms of moral hazard, the principal has the option of either investing in extensive information systems or of introducing outcome-based contracts. Information systems can cover budgeting and controlling systems, reporting procedures and supervisory boards. The systems reveal the agent's behavior to the principal and close potential information asymmetry[169]. An outcome-based contract rewards the agent based on his performance. However, performance variations can occur due to uncontrollable external factors, e.g., economic developments and competitive actions. Supposing the agent is risk-averse, the transfer of the outcome-related risk will incur a payment premium for the agent. Only in the case of a modest uncertainty will the risk costs be justified. In case of high uncertainty, a behavior-based contract will be more attractive. Besides increased payments, the

167 See Eisenhardt 1989a, p. 60
168 See Eisenhardt 1989a, p. 61
169 See Eisenhardt 1989a, p. 61

aforementioned different risk preferences of agent and principal can be solved by separating the outcome by endogenous, agent effort-related, and exogenous, uncontrollable factor-related, effects. The principal might consider separating both effects, e.g., delegating decisions concerning exogenous factors. Therefore, the agent's performance can be measured independently. However, it is nearly impossible for the principal to align the agent at no cost to make optimal decisions for the principal's payout. First, the principal will need to control the agent, incurring monitoring costs. Second, in some situations the principal will pay the agent bonding costs to guarantee that he will not take certain actions, which would harm the principal, or to ensure that the principal will be compensated if the agent does take such actions. Bonding costs include signaling and screening. The researchers refer to the remaining loss in wealth for the principal as residual loss.

The most efficient delegation model minimizes the interest conflict between principal and agent and reduces the so-called agency costs, consisting of the residual loss as well as monitoring and bonding costs. Often, the shareholders of a company suffer from residual loss due to empire building and extensive diversification by management. The governance structure and implied distribution of rights in a leveraged buyout is assumed to reduce the residual loss and decrease the cost of monitoring[170].

3.2.1 Agency Costs of Equity and Debt

In an idealistic model of a company hold completely by an owner-manager, the agent will operate the company to maximize both his pecuniary and non-pecuniary benefits. The utility of non-pecuniary aspects of entrepreneurial activities may cover benefits such as office attractiveness, charity contributions, personal relationships and other slack resources appealing to the manager's vanity. The share of pecuniary to non-pecuniary is determined by an equilibrium of the underlying marginal utility. If the owner-manager sells equity claims, monitoring activities will occur to limit the wealth reduction of non-pecuniary costs. However, the owner will have to bear the entire wealth effect of the monitoring costs, as long as equity markets anticipate these effects. Shareholders will discount the share price by the monitoring costs and losses due to divergence between the owner-manager's and their own interest[171]. Further, the decrease of the owner-manager's shareholdings will reduce his incentive to devote personal effort to increasing wealth, e.g., entering into new markets and developing new product ideas. Such managerial activities require risk-taking and

170 The distribution of rights and implied agency costs are discussed in detail in the following chapters.
171 See Jensen and Meckling 1976, p. 323

personal effort to learn about new market structures and technologies. In the corollary, agency costs of equity consist of (1) the wealth loss caused by non-pecuniary effects of owner-managers and other benefiteurs, (2) monitoring and bonding costs, and (3) residual loss due to a lack of managerial effort, and (4) opportunity wealth loss due to neglected growth opportunities.

The debt holders may also bear residual losses if the agent, the managers, reduce the likelihood of the fixed debt repayments. When the owner-manager has raised debt at a certain promised risk level, he may later choose a higher variance investment with a higher expected value of payout for his equity. However, the debt holders will anticipate the opportunistic behavior and pay only an adjusted price for the debt claims. Similar to non-manager equity shareholders, the debt holder can impose a number of monitoring and control instruments, e.g., detailed covenants for investment policy and dividend payments. These contractual agreements will though never be complete, so bondholders will balance their level of monitoring to their expected benefit. Further, costs arise in the case of bankruptcy. Debt holders will detail contracts with claims on the company, which delineate their rights for all possible contingencies, even though the contracts will always be incomplete[172]. In summary, agency costs of debt, therefore, consist of: (1) the opportunity wealth loss due to the threat of risk-increasing investments due to information asymmetry, (2) monitoring and bonding expenditures by bondholders and owner-managers, and (3) bankruptcy costs.

The consideration of agency costs of both equity and debt is at first an analysis of ownership structure, rather than capital structure. Further, agency conflicts arise between the external and internal equity of owner-managers. Jensen and Meckling argue that outside financing of debt and equity leads to increased agency costs, as the managers (agents) will take additional non-pecuniary benefits since their share of costs has fallen[173].

The model does not explain why in practice one finds public corporations with a separation of ownership and control, and a high share of both external equity and debt. Light is shed when one considers the individual risk tolerance of owner-managers (agent) and external equity shareholders (principal). Risk tolerance among managers is rare. The provided equity, however, is risk-neutral, and enables to invest

---

172 See Jensen 1986, p. 354, Easterwood 1998, pp. 147 et seqq.

173 Jensen, for his initial model, assumes that external equity has no voting right. A manager will, in the case of voting rights in particular, be concerned about the point at which external equity gains control over the corporation and can fire him. Equilibrium will exist where the benefits from reducing agency costs are higher than the costs of reducing the dispersion of ownership. See Jensen and Meckling 1976, p. 352

at a higher share[174]. Investors can diversify their risk over a number of investments. The higher the dispersion of risk in external equity is, the greater the increase in wealth is. Hence, the share of management is stepwise reduced, until management and ownership is quasi separated. A separation with a comparably small share of management equity can be sighted for most public corporations. To counter diverging interests of management and external equity, information and control rights are assigned to equity shareholders. Fama and Jensen propose that the modern corporation is based on the separation of management and ownership[175]. Shareholders as owners are entitled to the residual claims after the obligations to debt holders have been paid. Therefore, the owners bear the risk of zero or even negative returns. On the other hand, managers specialize in decision-making in the corporation and receive compensation. Owners may control the decision-making to some degree, but the separation of ownership and management allows specialization and is the nature of most public corporations.

3.2.2 Agency Costs of Free Cash Flow

Free cash flow is 'cash flow in excess of that required to fund all projects that have positive net present values when discounted at the relevant cost of capital'[176] and are, most notable, under managers' control. On the one hand, management may decide to return the free cash to the shareholders by increasing dividends or repurchasing stock, hence reducing their managerial power. On the other hand, they may invest in projects not earning their cost of a capital or in inefficient, slack resources. Further, they will pursue their individual utility function, e.g., to increase revenue on basis of the positive correlation between revenue and compensation[177], to reduce the risk of loosing their job[178] and other non-pecuniary benefits[179]. In the corollary, conflicts of interest arise between shareholders and managers over the payout policy for free cash flow[180].

Although debt incurs agency costs, it can have a positive, secondary effect on managerial motivation and organizational efficiency. Debt can work as an effective substitute for dividends. A substantial issue of debt binds the management to regular paybacks and reduces free cash flow. In addition, the enhanced likelihood of

174 See Then Bergh 1998, p. 163
175 See Fama and Jensen 1983, p. 302
176 See Jensen 1986, p. 324
177 See Hoskisson and Turk 1990, p.463
178 See Roll 1986, p. 212 et seqq.
179 See Jensen 1989a, p.66
180 See Jensen 1986, p. 324

bankruptcy forces management into disciplined spending and helps to overcome organizational resistance to retrenchment. Not surprisingly, Jensen calls debt 'a powerful agent for change'[181]. Finally, interest payments are tax deductible. The direct and indirect control effects of a high debt load reduce the agency costs of free cash flow and certainly influence the capital structure chosen. A high debt share further reduces the share of equity at a purchase and enhances the return on invested equity.

A potential downside of increased leverage is the greater risk of bankruptcy. The debt to equity-ratio should be limited where the marginal cost of bankruptcy offset the marginal benefits of control. Furthermore, the 'control hypothesis' of debt is, in particular, suited for companies with limited investment requirements. Companies with a need to finance growth will be hindered by debt payments and may have to relinquish value-adding investments.

3.2.3 Agency Costs during the Buyout

Candidates for a buyout regime operate in general in a mature industry[182]. They tend to have a higher level of free cash flow and limited investments with a positive net present value. In the corollary, the costs of monitoring and control enhance. Managers can more easily expand and diversify the business beyond its optimal point, causing residual loss.

Further, agency costs are negatively correlated with the concentration of ownership. The incentive of principals to invest independently in monitoring declines, since they bear the entire cost but have to share the benefits because of shared ownership[183]. Moreover, the enforcement through the board of directors is much easier with a higher equity share and less dispersed ownership. One may argue, that a high share of ownership leads to a risk sensitivity and, in the consequence, to more risk reducing diversification of the business[184].

In the regime of a leveraged buyout, the agency costs are significantly lessened. First, the term 'leveraged' implies a high share of financing with debt and, in the corollary, decreased costs of free cash flow. Further, ownership is concentrated in the hands of few investors, increasing the benefits from monitoring and control. The investors equip the managers with a large share of equity, therefore reducing the incentive for non-pecuniary benefits. Finally, the buyouts are often accompanied by a buyout

181 See Jensen 1989a, p. 12

182 Refer to the characteristics of buyouts as elucidated in chapter A2.2.

183 See Hoskisson and Turk 1990, p. 464

184 See Titzrath 1994, p. 103

investor. The specialists act as active outside investors, however engage closely in discussions on strategic direction and operational improvement programs.

Owner-managers

Considering the effect of increased managerial stockholdings, two hypotheses stand diametrically opposed to one other: (1) the alignment of interest- hypothesis and (2) the management entrenchment-hypothesis. The former hypothesis argues for lowered monitoring costs and residual loss, the latter for an increased residual loss.

The alignment of interest-hypothesis proposes reduced agency costs between owner (principals) and owner-managers (agents/principals). The latter group will reduce their non-pecuniary benefits, since they share the costs related to their percentage of share. An increased share is associated with an increased positive market valuation of the company[185]. The management entrenchment-hypothesis claims that managers with a substantial proportion of shares will reduce their personal risk of unemployment and ensure an attractive salary.

Beyond the related agency costs of managerial ownership, the risk tolerance of management is limited. The separation of ownership and management-rationale proposed by Fama and Jensen argue that risk-bearing capability of managers is limited. Managers with large personal stakes in a buyout have only limited opportunities to diversify their risk[186]. The preservation of their wealth may also prevent management from undertaking projects with higher risks[187].

Shareholders

Equity shareholders typically benefit strongly from the new governance structure. Yet they also have to invest more resources in general advice to and support of the management board in their role as active investors. The tight buyout governance structure reduces the agency costs of free cash flow substantially.

In public companies, a dispersed shareholder structure imposes free-ridership on monitoring the management board. Any efforts of an individual shareholder become a public good. The related return is distributed among the entire shareholder base. Hence, shareholders in a dispersed shareholder structure will under-invest in monitoring activities. In a buyout structure, the equity ownership is concentrated in fewer hands. The investors will participate to a higher degree in their monitoring efforts and, therefore, invest more in gathering information and actively participating

185 See Morck 1988, p. 294
186 See Morck 1988, p. 294
187 See Holthausen and Larcker 1996, p. 295

in decision-making. The so-called control hypotheses, therefore, proposes a reduction in agency costs by a substantially higher concentration of ownership[188].

Active investors are closer to strategic and operational decision-making, e.g., they discuss potential acquisitions and divestitures with the management and sometimes even manage the companies himself[189]. All these activities naturally incur apparently higher monitoring costs. However, without substitution by debt, the equity investors would have to invest a higher amount of capital for the same level of control, supposing the debt holders inherit only limited decision-making power. In addition, they would have to actively secure the excess free cash flow and ensure either increased dividend payments or value increasing investments.

Debt holders

The managers are typically owners and hold a significant share of equity. Further, the external equity investors, e.g., buyout investors, are closely integrated into management decision-making. Information asymmetry, therefore, occurs in particular between management and debt holders.

The debt holder receives fixed payments on his debt. The equity holder benefit only from the residual, and, in the corollary, is comparable to holding a call option, where the option price would equal the maximum loss in terms of the initial capital investment[190]. The asymmetric distribution of corporate profit motivates equity holders to pursue a risky corporate policy. The higher the variance of the profits and the share of debt holders are, the higher the risk is of choosing the 'second best' versus the 'first best' investment alternative[191]. Large creditors can play a similar role as the large equity investors. The debt covenants and related costs of violation give the banks significant power towards management. In Germany, the traditional weak equity market and legal environment favorable to creditors enhances the role of banks[192].

To avoid an increased corporate risk because of moral hazard, debt holders can implement disciplinary mechanisms. First, the debt holders may secure their claims on real property. The provision of collateral should be linked indeed to corporate assets, not to third parties, e.g., insurances. Second, normal debt is rationed. Junk bonds will allow closing the financing gap, yet at higher capital costs. Third, debt

188 See Admati, Pfleiderer et al. 1994, pp. 1124 et seqq., Hoskisson and Turk 1990, p. 464
189 See Jensen 1989a, p. 6
190 See Black and Scholes 1973, p. 649
191 See Green 1984, p. 116, Then Bergh 1998, p. 174
192 See Gorton and Schmid 2000.

holders will focus on buyout companies with the perspective of stable cash flows, revenue growth, low investment need, and sustainable market entry barriers. External factors only modestly affect such companies. Hence, a limitation of lending policy to certain risk classes may avoid having high-risk companies seeking low-risk debt. Fourth, debt holders will demand, besides control rights, decision-making rights over the corporate policy most crucial to their risk position. The buyout investors though are experienced in installing the right debt structure and providing sufficient collateralization[193]. They can use their reputation to find cheaper means of financing and further reduce the costs of debt.

Strip financing and convertibles

Investors, and in particular the debt holders, are often invited to acquire a mixture of debt and equity securities[194]. Both investors and debt holders expect to reduce thereby potential conflicts between debt and equity shareholders and to avoid bankruptcy in the case of temporary insolvency. A debt holder with an additional share in equity can participate in the upside of future value creation and is, therefore, more likely to decide to continue operations[195]. Such 'strip financing', for example by convertible bonds, is an appropriate instrument to reduce agency costs, in particular the costs of bankruptcy[196]. Furthermore, bankruptcy costs can be decreased since refinancing and reorganization do not have to be settled in law courts, but can be solved directly between debt and equity holders.

3.2.4 Agency Costs in the Post-Exit Period

Governance structure will change in dependency of the exit path chosen[197]. LBOs often return to public ownership through a secondary going-public. In this case, ownership will be handed over to new equity shareholders, with a high probability of a significant reduction of ownership concentration. The proceeds from going-public will allow repaying the liabilities and reducing debt leverage. Owner-managers will partially cash out their shareholdings, while reducing their closeness to the owners' interests. Alternatively, LBOs can be sold to strategic investors

---

193 See DeAngelo, DeAngelo et al. 1984, p. 373

194 See Arzac 1992, p. 19

195 See Jensen 1986, p. 326

196 For strip financing to have a meaningful role, the probability of default has to be evident. Investors may strive to detach and sell the individual components of the strip financing instruments. Even if secondary markets are present, theory shows that stripholders have limited incentive to sell separately their strips, as a potential decrease in the bonds in case of a potential crisis if more than offset by the potential increase in equity. See Arzac 1992, p. 20.

197 For a detailed discussion on the changes in the governance structure as an exogenuous factor to the change in agency costs, refer also to discussion and empirical evidence presented in chapter B5.3.4.2 (for going-public) and chapter B5.3.5.2(for trade sale).

through a trade sale, where the shares will be held by the parent company. In this case, the level of debt is subject to the financing policy by the parent company. Further, owner-managers will presumably sell their shares to the acquiring company. In a secondary buyout, the company is passed over to a further buyout investor. The investors endow the capital structure with a high debt share, since they benefit from a relatively small equity investment and the repayment of debt. Further, management remains aligned with owner interests' with managerial shareholdings. In principal, the governance structure remains unchanged. In a management buyback, the changes in governance are ambiguous, with no representative pattern. In some cases, management pays down debt through investment of private wealth. In other cases, managers invite outside industrial experts. For the case studies to be studied, the author will focus on trade sale and going-public as an exit path, since the changes in governance are (i) significant and (ii) homogenous within the exit path.

Debt holders

After the exit from the buyout regime, the positive function of debt as a disciplinary change agent will be substantially weakened, if not in some cases even omitted. Given that in the majority of cases the debt burdened is reduced considerably[198], the level of free cash flow will return to or even beyond prior-buyout levels due to organizational efficiency improvements. Inasmuch as management is not aligned with the interest of the owners, the new investors will have to monitor closely management's decision-making on the usage of the free cash flow. Further, the additional capital beyond the free cash flow[199] from a going-public at the disposal of management will impose further need for control and monitoring.

In contrast, the reduction of debt will lower the likelihood of bankruptcy and costs associated to hedge potential financial distress. The costs of financial distress are highest for firms with relatively unique products that may require future specific investments. In general, buyouts have assets with a high collateralizability[200]. Jensen and Meckling argue that equity holders of a buyout have incentives to expropriate the debt holders during the buyout restructuring[201]. In the consequence, the agency

---

198 Empirical evidence on the change of debt leverage throughout the buyout cycle is presented in chapter B2.1.1.

199 Free cash flow as generated by normal activities from operations, investing and financing.

200 Empirical evidence indicates that costs of financial distress can even deter firms from undergoing a buyout. In a comparison of buyouts and non-buyout, Opler and Titman report higher financial distress costs as an important determinant to undergo a buyout. See Opler and Titman 1993, p. 1996.

201 With appropriate covenants no wealth transfer from debt holders to shareholders can be observed. See the detailed discussion in chapter B2.1.1.

costs of debt will decline after the exit due to equity holders being less motivated to undergo riskier projects.

(Owner-) Managers and shareholders

The reduction of managerial shareholdings will lessen the alignment between ownership and control. Managers may engage less in severe restructuring activities, will stronger seek for non-pecuniary benefits, and may manipulate earnings to maximize short-term profits.

First, the reduction of shareholdings will make a severe restructuring more difficult and potentially demotivate management from a high level of personal efforts in the sense of shirking[202]. Empirical evidence measures that specific investment projects and operational changes require disproportional managerial effort. The management will only undertake such investments if it can capture a corresponding share of the related gains[203]. In addition, enhanced managerial shareholdings furnish management with the organizational power to undertake severe restructuring activities and simplify decision-making, for instance to sell-off underperforming business units and divest inefficient assets[204]. Both equity and debt holders will have to compensate for the decreased self-commitment of management by enhanced monitoring and bonding efforts.

Second, the utility function of a manager will be stronger influenced by non-pecuniary benefits and not be as closely aligned to value creation as during the buyout. In a trade sale, cross-subsidies to other business units and the result of the corporation in total will dilute management's compensation. In addition, the compensation will be tied to size effects, hence leading to an over-tendency towards external acquisition with limited focus on the effect on profitability and company value. Furthermore, management does not have to bear fully the costs of excessive staff and empire-building related to the social prestige of the manager.

Third, moral hazard may also be expected from the diverging planning horizons between principals and agents. During the buyout, management and non-management investors are jointly tied to the exit from the buyout. In the post-exit period, however, there is no deterministic synchronization between management

202 See Hoskisson and Turk 1990, Holthausen and Larcker 1996

203 Kaplan, for instance, consolidates for a sample of transactions in the 1980s that CEOs hold a average of 6.4% of a firm when going-private through a LBO, hence, achieving a personal wealth increase of 64 USD for an increase in equity of 1000 USD. In contrast, the CEO of a public company receives only 3,25 USD on an increase of 1000 USD, including all compensation payments, totaling to only 5.07% of the sum of a private firm (See Kaplan 1988, p. 121). Further refer to DeAngelo, DeAngelo et al. 1984, p. 373

204 See the review of empirical evidence of managerial shareholdings over the buyout cycle in chapter B2.1.4.

and investors investment horizon. Accounting-based financial results as basis for management compensation will lead to short-term profit maximization as opposed to long-term value creation[205]. Further, the top managers may fear to loose their position and, in the corollary, maximize current earnings[206].

On the credit side, the return to the stock market imposes the disciplinary effect of the market for corporate control[207]. A public company has to diligently report on strategic and financial changes, at no cost to the equity holders. If management fails to fulfill stock market expectations, the company may be acquired. Furthermore, the daily stock price is one, if not the most important source of information of the quality of management[208]. Still, myopic investment behavior from the stock market and atomistic ownership structure may dilute the direct and close principal-agent relationship[209]. In a trade sale, the parent corporate board will step in as new principal toward the management of the former buyout. Dependent on the alignment and motivation of the corporate board as the new principal, the monitoring may be more or less intense. Further, non-pecuniary benefits will influence the utility function of the corporate board members. Board members may seek to favor one specific business unit within the corporation and reallocate resources to the disadvantage of other businesses. However, the investment horizon of a strategic investor will be medium- to long-term, whereas a buyout specialist typically invests for a limited time[210].

Agency costs have been proven to decrease when entering into a buyout regime[211]. It is likely that a return to a governance system similar to the pre-buyout regime will again increase agency and weaken organizational performance[212]. Some prominent cases of insolvency and massive layoffs of former buyout companies have dominated the public discussion and lead to a conjecture of wealth transfer, e.g., excessive

---

205 See Rappaport 1978, pp. 82 et seqq.

206 The managers may for instance opt for a linear as opposed to a progressive depreciation and reduce R&D expenses at the cost of future earnings. See also Then Bergh 1998, p. 137

207 See Grossman and Hart 1983, p. 107, Jensen and Ruback 1983, pp. 29 et seqq., Morck 1988, pp. 101 et seqq., Rappaport 1978, p. 84

208 See Rappaport 1990, p. 3

209 The implications of the ownership structure and in particular of the concentration of ownership on the level of monitoring is discussed more closer in chapter A3.4.

210 A more detailed analysis of the motives of the different shareholders is provided in chapter A3.4 on the theory behind corporate governance.

211 The majority of studies on the performance during the buyout period indicate a positive development and a performance level of the buyout significantly above their industry competitors. See an overview in chapter B5.2.

212 For a detailed discussion of the performance implications in the post-exit period please refer to chapter B5.3. See also Muscarella and Vetsuypens 1990, Holthausen and Larcker 1996, as well as Bruton, Keels et al. 2002.

dividend payments, to the buyout specialist. At a closer look, the increase of agency costs due to an inferior governance system may be the cause for the decline in performance. Nevertheless, it is not a matter of course that the performance of a former buyout will deteriorate. The new principals may be able to install a new governance system with reasonable agency costs. The question is much more how the constituents of the governance system - the debt leverage, the concentration of ownership, the individual investor, and the managerial shareholdings - change when exiting the buyout and how they influence managers' decision-making in the long term.

3.3 Resource-Based View

The resource-based view relates the competitive advantage of a company to its idiosyncratic resources[213]. Two important assumptions are the basis for this view: (i) the heterogeneity of (strategic) resources within an industry, and (ii) the imperfect mobility of resources across companies[214]. The resource position may lead to a sustained competitive advantage. Sustainability is hereby understood as a competitive advantage with a strategy toward value creation that cannot be "simultaneously implemented by any current or potential competitors"[215]. Hence, RBV stands in contrast to the market-based view, where competitive advantage is achieved through seizing environmental opportunities and exploiting internal strengths. A change in governance, as throughout the buyout cycle, may change the resource position through changes in control over resources, through changes in funding, and changes in the allocation of funding among the resources.

Within the RBV, performance and strategy are not exclusively dependent on the industry structure as emphasized by industrial organization economics, but on the resource endowment and development of the company. The choice of the resource position is more fundamental to success than the strategic positioning[216]. The specific resource endowment may, for instance, ensure a cost advantage, e.g., by a superior process technology or the ownership of a low-cost source of material. In terms of the resource-based view, strategy is less a quest for monopoly rents based on market power than a quest for Ricardian rents[217]. Resources include all assets, capabilities,

---

213 See Penrose 1959, Barney 1991, Nelson 1991, Peteraf 1993, Prahalad and Hamel 1990, Wernerfelt 1984, Grant 1996

214 See Barney 1991, p. 101, Amit and Schoemaker 1993, p. 35

215 See Barney 1991, p. 102

216 See Grant 1991, p. 117

217 See Barney, Wright et al. 2001, pp.125 et seqq., Grant 1991, p. 117

organizational processes, information, and knowledge controlled by the company, to name but a few[218]. Barney postulates four attributes to resources that have the potential to contribute to sustained competitive advantage. Firstly, resources must be valuable in the sense that they enable the implementation of strategies leading to superior efficiency and effectiveness[219]. Secondly, resources must be rare in the sense that they are not retrievable by other companies and are not the source of the competitive advantage of competitors. Thirdly, resources must be imperfectly imitable in the sense that although observable to other companies they cannot obtain them. Companies with such resources are often innovators with first-mover advantages[220]. Fourthly, resources must be not substitutable in the sense that there must be no strategically equivalent resource[221].

3.3.1 Overview Resource Base

One may now question how changes in the governance structure influence the endowment and development of the resource-based view of a company. So far, the theory indicates that the changes in governance effect the way management develop resources in four aspects: (i) in terms of the strategic control over the resources; (ii) in terms of the funding and investment of resource building; (iii) in terms of the allocation of resources within company's boundaries; and (iv) in terms of the choice among different resources.

The closer alignment of management and ownership allows strengthening the control over the resources of the company. In a multi-divisional company, the business unit management will have a limited disposition over the resources, since the corporate managers will allocate both the resources and their funding to the optimum of the company in total[222]. Buyout researchers argue the re-establishment of control over company's resources to be a beneficial factor during the buyout period. The management can set a boundary and redirect the resources to corporate strategy. In contrast, the trade sale to a strategic investor will reduce the ownership and control over the resources of the company. The new corporate management may pull away the most valuable resources, for instance to a central, cross-functional

218 See Barney 1991, p. 101

219 Only those assets are valuable that help to exploit environmental opportunities and neutralize threats, otherwise they are not considered to be valuable or resources.

220 First, firms can rely on unique advantageous historical conditions, e.g. access to low-price supply. Second, the way the resources contribute to sustained competitive advantage is not well understood and non-transparent.Third, the resources cumulate in a complex social phenomenon, which is hard to manage and influence in a systematic way. See Barney 1991, pp. 105 et seqq.

221 In the case that two sets of resources can be directed toward an identical strategy, the specific resource can no longer be regarded as essential for the resource base. See Barney 1991, p. 111.

222 See Hitt 1991

department, to provide the related competitive advantage to other business units. Furthermore, the less tight control over the resources may diminish the ability to react quickly to changes in the business environment. As suggested earlier, the resource base requires a permanent adaptation, dependent in speed and efficiency on the dynamic capabilities of the management. In contrary to a going-public, where management will continue to have a strong grasp over the resources, a buyout in a multi-divisional corporation may suffer from the loss of control. In the opposite, the reduction of debt leverage in both trade sale and going-public will allow investing in new resources and will strengthen the resource base of the former buyout. During the buyout, the debt payments will limit investments, for instance installing new facilities or recruiting new employees. In many cases, such investments can be crucial to overcome former growth restrictions, in particular after divisional spin-offs. Bacon, Wright and Demina report that buyouts focus on the internal development of resources as opposed to external, in particular acquisitions[223]. Buyouts with a focus on entrepreneurial are, in contrary, often provided with a higher share of equity to permit additional investments. Furthermore, buyout investors increasingly implement a "buy & build" strategy to seize on rents from industry consolidation and increased economies of scale[224]. From a resource-based view, the alignment of managers and owners will determine, in addition, the decision of where to allocate available funds with different return prospects. Executives may favor to fund projects related to personal interest, e.g., questionable R&D projects, or to provide resources with an appreciation to their personal social prestige. Hence, the post-exit may lead to a less efficient allocation of available funding. Finally, the governance and strategy of the investor affect the choice of investing between diverging, yet equal valuable resources. Agency theory proposes that buyouts tend to follow cost leadership strategy based on the efficiency focus from tight debt payments. Hence, they may re-allocate funds for resources with the some prospects of return. Thereby, the direction of funding and developing of new resources will depend on the strategic intention of the new owner.

Some may even go so far to classify the governance of a corporation as a resource itself. Advisors on the supervisory board can be regarded as resources for corporate governance and are, therefore, a part of the managerial resources contributing to the competitive advantage of a company[225]. Barney, Wright and Ketchen argue that the skills to implement and conduct governance are, similar to other resources,

---

223 See Bacon, Wright et al. 2004, p. 327

224 For the specific characteristics on buy and build strategies in Germany, see Hoffmann 2008.

225 See Forbes and Milliken 1999

heterogeneously distributed among companies[226]. Buyout investors, in particular the operating partners, have a significant experience in overseeing companies from a supervisory board position and appoint industry experts to support the monitoring[227]. In the corollary, the investors can gain more insight and reduce the information asymmetry, while offering management a fairer share of the economic gains generated[228]. Even if governance itself is not a source of competitive advantage, "failure to implement the correct governance in a situation can lead companies to not fully realize the benefits of the resources they control"[229].

3.3.2 Categories of Resources and Capabilities

As outlined, research suggests that a buyout regime influences the build-up of specific resources, for instance in the sense of a positive emphasis of the management of human resources[230]. Still, the consideration of the resource based-view as a supporting theory for understanding the changes throughout the buyout cycle is still in its infancy, notwithstanding confirms that RBV has been instrumental in reasoning the increasing entrepreneurship during a buyout[231]. To derive hypotheses on the change of resources throughout the buyout cycle, the author will analyze categories of resources that serve diverse aspects of competitive advantage, whereby only few categories are relevant in the context of an LBO[232].

First, human resources determine how efficiently other resources, for instance technical equipment, are used and under what operational level of productivity a company operates. For the analysis during the buyout cycle one should differentiate between personnel resources and managerial resources. Personnel resources in general include the skills, the accumulated knowledge, and the abilities of non-managerial personnel. The sense of shared responsibility for corporate success and related motivation are thereby the key to superior performance. The increased

---

226 Falsely installed resources for corporate governance may lead to an under-exploitation of general resources under their control, e.g., in non-related diversification or unattractive investments. The resources of corporate governance are also critical to incentivize and control management to undertake the right actions. The effectiveness of supervisory boards is furthermore determined by the level of dedication and time commitment of board members, e.g. boards composed of managers' affiliates with limited access to information and irregular meetings not meeting expected governance contribution (See Barney, Wright et al. 2001, pp. 632 et seqq.

227 See Kester and Luehrman 1995, p. 123

228 See Barney, Wright et al. 2001, p. 633

229 Barney, Wright et al. 2001, p. 632

230 See Bacon, Wright et al. 2004, p. 334

231 See Wright 2001, Wright, Hoskisson et al. 2001, Bruining and Wright 2002, Wegner 2003

232 Barney introduces a broad categorization with physical, human and organizational resources (see Barney 1991, p. 101. Grant details the categorization into physical, technological, human, organizational and reputation resources (see Grant 1991, p. 119).

alignment with ownership and additional freedom in decision-making enhances in most case the motivation of the workforce[233]. Managerial resources refer to the skills, the innate and learned abilities, the expertise, and the knowledge of managers. Their skill set can be distinguished as generic, industry-specific, and company-specific[234]. The managers are the change agent during corporate restructuring. They plan and execute strategic changes, e.g. disposal of non-core businesses and assets. Further, it is their role to conduct severe restructuring and promote entrepreneurial orientation essential for strategic and organizational renewal. During buyouts, a change in the composition of the management board occurs towards profiles with both strong industry and restructuring experience. To strengthen the managerial resource base, buyout investors build typically a strong network of experienced senior managers with the support of the buyout specialist[235]. After the exit, the profile of managerial resources will alter toward industry- and company-specific skills, latter in particular for maneuvering in a multi-divisional corporation after a trade sale.

Second, physical resources comprise the plant with its machinery and equipment, the access to raw materials and the geographic location. Improvements and specifications of the machinery are continuously finetuned to the requirements of the operations of the company and its production processes[236]. Since buyouts in most cases occur in mature industries, efficient manufacturing processes are pivotal to success. Companies will seek to have a high level of automation, leading to specific assets. Buyout investors support the enhancement of operational productivity since these improvements can often be realized in a short period and directly strengthen the operating cash flow.

Third, technological resources initiate innovation in new products and processes. These resources comprise the abilities, skills and experience of the engineers and technicians, especially in R&D. The inherent knowledge of technology trends, new product/market combinations and potential innovations in allied industries are further part of the technological and innovation resources. High-performing organizations rapidly recognize changes in customer behavior and adapt their product offerings[237]. Other companies may opt to build resources to reinvent an idea and conduct a 'first follower'-strategy. Thereby, constant investments in technological resources are required to protect a targeted position within an industry

233 See Fox and Marcus 1992, p. 75

234 See Castanias and Helfat 2001, p. 662

235 See Baker and Smith 1998, p. 112, Kester and Luehrman 1995, p. 122

236 For instance, workers will adjust the setup time for the changeover for a compression mold to the production requirements and increase the operational efficiency.

237 See Peters and Waterman 1982

as new technologies and applications reach the market[238]. Dynamic capabilities related to technological resources are product development routines where managers and leading employees integrate various skills and functional areas to create new products and services[239]. For buyouts, the technological resources are often crucial to ensure the targeted growth momentum.

Fourth, superior financial resources are crucial for buyouts as they provide the means to restructure, and in many cases, to fund new growth, e.g., by entering new markets and developing new products. The buyout investors play an important role as their professionals reconfigure the debt and equity financing to optimize the costs of capital and risk profile[240]. Often, they use their own reputation to improve ratings and reduce debt payments[241].

Fifth, companies can differ in the extent and quality of organizational resources. These resources include routines of coordination and integration within an organization. Furthermore, they may cover the sales force and advertising department. Examples of highly sophisticated routines may be the quality and convenience with which customer requests and quotes are handled within the organization. The quality of planning can also improve organizational routines, e.g., how far the company plans its business, to what level of detail, and how much it anticipates future risks. Other examples may refer to the related speed and effectiveness of decision-making within the organization's hierarchy. Buyout investors support the increase in professional processes throughout the organization by transferring best practice, e.g., through their own expertise and through appointing industry experts[242].

Other resources mentioned[243], e.g., social and reputation, are less relevant in the field of a buyout. Reputation is especially critical for developing new products and entering into new markets. Established companies as the prominent target of buyouts typically have a sufficient level of reputation in place. A similar maturity can be related to social resources relying on the ability to establish close partnerships with external stakeholders, e.g., suppliers and strategic alliances.

The resource-based theory further lies at the heart of the entrepreneur who possesses different beliefs about the value of a resource when converted from input to output.

---

238 See Wernerfelt 1984, p. 174
239 See Clark and Fujimoto 1991
240 See Baker and Smith 1998, pp. 56 et seqq.
241 See Baker and Smith 1998, pp. 76 et seqq., Sharp 2003, pp. 55 et seqq.
242 See Burger-Calderon 2005, p. 49
243 See Grant 1991, p. 119, Brush, Greene et al. 2001, p. 69

Although the heterogeneity lies not with the resource itself but with the expected output, both the theory of entrepreneurship and the resource-based view concentrate on resources as the focal point for competitive advantage and corporate success. Entrepreneurial resources are therefore claimed to have the ability to discern appropriate inputs for future competitive action[244]. Heterogeneous outputs are then the basis for sustainable competitive advantage and require entrepreneurial cognition and discovery, the realization of market opportunities, and coordination of knowledge[245]. Rapid decision-making is key to commercialize business opportunities under uncertainty, often in a brief window of opportunity. Entrepreneurs make extensive use of their individual heuristics[246] and beliefs to assess future market trends. They rely on their personal experience, on their knowledge base, and broad absorptive capacity[247]. On the macro level of the company, resources have to be provided that invest a substantial amount of time and diligence to obtain the information for initiating innovation[248]. On the micro level, individuals in the company exhibit entrepreneurial alertness in the sense that they discover where current products and services do not meet demand. Most companies focus on exploiting current resources to create capabilities and neglect to explore future viability as the environment changes[249]. In a buyout regime, the increased managerial shareholdings may motivate the owner-managers to considerably invest their own time in acquiring new knowledge in unacquainted markets.

3.4 Corporate Governance-Related Perspective

The governance of a company is constituted of multiple interactions of different stakeholders. The corporate governance view seeks to acknowledge the complexity of such interactions on basis of agency theory. Stakeholders analyzed include management, employees, shareholders (to be differentiated between a going-public (direct) and trade sale (mostly indirect principal-agent relationship)), debt holders, and corporate level management (in case of a trade sale), to name the most prominent ones in the post-LBO period[250].

---

244 See Barney, Wright et al. 2001, p. 628, Conner 1991, pp. 133 et seqq.

245 See Alvarez and Busenitz 2001, pp. 757 et seqq.

246 The term 'heuristics' as used in this context refers to the ability to simplify strategies that individuals use to make strategic decisions in complex situations with less or incomplete information based on past experience.

247 See Barney, Wright et al. 2001, p. 628

248 See Mosakowski 1998, p. 627

249 See Levinthal and March 1993, p. 105

250 See Blair 1995, p. 21

3.4.1 Stakeholders in General and their Claims

The governance of a corporation encompasses a system of laws, rules, and factors that control the management and the operations of a company[251]. According to Shleifer and Vishny, the theory and discussion around corporate governance deals with "the ways in which suppliers of finance to corporations assure themselves of getting a return on their investment"[252].

The shareholders are the resident claimants to the company's returns. Debt holders receive fixed payments, employees predetermined compensation arrangements. On the other hand, the various parties make specific investments into the corporation. Employees invest in specialized skills and suppliers in dedicated assets and hence raise their claims to the company's return. Contractual agreements are complex and incomplete in reflecting accurately such investments and relationships[253]. To avoid a demotivation and hold-up of specialized employees, all parties contributing to company-specific investments have to participate in the distribution of the economic surplus[254]. The governance system decides where to spend resources on building organizational capabilities and how to compensate management and employees. Management decides how to use non-human assets given that the usage has not previously been contractually specified. In general, the governance system is a substitute for decision-making that has not been specified in the initial contracts[255]. The claims of the various stakeholders differ significantly, as elucidated in the following[256].

Employees

Employees carry substantial value of the company due to their specific knowledge and experience and are, therefore, co-owners of the company[257]. Their motivation and level of effort is detrimental to the productivity and success of the related company. They invest in trainings and other personal developments to increase their job-related know how. They may also threaten to leave the company with their company-specific training if their salary is below their opportunity costs. Company tenure for the relative salary level and decreasing turnover with higher tenure

---

251 See Gillan and Starks 1998

252 See Shleifer and Vishny 1997, p. 738

253 See Hart 1995, p. 680

254 See Blair 1995, p. 14

255 See Hart 1995, p. 680

256 Since the claims of the shareholders are the central objective to the formulation of a post-exit value creation hypothesis, they are presented in more detail in the following chapter A3.4.2.

257 See Blair 1995, p. 17

indirectly determine the value of company specific training[258]. Therefore, they have to be integrated into decision-making and the distribution of the economic surplus. If employees are confident that they will participate in wealth creation, they will be more likely be motivated und more likely to support any activities to cut costs, even at their own expense.

Supervisory board members

The non-executive, supervisory board members serve as both strategic advisors as well as corporate 'watchdogs'[259]. They face various interest conflicts hindering them from effective supervision. First, they can only contribute limited time and attention since they are typically active senior managers in other corporations[260]. Above the level provided by management, only little diligence is often invested in collecting information and reflecting on potential strategic changes. Second, the motivation to improve corporate performance is limited as they normally do not have a substantial financial interest in the company. Third, the non-executive directors are often closely related to the incumbent management and seek to be re-elected and maintain their presence on the supervisory board. Fourth, they may place too much focus on short-term performance and neglect investments in internal growth and corporate entrepreneurship[261].

The different parties involved in the governance systems of a company are to a certain degree interdependent in the sense of substitutability and complementarity of the various mechanisms in place[262]. A dominant institutional investor can substitute a vivid market for corporate control. Motivated owner-managers, for instance, can compensate for a large blockholder.

3.4.2 Large Investors

Larger owners have a strong incentive to monitor managers since they participate at a higher level in their monitoring efforts. A major blockholder may counteract over-diversification and refocus management on value creation[263]. In the case of a diffuse ownership with numerous small shareholders, the incentive for the individual to bear the costs of monitoring is limited. Furthermore, the incentive of a shareholder is

258 See Blair 1995, p. 16

259 See Short, Keasey et al. 1999, p. 339

260 See Hart 1995, p. 682

261 See the negative effect on corporate entrepreneurship, e.g. R&D expenses, as reported in Baysinger and Hoskisson 1990, Baysinger, Kosnik et al. 1991 and Zahra 1996.

262 See Short, Keasey et al. 1999, p. 346

263 See Berle and Means 1932, Fama and Jensen 1983, p. 306, Hoskisson, Johnson et al. 1994, p. 1212, Shleifer and Vishny 1997, p. 754

diluted when all other shareholders will benefit from his actions without incurring any costs, known as 'free-rider' problem[264]. In contrary, investors with large shareholdings easily exercise control through their voting rights and enforce manager to act in their interest. Thereby, minority shareholders also benefit from intensified monitoring[265].

Concentrated ownership by large investors can leverage up legal protection[266]. A small number of investors with a collectively large cash flow stake may simulate the control rights of a large investor. The increasing occurrence of club deals where multiple buyout investors line up for an LBO confirms the advantage of a collective large stake while diversifying risk. Still, the power of the large investor depends on the enforcement of the voting rights. When minority shareholder rights are strong, they may severely prevent an effective control.

However, various pitfalls from large investors have to be considered. First, enlarged ownership also increases the owner's portfolio risk. The optimal share of ownership will therefore depend upon the difference between the company-specific and private risk[267]. Since the optimal ownership structure is determined by the equilibrium of financing and controlling costs, financing will be more expensive the larger the investment is and the smaller the diversification is. Therefore, widely dispersed ownership structures may be more appropriate for larger, concentrated ownership structures for smaller corporations. Demsetz proposes that the right equilibrium is an "endogenous outcome of competitive selection in which various cost advantages and disadvantages are balanced"[268]. He promotes that diffuse ownership does not automatically fail to allocate resources efficiently and to maximize profit. Second, large investors may enjoy substantial private control benefits. Such benefits can include pecuniary benefits, e.g., assets expropriation, and non-pecuniary benefits, e.g., promoting close friends[269]. Third, large investors may treat themselves preferentially, in particular if their control rights are in excess of their cash flow rights[270]. In Germany, it is not uncommon to control companies with a comparatively small number of voting as opposed to non-voting shares. In addition, German companies repeatedly have power over other companies through pyramid

264 See Grossman and Hart 1981, Shleifer and Vishny 1986, Admati, Pfleiderer et al. 1994

265 See Alchian and Demsetz 1972, p. 778

266 See Shleifer and Vishny 1997, p. 753

267 See Thomsen and Pedersen 2000, p. 691; Kirchmaier and Grant 2005, p. 6

268 See Demsetz 1983, p. 384

269 The extent of private control benefit varies by country due to law jurisdiction. It may be noteworthy, that such benefits can count up to 29% of market capitalization (Italy), whereas the 4% share in Germany seems relatively low (see Nenova 2000).

270 See Grossman and Hart 1987

structures, in which the owner controls 51% of a company, which in turn controls 51% of its subsidiaries, hence minimizing their capital amount invested[271]. An example of preferential treatment may be a special dividend or targeted share repurchases[272]. The relatively small public stock market in Germany may be seen as a result of the weak protection of minority investors. Since they are targeted by expropriation by large, majority investors, they will be less willing to offer finance to the equity markets[273].

Large creditors can balance the power of large investors. If the company misses a payment, the bank can quickly take over control over the asset. Furthermore, the effective legal protection to a dispersed creditor base is likely to be greater than that enjoyed by a dispersed equity shareholder base. Any legal obligation of a company is an obligation to each and every creditor, so any creditor can take action individually[274].

Determinants of Ownership Concentration

Some theorists argue that ownership structures are path-dependent within their institutional context and reflect vested interests[275]. According to the arguments of Bebchuk and Roe, prvious ownership structures affect subsequent structures due to a potentially higher level of rent seeking and efficiency. Powerful interest group may shape the ownership at their own interest, not at the interest of the society. The frequency of an ownership structure, therefore, may not reflect its superior efficiency. Even if the external environment implies a change in ownership, the parties in control may have the incentive and power to impede any changes[276]. Prospective efficiency gains, from which also others would profit, may be more than deteriorated by the loss of private benefits.

However, if considering that the company's ownership structure reflects decisions by those who own it, shareholders will in all cases, whether concentrated or disperse, follow a profit-maximizing interest. Considering insider information of management and performance-based compensation, the performance is as likely to affect the ownership structure as ownership structure is to affect performance[277]. Therefore, this research stream argues that there should be no systematic relation between

---

271 See Franks and Mayer 1994
272 See Dann and DeAngelo 1983
273 See Shleifer and Vishny 1997, p. 760
274 See Shleifer and Vishny 1997, p. 764
275 See Bebchuk and Roe 1999
276 See Bebchuk and Roe 1999, p. 142
277 See Demsetz 1983, Demsetz and Lehn 1985

ownership structure and performance[278]. Much more, they consider a company's ownership structure as endogenous. Factors explaining the apparent differences in structure are scale economies, regulation, and stability of the environment[279].

Identity of Owner and Strategic Objective

Principal and owners will seek to maximize their utility from their shareholding of the company. Not in all cases will this be equivalent to maximizing the shareholder value, e.g., if they have different risk preferences or if they act as intermediate agents, e.g., for banks or institutional investors.

For different ownership categories, the related costs and potential benefits will differentiate strongly. Ownership may be attributed to any stakeholder, e.g., strategic investor, institutional investor, bank, management, government, who are willing to bear the costs of ownership and of market contracting. Further, the ownership may coincide with active involvement, e.g. management, or less active involvement, e.g. shareholders. Ownership implies costs of risk bearing, of monitoring, and with costs related to collective decision-making. The costs of market contracting cover information costs, transaction costs associated by the asset specificity, and potential losses from market power distortions.

Institutional investors differ significantly in terms of activity level and of investment horizon. The less active investors invest little time and leave the companies to a certain degree unmonitored[280]. They spend less time on strategic discussions and instead focus on monitoring financial results. They avoid investing in specific industry and market knowledge to provide independent advice to the management. They often pursue a short-term, myopic investment objective and divest as soon as the share price has passed a pre-defined threshold. More active investors, e.g., pension funds, mutual funds, debt providers and, of course, buyout investors, commit more time into strategic decision-making and urge management towards long-term value creation[281]. Such investors will have a lower risk-aversion and considerably long investment horizon. Since they typically are responsible for a portfolio of companies, they will be concentrated on financial reports. With their utility directed to maximize shareholder value, shareholders can expect a positive effect of ownership of institutional investors on profitability and on value creation.

---

278 See Demsetz and Villalonga 2001, p. 210
279 See Demsetz and Villalonga 2001, p. 231
280 See Short, Keasey et al. 1999, p. 343
281 See Kochhar and David 1996, p. 82

Family owners will seek to realize, beside company growth and profitability, to a higher extent private benefits. They make a long-term commitment to the survival of the company and invest in company-specific knowledge. Since they commit a significant part of their personal wealth into the company, they will be more risk-averse and fear losing control by obtaining equity from capital markets[282]. Therefore, they will be capital rationed and focus on niche strategies with a higher level of differentiation. Corporate ownership allows internalizing and simplifying highly specific transactions, e.g., transactions related to suppliers with high asset specificity and high frequency. An internal capital market may manage the financing. The corporate managers will support diversification and provide financial means for investment into new products. However, they may constrain flexibility and entrepreneurial freedom, with the risk of deficient monitoring. In Germany, a blockholder position of banks is not uncommon[283]. The companies have the advantage to internalize their financing relationships and to have easier access to capital. However, banks may be risk-averse and may have to bear increased costs of monitoring and decision-making from hiring industry experts. Further, they may not be toughest in negotiating with management[284]. Ownership from the government lessens only small parts of transaction costs. However, the government will seek to pursue political objectives, e.g., maintaining high employment and low output prices while protecting the company from market competition[285]. Finally, insiders play an essential role in the governance and performance relationship. Theorists have elaborated two balancing effects: increased ownership leading both to the convergence of interest leading and to management entrenchment.

3.5 Active Ownership and the Governed Corporation

The emergence of active investors such as Kohlberg, Kravis & Roberts and Clayton Dubelier & Rice who have shown tight corporate control has reinforced the idea of the 'active investor'.

Jensen refers to such investors as 'active' investors. They sit on the supervisory board, are involved in strategic and operational decision-making, and closely monitor management[286]. Due to unfavorable legislation and increasing costs of monitoring,

---

282 See Shleifer and Vishny 1997, p. 758

283 See Shleifer and Vishny 1997, p. 754, Thomsen and Pedersen 2000, p. 693

284 See Shleifer and Vishny 1997, p. 773

285 Since it is unlikely that former buyout firms will turn to governmental ownership, a closer analysis is therefore not required.

286 See the introduction to the 'governed corporation' in chapter A3.5 .

financial institutions have left their important role of being an active investor[287]. Jensen refers to the increasing control premium paid and diversification as witness for the low level of corporate control. Jensen enumerates the emerging buyout specialist from the private equity funds, large family funds and private investors as representatives for active owners[288].

The resurgence of the active investor is partially related to the high monitoring costs and unfavorable legislation that impeded financial institutions such as commercial banks from continuing to take on this role[289]. Private equity, e.g., buyout investors, and wealthy investors have instead stepped into the market for corporate control. They successfully lowered the costs of monitoring by increasing managerial shareholdings and installing debt. They are highly motivated by a high participation from the value creation and undergo a more frequent as well as detailed reporting than an external capital market would be able to do[290].

Constituents of governance
A. Resources: skills of supervisory board members
Financial expertise
Industry expertise
Operational expertise
B. Interaction intensity: time commitment of supervisory board members
Investment in strategy and business plan refinement
Regular interaction with board members (CEO and CFO)
Regular interaction with key personnel (e.g., in R&D, sales)
C. Interest alignment: shared objectives (e.g., business plan)
Explicit joint formulation of business/ value-creation plan
Continuous refinement of value-creation plan
Continuous controlling of plan (milestones, etc.)
Discussion on key operations policy making
Active information for shareholders
Usage / free access to (key) employees
Usage of financial key performance indicators
Usage of industry-related / customized performance indicators
D. Interest alignment: personnel policy and incentives
Diligent selection of management board members
Active replacement of management by supervisory board members
Independent (outside) review of board member performance
(Large) share and option packages for managers related to value creation plan
(Large) share and option packages for directors related to value creaiton plan

Table 2: Constituents of governance (author)

However, capital markets have started to duplicate the mechanisms applied by the buyout investors that apparently bridge ownership and management[291]. The extent of usage of the listed constituents of a governance system is dependent on the

287 See Jensen 1989c, p. 36
288 See Jensen 1989c, p. 37
289 See Jensen 1989c, p. 36
290 See Robbie, Thompson et al. 1991, p. 79
291 See Kaplan 1997, Holmstrom and Kaplan 2001

expected benefits of the effort-bearing investor. Since increased shareholdings decrease the likelihood of free-ridership, concentrated ownership is positively related to the activity level of the investor[292]. Furthermore, concentrated ownership is the precedent in terms of having sufficient control of company's assets and sufficient power against the management[293]. Still, concentrated ownership per se does not lead to best governance given the benefit from private control and the favor for control over liquidity and profitability. The differences in governance may be differentiated by the resources and skills provided, by the level of time invested, and by both the formal instruments and personnel policy installed for interest alignment between the agents and principals (see Table 2).

The LBO investors will offer the expertise of their general partners, their investment managers, and of their related advisors. During the transaction, they will commence an intense refinement of the current corporate strategy and long-term plan to their own investment objectives[294]. In many cases, the company has not used external equity prior to the LBO, and confronts the owner-managers with an intense monitoring and shared decision-making[295]. Out of intense discussion with management board members, key personnel and operational managers responsible the investors will develop a business plan detailing the expected business development and implied debt repayment, notably called a value-creation plan[296]. Within the value-creation plan, milestones will be defined, detailing the agreed-on measures and providing the basis for monitoring and management assessment. In addition, the buyout investors will implement a reporting system adapted to monitor cash flow generationand the development of the key underlying value driver. The milestones and reporting system provide the basis for the individual compensation scheme, arranged separately for each manager and combined with a high level of shareholding and variable payment. The buyout investors will assess current management and appoint new managers if required. They will offer outside industry "best practice" and provide constant market feedback[297]. This may include for instance mandating external experts to accelerate strategic and operational changes. Investors will rely upon the refined value-creation plan to follow with the restructuring.

---

292 See Shleifer and Vishny 1986

293 See Lehmann and Weigland 2000, p. 162

294 See Easterwood 1989, pp. 34 et seqq.

295 This change is expected to be more incisive in Germany, since the disciplinary force of corporate control by capital markets is far weaker due to the low level of publicly quoted companies (See Titzrath 1994, p. 176, Franks and Mayer 2001,p.965, Schmidt 2003, p. 14).

296 See Heel and Kehoe 2005a

297 See Pound 1995, p. 91

At a closer look, buyout investors will however strongly differ by the extent of governance and type of instruments they apply. One group of buyout investors may govern the company by simply monitoring the management against the developed value-creation plan. If the company seems to perform below expectations, they will dedicate additional resources to avoid a potential bankruptcy. A different group of investors may truly act as an owner, focusing on rapid operational improvement and providing their industry expertise. They appoint experienced managers to the board; however, they will also quickly exit a bad deal instead of continuing to improve profitability. Finally, buyout investors seeking to provide their in-depth operational knowledge will even go a step further and will actually move into management positions and substantially invest time and resources.

The Managed-Corporation Paradigm	The Governed-Corporation Paradigm
The board's role is to hire, monitor, and, when necessary, replace management.	The board's role is to foster effective decisions and reverse failed policies.
Board Characteristics	**Board Characteristics**
Power sufficient to control the CEO and the evaluation process	Expertise sufficient to allow the board to add value to the decision-making process
Independence to ensure that the CEO is honestly evaluated and that directors are not compromised by conflicts or co-opted by management	Incentives to ensure that the board is committed to creating corporate value
Board procedures that allow outside directors to evaluate managers dispassionately and effectively	Procedures that foster open debate and keep board members informed and attuned to shareholders' concerns
Policies	**Policies**
Separate the CEO and chair (or lead outside director)	Required areas of expertise that must be represented on the board, such as core industry and finance
Board meetings without the CEO present	Minimum time commitment of 25 days
Committee of independent directors to evaluate the CEO	Large options packages for directors
Independent financial and legal advisers to outside directors	Designated critic to question new policy proposals
Explicit yardsticks for judging the CEO's performance	Regular meetings with large shareholders
	Board members free to request information from any employee

Table 3: Managed versus the governed corporation (according to Pound)[298]

Pound introduced two oppositional profiles of governance activity in a company. The governed corporation seeks to reconnect shareholders and management through an intense, shared decision-making process. The shareholder representatives commit themselves to invest substantial time and actively participate in governing the company. They build distinctive expertise to add value to the decision-making process, foster open debate and closely inform management about their concerns[299]. Further, they pro-actively address open issues and take actions against malfunction. In principal, investors in the governed corporation have a significant share of equity

298 According to Pound 1995, p. 93
299 See Lehmann and Weigland 2000, p. 161

and control over the assets[300]. In the case of the managed corporation, the shareholders typically hold small equity stake. The incentive for monitoring is low due to free-ridership. The supervisory board concentrates on financial monitoring and the supervision of management (see Table 3).

A recent survey of Heel and Kehoe has extracted the practices of best governance of buyouts over a series of general partner interviews[301]. They report a consistent out-performance of specific private equity companies, indicating substantial differences in their activities and investment approach. The pattern behind the performance of best practice is referred to as 'active ownership'. The identified constituents of best practice are: (i) a continuous high level of time commitment by general partners in the preparation phase and decisive strategy changes along the '100 days' program[302]; (ii) close interaction with management board[303]; (iii) early changes in the management team if necessary[304]. Further, they report an extensive usage of external support bringing in best practice in operations and administration. Anslinger and Copeland even report a daily interaction between the buyout owner and the CEO through a gatekeeper, typically an investment manager from the financial investor[305]. However, some researchers limit the influence of governance by buyout investors. Pound argues that buyout investors may change the ownership structure but not the quality of decision-making[306]. Much more, the debt control and pressure of the financial sponsor may lead to a dispute and a defense budgeting behavior among board members. The executives could start refocus on internal policy-making.

---

300 See Lehmann and Weigland 2000, p. 161

301 See Heel and Kehoe 2005b

302 Among the best third performing buyout investors, 67% did a complete overhaul of the management plan versus 38% of the underperforming group. This included a significant time share of the leading general partner in discussions with the top management during the first 100 days (on average 50% versus 20% of time spent). Less successful are more reluctant to use external support to implement organizational change during and after the first 100 days. Best practice includes shaping key initiatives, e.g., efficiency improvement and product portfolio restructuring, and at the same time mandating external experts. See Heel and Kehoe 2005b

303 The frontrunners recognized the necessity for a refined performance management system (92%), whereas the laggers (46%) more often left the system unchanged. The best third strove for close interaction with board members and proactively took immediate action to counteract potential threats instead of merely spotting deviation through monthly reports and reacting only when the deviations turned serious. One of the reported key success factors is the close interaction with the CFO and other board members in addition to the CEO. See Heel and Kehoe 2005b

304 83% of the frontrunners appointed additional board members already at the pre-closing stage versus 33% of the laggers. The best third continuously interact with the management to gain a perspective on the managerial skills and commit themselves to tight deadlines for replacements. Further, they leverage their network of trusted advisors to integrate an external perspective and to source new positions. See Heel and Kehoe 2005b

305 See Anslinger and Copeland 1996, p. 106

306 See Pound 1995, p. 91

B Model Building and Hypotheses Development

1 Introduction to the Basic Model

Finance researchers have formulated and analyzed scores of hypotheses for a company going-private. However, only partial aspects have been discussed in the light of the handover to a new ownership regime after a buyout. The author will decompose the model into four levels of analysis: (1) post-exit changes in governance structure (hypotheses 1 to 5); (2) the effect of a new governance structure on management objectives (hypotheses 6 to 12); (3) the effect of a new governance structure on managerial activities and applied levers of value, both strategic and operational (hypotheses 13 to 28); and, (4) the effect of a new governance (post-exit) structure on corporate performance (hypotheses 29 and 30). The following figure illustrates the hypotheses and assumed relationships. These will be presented in the subsequent chapters and delved into in the upcoming case studies.

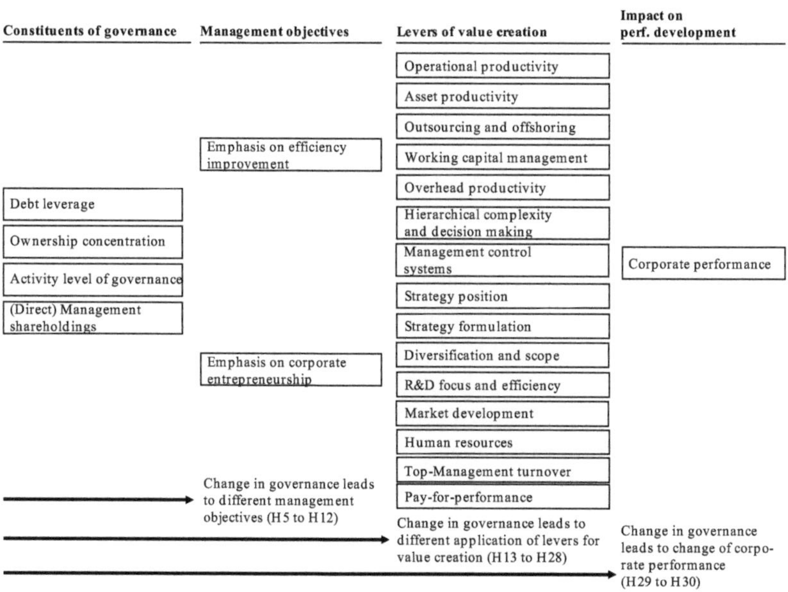

Figure 4: Basic model – impact of governance on management's objectives, on the applied levers on strategy and operations, and corporate performance

The author will elaborate four determining factors for the governance structure: debt leverage, ownership concentration, the activity level of governance, and management shareholdings. These factors will allow capturing the transformation from a buyout to a post-buyout governance structure. One should note that the activity level of governance is related positively to the ownership concentration, since free ridership is reduced. However, the owners can likewise choose the activity level of monitoring independently[307]. In a post-buyout governance structure, the intensity and quality of governance should decrease.

Further, one postulated effect is that the change in governance structure following the exit from the buyout will lead to a change in management objectives. The central assumption is Jensen's theory of free cash flow and the disciplinary and bonding effect of high debt. The author hypothesizes that companies are characterized by inefficiency and slack, and will benefit from improved governance. However, less intense governance after the exit of the buyout specialist with lower debt and less active investors may open the doors to managerial empire-building and lax budgeting. In contrast, the proceeds from a going-public or the broadened resource base from a trade sale will offer new room for entrepreneurial growth.

The changes in management's objectives and emphasis will lead to changes in strategy, structure and operations of the company. During the buyout restructuring, management emphasize efficiency in operations to maximize profitability and cash flow. Measures are implemented to maximize the productivity of the workforce, asset base, and to minimize working capital. Further, management strives to optimize the supply chain toward most cost-efficient production, hence, outsourcing non-core activities and leveraging advantages from low-cost countries. Managers introduce rigid planning and controlling processes, not only to fulfill the information requirements of the buyout investors, but also to increase the general quality of measuring the business. The question therefore arises whether the changes in governance at the exit will lead to a continuation of the focus on high productivity and optimized processes, or whether the changes invite the company to rebuild stepwise, consciously or unconsciously, organizational slack. The same may account for corporate strategy. In many cases, the former emphasis on growth has resulted in a high level of unrelated diversification, which the managers with support by the buyout investors reduce during the buyout restructuring to repay debt and to increase scale within the core business field. The recapitalization after the exit simplifies to again enlarge the strategic positioning and grow not only into related but also into unrelated businesses. Also likely is, that the re-scoping of R& program towards higher efficiency and a closer focus on the company's core growth market will be relieved. To achieve additional profitable growth, the executives will also

---

307 See Jensen 1989c and Pound 1995

seize growth opportunities in new markets, leveraging existing product strength and resources. An undiluted focus of the owners on strategic decision-making for long-term value creation will allow, in addition, the strengthening of the resource base, especially in the fields of key personnel. However, the change in governance at the exit may lead to a re-assessment of top managers and an increased turnover. It is also likely that the degree of pay-for-performance will in average be reduced.

Finally, the post-LBO governance will cause changes in corporate performance. The empirical evidence suggests that the buyout restructuring is beneficial to cash flow and operating profit. The increases in profitability thereby accrue not at the expense of long-term investments. Inasmuch as the governance structure of the buyout is beneficial, it remains open how the post-LBO governance influences corporate performance. Clearly, a decrease of debt and of managerial shareholdings will presumably increase agency costs and may weaken financial and operational performance.

Many of the postulated relationships have been verified by extensive surveys for the buyout restructuring, many, however, with inconclusive results. Buyout researchers have examined only a small number of relationships in the post-LBO period. It is an open question if the doubtless beneficial disciplinary effect of a buyout governance structure can be prolonged to the post-buyout period. Most research reports a decline towards higher agency costs and towards the lower pre-buyout profitability in a short time period after the exit, leaving an aftertaste of short-term financial gain by the buyout investors.

One should note that the model is relevant to companies regarded suitable for the benefits of a leveraged buyout governance structure, e.g., un-levered companies operating in mature markets with stable and predictable cash flows[308]. Non-appropriate candidates are believed to have weaker or even contradictory relationships between governance structure, management objectives, value levers applied and their influence on corporate performance.

In the following chapters, the author will detail the four levels of analysis according to their underlying assumed relationships. The current status of research will be discussed, and, if conclusive, a hypothesis formulated as the basis for the empirical part that follows.

308 See the details on criteria for buyouts in chapter A2.2.

2 Post-Exit Changes in the Governance Structure and Managerial Objectives

Singh, in his attempt to explain management's willingness for drastic changes, once concluded:

> "'The substantial change in governance of the company may be the new context in which entrepreneurial decisions are made. [...] The engine which drives the operational changes in companies undergoing buyout relates to radical changes in governance of the company - new incentive structure, increased ownership structure, a more focused board and a omplete reexamination of operational strategy"309.

In the following, the author will describe in detail how the constituents of the governance structure - debt leverage, ownership concentration, activity level of governance, and managerial shareholdings - change over the buyout cycle.

Buyout researchers have undergone only sparse research on the changes in the governance and the related agency costs at the exit of the buyout, both from a theoretical modeling and from an empirical research perspective. To close this gap, the author will review current findings on the changes in the governance constituents over the entire buyout cycle. On the basis of agency and governance theory and selected empirical evidence so far, the author will further formulate differentiated hypotheses for the proposed change of the individual constituents and, if indispensable, dependent on the chosen exit channels.

After a review of the financial performance of reversed buyout, Holthausen and Larcker report:

> "Our tests at least provide some evidence that there is a decline in performance subsequent to the reverse LBO and that this is related to the change in the ownership structure after the reverse LBO. [...] Our analysis indicates that [...] they (buyouts) retain some of the ownership structure of a typical U.S. corporation, as opposed to moving back toward an LBO-like structure."

The interesting question, therefore, will be whether the changes at the exit are a return to the prior-buyout structure or are the birth of a significantly different governance structure allowing post-buyout superior performance.

---

309 See Singh 1990, p. 127

2.1 Changes in Governance Structure at the Exit

2.1.1 Debt Leverage over the Buyout Cycle

Undoubtfully, the increase in debt leverage at the entry into a buyout transaction is significant. In the first wave of buyouts between the end of the 1970s to the mid 1980s, surveys report increases from debt to total capital from around 20 to 30% to 70 to 80% after the completion of the transaction[310]. In the mid- to end- 1980s, the leverage shifted to an average of 90%, caused by the emergence of specialized high-yield bond issuers and a prospering stock market[311]. After the overheating of the high-yield bond market, the lender's appetite for high leverage was appeased, leading to lower debt levels and remarkably reduced buyout activity. To the extent that debt increases in a buyout, one can expect it to decrease after the exit from the buyout governance structure.

A closer look at the key determinants of the debt level of a company will help to understand the changes and differences in the post-exit development of debt. The author will review the empirical evidence of the debt level over the buyout cycle.

Key determinants of debt level

Instead of referring to debt as exogenous, the author investigates how far debt is determined by endogenous characteristics. One key determinant is the company-specific risk. Higher earnings volatility increases the probability of bankruptcy and financial distress costs. The trade-off theory claims that the increased default probability reduces the debt capacity[312]. According to agency theory, owner-managers are more willing to engage in growth opportunities and increase their personal effort if the business is risky and offers them the possibility to participate in the upside[313]. Without risk, debt holders have no agency costs and managers benefit from value upside. Therefore, a company with higher risk leads to higher agency costs and decreases the extent of senior debt. A review of empirical studies shows an inconclusive picture, with a preference towards a negative relationship between risk and leverage as predicted[314]. A further determinant for leverage is the expected growth of the company. Growth opportunities are similar to options and bear substantial risk. In the case of default, the value of growth options are not tangible, consequently, excessive growth should be financed with equity. Monitoring of the

310 See Marais, Schipper et al. 1989, Kaplan 1989a, Baker and Smith 2000
311 See Muscarella and Vetsuypens 1990, Kaplan 1991, Kaplan and Stein 1990
312 See Johnson 1997, p. 54
313 See Myers 1977
314 See Jensen, Solberg et al. 1992, Friend and Lang 1988, Kühn 2006

choices among the growth options will be required, alongside with decreased bonding of debt[315]. Hence, the considerable growth options should be balanced with lower debt levels. The majority of empirical research confirms the negative relationship[316].Another prevailing factor for determining the right debt level is the company size. As persuasive as the fact that diversification increases with size, larger company are less volatile and therefore allow higher debt level. Larger companies may correlate with company age, and expect lower monitoring costs. The majority of studies have so far have p roved the positive relationship. Furthermore, profitability is a determinant for debt levels, if not presumably the strongest. The static trade-off theory argues that higher earnings are less likely to lead to bankruptcy and benefit from an increased tax shield. On the other hand, high free cash flows lead to higher agency costs and require stronger bonding. From both theories, a higher profitability comes along with higher debt levels. On the flipside, the pecking order theory proposes that higher internal funds lead to higher equity share[317]. The empirical evidence supports a negative relationship, confirming the pecking order theory[318].

In terms of the likelihood of a corporate default, fixed tangible assets enable a higher collateralization. The lenders have a higher liquidation value and will allow higher debt levels. Controversially, some theorist have claimed that higher depreciation of higher fixed assets reduce the benefit of tax-deductible interest[319]. Empirical research shows clear evidence for a positive relationship of fixed assets to debt level[320].

One may conclude that risk and growth enhance volatility and, in the corollary, reduce debt propensity. Increasing company size and profitability, however, endorse financing by debt. Further, a higher share of tangible assets allows higher debt levels. How these factors influence the chosen debt level at the exit of the buyout regime depends on the new owners and their strategic plan. The strategic plan or, to put in a more general context, corporate strategy has often been postulated and in many dimensions been proven to be a determinant of capital structure, with some researchers even proposing a 'strategy-capital structure' relationship analogous to the ‘structure follows strategy’ relationship[321]. However, in the light of the operations of the buyout being continued after the exit, some dimensions of strategy can be

---

315 See Smith and Warner 1979

316 See Lang, Ofek et al. 1996, p. 10, McConnell and Servaes 1990, p. 150, Kühn 2006, p. 116

317 See Friend and Lang 1988, p. 277, Titman and Wessels 1988, p. 6, Frank and Goyal 2003, p. 23

318 See Friend and Lang 1988, p. 278, Kühn 2006, p. 119

319 See Kim and Sorenson 1986, p. 137

320 See Rajan and Zingales 1995, pp. 22 et seqq., Philips and Mackay 2002, pp. 18 et seqq., Titman, Hovakimian et al. 2001, p. 12

321 See Barton and Gorton 1988, Balakrishnan and Fox 1993, Prasad, Bruton et al. 1997

assumed to remain constant, others to be adapted to the new governance structure and to the behavior of the owners. One of the major dimensions is the risk propensity of management. Empirical surveys indicate that management adapts the company's debt level to their individual risk profile. Gorton and Schmid, for instance, investigate different risk profiles and report a lower debt level for risk averse-managers, which is indicated by limited diversification[322]. At a given level of risk, managers may also align the asset structure with the debt level. Research reports an inverse relationship between financial and operating leverage, the latter determined by the level of fixed, dedicated assets in relation to the total capital base[323]. A lower share of the total value chain accomplishes a decrease in operating leverage, thereby implying a higher usage of outsourcing, and leads to reduced fixed and increased variable costs[324]. Since the risk propensity may differ between former and new owners, the capital structure ceteris paribus may change. Other dimensions, e.g. the preference for internally generated funds and contextual variables, are company-specific and more or less constant throughout the change in ownership.

Debt leverage over the buyout cycle in Germany

With respect to the empirical evidence for the debt level over the buyout cycle, the empirical evidence for Germany is scarce. In particular, no study has been conducted that analyzes the expected debt de-leverage at the exit. Thereby, the studies reviewing the change in leverage during the LBO restructuring offer an inconclusive picture.

Forst reports a significant increase of debt to total capital for succession-based, family buyouts, even though the increase is moderate in comparison to US-studies. For the spin-offs in his sample group, the leverage decreases. The high leverage is typical for spin-offs that operate as a business unit within a large corporation and benefit from the financing by the parent. Forst argues that the high pre-buyout leverage is related to the tax advantage of such a construction and does not reflect the result of an independent financing process[325]. For the observed buy-ins, the leverage enlarges notably from 60.5% to 80.0% in debt to total capital. The increase corresponds to the restrictive investment policy of the former owners, which yields a high level of equity and under-utilized debt propensity[326].

---

322 See Barton and Gorton 1988, Balakrishnan and Fox 1993,

323 See Prasad, Bruton et al. 1997, pp. 48 et seqq.

324 The extent of outsourcing will be discussed as lever of value creation in light of the buyout and in light of the post-exit changes. See chapter B3.2.3.

325 See Forst 1992, p. 23

326 See Forst 1992, pp. 45 et seqq.

Author	Year	Sample size	Observed time period	Data source / type	Geo-graphical focus	Total debt share (as debt to total capital[b])		Senior debt share (as debt to total capital[b])		Subordinated debt share (as debt to total capital[b])		Other debt share (as debt to total capital[b])	
						Before	After	Before	After	Before	After	Before	After
1. Change in leverage for US-based buyouts													
DeAngelo DeAngelo Rice (1984)	1973 to 1980	72	[t-20 to t] days	Public (de-listing)	US	*n/a*	*n/a*	*n/a*	*n/a*	14.4%	*n/a*	*n/a*	*n/a*
DeAngelo (1986)	1973 to 1982	64	[t-1] days	Public (de-listing)	US	*n/a*	*n/a*	*n/a*	*n/a*	18.1%	*n/a*	*n/a*	*n/a*
Marais Schipper Smith (1989)	1974 to 1985	113	[t-1 to t] days	Public (de-listing)	US	30.0%	73.8%	*n/a*	*n/a*	*n/a*	*n/a*	*n/a*	
Kaplan (1989a)	1980 to 1985	76	[t-1 to t] days	Public (de-listing)	US	20.7%	85.6%	*n/a*	*n/a*	*n/a*	*n/a*	*n/a*	*n/a*
Muscarella Vetsuypens (1990)	1976 to 1987	24	[t-1 to t] days	Public (de-listing)	US	41.4%	90.6%	*n/a*	*n/a*	*n/a*	*n/a*	*n/a*	*n/a*
Kaplan (1991)	1979 to 1986	33	*n/a*	Public (de-listing)	US	*n/a*	91.0%	*n/a*	*n/a*	*n/a*	*n/a*	*n/a*	*n/a*
Kaplan Stein (1990)	1980 to 1989	124	[t-1 to t] days	Public (de-listing)	US	*n/a*	89.1%	*n/a*	50.3%	*n/a*	*37.0%*	*n/a*	*1.8%*
Cotter Peck (2001)	1984 to 1989	64	[t-1 to t] days	Public (de-listing)	US	*n/a*	70.0%	*n/a*	44.5%	*n/a*	20.7%	*n/a*	4.8%
Wu (1996)	1980 to 1987	87	[t-1 to t] days	Public (de-listing)	US	*n/a*	*n/a*	*20.7%*	*n/a*	*n/a*	*n/a*	*n/a*	*n/a*
Kaplan (1991)	1979 to 1986	22	[t] day	Public	US	*n/a*	60.7%	*n/a*	*n/a*	*n/a*	*n/a*	*n/a*	*n/a*
2. Change in leverage for Germany-based buyouts													
Luippold (1991)	1983 to 1990	31	*n/a*	Survey	Germany	*n/a*	78.5%	*n/a*	54.6%	*n/a*	23.9%	*n/a*	*n/a*
Forst (1992)	1976 to 1991	14	*n/a*	Sucession-based/ family	Germany	69.0%	79.3%	*n/a*	*n/a*	*n/a*	*n/a*	*n/a*	*n/a*
Forst (1992)	1976 to 1991	14	*n/a*	Spin-offs	Germany	71.3%	69.9%	*n/a*	*n/a*	*n/a*	*n/a*	*n/a*	*n/a*
Graeper (1993)	1981 to 1989	36	*n/a*	Survey	Germany	*n/a*	69.8%	*n/a*	*n/a*	*n/a*	*n/a*	*n/a*	*n/a*
Vest (1995)	1985 to 1991	29	*n/a*	Survey	Germany	*n/a*	79.7%	*n/a*	59.4%	*n/a*	20.3%	*n/a*	*n/a*
Jakoby (2000)	1976 to 1996	62	*n/a*	Survey	Germany	*70.0%*	*63.7%*	*n/a*	*n/a*	*n/a*	46.3%	*n/a*	*n/a*
Wegner (2003)	1990 to 1999	31	*n/a*	Survey	Germany	*n/a*	67.7%	*n/a*	*n/a*	*n/a*	*n/a*	*n/a*	*n/a*

Table 4: Change in debt leverage and structure at the entry into the buyout

Jakoby rejects the hypothesis of a significant change in leverage and reports a slight decrease in leverage[327]. Potential reasons for the more or less constant leverage are not further detailed by the author, but may relate to the high share of retail and business services sectors among the buyouts[328], which traditionally have a lower propensity for collateral loan. In addition, the deal sizes seem rather small[329]. A more recent survey by Wegner for the German market reports a slightly lower leverage of 67.7% of debt to total capital. A possible explanation for the moderate leverage, assuming the debt market is more experienced and offers tailored instruments, is the higher share of growth-oriented buyouts also in Germany. Wegner compares the differences between growth and non-growth buyouts, and finds an average debt ratio of 56.8% for growth versus 74.5% for non-growth buyouts. Recent deals confirm a considerable increase in leverage. For instance, the investors raised debt by 236% from 2002 to 2001 at the auto parts retailer ATU, after the sale of 72% of equity by the founder family to Doughty Hanson[330]. A similar example is Peguform, a manufacturer of plastic parts and modules for the interior and exterior of automotive vehicles, which increased its debt by 191% from 2002 to 2001. Kloeckner Werke AG sold Peguform, which is now in the 100% ownership of Venture Holding Trust.

Nevertheless, no studies have systematically elucidated the change in leverage. The surveys on the capital structure of German buyouts of the late 1980s and early 1990s indicate a similar debt to total capital ratio of 70% to 80% during the buyout, similar to the ratio of the aforementioned US studies.[331]. What is noteworthy is that the studies indicate a strong correlation of subordinated debt and mezzanine capital with company size[332]. Implications on repayment schedules, governance structures and performance developments are limited due to the small sample size and data quality. Jakoby reports a higher share of mezzanine capital for successful buyouts[333].

---

327 Jakoby reports four separate measurements: (1) for less successful buyouts before the transaction an equity to total capital ratio of 32,8% (n=23); (2) for successful buyouts before the transaction an equity to total capital ratio of 26,9% (n=21); (3) for less successful buyouts after the transaction an equity to total capital ratio of 31,4% (n=30), and (4) for successful buyouts after the transaction an equity to total capital ratio of 41,0% (n=32). See Jakoby 2000, p. 262

328 See Jakoby 2000, p. 157

329 The BVK reports for the year 1996 (the last year of Jakoby's sample) total investments for 257 buyouts and buyins account for 1149,6 billion DM. Supposing a average equity to debt ratio of 1:3, the average deal size is 17.9 Million DM, approximately 39% (average deal size for the successful firms of 10.3 Million DM) and 74% (average deal size for the less successful firms of 12.9 Million DM). See Jakoby 2000, p. 302.

330 A debt to total capital at market value comparison is not available since ATU remained private.

331 The studies may be not representative due to the small number of buyouts at that point in time. See the comments in Hoffmann and Ranke 1990, p. 49. For the conducted surveys, see Luippold 1991, p.341, Gräper 1993, pp. 110 et seqq., Vest 1995, p. 245.

332 For smaller buyouts, Forst reports that 36.8% use mezzanine capital with an average share of 28.9%. Whereas Luippold reports that 61.5% rely on mezzanine capital, with an average share of 23.9%.

333 Jakoby reports a share of 56.6% (n=7) for mezzanine capital to total capital for successful buyouts versus

The decision to use mezzanine capital may reflect the level of experience, since it was a new instrument in the market and less-experienced managers may not have considered it[334]. The leverage is remarkable in light of the under-developed market for debt instruments in the 1990s. In addition, it is high in contrast to the conservative, in some cases even risk-averse attitude[335].

To summarize, the increase in leverage is significant for LBOs, with a clear indication for the US market, but also rather conclusive indication for the German market. However, the change seems to be less significant for smaller company sizes, whereas other factors, e.g., former investments restriction, partially require higher equity provision in a buyout ownership structure.

Change in debt level and exit channel

Empiricists have analyzed the change in leverage given the availability of public data for IPO. The surveys, which cover US companies, confirm the proposed decrease in leverage and intended reduction in financial distress for the buyouts going-public.

				Total debt share (as debt to total capital)		Senior debt share (as debt to total capital)		Subordinated debt share (as debt to total capital)		Other debt share (as debt to total capital)	
Author	Year	Sample size	Observed time period	Before	After	Before	After	Before	After	Before	After
Muscarella Vetsuypens (1990)	1976 to 1987	72	[t-1 to t] days	78.0%	56.0%	*n/a*	*n/a*	*n/a*	*n/a*	*n/a*	*n/a*
Mian Rosenfeld (1993)	1983 to 1988	40 (97)	[t-1 to t] days	*n/a*	*n/a*	*n/a*	*n/a*	55,2%	30,3%	*n/a*	*n/a*
Holthausen, Larcker (1996)	1983 to 1988	90	[t-1 to t] days	83.0%	56.0%	*n/a*	*n/a*	*n/a*	*n/a*	*n/a*	*n/a*
Jalilvand Switzer (2002)	1981 to 1992	200	[t-1 to t] days	83.7%	52.3%	*n/a*	*n/a*	*n/a*	*n/a*	*n/a*	*n/a*

Note: all surveys encompass IPOs with a geographical focus on the US

Table 5: Change in debt structure ownership from pre- to post-exit

From the investor perspective, the exit from the buyout via a going-public is motivated to monetize the value creation during the holding period, after having resolved the problems of high agency costs. From the company perspective, the return to stock market is motivated to reduce the financial distress costs and to raise new capital. A highly leveraged capital structure often limits investments to those necessary to maintain competitiveness and adapt to changing business environments[336], however, prevent the company from entering into growth investments (so-called under-investment hypothesis)[337].

36.0% (n=7) for less successful buyouts. See Jakoby 2000, p. 267

334 Jakoby relates the success to the increased liquidity during the buyout for the companies (see Jakoby 2000, p. 266. A correlation of the participation of buyout investors versus the usage of mezzanine capital is not provided.

335 See Jakoby 2000, p. 259

336 See Rappaport 1990, Kester and Luehrman 1995, Jalilvand and Switzer 2002, p. 4

337 See also the discussion on the change in capital expenditure in B3.2.2.

Companies that are severely suffering from the financial inflexibility show a positive correlation performance development after a greater decrease in leverage than their competitors do. During the buyout, the companies repay a substantial amount of their debt, as measured by Muscarella and Vetsuypens with a decrease from 90.6% to 78.0% of debt ratio from the entry to shortly before the exit from the buyout[338]. The proceeds from going-public allow repaying a considerable debt amount, with the surveys reporting a decrease in the debt to total capital ratio from around 80% to 55% (see Table 5). Holthausen and Larcker, for instance, report that 57% of survey participants used their entire proceeds for repayment[339]. The authors also elucidate that the companies continue to carry an above average leverage, even after their de-leveraging. Jalilvand and Switzer measure similar magnitudes of decrease in leverage at the exit. In addition, the authors find proof for the costs of financial inflexibility, since those LBOs with the greater decrease in leverage have the smallest decrease in performance[340]. One explanation is the usage of secondary offerings from the buyout investors at the exit that do not result in proceeds to the company. A de-leverage only occurs if the company brings a primary offering to market after a capital increase. Notwithstanding the latter observations, the hypothesis should be formulated as:

Hypothesis 1a: The debt leverage after the going-public of a buyout is expected to decrease.

A trade sale is a feasible instrument to increase the revenue base of the acquiring company. Further, the acquisition of a new company is intended to accelerate the growth of the acquirer, by accessing new customer groups and adding valuable resources and technologies, to name but a few[341]. Beside growth endorsement, the acquisition will enable the achievement of economies of scale and scope, resulting in considerable cost savings. Therefore, the investment objectives differ substantially from a financial investor. A buyout investor places equity to achieve a substantial value creation through both deleveraging within a short- to medium-term period and growth of underlying cash flow in terms of exit valuation. The investors focus - from the day they screen the potential candidate - on the exit. On the other hand, a

338 See Muscarella and Vetsuypens 1990, p. 1408 to 1409

339 Other purposes reported for the proceeds are investments into working capital, general corporate purposes, capital expenditure, retirement of preferred stock and acquisitions. See also Holthausen and Larcker 1996, p. 302.

340 See Jalilvand and Switzer 2002, p. 10

341 See the importance of revenues and growth as performance indicators at corporations versus financial investors (See Schmalenbach-Gesellschaft 2006, p. 242 and p. 259)..

strategic investor is interested in the long-term survival of his own company[342]. They will dedicate the cash flow to NPV-positive projects within the company and retain profit for future investment. An important determinant of the debt level is the capital structure on the corporate level. Often, the capital structure of a business unit is to a lesser extent optimized to the unit-specific risk level and growth expectations, but to a larger extent installed to duplicate the corporate capital structure. Furthermore, the business unit capital structures are diluted by short-term tax and legal concerns, even when the units are separate legal entities. Consequently, the capital structures do not fully reflect an independent financing decision. Further, growth by acquisition is more likely from management with low disciplinary power, high free cash flow and entrenchment. Research indicates that high managerial entrenchment leads to lower debt leverage, as the responsible managers avoid high risk and dislike performance pressure by debt holders[343]. The risk aversion against financial distress and high leverage is an untypical situation for non-buyout investors and will lead to a certain level of discomfort by management. The new owners may fear that they will have to control frequently the liquidity.

To summarize, one would expect, besides reduced volatility that the growth perspectives and long-term investment horizon lead to decreased debt leverage in a trade sale. Empirical research indicating the assumed relationship is sparse, since a trade sale typically does not require a disclosure of the deal terms. Still, a higher relative debt level in the post-exit period in a trade sale is reported to be beneficial to value creation[344]. Balancing the arguments and evidence, one should propose:

Hypothesis 1b: The debt leverage after a trade sale of a buyout is expected to decrease.

Debt Structure and Maturity

The total amount of debt is, however, not the primary indicator for the disciplinary force of debt on management, much more it is the actual debt service payments per period[345]. Debt with a short maturity will impose higher debt payments per period, while subordinate debt will have a longer lifetime and require lower payments. Private and senior bank loans are more likely to have restrictive covenants than publicly traded corporate bonds and junk bonds[346] Private lenders will monitor

342 For instance, the survey of the Schmalenbach-Gesellschaft 2006 report that over 84% of the spin-offs of large corporations have a holding period of more than 9 years.

343 See Fama 1980, Berger, Ofek et al. 1997

344 See Seth 1990, pp. 443 et seqq.

345 See Jensen 1986, p. 324, Cotter and Peck 2001, p. 102

346 See Smith and Warner 1979,

management much more closely than representatives of public issues of subordinated bonds. Hence, a higher share of short-term and senior debt imposes a higher disciplinary effect of debt on a buyout structure than subordinated and long-term debt[347]. Buyout investors have a strong reputation of closely monitoring management and positively affect the monitoring costs of debt. Their active monitoring may be regarded as a substitute for tighter debt terms and shorter maturities. Consequently, the optimal capital structure changes towards more long-term debt. Empirical research has proven that buyout without experienced buyout investors engaged have a lower average maturity of debt[348]. A possible interpretation may be that the buyout investors regard their own monitoring efforts as more efficient than installing disciplinary debt. The disciplinary forces of debt to performance are proven to be independent of the maturity, whereas the use of senior and short-term debt in non-buyout specialist-controlled buyouts improves operating performance.

Over time, different types of debt tailored to the specific requirements and securitization possibilities have emerged. 'Hard' physical assets of the company secures senior debt, which typically comes in two different forms. First, senior term debt is placed against the assets (property, plant and equipment) and takes priority over all other sources of finance for servicing. Notably called 'term' loan, the repayments follow a fixed interest and schedule, similar to a mortgage. It often covers the biggest share of debt and will have, due to the seniority, the lowest interest rate. Second, working capital flows, e.g. accounts receivable and inventory secure overdrafts and working capital revolver as a subset of senior debt. It is also typically contracted with a fixed term, but may be adjusted to changing requirements from working capital. Future cash flow and equity-like supplements secure the mezzanine financing. The repayment is subordinated to the senior debt and therefore has longer terms, e.g., from 5 up to 15 years. A higher premium to the prime rate than senior debt, often combined with an equity kicker in the form of a convertible bond or income adjustment bond, reflects the advanced risk[349]. The form of placement, either in private or public capital markets, characterizes mezzanine

---

347 See Cotter and Peck 2001, p. 102

348 In a review of transactions in the late 1980s, Cotter and Peck compute an average maturity of 9.19 years for buyouts controlled by specialists, while management-controlled (7.82) and investor-controlled buyouts (6.59) have a significantly shorter maturity, indicating a lower share of disciplinary senior debt. Further, the authors find within the group of buyout investors-controlled firms no correlation between the debt structure and performance within the group of buyout specialist-controlled firms. They propose that firm performance under this investor group will improve – with or without using senior debt. See Cotter and Peck 2001, p. 129

349 See Becker 2000, pp. 45 et seqq.

capital. In Germany, the former group is equivalent to subordinated debt and may cover seller's note and options for participating in capital increases[350]. The latter group, the high yield bond market, includes such instruments as convertible bonds, going-public warrant bonds or participation certificates[351]. High yield bonds are tradable securities, underwritten by an issuing investment bank, and traded in the open bond market. Securities are less risky, which entitle the purchaser to charge over the company's cash flow. Investment banks sell these into the market. In Germany, the participation certificate is very common since, under certain circumstances, the tax authorities treat them as debt for tax accounting[352]. If equity is sparse, cash-flow minimized securities may yield the necessary financial flexibility. Zero-coupons bonds and payment-in-kind securities defer the debt service obligations past the critical transaction period. These arguments should be well balanced against Myers contracting-cost hypothesis. The hypothesis proposes that long-term growth options of a company's investment opportunity may inspire debt providers to require a higher share and to increase their prices. Hence, companies should carefully balance short-term debt to avoid over-pricing[353]. As argued, debt-deferred securities are positively correlated with higher growth[354]. Such debt-deferred securities are in particular used when acquisition premiums have been high and incur immediate debt repayment[355]. Beyond company-specific reasons, Kaplan and Stein as well as Roden and Lewellen report an increasing use of subordinate, debt-deferred securities in 1980s reflecting a general trend toward more flexible financing[356].

When anticipating the maturity structure at the exit of a buyout, the implications seem inconclusive. On the one hand, the departure of the buyout investors may lead to an increase in short-term debt to install a bonding agent to keep the focus on

---

350 A seller's note, for instance, allows the acquirer to delay the payment of the purchase price, therefore, increasing the trust of the investors in the deal. As compensation, the former owner may participate if the cash flow achieves a certain threshold in the form of an 'equity kicker'.

351 See Becker 2000, p. 45

352 The leveraged and leveraged-finance debt market has grown significantly in Germany over the last few years. The increase was driven by (i) the high debt to equity ratio, (ii) the withdrawal of financing from the German 'Hausbanks' due to increased regulatory requirements by Basel II and (iii) increasing buyout activity. In the 1990s, the difficulties for buyouts to find appropriate financing means, as soon as the rating is non-investment grade, have been more than compensated by competing financing institutions seeking to provide profitable debt capital (See Forst 1992, pp. 98 et seqq., Becker 2000, pp. 35 et seqq., , p. 99, EVCA 2004, p. 2).

353 See Myers 1984, pp. 586 et seqq., Barclay and C.W. 1995 p. 610

354 See Roden and Lewellen 1995, p. 86

355 See Kaplan and Stein 1993, Roden and Lewellen 1995

356 They relate the increase to the emerging supply of creative finance instruments, since financiers have gained substantial experience with highly leveraged buyouts in the mid 1980s. See Kaplan and Stein 1993, Roden and Lewellen 1995.

monthly cash flow. On the other hand, growth-oriented exits, especially trade sales, would benefit more strongly from debt-deferred instruments. Further, short-term debt may overstretch management's willingness to shoulder the increased likelihood of bankruptcy.

2.1.2 Ownership Structure and Performance

Researchers have empirically analyzed the effect of different levels of concentration in ownership and different ownership objectives on performance. The results reveal a complex relationship between ownership and performance, requiring to take the historic governance structures and the identity of the respective owners into account.

The empirical findings support the hypothesis that a concentration in ownership reduces moral hazard of managers, in particular unprofitable empire building and unrelated diversification[357]. Shareholdings from outsider investors who are not board members amend the disciplinary force and further pressure management to reduce unrelated diversification[358]. The form of the relationship between concentration in ownership and performance, however, remains ambiguous, with contradicting empirical evidence. The majority of studies confirm a linear, positive ownership concentration effect. Empiricists report that indicators such as market-to-sales, Tobin's Q, and price-earnings increase with concentrated ownership[359]. Others studies report an equilibrium between financing and monitoring costs of high ownership concentration, as proposed by Demsetz[360]. Beyond this point, the concentration of ownership is detrimental to performance.

A different stream of researchers finds evidence for the superior performance of widely dispersed ownership structures, following the proposition of a path-dependency of the optimal ownership structure (and concentration). Further, several studies substantiate the importance of the owner identity as a determinant for the ownership concentration-performance relationship[361]. Researchers measure the strongest positive relationship for institutional investors and financial institutions, the weakest and, in most cases thereby in negative direction, for the government as

357 See Amihud and Lev 1981, p. 615. For the detailed elucidation of the costs and benefits of ownership concentration see A3.4.2.

358 See Bethel and Liebeskind 1993, p. 29, Hoskisson, Johnson et al. 1994, p. 1213

359 See Lloyd, Hand et al. 1987, Leech and Leahy 1991, Zeckhouser and Pound 1990, McConnell and Servaes 1990, Coles, Lemmon et al. 2002

360 See Pedersen and Thomsen 1999, Gedajlovic and Shapiro 1998

361 In the subsequent chapter, the relationship between owner identity and activity level of monitoring is discussed in detail. Further, the costs and benefit of concentration for different investor groups is elaborated in chapter A3.4.2 (See further Thomsen and Pedersen 2000, pp. 699 et seqq.).

owner. For the effect of family ownership, they report contradicting findings[362]. For insider ownership, the empiricists suggest that above a certain level, insider owners and managers expropriate wealth in an excessive way[363].

However, as a primary concern to resolve the contradictory findings, some researchers have sought to find potential causes, not only related to diverging measurement of company performance and ownership structure, but also related to endogen factors[364]. In a review of the status of the field of ownership-performance relationship, Demsetz and Villalonga propose to distinguish ownership structure by outside shareholders and management, and analyze their impact separately. Due to the critical role of management, one should further analyze the shareholdings of management (insiders) and non-management separately.

Ownership Concentration and Performance in the German Market

Similar to the international surveys, the empirical results for the relationship of ownership concentration and performance in Germany are to some degree inconclusive[365].

First, the German market is characterized by a high level of ownership concentration. More than half of the listed German companies have a dominant owner with 50% equity stake or more[366]. The concentration is further reinforced when taking into account the controlling power throughout chains of direct stakes, typical for the high level of crossholdings in Germany. A small number of large, complementary shareholders balance the concentration of ownership[367]. Lehmann and Weigand

362 On the one hand, the family-owned companies showed the highest sales growth, confirming the 'empire-building' hypothesis. On the other hand, they value liquidity, but are, however, cash-constrained and more suited to capital-light businesses (See Thomsen and Pedersen 2000, p. 703).

363 Morck 1988 report that management with effective control over the corporation will even indulge their own preference for non value -adding behavior. The authors find a less unambiguous relationship between management holdings and market valuation measured by Tobin's Q. Between 0% and 5%, a positive relationship is reported, between 5% and 25% the relationship is negative. After 25%, the effect returns to being slightly positive. The authors consolidate their findings in that the conditions necessary for entrenchment, e.g., voting power or control of the board of directors, significantly increase over 5%, however do not differ beyond 20%-25%. See in addition McConnell and Servaes 1990, Loderer and Martin 1997

364 See Demsetz and Villalonga 2001, p. 211

365 See Frick and Lehmann 2004. For a detailed overview, see also Goergen, Manjon et al. 2004.

366 For instance, Franks and Mayer report that in 1990, 85% of 171 large listed companies in Germany had a dominant shareholder with an ownership shareholdings of more than 25% of the capital and 57% had a single shareholder owning more than 25% (see Franks and Mayer 2001). See further La Porta, Lopez-de-Silanes et al. 1999, Edwards and Nibler 2000, Lehmann and Weigland 2000, Goergen, Manjon et al. 2004, and Faccio and Lang 2002.

367 Becht and Boehmer report an average size of 7.4% of shareholding for other large owners, whereas only a second shareholder is found for only 20% of the companies with a concentrated owner. See Becht and Boehmer 2003.

claim that many German companies seem to come close to the model of the 'governed corporation'[368]. One may hypothesize, therefore, that the expected reduction of agency costs of equity will be less than for a more dispersed shareholder structure in non-German (buyout) companies[369].

Nevertheless, one finds evidence for (i) a positive linear and bell-shaped, (ii) a negative as well as (iii) a non-existent relationship between ownership and company performance. First, the majority of research indicates a positive, linear relationship. Weigand and Edwards find a higher return on assets for companies with a concentrated as opposed to a dispersed ownership structure[370]. Further, Cable as well as Gorton and Schmid measure a positive control-performance relationship, focusing on banks in the dominant shareholding position[371]. Edwards and Weichenrieder review the separation of control versus cash flow rights, typical for many family-owned corporations in Germany, and attribute a positive effect of concentration in ownership if cash flow rights are in line with the control rights[372]. Is this case, the presence of a controlling shareholder is beneficial for minority shareholders. On the flipside, higher control rights lower in most cases the market value of equity. Such constellations are typical for family-controlled companies which seek to maintain control while raising additional capital and diversifying their risk. Lehmann and Weigand report similar negative effects of control versus cash flow-rights concentration for market-to-book and return-on-assets ratios. Lehmann and Weigand, however, report that in the long-term ownership concentration is beneficial to corporate performance[373]. In addition, company characteristics, e.g. company size and growth, and industry, e.g. industry consolidation, explain most variation of the relationship of ownership concentration to performance. A recent survey of Köke and Renneboog confirms the positive influence of ownership concentration on the productivity growth in Germany (in comparison to the UK). However, for blockholders that are not banks, insurance, or governments, researchers have not found a relationship of ownership concentration and performance. Further, Januszewski reports higher rates of productivity growth for companies with tighter control[374]. On the contrary, some empirics indicate a non-linear relationship. Gedaljovic and Shapiro find a non-linear relationship in the form

368 See the detailed discussion of the governed corporation in chapter A3.5.
369 See Titzrath 1994, p.180
370 See Lehmann and Weigland 2000, Edwards and Weichenrieder 1999
371 See Cable 1985, Gorton and Schmid 2000
372 See Edwards and Weichenrieder 1999
373 See Lehmann and Weigland 2000, p. 190
374 See Januszewski, Köke et al. 2002, p. 326

that for low level of controls, the effect on return on assets is low, whereas high levels of control incur a higher return on assets. They argue that the ownership concentration "limit both managerial cost padding and the negative consequences of excessive diversification". Finally, some latest surveys indicate a negative relationship. In a recent comparison of ownership structures in Europe, Kirchmeier and Grant find that the group of German companies under control of a dominant shareholder is the worst performing of all[375]. The authors argue that minority investor protection is still low, leading to expropriation by larger shareholders. They confirm rent-seeking behavior of large shareholders, following sub-optimal corporate strategies. Still, they find the private control benefits to be lower in Germany than in other comparable European markets. Becht confirms in a survey the hypothesis of reduced liquidity through ownership concentration, as he reports a negative relationship of turnover to market capitalization versus concentration[376].

Only limited focus has been directed on revealing the potential underlying causes for the different results beyond those related to agency theory. One explanatory thrust comes from Frick and Lehmann on a time series-perspective, where the authors claim a positive effect of ownership concentration for the 1970s and 1980s, however, turning to negative in the 1990s. Lehmann and Weigand argue that the liberalization of markets and increased international competition in the 1990s caused to enhanced failure of risk-averse large blockholders. The explanations do not unravel the controversial results for the latest studies analyzing the late 1990s.

Changes in Ownership Structure and Concentration during and after the Buyout

At the entry into the buyout structure, the shareholdings from both management and active insider investors increase (see Table 6)[377]. The reported shifts are considerable, e.g., an increase in management shareholding from 5.0% to 22.3% measured by Kaplan and Stein.

In total, the shareholder base is more focused, with clear governance by three constituents: the equity investors, management, and senior lenders[378]. The influence

375 See Kirchmaier and Grant 2005, pp. 19 et seq.

376 See Becht 1999

377 It may be noteworthy, that companies undergoing a buyout already have a higher level of ownership concentration prior to their existence as abuyout. In a survey of the first buyouts in the US, Maupin, Bidwell and Ortegren report that the share of equity in the hands of the management and directors was already higher (56%) compared to the non-buyouts (38%) before the transaction. The ownership concentration is argued as pre-determinant for buyout since the execution of the buyout is simplified. The authors also claim that potential additional funds are less and, therefore, more affordable (see Maupin, Bidwell et al. 1984).

378 See Singh 1990, p. 122

of other shareholders, e.g., representatives of other corporations, specialists such as lawyers, or bankers, etc., diminishes according to the lessening of ownership.

Equity investors participate in the majority of buyouts, with a positive correlation of their participation level to size. In Germany, the surveys report a share of on average 70-80% of buyouts where outside investors engage in at least 25% of equity[379]. In most cases, the investors have an equal or even higher share in equity than the management team. Forst reports that the share of management shareholdings is higher for spin-off than for family-/succession buyouts[380]. Interestingly, the buyout firms have been reluctant to use external equity prior to the buyout. The founder, his relatives, and the house bank as the major lender characterize the former ownership. Their resistance to external equity relates to the intention to preserve entrepreneurial freedom. Further, the entry of external equity requires higher transparency on business development and profitability[381]. Not surprisingly, the information asymmetry leads to high external financing costs, both for debt and equity.

The raising of new equity through a buyout is, in many cases, the key enabler for overdue investments and expansions. However, some empirical research indicates a less prominent role of buyout investors than expected. Jacoby reports that the likelihood for success diminishes significantly if specialists participate in a buyout[382].

At the exit from the buyout, the surveys again confirm the anticipated decrease in ownership concentration, however, with some differential nuances to their industry peers and limited to public data from buyouts exiting via the stock market. As a caveat, one should note that there is no long-term empirical research on the change in ownership through the entire buyout cycle[383]. The implications presented on the cycle are more or less a logical addition of the evidence from changes at entry and at exit. The research indicates that the level of management ownership and ownership of non-management insiders decreases significantly at the exit. As noted by Holthausen and Larcker, the aligned parties of managers and investor lose the majority to a dispersed shareholder base[384]. However, the authors also report that in 59% of companies observed, the management does not sell any shareholdings.

---

379 In the survey by Forst, private equity investors engage in 32 of 36 buyouts with at least 25% of equity. Luippold reports that from 18 buyouts, financial investors acquire a substantial share in 14 buyouts, with similar results confirmed by Vest (13 out of 16 buyouts). See Forst 1992, p. 30, Luippold 1991, p. 342, Vest 1995, p. 248

380 See Forst 1992, p. 72

381 See Forst 1992, p. 53

382 See Jakoby 2000, p. 279

383 See Bruton, Keels et al. 2002, p. 711

384 See Holthausen and Larcker 1996, p. 302

Author	Year	Sample size	Data source / type	Geo-graphical focus	Management (as percentage of total shares)			Investors, non-management (as percentage of total shares)			Others (as percentage shares)	
					Pre-Buyout	*Buyout*	*Post-IPO*	*Pre-Buyout*	*Buyout*	*Post-IPO*	*Pre-Buyout*	*Buyout*
1. Change in equity ownership for US-based buyouts												
Maupin Bidwell Ortegren (1984)	1972 to 1983	63	Going private	US	38.8%[1]	56.1%	n/a	n/a	n/a	n/a	n/a	n/a
DeAngelo DeAngelo (1987)	1973 to 1982	33	Going private	US	n/a	24.5%[2]	n/a	n/a	n/a	n/a	n/a	n/a
		31	Going private	US	n/a	50.1%[3]	n/a	n/a	n/a	n/a	n/a	n/a
Kaplan (1989a)	1980 to 1985	76	Going private	US	22.9%	31,0%	n/a	n/a	n/a	n/a	n/a	n/a
Singh (1990)	1980 to 1987	65	Going private	US	37.8%	39.3%	n/a	2.5%	35,7%	n/a	59.7%	25.0%
Kaplan (1991)	1979 to 1986	33	Going private	US	n/a	39.0%[8]	n/a	n/a	n/a	n/a	n/a	n/a
Kaplan Stein (1991)	1980 to 1989	124	Going private	US	5.0%	22.3%	n/a	n/a	n/a	n/a	n/a	n/a
Phan Hill (1995)	1986 to 1989	33	Going private	US	14.2%	35.7%	n/a	n/a	n/a	n/a	n/a	n/a
Wu (1996)	1980 to 1987	87	Going private	US	34.8%	n/a	n/a	n/a	n/a	n/a	n/a	n/a
Cotter Peck (2001)	1984 to 1989	64	Going private	US	n/a	20.0%	n/a	n/a	51.6%	n/a	n/a	28.4%
Peck (2004)	1984 to 1989	59	Going private	US	n/a	20.0%	n/a	n/a	54.3%	n/a	n/a	25.0%
Muscarella Vetsuypens (1990)	1976 to 1987	24	Going public	US	n/a	57,2%	41.3%	n/a	n/a	n/a	n/a	n/a
Mian Rosenfeld (1993)	1983 to 1988	85	Going public	US	n/a	36,7%	23,8%	n/a	35.3%[4]	22.7%[4]	n/a	28,0%
								n/a	64.6%[5]	41.6%[5]		36.4%
Holthausen, Larcker (1996)	1983 to 1988	90	Going public	US	n/a	36.0%	23.7%	n/a	38.7%	25.1%	n/a	25.3%
Bruton Keels Scifres (2002)	1980 to 1988	39	Going public	US	n/a	22.0%[6]	16.0%[6]	n/a	46.0%[7]	33.0%[7]	n/a	n/a
2. Change in equity ownership for Gernany-based buyouts												
Graeper (1993)	1981 to 1989	36	Spin-Offs, Succession	Germany	n/a	25.4%	n/a	n/a	n/a	n/a	n/a	n/a
Luippold (1991)	1983 to 1990	31	Spin-Offs, Sale of family business	Germany	n/a	39.3%	n/a	n/a	39.3%	n/a	n/a	n/a
Vest (1995)	1985 to 1991	29	Spin-Offs	Germany	n/a	51.7%	n/a	n/a	38.9%	n/a	n/a	n/a
Jakoby (2000)	1976 to 1996	62	All buyouts types	Germany	n/a	74.4%	n/a	n/a	n/a	n/a	n/a	n/a

[1] Industry average of firms still quoted
[2] With participation of third-party equity investors (buyout specialists)
[3] With no participation of third-party equity investors (buyout specialists)
[4] Share of other insider investors, no active investors
[5] Share of other insider investors, with active investors
[6] Only includes shareholdings of CEO
[7] Includes shareholdings of non-CEO management and non-management insiders
[8] Includes shareholdings of management and non-management insiders

Table 6: Overview change in equity ownership concentration and management shareholdings from pre- to post-buyout

Consequently, the decrease is largely related to the sell-out of the buyout investors who cash out. However, the buyout governance regime partially stays in place. Holthausen and Larcker report that the composition of the supervisory board remains constant, with only few changes. Although the concentration of ownership is reduced, the post-exit ownership of insiders is significantly higher than the industry norm. Holthausen and Larcker report that for the sample observed the share of average insider ownership (management and non-management) counts up to 48.8% (11.8%) for the former buyouts (stock market average)[385]. An important observation is thereby that the change in ownership is independent of the change in leverage, confirming the separation of the hypothesis in the research model[386]. However, the empirical research lacks a survey that investigates the long-term development of the ownership structure in the post-exit period.

The evidence for the post-exit development in Germany is scarce and has not been the object of a systematic academic analysis, not even the publicly available data from reverse buyouts. Anecdotal evidence points to similar reduction of ownership concentration as in the US studies presented, with the nuance that insider ownership is still above average.

Ehrhardt and Nowak, for instance, report for a sample of German IPOs that former family-controlled firms remain in the ownership of the families[387]. Hence, the hypothesis should be formulated as:

Hypothesis 2a: The concentration of ownership of a buyout decreases following a going-public and reversal of its buyout.

In the case of a trade sale, the acquiring company will seek to incorporate the majority of equity. Therewith, they strive to implement their strategic and operational plan and maximize the expected benefits. Further, the strategic investor will strive to acquire the highest share possible to consolidate the business into their own accounting and to reduce the efforts of a (separate) public listing. There are some reasons to believe that the concentration in ownership might, at the exit of the financial investor, even increase in some selected cases. First, the extent of club deals with multiple participating financial investors especially for larger deal sizes has increased. Second, financial investors have increasingly invited strategic investor to participate in buyouts, incorporating the advantages from both a rigid governance

---

385 See McConnell and Servaes 1990

386 See Holthausen and Larcker 1996, p. 303

387 See Ehrhardt and Nowak 2003, pp. 225 – 228. See also the summary on changes in ownership and the impact on performance in chapter B5.3.4.2.

and industry expertise. A trade sale will consolidate the non-management equity shareholders. The level of concentration will at least not decrease. Thus,

Hypothesis 2b: The concentration of ownership of a buyout remains constant following a trade sale of the buyout.

Whilst different ownership structures among equity have received attention in academic research, the consideration of debt holders and their influence on corporate performance has been rather modest. Regardless of the fact that public data on the specific debt structure is intransparent, the analysis of ownership structure without debt is incomplete.

Further, similar conclusions about the concentration may also apply to debt[388]. In a disperse structure of several debt holders, free-ridership of smaller lenders taking advantage of the monitoring efforts of larger lenders will occur. Therefore, lenders will underinvest. Agency costs of debt will be reduced if a single debt holder or a group of debt holders acts cooperatively in the form of a syndicate. Further, the risk of bankruptcy is smaller with a concentrated debt holder structure, since they feel more committed and are able to monitor more closely the operations of the company. A higher level of ownership concentration on the management side may also reduce the agency cost of debt, since lenders will expect management to be more willing to negotiate and potentially more willing to contribute additional capital. However, the relationship to corporate performance is subject to a different rationale. Debt holders are primarily interested in the probability of default and the liquidity worth of the company[389] and less in a long-term value creation. Therefore, one might expect a diluted relationship to financial performance indicators, e.g. net profit or operating cash flow. What is also found is a positive relationship between leverage and management shareholdings, with some contradictory results[390]. At low levels of managerial shareholdings, empiricists observe a positive linear relationship. High levels of debt spur the probability of bankruptcy what owner-managers may want to avoid due to their risk.

2.1.3 Owner Identity and Activity Level of Investors

The empirical research reinforces the relevance of the owner identity and sheds further light on the implications for the performance of the company after the change of the governance. The author will briefly discuss the different investment objectives

388 See Stiglitz 1985, p. 140
389 See Short 1994, p. 230
390 See Short 1994, p. 243

of the owner identities and, in the following, discuss how the activity level of governance evolves over the buyout cycle.

Ownership Identity to Performance-Relationship in the German Market

First, family control is an important determinant for German corporate ownership, especially for the small and medium-sized companies[391]. They typically have a long-term investment horizon and allow the retention of earnings within the company. However, they also benefit the most from private control benefits. Edwards and Weichenrieder report that family-owners expropriate wealth less with increasing control rights than bank or non-bank companies[392]. Edwards and Niebler provide empirical evidence that the family and individuals with a minority stake of less than 50% show the strongest, positive effect on market-to-book valuation[393]. Considering that shareholders in Germany already have significant control with 25% of voting rights, the positive effect may be extended, especially since the group of family-owners of listed companies with over 50% of voting rights is limited. In the survey 'Entrepreneurship in Germany', the family-controlled companies are not more or less likely to be successful than non-family companies[394]. Lower profitability compensates the above average sales growth. In a recent survey, Barontini and Caprio also report a positive relationship between family control and Tobin's Q[395]. In particular, the authors analyze the performance effect of the involvement in active management and find a positive performance implication for the founder serving as CEO and less for him taking a non-executive seat on the board. The researchers admit that a part of the positive effect is wasted by private control benefits, but argue that the residual effect is clearly positive. In a large survey of German ownership structures and their performance implication, Lehmann and Weigand contradict the beneficial effect for family ownership, leading below average return-on-assets[396]. The authors argue that the advantages of concentrated ownership apply strongly for quoted firms, while for non-quoted firms the concentration has an opposite effect on profitability. Lehmann and Weigand interpret that the owners favor control over both the liquidity of public capital markets and potential higher profitability by

---

391 Faccio and Lang report that of the 704 firms analyzed in Germany, 64.6% are under family control, defining the control above a threshold of 20% of voting shares. The share of family control increases to 81.0% for the sub-sample of the 50 smallest firms in the sample (See Faccio and Lang 2002,p. 382)

392 See Edwards and Weichenrieder 1999, pp. 23 and 24

393 See Edwards and Nibler 2000, p. 255

394 See Meffert, Radtke et al. 2005, Meffert and Klein 2007

395 Although family control is related to control-enhancing devices associated with lower performance, Barontini and Caprio reveal that family control leads to superior performance for any cash flow and voting rights combination of the owner (See Barontini and Caprio 2005, p. 52).

396 See Lehmann and Weigland 2000, pp. 185 et seqq.

exploiting investment opportunities better. Not surprisingly, the share of non-quoted firms for family control is significantly higher than for non-family controlled firms.

To conclude, the ownership by a family seems favorable, however, not always superior to other owners, as also detailed in the following comparisons. Privately held corporations especially have carefully to balance the advantage of a long-term investor versus the disadvantages of restricted capital access and of private control benefits.

Second, financial institutions, notably the German 'hausbank', play a crucial role. At a first sight, their reported voting blocks may appear to be comparably small with an average of 1.2% in shareholdings[397]. On the flipside, the banks control much more voting rights than their own stakes through excessive proxy votes[398]. They are lenders to the company and often provide the majority of capital due to the traditionally high debt-to-equity ratio in Germany. Further, they often take a position on the supervisory board. Not surprisingly, the enormous power related to German banks is highly controversial discussed, often accompanied by the notion of abuse[399]. However, these conjectures are not confirmed from an ownership-performance relationship perspective, as most research indicates a neutral to positive relationship. Weigand, for instance, provides evidence that in the long-term, bank-controlled companies outperform management-controlled ones. Gorton and Schmid report that company controlled by banks also outperform non-bank blockholders[400]. The authors also report that the criticized proxy voting rights do not interfere between the shareholders' and the company's interest. Much more, the companies benefit from reduced information asymmetry. Further, Gorton and Schmid refer to the quasi public-status of the German banks, therefore, limiting the extent of extracting private control benefits[401]. Köke and Renneboog report a positive role of banks, notably the German 'house banks', in monitoring poorly performing companies and stimulating productivity growth. Strong competition from product markets, however, serves as a supplementary disciplinary mechanism and weakens the relationship between

---

397 Among the voting stakes above 5%, banks in Germany hold 5.8%. See Goergen, Manjon et al. 2004, p. 45

398 See Gorton and Schmid 2000

399 For instance, Wegner and Kaserer claim that "German banks do not only provide industrial companies with loan but also exercise considerable voting power in stockholder meetings [...]. This is partly due to proxies of their clients and partly due to stock ownership [...} We would argue that the specific environment does not reduce agency problems; on the contrary, this situation is prone to enlarge and perpetuate these problems". See Wegner and Kaserer 1998, pp. 509 et seqq.

400 See Gorton and Schmid 2000, p. 61

401 See Gorton and Schmid 2000, p. 69. Also noteworthy is the negative effect of codetermination the authors measure: a switch from no-/one-third codetermination to equal representation reduced market-to-book by 15.9% and return-on-equity by 3.25 base points, respectively (See Gorton and Schmid 2000, p. 62).

ownership concentration, owner identity and performance[402]. Köke and Renneboog further claim that the positive role of bank is also related to the active supervisory role, since the bankers use their presence on the supervisory boards to enforce strategic decision-making. The results of Lehmann and Weigand are along the same lines as they find a positive impact of concentration in bank ownership on return-on-assets, arguing that banks are the more efficient monitors and, therefore, reduce agency cost[403]. Edwards and Nibler also report a similar positive effect of bank ownership, however, limited to the largest 3 banks[404]. However, they find no superior ownership of bank to other owners, e.g., family-controlled companies with minority stakes below 50% of voting equity. Contrary to Gorton and Schmid, they found limited evidence of a negative effect of proxy votes to company performance. Goergen, Correia da Silva and Renneboog argue that superior bank ownership performance is related to reduced informational asymmetry and agency costs. They found, for instance, a higher flexibility with dividend payments, whereas widely dispersed companies show reluctance to cut dividends. One should note that the 'house banks' benefited from an underdeveloped private equity market up into the 1990s. Through their strong power position as debt providers, they could act unchallenged as active investors, participating in corporate decision-making and placing confidants to the management board.

Critiques of the 'housebanks' bring forward that they are too inflexible and that their relationship is too intransparent and outdated in comparison to the Anglo-Saxon market-oriented banking system[405]. Januszweski reports lower productivity growth for companies where banks and other financial institutions form the majority shareholder[406]. He analyzes the role of product market competition and corporate governance as a predictor for the productivity growth of German manufacturing companies. On the flipside, Januszewski provides evidence that for companies with financial institutions as the ultimate owner, productivity growth rates are lower, while remarkably the level of competition does not influence the correlation. The author limits the results to the owning banks, which where in the period of the survey of the traditional German banks less aggressive than pension funds and investors.

402 See Köke and Renneboog 2003, p. 5
403 See Lehmann and Weigland 2000, p. 190
404 See Edwards and Nibler 2000
405 See Hellwig 2000
406 See Januszewski, Köke et al. 2002

To summarize, the evidence appears to be balanced, with a slight majority confirming the positive role of 'hausbanks'. As an owner, they seem to reduce information asymmetry and actively engage in corporate policy-making. However, this positive role is related largely to the historic weakness of the German equity market and the strong debt culture.

One should also take a stake from the empirical research of the role and efficiency of shareholder activism by institutional investors, which is admittedly focused on the U.S. capital markets. Short-term stock market reactions have not revealed a consistent result, instead studies find significant responses for specific proposals, e.g., negative abnormal returns for proposals addressing poison pills or board diversity[407]. For long-term performance following shareholder activism, the evidence is balanced, with a slight majority for the positive[408]. Bethel, Liebeskind and Opler report that company performance improves after an investor with a large block shareholder enters[409]. Other surveys delineate that especially large institutional investors seem to affect significantly the investment, with a positive relationship of activism by CalPERS and by companies on the Council of Institutional Investor to shareholder wealth[410]. Other aspects correlated to an active shareholder are found in the reduction of diversification and in the increase of corporate restructuring[411]. Further, management turnover increases and executive compensation is tightened with the presence of large shareholders[412]. Finally, the proposed incentive of relationship investing has been analyzed by Martin Gillan and Kensinger, offering mixed results[413]. However, since the increase in ownership has started to surge just in the last few years, long-term evidence remains to be proven.

Other owners are more difficult to identify and to analyze. On the one side, the governance system is Germany characterized by a high level of crossholdings of industrial companies. Although the tax-exemption of capital gains introduced in 2001 spurred the dissolution of the German crossholdings system, a large amount of crossholdings remained[414]. Januszewski, Köke and Winter report that companies

---

407 See Gillan and Starks 1998, Carleton, Nelson et al. 1998

408 See the overview by Gillan and Starks 2003

409 See Bethel, Liebeskind et al. 1998

410 See Smith 1996, Opler and Sokobin 1998

411 See Guercio and Hawkins 1999

412 See Kang and Shivdasani 1995, Kaplan 1995

413 Only the performance of Sears improved significantly, the closer relationship with the other firms does not seem to have led to superior performance. See Gillan, Kensinger et al. 2000.

414 Goergen, Manjon and Renneboog report that holding and industrial companies held on average 21% in other German listed companies in 2004, based on a sample of 402 companies. See Goergen, Manjon et al. 2004, p. 45

controlled by other companies tend to have a higher level of productivity, further, Köke notes less likelihood for acquisitions[415]. Some theorists hypothesize that the dominant shareholders may use their controlling rights for private benefits, however, no recent empirical evidence for German capital markets has been provided. On the other hand, insider ownership by managers and directors play an important role. Since hardly any information is disclosed about insider control, only limited research is available. Gorton and Schmid report that in 8% of companies, the management team is the largest shareholder, carrying at least 50% of shareholding[416]. Even higher shares are measured by Köke who reports a 22.5% share for directors for quoted and a 12% share for unquoted companies. However, limited research has been conducted for Germany on understanding the relationship of insider, non-family shareholding to performance.

Although the identity is a good predictor for classifying different investment objectives and incentives for private control, the relationship to performance is to some degree inconclusive. The suitability of an owner category will depend on the specific company situation. For a management that was capital-restrained and used the buyout to finance the succession of a company, a return to family-control may be the most promising way. However, a former family-controlled company with excessive private control benefits should maintain a non-insider, monitoring shareholder on the board, for instance, the 'hausbank', to ensure an objective control of management. Nevertheless, a more suitable classification of the owner can by found by the level and type of monitoring activities he is willing to invest.

Change in Governance Activity Level after Exit

At the exit through a going-public, the time commitment of supervisory board members is expected to decline substantially. According to the change in ownership, the governance is transferred to a new supervisory board. The dedication and commitment of the new board members will at best be shared with other businesses, even in the situation of a severe crisis. While the board members in the buyout were highly motivated by their own shareholdings or at least by strong second level performance-related compensation, the new representative only partially benefit from their efforts. First, supervisory board members often receive fixed payments for effort spent. Second, the second level of performance-related compensation is much less. Appointed industry experts are often representatives of companies with little or no crossholdings in the monitored company. Even in the case of shareholdings, the

415 See Januszewski, Köke et al. 2002, Köke 2002
416 See Gorton and Schmid 2000

effect is not comparable to a buyout investor share of the target company in their portfolio. Kaplan reports that the level of equity-based compensation for directors is significantly increasing as a direct outcome from the superior buyout governance[417]. Further, the time available for monitoring is much less. The survey of Heel and Kehoe reports an average share of around 10% of total time of the deal partner throughout the investment period, in contrast to the commitment of an average supervisory board member of approximately 4.4 board meetings per year[418]. In addition, the investment objectives change. A value-creation plan directed at maximizing cash flow is, as opposed to the buyout regime, not the focus of a quoted company. Much more, a plan comprising the strategy outlook will be formulated as a business plan focusing on revenue growth and innovation. In addition, there will be less access to the network of industry experts and advisors of the buyout specialist. Hence, the supervisory board will only be in a restricted manner able to develop an independent view on the right strategic initiatives to follow. In most cases, the management board will make a proposal that will be benevolently passed by the supervisory board. Instead of a reciprocal discourse between managers, shareholders, and the board, it is likely that a governance structure dominated by the management will be installed, referred to as the 'managed corporation'[419].

The picture for the activity level and necessary monitoring in Germany may be in respect to to product markets and internal control systems different. German companies have from early on faced competitive pressure beyond domestic markets. Concerning the internal control system, Germany has installed a system of reciprocal system of shared interests. The mandatory co-determination and the traditional strong role of the hausbanks[420] lead to a triumvirat of influential stakeholders, namely blockholders, employees and banks. Each group benefits from the private control differently. Further, they all carry shared interest in largely simlar long-term objectives[421] and favor control above liquidity[422]. Capital markets have been handicapped since only a little share of companies is subject to the market for corporate control. Further, corporate taxation has favored the interests of debt

---

417 See Kaplan 1997, p. 11

418 See Heidrick and Struggles 2007, p. 7

419 Please refer to chapter A3.5 for a detailed discussion on the differences between the 'governed' and 'managed' corporation.

420 The strong role is related to (i) High share of debt of long-term external funding (over 80%), (ii) depository rights representing their clients, (iii) direct shareholdings and (iv) extensive board representation. See Schmidt 2003, p. 11

421 The banks are interested in secure loans, the employees and union repreentatives in job security and the management in stable market structure and continuous growth.

422 See Schmidt 2003, p. 13

holders and restricted the attractiveness of equity. In the corollary, Germany has in terms of forces controlling management and alleviating conflicts suffered from weak internal control systems and under-developed capital markets.

A moderating effect to the level of monitoring and governance intrinsic to the post-exit period is the general business risk associated to the company. Theory and empirical evidence suggests that companies with a higher business risk from both internal, e.g., a business crisis due to management failure, and external factors, e.g., a highly dynamic environment, are likely to be monitored more closely[423]. The sheer fact that a company considers going-public or is acquired is most likely related to a successful management of the internal factors at least. Therefore, a reduction of the level of activity level should be accounted for the success of the restructuring during the buyout period. Further, monitoring will be substituted from the return to capital markets. The disciplinary force of potential hostile takeovers serves as a good interventionist mechanism and counters excessive wealth expropriation by managerial control. Stock price decreases and hostile takeovers will punish the executives for managing the company in a too strong favor of their own interest. A positive effect may also be expected from buyout investors who often remain on the board for a substantial time after their exit. Holthausen and Larcker elucidate the composition of the board at the going-public, and report that operating managers and non-management insiders account for 67% of the total board, versus 37.5% at other comparable companies[424].

In the corollary, one would expect, despite the aforementioned positive arguments, that:

Hypothesis 3a: The activity level of the governance system of a buyout decreases following a going-public.

The change of governance at a trade sale leads to a substantial transfer of supervisory power to the corporate level of the acquiring company[425]. The management at the corporate level may seek to participate in decision-making, access valuable resources, and reallocate capital if it seems more value creating.

The acquiring company typically has similar operations as the acquired company, and, consequently, will be able to provide some substantial industry and operational

---

423 See Barney, Busenitz et al. 1994, Sapienza and Gupta 1994

424 See Holthausen and Larcker 1996, p. 303

425 The author will focus on trade sales to non-financial investors, e.g., trade sales leading to control by a strategic investor either under (i) dispersed ownership or (ii) concentrated ownership of the acquiring firm, e.g., the founder and their heirs.

insight, accompanied by additional managerial resources. Since the integration is closely related to the core business, at least in the joint context of the proposed operational integration, the management at the corporate level will invest substantially in the governance of the acquired company on the level of time commitment. However, a strategic investor will have a different investment objective than a buyout specialist. Whereas the latter investor will focus on cash flow maximization and rapid debt repayment, the former will focus on realizing proposed cost savings and revenue increases, and on strengthening the resource base for long-term competitiveness. Notwithstanding, the entry into the ownership of a larger corporation will lead to a decline in monitoring activities[426]. The majority of studies report a high likelihood of an unsuccessful acquisition in terms of the expected synergies (cost savings and revenue growth)[427]. In many cases, the acquirer fails to formulate a clear joint strategy and conduct successfully the intended restructuring. It seems that the management of the acquirer often hesitates to apply their governing power to avoid turmoil in the organization. Thereby, they loose the best talents and distract the employees from the customers towards internal policy-making.

The incentive alignment by managerial shareholdings is, in addition, weakens. The compensation of the managers at the corporate level is only partially related to the performance of the formerly independent company. In addition, the shareholdings of the former managers now serving on the business unit board are reduced[428]. In the consequence, one would expect:

Hypothesis 3b: The activity level of the governance system of a buyout decreases following a trade sale to a strategic investor.

2.1.4 Change of Management Shareholdings

The manager plays the central role during the entire buyout cycle. As the agent of change, their motivation in terms of personal efforts and their alignment with the principal's interest are essential for the buyout's success. Through their shareholdings, they transform to true entrepreneurs of the company. They can achieve a considerable increase in their personal wealth, but also bear significant risk from a failure.

---

426 In chapter A2.3.3 the intensity of governance in the different organizational form - U-Form, H-Form and M-Form - is discussed. The buyout is a vehicle to align the interests of management and ownership and install an intense governance. In any case, the level of monitoring after a trade sale will presumably decrease .

427 See Anslinger and Copeland 1996, Bekier, Bogardus et al. 2001, Christofferson, McNish et al. 2004

428 See B2.1.4.

At the entry into a buyout, the incumbent management obtains a significant share of equity. The increased participation is supposed to increase the personal efforts of the managers and align the interest between the owners (principal) and managers (agent), substantially reducing the agency costs of equity for the principal[429]. On the other hand, managerial opportunism may lead a manager to buy a significant share of equity if they believe the company is undervalued. Since they possess an information advantage towards external investors, they will realize a gain if the price for the shares is lower than their expected intrinsic value[430]. The managerial opportunism argument though alone does not justify the engagement of managers in the buyout. It is questionable if the observed value creation is only related to the information asymmetry. Value creation is far more related to the restructuring and renewal undertaken during the buyout period. Further, the existence of large, informed shareholders who do not participate in the buyout weaken the argument of opportunism, since one would expect them to hold on to their shareholdings[431].

Empirical evidence confirms significant increases in management shareholdings at the entry for buyouts[432], though with limited evidence for Germany[433]. Beside the increase of equity shareholdings of already participating management, the circle of insider investors is often extended to middle management and key personnel. In total, leadership and employees participate much more strongly in a potential value increase during the buyout period. Without a significant ownership stake, management will utilize the private control benefits and impose costs of their leisure, status, etc., on the shareholders. Empirical evidence reports an increase in personal effort from higher shareholdings at buyouts[434]. Additionally, increased equity evens out the risk of failure and potential loss of position to the expected benefits from innovation[435]. On the flipside, managers are restricted in the diversification of their personal wealth[436].

---

429 See Jensen 1986, Thompson and Wright 1991

430 See Kaplan 1989a, p. 244, Singh 1993, p. 158

431 See Kaplan 1989a, p. 243

432 The results of empirical studies on changes in managerial shareholding details are outlined in Table 6 in chapter B2.1.4. For Germany, no study to the knowledge of the author has so far systematically investigated the change of shareholdings at the entry or exit from a buyout.

433 The surveys in Germany do not report the change at entry. For the buyout, the survey further lack a consistent picture of the ownership structure, with management shareholdings varying between 25 and 52% (39% (Luippold 1991), 25.4% (Gräper 1993), 51.7% (Vest 1995), 43.5% (57.1%) spin-off (family-succession) -buyouts with management shareholdings above 50% (both Forst)). The actual decision-making power will, in reality, be even higher for the management, since other capital providers only take dormant equity holdings.

434 See Green 1992, p. 528

435 See Green 1992, p. 516

436 See Fama 1980, p. 291

To note, although the relative share increases, managers often increase their liquidity at the entry into the buyout. Since the total amount of new equity in the buyout is much less, the new shareholdings, even with a substantial higher relative share, is in absolute terms cheaper. Kaplan and Stein report an average ratio of absolute new to old capital invested of 46%. The relevant data was gathered for the period 1980 to 1989 and should however be relativized for the German market. First, the increase in leverage was far bigger than recent buyouts, e.g., the reported increase from debt to total capital from 20.7% to 85.6% reported by Kaplan for buyouts between 1980 and 1985. Consequently, the absolute amount of equity capital decreased. Recent increases of debt are much more modest, especially in the German market[437]. Second, the ratio of new to old capital applies only for managers in position both before and during the buyout. Nevertheless, the liquidity increase for selected cases may lead to an adverse ex-ante incentive, where managers will pursue a buyout regardless of price and structure, since their shares equal more or less a free option[438]. Within the group of management, both CEOs, top managers, and middle managers participate in the increase. Especially the middle management takes advantage of increased participation[439]. Kaplan reports that the increase in shareholdings for the top two managers is significantly lower than for other managers[440]. On the flipside, the necessary capital may stretch the financing capability of the management. For a smaller buyout, management obtains in most cases the majority of equity[441]. In a larger transaction, specialists and other active investors will step in and take a larger share of equity[442].

During the buyout, no significant changes are reported. Management turnover may lead to modest shifts in the shareholdings. Further, new managerial personnel may be entitled to join the equity participation program. Since the debt is stepwise repaid, the value of equity and, as a consequence, the value of the managerial shareholdings will increase. In many cases, management is obliged to remain on the board until the exit from the buyout, or even for a specific time. Since liquidity is low and shareholdings are typically not sold during the buyout period, one would not suppose a substantial change in managerial motivation and rent-seeking. To avoid an adverse selection of managers entering into the buyout and subsequent shirking, the

437 See Forst 1992

438 See Kaplan and Stein 1990

439 Kaplan reports a sixth fold increase by 10.79% point from pre-buyout 1.70% in shareholdings. See Kaplan 1989a

440 See Kaplan 1989a, p, 245

441 See Robbie and Wright 1995, p. 528

442 See Green 1992, p. 515

shareholdings are often combined with equity ratchets, in the sense of performance-related compensation. Equity ratchets bond the management to the buyout with their shareholdings determined by the medium-term cash flow development and profitability achieved[443]. The ratchets scheme adopted vary, with some schemes related to passing a performance threshold, others penalizing weak performance and not meeting debt payment[444].

At the exit from the buyout, the level of management shareholdings changes significantly. First, managers will strive, after a period of high personal effort, to cash out a substantial part of their shareholdings (cash-out effect). Second, new investors may seek to obtain a majority of shares (control effect) acquiring all available shares. Third, the management will want to reduce their financial exposure subject to the high level of personal wealth committed to the buyout (diversification effect)[445]. Fourth, new managers may want to join the board. Often, the exit closes a phase of severe restructuring within the company, requiring new entrepreneurial personalities. Therefore, existing management may choose to leave the board and offer equity to new managers.

In both cases of exit - going-public and trade sale - the arguments seem reasonable. The empirical research on going-public reports decreases in management shareholdings at the same level as decreases in the participation of buyout investors. Still, the post-exit governance is noted as characterized by an above-average level of management shareholdings versus the average of other corporations[446]. Similar to the initial going-public of young venture capital firms, lead investors of the flotation will, in some cases, request management to continue taking responsibility, especially for the first steps after the flotation and to steer the company through the initial phase of expansion with the newly raised capital. Despite the tendency to retain the experienced management in place, the author supposes the cash-out effect of both management and investors to result in:

Hypothesis 4a: Management shareholdings of a buyout decrease following a reversal of its buyout.

For the exit by a trade sale, the acquiring company may have to obtain a significantly high share of equity for control and accounting reasons, and reduce the level of managerial shareholdings. The current compensation scheme within the acquirer

443 See Thompson and Wright 1991, pp. 17 et seqq.
444 See Thompson and Wright 1987
445 See Bruton, Keels et al. 1999, p. 403
446 See Holthausen and Larcker 1996, p. 302

may also hardly make it feasible to retain a management in position with such a high share of equity. For the incumbent management, a trade sale represents a significant loss of entrepreneurial freedom and independence (demotivation effect). It is not surprising that shareholdings will also decrease as management chooses to leave the company, even if the prospective value-creation continues to be appealing[447]. The same argument also holds for the middle management and key personnel with shareholdings during the buyout period. We, therefore, hypothesize that this secondary, demotivation effect will, together with the primary control and cash-out effect, imply that:

Hypothesis 4b: Management shareholdings of a buyout decrease following a trade sale of its buyout.

The decrease in management shareholding will presumably be higher at a trade sale, since a going-public will have a much less dampening effect on management and on employees.

The hypothesized decreases for both a going-public and trade sale only hold if the management stays in place. Otherwise, the proposed relationship has to be further differentiated by the entering and departing management. The research on management turnover at the exit so far reports only modest changes. Holthausen and Larcker delineate that at the time of the going-public, only 12.5% of the board member had been appointed within the last six months, whereas the new board member are more likely to complete the board, not to replace incumbent managers[448]. Further, only 3 out of 90 CEOs changed within six months prior to the going-public. As long as the following case studies are limited to management buyouts, a potential change in the management board may be neglected in the first approximation[449].

2.1.5 Concluding Remarks

The governance structure at the exit from the buyout changes substantially. The proceeds from going-public strengthen the equity base and reduce debt. The entry into the capital market will lead to a more dispersed shareholder base. At a trade sale, the aversion against higher financial distress will also lead to a decrease of leverage. However, the exit channels differ in the role of management. In a trade sale, management is in most cases forced to return their shareholdings and aligned with

447 See Jensen and Murphy 1990, Leschke 2003, p. 251

448 See Holthausen and Larcker 1996, p. 304

449 A more detailed analysis is required for the shift at the entry, where studies indicate a significant turnover of management (see Kaplan 1989a, p. 250).

an accounting-based pay-for-performance. Even if they can keep some shareholdings, they will consider reducing their shareholdings due to the diminishing entrepreneurial freedom. At a going-public, the management has the choice to retain shares without facing considerable compromises on the entrepreneurial freedom.

In decomposing the governing constituents and postulating their change by the exit channel chosen, the assumption is implicitly made that the constituents are sufficiently independent of each other[450]. However, selected empirical evidence raises the concern for some degree of bi-correlation that should be taken into account.

The relationship between the constituents depends on the characteristics of the capital markets and financial institutions. Strong financial institutions with undeveloped capital markets are most suitable for a corporate governance with combined high debt and concentrated ownership[451]. Where both financial institutions and capital markets are well in place, the governance is most efficient with takeovers, however least for debt and concentrated ownership. Where no institutions and markets are installed, concentrated ownership enables the best governance. The alignment of management and owner compensates for a weak takeover environment and a supposedly inefficient banking sector. John and Kedia resemble the governance regimes to the three most prevalent governance systems: family-based, bank-based, and takeover-based governance. The German corporate market is characterized by a small share of publicly quoted companies and an only slowly evolving market for takeovers. Since financial institutions, notably the 'hausbank', are in a strong position in Germany, both debt and ownership concentration are expected to maintain their strong influence as governing agents in the company.

2.2 Changes in Motives and Potential Wealth Transfer

The succeeding measures taken during and after a buyout are assumed to be related to the changes in corporate governance. Between the changes in corporate

450 The author had previously outlined that the level of governing activity correlates with the level of ownership concentration. Higher benefits from monitoring spur the intensity of governance. Still, at the same level of relative shareholding, the individual investor possess different investment objectives, resulting in different activity patterns. Besides positively affecting the level of monitoring, ownership concentration also influences the level of management shareholdings. Empirical evidence indicates that an institutional investor with higher shareholding places stronger emphasis on equity-based compensation for managers. If the investor however is able to apply their own monitoring on the board, the demand for equity-based compensation is less.

451 See John and Kedia 2002, p. 6

governance and the managerial activities stand multi-faceted relationships of the stakeholders and parties involved. The multiple stakeholders – the new post-exit investors, the buyout investors, debt holders, owner-managers and employees - follow different utility functions adherent to the individual gain during and after the buyout. Hence, the differences in utility will imply varying motives and, most likely, lead to more or less severe interest conflicts.

The changes in the governance at the exit will accordingly change the individual motives. The individual stakeholders may abuse their bargaining position and information advantage to their personal benefit. Amongst the stakeholders, the buyout investors are often accused of abusing their position both at the entry and at the exit from buyout, resulting in a one-sided wealth transfer[452]. In the corollary, the value creation of the post-exit shareholders has to be elucidated while factoring out any wealth transfer to their advantage and to the disadvantage of other stakeholders.

The motives of the different parties involved will alter due to change in the ownership structure and related cash flow and control rights. Further, the relative organizational power and bargaining position will shift between equity and debt holders, management and employees. For instance, the management in a going-public with significant ongoing shareholdings will continue to be closely related to the interests of the owners, with a high overlap with their self-interest. However, the consolidation of shareholdings in the hands of the acquirer in a trade sale will de-couple the interests of both management and ownership and lead to potential conflicts. A potential wealth loss could occur for the prospective acquirer to the benefit of the former buyout investor. The selling party, e.g. the buyout management or the buyout investors, might exploit their information advantage and withhold important assessments on future income and cash flow from the prospective acquirer.

The changes in motives have, at least in some aspects, to be differentiated by the exit channel chosen from the buyout. Theory building and research on the change in motivation at the exit from a LBO is sparse[453]. To complete the prediction on the changes in motives, the author will mirror some assumptions from the entry into the buyout.

---

452 See DeAngelo, DeAngelo et al. 1984, pp. 371 et seqq., Lowenstein 1985,pp. 748 et seqq., Palepu 1990, pp. 251 et seqq., Smith 1990a, pp. 20 et seqq., Frankfurter and Gunay 1992, pp. 83 et seqq.

453 See Bruton, Keels et al. 1999, p. 404

2.2.1 Buyout Investors

The utility function of the buyout investors is almost exclusively related to the residual value creation and cash generation between the point in time of investment and exit. Pre-agreed scheduled repayments of principal and any contractually agreed additional cash flows only form a small part of the total return. The major part is related to the achieved sale's price at the exit[454]. The investor will seek to minimize his equity investment at the entry, thereby maximizing his leverage and ensuring additional benefits from tax shield[455]. During the restructuring period, the buyout investors are confronted with a lack of an organized secondary market. As an investor, they face low liquidity or even illiquidity[456]. They are locked into the investment until the company can either float on the public market, be sold to a third party, or refinanced. The investments are provided from a fund, most commonly a limited partnership, and have a fixed life during which the investors expect the general partner to invest and realize the targeted gain[457].

Since the transaction leads to private ownership, the contractual and reporting agreements are directly negotiated between management and the buyout investor. The buyout investors will seek representation on the supervisory board of the buyout company. They will close follow and actively participate in discussions on strategic actions, e.g., acquisitions and divestments, and on major investments[458]. Appointments to the management board and employment contracts are thereby of particular interest. The format and frequency of reporting will be directly agreed between management and buyout investor, and is typically more intense due to the necessity for debt servicing.

A going-public typically achieves the highest gain for the equity investors during the buyout[459]. Therefore, the buyout investors, further equity investors, and management will in general favor this exit channel[460]. However, a trade sale is a more predictable exit option and in times of an unstable stock markets the only feasible one[461].

454 See Sharp 2003, p. 43

455 Leveraged buyouts do benefit from the tax shield, e.g., as measured by the premium at buyout takeovers. See Kaplan 1989a.

456 See Kaserer, Wagner et al. 2003, p. 19, Jugel 2003, p. 20

457 See Sharp 2003, p. 45

458 See also the detailed discussion on changes in the activity level of governance in chapter A3.4.

459 See the review of post-exit performance of stock market listings in chapter B5.3.3. See also Achleitner 2001, p. 527 – 528, and Weitnauer 2001, pp. 296 et seqq.

460 A detailed discussion of the favorability of the different exit channels is provided in chapter B5.3.2.

461 See the review of post-exit performance of trade sales in chapter B5.3.5.

The investors can take advantage of the broad liquidity of capital markets during a going-public. However, stock markets are not always receptive to a flotation and may limit the feasibility of achieving an attractive sales price[462]. Further, a going-public requires a strenuous process with onerous disclosure and due diligence requirements[463]. The stock exchange requirements are standardized and offer less scope for specified negotiations and terms. Further, the prescribed information and transparency to the capital markets requires substantial managerial time and limits independent decision-making. In comparison to a trade sale, not only one investor has to be convinced, but the entire capital markets, requiring broad management commitment in the pre-flotation period. The buyout shareholders will also have to balance the upside from flotation as opposed to share retention required. The new investors will often require a lockup period to ensure risk sharing and to bind in the buyout investors for some time to the company. Hence, the buyout investors will be dependent on market conditions and management performance while being subject to limited influence on corporate policy. It is worth noting that the investor might not be able to seize the potential value from control rights (premium) if no major blockholder engages during the book-building period. In many cases however, a going-public can indeed attract potential strategic investors[464]. Further, a buyout specialist can opportunistically seize a window in stock market appetite, while continuing to hold a substantial share in the company and participate in stock price gains.

When liquidity for a going-public is low, a trade sale may be the only option to exit from the buyout. However, a trade sale may also be the only way to monetarize the control premium related to strategic and synergistic benefits for the acquirer[465]. Any buyout investor will seek to anticipate the most viable exit option in the due diligence period, and adjust the restructuring and value-creation plan towards the highest possible exit valuation. Further, a trade sale enhances the likelihood of a cash consideration. The objective to maximize the sales price leads frequently leads to an auction, with multiple interests bidding for the target company. Often, this can lead to an interest conflict between management and buyout investor. The management will consider, beyond the mere sales price, the strategy intended by the acquirer for

---

462 In a depressed market, the going-public route is unviable, even for the most promising businesses. Sometimes, the acceptance for flotation differs by sector and by the individual risk/return profile. Even if the flotation is decided-upon, the buyout investors will have to bear some risk if the IPO has to be aborted at short notice due to unfavorable market conditions (See Ritter 1991).

463 See Sharp 2003, p. 114

464 See Leschke 2003, p. 250

465 See Sharp 2003, p. 111

the target, since this closely relates to their prospective role in management and future compensation.

2.2.2 Post-Exit Shareholders

The shareholder structure and the related motives will differ significantly according to the exit channel. Although weak governance was in many cases the antecedent and cause for the buyout, the exit and return to stock market should indicate that governance has been re-adjusted and the company has returned to a viable and healthy condition. Therefore, the post-exit shareholders should not per se fear that the company would return to a pre-buyout state of performance[466]. However, in the long-term the shareholders should not expect an above-average performance as observed during the buyout and in the initial years after exit[467]. Although empirical evidence for the first years after the exit report higher debt level and managerial shareholdings[468], the company will presumably converge to industry-average capital structure, if other factors do not intervene. A stock market listing offers thereby multiple advantages to the investors as opposed to private ownership: a nearly continuous fungibility to sale and buy, an ongoing current market price, and the option to increase or to decrease the share within certain boundaries.

A trade sale will, similar to a going-public, lead to a shift in governance and monitoring to the new shareholders. Depending on the acquisition rationale, the acquirer will either seek to integrate the operations and seize cost and revenue synergies, e.g., in particular after a horizontal acquisition, or to further create value at the acquired company as an independently operating unit. The acquirer will strive, in most cases, to incorporate the entire ownership, therefore limiting the participation in value creation to the owner-managers. As elucidated for a going-public, the post-exit shareholders at a trade sale may believe that the buyout will continue to outperform permanently its industry peers as demonstrated during the LBO. However, it is more than questionable whether the former buyout will be able to continue to outperform. Conflicts of motives will likely emerge between the incumbent management and the corporate management of the acquirer. The corporate management as new good shepherds of the company will expect a similar level of personal effort by the incumbent management. With decreased shareholdings however, the former management will be less motivated due to lack of

---

466 In chapter B5.3.4.3 the post-exit performance development for going-public is elucidated in detail.

467 See details on empirical evidence on performance development after exit in chapter B5.3.

468 See details on changes after exit in both debt in chapter B2.1.1 and in managerial shareholdings in chapter B2.1.4.

entrepreneurial freedom and organizational power. Further, the incumbent management will be in the difficult situation of having to justify and fulfill the expectations attached to the purchase price. Nevertheless, the trade sale avoids the costs and necessity for information disclosure related to a going-public. The non-transparency in financial performance may be beneficial in supplier and customer negotiations. A trade sale can, if not openly discussed and negotiated, lead to a disappointment for the post-exit shareholders. They might have to accept that the purchase coincided with a peak in performance. Further, the new governance structure per se will make it more difficult for the incumbent management to extend the high level of beneficial restructuring.

A potential wealth loss could occur for the prospective acquirer to the benefit of the former buyout owner. The selling party, e.g., the buyout management or the buyout investors, might exploit their information advantage and withhold important assessments on future income and cash flow from the prospective acquirer. In the case of a going-public, the required fiduciary duties and regulatory requirements minimize potential information asymmetries.

2.2.3 Management

In the case of a successful development of the company, the owner-managers can achieve during an LBO a substantial increase in private wealth out of the range of comparable board salaries. Further, they will gain in social and professional reputation, as they are now owners of the company they manage. They benefit from increased organizational power, partially related to their increased shareholdings, and partially related to the relief from former corporate management or autocratic company founders. Even though the professionals of the buyout investor and representatives of debt holders will closely monitor their work, they have no corporate board to report. They can focus on discussions on strategic issues instead of reporting in the formats of standardized budgets and profit & loss statements required by the corporate[469]. The empirical evidence indicates that entrepreneurial freedom and independence is the most important motivator, long before the prospective increase of personal wealth[470]. However, the high commitment of personal wealth in the company may lead to risk-averse behavior, as the ability to diversify their risk is often limited[471]. In addition, there might be some conflict

469 See Gräper 1993, p. 34. For the change to strategic vs. financial control, also refer to chapter A3.3.1 and B3.3.

470 See Hanney 1986, p. 123

471 Refer to the changes in managerial shareholdings as elucidated in chapter B2.1.4. See in addition Bruton, Keels et al. 1999, p. 403.

potential between management and the buyout investors, since management will have a long-term perspective on the investment, often surpassing the investment period of the buyout and institutional investors who seek for a fast exit.

The level of management shareholdings will decrease significantly in a going-public related to the intended cash-out by management. In contrast to a trade sale, the demotivation effect is less, since management can continue to strongly participate in upsides in value creation and continue to steer the company at a high level of entrepreneurial freedom. Still, the level and direction of intrinsic motivation will change. Only in few cases will a concentrated ownership structure with a dominant blockholder continue. It is far more likely that management will be monitored by a dispersed shareholder structure. Their incentive to undertake high monitoring efforts and to enter into mutual enforcing strategic discussions decreases. Further, a reverse of the strong alignment by reduced managerial shareholdings accompanies the less intense monitoring. Bruton, Keels and Scifres comment: "manager's self-interest deviates from the company's."[472] A primary concern for the motivation and effort level is furthermore the expected increase in personal wealth and the managerial challenge ahead. Due to the debt deleveraging, the returns of a buyout can hardly be duplicated in the post-exit period. In addition, the challenge of management will as a tendency after the intense restructuring period, more of an administrative than entrepreneurial nature. Hence, the post-exit period will attract different management characteristics in terms of risk propensity.

In a trade sale, management will fear the loss of independence and self-determination. Since management will have to sell the majority of their shares to the acquirer, they will benefit only modestly from future value creation. Even if the management receives shares from the acquiring company, the participation and their personal efforts will be diluted by the efforts and success from the other business units of the parent company. On the other hand, they will be able to cash out and, in the case of a strategic acquirer, also obtain the premium related to the control of the company. The incumbent management will now have to report to a corporate board and ask for the board's approval for major investments. The intensity of monitoring will depend on the organizational form chosen and level of internal governance applied by the parent company[473].

---

472 See Bruton, Keels et al. 1999, p. 406

473 In an H-Form setting, the incumbent management can continue to operate independently, as long as the performance requirements are fulfilled. The monitoring will center around financial reporting and meeting an agreed-upon budget. However, a U-Form company will aim to integrate overlapping operations and to gain synergies. Therefore, senior managers will have to cooperate very closely with the

2.2.4 Employees

In general, a successful restructuring of a company during an LBO will be in the interest of the employees because it will increase profitability and reduce stability. The workforce will seek to secure their wages and terms of employment contracts if they are favorable in their eyes. If employees were laid off and wages renegotiated during the buyout period, it would indicate a potential wealth distribution from employees to shareholders. The implicit contracts between shareholders, management and employees would be broken which reflect the bargaining power of the workforce and imply a certain level of productivity and wages[474]. There is evidence for both industry-adjusted employment reductions and increases. For the observed decline in employment, the reductions were in all cases not significant. Only few empirical studies have analyzed the development of wages, mostly indicating a modest growth or a slight increase[475]. A possible examination is that the buyouts grow, at least in the initial phase, more slowly in sales than their competitors and sell substantial parts of their assets[476]. An employee wealth transfer hypothesis is not confirmed, due to the limitation that the observation of level of employment and wages may not be sufficient. The significant increase in operational productivity for various studies is noteworthy[477]. The buyout structure may therefore have a positive effect on reducing existing organizational slack in resources. Wealth transfer is more unlikely for Europe and especially Germany as the countries have a more rigid protection of employee rights then in the US[478].

The urgency of restructuring to more competitive cost structure and higher productivity will be diminished by both a going-public and a trade sale. In the case of a going-public, liquidity will increase, making it more difficult for management to argue any reduction in wages. Further, management will lose substantial organizational 'power' due to a more dispersed investor base and will be less able to pursue any workforce cutbacks. During a trade sale, the contractual agreements of the parent company with its employees have to be considered. Larger corporations may have more generous payments and will, in worst case, avoid any substantial cutbacks and, in best case, lead to stepwise improvements. The ongoing pressure on

---

management of the other business units. Former strategies directed to independent growth will have to be reversed and valuable resources shared across the business units. The integration into a M-Form company is a little less likely to lead to conflicts between parent and buyout management. For a detailed discussion about the distribution of control rights and the allocation of resources see also chapter A2.3.3.

474 See Shleifer and Summers 1988, p. 37

475 See Lichtenberg and Siegel 1990, p. 192

476 See Kaplan 1989a

477 See the detailed review of the empirical studies on operational productivity in chapter B3.2.1.

478 See the detailed review of the development of workfocr in chapter B3.2.1.

the labor force to compromise on employment level and compensation will most likely decrease[479]. The reversal of the buyout will lead to a more stable environment with increased routine and predictability. Under a buyout, the employees often suffer from the uncertainty and instability, making it more difficult for them to understand how they are expected to perform. In contrary, the same 'de-motivation effect' on management will also apply to the employees who participated in shareholdings and incentive schemes during the buyout. Radical organizational changes will be much harder to implement. Depending on the corporate culture, some employees will memorize the organizational processes and slack in the pre-buyout period and will feel tempted to fall back into old routines.

In total, the employees will sense an increase in job security. They will most likely favor the ownership in a larger parent shell or listing on a stock market as opposed to the increased likelihood of bankruptcy during the buyout.

2.2.5 Debt Holders

The largest share of financing is provided by the debt holders. They receive contractually fixed payments and claim for loan agreements. If the buyout company breaches financial performance undertakings, they are entitled to renegotiate their debt terms.

Most common, debt is often restructured at the entry and during the buyout, as some debt may be redeemed, partially due to better conditions if backed by a buyout investor, others may be renegotiated or converted into other securities[480]. A buyout is subject to high uncertainty of the outcome of the restructuring period - e.g. proposed operational improvement, management changes, and investment cutbacks - and feasible exit. The debt holders will require a compensation for the increased risk by a higher level of collateralization and premium spreads. To advance the risk diversification, the debt is distributed among several institutions, on the debt side by syndications, on the debt/equity side by strip financing[481].

The debt holders, especially the senior debt providers, will welcome the exit, as a substantial amount will be paid back due to the primary offering. Mezzanine capital providers will also participate in the going-public, by either taking equity shares or receiving contractually fixed cash payments. The buyout owners and the subsequent

---

479 See Bruton, Keels et al. 2002, p. 720

480 See Renneboog and Simons 2005, p. 11

481 For the growing importance of syndication in the German market, see Becker 2000, p. 34. For the advantages of strip financing, see Arzac 1992, p. 19 and the related reduction in agency costs in chapter A3.2.1 and A3.2.2.

shareholders of the floated company may be reluctant to raise equity if the reduced likelihood of bankruptcy is not passed to them by reduced premium[482]. The debt holders who anticipate the price increase should be willing to trade in some of their rights and premium in return for the expected risk reduction. Since the expensive high yield senior debt will be repaid first, the degree of overpayment is limited, though still present. A trade sale should also reduce financial distress. Diversification through related and unrelated businesses will decrease earnings volatility and risk. It is unlikely that the basic risk of the parent company is higher than the former buyout, in particular due to the lower corporate-level debt leverage. A brief study of DeGeorge and Zeckhauser reports a modest, yet insignificant relationship between performance increase and bond ratings[483]. The authors argue that some anecdotal evidence confirms a wealth transfer hypothesis, however, that the bargaining power and experience of buyout investors impedes debt holders from increasing wealth at the exit.

2.3 Changes in Management Objectives at the Exit

The change in the governance structure of the company will lead to a change in the goals and objectives of the management, as proposed by agency theory[484]. Under an open shareholder structure with weak monitoring and low managerial shareholdings, managers will maximize their status and power, incurring the build-up of slack resources and non-value-creating growth. Further, tight financial budgets and limited participation in value increase will prohibit management from undertaking risky long-term investments and entering into new markets.

The research on buyouts, so far, has reported significant changes in the goals of management, with strong evidence for the entry and some first findings for the exit[485]. At the exit, first empirical evidence indicates a re-entry of inefficiencies through loosened governance and less emphasis of efficiency by management[486]. The relationships between governance structure and management objectives will be discussed and consolidated into distinctive hypotheses (see Figure 5). Even though management objectives per se only offer limited detailed insight into the actual changes in strategy and operations of the company, they summarize the overall re-direction and may serve as a proxy indicator.

---

482 See DeGeorge and Zeckhauser 1993, pp. 1331 et seqq.
483 See DeGeorge and Zeckhauser 1993, pp. 1339 et seqq.
484 See Jensen 1986, Phan and Hill 1995, Easterwood 1989
485 See Easterwood 1989, Phan and Hill 1995, Zahra 1995, Bruton, Keels et al. 2002, Bruining and Wright 2005
486 See Bruton, Keels et al. 2002

2.3.1 Emphasis on Efficiency by Management

Agency theory places debt as a disciplinary agent for management at the heart of the buyout. With increased debt, management will seek to maximize the productivity of the operations to increase the level of available cash flow. Management will furthermore seek to reduce the risk of financial distress.

One of the determinants of the emphasis on efficiency is the level of monitoring and type of control applied by the leading investors. In contrary to entrepreneurship, the information asymmetry of the productivity for operations is low, since a measurement solely demands to determine current input and output levels (instead of understanding market dynamics and assessing potential business opportunities)[487]. Even financial control, as the less-intense type of control, allows revealing potential differences in productivity and efficiency. Therefore, the attention for efficiency should not be as dependent from the governance as for entrepreneurial activities. This will account for the operations functions, however, will not account in the same level for the administrative functions that require a much more fine-tuned measurement of efficiency[488]. Notwithstanding, the level of monitoring will considerably diminish due to free ridership.

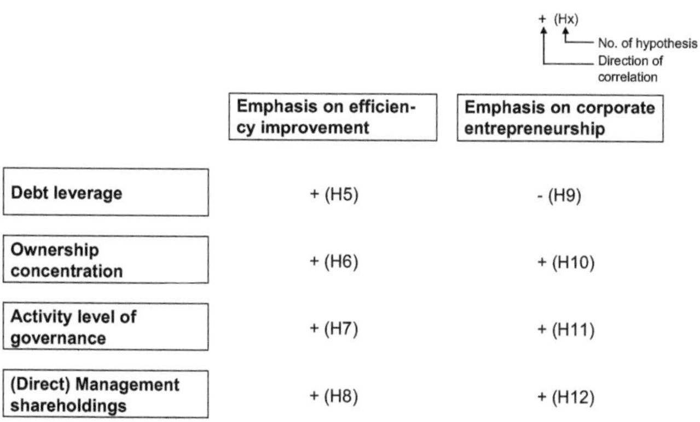

Figure 5: Changes in management objectives

A strong facilitator for the emphasis of management is the managerial shareholdings. Since they will participate in increased profitability through their own shareholdings, it will be in their own interests to reduce inefficiencies. The increased equity share of

487 Please refer to the discussion in the following chapter B2.3.2.

488 The level of repetitiveness and comparability is often much lower and makes a direct productivity comparison more diffcult. See also the discussion in chapter B3.3.1.

the buyout investors will also impose pressure on management to review current practices and increase productivity to industry benchmarks. In addition, the embedding of a buyout specialist will lead to an opening to outside best-practice and benchmark. Further, the bargaining power within the organization is much higher, simplifying the pursuit of such unpopular measures as dismissals and closures of production plants[489]. However, since they invest a large amount of private wealth in the company, they have a much lower level of risk diversification. Not surprisingly, the fear of financial distress leads to a build-up of slack resources to counter potential crises[490]. In theses cases, a share of risk through redistribution of risk is much more appropriate to reduce slack and increase efficiency.

The surveys and case studies on the change in management's agenda at the entry to the buyout confirm the increase of efficiency as management objective[491]. The major part of value creation is related to the increase in operational performance throughout the buyout period[492]. The limited research on Germany hypothesizes that the force of redirection by debt and by concentrated ownership is though less prevalent than in the US. German corporations, especially the medium-sized family-run businesses, typically have a rather high level of debt and ownership concentration.

At the exit from the buyout, some of the major disciplinary forces on management are in danger. First, management has less urgency to service high debt payments and, therefore, has higher disposition of the cash flow. Second, the decrease in ownership and governance will reduce the intensity of justifying investments and of comparing internal practices with external best-in-class. Due to free ridership, the owners will considerably decrease monitoring and be less able to provide an independent view on the targeted level of efficiency they expect. Third, lower profitability will less affect management's compensation, but rather their addiction to empire-building through slack resources, etc., may get the upper hand. Not surprisingly, the performance-based remuneration is much weaker in large corporations, and diluted by the contributions of other multiple divisions[493]. Since a buyout is often related to a dramatic down-scoping, management will feel disposed

489 A more concentrated ownership will simplify the decision-making and support managers in such unpopular measures. However, since management is responsible for executing and further detailing these measures, the influential power of managerial shareholding on operational productivity is the dominant relationship to be proven.

490 See Titzrath 1994, p. 181

491 See Muscarella and Vetsuypens 1990, Long and Ravenscraft 1993a, Phan and Hill 1995, Baker and Wruck 1989

492 See Sharp 2003, p. 43

493 See Jensen and Murphy 1990

to reestablish the former size. Still, some of the disciplinary instruments will keep an eye on management. Hence, one should formulate for the exit of a buyout:

Hypothesis 5: The emphasis on efficiency improvement decreases with a reduced debt advantage after the exit from the buyout.

Hypothesis 6: The emphasis on efficiency improvement decreases with a reduction of ownership concentration after the exit from the buyout.

Hypothesis 7: The emphasis on efficiency improvement decreases with a reduced monitoring and bonding activity level (governance) after the exit from the buyout.

Hypothesis 8: The emphasis on efficiency improvement decreases with a reduction of management shareholdings after the exit from the buyout.

As the ownership stays concentrated in a trade sale, the reduction of the focus on efficiency might be modestly weaker. Further, the transparency of performance after the going-public will make a comparison of productivity and efficiency much more difficult and less obvious. Otherwise, there is no indication for a difference in the change of efficiency improvement between the exit options as part of the management agenda.

2.3.2 Emphasis on Corporate Entrepreneurship by Management

The success of buyouts in seeking investment opportunities and stimulating innovation has directed the view on corporate entrepreneurship as an additional source for value creation. Efficiency improvement has been in the past the major contributor to value creation within the company. However, buyouts have increasingly built on their ability to innovate, engage in new ventures and renew their strategy. After a review of the determinants of financial performance of buyouts, Bull consolidates his findings of the complementary sources of value - efficiency and entrepreneurship - as[494]:

> "The evidence is convincing that management does change significantly after an LBO. The management change is interpreted as one of becoming entrepreneurial, subject to the severe constraint that a high level of debt must be serviced".

One of the facilitators of refocusing on corporate entrepreneurship (CE) is management shareholdings. An increase in the participation in long-term growth will redirect the attention of management to invest in innovation and seek new business opportunities[495]. Further, the increased ownership may provide

494 See Bull 1989b, p. 69

495 See Keels, Bruton et al. 1998, p. 64, Zahra 2000, p. 967

management with the power and freedom to undertake the strategic changes required for renewing the company[496]. To learn and manage new technologies often requires substantial personal costs for managers, costs they will be more willing to bear if they participate in the upside[497]. Another facilitator is the type of control applied by the leading investor. The information asymmetry is explicitly high for investments in entrepreneurial activities, since they often require the entry into a new business field related with a high level of uncertainty. Less active investors will typically control the company with a set of financials. Investments in projects with insecure returns and long-term horizons are difficult to measure and will not match with traditional financial incentive systems[498]. In an ownership structure with a higher level of concentration, the representative will be more willing to invest in discussions with the top management about corporate strategy since they benefit strongly in the value creation[499]. Furthermore, the high level of ownership may give them first the power to promote their interest into long-term value creation.

An additional determinant for CE activity may be the actual investment objective of the majority owner. If an investor is directed to an exit in the medium-term, they may discourage management to pursue investments with a long period until payback. On the flipside, a potential vendor at the exit of the buyout will question the long-term validity of the business. More long-term buyout investors will supposedly encourage management to follow venture with a higher risks[500]. Debt is rather a hindrance than a facilitator to the emphasis on CE by management. The aforementioned asymmetric information between the company's management and external lenders can lead to underinvestment in new projects. Furthermore, debt holders are usually risk-averse and will avoid non-secured investments. A change of ownership, especially at the succession of management, may relieve the corporation from a more risk-averse management and allow an entry of management with more entrepreneurial capabilities[501].

Since the influence of debt on entrepreneurship is apparently detrimental, the research on the relationship of changes in CE at the entry and during a buyout has been quite extensive. However, research so far has focused on single aspects of an entrepreneurial orientation after buyouts, e.g., innovation by the level of R&D expenditure or strategic renewal by corporate diversification. To summarize,

496 See the example of Duracell in: Wright 2001, p. 114; Westhead and Wright 1998, p. 175
497 See Jensen and Meckling 1976, p. 313, Wright, Kroll et al. 2002, p. 443
498 See Baysinger and Hoskisson 1989, p. 327, Wright 2001, p. 112
499 See Baysinger, Kosnik et al. 1991, p. 211
500 See Jensen and Meckling 1976, p.244
501 See Wright, Hoskisson et al. 2001, p. 250

management increases their emphasis on CE during a buyout, while balancing the opportunities of CE with the constraints from limited financing and resources[502]. The surveys report an increase in CE after the buyout, both for buyouts in the US[503] and in Germany[504]. Typically, buyouts in Germany were constrained in the pre-buyout period by limited capital, restrictions on market growth, and a weak orientation towards entrepreneurship[505].

The emphasis on CE at the exit of a buyout is however largely an unanswered question. Further, the empirical evidence is, to some degree, inconclusive. The few studies available have focused primarily on changes in R&D and capital expenditure, and ignored other activities related to CE. Holthausen and Larcker report that subsequent to the going-public, R&D expenditures decline[506]. By contrast, capital expenditure returns to the industry level after the going-public, after being significantly below industry average prior the going-public. Muscarella and Vetsuypens report a different post-exit change in the sense that all reverse buyouts reduce their capital expenditure more strongly than their industry peers do[507]. To the knowledge of the author, there are no studies analyzing the change on CE on the level of portfolio companies. Paffenholz reports that, regardless of the exit channel, the growth potential of the company is the most important factor for the success of the exit[508]. Leschke argues that for a going-public, an emphasis on corporate entrepreneurship is essential to attract potential investors[509].

---

502 The detailed effects on the constituents of CE, e.g., investment into R&D, venturing into new markets, etc., will be discussed in chapter B4. See the following papers with a good overview of changes related to buyouts: Zahra 1995, Wright, Hoskisson et al. 2001, Bruning and Verwaal 2005.

503 In a survey of 47 manufacturing companies, Zahra analyzes the entrepreneurial activities of LBOs (See Zahra 1995, p. 225). He finds evidence for an increase in commercialization, product innovation and modification, R&D quality and venturing, with only R&D expenditures remaining at the same level. He confirms a positive EO-performance relationship with a narrow time lag of three years after buyout. (See Zahra 1995). Bruining and Wright examine the change in entrepreneurship activities and in the contribution of the venture capital to the EO of LBOs. The authors summarize the findings as proof for both innovation and new business venturing during the buyouts restructuring period (See Bruining and Wright 2002, p. 148).

504 Wegner analyzes the extent of corporate entrepreneurship among German buyouts. For the group of growth buyouts, he finds a significant higher focus on innovation and corporate venturing, for strategic renewal less significant as opposed to non-growth buyouts. Among the respondents, 58% (44%) of the managers of the growth (non-growth) buyouts note that the extent of entrepreneurial activities has increased. Wegner further reports that the CE is related to an increase in financial performance (See Wegner 2003). Other research in Germany has focused on single aspects of CE, e.g., Vest who reports that 20 of 29 buyouts increase the activities around product innovation (See Vest 1995, p. 291).

505 See Forst 1992, pp. 36 et seqq., Gräper 1993, pp. 126 et seqq., Vest 1995, p. 327

506 See Holthausen and Larcker 1996, p. 311

507 See Muscarella and Vetsuypens 1990, p. 1405

508 Only for share buy-back, the liquidity and openness of the buy-side is more important than the growth potential. See Paffenholz 2004, p. 166

509 See Leschke 2003, p. 250

Among the changes in the constituents of governance, the interaction of management shareholdings and debt will influence, at most, the emphasis on CE after the exit. Apparently, the expected decrease in debt will allow an increase in the financing of CE-related resources and the undertaking of new ventures. However, reduced managerial shareholdings and less close governance might lead to less efficient allocation of the available resources[510]. Although the apparent level of CE activities might increase, the extent of efficiency and efficacy is questionable[511]. The incumbent managers may follow their personal favored projects that had been put on the back during the buyout. Hence, one should formulate for the exit of a buyout:

Hypothesis 9: The emphasis on corporate entrepreneurship increases with a reduced debt leverage after the exit from the buyout.

Hypothesis 10: The emphasis on corporate entrepreneurship decreases with a reduction of ownership concentration after the exit from the buyout.

Hypothesis 11: The emphasis on corporate entrepreneurship decreases with a reduced monitoring and bonding activity level (governance) after the exit from the buyout.

Hypothesis 12: The emphasis on corporate entrepreneurship decreases with a reduction of management shareholdings after the exit from the buyout.

3 Post-Exit Changes in Efficiency-Focused Management Activities

3.1 Introductory Remarks

The changes in management's focus on efficiency will undoubtfully lead to changes in structure and operations of the company. As elucidated in the introductory to the basic model, management implements various measures to maximize profitability and cash flow during the buyout restructuring. The following discourse will answer the question how the changes in governance will affect the activities of management

510 Robbie, Thompson and Wright polarize the commitment of management to efficiency as opposed to other objectives: "... Consider a typical cash cow division, perhaps with high returns, but little scope for profitable re-investment: as a debt-laden independent business it must pursue efficiency; as a cash generating division its managers may prefer to pursue alternative goals." See Robbie, Thompson et al. 1991, p. 79

511 Zahra, Neubaum and Huse report an increase in CE orientation with increased executive ownership, and argue for firms with low ownership: "Lack of stock ownership may cause executives to behave opportunistically by supporting projects that increase their own wealth and further ensure their job security. Lack of ownership may also discourage executives from supporting CE projects that put their salaried positions in jeopardy". See Zahra 2000, p. 950

in the post-exit period. In detail, the changes in governance are decomposed into their constituents and separately discussed by their effect on the individual levers. The author will divide the efficiency-focused management activities into those directed to operations (hypotheses 13 to 16) and those directed to organization and administration (hypotheses 17 to 19). In contrast to the entrepreneurial growth-focused management activities, the following relationships of governance to levers of value creation do not need to be differentiated by the exit channel.

3.2 Changes in Operations and Manufacturing

As discussed before, the success of a buyout increasingly depends on the value creation from strategy and operations in the company itself. One would predict that the disciplinary force of debt and managerial shareholdings would direct management's attention to apply best practices and to reduce slack resources. Management plays the most important role, as it is the change agent and has to overcome organizational hindrances.

Not surprisingly, the empirical evidence reports a significant upswing in productivity at the entry into the buyout. The buyout apparently serves as a catalyst for restructuring, enabling (and motivating) management to undergo changes, which are often already known to be necessary.

+ (Hx)
No. of hypothesis
Direction of correlation

	Operational productivity	Asset productivity	Out-sourcing and Off-shoring	Working capital mana-gement	Overhead productivity	Hierarchical complexity	Mana-gement control system
Debt leverage	+ (H13a)	+ (H14a)	+ (H15a)	+ (H16a)	+ (H17a)	- (H18a*)	+ (H19a*)
Ownership concentration	+ (H13b)		+ (H15b*), o (H15c**)				+ (H19b*)
Activity level of governance			+ (H15d)	+ (H16b)			
(Direct) Management shareholdings	+ (H13c)	+ (H14b)	+ (H15e)	+ (H16c)	+ (H17b)	- (H18b*)	+ (H19c*)

* Only for trade sale
** Only for going-public

Figure 6: Overview of hypotheses for efficiency-related management activities

If, as reported, the disciplinary force is so prominent from the buyout structure, the question has to be answered to what extent the beneficial effect can be transferred when exiting the buyout. The evidence of managerial activities after the exit is, however, sparse. Only a short post-exit time span is covered and lacks of detailed understanding of the underlying activities. The productivity of labor and assets employed will depend on the exit channel chosen and the new owner. A trade sale may lead to substantial changes in the resource allocation and operations between the former buyout and the existing business units. The availability of cash from a going-public will increase the likelihood of more asset-intense operations and a higher share from the value chain.

3.2.1 Operational Productivity and Employment

In the introductory part, the hypothesis was already discussed whether a buyout leads to a value transfer from the employees to the investors during the entry and the exit period of the buyout. The empirical research so far has confirmed a reduction of slack resources, however, it has also reported a beneficial increase in employment at the buyout firms. Notwithstanding, the public discussion, especially in Germany, has associated buyouts with off-shoring of manufacturing activities to low-cost countries and massive dismissals[512]. Highly efficient processes in operations and administration require the flexibility to adjust the workforce in a short term. The flexibility to adjust the workforce is, however, often restricted by long-term labor contracts. Further, many entrepreneurs feel responsible for their workforce in the sense that they want to offer secure job position. Finally, any dismissals are naturally highly unpopular activities, which no manager will seek to take the responsibility. An additional argument for high pre-buyout labor resources is the objective of managers to build up resources as a sign of their status, e.g., through employing relatives and friends.

First, managerial shareholdings should refocus management on increasing operational productivity at the entry into the buyout. The bargaining power within the organization is much higher, simplifying the pursuit of such unpopular measures as dismissals and closures of production plants[513]. Empirical evidence denotes significant productivity increases from managerial shareholdings and ownership that is more concentrated after breaking unfavorable contracts between unions, employees and the company due to known substantial slack in resources[514]. Under the managerial freedom of a buyout, operational managers will more closely analyze

---

512 See the examples in the introductory chapter A1.1.

513 A more concentrated ownership will simplify the decision-making and support managers in such unpopular measures. However, since management is responsible for executing and further detailing these measures, the influential power of managerial shareholding on operational productivity is the dominant relationship to be proven.

514 See Shleifer and Summers 1988

the current level of inputs, reflecting the level of staffing, wages, and the efficiency of the organizational system. At the entry into buyouts, the revised contracts may lead to reductions in the level of employment and wages. Second, the necessity to service the high debt payments will also direct management's attention to the high cost position of personnel and potential measures to reduce it. Next to decrease inefficiencies of processes, management will consider refining labor contracts in the sense of reducing above average contracts.

Author	Geographical focus	Operational productivity and employm. changes	Asset productivity and capital expenditure	Outsourcing and offshoring	During buyout	Post-exit
Bannock (1989)	UK	x	x		x	
Bull (1989)	US		x		x	
Kaplan (1989a)	US	x	x		x	
Malone (1989)	US		x		x	
Lichtenberg Siegel (1990)	US	x	x		x	
Mohan (1990)	US	x	x			x
Muscarella Vetsuypens (1990)	US	x	x		x	x
Smith (1990)	US	x	x		x	
Opler (1992)	US	x	x		x	
Forst (1992)	Germany	x	x		x	
Wright Thompson Robbie (1992)	UK	x	x		x	
Graeper (1993)	Germany	x	x		x	
Mian Rosenfeld (1993)	US		x			x
Verma (1993)	US	(x)	(x)		x	
Denis (1994)	US	x	x		x	
Lei Hitt (1995)	US			x	x	
Vest (1995)	Germany	x	x		x	
Holthausen, Larcker (1996)	US	x	x			x
Wright Wilson Robbie (1997)	UK	x	x		x	
Jakoby (2000)	Germany	x	x		x	
EVCA (2001)	EU	x			x	
Amess (2002)	US	x	x		x	
Harris Siegel Wright (2002)	UK	x	x	(x)	x	
Bruton Scifres Keels (2003)	US	x				x
Wegner (2003)	Germany	x	x		x	
EVCA (2005)	EU	x			x	

Table 7: Surveys on the impact of buyouts on manufacturing and operations

The direction of managerial action to operations is unspecific, yet determined by the objective to maximize cash flow. Operational managers will strive to apply current best-practice production processes, e.g., principles of lean management that focus on reducing any unnecessary wasteful activities. Hence, shop floor managers might reassess current tact times, extend the level of standardization, and undertake detailed task analysis to find waste in movements, etc. Management could also revise the level of automation. However, the pressure to avoid investments might inhibit management from implementing new production processes with higher efficiency and they may substitute, for the short term, these processes with manual labor.

Often, the variety of tasks and flexibility of production workers is constrained by long-term contracts with the union and workforce. For instance, the time for any movements in assembly is in most European, and especially German manufacturing companies, regulated by industry norms and individual company agreements. Debt discipline and managerial freedom may allow breaking up the aforementioned slack and the optimal readjustment of the work force level to the process in question. Executives may also consider changing the composition of employment. They could feel inclined to substitute older employees with new employees, who might be cheaper. Managers may also be shortsighted and reduce the workforce related to long-term operational productivity and to performance, for instance cutting staff that control product quality, undertake extensive documentation or conduct continuous machine maintenance. There is also a growing body of evidence relating to enhanced employee ownership and variable remuneration. The increased co-ownership of employees offers the same positive effect as the introduction of owner-managers[515]. Additional efficiency improvements may also be expected if the buyouts are spin-offs of former multi-divisional companies. The workforce in is often controlled by multi-layered hierarchies with additional coordination activities and complex internal remuneration packages[516].

Since the potential threat of one-sided wealth transfer to the benefit of the buyout investor has been widely discussed, the empirical evidence is rather rich, however limited to the entry into and the period during the buyout. The absence of analyses of non-financial output is a dilemma when examining operational productivity. Most surveys link labor input to financial output, e.g., operating return or cash flow[517]. The authors often intend to normalize productivity changes from pre- to post-buyout for which the indicators are appropriate. The indicators, however, are diluted by potential changes in other cost positions, for instance in the level of material cost or expenditure for R&D and advertising.

The first series of studies of buyouts in the 1980s in the US report that the majority of buyouts increase their employment while improving their operational productivity[518]. However, the increases in employment are below industry average,

---

515 See Wilson 1992

516 See Thompson, Wright et al. 1992

517 For instance, Bull limits his conclusion by the shortcomings of using financial and accounting variables to measure performance improvements. See Bull 1989a, p. 277, Kaplan 1989a, p. 224, Smith 1990b, p. 147, Muscarella and Vetsuypens 1990. Only Lichtenberg and Siegel 1990 and Amess 2002 have used non-financial output variables,e.g., total factor output in the unit of produced units, etc.

518 Kaplan notes an increase by 61.5% of sampled firms, leading to an average absolute increase of 0.9%, and rejects the hypothesis that "buyouts gain from firing a large number of employees" (See Kaplan 1989a, p. 241) However, the increase is still 6.2% points below industry average. Kaplan excludes buyout firms with

although not significantly below. The increase in operational productivity is proven not to be related exclusively to the divestment of underperforming business units, but also to actual improvements in the processes in operations and administration. Similar results are reported by research on buyouts in the United Kingdom[519]. In two longitudinal analyses, the researchers report that the increase in operational productivity occurs with some time delay (year 2) and that the achieved efficiency advantage declines at the end of the buyout (year 6). The authors relate the increased efficiency to some degree to the increased level of management shareholdings. A study by Thompson and Wright investigating the change in labor claims that although the bargaining position of organized labor appears to be weakened, the work conditions and compensation are not severely damaged during the buyout restructuring[520]. However, a survey rejects the hypothesis that union recognitions declines dramatically and that unions are highly resistant against a buyout[521].

The studies based on the actual factor output confirm the increase in productivity for buyouts as opposed to non-buyouts. Lichtenberg and Siegel have analyzed the impact of ownership change on manufacturing plants and their productivity. They argue that buyout transactions coincide with a low level of efficiency in relation to

---

significant divestiture or acquisition activities (over 10% of capital). The reported decrease in comparison to industry average is not significant. Bannock confirms the increase with a share of 78. 5% of buyouts reporting an increase in employment, whereas 49.3% report an increase of at least 10% (See Bannock 1990, p. 19). The decline of employment in a few buyouts is recurred to the increase in operational productivity. Smith observes a strong increase of 71% of operating cash flow to employee for the first 2 years after the buyout (See Smith 1990b, pp. 150 et seqq.). Similar to Kaplan, the changes in employment are not significantly different from the industry average, although the number of employees as in the survey by Kaplan, declines. The comparison of the group of buyouts with substantial divestments does not reveal any significant differences in increases in operating cash flow. A long-term analysis of employment between the buyout transaction and the going-public by Muscarella and Vetsuypens indicate an average increase of employment for 17%. This increase outpaces the random sample. (See Muscarella and Vetsuypens 1990, p. 1405). Smith argues that the improvements of efficiency are related to some degree to improved operations and increased productivity. Opler confirms the results of Smith (a rise of operating cash flow per employee of 40% in year 2 after the buyout) and relates the increases in improvements to operational productivity (See Opler 1992, p. 33).

519 Wright, Thompson and Robbie measure for UK that 24.7% reduce employment at the buyout and 17.6% in the years following the divestments are treated separately (See Wright, Thompson et al. 1992, pp. 64 et seqq.). In a review of productivity changes, Wright, Wilson and Robbie report strong improvements in profit per employee and productivity, with initial transaction. In total, employment decreases by 6.3% at the entry into the LBO, but recovers to 1.9% above the number of employee at the time of the transaction. Changes through acquisitions or a time lag of 2 years to transaction. The authors argue that the incentives and control mechanisms take their time until they fully apply. After year 5 years post-buyout, the efficiency advantages of buyout to non-buyout however decline to insignificance. (See Wright 1997. p. 564).

520 See Thompson and Wright 1987, pp. 15 et seqq.

521 In a buyout, managers are reported to recognize the need of trade unions in industrial relations. The researchers comment that the buyout leads to some degree to a decoupling of unions from the employees, limiting their power and making a removal of recognition not necessary (See Wright, Coyne et al. 1984, p. 52).

the industry average[522]. The increase in the first two years is significant and is reported to continue. In addition, the empirical evidence suggests a strong decline in wages and the staffing level of non-production workers, while the wages of production workers slightly increase. The authors conclude that the management of buyouts tends to motivate the workforce more by wage premiums than by intensifying supervision. A more recent survey by Amess reports a one-time ('Hicks-Neutral') shift in output productivity by 16.1% (labor and capital), and a marginal increase of operational productivity by 32%[523]. Amess argues that the governance structure - in detail, the debt bonding, the management shareholding, and the governance activity of the buyout investor - shows an apparently unambiguous positive effect on the motivation of divisional managers and leads to significantly higher operational productivity. For instance, managers refused to employ full-time employees in the case of O.M. Scott for temporary peaks, but instead hired part-time workers, therefore, increasing productivity and reducing personnel costs[524]. A more recent survey confirms the increase in operational productivity and argues that the increase is based on improved processes and on reduced labor intensity of production[525]. A survey by Verma investigating the change in total factor productivity reports, in contrast to the other surveys presented, a significant decline in the first two years after the buyout[526].

---

522 Lichtenberg and Siegel report that factor productivity increases. The increase is related to the 'matching theory', proposing that a firm with a lack of best managerial and technical skills will sell the manufacturing plant to another corporation who is able to operate the plant at best level. Therefore, the plants sold are among those with low levels of efficiency (See Lichtenberg and Siegel 1987, p. 665). Lichtenberg and Siegel continued their research and conducted a thorough analysis of over 1100 US LBOs and MBOs between 1981 and 1986. For the separation of productivity effects of labor and capital the researchers apply a standard Cobb-Douglas production function. The buyouts observed reveal average total productivity differences in the first 2 years post-buyout of 2.7 percentage points for LBOs and 5.9 percentage points for MBOs against non-buyouts. The plants involved in buyouts show above-average levels of productivity 10 to 12 years prior to the buyout, then decline strongly in subsequent years. Based on the earlier survey of productivity variations after ownership changes, the authors propose a 'u-shaped' path for productivity development. On the basis of the first two years after the buyout transaction, they predict a continuous productivity increases in the following years (See Lichtenberg and Siegel 1990, p. 180).

523 Separating the productivity shift between labor and capital base, Amess assigns a marginal increase in operational productivity on average of 32% and of minus 71% to capital to post-buyout. On a closer look at year 1 post-buyout, he derives an even higher increase of 41% to non-buyouts (see Amess 2002, pp. 312 et seqq.).

524 See Baker and Wruck 1989, p. 187

525 Harris, Siegel and Wright conduct a decomposition of the post- to pre-buyout changes in total factor productivity on plant level by a Cobb-Douglas function. The reported buyouts between 1994 and 1998 experience a substantial increase in productivity (+70.5% in the short run and +90.3% in the long run). The authors further measure the changes in the ratios of capital to labor and materials to labor, and conclude that both the increased share of material costs and less capital presumably imply a higher share of outsourcing (See Harris, Siegel et al. 2002).

526 Verma applies a Leontief production function to analyze the change in TFP on firm level. Although the

The research in Germany has also focused on the change at the entry into and during the buyout. Forst consolidates his findings from interviews with managers and buyout executives that both recapitalization and management turnover often lead to significant improvements in the efficiency of manufacturing and working processes[527]. Often, the founder-CEO neglects investments in new facilities and machines. Therefore, the workforce has outdated machinery at their disposal associated with lower productivity than their direct competitors have. Forst observe that employment decreases at spin-off buyouts, but increases at succession-buyouts[528]. Vest confirms a modest increase in employment over the buyout cycle for the majority of spinoff-buyouts investigated. If employment is cut back, this happens in most cases in an balanced manner over all functional areas. One exemption is manufacturing, where workforce adjustments occur more rarely[529]. Vest further points out that management in such a corporate setting is often risk-averse to purchasing and, therefore, prefers to in-source. Nevertheless, increasing revenues lead to a continuation of the high staffing level. Gräper confirms, on the one hand, the necessity for reduction of over-capacity at spinoff-buyouts but on the other hand, the necessity for impressive growth at succession-buyouts[530]. More over, the author observes a notable increase in operational productivity after the entry into the buyout structure[531]. Jakoby argues that the reduction of personnel costs in terms of salary cuts are limited, since workers benefit from a safeguard of existing labor contracts for at least for 1 year after the buyout [532]. Jakoby analyzes employment of successful and less-successful buyouts before and during the buyout, and

---

sample is to a large part identical to the one analyzed by Kaplan, Verma relates the decline in both operating margin and total factor productivity to the manufacturing part of the sample. He argues that the observed time period of two years may be too short to implement successful cost reduction programs (See Verma 1993).

527 See Forst 1992, pp. 35 et seqq.

528 Forst reports that 37.5% of succession buyouts increased their employment more than 5% in average. For spinoff buyouts the share was only 21.4%. After the spin-off, resources dedicated to the former administration and coordination with the parent divisions were reduced. See Forst 1992, pp. 73 et seqq.

529 See Vest 1995, p. 307. In a detailed time series, Vest further reports that in going-concern buyouts employment is reduced by 1.1% in the first year, however increases cumulated by 34.8% in year 6 after the buyout transaction. For turnaround buyouts, mass dismissals were necessary in 4 of the 11 cases analyzed. On average, employment had to be reduced to 73.35% of the staffing level at the transaction, and only slowly recovered to 94.25% of the original level in year 6. The primary reasons for partial reductions in employment are the decrease in manufacturing penetration (18 of 29 buyouts) and the increase in the level of automation (reported by 9 of 29 buyouts). The author argues that a substantial part of the reduction is related to prior ownership in a multi-divisional corporation, where due to inflexible personnel policy production overcapacities and a high share of value creation were prevalent (See Vest 1995, p. 307 to 313).

530 Gräper reports that employment at spinoff-buyouts decreases to 96.8% (year 2) of the staffing level at the buyout (year 0). In sucession-related, buyouts enlarge workforce to by 12.35% (year 2) to the original staff level (See Gräper 1993, p. 140 – 141).

531 See Gräper 1993, p. 147

532 See Jakoby 2000, pp. 318 et seqq.

summarizes that the more successful buyouts have substantially decreased personnel already prior to the buyout, however, but also increase personnel more strongly during the buyout[533]. The recent survey of Wegner reports that operating inefficiencies and low productivity are not the prevailing issues in the pre-buyout period[534]. Even for non-growth, efficiency and turnaround-focused buyouts, other factors, e.g., reduced entrepreneurial freedom due to a dominant founder, an inefficient capital structure and bureaucracy are more prohibitive for improvements. Wegner reports an increase in employment for the growth (non-growth) buyouts of 19.6% (1.8%) per annum, accompanied by a revenue growth of 22.3% (a decline of 2.6%)[535]. The author claims that the buyouts, therefore, increase productivity[536]. Two surveys by EVCA confirm that the majority of buyouts increase the number of employees, with the strongest increase related to family-controlled buyouts[537]. A decline in labor compensation is reported for employee buyouts. Chaplinsky, Niehaus and de Gucht find evidence that in such cases the employees trade in favorable labor contracts for shareholding participation[538]. Often, the funding of a buyout would not have succeeded without significant changes in labor contracts. On the flipside, employee ownership does not prevent a reduction in employment[539].

To conclude, the entry into the buyout structure leads to an increase in productivity as consistently reported by both recent and older research. The question about the speed with which the increase occurs and how long it persists remains unanswered. Changes in wages and share of production to non-production workers have only been reviewed in a single survey: Further derivations and implied conjectures should be handled, therefore, carefully. The publicly discussed threat of substantial layoffs in comparison to the industry average can be rejected.

---

533 In total, the more successful buyouts increase their average employment by 10%. Interestingly, the fluctuation rate of personnel significantly reduces after the buyout, indicating a higher level of satisfaction among the staff. See Jakoby 2000, p. 318

534 See Wegner 2003, p. 178

535 See Wegner 2003, pp. 196 et seqq.

536 This is only true as long as the share of value creation remains constant. Other studies, e.g. Gräper 1993 and Vest 1995, report that share of value is decreased. Therefore, a closer analysis of the buyouts studied by Wegner would be required.

537 A survey of the EVCA reports that 60% of sampled companies increased their employment, whereas 25.5% reduced. Interestingly, the authors of the EVCA survey further note that both at top management, middle management and for other employees total remuneration increased in around 60 to 70% of cases (See EVCA 2001, p. 14). A very recent survey of the EVCA with an enlarged sample base reports that employment rose by on average 2.4% per annum during the buyout period. Further, the majority of buyouts reported a constant or significantly increasing level of staff. Among the different buyout types, the family-controlled buyouts achieved with on average 7% the highest growth in employment (See EVCA 2005, p. 4).

538 See Chaplinsky, Niehaus et al. 1998, pp. 300 et seqq.

539 See Chaplinsky, Niehaus et al. 1998, p. 315 and 316

The question of the development of employment and operational productivity at the exit and in the years following the buyout is, not surprisingly, largely unanswered. With a decrease in managerial shareholdings, the bargaining position and independence of management will be weakened. The unambiguous support of a large owner will also, in the case of a going-public, decrease. Further, the liquidity increase and reduced debt payment through a going-public will make it more difficult for management to justify any reduction in wages. For a trade sale, the contractual agreements and working standards of the acquiring company have to be considered. Larger corporations may have payments that are more generous and will have to increase the provisions to the general standard. One, therefore, expecta management to be less able to pursue any workforce cutbacks. On the other hand, management will feel less motivated to minimize the workforce and seek to employ relatives and friends as a sign of status, re-establishing slack resources. However, from the reported empirical evidence, one may hypothesize that some changes are long-term and will survive the exit from the buyout. The measures taken to modernize the manufacturing facilities and to introduce best-practice, lean management principles may continue to keep operational productivity high, for at least one investment cycle. Further, the reduction of the share of value creation will, at least short to medium-term, not be revised. If employees' compensation has been enriched by stock plans and other performance-related constituents, one would also expect them not be revised, as they are to the benefit of both the owners and the workforce. Finally, a trade sale through an acquirer in a related industry should be able to seize significant economies of scale. The surveys on reverse buyouts report a continuation of the high level of operational productivity after the exit. In a review of reverse buyouts in the 1980s, Mohan reports that the ratio of sales to employees remains significantly above industry average and even increases from year 1 to year 2 after the exit[540]. Holthausen and Larcker report a decline in the number of employees at company level, but not below the relative development of the industry[541]. Bruton, Keels and Scifres observe that the share of companies following restructuring activities to lower operational inefficiencies drops from 54% to 36%[542]. The authors also report that the reorganization of production facilities become even more prominent in the public period. The research from related surveys on the post-acquisition changes from trade sales does not provide a conclusive picture of the

540 See Mohan 1990, pp. 96 et seqq.
541 See Holthausen and Larcker 1996, p. 315
542 See Bruton, Keels et al. 2002, p. 719

effect on operational productivity[543]. In the corollary, the author concludes the following hypotheses:

Hypothesis 13a: The focus on improvements in operational productivity decreases with a reduced debt leverage (after the exit from the buyout).

Hypothesis 13b: The focus on improvements in operational productivity decreases with a more disperse shareholder base (after the exit from the buyout).

Hypothesis 13c: The focus on improvements in operational productivity decreases with reduced managerial shareholdings (after the exit from the buyout).

A high share of performance-related payment of employees, e.g., by employee stock ownership programs, may encounter a reduced focus on operational productivity and ensure high motivation among the employees to continue seeking efficiency. Since employees and management often strongly benefit from a going-public, the likelihood for operational productivity improvements may be higher at a going-public.

3.2.2 Asset Productivity and Capital Expenditure

A shortcoming in interest alignment of principal and agents may result in a residual loss related to the asset base and capital expenditure[544]. Managers may abstain from divesting underperforming assets that were in former times an essential part of the business and whose disposal would result in severe changes and even layoffs.

The alignment of interest through managerial shareholdings and the aforementioned strengthening of the organizational power of managers will stimulate a reassessment of the level and the scope of the current asset base. Owner-managers will diligently ask themselves which assets are truly necessary to operate the business and which are dispensable[545]. Further, they will compare their productivity with the industry benchmark. In addition, the necessity to service the debt payments will motivate management to consider divesting dispensable assets and to reduce budgeted capital expenditure to a feasible minimum. For short-term liquidity, a sale and leaseback of

543 For instance, Seth reports a positive increase in the ratio of production costs of goods sold to net sales for the combined equity for each of the two years following the acquisition. However, the increase is not significant. It may be noteworthy that the level of value creation in operations correlated strongly with the relative firm size in the sense that if the acquisition target was of significant size the expected effect on relative costs was stronger. See Seth 1990, pp. 440 et seqq.

544 See Jensen and Meckling 1976, pp. 5 et seqq., and details on agency theory in chapter A3.2.

545 The author differentiates between asset disposal and corporate downsizing. The former embodies the disposal of assets not absolutely required for the operation of the firm or no longer relevant due to substitution. Corporate downsizing embodies divestments of fields of business no longer in the focus of management and covers entire business units and divisions. The author will detail corporate downsizing as a lever for value creation within strategic renewal in chapter B4.2.

assets may seem appropriate. Management could also consider outsourcing substantial parts of the value creation and avoiding the risk of investing in specific assets[546]. Furthermore, operational managers will strive to reduce current assets, in particular the work-in-progress to minimize working capital in manufacturing and inventory[547]. Investments in the asset base will be limited to basic renewals of machinery and to projects most relevant for growth and profit increase. Any non-vital investments will be postponed. In addition, management could revise the level of automation. The pressure to avoid investments might inhibit management from implementing new production processes with higher efficiency and, at least in the short term, endorse substituting low automation with manual labor. To maximize utilization and avoid expansion investments, they might increase machine hours and move to multi-shift schedules. Optimized arrangements of workflow and increased standardization could help to reduce the tact time required and, therefore, raise asset productivity.

A caveat, once again, has to be placed on the measurement of the variables, in this case the asset base itself. Most research lacks the stringency of comparing nominal output to a nominal asset base with the same accounting principles. Further, insufficient data directs most researchers to measure asset productivity using accounting terms[548], e.g., operating return or cash flow to asset bases. In addition, any comparisons of asset productivity are complicated by revaluation of assets after the transaction[549]. Since some companies divest a substantial part of their business, the comparability of pre- to post-buyout asset productivity even within a company may be limited. For instance, companies might dispose underperforming assets, while not optimizing the remaining operations. Most researchers normally take this dilution of cause and effect into account and define different groups of companies to conduct separate analyses.

From bird's eye perspective, the efficiency hypothesis for improvements in asset productivity and reduced capital expenditures at the entry and during the buyout is confirmed. The surveys conducted on buyouts in the US and UK confirm in the majority a significant increase in asset productivity and a decrease in capital

546 The lever of outsourcing will be discussed in the light of concentrating on core capabilities in chapter B3.2.3.

547 The reduction of working capital will be discussed in more detail in chapter B3.2.4.

548 For instance, Kaplan uses cash flow to assets as proxy for the efficiency with which the buyout uses its given asset base (See Kaplan 1991, p. 230).

549 For instance, hidden reserves may induce a revaluation and apparently lead to reduced productivity (or an impairment an increase in productivity). A change in accounting methods associated with the buyout furthers dilutes any apparent changes in income and productivity.

expenditures[550]. Kaplan argues that the decrease is related to a more efficient capital allocation and to the deferral of investments with negative net present value[551]. Further, studies measuring the actual factor output also report an improvement in asset productivity[552]. In many cases, sale and leaseback are used to maintain the assets, however, and to increase short-term liquidity[553]. The improvement of asset productivity is not related to a disposal of underperforming assets, as reported by a study from Smith[554]. In a study by Amess, the author measures a strong decline in asset productivity. Since the revaluation of assets are taken into account, Amess argues that the adjustments after accounting audit at the point of transaction dilute the effect, e.g., by using different depreciation rates. Second, the author calls the assets 'lumpy' and 'not malleable' to the desires of managers. Third, Amess makes

550 Bull shows a strong increase in EBIT and sales to the initial asset base and a reduction in capital expenditure as quota to sales from pre- to post-buyout. The author relates the increase to real gains in productivity and efficiency improvement. However, the asset base is not consolidated for substantial divestments or acquisitions. Further the author does not detail the nature of assets sold and the related management's intention (See Bull 1989a, pp. 273 et seqq.). In a broader study, Kaplan also confirms substantial productivity increases. Operating income to assets increase by 16.6% (36.1%) industry-adjusted from year t before to year 1 (year 2) after the buyout transaction, net cash flow to the same relative time period by 50.5% (85.4%). In the light of write-ups of inventory and assets, the author comments that the changes observed underestimate the level of improvement. Also, capital expenditure normalized to assets and sales decreases, with a drop of -5.7 % (-19.3%) for year 1 before to year 2 (year 3) after the buyout transaction, and remains below industry average. Kaplan quotes postponed maintenance as a potential causes and leaves it open as to whether the capital expenditure reductions increase or decrease value. However, he consolidates the findings as the result of operational improvements and the aligned interests of managers and owners (See Kaplan 1989a, pp. 227 et seqq.). Similar results on declining capital expenditures are also reported by Opler, with an industry adjusted decline of 50.7% of capital expenditure to sales in year 2 after year 1 prior to the buyout (see Opler 1992, p. 32). Malone observes that 34% of small and medium-sized buyouts have liquidated or sold unnecessary assets, as opposed to 4% who have invested (See Malone 1989, p. 358). In contrast, Bannock reports that 36.3% of thje surveyed buyouts increase their investments in the three years after entering the buyout, as opposed to 3.0% that reduce their expenditure (See Bannock 1990, p. 15).

551 See Kaplan 1989a, p. 229

552 Lichtenberg and Siegel report a strong decrease in the capital base and improved asset productivity (See Lichtenberg and Siegel 1990, pp.182 et seqq.). In a similar research approach, Wright, Wilson and Robbie decompose the effect on total outcome by using a Cobb-Douglas production function. Asset productivity is significantly enhanced after a 2-year lag and remains superior until 6 years after initial transaction (See Wright 1997, pp. 564 et seqq.).

553 Wright, Thompson and Robbie report a high share of companies to sell surplus equipment and refinance fixed assets in terms of sale and leaseback. The authors also measure that 44% of respondents admit asset purchases that would not have occurred without the buyout, since no capital was available (see Wright, Thompson et al. 1992, pp. 313 et seqq).

554 Smith confirms the asset productivity increase, with an upside for year 1 to year 2 post-buyout of 5.9%. The author assumes, therefore, the longevity of increase in asset productivity. Smith further compares the asset with the non-asset sale sub-sample. Productivity increase is confirmed for all cases and rejects the hypothesis that the improvements are solely caused by disposal of underperforming assets. Moreover, Smith also restates a significant decrease in capital expenditure to sales by 9.2% for year 1 prior to post-buyout. A further interesting insight is developed by testing the correlation of short-run increases in asset productivity to reduced capital expenditure. By comparing beginning-of-year assets, the increase in asset productivity can be linked to operational improvements, not to reduced capital expenditure and in the following depreciated asset base (See Smith 1990b, pp. 149 et seqq.).

potential revaluations to justify that the premiums and goodwill paid are responsible for the low asset productivity. Since no further details are provided on the industry or on other indicators to explain the decrease, the potential causes could apply to the former studies and offer only a limited prediction to resolve the contradiction. Other researchers have circumvented this problem by either introducing a mean-reversion or comparing only relative changes while omitting the fiscal year of the buyout[555].

As reported in chapter 3.2.1, underinvestment is often a characteristic of the pre-buyout period for German companies. The surveys support the necessity for capital expenditure in the first years after the buyout. Forst reports that 46.8% of the buyouts analyzed increase their machinery investment by at least 5% per annum[556]. The survey respondents of the study by Vest also indicate investments in manufacturing capacity[557]. On the other hand, the companies sell non-required business assets and reduce overcapacities[558]. Sale and leaseback as a means of increasing liquidity is only moderately used[559].

It seems that residual loss and cumulative slack of resources are lastingly trimmed down. Alongside increased output to input, the investments in the asset base are diminished. A detailed analysis over a longer period of the effect of reduced capital expenditure on asset productivity though would be necessary to find a satisfactory answer. Some authors are right when they question whether the reduced investments are detrimental to or supportive of value creation. Finally, the high level of analysis does not provide any insight into which managerial activities are actually undertaken. It would also be of interest to understand the tradeoffs of management between investing capital for capacity and efficiency improvements against reducing expenditure to service the debt payments.

Again, the question of activities in the years following the buyout is largely unanswered. After the exit from the buyout, and with a decrease in managerial shareholdings, investments in non-value creating activities may increase. The infusion of cash through the going-public and to some extent from a less leveraged new parent company may lead to more asset-intense investment policy. On the contrary, the change in ownership may lead to an increase in capital expenditure, if investments have been postponed to the post-buyout period but are regarded,

---

555 For mean-reversion adjustment due to asset inventory revaluations, see Holthausen and Larcker 1996. For the omission of the fiscal year of buyout, see Kaplan 1989a.

556 See Forst 1992, p. 75

557 Of 29 buyouts analyzed, 13 report an increase in capacity, whereas only 4 will reduce capacity (See Vest 1995, p. 307)

558 See Vest 1995, p. 274

559 See Gräper 1993, p. 153, Vest 1995, p. 280

nevertheless, as necessary. As in the case of operational productivity, some changes will last throughout the change in ownership. For instance, the improvements to asset productivity, e.g., the enlarged working shifts and capacity consolidation, will most probably last. Further, it is unlikely that the management will buy back former divested non-core assets. On the flipside, the increased asset base of the acquirer after a trade sale may lead to an increase in slack resources, especially in the case of a horizontal acquisition with overlapping businesses[560]. Empirical evidence suggests that after an acquisition significant divestments follow to gain scale efficiencies. Other researchers argue that an acquisition helps the acquirers to enhance their resource base. Simple scale increases can be conducted much more cheaply[561]. Nevertheless, a potential decline in productivity will probably be much likely in the arena of a going-public than in a trade sale.

The results of a survey of reverse buyouts from Mohan confirm the hypothesis of postponed investment. In year 1 after the IPO, the capital expenditure to total capital ratio is 4.3 percentage points above industry average, however decreases to 3.4 percentage points below the industry average in year 2[562]. The author argues that the switch in sign is related to expenditures that have been delayed during the period of being private. A similar indication is reported by the survey of Holthausen and Larcker. The authors measure a strong increase in capital expenditure to assets in the year and in the subsequent year of going-public (both +12%)[563]. Afterwards, the modest increases are statistically not significant. The relative capital spending intensity, however, remains at or slightly below industry average. Again, the authors argue that the increase is related to the cash infusion of the going-public. The asset productivity is at the year prior to going-public 92% (cash flow to assets) respectively 65% (operating income to assets) higher than the industry average. The ongoing high productivity continues for the four years reported. Nevertheless, there is also a slight decline in performance relative to the industry. The higher the managerial ownership in the post-IPO period is, the more likely it is that the asset productivity remains at the ante-IPO period[564]. To conclude, the asset productivity is likely to decrease at the exit of a buyout:

Hypothesis 14a: The focus on improvements in asset productivity decreases with a reduced debt leverage (after the exit from the buyout).

---

560 See Hoskisson, Johnson et al. 1994, pp. 1212 et seqq.

561 See Capron 1999, pp. 990 et seqq., Capron, Mitchell et al. 2001, pp. 819 et seqq.

562 See Mohan 1990, p. 96

563 See Holthausen and Larcker 1996, pp. 312 et seqq.

564 See Jain and Kini 1994, pp. 1711 et seqq.

Hypothesis 14b: The focus on improvements in asset productivity decreases with reduced managerial shareholdings (after the exit from the buyout).

Since the going-public will raise new capital for the company, the discipline to withhold capital and emphasis on asset productivity will be probably less than in a trade sale.

3.2.3 Outsourcing, Offshoring and Partnering

Additional efficiency gains may be associated with the refinement of the value chain[565]. A lack of organizational power, a lack of management focus, and a lack of expertise on the part of suitable partners can misguide a company in choosing which activities to make and which activities to buy.

Over time, the initial optimal share of 'make or buy' and the company's boundaries will change, dependent on the relative competitiveness[566]. Some companies specialize in a particular business function by developing advanced expertise and gaining economies of scale. Outsourcing will allow the buying company to seize the economic advantages from higher specialization, to externalize the risk of demand uncertainty and increase flexibility, to access the skills, competencies, and resources of other more advanced companies[567].

Outsourcing of selected activities can serve the needs during the buyout period from a multiple perspective: to improve profitability and increase cash flow from operations; to reduce the fixed assets base and increase cash flow from investing; and to acquire rare resources that allow to access know how and improve competitiveness. Further, management can control its costs more short-term and reach earlier break-even[568]. The increased cost flexibility reduces the risk exposure, e.g., during an economic crisis, and lessens the likelihood of financial distress[569]. Even further, not only operating risk is reduced, but also investment risk. Investments in new technologies are, especially for smaller to medium-sized companies, related with significant investments at a high level of uncertainty. To access the latest technology and to share the risk of, for instance, new product development, managers in a buyout may choose to increase the level of partnering

---

565 The author will elucidate potential changes in the share of value creation within one existing business line. The influence of a buyout on the diversification of a business over multiple business lines (horizontal diversification, related and unrelated) will be discussed separately as part of strategy refocusing in chapter B4.2.

566 See McCarthy and Anagnostou 2004, p. 62

567 See Bettis, Bradley et al. 1992, Abraham and Taylor 1993, Kakabadse and Kakabadse 2000, Gilley and Rasheed 2000

568 See Gilley, McGee et al. 2004, p. 119

569 See Domberger 1998

and form alliances. From a capital-constrained buyout perspective, the company can substitute its own investments by hiring external development partners.

A disaggregation of the value chain may also occur by geography, leading to off-shoring – while operating the activity still within the company's boundary - to low-cost countries. This may enable the company to maintain control, while seizing the advantage from lower factor costs in labor and natural resources. Further, the company can more easily bundle its resources from worldwide operations and increase economies of scale and scope[570]. Often, middle management is reluctant to offshore since they fear giving up responsibility and reducing their organizational power. Not surprisingly, a buyout, therefore, may serve as a catalyst that leads to increased outsourcing, offshoring and partnering in general[571].

A refinement of make or buy requires the flexibility to adjust workforce. As discussed in chapter 3.2.1, managers in a pre-buyout setting often do not have enough organizational power and enough incentive to undertake unpopular layoffs and to divest former parts of the businesses. Higher managerial shareholdings and increased debt at the entry into the buyout should refocus management on producing every activity at the lowest cost and redesigning value creation in terms of the cheapest 'make and buy'. The concentrated ownership will further support the management in undertaking severe measures, e.g., closing plants. In addition, a more active board will spur decision-making and bring industry-related expertise to the company. The experienced board members may suggest alternative partners, leveraging their social network within the industry, and point to the latest knowledge the company could find access[572].

An efficiency-driven restructuring, initiated by the buyout, may accentuate the tradeoff between make or buy to suppliers and partners. However, a one-sided, blindfold reduction of the share of value creation holds severe risks for the company. From a resource-base and growth-potential perspective, outsourcing might weaken in the long-term the ability to cope with new technologies and develop new capabilities. Knowledge and skill building is a path-dependent process[573]. Investments in a certain time span result in new growth and efficiency measures in the following period. Without understanding significant parts of the production process and through relying on external partners, companies will put their ability to

570 See Farrell 2004, p. 86
571 See Lei and Hitt 1995, p. 835
572 See Dyer and Singh 1998, p. 672
573 See Barney, Wright et al. 2001

shape future industry evolutions at risk[574]. Furthermore, competitive advantage also increasingly depends on the ability to coordinate and integrate complex, cross-functional processes and routines[575]. Without distinctive skills in coordination and integration, companies will lose ground against competitors. The alliance partner can turn into a competitor, and, once the alliance is dissolved, leave outsourcing as the only viable option[576]. Managers have to differentiate skills and products that are essential for competitive advantage and for core competencies, and avoid transferring critical functionality[577]. Offshoring is also detrimental if the related logistics costs turn out to be too high. Relative advantages in labor cost are also often less durable than expected, since an increased share of the value chain leads to significant salary increases. Finally, the related governance costs and costs of co-developing the skills required to control and manage a distant location are often underestimated.

To conclude, the positive effect of increased outsourcing and offshoring is questionable. From a financial asset-based perspective, a concentration on the most differentiating activities seems feasible. Further, the ability to minimize the capital employed and maximize the level of variables to consolidate the business is highly attractive for a buyout. Yet, from a competence-based view, the disposal of core, and to some degree, non-core activities may endanger the company's ability to develop its resource base. The effect is dependent on the specific context of the company, on the current relative share of value creation to its industry competitors and on the strategy chosen. The empirical studies so far have not confirmed a direct, linear relationship between outsourcing and performance[578]. Companies pursuing a strategy towards cost leadership and excellence in operations and manufacturing, however, have a positive correlation between a high share of outsourcing and offshoring, and performance[579]. In addition, the preference for outsourcing may seem more beneficial for smaller and growth-oriented companies to access sparse resources, however with contradicting empirical evidence[580]. In mature industries,

---

574 Hamel, Doz and Prahalad report that Western manufacturing firms, after outsourcing important activities to Far East producers, lost their ability to take advantage of new technologies and to develop their own, ground-breaking products (See Hamel, Doz et al. 1989.

575 See Domberger 1998

576 See Lei and Hitt 1995, pp. 849 et seqq.

577 See McCarthy and Anagnostou 2004, p. 64

578 Gilley and Rasheed analyze the extent of outsourcing at fourteen different functional level activities, with no significant indication for a linear effect on performance. Outsourcing interacted with firm strategy and environmental dynamism, indicating that a cost leadership and innovative differentiation strategy can benefit from outsourcing (See Gilley and Rasheed 2000).

579 See Meffert, Radtke et al. 2005, p. 80, Meffert and Klein 2007, pp.140 et seqq.

580 See Arbaugh 2003, p. 102

the intensity of cost competition increases and strategies based on cost leadership become more attractive. Therefore, outsourcing and off-shoring should become more prevalent in a buyout context.

Still, the empirical evidence on the change in outsourcing and offshoring and the level of partnering throughout the buyout cycle is sparse. Research has mostly focused on the share of value creation in total, as opposed to testing in more detail whether the activities were core or non-core, and what kind of motivation was related to the decision. Lei and Hitt elucidate multiple initiating factors following a buyout deal that lead to increasing outsourcing[581]. The authors consolidate their hypothesis in the sense that a buyout is detrimental to the company's human capital and skills. Malone reports that a higher share of small and medium-sized buyouts prefers to increase the number of suppliers as opposed to decreasing them during the buyout period[582]. A recent survey by Harris, Siegel and Wright on factor productivity changes during a buyout find a substantial increase of material to labor cost and a decrease in capital to labor, and conclude that the share of outsourcing is enlarged[583]. The admittedly even sparser research in Germany has confirmed a reduction of the share of value creation to substitute fixed by variable cost structure. Since Germany historically has a high share of processing industries, outsourcing and offshoring to manufacturers in low-cost countries should occur rather often, especially when a buyout can serve as the change agent. Vest reports that both turnaround-buyouts (9 from 11 respondents) and going-concern buyouts (9 from 18 respondents) significantly reduce the share of value creation[584]. The higher share among the turnaround-buyout is, according to the author, related to impending sales and capacity decline and the resulting feared increased share of fixed costs.

Only conjectures based on related research are able for the post-exit period, since no empirical evidence is known to the knowledge of the author. First, one may predict that the capital inflow from going-public increases the likelihood for activities remaining within the company's boundaries. Second, one may consider less managerial risk aversion as an indicator towards less outsourcing and offshoring. The reduced debt will decrease the likelihood of financial distress, decreasing the

---

581 First, the authors hypothesize that managers during a buyout are more risk-averse and restrict capital expenditure in technologies and skills development where the result is questionable. Second, they argue that stronger financial controls may lead to a redirection into more mature investments. Third, risk aversion motivates management to expand the level of formal alliances and long-term supply contracts (See Lei and Hitt 1995, pp. 838 et seqq.).

582 See Malone 1989, p. 358

583 See Harris, Siegel et al. 2002, p. 15

584 See Vest 1995, pp. 305 and 306

necessity to keep costs as variable as possible. Research has confirmed that more risk-averse top executives choose to outsource their manufacturing-related activities more[585]. Additionally, a less committed board with an experienced executive will reduce their engagement, for instance in the sense of leveraging their social network, and simplify identifying and contracting with potential partners[586]. Less strategic control may nurture less effective outsourcing. Without a well-defined strategy and related organizational advantages, the company may decide on outsourcing more in opportunistic, functional isolation rather than in a strategic context[587]. For a trade sale, increased outsourcing - besides the proposed effects of debt, management shareholdings and reduced governance - may reduce the necessity to access resources for growth from other partner companies[588]. An acquisition is, in many cases, motivated by the expansion of the horizontal or vertical share along value creation and by the internalization of certain assets and activities. On the other hand, the evidence suggests that management's attention and industry knowledge is diluted over a wider span of businesses[589]. Porter, for instance, argues that acquisitions primarily center on market leadership and industry position, as opposed to developing new relationships between the business units to take advantage of internal resources sharing[590]. One may conclude in terms of the level of outsourcing, offshoring and partnering as:

Hypothesis 15a: The level of outsourcing, offshoring and partnering decreases with a reduced debt leverage (after the exit from the buyout).

Hypothesis 15b: The level of outsourcing, offshoring and partnering decreases with a reduced concentration in ownership (after the exit from the buyout).

Hypothesis 15c: The level of outsourcing, offshoring and partnering decreases with a reduced governance activity level (after the exit from the buyout).

Hypothesis 15d: The level of outsourcing, offshoring and partnering decreases with reduced managerial shareholdings (after the exit from the buyout).

3.2.4 Working Capital Management

A further source of efficiency improvement is related to the management of working capital. The resulting inefficiencies are materialized in higher capital employed and,

585 See Gilley, McGee et al. 2004, p. 126
586 See Arbaugh 2003, p. 93
587 See Quinn 1999
588 See Arbaugh 2003, p. 97
589 See Lei and Hitt 1995, p. 839
590 See Porter 1988, pp. 61 et seqq.

therefore, higher capital costs and interest, respectively. However, the related costs are often disguised in the financial accounting and not appropriately penalized by the supervising executives.

The necessity to service debt will motivate the management to reduce working capital as a short-term measure for financing. Further, the cash flow can be increased through reduced capital costs. The three main constituents of working capital - accounts receivable, inventory, and accounts payable - can account for up to the half of yearly revenues, but are too often neglected by management. A rigid management of collection, holding, and payable period is regarded as one of the first steps taken during restructuring. However, the reduction in working capital is a one-time cash flow improvement, since the relevant time periods can only be reduced to a certain limit. In particular, companies with access to cheap capital may carry too high a level of working capital since the opportunity costs are low. This is most likely for subsidiaries with inefficient internal capital allocation.

The majority of empirical research confirms an increased focus of management on working capital and a tightening of the control of inventory, receivables, and payables at the entry into the buyout. The ratio of working capital to sales decreases significantly in the first years after the deal and afterwards remains at an optimized level[591]. Baker and Wruck for instance report that after the buyout of O.M. Scott & Sons , working capital fell from 37.5% to 18.4% of sales, equaling to a cash generation of USD 23.1 million[592]. Most researchers classify the efficiency increase as a one-time effect[593]. Further, the increase in efficiency of working capital management is observed to be more prominent for corporate spin-offs than for prior stand-alone

---

591 Smith reports a significant industry-adjusted increase of overall working capital productivity, defined as sales to working capital, by 19.3% from year 1 pre- to post-buyout. Similar results are observed for accounts receivable (-8%) and the inventory holding period (-8%). The operating cycle, defined as the time period between payment of suppliers and receipt of cash from customers, declines by 18% on an industry-adjusted base. However, the period for paying suppliers is not significantly lengthened (See Smith 1990b, p. 152). Muscarella and Vetsuypens note that only 6.9% of buyouts observed improve inventory control and actively manage their account receivables, therefore relativizing the importance of working capital management (See Muscarella and Vetsuypens 1990, p. 1397). In a review of financial changes during buyout restructuring, Wright, Thompson and Robbie report that 43% of companies reduce their debtor days and 31% their creditor days. It seems noteworthy that both changes are the first and second most frequently reported changes (See Wright, Thompson et al. 1992, p. 65). Weir finds ambiguous results on performance changes from the moment of the buyout to two years post-buyout. Neither the hypothesized increase in creditor nor the decrease in debtor days is significant (See Weir 1996, p. 27).

592 See Baker and Wruck 1989, p. 165

593 Smith classifies the effect of working capital management as an aforementioned one-time effect. He observes an increasing ratio of working capital from operations to operating assets, confirming the one-time characteristic. In addition, the effect of working capital management on operating cash flow is fairly small with a 1% increase (See Smith 1990b, p. 163).

companies[594]. Independent ownership apparently creates stronger incentives for tighter control of inventory days and operating cycle than ownership in a multi-divisional organization. For German buyouts, the reduction of working capital plays a similar prominent role in raising capital for debt service and improving efficiency. Gräper measures a modest decrease of the inventory to sales ratio[595]. He argues that a decrease is related to organizational resistance, e.g., consolidating part variety and refining the supplier and customer supply chain, and, therefore, can only be overcome by a newly motivated management team[596]. Further, Vest confirms that management in German buyouts reduces the inventory and work-in-progress, respectively, both in purchasing, production, and distribution[597]. The reduction is based on a closer alignment of the planning and controlling of sourcing, production, and sales through a just-in-time production. As a result, the lead time in production is reduced[598]. In a more recent survey, Wegner reports that as a part of financial reengineering, improved working capital management is, as a value driver, more prevalent for non-growth buyouts, e.g., turnaround, than for growth buyouts[599].

Whether working capital remains lower to industry average after the exit from a buyout, has not been in the focus of empirical research. Holthausen and Larcker confirm a significant low level of working capital to assets of reverse buyouts to non-buyouts[600]. The authors measure that the LBOs analyzed carry approximately half of the working capital of their competitors. After the going-public, working capital remains significantly below industry average, up to the last year (year 4) reported. However, the industry-adjusted ratio of working capital to assets increases. In addition, Holthausen and Larcker measure in a regression analysis the sensitivity of working capital to (i) leverage, (ii) management equity, and (iii) non-management insider equity[601]. Surprisingly, non-management insider ownership after the exit, e.g., by buyout investors, highly determines the level of working capital, with the

---

594 Long and Ravenscraft report that firms that were, prior to their buyout, a division of a conglomerate company carried 14% above industry-average inventory levels, and, during restructuring, cut their levels to 3% above average. Second, no significant levels and no significant changes can be reported for independent companies. The authors conclude that independent ownership and debt create incentives apparently lacking in multi-divisional organizations, however, not in stand-alone corporations (See Long and Ravenscraft 1993c, pp. 218 et seqq.). A later study of Long and Ravenscraft confirms that independent companies do not change their level of inventories and accounts significantly different than their competitors (See Long and Ravenscraft 1993b, p. 30).

595 See Gräper 1993, p. 148

596 See Gräper 1993, p. 142

597 See Vest 1995, p. 302 and 303

598 See Vest 1995, p. 304

599 See Wegner 2003, p. 235

600 See Holthausen and Larcker 1996, pp. 312 et seqq.

601 See also the results of the regression analysis on cash flow and operating income in chapter B5.3.4.3.

average decrease of 13% percentage points of ownership of non-management insiders leading an increase of 20% of working capital to assets[602]. In an additional analysis, the correlation between ownership and working capital was proved not to have been induced by the cash infusion from the IPO. Singh analyzes the working capital management preceding a going-public[603]. He reports that the inventory management is strikingly more efficient, measured by an ongoing below industry-average reduction of day of inventory[604]. Similar results are pointed out for accounts receivable, where most efficiency improvement has already been pursued before the going-public year.

Once again, the buyout structure seems to be a catalyst for change. Management shifts its focus to reduce inventory by best-practice supply chain management and by close control of receivables. A substantial part of the measures taken may sustain and allow working capital to stay below industry average. The empirical results confirm the longevity, however, they also show the importance of an ongoing, active control, not only by management, but also by non-management, active representatives on the board. However, the level of ownership concentration is of less importance. Hence, the relative level of working capital will, after the exit through either a trade sale or a going-public, change in relation to the following hypotheses:

Hypothesis 16a: The relative level of working capital decreases with a reduced debt leverage (after the exit from the buyout).

Hypothesis 16b: The relative level of working capital decreases with a reduced activity level of governance (after the exit from the buyout).

Hypothesis 16c: The relative level of working capital decreases with reduced managerial shareholdings (after the exit from the buyout).

3.3 Changes in Administration and Organization

The changes related to the governance structure will also affect the administration and the organizational processes. The disciplinary force or debt and management shareholdings will direct management's attention to apply best practices and to advance outdated procedures. Since the processes in administration are hardly measurable and, therefore, to a limited extent comparable. It is, in the corollary, not surprise that the build-up of slack resources is in particular observable in

602 The reduction is ceteris paribus constant management equity shareholdings and leverage. See Holthausen and Larcker 1996, p. 320 and 321.

603 See Singh 1990, pp. 124 et seqq.

604 See Singh 1990, p. 124

administration. Hence, the agency costs and residual loss will be present throughout the buyout cycle, perhaps even more prominently than in operations.

The attention on efficiency will initiate an optimization of the hierarchy and of the decision-making procedures, in particular for the spin-offs from multi-divisional companies with overhead-burdened staff. Further, independence may also positively affect the conformity of the management control systems towards the specific reporting needs of the business, e.g., tracking more closely the operational performance indicators.

The continuation of efficiency improvements in the post-exit period should be questioned and differentiated by the nature of change. Presumably, changes related to applying best-practice processes, e.g., in customer service or marketing, will survive changes in the governance structure. Nevertheless, reduced ownership by management may endanger the reduction of slack resources, especially if family-controlled businesses use the resources to offset their risk. In addition, beneficial effects of the buyout period, e.g., a closer conformity of the management control system to the business environment, will be dependent on the owner identity. In a trade sale, the acquiring company may feel inclined to impose its own controlling systems and techniques, and, therefore, reduce both efficiency and participation during the planning and budgeting process.

3.3.1 Overhead Productivity

The costs of overhead[605] and related productivity highly correlate with management's attention for efficiency. The measurement of the output and productivity of activities in administration is more difficult in non-operations than in operations, since the tasks are less standardized and repetitive. Hence, management may more easily build up resources associated with their personal interests, e.g., activities related to their status and their organizational power. The costs related to the company's overhead may, therefore, serve as a rough indicator for the level of agency costs and, in particular, the residual loss[606].

Consequently, the positive control effect of increased debt and the incentive effect of increased managerial shareholdings should be at least as strong on the overhead productivity as on the operational and asset productivity of non-overhead activities. Beside the reduction of organizational slack, increased attention on efficiency may

---

605 For conceptual simplification the term 'overhead' may subsume activities and costs related to sales, marketing, accounting, controlling, corporate planning, and general administration within the firm.

606 See Bruton, Keels et al. 2002, p. 719

initiate profound changes in the processes and practices applied within the different overhead departments. Similar to operations, a management with organizational power may overcome hindrances to introduce newer, more efficient processes inducing significant learning of the individual employees. Examples of such significant changes may be the transfer of paper-based work to an entirely computer-based processing, the introduction of principles of lean management to administration, or the introduction of customer segment-based marketing instruments based on detailed behavioral data. In some cases, the efficiency-driven changes will also lead to layoffs.

Author	Geographical focus	Overhead productivity	Hierarchical complexity	Efficiency of management control systems	During buyout	Post-exit
Bannock (1989)	UK			(x)		
Baker Wruck (1989)	US (case study)	x				
Easterwood Seth Singer (1989)	US		x		x	
Malone (1989)	US	x			x	
Muscarella Vetsuypens (1990)	US	x	x		x	
Smith (1990)	US	x				
Luippold (1991)	Germany			x	x	
Wright Thompson Robbie (1991)	Europe		x		x	
Forst (1992)	Germany		x			
Fox Marcus (1992)	US		x		x	
Jones (1992)	UK			x	x	
Bruton Scifres Keels (2002)	US	x			x	x
Graeper (1993)	Germany	x			x	
Baker Smith (1998)	US	x		x	x	
Mian Rosenfeld (1993)	US	x			x	
Phan Hill (1995)	US		x			
Vest (1995)	Germany	x		x	x	
Holthausen, Larcker (1996)	US	x			x	x
Mitchell Reid Terry (1997)	US			x	x	
Samdani Butler McNish (2001)	US, Europe	x			x	
Wright Hoskisson Busenitz (2001)	No focus					
Bruining Bonnet Wright (2003)	Europe		x	x	x	
Wegner (2003)	Germany		x		x	
Berens Brauner Högemann (2005)	Germany			x	x	
Burger Calderon (2005)	Germany			x	x	
Schulze Wickerath (2005)	Germany			x	x	
Arbeitskreis Schmalenbach (2006)	Germany			x	x	

Table 8: Surveys on the impact of buyouts on administration and organization

At the entry and during a buyout, the empirical evidence reveals that the total costs related to overhead[607] decrease[608]. Especially, restructuring activities associated with

607 The author will exclude costs related to R&D, since the considerations for entrepreneurial growth are more prominent when discussing the impact of the buyout. For the review of the level of R&D expenditure,

marketing and sales lie in the focus during the buyout[609]. In selected cases, the expenditure for such marketing and advertising activities increases[610]. Growth buyouts may invest in strengthening their market presence as part of their entrepreneurial growth strategy, e.g., introducing new products and introducing a new corporate design. From a broader perspective, the level of expenses in the overhead is highly dependent on the pre-buyout situation and chosen strategy, which may change under the restructuring of a buyout[611]. A strategy based on differentiation by product quality and innovation will incur higher expenses related to marketing, sales, and R&D[612]. To illustrate, the spin-off from the parent company or the establishment of customer contacts after a founder has left the company induce additional costs. However, in many cases, the increase in overhead productivity implied significant workforce reduction[613].

---

refer to chapter B4.3.1.

608 Bruton, Keels and Scifres report a decrease from 19.1% to 17.6% for selling, general, and administrative (SG&A) expenses to sales in the private period of a buyout (See Bruton, Keels et al. 2002, p. 717). Malone finds evidence for increased marketing and sales effort in the buyout period for over 64% of respondents. However, no related changes in costs are reported. Further, Malone reports that 41% of company conduct a reorganization of their administration unit (See Malone 1989, p. 13). Gräper finds for German buyouts that sales and marketing were often too related to the founder themselves. If the founder left the firm, significant resources had to be invested and new relationships to customers established (See Gräper 1993, pp. 36 and 37). In the case study of the buyout of Safeway, headquarters staff were reduced by 20 % (See Baker and Smith 1998, p. 109).

609 Muscarella and Vetsuypens report that 44.4% of all responding buyouts undertake changes in marketing related to pricing, product quality, customer service and product mix (See Muscarella and Vetsuypens 1990, p. 1397). Mian and Rosenfeld confirm the results, with a ahare of 39.4% (38.5%) for the buyout period for buyouts acquired after their going-public (not acquired after their going-public) (See Mian and Rosenfeld 1993, p. 55). Bruton Keels Scifres even find a higher share, with 62% of buyouts undergoing changes in marketing (See Bruton, Keels et al. 2002, p. 719)

610 Holthausen and Larcker measure a higher ratio of advertising to assets for the time period during buyout restructuring before going-public (See Holthausen and Larcker 1996, p. 313). However, Smith does not find significant results analyzing the effect of buyouts on advertising expenditures as quota to sales. The direction of industry-adjusted change is negative for year 1 and positive for year 2 compared to year 1 prior to buyout (See Smith 1990b, p. 155). Bannock measure a share 27.3% as opposed to 1.1% of buyouts that increase their marketing expenditure (See Bannock 1990, p. 15). Vest reports mixed results, with both an increase and a decrease in advertising expenses after a buyout. The increase is more prevalent among the spin-off buyouts, since they often have to introduce an independent corporate design, accompanied with investments into branding. In 10 of 29 buyouts a customer segment-based marketing was introduced (See Vest 1995, pp. 297 et seqq.). Baker and Wruck report in the case of O.M. Scott that advertising expenses increased during the buyout by 21%, which is, considering the sales increase of 25%, a slightly smaller, but more or less constant ratio (See Baker and Wruck 1989, p. 165 and 166). Baker and Smith refer to increased marketing expenses in the Duracell buyout, related to the necessity to introduce new products to the market, to improve the brand image and increase domestic market share (See Baker and Smith 1998, p. 120).

611 See the relationship of buyouts and strategy renewal in chapter B4.2.

612 For example, Conant, Mokwa and Varadarajan report that different Miles Snow-strategy types have different strengths in marketing and sales, and also invest different percentages of their sales in related activites (See Conant, Mokwa et al. 1990, pp. 376 et seqq.).

613 Vest measures that layoffs among administration were conducted in 7 of 29 buyouts. In most cases, the layoffs were related to the high coordination tasks with the former parent, e.g., preparing investment

To conclude, the entry into the buyout leads to an increase in overhead productivity, with the differentiation that the increase in productivity will not be related in all cases with a decrease in spending on overhead-related activities. Managers feel motivated to increase efficiency and introduce best practices in administration, sometimes leading to layoffs. On the other hand, the necessity for renewal of market presence may incur investments in sales and marketing.

Strategy adjustment, shifts in the emphasis of management focus, and misalignment of management and ownership may also lead to changes in overhead productivity in the post-exit period after the buyout. Again, the question of the development of overhead productivity at the exit and in the years following is largely unanswered. Considering the decrease in debt and, in the case of going-public, the notable cash infusion, it will be more difficult for management to pursue any workforce cutbacks[614]. The diminished alignment of management and ownership will increase agency costs and may reinforce managers' desire for empire-building and spur additional, non-value adding resources in the overhead. Further, the 'risk-buffering hypothesis' related to the high share of personal wealth invested by German family-controlled companies might suggest that the share of slack resources increases, since overhead activities are less transparent than operational activities[615]. Still, some changes undertaken, e.g., introducing best-practice processes and revitalizing corporate marketing and sales strategy, are of a long term-nature and potentially survive the exit from the buyout. As argued before, the contractual agreements and working standards of the acquiring company in a trade sale may increase average salaries. Further, the acquirer may want to build up some resources for coordination among the business units, if synergies from operations can be expected. In addition, some resources may be required to serve the reporting and accounting requirements of the acquirer. In a going-public, the expenses for marketing and sales will at least remain constant or even increase modestly, since management will want to signal an attractive growth outlook. Depending on the size of the corporation, the activities required for investor relations and capital markets reporting may lead to additional costs[616].

The empirical research is sparse, and more of a qualitative, sometimes even anecdotal nature. In the post-exit period, Bruton, Keels and Scifres report that SG&A

decisions and corporate accounting (See Vest 1995, pp. 307 and 308). Samdani, Butler and McNish cite as a typical example for improving productivity a buyout in the chemical industry where the corporate center was downsized from 300 to 180 people (See Samdani, Butler et al. 2001, p. 99).

614 See also the assumptions on the development of operational productivity at the exit in chapter B3.2.1.

615 See Titzrath 1994, p. 181

616 See also the discussion of costs and benefits related to a stock market listing in chapter B5.3.2.

expenses to total costs rise from 17.6% to 20.4%, similar to pre-buyout level, however, with statistical significance against industry peers only in year 3 after going-public, the last year observed. The lagged effect of the increase in agency costs is also indicated by the development of sales[617]. The authors argue that this is a result of several self-serving choices of management over the time. Bruton, Keels and Scifres conclude that the reappearance of inefficiency due to increased agency costs does not occur suddenly, but requires a substantial span of time. The authors further measure changes in the restructuring activities chosen by management, and report a decrease in the number of companies pursuing changes in marketing from 62% pre-exit to 49% post-exit. Holthausen and Larcker observe that the enhanced expenditure during the buyout continues beyond going-public, and remains significant up to year 4, the last year observed. Further, no significant changes in relation to industry average are measured[618]. No remarkable research work has been undertaken in Germany to analyze the changes in overhead after the exit from a buyout. To broaden the picture, the empirical evidence on changes in overhead productivity from acquisitions and mergers reports that - although overhead cost reduction is on the top of the agenda of an acquisition – improvements are sparse. Often, resources are liberally duplicated, e.g., resulting in two separate brands, two separate customer service facilities, and two sales forces[619]. Any changes in the post-exit period seem to be related to the manager itself. No observations have been made for an enhanced activity level of the supervisory board toward improving overhead efficiency. Hence, the relative level of overhead productivity will, after either a trade sale or a going-public, change in relation to the following hypotheses:

Hypothesis 17a: Overhead productivity decreases with a reduced debt leverage (after the exit from the buyout).

Hypothesis 17b: Overhead productivity decreases with reduced managerial shareholdings (after the exit from the buyout).

3.3.2 Hierarchical Complexity and Decision-Making

Management with weak alignment to owners tends to install organizational structures with too small spans of control and too many hierarchical levels. Further, former subsidiaries of large corporations typically have a complex, multi-level

---

617 The authors hypothesize a decrease in strategic focus after the exit and, therefore, assume a significant increase in sales growth. Whereas the strategic focus remains close to the core competencies, the evidence suggests an increased focus on sales increase (See Bruton, Keels et al. 2002, p. 717 and 718).

618 See Holthausen and Larcker 1996, pp. 313 et seqq.

619 See Weber and Dholakia 2000, pp. 158 et seqq.

hierarchy. Williamson argues that managers without control tend to maximize the size of the departments and headcounts under their control[620]. Hierarchical complexity reduces the speed of decision-making and provides ground for resistance to adapt to any changing external factors.

Owner-managers will presumably initiate an evaluation of the number of necessary hierarchy levels and managerial resources. An increased control span and a flattening of hierarchy spur organizational efficiency. First, the extent of management necessary, especially in the middle management levels of the organization, can be reduced. Lines of authority will be shortened to improve efficiency[621]. Second, the information flow is simplified due to fewer interfaces and gatekeepers between individuals responsible. The quality and speed of decision-making improves. Third, the level of autonomy is enlarged since fewer managers take responsibility and accountability moves to the most knowledgeable individuals.

With excessive managerial resources, companies tend to centralize decision-making and have responsibility rest within the management group. Executives of buyout companies will grant, in general, more autonomy to management. Strategic decisions will remain with top management, while operating decisions will be decentralized to the line organization and employees responsible[622]. Hence, the individuals closest to the operations and with the most complete information will more often make the decisions. Furthermore, delegation has beneficial effects on motivation and the level of personal effort. The individuals and working groups will feel more responsible and monitor their own performance. Therefore, the managerial control can be focused on measuring the output instead of discussing the underlying facts in detail.

Concluding the arguments, the entry and the restructuring activities during the buyout should lead to a reduction in hierarchical complexity, e.g., in the number of managers and in increased decentralized decision-making. The empirical evidence suggests a reduction in hierarchical complexity and an increase in decentralization, especially for former corporate spin-offs[623]. In most cases, the focus lies on a change

620 See Williamson 1964

621 See Fox and Marcus 1992, p. 75

622 See Easterwood 1989, p. 41

623 Phan and Hill analyze in detail the change of hierarchical complexity and the level of decentralization during a buyout. First, the authors report that both increased debt and management shareholdings positively influence the level of operating decentralization, e.g. decisions regarding advertisement, marketing, production, pricing, buying, product mix and business unit strategy. Management shareholdings also influence strategic decentralization, e.g., acquisitions, capital investment, and financial goals (See Phan and Hill 1995, pp. 722 et seqq.). Easterwood Seth Singer confirm that during the buyout, strategic decision-making is centralized, while operating decisions are decentralized to the units responsible (See Easterwood 1989, pp. 34 et seqq.). Bruining Bonnet Wright consolidate their analysis of

in the role and capacity of middle management[624]. Many buyouts are characterized by excess managerial capacity[625], which is reduced during the restructuring. On the other hand, the increase in entrepreneurial responsibility, e.g., to introduce new products and acquire new market share, are tasks unfamiliar to many managers who formerly worked in subsidiaries. Therefore, many buyouts compensate for the lack of capacity by hiring new managers[626]. Especially for German buyouts, where managerial responsibility is concentrated in the founder, the development of a middle management level is required[627]. In addition, the empirical evidence for buyouts reports, for both Anglo-Saxon and German transactions, an increase in the quality and efficiency of decision-making during the holding period[628]. However, the dramatic change in management personnel and communication structures may lead to a high level of uncertainty and disruption in the traditional decision-making routines, and therefore, at least in the short term, decrease productivity[629].

Not many studies have analyzed the determinants of hierarchical complexity and decision-making related to the characteristics of a post-exit period to a buyout. From an agency theory perspective, hierarchy reduces the agency costs between the

---

four case studies in terms of decision-making and state that through the buyouts the delegation of decision-making wanders to lower levels in the organization (See Bruining, Bonnet et al. 2003 p. 21).

624 Muscarella and Vetsuypens report that 4% of buyouts observed reorganize their managerial structure during the buyout (See Muscarella and Vetsuypens 1990, p. 1397). Malone analyzed the operating changes in entrepreneurial-buyouts and reports that 27% reduce the number of managers (See Malone 1989, p. 358).

625 See Phan and Hill 1995, p. 713

626 Wright, Thompson and Robbie, by contrast, argue for the need for both rationalization and growth in managerial capacities. First, they report that 9% (buyouts before mid 1983) and 4.4% (buyouts between mid 1983 and 1986) of buyouts remove a tier of management. Second, they also report that 11.7% (buyouts before mid 1983) and 12.6% (buyouts between mid 1983 and 1986) of buyout introduce a new tier of management. The authors argue that the expansion of management levels is related to the necessity for managers able to manage an independent organization with the challenge of growth and new product development (See Wright, Thompson et al. 1992, p. 313).

627 Forst argues that the dependence and focus on the founder in German companies make the growth of an experienced middle management more difficult. Therefore, it is not surprising that the share of buy-ins among all family-owned buyouts/-ins is fairly high with 41.7%. The level of delegation is low, most decision-making lies with the founder (See Forst 1992, p. 34 and 35).

628 Baker and Wruck report an increase in decision-making through decentralization for the O. M. Scott case (See Baker and Wruck 1989, p. 189). Bannock measure a share of 63.3% (57.7%) of buyouts favouring the significant increase in internal (external) communication and decision-making (See Bannock 1990, p. 16). Wegner computes that among the inefficiencies in the pre-buyout period, 39.3% of buyouts respondents name inefficiencies related to bureaucracy and complex hierarchy as prevalent. Therefore, it is not surprising that 71.0% of survey participants call improved and faster decision-making an improvement during the holding period. Further, 58.1% of the respondents state that the quality of decision-making has improved through increased participation after the buyout. Among the factors driving the value increase during the buyout, the improved decision-making is placed 9th in a Top-10 list, and is slightly better positioned in the group of growth buyouts (See Wegner 2003). Bruining, Bonnet and Wright report improved decision-making in a case study after installing decentralized self-managing teams (See Bruining, Bonnet et al. 2003, p. 18)

629 See Rieley and Leahy 1998, pp. 58 et seqq.

individual, multiple principal-agent relationships, e.g., between managers and subordinates, within a company. The agency costs are related to the principal's intention of efficient coordination and cooperation as the two objectives of an organizational structure[630]. From a knowledge-based view, a hierarchical system with centralized decision-making under-utilizes the dispersed knowledge residing in different individuals within the company[631]. Since competition is increasingly determined through knowledge-related and entrepreneurial resources, efficiency improvements in hierarchy will be better accomplished by a closer fit to changing external factors, and less with an increase in the number of hierarchical levels.

Phan and Hill decompose the determinants of a buyout into the changes in debt and management shareholdings[632]. First, they only find a relationship between hierarchical complexity and management's emphasis on growth, but not with debt (negative relationship) and shareholdings (negative). Second, in contrast with the implications from the knowledge-based view, Phan and Hill find a relationship between decentralized decision-making - both strategic and operational - and management's emphasis on growth (negative) and efficiency (positive) alike, as well as debt (positive) and management shareholdings (positive). In their argumentum, diminished debt and management shareholdings may lead in a trade sale or going-public to an increase in hierarchy and centralized decision-making. However, the implications have to be relativized because they are based on a single survey and on buyouts occurring between 1986 and 1989. Since then, the intensity of knowledge-based competition has increased, as well as the share of growth-based buyouts. More general research on the decision-making process after a going-public reports a positive relationship of increased delegation and participation on company performance[633].

An industry buyer of a buyout may have a significantly higher level of hierarchy to accomplish the greater need for cooperation and coordination. The acquirer will consider implementing their organizational structure in the buyout to increase consistency in the organizational setup over all business units. For a going-public,

---

630 See Jensen and Meckling 1976, Lawrence and Lorsch 1967, Grant 1996

631 Competition that is increasingly dependent on knowledge resources requires a more flexible, differentiated hierarchy. First, decision-making has to be close to the owner of the knowledge, the individual employees with specific knowledge. Hierarchy may enforce cooperation and also, however, allow independent coordination. Second, knowledge that is explicit and, therefore, transferable should be collocated and processed at a central institution, e.g., the management board. Knowledge that is implicit, and, therefore, costly to transfer should be processed through the individual owner of the knowledge (See Grant 1996, pp. 118 et seqq.).

632 See Phan and Hill 1995, pp. 722 et seqq.

633 See Zwaan, Eije et al. 2002, pp. 131 et seqq.

the incentive to rebuild hierarchical complexity is expected to be modest. Again, any changes in the post-exit period seem to be related to the manager itself. No observations have been made for an enhanced activity level of the supervisory board toward improving hierarchical complexity and decision-making. Hence, the level of hierarchical complexity should change corresponding to the following hypotheses:

Hypothesis 18a: Hierarchical complexity will increase with reduced debt leverage at a trade sale.

Hypothesis 18b: Hierarchical complexity will increase with reduced managerial shareholdings at a trade sale.

3.3.3 Efficiency of Management Control Systems

A change in the ownership and in the governance may serve as a catalyst for efficiency improvement of the management control systems of a company[634]. Inefficiencies occur through a mismatch and non-conformity between the business environment on the one side and the control instruments and methods chosen on the other side[635]. If the performance indicators chosen do not reflect the value driver of a company's operations, the management control system will not be able to give a realistic picture of the current health of the company and provide a misleading decision base for both management and investors.

A management control system should reflect the company's strategic intent and serve as a change agent if strategic attributes alter[636]. In the pre-buyout phase, managers may encounter inefficiencies of the management control system induced by the conformity with the management control system practice of a parent, by highly formalized and bureaucratic budgeting, and by limited discussion on business aspirations and competitive environment[637]. In a family-controlled company, management may face a low degree of formal planning, with unclear performance-related compensation schemes.

After the buyout transaction, the management can use its independence to adapt the control system more closely to the business environment. Further, necessary investments in growth can be more easily discussed since management is much more

---

634 The management control system is understood as consisting of (i) the (strategic) planning system, (ii) the budgeting system, (iii) the performance management system, (iv) capital expenditure and investment procedures, (v) systems based on variance, e.g., budget, information and (vi) a system of operational performance indicators (See Goold and Quinn 1990, p. 44, Langfield-Smith 1997, p. 209, Nilson 2002, p. 42).

635 See Govindarajan 1988, Langfield-Smith 1997

636 See Nilson 2002, pp. 41 et seqq.

637 See Jones 1992, pp. 152 et seqq., Vest 1995, p. 319, Wright 2001, p. 118, Bruining, Bonnet et al. 2003, p. 9, Schmalenbach-Gesellschaft 2006, p. 253,

knowledgeable about the business opportunities. The quality of budgeting will increase, fostered by motivated management and employees alike, and requested by the buyout investors. The latter investors will require close reporting of cash flow development to track the diligent repayment of debt and to ensure the implementation of the value-creation plan. Empirical research indicates a significant change in the management control system after entry into the buyout[638]. As discussed before, the control and reporting systems are, especially after a spin-off, adapted to correspond with the business environment and the competitive context of the company[639]. The number of reports related to the monitoring as a subsidiary in a multi-divisional company is reduced, if not even omitted[640]. Further, different instruments and techniques are adapted to the reporting requirements of a buyout: improved liquidity and cash flow-related reporting[641] and improved reporting directed to operational efficiency[642]. The former changes are introduced at the request of the buyout investors urging strict fulfillment of the debt covenants, but also from the newly motivated owner-managers interested in the current debt repayment[643]. The management starts to introduce more detailed measurement systems, e.g., product calculations, profit and cost center structures, and productivity reports[644]. The increased emphasis on efficiency, related with a higher level of ownership, spur quality and commitment to the control systems, in particular the budgeting and capital expenditure appraisal. For instance, Vest reports that of 29 buyouts, 16 mentioned having increased controlling, 11 having enhanced the

---

638 For instance, the change in the management control and accounting system was the most often reported change (69.5% of all respondents) in Forst's the survey on German buyouts (See Forst 1992, p. 39).

639 Jones observe that the accounting control systems are adapted to the business environment and, in particular, the level of competition. Management developed a more favorable attitude towards planning techniques, although the environmental dynamism remained largely unaltered (See Jones 1992, pp. 158-160). Bannock reports that 82.5% of surveyed buyouts enjoy the increased freedom in financial planning as required by the business environment (See Bannock 1990, p. 16). Baker and Smith elucidate the advice of KKR on changes in internal financial controls, especially for corporate spin-offs (See Baker and Smith 1998, p. 101). On German buyouts, see also Luippold 1991, pp. 220-221

640 Jones points out that managers reduce the usage of formal reports used for steering large corporations, e.g., highly formalized investment (See Jones 1992, p. 157)

641 Jones notes that in many companies cash flow reporting was extended from a monthly to a daily basis (See Jones 1992, p. 158).

642 Forst reports that in German buyouts the control system was often limited to the tax and legal requirements. The management of the firm was often rather based on heuristics and intuition by the founder than on objective planning and measurement systems (See Forst 1992, p. 37). See also Jones 1992, p. 161

643 See Mitchell, Reid et al. 1997, Bruining, Bonnet et al. 2003, Berens, Brauner et al. 2005, p.72

644 Bruining, Bonnet and Wright point out that one of the case study companies expanded its controlling to the quality of working relationships with its core customers, acknowledging the importance of more accurate scheduling and just-in-time delivery (See Bruining, Bonnet et al. 2003, p. 17). See also Jones 1992, p. 162

efficiency of the controlling system, and 6 having raised the quality of budgeting[645]. Further, the researcher reports management shifted the capacity related to the reporting to the former corporate board to fulfill the requirements from the buyout investors. Managers take the budget planning process more seriously, provide more accurate data and commit themselves more strongly to the projected business forecast[646]. Intensive discussions on non-financial information, especially on the related business outlook and market environment, not at least required by the buyout investors to understand in more detail the underlying business risks, enhance the quality of the control system[647]. To obtain detailed data the employees were integrated closely in the data gathering[648]. Therefore, the feedback can be disaggregated and more closely directed to the individual responsible within the organization. The participation of employees in setting and planning the budgets facilitates a broader discussion on the corporate strategy, while reducing the power of private information[649].

A recent survey of the success factors in large German medium-sized companies reports a significant higher profitability for companies with a higher level of professionalism in their management control system, covering finance and risk management processes[650]. The better practices included having a regular strategy and business planning process, actively managing the capital structure, frequently measuring the underlying business risks and actively hedging these if necessary. Interestingly, the level of professionalism was not dependent on whether the company was family-controlled or whether it was a subsidiary. However, the authors report that the companies under ownership of a buyout company had a significantly higher level of professionalism. The investment partners of the buyout companies note that the introduction of a higher level of professionalism, in respect

---

645 See Vest 1995, pp. 319-320

646 Baker and Smith detail for the buyout of Safeway through KKR that monthly reports were commented by business development and served as the basis for discussions within the management and between the board and KKR (See Baker and Smith 1998, p. 106). Schulze and Wickerath report, in a review of best-practice investment controlling, that, next to the accounting-related reporting, a buyout investor often introduces a report on the monthly development of the key performance indicators with a detailed listing of customer/market data, capacity/utilization status, quality-related costs, employed labor, and net working capital (See Schulze and Wickerath 2005, pp. 434-436). See also Jones 1992, p. 158, Bruining, Bonnet et al. 2003, p. 17.

647 See Jones 1992, p. 159, Bruining, Bonnet et al. 2003, p. 19, Sharp 2003, p. 98

648 Forst argues that the low delegation of decision-making hinders the information flow from operational units and employees to management (See Forst 1992, p. 37). See also Easterwood 1989, p. 42, Jones 1992, p. 161, Bruining, Bonnet et al. 2003, p. 21

649 See Jones 1992, p. 164

650 The survey reports that firms of the same size differ significantly in profitability by the level of professionalism. For instance, companies between 0 and 100 Million EUR sales with a higher (lower) professionalism achieve an average EBIT of 7.1% (4,0%) (See Meffert, Radtke et al. 2005).

of both financial planning and other administrative processes, is one of the top priorities during the restructuring phase[651]. The entry of an experienced buyout investor and their related network will not only motivate managers to reassess the organization from an efficiency perspective, e.g., by reducing the level of staff, but will also question the quality and professional level with which the organizational and administrative processes are executed. Often, the buyout companies have been reluctant to employ outside comparisons and benchmarks with best practice, in many cases due to the dominance of the former founder and a publicity-shy family. Further, a recent survey on German buyout reports that the buyout investors strive to introduce the Anglo-Saxon one-tier system to reduce the information transfer in the German two-board system. The investors increase the frequency of meetings of the management board, while separate committees, e.g., for strategy and personnel, are formed to make the discussions more focused and efficient[652].

To conclude, the efficiency of the management control system during the buyout period is increased, not only imposed by the requirements of the buyout investors, but also self-motivated through a management interested in understanding in more detail the risks and underlying operational value drivers.

The changes are significant, however to be questioned concerning their survival beyond the exit from the buyout. First, the decrease in debt will reduce financial distress and the urgency to monitor the cash flow at the same attention level as during the buyout. Second, a more remote management with lower shareholdings may feel less motivated to challenge budget proposals and enter into conflicts with their peers and subordinates. Third, the expertise of the buyout investors and their industry network will not be available to that extent. Anyhow, the expansion of the control system into single performance cells, e.g., profit centers, and towards operational value drivers will presumably continue to be regarded as beneficial. However, potential reentry into a corporate dependency as opposed as to capital markets-based control requires a differentiation between the exit channels.

In a trade sale, the conformity effect, formerly observed from the pre-buyout phase, may tend to impose the management and accounting control system of the acquirer on the acquired buyout[653]. From the viewpoint of the acquirer, an effective monitoring and control is ensured at best by implementing the existing controlling

---

651 Other administrative processes encompass for instance the top management development and talent retention, discussed in detail in chapter B4.5. For quotes of the buyout managers, see Burger-Calderon 2005 , p. 49.

652 See Schmalenbach-Gesellschaft 2006, p. 254

653 See Jones 1985, Nilson 2002, pp. 42 et seqq.

system. However, the efficiency of the management control systems depends on the match between the corporate strategy of the acquirer and the business strategy of the company to be acquired[654]. For instance, a portfolio-management strategy approach tightly controls the acquired companies through their financial performance, e.g., budget and capital expenditure, while allowing a high level of diversification in the portfolio[655]. The surveys indicates that the best fit between the control systems is accomplished if the control of the acquired company is also characterized by financial measures, e.g., when the company operates in a stable environment with a large-scale production and highly formalized principles of transfer pricing[656]. If the acquirer follows an activity-sharing strategy - seeking synergies between the portfolio companies and engaging in a close and more informal strategy planning process - the control system would presumably be too weak and too non-binding. Jones reports that in 60% of acquisitions, the acquirer transferred his management control system to the acquired company[657]. To avoid a misfit of corporate and business strategy and, therefore, risking a less effective control system, management has to be aware of potential inefficiencies and balance the needs of both integrated control by the parent and conformity to the business environment of the subsidiary. The empirical evidence of the efficiency of the management control system and its dynamic adaptation is still sparse, in particular with respect to the changes in the post-exit period of a buyout[658]. Further, management may reduce the efficiency also by a change in business strategy. It may be that the acquirer provides the company with resources to outgrow a differentiation-based niche strategy and to pursue a more mass-market, cost leadership strategy. Porter argues that a niche strategy does not require the tight and detailed cost controlling of a company pursuing a cost leadership position and reliant on exploiting economies of scale[659]. To summarize, it is more than questionable whether the efficiency of the management control system can be upheld in a trade sale after exiting the buyout structure.

In a going-public, the requirements of stock market listing determine the changes in the management control system. Although the stock markets regulations require

---

654 See Nilson 2002

655 The necessity to align the acquired firm is dependent on the corporate strategy of the acquirer, in particular the intent for coordination and integration. Porter formulated four distinct corporate strategies, whereof the portfolio management strategy (low coordination) is the antithesis of the activity sharing strategy (high coordination) approach (See Porter 1988, pp. 50 et seqq.).

656 See Nilson 2002, pp. 67 et seqq.

657 See Jones 1986

658 See Langfield-Smith 1997, pp. 228 and 229, Nilson 2002, p. 68

659 See Porter 1985. For other surveys arguing for strategy-adjusted control systems see also Simons 1987 and Anthony, Dearden et al. 1992.

frequent and detailed reporting, they are no match for the intensity of discussions between management and buyout investors during the buyout[660]. Since, similar to a trade sale, the likelihood of bankruptcy is reduced, the focus will be less on cash flow and repayment than on a continuous business outlook and an assessment of the related risks and opportunities. In some cases, the reporting required for stock markets listing may distract management's attention from the control of operational performance indicators. Although some inefficiency may be expected from the going-public, they will be far less than in a trade sale. Hence, the efficiency of management control systems should change corresponding to the following hypotheses:

Hypothesis 19a: The efficiency of the management control systems will decrease with reduced debt leverage in a trade sale.

Hypothesis 19b The efficiency of the management control systems will decrease with a reduced activity level of governance in a trade sale.

Hypothesis 19c: The efficiency of the management control systems will decrease with reduced managerial shareholdings in a trade sale.

4 Post-Exit Changes in Entrepreneurial Growth Focused-Management Activities

4.1 Introductory Remarks

Mitton once claimed that buyouts are the "less risky route to becoming an entrepreneur"[661]. Former managers transform after the acquisition of significant shareholdings to entrepreneurs. They can achieve a significant increase in personal wealth while enjoying their entrepreneurial freedom and increasing their organizational power within the company. Further, they overcome former hurdles of initiating long-term changes in privately- and family-owned businesses against highly risk-averse owners[662].

Hence, they steer the company in a new dimension of self-responsibility and entrepreneurship at a higher level of managerial freedom[663]. The changes in management's focus will initiate significant changes in strategy, innovation, market

660 See Robbie, Thompson et al. 1991, p. 79

661 See Mitton 1982

662 See Malone 1989, p. 350

663 See Malone 1989, Bull 1989a, Fox and Marcus 1992

development and resource management of the company. Management will seek for value creation in refining the strategy position, maximizing synergies between the existing resources, and enhancing growth in the core businesses. The following section examines how this verve from the buyout restructuring will outlast and develop in the post-exit period. The author decomposes the changes in governance thereby into their constituents and discusses them separately by their effect on every individual lever. The author divides the management activities into those directed to strategy (hypotheses 21 to 23), to innovation (hypothesis 24), to market development (hypothesis 25), and those directed to human resource management (hypotheses 26 to 28). As indicated by the asterisks, the relationships between changes in governance and changes in the lever for value creation are disjointedly discussed between going-public and trade sale. Even though the direction of relationship may be alike, the underlying cause and effect can differ.

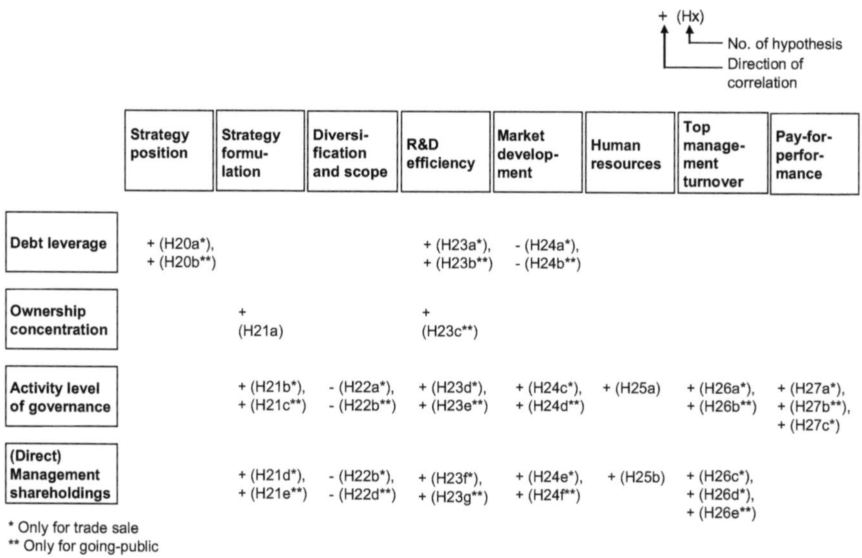

Figure 7: Overview of hypotheses for entrepreneurial growth-related activities

Constituents of Corporate Entrepreneurship

Although attention is stunning, there is still a lack of consistency in the way company-level entrepreneurship is defined[664]. At the heart of entrepreneurship, as

664 See Covin and Slevin 1991, Morris and Sexton 1996, Dess, Lumpkin et al. 1997, Sharma and Chrisman 1999, Zahra 1999

introduced by Schumpeter and later Kirzner, is a new combination of resources, leading to new products, new markets, new product-markets combination, and new organizational structures, to name but a few[665]. An entrepreneurial orientation on company-level describes the conduct of entrepreneurship in association with an organization that leads to activities that characterize the entire corporation as entrepreneurial[666].

Still, the way corporate entrepreneurship (CE) is operationalized and measured remains inconsistent. One strand of researcher refers to the different processes of altering the pattern of resource redeployment[667]. The different patterns, as presented by Guth and Ginsberg, are grouped around: (i) innovation as commitment to create and introduce products, productions process and organizational systems; (ii) market venturing as activity of company expanding the existing operations into new markets and entering into new business; (iii) strategic renewal as revitalization of operations by refocusing the scope of the business or its competitive approach[668]. Another group of researchers understands CE in the sense of the activities and attitude related to entrepreneurship. Miller and Friesen introduce CE as a multidimensional concept embodying the company's activities in product-market and technological innovation[669]. He categorizes the activities as (i) related to an engagement in product-market innovation, as (ii) related to a high risk-taking propensity of the decision makers, and (iii) related to the proactiveness in terms of being first to the market. Recent researchers have refined the concept[670], and hereby sought to integrate both schools of thought[671]. Zahra argues that the Miller and

---

665 See Schumpeter 1934, Kirzner 1973

666 See Covin and Miles 1999, p. 49, Sharma and Chrisman 1999, p. 18, Guth and Grinsberg 1990, p. 6

667 Guth and Ginsberg propose a concept of CE directed to external activities. They define company-level entrepreneurship as consisting of all types of innovation and new business creation through venturing (See Guth and Grinsberg 1990. They further extend the conceptualization by strategic renewal, focusing on internal entrepreneurial activities (see Guth and Grinsberg 1990, Zahra 1996). Covin and Miles continue this line of thought and claim a company's objective to sustain high performance and to improve competitive standing as the basis for entrepreneurship. Underlying activities have to shake up the markets and industries the company is engaged in (See Covin and Miles 1999. Thus, all efforts lead to rejuvenation, renewal and the redefinition of organizations, their markets and industries. Covin and Miles differentiate between strategic renewal and organizational rejuvenation, the latter covering policy changes in operations, administration and human resources (See Covin and Miles 1999. Although the concept is persuasive because it links entrepreneurship to the strategy making process and competitive standing, Covin and Miles' definition of entrepreneurship is fairly broad and in practice difficult to prove.

668 See Guth and Grinsberg 1990, Zahra 1991, Covin and Slevin 1991, Block and MacMillan 1993, Lumpkin and Dess 1996, Zahra 1996

669 See Miller and Friesen 1982, Miller 1983

670 Lumpkin and Dess expand this conceptualization by adding two further dimensions, autonomy of management and competitive aggressiveness, to entrepreneurial orientation (See Lumpkin and Dess 1996)

671 Zahra, Jennings and Kuratko strive to integrate both Miller's and Guth and Ginsberg's line of thoughts. They distill three distinct factors of CE: content(embodies innovation as new product-market

Friesen construct captures the disposition as opposed to the actual engagement in entrepreneurship, and ignore less formalized efforts, e.g., activities from individual creativity or self-interest[672]. Still, Zahra, Jennings and Kuratko consolidate that researchers prefer the Miller and Friesen conceptualization[673].

From the author's perspective, the concept by Guth, Ginsberg and Zahra, respectively, serves best the task of analyzing the change in CE at the exit and subsequent years of an LBO[674]. The focus rests on the changes in the emphasis and related levers for value creation. The levers are related to actual measures within the organization, e.g., R&D efficiency, number of markets served, and actual changes in the organizational setup. Further, market development (corporate venturing) is an important optimization lever during the buyout cycle[675], though not explicitly operationalized in the concept of Miller and Friesen[676]. However, even most recent research investigating the potential influence of a buyout regime on the nature and extent of CE has applied different concepts for operationalization[677].

Corporate Entrepreneurship – Financial Performance Relationship

The paucity of a consistent definition of CE is reflected in its blurred impact on financial performance. Different entrepreneurial postures may influence the

---

combinations, new technologies and new business creation), locus (internal and external entrepreneurial activities) and source (level of formality) (See Zahra 1999).

672 See Zahra 1991, p. 272

673 Studies applying the concept of Miller and Friesen are (not complete): Stopford and Baden-Fuller 1994, Covin and Slevin 1991, Barringer and Bluedorn 1999, Covin and Miles 1999, Kemelgor 2002, Goosen, de Coning et al. 2002, Jennings and Hindle 2004, and Wiklund and Shepherd 2005. Studies applying the concept of Guth Ginsberg and Zahra are: Zahra 1996, Zahra 2000, Wegner 2003.

674 Following Guth and Ginsberg's definition of CE and the strategic imperative of Covin and Miles, an entrepreneurial orientation will be understood as: any entrepreneurial activities within the context of an organization that lead to a competitive advantage on the basis of either (i) innovation, (ii) market development/venturing or (iii) strategic renewal. Hence, activities and policies of CE embrace: (a) developing and producing new products, installing new technologies or systems, creating new resources and capabilities distinctive from competitors, (b) entering into new businesses by expanding operations in existing or new markets and (c) redefining corporate structure or strategy while in parallel substantially changing relationships within the organization or to the external environment.

675 See Wegner 2003, p. 217

676 See also the critique from Zahra 1999, p. 51

677 Bruining and Verwaal analyze how CE positively affects performance. The researchers apply a concept of Stevenson, which measures CE as a set of opportunity versus administrative based management practices (See Stevenson 1983, Bruning and Verwaal 2005). A survey on the differences between growth as opposed to non-growth buyouts details CE by the concept of Guth and Ginsberg (see Wegner 2003). Wright, Hoskisson and Busenitz introduce a framework related to the mindset of managers, which may either by entrepreneurial or managerial-oriented. An LBO may serve as a vehicle for unleashing the entrepreneurial mindset and fostering renewal, leading to revitalization and strategic innovation. Along the dimensions 'mindset' – entrepreneurial as opposed to managerial and 'buyout type' – efficiency as opposed to innovation – the authors classify four categories of buyout opportunities, which are: efficiency, revitalizational, entrepreneurial and failure. The categorization has however not yet been empirically tested (see Wright 2001).

individual dimensions of performance quite differently and assumingly at different points in time[678]. Even the latest research admits unclear results, taking into account modifying moderating variables[679].

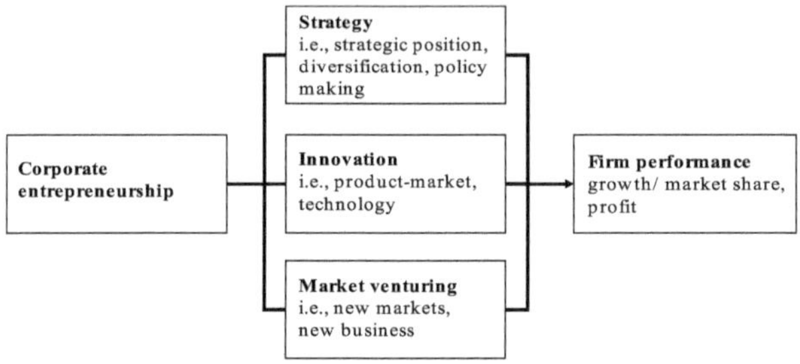

Figure 8: Constituents of entrepreneurial orientation[680]

Nonetheless, a theoretical link between CE and performance can be decoded. Companies introducing new products and technologies benefit from their pioneer position. They target premium segments at high prices, establish industry standards to their own benefit and dominate distribution channels[681]. With their robust profits, the pioneering companies can often sustain and expand their market position. They capitalize on their strong products with increasing reputation and customer loyalty. If performance increase cannot be observed, Zahra argues that at least entrepreneurial activities secure the survival of companies in hostile environments[682]. Foster and Kaplan reason that companies survive if they follow closely their markets and are willing for decisive revolutions, notably called 'creative destruction'[683]. McGrath, Venkatraman and Macmillan argue that CE creates superior value for customers and insulates the company from intense competition[684]. The different dimensions within corporate entrepreneurship are related differently to performance. Bruining and Verwaal investigate the different factors of CE used from a conceptualization of Stevenson.Only an entrepreneurial posture to strategy and to

678 See Zahra 1993b, p. 11

679 See Wiklund and Shepherd 2005, p. 71, Wiklund 1999, p. 38, Morris and Sexton 1996, p. 8, Zahra and Covin 1995, p. 47, Zahra 1993b, p. 12, Zahra 1993c, p. 321

680 For the purpose of mutual exclusivity, a precise distinction of efforts toward efficiency is necessary. Any activities that lead to enhanced efficiency which are not decisive for strategic position and uniqueness will be regarded as part of an efficiency-focused value creation. In contrast, innovation in new manufacturing technologies leading to significant cost leadership and a distinct competitive advantage should be considered as a part of entrepreneurial growth-focused value creation.

681 See Zahra and Covin 1995, p. 47, Wiklund 1999, p. 39

682 See Zahra 1993b, p. 12

683 See Foster and Kaplan 2001, pp. 8 et seqq.

684 See McGrath, Venkataramann et al. 1994, p. 364

compensation scheme contributes significantly to the company's operating profit relative to competitors. An administrative rather than en entrepreneurial focus on resources, growth and entrepreneurial culture spurred success. Otherwise, the latter factors contributed to a decline in performance[685].

Research has proven the positive relationship of CE on various performance indicators. Revenue and sales seem to be increased by higher CE activities, induced by increase of customers[686]. A time lag may occur through lead times when developing new products and realizing the gain in revenues and profits. Further, time lag may derive from learning and experience curve effects. Companies who continue to act aggressively on new product-market solutions and exploiting new market niches should be able to improve their market strategy and operate more efficiently. The strength of the CE-performance relationship will increase, therefore, over time, what is confirmed by empiricism[687]. Therefore, CE is a mean to deliver long-term superior performance, both on growth and profitability[688]. Executives have to understand that the relationship is long-term and may require a severe short-term sacrifice of resources and liquidity. A preference toward corporate entrepreneurship may though also be associated with some downsides. Kind-hearted efforts can fail, not due to management failure, but due to the inherent market risk. In a severe crisis, such a failure can be detrimental to short-term liquidity. Without a clear strategic focus and functioning administration policies, entrepreneurial activities might not be able to develop their positive impact[689].

In addition, the relationship between corporate entrepreneurship and performance is contingent on multiple external factors[690]. The results indicate the necessity to select

---

685 See Bruning and Verwaal 2005

686 See Wiklund 1999, p. 45, Morris and Sexton 1996, Zahra 1991

687 Ravenscraft and Scherer document the strongest relationship between R&D expenditure and profitability indicators at year 4 to 6 after initial investment (See Ravenscraft and Scherer 1982). Franko finds evidence for long-term effect of R&D expenditure on both profitability and growth (Franko 1989). Zahra reports an increasing association from the contemporaneous year to a two-year lag (See Zahra 1991). Zahra and Covin detail the relationship and prove the increasing relationship up to a seven year time lag (See Zahra and Covin 1995). Morris and Sexton could not prove the profit implication, arguing that entrepreneurial activities and their related financial performance are not always concurrent (See Morris and Sexton 1996, p. 11).

688 See Zahra and Covin 1995, p. 55

689 See Fast 1981, p. 23

690 CE is more influential in an environment with high growth, high degree of innovation speed and technological opportunities, and with the degree of dynamism. Opportunities emerge where modifications can enrich the niche in which the company operates (See Zahra 1991, p.263). In the case of massive deregulation, companies will profoundly revise current business practice, undergo a renewal, and may strive to regain competitiveness with new products. Firm-level entrepreneurship to performance-relationship is also moderated by the level of hostility and competitive rivalry (See Zahra 1993c, p. 324). A at a high level of rivalry, companies have to innovate to find novel ways to differentiate themselves from

the dimensions of entrepreneurship efforts carefully to address the competitive and technological environment[691]. A dynamic and growth environment leads to a stronger focus on new business creation and innovation, whereas a hostile environment fosters redefinition of business through venturing activities. Increased hostility has proven to strengthen the relationship, benign environments to weaken the relationship[692]. However, the level of predictability of the CE-performance relationship is not satisfactory when merely considering environmental factors[693]. Access to resources seems to explain additional variability in performance to CE. Especially sufficient access to financial capital apparently strengthens the performance implication of a CE. This observation thereby corresponds to the aforementioned underinvestment hypothesis[694].

4.2 Changes in Strategy

The change in the ownership and governance structure, both at the entry and the exit from the buyout, will initiate an intense debate about the right strategy. Without a close alignment of the managerial compensation scheme and long-term value creation, the responsible managers may overinvest and diversify the company to a level where the survival is at risk.

An adjustment of the corporate strategy will be facilitated by the change in the ownership over the buyout cycle. First, the efficiency emphasis and the entrepreneurial orientation towards growth alike will initiate a discussion about the general strategic position. The strategic position is determined by the relative weighting of key variables such as cost leadership, market leadership or technology leadership. Second, the necessity for an increase in efficiency will motivate managers to question the strategic scope of the company. A buyout may lead to a narrowing of the strategic scope to the core business of the company and to considerably reducing

---

competitors.

691 Zahra found strong empirical support of the CE-performance relationship in different identified environmental clusters. Strategic renewal, venturing and innovation have to be closely adapted to industry growth, the level of technological opportunity and dynamism. Further, competitive rivalry and hostility influence the CE-performance relationship (See Zahra 1993c, p.333). Lumpkin and Dess propose an independent effect of both environmental munificence and entrepreneurial orientation on organizational performance (See Lumpkin and Dess 1996, p. 158).

692 See Zahra and Covin 1995, p. 54, Covin and Slevin 1989, pp. 80 et seqq.

693 For example, Zahra and Covin notice the possibility of various other factors influencing the CE-performance relationship (See Zahra and Covin 1995).

694 Since financial capital enables the acquisition of generic resources, it is to some extent a proxy for resources in general (See Dollinger 1999). From a theoretical perspective, sufficient resources provide a buffer to experiment with innovative projects with high uncertainty in a resource-constrained environment (See Cooper, Gimeno-Gascon et al. 1994, p. 384). In particular, small firms will exhibit limited growth due to capital constraints.

the level of diversification. The necessity to divest and reduce the corporate scope though may lead to a downsizing below a critical scale required for a competitive efficiency. Debt may hinder to gain the resources needed for long-term growth. The appetite for growth in new businesses may increase, therefore, significantly after the exit from the growth, in particular after reducing the debt service and infusing new cash. An enhanced focus may serve as a platform for growth within a much more well-defined market. Manager's personal utility of growth and size once against becomes more prominent, since their compensation is often less dependent on stable cash flows than on revenue growth.

4.2.1 Strategic Positioning

How a strategy is chosen is determined by a series of factors: the business environment and competitive forces the company is confronted with; the capabilities and resources available and sought for in the company; the capital structure; and the utility function of the senior in the company, to name but a few. The entry in and the exit from a buyout will influence several of the listed factors. Hence, questions may circle around: How does debt and financial distress invite a risk-reduced strategy around mass-market cost leadership? Will the promise for synergies in a trade sale incur massive scale efficiency improvements, accompanied to an augmented emphasis on a volume strategy over multiple markets? Will the growth expectations of the stock market in a going-public promote a high-risk strategy?

The author will briefly review theory and empirical evidence on strategy positioning and generic strategy types with the perspective on how LBO and exit may be related to a preference to one or the other strategy. Secondly, the author will elucidate some additional related literature on strategy-implied changes during a turnaround, whereby the changes are reviewed in the light of an LBO entry and exit. Thirdly, the empirical evidence of both LBO and exit is discussed. Finally, theoretical discourse and evidence are consolidated in hypotheses for analysis and testing in the following case studies.

Basic Link between Strategy, Resource-Based View and Product Life Cycle

Based on the resource-based view of the company, the essence of strategy formulation and adjustment is to make the most effective use of core resources and capabilities[695]. Designing the strategy around these critically resources and capabilities may imply that management restricts its strategic scope to those activities where it possesses a clear competitive advantage. If resource base lacks of durability

695 See Grant 1996, p. 129

or are easily transferable, the company should seek to either adopt a strategy of short-term harvesting or investment in new sources of competitive advantage. Strategy researchers have searched for a construct of contingency variables to predict a company-specific suitable strategy besides the marching with the resource base. Attention within contingency has been devoted to product and business life cycles. Most buyouts take place in the situation of a mature industry and intense competition[696]. A company is more likely to achieve stable cash flow if a substantial part of the products is in the maturity phase[697]. Besides having already invested in the development and introduction of the products, the products have proved that the customers accept them. Thereby, management has to advance and to align continuously the resource base with the business environment. Miles and Snow propose that this process of alignment defines company's strategy. Such a strategic fit is however temporary, and requires to some degree intentional realignment or superior resources and capabilities to remain in inertia. Zajac, Kraatz and Bresser opened the question on the nature and extent of change in strategy under different levels of misalignment between strategy and the company's environment[698].

As outlined, management's objectives change considerably over the buyout cycle. Thereby it seems likely that the preferences towards strategic objectives will evolve. Further, the changes in the governance system may induce a change in the fit of resource base and capabilities with the company's environment. In mature industries where buyouts typically occur, management finds it hard to initiate strategic change due to established managerial views on corporate strategy[699]. A buyout may dissolve a potential strategic misfit between external factor and internal strengths. To analyze the changes in strategic objectives the author will discuss the concept of generic strategies and strategy groups[700] that incorporate a consistent set of strategic attributes and investigate whether the preference such groups alter in the course of the exit.

Strategy Types

A review of companies moving in the maturity phase of their industry with intensifying competition, analogous to a typical pre-buyout situation, reveals that companies do not have to follow a pure cost leadership strategy to be successful. Hall

---

696 See Anderson and Zeithaml 1984, p. 22
697 See Ballwieser and Schmid 1990a, Ballwieser and Schmid 1990b
698 See Zajac, Kraatz et al. 2000, p. 432
699 See Leonard-Barton 1992, p. 112, Bettis and Prahalad 1995, pp.5 et seqq.
700 See Porter 1980, Miles and Snow 1984, Hambrick and Schecter 1983

identifies two distinct strategies for success[701]. In the first strategy, the company seeks to achieve the lowest delivered cost position relative to competition, both with an acceptable delivered quality and aggressive pricing to gain market share. The company relies on efficiency advantages from a highly specialized asset base. In the second strategy, the company seeks to achieve the highest product/service/quality differentiated position relative to competition, with both an acceptable delivered cost structure and pricing policy. Thereby, the company has a flexible, "light" asset base. Hall reports that the successful companies aim to re-invest in their asset base in their core industry, as opposed to diversify into other businesses. Further, companies operating in mature markets are not obliged to cost leadership strategy. They may choose to combine a differentiated product or quality position with a reasonable cost structure[702]. A similar study by Anderson and Zeithaml details the strategy position in the mature period and potential changes when turning into the decline period of the industry[703]. As maturity turns into decline of the industry, the emphasis on efficiency and restrictive investments continues. In particular, operational excellence and a high efficiency in product and process R&D, sales force and general marketing becomes more important, spurring employee productivity and asset utilization. The strategic approach turns to a higher level of standardization, as products are perceived as commodities. Quality service is still relevant, however does not differentiate. Porter introduces a framework with generic strategies. He emphasizes a strong link between differentiation strategies and entrepreneurial-type activities[704]. Companies following a differentiation strategy rely on strong marketing capabilities and product engineering skills. Companies following a cost-leadership strategy concentrate on process engineering skills, as well as on an efficient distribution system and tight cost control. According to Porter, LBOs seeking for strategy renewal with increased CE should adopt a differentiation-type strategy.

A research paper by Dess, Lumpkin and McGee reject this clear differentiation[705], finding cost leadership strategies to be associated with elevated performance where managers tend to an entrepreneurial approach in decision-making. Understanding entrepreneurship as a profound renewal, they esteem the strategic initiative to both lowering costs and introducing new products as superior[706]. Zahra and Covin

701 See Hall 1980, p. 79
702 See Hall 1980, p. 82
703 See Anderson and Zeithaml 1984, p. 15
704 See Porter 1980, pp. 40-41
705 See Dess, Lumpkin et al. 1999, p. 89-90
706 A linkage may exist when, for example, management introduces state-of-the-art technologies in inventory and information systems, addressing productivity increases and quality enhancements. Moreover, the

confirm the former empirical results with a positive relationship between cost leadership strategy and new product development[707]. Murray argues that the combination of a differentiation and a cost leadership strategy may result in superior performance[708]. Since both preconditions, the industry structure as well as customer preferences, may occur independently in the same environment, a combination can be feasible. Empirical investigations show that for company with high quality products, costs declined more rapidly[709]. Other research more generally finds high product quality negatively related to direct costs. Therefore, external factors can allow a combined efficiency and entrepreneurial growth-oriented strategy to be superior to traditional strategies. Miles and Snow have also enriched the theoretical discussion about dominant strategies and organizational setups[710]. The key design factor differentiating their 'strategy types' is the speed at which the organization changes to altering customer needs, competition, and technologies[711]. The likelihood of success differs by the environment and in particular by the product life cycle stage. The moderate 'analyzer' strategy is measured to be superior in the maturity, non-innovative period to the both extreme strategy positions– the 'defender' and the 'prospector'[712]. The prospectors have to bear high costs for the development and marketing of new products. Hambrick concludes that the prospector strategy is a viable temporary strategic positioning "in a period of growth and rapid technological change", however, not in the long term[713]. On the other hand, intense price competition scrutinizes the defender strategy. Hence, the analyzer is able to buffer the intense competition with a modest level of quality and/or product-based differentiation. In an innovative industry, the prospectors gain the highest market change, however, are not considerably more profitable. The strategy tends to have complex coordination and communication skills. The prospectors rely on participative and decentralized decision-making processes. Marketing and product

---

authors argue the advantage of entrepreneurial orientation, with urging the organization to undertake a range of strategies and to strive to be performer in all of them (See Dess, Lumpkin et al. 1999, p. 91)

707 See Zahra and Covin 1993

708 See Murray 1988, p. 395

709 See Fine 1983, p. 213, Philips, Chang et al. 1983, p.40

710 See Miles and Snow 1984, pp. 45-60

711 Defenders are organizations that undertake little or no new product and market development. Defenders tend not to search outside their domains for new opportunities; they rather focus on niches within their industries. Prospectors continually search for market opportunities and tend to be pacemakers of industry change. They excel on product and market development. Analyzers are an intermediate type, operating in both relatively stable and volatile markets. They undertake fewer product and market changes than prospectors do, however feel less committed to stability and efficiency than defenders. Reactors lack a consistent strategy and merely respond to external forces (See Miles and Snow 1984, pp. 45 et seqq.)

712 In a survey by Hambrick, the return on investment is highest for the analyzer (31%), followed by the defender (23%) and prospector (13%) (See Hambrick 1983, p. 18).

713 See Hambrick 1983, p. 19

development function dominate their strategy. By contrast, defenders have simple, centralized and hierarchical coordination mechanisms. They focus on permanent rationalization throughout the entire value chain. Typically, production and finance executives dominate the defender strategy. Hambrick synthesizes that the "strategy should be a function of the nature and requirements of the environment and the type of performance being sought at the time"[714]. The empirical research attributes a high level of explanatory power to the Miles Snow typology[715].

One may also find guidance for strategy after exit when referring to the situation during a strategic turnaround[716]. In particular, the companies undergoing a turnaround typically operate in mature industries, suffer from intense competition with tight margins, and have a high share of debt, similar to the profile of an LBO company[717]. Hambrick and Schecter propose two directions of turnaround strategies: efficiency-oriented and entrepreneurship-oriented[718]. Cost cutting or an asset reduction strategy (a disposal of primarily fixed assets) may realize the intended efficiency improvements. The entrepreneurial strategy covers strategic activities for revenue generation and product/market refocusing. The researchers identify three different patterns of managerial actions which they name successful 'turnaround gestalt'[719]. The turnaround strategies are dependent on their contingency factors, such as the current market share and the degree of capacity utilization. Nonetheless, Hambrick and Schecter find only modest evidence for entrepreneurial growth

---

714 See Hambrick 1983, p. 25

715 In an extensive research, Doty, Glick and Huber predict, using the Miles and Snow typologies, 24% of the overall variance in organizational effectiveness (See Doty, Glick et al. 1993, p. 1236)

716 A strategic turnaround is, following the categorization of Hofer, necessary if the company has a weak position (i) from a product/market perspective, (ii) in its technological and production capabilities, and (iii) in its financial capabilities. Unter (i), the company will not have enough scale to compete. Further, an increase in market share without a unique competitive advantage can be detrimental. Under (ii), the company will have to closely assess potential changes in production capacity and adjust the location to the most appropriate labor markets, sources of raw material, or markets. In addition, the management has to understand how important the experience curve effect is and how to compensate for a undercritical size. Long term investment needs have to be balanced again the expected growth rate and intended asset structure. If the financing capability is limited as in (iii), the company has to re-configure the capital structure (See Hofer 1980, pp. 22-24)

717 See Barker and Duhaime 1997, p. 30

718 See Hambrick and Schecter 1983, p. 233-234

719 The 'asset and cost surgery turnaround strategy' focuses on increased employee productivity, capacity utilization, and asset disposal as well as decreasing R&D expenses. The companies return to profit with no damage, e.g., a detrimental loss of resource base, to their market position. The 'selective product/market pruning' strategy sustained their R&D and product development activities. They increased their product quality, while reducing working capital and increasing employee productivity. The decline in capacity utilization can be seen as focus on high margin instead of volume business. Hambrick and Schecter interpret this strategy as consolidating towards the most profitable businesses lines. The 'piecemeal productivity' does not prompt significant strategic actions. The observations indicate selective enhancements of capacity utilization and employee productivity (See Hambrick and Schecter 1983, p. 241-242)

strategies in mature industries. According to their results, the market shares in stagnating industries are relatively fixed, with limited opportunities for ambitious market share expansion. An additional aspect is the availability of slack financial resources. In a decline, companies will stepwise loose the ability for undertaking necessary investments in new resources and businesses. A recent survey by Barker and Duhaime confirms that slack resources enhance an organization's ability to innovate and to implement significant strategic changes[720].

A recent survey in Germany identifies four idiosyncratic strategies for the medium-sized to large corporations, differentiated by the extent of innovation and market/volume focus. The successful companies encompass a specific set of capabilities and resources, dependent on the individual strategy. All strategies in general, except the strategy of cost leadership, can direct the company to success[721]. However, the distribution of strategy types is reliant on the industry sector, e.g., the share of 'innovation champions' is significantly higher for the high-tech than for the construction industry. Further, the 'specialist' strategy allows a higher profitability at lower growth rates, whereas the 'innovation champion' allows out-growing the competitors while compromising on profitability. In addition, the strategy type correlates with company size. Larger companies tend to choose the 'innovation champion' or the 'competence leadership' strategy, since they can afford to build-up the variety of resources required for the position. Smaller companies are limited in their resources and pursue the 'specialists" strategy focusing a market niche. An additional publication on the same survey reports that the innovation-oriented strategies comprise a significantly lower share of debt to total capital, whereas the cost-oriented strategies, in particular the 'cost leadership', have a higher share of debt. In contrast to Porter's generic strategies, the survey also suggests that an organizational design with both capabilities in efficiency management as well as entrepreneurial growth through innovation is feasible. Such a strategy type, named as 'competence leader', is the most challenging and requires superior managerial expertise[722]. Porter proposes that there are differences in the organizational arrangements and procedures for the formulated generic strategies, and excludes concurrent organizational designs for cost leadership and innovation[723]. However,

---

720 See Barker and Duhaime 1997, p. 33

721 The decreased average profitability and growth of the "cost leadership" strategy is claimed to be a result of the high factor costs in Germany. The authors argue that firms located in Germany choose to compete more by quality and technology leadership enabling to achieve price premiums (See Meffert, Radtke et al. 2005, p. 43)

722 See Meffert 2007, p. 72-73

723 See Porter 1980, p. 40-41

Murray argues in extension of his critique on Porter's exclusive strategies that organizational design can also fulfill requirements of both differentiation and cost leadership[724]. In extension to the aforementioned German survey, he admits that the integration task within the organization is an exceptional challenge for management[725].

To conclude, the observations predict that the entry and exit from a buyout structure will induce changes in strategy. The available capital, the resource base, and the company size appear to be an indicator for the right strategic position. Companies seeking for a strategy based on a relative cost advantage require significant investments and bind capital in specified assets. The survey of German companies' reports that small companies should concentrate on a niche strategy with a limited set of attributes, otherwise they are highly penalized and likely to fail. Larger companies, however, have sufficient resources to build simultaneously distinctive capabilities in both cost- and market-leadership. Further, larger companies possess more capital to invest into entrepreneurial projects, for instance, to enter into a new market. Hambrick argues that a moderating strategy ('analyzer') with a modest level of differentiation, combined with a competitive cost structure, leads to superior performance in mature industries. Such a mixture of efficiency- and entrepreneurship-oriented strategic positioning is highly challenging, and demands a strong resource and skill base. The research around strategic turnarounds claims that management should decide between an efficiency-oriented or an entrepreneurship-oriented strategy.

Empirical Evidence for Buyout Period

The research has been sparse on investigating changes in key strategic variables during the buyout restructuring. Firstly, the empirical data suggests a shift towards cost leadership strategies[726]. Secondly, supplementary surveys, especially on most recent data from the late 1990s, indicate some contradictory strategy adjustment to

---

724 See Murray 1988, p. 397

725 Murray refers to the two main tasks of differentiation and integration proposed by Lawrence and Lorsch 1967. Whereas differentiation can serve both competencies in product design and cost leadership, the degree of integration is dependent on the scope of tasks.

726 Green reports a preference to cost-cutting over growth during the LBO. External financial claimants urge managers to pursue a rigid consolidation path (See Green 1992, p. 517). Anslinger and Copeland stress the need for LBOs for innovative operating strategies above all other strategic modifications. They report a contribution of strategic cost leadership-initiatives for up to 60% of value creation in the post-exit phase (See Anslinger and Copeland 1996, p. 99). Baker and Smith, along the same line of thought, also report the prominent focus on cost initiatives of past LBOs by KKR. In the case of Safeway, the major improvement levers were found in enhanced employee productivity, rationalized distribution systems and divestments of underperforming units (See Baker and Smith 1998, p. 92-113).

growth-related strategies, focusing on market expansion and new product development[727]. Thirdly, the strategy formulation process seems to be professionalized, with a higher share of participation and frequency[728].

The results for German buyout correspond to these observations. From the perspective of the product life cycle, German buyouts do not seem to resemble the ideal picture of a company focused on the maturity stadium[729]. For instance, Vest measures the relative position of the spinoff-buyouts in the product life cycle. Although the majority of products (55%) are positioned in the maturity stage, a considerable part of the products (40%) is situated in the early cycle[730]. Wegner questions how the strategy focus, categorized by Porter's competitive strategies[731], contributes to the success of the buyouts. The managers of the buyout related the success to a high share to a differentiation-based strategy (66,7%), a niche-based strategy (50,0%) and a cost leadership-based strategy (50,0%)[732]. A strategy founded on technology-based leadership is, however, much less likely to lead to success (26,6%). The low share of technology-based leadership is surprising, since German companies are known for their focus on innovation and technology leadership[733]. With respect to strategic decision-making, surveys indicate an increase in the quality for German buyouts. For spinoff-buyouts, the Arbeitskreis Schmalenbach suggests on basis of empirical evidence a high share of buyouts (84%) revising their strategy. The buyouts leverage their stand-alone position through reinforcing external growth through acquisitions, in particular to expand the current product portfolio in the core market[734]. Notwithstanding, the existence of a strategy does not seem to be too

727 Bruining, Bonnet and Wright report an increased growth focus after the entry into the LBO through international acquisitions and entry into cross-border alliances. The growth focus is related with a strong focus on specific customer needs (See Bruining, Bonnet et al. 2003, pp. 12- 14). A survey on European LBOs confirms the growth focus, e.g., by increasing the range of markets and products, and stronger emphasis on customer needs. (See EVCA 2001, p. 9. See the analysis on changes in market development in chapter B4.4.

728 Green analyzes the strategic decision-making process by the activity level of investors and speed of implementation. The emphasis on strategy formulation is most important during the LBO preparation, and requires only modest adjustment in the holding period. Owner-managers focused rather on a stringent implementation of existing strategies than on the implementation of new growth plans. Further, the author esteems ownership over debt as the facilitator for enhanced strategy making (See Green 1992, p. 530) Bruining, Bonnet and Wright observe a stronger emphasis on explicit strategy formulation in close interaction with the supervisory board and buyout investors (See Bruining, Bonnet et al. 2003, p. 14).

729 See Hoffmann and Ranke 1990, p. 50, Titzrath 1994, p. 214. The two references though are biased by the high occurrence of buyouts in former East Germany with a significant part of Venture Capital-based seed and early stage financing.

730 See Vest 1995, p, 147

731 See Porter 1996, pp. 62 et seqq.

732 See Wegner 2003, pp. 210 - 211

733 See Meffert, Radtke et al. 2005, p. 43

734 See Schmalenbach-Gesellschaft 2006, p. 254

important for the decision to enter into a buyout negotiation by commercial banks in Germany, according to a survey by Luippold[735]. Only 12% report an appropriate strategy as mandatory, while for instance a qualified management (85%) or an attractive product and market position (69%) is honored more valuable. Further, surveys analyzing the changes of German buyouts have investigated the changes in the determinants of the key strategic variables on basis of Porter's model of competitive forces[736]. In summary, the competitive forces remain throughout the buyout to be of a middling strength, allowing the individual company to come across a profitable strategic position[737]. Since the buyouts typically operate in mature industries, the rivalry among competitors is high[738]. In total, the risk related to the cash flows of the buyout company is located around customer relationship and the rivalry with established competitors. Therefore, the shift of focus to customer needs and services, as reported for instance by Bruining, Bonnet and Wright and for German buyouts by Gräper[739], seems more than reasonable. Gräper concludes that one of the reasons for the divestment was the 'strategic failure' to integrate the buyouts into the parent company. Nevertheless, the change in strategic focus is more far-reaching for a former division unit than for a former stand-alone enterprise[740].

Empirical Evidence for Post-Exit

The indication for a post-exit strategy, beyond the relative position of the industry over the product cycle and the level of asset intensity, is limited, with modest guidance to relate the choice of strategy with the changes in the governance.

After going-public, debt decrease should simplify a stronger emphasis on a growth strategy. Management can benefit from higher freedom in the investment policy. Further, an increase in company size through a trade sale, accompanied with a broader access to resources, enables a broader strategy approach, e.g., developing

735 See Luippold 1991, p. 313

736 See Vest 1995, pp. 133 et seqq., Porter 1980, pp. 36 et seqq.

737 For the discussion of the relationship between competitive forces, strategic positioning and profit pool see chapter A2.2.1.

738 Vest argues that LBOs operate in niches with specialized products and small lots (See Vest 1995, p. 138). In particular, former divisions may suffer from loss of internal delivery and performance relationships with their parent company. In a survey by Gräper none of the studied spinoff buyouts had more than 10% of revenues with the former parent (See Gräper 1993, p. 127). The fear for substitute products is low, since new service and product solutions are apparently regarded as improvements of the incumbent producers, rather than a threat. The threat of market entry by potential new competitors is regarded as modest. Buyout managers argue that the customer relationships are of a long-term quality. Vest also reports that narrow niche market segment where the LBOs are positioned have limited attractiveness for new entrants (See Vest 1995, p. 140).)

739 Gräper reports that for 39% of buyout the customer relationship improves through increased acquisition activities and the termination of unprofitable customer (See Gräper 1993, p. 126).

740 See Titzrath 1994, p. 239

capabilities either around volume/market penetration or innovation. However, decrease of managerial shareholdings may harm management's risk propensity towards entrepreneurial activities. Further, management may reduce their commitment to strategy formulation. In addition, the intensity of strategic discussion and decision-making may decrease after the departure of the buyout investors from the board.

For an exit through a trade sale, most acquisitions are argued to be motivated by economy of scale and scope[741]. In this case, asset disposals and layoffs allow diminishing excess capacity. The acquirer can increase his market power, for instance, by enlarging his purchasing volume (against his suppliers) and his market share (against his customer base)[742]. In addition, an acquisition can serve as a 'catalyst' to restructure the business system. Bowman and Singh note that an acquisition allows "to develop a new configuration of the lines of business of the corporation"[743]. The product portfolio and mix of goods and services will be refined, the organizational structure reviewed and processes adapted. Beyond seeking scale efficiency, an acquisition accompanied by a restructuring allows to change the basic concept and the way the business is performed[744]. The restructuring is not limited to the target, but also covers the acquiring company itself. Salter and Weinhold analyze the strategy implications of an acquisition. They differentiate the strategic fit into four categories and grant a more detailed differentiation of post-acquisition strategic modifications (see Figure 9)[745]. The basis is strategic intent of the bidding company and the relatedness between the bidder and the target, e.g., how markets and customers, assets and resources, and products match. The strategic adjustments and the potential value creation will be higher the closer the strategic fit is. Empirical evidence confirms that value creation is highest for a strategic fit between products and customers by strategies permitting to expand into new markets (related-supplementary) and by strategies permitting to expand within the same business (identical)[746]. A low strategic fit will require significant adjustments to align the strategies and may overstretch existing management capabilities and resources. Alternatively, the management may decide to concentrate either horizontally, e.g., consolidating the product portfolio, or vertically, e.g., focusing on a distinct number of markets.

---

741 See Jensen 1986, Dutz 1989, Seth 1990
742 See Heflebower 1963, Hartman, Teece et al. 1994
743 See Bowman and Singh 1993, p. 6
744 See Bowman and Singh 1993, Bethel and Liebeskind 1993
745 See Salter and Weinhold 1979
746 See Singh and Montgomery 1987, pp. 382 et seqq., Shelton 1988, pp. 283 et seqq.

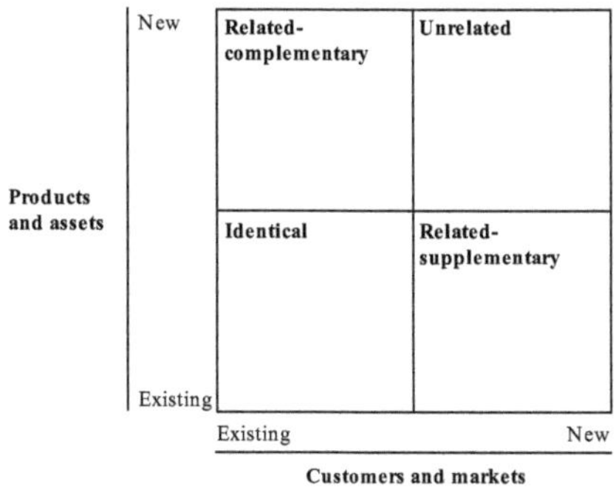

Figure 9: Strategic fit between a target and a bidder business[747]

A further conceptualization of acquisitions is associated with the exchange and redeployment of resources. Strategy researchers argue that acquisitions support the acquiring company to reconfigure their own and the target business as part of a transformation. The acquisition concedes the companies to exchange firm-specific resources that are difficult to develop. The resource-based view argues that companies have frequently to reconfigure their resources to respond to changes in their competitive environment and to improve existing operations[748]. However, the internal development of new resources often fails. The development may be impeded by a bounded rationality in decision-making, by the tendency to develop new resources only in areas where the company already has prior knowledge, and by a diminishing response capability[749]. Therefore, management turns to external markets to acquire new resources. The market for discrete resources though often fails due the difficulty of correctly valuing the resources, of disentangling the resources from the remaining operations, and of opportunistic behavior in the post-contract period[750]. Hence, business acquisitions play a pivotal role in the transformation of the company and a strategy-linked resource development. The empirical research suggests that resources are redeployed, as expected, between the bidder and target[751]. The direction of redeployment is thereby dependent on the relative strength and quality of the resources. Interestingly, the redeployment is

747 See Salter and Weinhold 1979

748 See Teece 1982

749 See Nelson and Winter 1982, Teece, Pisano et al. 1997, Singh and Montgomery 1987, Levinthal 1997

750 See Nelson and Winter 1982, Peteraf 1993, Connor and Prahalad 1996

751 For instance, Larsson and Finkelstein report that the redeployment of complementary resources (and operations) increase the probability of success; acquisitions with similar production and marketing operations tended to elicit more resistance (See Larsson and Finkelstein 1999, pp. 10 et seqq). See also Capron, Dussauge et al. 1998, pp. 641 et seqq., as well as Capron 1999, pp. 1000 et seqq.

observed, at equal probability, in acquisitions intended either to increase market power or to enhance scale efficiency. The problem of market failure will also concern the resource exchange in the post-acquisition period. A difficulty to value a resource adequately may lead to suboptimal redeployment[752].

Post-acquisition strategies targeted on integrating resources and processes are the most successful. The theorist hypothesize that the performance improvement inherent in either horizontal or market expansion is only obtainable if the target is completely integrated within the acquirer's structure[753]. In this case, the performance enhancement from integrated operations compensates by far the costs of disruptions and frictions. In contrast, Hoskisson, Hitt and Ireland argue that differences (unrelatedness) in the resource base result in valuable synergies, while similarities in the resource base (relatedness) are less likely to lead to success. The researchers conclude that strategy changes and changes in the resources during acquisitions should be analyzed not by generic strategy types but by the individual resource category[754]. Supplementary researcher reports that the resources related to market coverage and development have the most direct positive impact on acquisition performance, while innovation related resources are less important[755]. The resource redeployment is primarily used for capability enhancement, in some cases also for cost savings through shared resources. The usage of the target's resources for the acquirer is more problematic as the usage of the acquirer's resource for the target.

In principal, the decrease in debt will allow a broadening of the strategic position. The former LBO may move out of market niche and choose a broader market strategy with a differentiation on product, quality, service, or other. The broad resource base and capital from the parent will support the strategic changes potentially not feasible in the tight cost regime during the LBO. The acquirer will seek to close any strategic gaps through a leverage and redeployment of the resources to the most valuable place within the company. Nonetheless, the management of the acquiring company will continue with a strong focus on cost cutting and operational excellence in the target to justify the paid premium. The decreased participation in value creation of management through reduced shareholdings will dampen, however, the motivation of the top managers to pursue decisive strategic changes against the employees' will. Further, the departure of the

---

752 See Capron, Dussauge et al. 1998, p. 655

753 See Singh and Zollo 1998b, p. 4

754 See Harrison, Hitt et al. 1991, pp. 186 et seqq.

755 See Capron 1999, pp. 1000 et seqq.

buyout investors will lessen the independence of strategic discussion and decision-making. For the strategic position, the following hypothesis is formulated:

Hypothesis 20a: After a trade sale, reduced debt leverage will lead to a decrease of niche market and product-differentiated strategies. For a related-complementary strategic fit between the acquirer and the former buyout, the strategy will shift to a broader offering of products and sharing of assets and resource base. For a related-supplementary strategic fit, the strategy will shift to a broader penetration of markets and customer bases. In both case, the strategic position will be broadened. No significant changes will be expected for an identical strategic position. The extent of companies pursuing cost leadership strategies will remain, however, unchanged.

Concerning the strategy policy-making process, the changes in governance at the exit through a trade sale may change in the following way:

Hypothesis 21b: After a trade sale, a reduced activity level in governance of the owners will lead to a less intense and open strategy discussion and formulation.

Hypothesis 21d: After a trade sale, reduced management shareholdings will lead to a decrease of management commitment to an intense strategy formulation. Further, management will be less willing to pursue decisive strategic changes.

For a going-public, the changes in the strategic focus will not be related to any considerations of strategic fit with other neighbored business units or of redeployment of resources. The changes of debt, managerial shareholdings, the prospective ownership dispersion and the reshuffling of the supervisory board determine the modifications of the key strategic variables.

Firstly, the decline in management shareholdings will presumably dampen, in analogy to a trade sale, the motivation of the top managers to pursue decisive strategic changes, which may be painful to the organization. As discussed in the introductory chapter about the motivation of the different parties involved[756], the agency costs will increase considerably. Management will have to justify its strategic position and any related changes to the new shareholders and stock market[757]. Ongoing high levels of managerial shareholding can compensate for the increased conflicts of interest. Empirical research reports that post-IPO performance is in those cases superior in which management retains a high ownership[758]. On the other hand,

---

756 Refer for details to chapter B2.2.

757 See Jensen and Meckling 1976, Leland 1977

758 Jain and Kino, Holthausen and Larcker, as well as Roosenboom and Van der Goot report a positive relationship of post-IPO managerial ownership with performance (See Jain and Kini 1994, pp. 1700, Holthausen and Larcker 1996, p. Roosenboom and Van der Goot 2005, pp. 51 et seqq.). Mikkelson, Partch

the cash infusion through the reduced debt will unleash management to follow a stronger growth focus in strategy with a presence on multiple markets, and less niche-oriented strategy. Therefore, the focus on tight cost control and operational excellence may be less prominent than in the ownership of a larger corporation. Secondly, the dispersion of the ownership structure into a scattered shareholder base will reduce the quality and intensity of monitoring. Buyout investors follow a more balanced investment objective based on actual cash flow increase as opposed to long-term growth prospects. In terms of a balance between cash flow-oriented profitability and growth outlook, the disperse ownership structure of the stock market will induce a stronger emphasis on growth. Therefore, investors can justify holding shares in the company and will actively promote a growth and broad market strategy, with a reduced focus on differentiation by products, service, or quality. Again, empirical research for the post-IPO in general confirms the beneficial effect of the monitoring by a dominant shareholder[759]. Thirdly, as already elucidated for the exit through a trade sale, the departure of the buyout investors will most likely reduce the quality and intensity of strategic discussion and related decision-making on the management board.

Thus, the hypotheses are identical for the expected influence on the strategic as for a trade sale, with changes in the foresight by the decrease of debt and in the importance of the de-concentration of ownership supplemented.

Hypothesis 20b: After going-public, reduced debt leverage will lead to a decrease of niche market and product-differentiated strategies. The strategic position will be broadened. Further, the extent of companies pursuing cost leadership strategies will decrease.

Hypothesis 21a: After going-public, the dispersed ownership structure of stock market will in lead to a decrease of niche market and product-differentiated strategies. The focus on less-differentiated strategies with a broad market approach will increase.

Concerning the strategy policy-making process, the changes in governance at the exit through a going-public may change in the following way:

---

and Shah, in contrast, only finds modest evidence, in particular only in year 1 post-IPO, for a positive significant relationship (See Mikkelson, Partch et al. 1997, pp. 297 et seqq.. See detailed discussion in chapter B5.3.3.

759 See Roosenboom and Van der Goot 2005, pp. 53 et seqq.. See detailed discussion in chapter in chapter B5.3.3..

Hypothesis 21c: After going-public, reduced activity level in governance by the former buyout investors will lead to a less intense and open strategy discussion and formulation.

Hypothesis 21e: After going-public, reduced management shareholdings will lead to a decrease of management commitment to an intense strategy formulation. Further, management will be less willing to pursue decisive strategic changes.

4.2.2 Diversification and Scope

Beyond the strategic position the strategy will be further determined by the level of diversification, in particular the number of related and unrelated markets the company is operating in. In related businesses, the diversification can be beneficial by sharing resources and assets, and hence increase company value[760]. Diversification in unrelated businesses, however, is uncertain to increase company value[761]. In such a case, the likelihood of gaining synergies from shared resource and enhancing company's competitive advantage is lower. Further, the increased strategic and business scope incurs organization costs by high coordination and consumption of scarce management attention[762]. The diversification into other related to a smaller and into unrelated markets to a larger extent allows to reduce the systematic business risk. Managers tend to diversify beyond the optimal level for the company, given that their compensation and status is often too strongly linked to revenue size and growth[763]. To reduce non-value creating diversification, debt may serve as a bonding agent to management. Further, active investors with close monitoring may hold back management from any unnecessary acquisitions or mergers.

Diversification is further correlated to the prevalent debt leverage and hence, requires some brief, separate analysis for the post-exit period. Level and direction of diversification reflect the risk attitude of management and should be, therefore, closely subject to the capital structure[764]. Risk-averse strategies of companies operating in a single or related business field are argued to have lower level of debt, while companies with a more risk-affined strategy operate in unrelated business fields have higher level of debt[765]. In equilibrium, a substitution of equity by debt turns management to maximize cash flow, in particular by enhancing operational

760 See Teece 1980, Montgomery and Wernerfelt 1988
761 See Palepu 1985
762 See Bhide 1990, Hoskisson, Johnson et al. 1994
763 See Jensen 1986, p. 323
764 See Rumelt 1974, Barton and Gordon 1987, Barton and Gorton 1988
765 See Barton and Gorton 1988, p. 631

efficiency and by divesting business units and non-core assets[766]. Management will therefore, while entering an LBO, consider to actively downscope the company. Ansoff classified divestment strategies by either (i) reducing geographical coverage, (ii) reducing lines of businesses unrelated to those retained, or (iii) reducing the lines of business related to those retained[767]. Since the divestments are a viable option to raise cash, the contractual partners often explicitly note them in debt contracts for the LBO[768]. Beside the risk preferences of the acting managers, debt will be required to fund acquisition-based growth strategy[769].

The reduction of over-diversification has always been one of the major value creation levers of corporate restructuring, and in particular restructuring during a LBO[770]. Conglomerates and larger multi-business companies with limited advantage from shared resources and capabilities will question to increase strategy focus, finally yet importantly initiated by the shareholders[771]. A further rationale for downscoping is related to strategic errors of management while poorly formulating and implementing a strategy[772]. The failure of strategy formulation occurs when the shareholders exert the wrong type of control, and when management becomes too evidentiary on financial control and looses strategic control over the business units[773].

Managerial shareholdings, beside debt, determine largely the level of diversification. In general, managers are confronted with a company-specific risk associated with their expected income. Without substantial shareholdings or equity-related compensation, they will seek to reduce the systematic risk of the business by acquiring companies and increasing diversification to achieve stable earnings[774]. Management may opt to follow such risk reducing, even if the acquisitions are not value adding. Corporations with high free cash flow and weak governance simplify

766 See Hoskisson, Johnson et al. 1994, p. 1217

767 Diversification in the same line of business is referred to as related diversification and in areas not related to the core line of business it is termed unrelated diversification. Research has shown that the performance of related diversification is higher than that of unrelated diversification due to more shared resources. See Ansoff 1957, pp. 114 et seqq.

768 See Seth and Easterwood 1993, p. 256, Phan and Hill 1995, p. 710

769 See Hitt 1990, p. 32

770 Kohlberg, Kravis and Roberts explicitly call a pre-buyout diversification strategy one of the top 3 selection criteria for buyouts. See in addition cites from Liebeskind 1992, p. 74, Bethel and Liebeskind 1993, p. 15, and Baker and Montgomery 1994, p.2.

771 See Seth and Easterwood 1993, p. 256

772 See Hoskisson, Johnson et al. 1994, pp. 1209 et seqq.

773 See Shleifer and Vishny 1991, pp. 53 et seqq.

774 See Amihud and Lev 1981, pp. 606 et seqq., Baysinger and Hoskisson 1990, p. 80, Bethel and Liebeskind 1993, p. 17, Easterwood 1989, p. 35, Denis, Denis et al. 1997a, p. 141

such non-value adding acquisitions[775]. Since management objectives and compensation schemes remain closely tied to sales growth, managers have the incentive to expand the business beyond the optimal size, leading to decreased resource utilization and productivity[776]. The heart piece of Jensen's theory is that management in many cases diversifies beyond optimal efficiency when the monitoring costs of free cash flow are apparently high[777]. Increasing managerial ownership may lead to value-creating, but risk-enhancing acquisitions[778]. In addition, the right incentives embedded in management's compensation scheme, e.g., stock options, can facilitate a value-increasing strategic downsizing[779]. However, if the personal wealth accompanied with higher managerial shareholdings becomes substantial, managers will opt to undertake more risk-reducing strategies. Empirical evidence confirms such curvilinear relationships[780]. Managers will thereby seek to move the capital structure away from debt to increase the value of their equity[781].

In addition, the composition of the board may influence the level of diversification. First, a higher share of independent, outside directors will be more effective and limit managerial opportunism[782]. For instance, outside director and representatives of investors are most likely to replace underperforming top managers. Empirical evidence reports that corporate downsizing is in many cases preceded by a change in the CEO[783]. Further, the more powerful the outside directors are, the more likely a portfolio restructuring is[784]. The second factor moderating the agency costs is associated with more active and experienced board members. Typically, they will intensify strategic discussions and force management to justify any investment decisions. They exercise their authority given their shareholdings[785].

---

775 See Gibbs 1993, p. 51

776 Excess cash flow leads to an expansion into unrelated business with limited or no synergies. Further, diversified companies cross-subsidy between different businesses, continuing unprofitable businesses and lagging necessary restructuring. Also, management of diversified firms implies higher administrative overhead cost (See Hoskisson and Turk 1990, p. 468). Also refer to Jensen 1986, Belkaoui and Pavlik 1992, Liebeskind 1992, Wiersema and Liebeskind 1995

777 A diversification is non-efficient if the risk reduction is outweighted by the costs of managerial resources required for steering a non-core business. See Jensen 1986, p. 11, Hoskisson and Turk 1990, p. 463

778 See Hill and Snell 1989, Bethel and Liebeskind 1993, Grossman and Hoskisson 1998, Phan and Hill 1995

779 See Berger and Ofek 1999, p. 319

780 See Gibbs 1993, p. 63, Wright, Kroll et al. 2002, pp. 47 et seqq.

781 See Phan and Hill 1995, p. 710

782 See Hoskisson, Johnson et al. 1994, pp. 1212 et seqq.

783 See Berger and Ofek 1999, p. 319

784 See Gibbs 1993, p. 65

785 See Johnson, Hoskisson et al. 1993, p. 36

A concentrated ownership can also induce a decrease in diversification. Opposite to the principals in an atomistic shareholder group[786], major blockholders have the power to oppose management and influence strategy policy-making[787]. Such blockholders will be attracted to companies and LBO candidates with such potential value creation. The empirical evidence suggests that market disciplinary events enhancing the concentration of ownership, e.g., from the purchase of large block or takeover threats, lead to a significant reduction of diversification and strategic refocus[788]. Observations confirm that majority shareholders force managers to revise their strategy[789]. However, the effect of bundled ownership is contingent on the activity level and strategic intent. A short-term investor will seek to gain value increase from inefficiency in capital markets even though he possess the power to induce major strategy adjustments, whereas the same investor with a long-term investment horizon may opt to actively engage in corporate policy and strategic decision-making[790].

A recent survey by Lane, Canella and Lubatkin contradicts the findings of Amihud and Lev, and other agency theory-related research[791]. First, they argue, against the common findings that management-controlled companies follow strategically inferior levels of diversification, and that the agency theory is not suitable to analyze the complex interactions related to the governance of a company. Second, they demand to regard managerial discretion as a frequent and natural behavior. Much more, they insist on a more flexible theory with a balanced view on managerial behavior, as in particular proposed by stewardship theory. Amihud and Lev balance the critique and argue that further instruments related to governance, for instance a performance-based compensation and a high share of institutional investors, help reducing potential conflicts from agency[792].

The empirical evidence at the entry in the buyout is to some degree inconclusive on the decrease in diversification and related corporate downscoping during the buyout restructuring. One group of surveys confirms the decrease of the level of total

786 See Hill and Snell 1989, p. 27

787 See Bethel and Liebeskind 1993, p. 18

788 See Bethel and Liebeskind 1993, p. 27, Denis, Denis et al. 1997a, p. 150, Berger and Ofek 1999, p. 319

789 See Hoskisson, Johnson et al. 1994, p. 1212

790 A study by Bethel and Liebeskind reports that ownership by blockholders has a negative correlation to firm growth, and build up pressure against managers to restructure. Interestingly, the same survey also reports that institutional investors spur growth and support managersin developing growth strategies. (See Bethel and Liebeskind 1993, p. 27). See also Gibbs 1993, p. 54

791 See the critique of Lane, Cannella et al. 1998, pp. 568 et seqq., against the research by Amihud and Lev 1981, Jensen 1986, Bethel and Liebeskind 1993, Hill 1988 and Hill and Snell 1989.

792 See Amihud and Lev 1999, p. 1068

diversification[793]. Phan and Hill report that the incentive force from enhanced management shareholdings, not from debt, dominates the changes[794]. The other group of surveys report a more inconclusive picture, with significance of a decrease in related, however, not in unrelated diversification[795]. The extent of decrease in diversification appears thereby to be dependent on the pre-buyout situation, with former conglomerates demonstrating a higher divestment activity[796]. Buyout investors apparently support the divestment intensity, as the likelihood of a backing by specialists increases with the level of diversification[797]. However, researchers also find strong evidence for acquisitive activities after buyouts, both in related and unrelated businesses[798].

Empiricists have not investigated the changes in diversification of German buyouts in detail. Vest measures a small share of buyouts that follow a diversification strategy (4 of 29) during the buyout[799], however, without questioning the option whether buyouts decrease their diversification. Wegner reports an increase in diversification as part of a growth strategy, while the non-growth buyouts do not focus on

---

793 See Phan and Hill 1995, Seth and Easterwood 1993, Wiersema and Liebeskind 1995

794 Phan and Hill conduct a long-term research of the changes of 214 firms on pre- to post-buyout in goals, strategy, structure und productivity. Increase in management stockholdings advances the decrease in diversification. Increase of debt and growth goals however do not incur decrease in business scope. Further, decreased diversification enhance productivity, but not profitability. Hence, the authors conclude that "debt plays an important role, but in the long run the changes with management shareholdings may have the most enduring impact upon firm efficiency" (See Phan and Hill 1995, p. 704).

795 Liebeskind, Wiersema and Hensen can not confirm any change in the level of diversification and portfolio reorganization. LBOs decrease related diversification, however not significantly, and even slightly unrelated diversification. The authors conclude that downsizing is apparently not linked with an increase in strategy focus. Further, the authors can not confirm increased corporate divestment. Although the LBOs demonstrate a higher number of divestments, the associated size of divested revenues is below the comparables. (See Liebeskind 1992). A similar survey by Wiersema and Liebeskind suggests a modest, but insignificant increase in unrelated diversification. The authors measure lower sales growth rates for the periphery and core business. The latter measure is related to the number of businesses, whereas the former measure is related to the share of sales in the relevant business. (See Wiersema and Liebeskind 1995, pp. 452 et seqq.)

796 Seth and Easterwood reject the proposition that buyouts are typically former conglomerates with excessive diversification. To understand better the direction of change in focus, the authors differentiate whether the strategy is intended to (i) reduce geographic coverage (market focus), (ii) reduce lines of business related to those retained (business focus), and (iii) reduce the lines business unrelated to those retained (corporate focus). Not surprisingly, conglomerates extensively follow a corporate refocussing strategy, while in contrast, buyouts with former single businesses or related diversity pursue a more modest divestment strategy with a business and market focus (See Seth and Easterwood 1993).

797 Buyout investors were overrepresented at firms with a high level of diversification. The efforts and steps necessary lead to a longer time under private ownership for buyouts having to increase their focus much stronger than other competitors (See Seth and Easterwood 1993)

798 See Bowman, Singh et al. 1999, pp. 37 et seqq., Wright, Hoskisson et al. 2000, pp. 596 et seqq.. The buyout investor Clayton & Dubelier for instance advised the owner-managers of Borg-Warner after the buyout to actively seek for new investment opportunities, leading to an acquisition in the fastest growing segment (See Kester and Luehrman 1995, pp. 121 et seqq.).

799 See Vest 1995, p. 283

diversification as part of the buyout restructuring[800]. The Arbeitskreis Schmalenbach briefly details that strategic reorientation is typically related to growth in the core business and extension of the presented product line[801].

In total, the evidence of changes in diversification after an LBO is inconclusive. First, the intensity of divestment is dependent on the pre-buyout situation. Second, debt is apparently a less powerful "change agent" as opposed to management shareholdings. Third, in some cases buyouts even extend the level of diversification, heading for new markets or products.

Strategy changes to diversification have not been analyzed, to the knowledge of the author, in the post-exit period for a subsample of prior buyouts after a trade sale. However, changes in diversification have been investigated while analyzing post-acquisition divestments and the impact of capital structure to strategy. An acquirer may consider divesting some parts of the target company to finance the acquisition[802]. It is unlikely that significant business units survive the Hoskisson and Johnson outline that companies with an unclear strategy of both related and unrelated business units suffer from organizational and control inefficiencies in managing both categories. Corporate restructuring, if applied, leads in most cases to a lower level of diversification and to a decrease of debt. An increase in R&D expenditure accompanies the reduction in diversification. Hoskisson and Johnson conclude that management focuses on internal growth and, therefore, substitute diversification with R&D. The authors further stress the significant major risk the managers take[803]. Managers may avoid, without an initial stimulus, to conduct a re-diversification that grants to reduce the systematic business risk, even if the expected value creation is apparently positive. Among the divestments of an over-diversified company, a divestment of the smallest segments is most likely[804]. Further, the illiquidity of asset markets and market for corporate control grow with size, enhancing the likelihood of divestments of smaller units. Further, management will choose to divest units with the least impact on company value, in general non-core business segments. Researchers elucidate that investments are excessively directed to business units with low Tobin's Q[805]. The problem is accelerated if management shareholdings are low. Meyer and Lieb-Doczy analyze different strategies towards integrating an acquired business. They find evidence that a defensive focus of the

800 See Wegner 2003, p. 227
801 See Schmalenbach-Gesellschaft 2006, p. 254
802 See Bhagat, Shleifer et al. 1990, pp. 8 et seqq.
803 See Hoskisson and Johnson 1992, p. 630
804 See Schlingemann, Stulz et al. 1999, pp. 7 et seqq.
805 See Scharfstein 1998, Rajan and Zingales 2001

acquirer on purely short-term efficiency improvement, e.g., through downsizing, is less likely to materialize the long-term growth and profit potential of the organization. Such strategies may improve productivity, but fail to initiate strategic renewal. The empiricists report an evolutionary development of the target to be the more successful strategy, providing target's management autonomy and complementary resources where available. The heartpiece of a successful integration is the facilitation of knowledge transfer paralleled with high absorptive capacity of both organizations. From the perspective of the management of the acquired company, the ownership by a parent company may provide the financial means to pursue a more acquisitive strategy. Especially if the major blockholder reduce the intensity of monitoring and detain shareholdings for management, the executives may pursue acquisitions to reduce their risk and acquire new businesses even if they do not create value. Since the empirical evidence on related as opposed to unrelated diversification was unclear, the hypotheses are formulated for the level of total (both related and unrelated) diversification:

Hypothesis 22a: After a trade sale, reduced governance and monitoring activity will lead to an increase in total diversification.

Hypothesis 22c: After a trade sale, reduced managerial shareholdings will lead to an increase in total diversification.

LBOs exiting through a going-public may accelerate the level of acquisitions to foster growth based on the cash infusion and, therefore, increase diversification. A survey measures a share of 28% of companies planning the acquisition of another company[806]. At the same time, 32% of the companies list their dependence on a single product line. The data is based on the IPO prospectus, where planned acquisitions have to be disclosed in the risk factor section[807]. These results are biased because of young companies pursue an initial public offering, whereas established company who seek a reverse going-public are less likely to be dependent on a single product line.

Empirical evidence of disciplinary events on corporate control implies, in the reverse, that the diffusion of the shareholder base will make control more difficult and increase management's discretion[808]. Without a strong blockholder among the group of shareholders, there may only be limited incentive to monitor closely the right

806 See Martens 2003, p. 157

807 This is a mandatory information for an IPO by SEC. For the German stock market, [...]

808 See Bethel and Liebeskind 1993, p. 27, Denis, Denis et al. 1997a, p. 150, Berger and Ofek 1999, p. 319, Amihud and Lev 1999, pp. 1066 et seqq.

diversification strategy and to oppose management to refine the strategy toward diversification[809]. Disciplinary effects from competitive markets for factors, products and managers may compensate[810]. McConaughy, Dhatt and Kim conclude their analysis of post-IPO operating performance and outline that the diffusion of ownership does not result in increased agency costs[811]. Bruton, Keels and Scifres argue that management follows the strategy orientation in terms of diversification and position as established during the buyout, and only conduct stepwise any strategic changes[812]. In both cases, the deleveraging of debt is less important than the decrease of management shareholdings to the level of divestment.

To conclude, a significant decrease of management shareholdings will presumably have management focus less on value creation and pursue a risk-averse strategy, leading to an increase in diversification. Further, the departure of active shareholders with a significant share of equity from the board will reduce the disciplinary effect on management.

Hypothesis 22b: After a going-public, reduced monitoring activity will lead to an increase in total diversification.

Hypothesis 22d: After a going-public, reduced managerial shareholdings will lead to an increase in total diversification.

4.3 Changes in Innovation

Finance researchers still controversially discuss the potential effect of LBOs on a company's ability to innovate and to support entrepreneurial projects. Zahra and Fescina once titled a research paper with: "Will LBOs kill US corporate research and development?"[813]

From an acuminated view of debt, innovation-related activities are not suitable for an LBO: innovation is (i) of a long-term nature; (ii) of high-risk in terms of the probability of failure and the potential for high returns; (iii) unpredictable in the sense of multiple possible outcomes, which are unspecified; (iv) labor-intensive; and (v) idiosyncratic[814]. In total, the initial contracting and cumulated agency costs are high. On the other hand, innovation is one of the key success factor for growth and

809 See Bethel and Liebeskind 1993, p. 18
810 See Fama 1980, Demsetz 1983
811 See McConaughy, Dhatt et al. 1996, pp. 55 - 56
812 See Bruton, Keels et al. 2002, p. 720
813 Sse Zahra 1991
814 See Holmstrom 1989, pp. 309 et seqq.

above average profit. Successful companies understand to innovate, to protect (intangible) knowledge assets and to use knowledge assets[815]. Within innovative markets, growth and survival rates are higher[816]. Any allocations to R&D are primary predictor of sales growth performance relative to competition, and therefore future profit.

It seems likely that the exit from the LBO spurs investments into innovation-related resources. Still, the beneficial re-investment may be countered by a decrease in productivity by investing in projects with negative NPV. After the exit through a trade sale, corporates may substitute organic growth from R&D, with external acquisitions. The exit through a going-public will require to show long-term growth potential. The stock market will however also reward high short-term earnings. It is therefore open how management's focus and funding of innovation will change after exiting the LBO.

4.3.1 R&D Spending and Efficiency

At first sight, numerous reasons exist why debt might prevent a company from engaging in value-adding R&D. The pressure to meet debt obligations creates an incentive to emphasize investments that generate high levels of current cash flow. Long-term capital-forming R&D projects will be neglected, short-term cash flow generating operations favored[817]. Even within the portfolio of R&D projects, management may feel inclined to choose the project with the highest NPV, leading to a misallocation of the company's investment policies[818]. Executives may trade R&D cutbacks against operating cash flow improvements[819]. The urgency of management to reduce the asset and raise funds to repay debt may also lead to an extensive outsourcing, therefore, transferring critical activities to outside partners. In the long-term, the company looses important know how, in particular related to crucial processes within R&D. Further, the substantial personal costs of financial distress that managers face will foster a selection of investments that maximize the cash flow of the company at the lowest risk, however, not absolutely at highest value. The asymmetric information between the management and external investors is an additional counterforce to R&D investments subject to debt leverage. In general, insiders find it difficult to reveal their superior information related to the prospects of an R&D investment and communicate the strategic benefit to outsiders. The

---

815 See Teece 2000
816 See Audretsch 1995
817 See Singh and Faircloth 2005, p.880, Rappaport 1978, p. 82, Zahra 1991, p. 9, Hitt 1990, p. 35
818 See Peyer and Shivdasani 2001, p. 513, Baysinger, Kosnik et al. 1991, p. 211, Bruton and Scifres 1992, p. 8
819 See Lei and Hitt 1995, p. 837, Long and Ravenscraft 1993a, p. 120

apparent information disadvantage implies high external costs of financing[820] and can lead to an underinvestment in new projects and R&D. Furthermore, debt holders are usually risk-averse and will avoid non-secured investments. Transaction cost economy argues that deployable assets are preferably financed by equity[821]. Typical investments in R&D are generally highly specific and difficult to liquidate[822]. In addition, investments in human capital are hard to secure, as researchers can easily leave the company. Meeting debt payments also distracts management commitment to innovation. Building and developing core competences in R&D requires not only investment, but also rigid and focused management attention[823]. If management has the choice, they might even 'safeguard' their high R&D with low debt to keep flexibility in financing high[824]. Reductions in general capital spending[825] may also handicap R&D since they lead to increased deterioration of facilities, equipment, and support systems essential for innovation[826].

At second glance, the necessity to meet debt payments may also have a positive effect on R&D. As argued before for resources related to administration, routines and procedures related to R&D are difficult to measure in terms of their productivity. Development lead times and trial-and-error learning diffuse a linear relationship of R&D outputs to inputs. Thereby, the R&D department is often regarded as a 'black box', with even senior management being insecure about where and to what amount to invest. Hence, the management of R&D often lacks the level of rigidity in productivity analysis and comparison to other departments. Frequently, managers follow personal interests in specific R&D projects of only low value to the company[827]. The control effect of debt will force the reevaluation of the current R&D project portfolio, and will cause the termination of the least promising projects[828].

Obviously, further changes in the governance structure may be beneficial to the level of R&D expenditure. The disentanglement of a prior risk-averse owner offers a previously unknown entrepreneurial freedom for management. Motivated by their

---

820 See Myers 1984, p. 584, Palepu 1990, p. 257

821 See Hall 1992

822 See Williamson 1988, p. 580, Smith and Warner 1979, p. 250

823 See Ravenscraft and Scherer 1987, p. 155, Long and Ravenscraft 1993a, p. 122, Hitt 1991, p. 703

824 See Bhagat and Welch 1995, p. 468

825 For details on changes in capital expenditure please refer to chapter B3.2.2. See also Kaplan 1989a, p. 228

826 See Zahra 1991, p.8; Smith 1990a, p. 22

827 See Long and Ravenscraft 1993a, p.122

828 Lang, Ofek and Stulz report that debt prohibits spending in non-value creating investments (Lang, Ofek et al. 1996. Further, Denis and Denis report that total investment is reduced, however with a focus on reversing poor investment decisions (Denis and Denis 1993). McConnell and Servaes measures that debt load is positive to R&D related value creation for low growth firms, though detrimental to high growth firms (see McConnell and Servaes 1990).

equity stake, management will view R&D expenditure as mean to competitiveness and performance improvement[829]. The management's background and experience is crucial, as a revamping and revitalization of R&D requires a substantial level of industry understanding[830].

Supposedly, the concentration of ownership spurs the level of R&D expenses and overall R&D strategy. First, larger stakeholders have a substantial incentive to monitor management and promote activities leading to long-term value creation. Second, the high share in equity gives them the power to direct the company and to encourage management to undertake the risk of increased investment into R&D. Third, a widely held company will prefer external growth through acquisitions as opposed to internal growth through R&D related activities. Recent surveys have reported a correlation of higher concentration of equity ownership to R&D expenditures[831]. The observations have been contradictory with relation to the different owners, with some inconclusive results in particular related to institutional investors[832]. A further indication of reduced agency costs associated with R&D activities is the observation that dispersed stock ownership is related to a reduced R&D efficiency measured by a lower level of patent activity and by higher R&D spending per patent among industry peers[833].

The increase in leverage and associated financial distress will draw management's attention to meet debt payments. The absorption of attention, however, may harm the decision-making and learning around initiating and managing R&D projects[834]. Active ownership and intense monitoring encounters the distraction and forces management into strategic discussions, re-directing management's focus on non-financial and, in particular, R&D related decision-making.

To conclude, several arguments may favor or disfavor the emphasis on R&D resulting from the changes in governance after the entry into a buyout. If management has enjoyed a limited level of monitoring, the positive effect of debt

829 See Zahra 1991, p. 14

830 See Zahra 1991, p. 18

831 See Hill and Snell 1989, Graves 1988, Baysinger, Kosnik et al. 1991, Francis and Smith 1995

832 In the survey by Hill and Snell, internal directors as opposed to external directors seem to have the strongest positive effect on the level of R&D expenditure (See Hill and Snell 1989). Further, institutional investors are determinental to R&D expenses, as reported by a survey on manufacturing firms by Graves (See Graves 1988. However, Baysinger, Kosnik and Turk report that institutional stockholders positively value capital investments in long-term R&D projects (See Baysinger, Kosnik et al. 1991, pp. 210 et seqq.).

833 See Francis and Smith 1995, pp. 395 et seqq.

834 Burgelman and Maidique stress the necessity of management to champion new products and process ideas if they are to be transferred into a commercial success (See Burgelman and Maidique 1988. See also Hitt 1991, p. 703

control may predominate on the decision on R&D expenses. If, however, management has allocated their R&D resources in a disciplined manner, the negative effect of debt may indeed outweigh and pare down R&D expenses. Empirical evidence has disclosed a negative relationship between debt and R&D expenses over all industries (and is not just not limited to LBOs)[835]. A country comparison has further revealed that the relationship between debt and R&D is weaker for European companies than for the US, since they typically have a higher basic level of debt[836]. The increased ownership concentration and activity level of governance, however, should prevent an adverse selection of value-adding R&D projects due to risk aversion and capital constraint. One should also note that considerations of the late 1980s and early 1990s, where the efficiency paradigm was prevalent, and entrepreneurial-based buyouts in the minority, have dominated the hypotheses formulation and related research.

Empirical evidence for buyout period

The empirical research on the effect of a buyout on R&D intensity and efficiency at the entry and during the restructuring of the buyout offers evidence for a negative, a neutral and a positive relationship. The research results indicating a decline in R&D intensity argue that the cutbacks do not impair the R&D output, but foster R&D efficiency[837]. The cutbacks do not harm short- and long-term performance, but rather have a beneficial effect on marginal, low productivity R&D[838]. Further, moderating

---

835 Bhagat and Welch confirm a bidirectional effect on debt and R&D expenses. On the one hand, debt holders have a risk aversion towards specific R&D expenses. On the other hand, firms with higher R&D choose to hedge their R&D with a lower leverage. For similar results on a negative effect of debt to R&D, see Hall 1990, pp. 113 et seqq., Bhagat and Welch 1995, p. 468, Peyer and Shivdasani 2001, pp. 494 et seqq., Singh and Faircloth 2005, pp. 880 et seqq.

836 Bhagat and Welch report that the relationship of debt to R&D is insignificant for European firms. The level of available internal funding, approximated by the level of operating cash flow, is also not statistically significant for the level of R&D expenditure (See Bhagat and Welch 1995, pp. 457 et seqq.)

837 Lichtenberg and Siegel confirm that buyouts occur more often in firms with a lower R&D intensity. Average R&D expenditure to sales for the buyout sample was 1,0% versus 3,5% industry average. They measure an even larger difference of 3.2% in the buyout versus non-buyout R&D intensity in the three years following the transaction. Average employment in R&D is reduced by 0.7%. Still, the differences are not statistically significant. Interestingly, the R&D to sales ratio declines in the 7-year period observed before the buyout, from 1.0% to 2.4% below industry average. The authors conclude their observations with the rejection of the hypothesis of no change in R&D intensity, despite the weak significance (See Lichtenberg and Siegel 1990, pp. 187 et seqq.). Long and Ravenscraft elucidate the impact of debt on R&D intensity for firms undergoing a buyout in the manufacturing industry. They find that R&D intensity of LBOs is less than half the respective industry average. They measure a significant cutback in R&D expenditure to sales by about 40%. However, the authors argue that cutbacks in R&D do not harm short- and long-term performance. In contrary, the authors relate the missing relationship to performance with a beneficial cutback effect on marginal, low productivity R&D (See Long and Ravenscraft 1993a, pp. 131 et seqq.).

838 See Long and Ravenscraft 1993a, p . 131 - 132

factors are found. First, the decrease in productivity is less for larger buyouts[839]. Second, the decrease is partially linked to the divestment of business units with a higher R&D intensity and an expected lower suitability for an LBO[840]. Third, the individuals amongst the management team are not key. One of the studies further questions whether the decline in R&D is contingent on the past commitment of management to specific R&D projects, using the R&D department as 'personal playground". Researchers do not find any evidence for differences in changes in R&D related to the continuation or discontinuation of management[841].

The second group proposes a neutral effect of buyouts on the R&D intensity, while agreeing with the former researchers that the R&D efficiency is increased[842]. They differentiate the effect by size and by strategy position. From selected case samples Bruton and Scifres conclude that an LBO leaves a company's posture towards R&D largely unchanged. At high levels of R&D, they admit that cutbacks to meet debt payments are not unlikely. Still, they find evidence that the cutbacks did not fundamentally change the strategy of the buyouts[843]. Fox and Marcus claim that if LBOs become focused around a core business, it is likely that they become more R&D-intensive. The finance researchers assume the higher strategic focus to be more in the interest of the investors, to be more long-term oriented in performance improvement, and to yield a higher willingness to take risk. Hence, finance empiricists consider the commonly observed low research intensity to be short-term in nature and subject to the high level of diversification[844]. Finally, there is also a group of researchers providing evidence for a positive effect of LBOs on R&D

839 See Long and Ravenscraft 1993a, p. 131

840 Lichtenberg and Siegel measure a relatively higher decline in R&D expenditure in the first 2 years after the LBO, correlating with higher asset divestiture. They assume that LBOs typically divest assets and business units with higher than average R&D (See Lichtenberg and Siegel 1990, p. 190 – 191 and p. 193).

841 See Long and Ravenscraft 1993a, p. 131

842 Smith investigates multiple discretionary expenditures and their effect on cash flow during the LBO. For the 7 firms with substantial R&D expenses, the author measures a increase in the first year and a substantial decrease in the second year in R&D to sales. Still, the results are insignificant and too small to affect cash flow generation (See Smith 1990b, pp. 154 et seqq.). Bruton and Scifres report that buyout related restructuring does not harm or help R&D (See Bruton and Scifres 1992, pp. 15 et seqq.). Fox and Marcus formulate multiple propositions around causes and consequences of buyouts. They propose that R&D does not decline after the transaction, since buyouts take place in less R&D-intense industries. Second, if a decline occurs, it may be related either to a halt in unprofitable, non value-adding projects (positive) or to cash flow-oriented, short-sighted termination of value-adding projects with, however, a high level of uncertainty. The authors conclude that the second argument based on a behavioral view will dominate managers' rationale (See Fox and Marcus 1992, pp. 76 et seqq.). In a broader survey of the changes of CE during a buyout, Zahra does not confirm that R&D spending significantly increases. However, Zahra does confirm a rise in R&D staff size and quality of staff. Further, the author reports a rise in the number of new products and commercialization. Zahra does not find an interpretation for the to some degree contrasting results (See Zahra 1995, p. 238 – 239)

843 See Bruton and Scifres 1992, pp. 15 et seqq.

844 See Fox and Marcus 1992, pp. 76 et seqq.

intensity[845]. For instance, during the buyout of Duracell, R&D expenditure is reported to have increased to develop a new series of products and to accelerate the commercialization from concept stage to mass market[846].

Author	Geographical focus	During buyout: Negative	During buyout: Neutral	During buyout: Positive	Post-exit period: Negative	Post-exit period: Neutral	Post-exit period: Positive
Hall (1989)	US		x				
KKR (1989)	US			x			
Lichtenberg (1989)	US			x			
Malone (1989)	US			(x)			
Lichtenberg Siegel (1989)	US	(x)					
Smith (1990)	US		x				
Long Ravenscraft (1991)	US	x					
Bruton Scifres (1992)	US		x				x
Forst (1992)	Germany			x			
Fox Marcus (1992)	No focus		x				
Opler (1992)	US			x			
Wright Thompson Robbie (1992)	UK			(x)			
Vest (1995)	Germany				(x)		
Zahra (1995)	US		x				
Holthausen, Larcker (1996)	US				x		
Wegner (2003)	Germany		x				
EVCA (2001)	Europe			x			
Arbeitskreis Schmalenbach (2006)	Germany			?			

Table 9: The Impact on R&D Intensity during the Buyout and in the Post-Exit Period

Independent on the basic relationship of a buyout to R&D intensity and efficiency, most of the empirical evidence suggests that buyouts occur in less R&D-intense industries[847]. Hall notes that buyouts facilitate 'the shrinkage of an older, low-technology industry'[848]. Blair and Schary investigate R&D intensity from the perspective of an explanatory variable for industry-level restructuring. They find that technological intensity, approximated by the ratio of R&D to sales, is a statistically

845 Malone reports a shift towards R&D, with over 50% of interviewees admitting a higher emphasis on new product innovation (See Malone 1989, p. 358). KKR reports an increase in R&D expenses of 15%, however, with no correction for any industry-related effects (See Kohlberg, Kravis et al. 1989). For a small sample of 8 buyouts, Opler reports an industry-adjusted increase in R&D expenditure of 6.6% (See Opler 1992, p. 32) In a survey of British buyouts, Wright, Thompson and Robbie propose that strategic changes around product development are part of the testimonial for increased entrepreneurial freedom. They report that 62,3% of buyouts introduce new products they would not have not introduced in a non-buyout situation. Among other activities, the development of new products in the core market area is with 19,1% of the respondents the most prominent single measure (See Wright, Thompson et al. 1992, p. 312).

846 See Baker and Smith 1998, p. 119 and 120

847 Smith counts approximately 80% of the sample with no disclosure for expenses related to R&D since the expenditure was insignificant from zero (Smith 1990b, pp. 154 et seqq.). Interestingly, the correlation is only significant for the time period between 1979 to 1985. For buyouts between 1986 to 1989, the coefficient is much lower and not significant (See Blair 1993, pp. 175 et seqq.). See also Lichtenberg and Siegel 1990, p. 190, as well as Long and Ravenscraft 1993a, p. 131

848 See Hall 1990, p. 101. Among the 76 buyouts Hall analyzed in a later study, only 7 occur in technology-intense industries with a R&D to sales ratio above 3,5% (See Hall 1990, p. 99).

significant and negative indicator of private buyout activity on an industry level[849]. Bruton and Scifres contradict the belief that buyouts typically occur in less R&D intense industries. They report an occurrence of 61% of buyouts in industries with significant R&D activity[850].

The results for German studies are quite similar, with the exception of indication for a negative relationship. Forst and Vest report that the majority of LBOs increase R&D expenditures[851]. Further, Forst measures no difference in R&D between spin-off and family-buyouts[852]. Wegner finds evidence for a neutral effect of buyouts on the R&D intensity[853]. Interestingly, he reports that the majority of growth buyouts assess external growth as important for their success (54,5%), while pursuing a relatively high R&D intensity[854]. The conclusion that external growth can also relate to significant investment in R&D stands in contrast to the majority of findings of either a 'make or buy' strategy[855]. For a further analysis, a separation of the growth buyouts by the importance of external growth would be necessary[856]. One should bear in mind that the average debt level in Germany is significantly higher in comparison to other European economies and the United States. Therefore, the impact of debt on R&D should be less prominent. A recent survey of European buyouts by the EVCA even clearly indicates an average increase, with R&D expenditure (as a percentage of sales) rising by 66% (from 1.8 to 3.0%) for the last year (either the last buyout year or the current of the survey) compared with the year before the buyout[857]. The survey

---

849 See Blair 1993

850 See Bruton and Scifres 1992, p. 15

851 For 33.3% of buyouts analyzed, Forst counts an annual rise of over 5% of R&D expenses, for another 58.8% still an rise of between 0 and 5%. Only 2.8% of buyout state that they reduce R&D. The author consolidates his findings as a proof for the in average sufficient equity provision of German buyouts. (See Forst 1992, pp. 25 et seqq.). For 20 of 29 buyouts, Vest notes an increase in product innovation, however, with no quantitative measurement (See Vest 1995, p. 291).

852 Weir argues that former parent companies may have restricted investments as the business was outside their core business, indicating that a spinoff-buyout may require more funding than a former stand-alone company (See Weir 1996, p. 25). Forst further reports that the probability of a rise of over 5% in annual R&D expenses is similar for spin-off (35.7%) and family-buyouts (31.8%). The larger increase for spin-off buyout is argued as a result of investment reservation by the former parent in the pre-buyout period (see Forst 1992, p. 74 and 75).

853 Wegner questions whether buyouts invest above average in R&D. In total, 29.0% claim that investments above average are important, however, the majority (51.6%) claim that they do not invest above average. Investments above average are higher for the sub-sample of growth buyouts (50%). The indifference towards R&D investment in the buyout period is confirmed by the answers to the change in relative innovation intensity as part of corporate entrepreneurship.(See Wegner 2003, p. 218)

854 See Wegner 2003, p. 203)

855 See Hall 1990, Hitt 1991, Blonigen and Taylor 2000

856 See Wegner 2003, p. 203 and 204

857 See EVCA 2001, p. 10

further reports that in 33.2% of cases the increase was associated with the involvement of private equity investors.

The empirical evidence is inconclusive. Potential moderating factors, e.g., industry, technological opportunities, company size, level of diversification, do not add sufficient explanatory content to generalize the most likely change in R&D intensity and efficiency. Still, the surge of entrepreneurially-oriented buyouts will turn increasing focus on R&D management, not only from a growth, but also from an efficiency perspective. The most recent surveys by EVCA and Wegner confirm the positive relationship for the restructuring period. For the post-exit period following a buyout, there is practically no available empirical evidence except the study of reverse buyouts by Holthausen and Larcker, and some brief case studies presented by Bruton and Scifres.

Post-LBO Evidence

Some basic observations on acquisitions on R&D intensity may serve as an indicator for potential changes in a trade sale. In the aftermath of an acquisition, the synergistic motive will most likely influence the level of R&D in both the acquiring and acquired company. An acquirer will strive to increase the efficiency of the integrated R&D department and leverage the R&D output to the joint customer bases. The research so far confirms a modest decrease in R&D intensity after an acquisition[858]. Hall argues that the decrease may be the result of a strategy change rather than subject to a short-term efficiency improvement, since the effect grows with the increasing time lag to the acquisition[859]. For acquisitions not subject to a synergistic motive, e.g., motivated by obtaining exclusive access to a customer segment, the empirical evidence rejects any influence on R&D expenditure[860]. In addition, the relative size of the companies may play a role in subsequent R&D efficiency. If the R&D resource base is much larger than that of the acquired company, the acquirer will be largely occupied with aligning the routines and installing new joint teams[861]. The R&D level may also be associated with whether the acquiring company follows a 'make or buy' strategy towards growth. An internal growth strategy will choose a higher, relative R&D intensity, whereas a company seeking for external growth will invest much less in R&D. The empirical evidence analyzing the probability of an acquisition confirms the

858 Hall reports a modest decrease in R&D intensity of the acquired firms in the three years after the acquisition. The effect is significant for the group of R&D performers with a relatively higher R&D intensity (See Hall 1990, pp. 107 and 108).

859 See Hall 1990, p. 111

860 See Ahuja and Katila 2001, pp. 209 et seqq.

861 Ahuja and Katila report that the innovation output decreases with increasing relative size of the acquired firm (See Ahuja and Katila 2001, pp. 210 et seqq.)

negative correlation to R&D expenditure[862]. Finally, researchers point to the probability that an acquisition will lead to a higher debt leverage of the acquirer. Therefore, the necessity for debt payment will set pressure on the R&D expenses[863].

So far, the evidence from post-restructuring activities at acquisitions indicates increased pressure on the R&D budget. However, most efficiency gains will have been seized already during the LBO restructuring. Intense monitoring and control by debt will have disciplined managers in a manner at least as effective as in a multi-divisional company. It is, therefore, unlikely that management can advance the efficiency of R&D much further. Much more, management may return to pursue less value-adding R&D projects with high personal utility. In addition, the shift towards financial control with a declining intensity of monitoring may also negatively influence management commitment to R&D. Still, there may be a positive effect from the deleverage for NPV-positive R&D projects suffering previously from underinvestment. However, evidence during the LBO has proved that even restricted free cash flow does not hinder management from investing. If an increase in R&D is crucial for the company, management has been able to allocate resources to R&D. Hence, the most likely development of R&D intensity and efficiency after a trade sale is:

Hypothesis 23a: After a trade sale, reduced debt leverage will lead to a decrease in R&D efficiency, while leaving the R&D intensity unchanged.

Hypothesis 23d: After a trade sale, a reduced activity level of the owners will lead to a decline in R&D efficiency.

Hypothesis 23f: After a trade sale, reduced management shareholdings will lead to a decrease in R&D efficiency.

After going-public, the level of R&D intensity is, next to management's rationale, under the influence and scrutiny of the stock market. The level of R&D expenditure may be a convenient variable to steer the IPO offer price. If potential investors esteem R&D as beneficial to the company's long-term performance, the owner-managers may consider over-investing to signal growth potential to the stock market. If potential investors however prefer current reported earnings as indicator for long-term performance, the owner-managers will underinvest. Recent research confirms the latter argumentation, inasmuch as those changes in R&D in the offering year are

862 See Hall 1990, p. 109, Hitt 1991, pp. 699 – 701, Blonigen and Taylor 2000, pp. 60 et seqq.
863 See Hall 1990, p. 112

negatively related with managerial share sales during the going-public[864]. Hence, the first subsequent years of a going-public are an inappropriate indicator for the actual long-term commitment to R&D. A further argument proposes that financial markets are myopic and do not value long-term investments such as R&D properly. R&D intense companies are likely to be undervalued and provide an attractive takeover candidate[865]. Finally, research has confirmed that concentrated ownership and shareholder monitoring are best at reducing the high agency costs related to R&D[866].

As elucidated before, the empirical evidence on the influence of institutional investors on R&D is to some degree inconclusive. Bushee measured a higher tendency of myopic R&D behavior by institutional investors that have a high turnover and engage in momentum trading[867]. In a review of R&D intensity of reverse buyouts, approximated by the ratio of R&D expenditure to total assets, Holthausen and Larcker report that both the median and industry-adjusted level is insignificantly different from zero[868]. The examination of changes, however, reveals a decrease in R&D relative to the last year prior to the going-public. The decrease is significant only when the four year average (t+1 to t+4) is compared with the last year prior to the going-public (t-1) At first glimpse, this is somewhat surprising since, as discussed before, the statistical significant increase of capital expenditure associated with the cash infusion would indicate a certain level of investment lag[869]. One would assume that the result for R&D expenditure would be at least neutral if the denominator were not be the asset base, which enlarges due to an increase in capital expenditure, but total sales. Bruton and Scifres investigate the R&D intensity of five case studies in the manufacturing industries, and report in three cases an increase, in one case a decrease and in one case no change in R&D intensity[870]. The authors conclude that the both the entry and exit from the buyout does not affect the basic R&D strategy, e.g., the aspiration whether or not to be technology leader.

To summarize, the cash infusion related to a going-public does not increase R&D intensity. Most likely, management is able to raise the capital for promising R&D projects already during the LBO. Therefore, the beneficial effect of proceeds will not significantly increase R&D expenditure. Rather, the dispersion of the shareholder with potential investors seeking for short-term gains could set pressure on a myopic

---

864 See Darraugh and Rangan 2005, p. 15
865 See Hall 1990, p. 87
866 See Francis and Smith 1995, pp. 395 et seqq.
867 See Bushee 1998, pp. 318 et seqq.
868 See Holthausen and Larcker 1996, pp. 311 et seqq.
869 See for further details in chapter B3.2.2
870 See Bruton and Scifres 1992, p. 16

R&D policy towards the maximization of current earnings. Further, the reduction of management shareholdings and the shift to financial control may reduce management's commitment for ongoing reviews of R&D projects and intense discussions, similar to the post-exit development in a trade sale. Thus, the following hypotheses are stated:

Hypothesis 23b: After a going-public, reduced debt leverage will lead to a decrease in R&D efficiency, while leaving the R&D intensity unchanged.

Hypothesis 23c: After a going-public, a more disperse shareholder base will lead to a decline in R&D intensity.

Hypothesis 23e: After a going-public, a reduced activity level of the owners will lead to a decrease in R&D efficiency.

Hypothesis 23g: After a going-public, reduced management shareholdings will lead to a decrease in R&D efficiency.

4.3.2 R&D Focus and Cooperation

Following the previous arguments and evidence, the effect of debt increase has not been as detrimental on R&D intensity as potentially expected. The restructuring during a buyout seems to have a beneficial effect on R&D efficiency while having a more or less neutral effect on the R&D budget in total. Is then the efficiency gain only prompted by canceling non-value adding projects, or caused by re-orientation of the R&D program? Do for instance external corporations strengthen the resource base?

Sparse empirical (and more anecdotal) evidence indicate considerable alterations in the R&D program. Concerning the focus of the R&D program, most LBOs seem to direct their resources to applied and developmental R&D, while reducing allocations to more basic R&D[871]. Managers lessen internal staff and resources dedicated to long-term, basic R&D. They reduce the scope of R&D projects and re-direct R&D to market-oriented product development to yield a higher level of commercialization and reduced time-to-market[872]. The re-direction thereby often coincides with

871 Zahra measures for LBOs a decrease in the R&D spending factor, consisting of management commitment to (i) basic and to (ii) applied R&D (See Zahra 1995, p. 241). In five case studies, Bruton and Scifres elucidate the change of firm's strategic posture toward R&D as a source of competitive advantage. They report that resource reallocations were also directed to increase developmental R&D to exploit existing technologies and increase the number of new products (See Bruton and Scifres 1992, p. 17). Zahra and Fescina conduct a series of interviews with LBOs about their R&D policy. They report a shift towards applied and developmental R&D with a shortened lead time, e.g., 3 to 5 years, to yield actual revenues (See Zahra 1991, p. 15).

872 Zahra relates the improvements in time-to-market with reduced agency costs from improved managerial incentives and discretion in initiating strategic changes to R&D (See Zahra 1995, p. 241)

corporate downscoping and refocusing from a strategic business unit perspective[873]. For German buyouts, only Wegner has conducted some preliminary research and reports a rather low activity level for basic and applied R&D during the LBO restructuring period[874]. Further, the aspiration to have a high caliber R&D department was esteemed even less important.

Further, the empirical evidence proposes that the buyouts expand their cooperation with other companies, suppliers, and customers seeking to share costs and risks to mutual benefit[875]. The R&D managers expand the links to research centers and university labs. As discussed in chapter 3.2.3, the necessity for debt repayment and for reduction of business risk leads to a tendency for outsourcing and partnering. In particular, a shortsighted management could opt to outsource activities with a high level of uncertainty of outcome and which are long-term, such as R&D[876]. Internal development of core competences and distinctive R&D skills increases short-term costs whereas outsourcing to external suppliers reduces the fixed asset base[877]. With reduced internal sources, the knowledge base is likely to erode. However, coordination between different disciplines and functional teams is essential for an efficient development process[878]. Zahra and Fescina express their fear of the effect of buyouts on basic research. Since basic research is the foundation of applied and developmental R&D, the cutbacks may in the long term slow down the development and weaken the company's competitiveness[879].

The exit from the buyout in a trade sale may have multiple effects on the R&D program and the intensity of cooperation with external partners. An acquirer with potential synergies through shared operations and markets may redirect R&D to research that is more basic. First, the enlarged customer base and wider market reach will presumably lead to increasing sales and, therefore, a higher volume to offset R&D expenses. An increased budget will make management reconsider the necessity for basic R&D. Second, the acquirer will have a longer investment horizon as opposed to the buyout investor and will avoid cutting back basic R&D in the short term, which may risk long-term competitiveness. However, acquisitions seeking a substantial efficiency gain may further reduce R&D intensity through downscoping R&D to a pure application development. For cooperation, there are few indications

873 See Zahra 1991, p. 15
874 See Wegner 2003, p. 227
875 See Zahra 1995, p. 241, Zahra 1991, p. 14
876 See Lei and Hitt 1995, pp. 841 et seqq.
877 See Lei and Hitt 1995, p. 842
878 See Grant 1996, p. 118
879 See Zahra 1991, p. 15

for any change after the ownership transfer to an industrial buyer. The acquirer will compare current partners and consolidate with their own R&D partner.

Changes related to an entry on the stock market through a going-public will only modestly affect the focus of the R&D program and the level and direction of partnering. Since it remains unclear to what degree the shareholders are myopic or long-term oriented, the necessity for a long-term R&D focus also remains unclear. Similarly, motivation will be low to assess the level of cooperation with external partners. If the buyouts operate in an industry with a medium to high R&D intensity, capital markets may be more interested in details of the R&D program, and demand a sufficient access to crucial knowledge, partially located in external partners. Further, they will require some investments in long-term basic R&D.

Since to the knowledge of the author no studies have analyzed the changes in the actual R&D program, there is little orientation for hypothesis building. Rather, the investigation of the case studies will focus on understanding the rationale and arguments outlined by the senior management in the post-exit period.

4.4 Change in Market Development

The increase of penetration in existing markets and the entry into new markets, from both a sales and an operations perspective, offers several advantages. From a resource-based view, the existing resources, both tangible and intangible, can be better utilized. Further, resources build barriers against market entry and positively influence performance[880]. Companies with a strong market position in their core market will be able to reduce the efforts related to market entry and to absorb monopolistic rents[881]. With a sales base distributed in multiple national and international markets, the company will potentially be able to diversify its risk[882].

The relationship of venturing into new markets and economic performance is nothwith-standing inconclusive[883]. One stream of research proposes different

880 See Barney 1991, pp. 99 et seqq.

881 See Hamel and Prahalad 1985, pp. 139 et seqq.

882 See Kim, Hwang et al. 1993, pp. 275 et seqq.

883 A series of studies reports a positive, linear relationship (e.g., Grant 1987, pp. 84 et seqq.). Further, there is empirical evidence for a non-linear, inverted U-shaped relationship indicating a turning point in the beneficial effect of international expansion to performance. The turning point is determined by increased costs in coordination, communication and controlling of international operations. Coordination of multiple transactions among many international business units may start to costs more than the benefits from sharing resources and exploiting market opportunies (See Hitt, Hoskisson et al. 1997, pp. 783 et seqq., Gomes and Ramaswarny 1999, pp. 174 et seqq.). Some researchers, therefore, argue that the optimal level of internationalization is industry-specific due to different market entry barriers and cost degressions (See Daniels and Bracker 1989, pp. 50 et seqq.). Others contradict the view that an individual firm is able to

patterns and entry modes per country[884]. For Germany, the empirical evidence suggests an inverted U-Form relationship of the level of internationalization to performance[885], similar to the caveat of a too high level of CE[886]. A determinant for the internationalization-performance relationship is the organizational structure. A centralized decision-making structure hinders entrepreneurial growth[887]. Since decentralization increases during an LBO[888], the impact of internationalization on performance will increase. Further, international growth and innovation have a positive relationship to each other, supposedly in both directions. On the one side, intense innovation allows building a competitive advantage required for the presence in global markets[889]. Further, a highly innovative company will be able to a build a brand and, therefore, be able to increase customer awareness and reduce costs of market entry. On the other side, broad presence in multiple markets helps to access resources necessary to build innovation capabilities[890]. The company can leverage the resource base over higher volumes and achieve a higher return on investment. Without international presence and enlarged potential customer base, the company may find it difficult to commit considerable investments in R&D[891]. Kotabe, Srinivasan, and Aulakh even go so far to propose that companies "focus on their R&D and marketing activities in order for their oversea expansion to be successful"[892].

To conclude, penetration of existing markets and entry into new markets seems to be to a certain point beneficial to performance. A high level of innovation enhances the success, while an international presence vice versa allows significant investments in innovation. However, a resource-constrained company may overstretch its own

extend the beneficial effect by organizational learning (See Gomes and Ramaswarny 1999, pp. 184 et seqq.).

884 See Johanson and Vahlne 1990

885 Companies have to undergo a learning period and develop appropriate structure and mechanisms to effectively exploit the advantages from global factor markets. The findings imply that companies operating in multiple markets reach superior performance with a high degree of internationalization after significant internal reconfiguration. Many firms retreat and reduce the level of internationalization before reaching the turning point (See Ruigrok and Wagner 2003, pp. 74 et seqq.).

886 See Miller and Friesen 1983

887 Efficient and open communication is required to process the intense data related to an international business. Local managers often have to make a rapid decision with limited time for intense discussions with the corporate head. High level of standardization and formalism hinders the motivation of local managers (See Covin and Slevin 1990, Zahra 1993b, Altinay and Altinay 2004).

888 See the detailed discussion in chapter B3.3.2.

889 See Kotabe, Srinivasan et al. 2002, pp. 82 et seqq.

890 See Kotabe 1990, p. 624

891 See Hitt, Hoskisson et al. 1997, p. 770

892 See Kotabe, Srinivasan et al. 2002, p. 92

management and organizational capabilities in coordinating international activities if the extent of internationalization is not carefully tracked.

From a buyout perspective, the entry into new markets seems prudent, since the company can generate new sales and leverage existing resources. With increased equity, management will use the entrepreneurial freedom to launch new sales and market initiatives. In addition, the buyout specialists will consider the expansion of market presence and customer base as highly attractive to ensure long-term growth potential that is imperative for a successful exit. Inasmuch as internationalization is attractive, it faces significant obstacles within an LBO governance structure. First, entry into new markets requires substantial cash-related investments in new resources, e.g., hiring local experts, starting local joint ventures or acquiring companies. Second, the investments are subject to uncertainty, similar to the investments in R&D. When entering a new market, the incumbent management is typically unfamiliar with the specific market environment, e.g., local distribution channels and customer needs. Thus, new entrants often fail to penetrate the market as planned, even if they have invested significant resources and adapt their entry and expansion strategy to the local conditions.

Wright, Hoskisson and Busenitz report that LBOs frequently change to more growth-oriented strategies during the buyout. They delineate two different entrepreneurial buyouts types with the strategic intent of market growth from their observations: (i) revitalization and (ii) entrepreneurial buyouts. In a revitalization buyout, the mindset is based on predictable, managerial procedures to stifle innovation. The risk is moderate, the markets are known and the innovations have already proven to be successful. They occur often after a corporate spin-off[893]. Although the increase of management shareholdings will be beneficial to the interest alignment, a stronger positive effect is expected from the increased entrepreneurial freedom. Typically, such LBOs are financed with a higher share of equity to offer flexibility for riskier investments. In an entrepreneurial buyout, the growth plan is more radical and revolutionary. Little is known about the market acceptance and success of new products. Managers rely in their decision-making on heuristics, less on facts. Wright, Hoskisson and Busenitz argue that such buyouts may occur when there is a misalignment between incentives and management prior to the buyout, or when monitoring in terms of strategic advice has been weak prior to the buyout. Such an entrepreneurial buyout demands a more specific insight for monitoring than in the

893 In the pre-buyout period, the management will supposedly face severe investment restrictions from the corporate headquarters. The businesses are most likely to be peripheral to the strategy, market and product portfolio of the parent companies (See Wright 2001, pp. 116 et seqq.)..

case of the traditional efficiency-oriented buyout, or even the aforementioned revitalization buyout[894].

As a moderating factor, one should note that the empirical observations of the market development during the buyout have to be adjusted by the strategy-related corporate downsizing in unrelated business fields. Two effects should be differentiated: a decrease in sales in unrelated, non-core businesses, and an increase in sales in related, core businesses. Interestingly, no empirical research on buyouts has differentiated the sales development in these two effects.

The surveys find broad support for growth in LBOs in both domestic and non-domestic markets[895]. Growth positively influences financial performance[896]. Higher management equity appears to stimulate growth around the core business and to balance the funds against cash flow limitations. Further, researchers observe a higher level of growth for buyouts with backing of a buyout investor [897]. The focus on market development and international expansion is prevalent for so-called 'buy and build' buyouts. They pursue both internal growth, e.g., penetration in home markets and entry into new markets, and external growth, e.g., selected add-on acquisitions[898]. The buyout investors thereby play a much more active role in

894 Buyout investors must understand the underlying technology and customer needs sufficiently. Often, the former parent of the buyout did not have the capability to control and manage the technology involved. To offer flexibility for growth, leverage will also be lower than in a normal buyout. Still, an entrepreneurial buyout requires the traditional financial control implemented by buyout professionals, accompanied by intense strategic discussions and industry expertise (See Wright 2001, pp. 116 et seqq.).

895 Bruining, Bonnet and Wright investigate the strategy changes related to a buyout. They find clear evidence for international expansion, partially through installation of operations and sales alliances with other companies (See Bruining, Bonnet et al. 2003, pp. 13 et seqq.). Bannock measures an accelerating share of LBOs persuing a widening of their geographical scope (See Bannock 1990,p. 15). By year 3 during the buyout, 35.8% report an enlargement of foreign markets served. Bannock further reports that the share of LBOs not interested in exported sales drops from 37.4% prior to 21.9% after year 3 during the buyout (See Bannock 1990,p. 20).

896 Bruining and Verwaal explore the change of CE during an LBO and its impact on financial performance. Growth orientation, subsuming the posture toward rapid internal and external growth as well as risk acceptance correlates positively with buyout performance (See Bruning and Verwaal 2005, pp. 21 and 22)

897 Bruining and Verwaal report that "the perspective of big and fast growth as a top priority [...] is not attractive for successful buyout managers". Moreover, senior managers in a buyout context should follow (opportunistic) growth opportunities around their core business. In alignment with the hypotheses of growth orientation, Bruining and Verwaal admit that their sample is biased by insider dominated employee buyouts (62% of the firm's equity is in the hand of managers and employees, only 30% in the hand of private equity and investors), therefore, expecting different results for investor-led and larger PE-backed buyouts (See Bruning and Verwaal 2005, p. 25)

898 See Wright, Hoskisson et al. 2001, p. 248, and Allen 1999, p. 717. In addition, Trottier reports so-called 'platform investments' and 'leveraged build-ups'. They prompt subsequent acquisitions to complement and expand the initial platform (See Trottier 1995, pp. 37 et seqq.).

developing and implementing the growth strategy[899]. For such cases, the investors provide a higher amount of equity.

Growth plays an even more prominent role in the advancement of German buyouts. Vest analyzes in detail the source and direction of growth during the buyout. Of 29 observed buyouts, the majority of 21 report a market growth strategy of introducing existing products to new markets. Only 7 of 29 buyouts, however, report that they concentrate on further penetrating their existing markets. Further, 4 buyouts choose to follow a strategy of diversification of entering new markets with new products[900]. From the buyouts seeking to further expand their market area, 5 focus on their national market, while 11 on new international markets[901]. Vest further investigates how the buyouts develop and position their products within the relevant markets. He differentiates whether the buyouts focus on a preference-based product differentiation, e.g., by offering superior product attributes with best performance, or on a price-volume based product differentiation, e.g., by offering the lowest sales price. Among the buyouts, the majority (16 of 29) of buyouts choose a preference-based strategy, whereas only few (2 of 29) choose a differentiation based on price-volume advantages. Vest argues that the buyouts as former subsidiaries likely did not have enough capital either to develop advantages from economy of scale (based on investments in machinery) or to develop advantages from distinctive product innovation and marketing capabilities, confirming the previous underinvestment hypothesis. The 2 buyouts following the price-volume strategy argued that the price reductions were short-term and gave them some time to develop the capabilities related a preference-based strategy. From the 16 buyouts following the preference-based strategy, 14 reported the introduction of a niche strategy with the intention of increasing customer loyalty and retention[902]. Gräper elucidates that 35% of the German buyouts studied entered into new markets not served before[903]. The majority entering into new markets introduced new products. Wegner confirms the importance of entering new markets and businesses during the buyout. The expansion of international sales and presence is the most important operational measure chosen, from among other measures such as product development or

---

899 From an analysis of three case studies, Bruining and Wright note a significant contribution from venture capitalists to broadening market focus. See Bruining and Wright 2002, p. 15

900 The different strategies are not exclusively, they may be followed in parallel (See Vest 1995, pp. 282 and 283).

901 See Vest 1995, pp. 287 and 288

902 See Vest 1995, pp. 284 et seqq.

903 See Gräper 1993, pp.125 and 126

external acquisitions among the group of growth-buyouts[904]. Further, the development of new customer segments is the second most prominent measure applied by management. The majority of buyouts (62,5%) pursue expansion into new markets. A recent survey of European buyouts by the EVCA underpins this observation[905].

In summary, the pursuit of market development is a major part of the restructuring during the buyout for German buyouts, similar to US where it is apparently even more prevalent. Corporate spin-offs in particular benefit from the entrepreneurial freedom and turn to growth-oriented strategies.

With the exit of through a trade sale, there will be some countervailing effects determining the emphasis on market development. Reduced managerial shareholdings and decreased self-determination may demotivate top management to undertake risky and strenuous entries into new markets. In contrast, increase in free cash flow will allow management to allocate significant resources into market expansion. From a transaction cost theory perspective, the rationale for the acquisition of a company with a strong international presence is the transfer of resources and knowledge in an intra-corporate context. Researchers have argued the advantage of the acquisition of a company with international operations from three synergistic aspects[906]: (i) from ownership, e.g., the possession of proprietary assets; (ii) from international growth opportunities, e.g., access to geographically distributed resources; and (iii) from the organization, e.g., capability to coordinate and manage intra-corporate knowledge transfer. These three sources will influence the post-exit strategy. The acquirer will be able to obtain and transfer these resources, rather than to purchase them through discrete factor markets[907]. Combined market presence and business fields will motivate management to redeploy resources over regions, businesses, and functions in the most effective manner. Acquirer and acquired company can seize opportunities to increase differentiation of existing products to new markets. A survey by Anand, Capron, and Mitchell elucidates that advantages from market expansion typically occur for the acquirer, whereas the product extension advances the former buyout[908]. Further, a high level of internationalization at an acquisition will spur the need for capability building. The aforementioned product line extension requires significant investments in marketing and product

904 See Wegner 2003, p. 227
905 See EVCA 2001, p. 9
906 See a summary in Anand 2005, pp. 194 er seqq.
907 See Wernerfelt 1984, Dierickx and Cool 1989
908 See Anand 2005

development in new market and customer segments. A domestic-oriented company however has presumably much lower capabilities in knowledge creation and absorption[909].

In total, it is likely that the emphasis on market development will at least remain at the same level and, in some cases, increase. For the separate changes in the corporate governance, one would therefore expect:

Hypothesis 24a: The emphasis on market development will increase with reduced debt leverage in a trade sale.

Hypothesis 24c The emphasis on market development will decrease with a reduced activity level of governance in a trade sale.

Hypothesis 24e: The emphasis on market development will decrease with reduced managerial shareholdings in a trade sale.

The argument of increased resource redeployment is obviously not prevalent for the exit through a going-public. However, the relief from predetermined cash flow will most likely stimulate increased investment in market expansion, both national and international. Results from post-IPO performance indicate a high growth in sales, in particular if managerial ownership remains high[910]. Further, the stock market will reward any prospects of growth. Therefore, management will be motivated to continue (or to initiate) with market growth. Even the dispersion of the shareholder base should not negatively affect management's focus on market.

Empirical evidence of reverse buyouts, although sparse, confirms such a hypothesis of market growth orientation. Mohan investigates the sales growth of reverse buyouts and finds a significant positive increase in sales per employee in the second year after the going-public[911]. Bruton, Keels and Scifres analyze the sales growth of buyouts after a going-public. The reverse buyouts outperform industry in sales growth in all 3 years observed, even though at a decreasing rate (22% to 18% to 7%)[912]. The authors do not further detail the sources and operational measures behind the sales growth. However, they report that in the years of public ownership covered, the strategic focus remains constant with no significant increases in the level of diversification. Therefore, market growth observed can be accounted to an expansion in core markets. In the corollary, the author expects the dispersion of the shareholder base to spur notably the emphasis on market development:

---

909 See Lane and Lubatkin 1998

910 See Jain and Kini 1994, p. 1708

911 See Mohan 1990, p. 96

912 See Bruton, Keels et al. 2002, pp. 717 and 718

Hypothesis 24b: The emphasis on market development will increase with reduced debt leverage in a going-public.

Hypothesis 24d: The emphasis on market development will decrease with a reduced activity level of governance in a going-public.

Hypothesis 24f: The emphasis on market development will decrease with reduced managerial shareholdings in a going-public.

4.5 Change in Human Resource Management

Changes in the management of human resources during and after an LBO are subject to agency and resource-based theory. From an agency theory perspective, human resource management will be subject to enhanced emphasis on cost efficiency[913]. From a resource based view, human resource management will be intensified at it is expected to enhance the performance of the individual employee and to improve financial performance. The positive effect supposedly contributes to the performance through three levers: (i) by enhancing the skills and ability of the employees, (ii) by increasing the motivation of the employees, and (iii) by improving the way the work is organized[914]. Even companies following a cost-leadership strategy can benefit from high performance in human resource management[915].

Theoretical discussions and related empirical research on human resource management after changes in the ownership structure are sparse, in particular for the time after an LBO. This is as more surprising as the fragmented research on changes during LBOs and on changes subject to acquisition (trade sale) indicates that integration of human resources is highly challenging[916]. Top management is subject to a close assessment by investors and post-exit owners. Investors will optimize compensation to achieve optimal interest alignment and to maximize personal commitment. Further, they closely assess the track record and experience background, and perhaps decide to change the composition of the board. Consequently, the author discusses the managerial resources as a part of the human resources separately[917].

---

913 See the outline in chapter B3.2.1.

914 See Delaney and Huselid 1996, p. 950

915 See Huselid 1997, p. 146

916 For instance, see: Baker and Wruck 1989, pp. 172 to 176, Greenwood, Hinings et al. 1994, p. 253, Larsson and Finkelstein 1999, p.6, Bacon, Wright et al. 2004, pp. 335 et seqq., Peck 2004, p. 5,

917 On the nature of managerial resources and the differentiation to general human resources refer to the introduction in chapter A3.3.1.

4.5.1 Human Resources

Human resources include skills, knowledge, and abilities of the company's employees. Employees' motivation determines the level of personal effort and how human resources contribute to (intangible) company value and performance development. Changes in governance lead to considerable changes to these resources. Uncertainty of future prospects of the company may spur turnover and lead to a loss of experienced employees. Unclear compensation schemes and participation programs may result in a loss of employee motivation. Further, complex management structure and multi-layered decision-making may hinder speed and efficiency of an organization. Focus on cost efficiency may impede necessary investments in knowledge development and mutual learning.

From a resource-based view of the company, the owners, both during the holding period and after exiting the buyout, will consider internal resources as essential for revitalizing the business and gaining competitive advantage. Increase in managerial shareholdings and organizational power will reestablish the control of management over resources[918]. Strategic control should facilitate a closer alignment of strategy related to human resources with overall corporate and business strategy[919]. In a spin-off, management had before the LBO to compromise on knowledge development and mutual learning with former business units from the parent company. Employee-led buyouts will focus on introducing human resource programs, therefore granting relief from demanding working procedures. They will expand training and increasing employee participation[920]. A growth buyout intended to create value by extensive market growth and new products will doubtless invest in human resources, e.g., experienced sales representatives and researchers. Practices will have to be implemented allowing fast learning and knowledge transfer to keep talents motivated and retention high.

Empirical research has concentrated on analyzing the impact of LBOs on the employment level[921]. The sparse research on changes in the management of human resource reports a positive emphasis[922]. LBOs prompt progressive compensation schemes, while enlarging the degree of employees eligible to such programs[923]. In

---

918 See the discussion on the reestablishment of control over resources in chspter A3.3.1.

919 See Phan and Hill 1995, Bacon, Wright et al. 2004, p. 327

920 See Bacon, Wright et al. 2004, p. 330, Wright 1989, pp. 412 et seqq.

921 See the discussion on changes in operational productivity and employment level in chapter B3.2.1.

922 See Bacon, Wright et al. 2004, p. 334

923 Fox and Marcus report that the use of performance-based compensation system increases. Incentive systems are supposed to be modified by means of employee stock ownership plans and enhanced profit-sharing schemes. The authors claim that management as well as employees increase their exposure

addition, research also reports that buyouts increase the level of training towards customer and business concerns[924]. The investments lead to valuable resources, which are regarded as crucial to the success of the buyout[925]. The observations do not confirm a detrimental role of buyout investors and financier on commitment to and investment in human resources[926]. The investors support a distinctive strategy for human resource management and increase the importance of related issues. Further, the approach of human resources is related to the challenge and type of buyout. For growth buyout, Bacon, Wright and Demina confirm a strong focus to accomplish 'buy and build' strategies and strategies related to market and product enlargement[927]. For efficiency buyout, the study records a 'hard' approach to the management of human resources.

After a trade sale, the integration of human resources of two entities is challenging. Changes in human resources will depend from the general strategic intent and fit of the acquiring with the acquired company[928]. If businesses are rather similar as opposed to complementary[929], resistance will be higher, since significant layoffs are expected. With a high overlap, overcapacities are likely and result in layoffs, what supposedly may have justified the control premium paid. Top management turnover will be higher, since the acquiring management is presumably familiar with the business of the former buyout[930]. Within the joint management, conflicts of control and responsibilities arise[931]. Resistance will also arise from the convergence of processes. The managers have to integrate pay differentials and employment benefits

---

towards risk (See Fox and Marcus 1992, p. 75). Vest observes that management reported not to have increased personnel costs, but to have succeeded in enforcing performance-related salaries and increasing the alignment of both owners and employers' interest. In 13 of 29 buyouts analyzed, the introduction of pay-for-performance related incentive system. The respondents named management bonuses for the extended circle of managers, a profit-dependent 13th salary, and the distribution of a fixed share of the profit to the workforce as new instruments. Vest further measures that 9 of 29 cases modified their existing performance-related compensation to a stronger emphasis on variable share. An additional 5 of the 29 reduced the share of salaries paid above tariffs (See Vest 1995, p. 314 et seqq.). A survey by EVCA finds an increased usage of performance-related pay by 28% of respondents. Employees receiving performance-related pay doubled from 16% to 38%, while the participation in a share option scheme rose from 2% to 11% (See EVCA 2001, p. 14. See also Wright, Coyne et al. 1984, Bradley and Najed 1989, and Wright 1989.

924 See Neerven, Bruining et al. 1996

925 See Wright, Hoskisson et al. 2000, Wright 2001

926 See Bacon, Wright et al. 2004, pp. 336 et seqq.

927 See Bacon, Wright et al. 2004, p. 341

928 For a detailed discussion on different acquisition strategies refer to chapter B2.2.2.

929 Larsson and Finkelstein investigate the relationship between employee motivation and resistance versus combination potential. This is related to synergies from combined operations, market and purchasing power, managerial resources, and from increased financial diversification. The authors measure the effect of the similarity and complementarity of the business on employee resistance. Similar businesses lead to high levels of employee resistance, while complementary businesses are less detrimental (Larsson and Finkelstein 1999, p. 17).

930 See Walsh 1988

931 See Vlasic and Stertz 2000, pp. 319 et seqq.

and to align trade union policies, to name but a few. The former buyout may find its cultural traditions and existing routines challenged[932]. Human resources are most apt, at least in the immediate period after the exit from the buyout, to suffer from the integration task and notably decrease in value. Above all, employees may have to return their shareholdings if the acquirer seeks to consolidate the former buyout, leading to a significant decrease in motivation. In total, the empirical evidence reports a high potential for uncertainty among employees about future roles and hierarchy systems as well as increased employee turnover[933]. Dislike for an acquisition may incur loss of productivity and performance[934]. However, management of human resources is often not a priority task on the management agenda. Typically, management does not formulate a strategy on how to align the organizations and retain key employees[935]. For the case of an acquisition motivated by product or market expansion, the focus will lie more on retention than on layoffs. Researchers report that there is a higher degree of variation and flexibility toward practices and systems, e.g., compensation schemes[936]. Processes will be transformed more slowly if the acquiring company is experienced and comparably larger than the former buyout. For acquiring companies seeking to acquire valuable resources, e.g., R&D capabilities, the emphasis will lie on retention[937]. Senior managers will strive to keep the best talents. To increase retention will require significant salary rises, since the key employees typically hold shareholdings and will cash in at the exit. Managers from the acquirer will align the underlying processes, with focus of knowledge transfer from the acquired to the acquiring company[938]. However, if highly appreciated compensation schemes are in place, the acquirer will be careful about assimilating them too fast. Best-practice reports that early employee involvement

---

932 See Larsson and Finkelstein 1999, p. 6

933 Mirvis reports that mergers and acquisitions lead to retrenchment and unplanned labor turnover. Employees experience a loss of former status and identity, and are unwilling to fit into to the new organization (See Mirvis 1985, p. 82). See also Greenwood, Hinings et al. 1994, p. 253

934 See Hambrick and Cannella 1993

935 Price confirms the lack of a clear transformation strategy for human resources after an acquisition. The ambivalence leads to role conflicts and weakened internal communication (See Price 1999, pp. 37 et seqq.). Horwitz et al conduct a detailed analysis on the integration strategy. First, they note a lack of an implementation strategy to integrate the firms' cultures and systems. Second, they observe a difference in the perception of such a strategy between managers and employees. Latter group claims a lack of strategy, while management reports a broad strategy to be in place. Third, employees accuse management of neglecting a cohesive organizational culture (See Horwitz, Anderssen et al. 2002, pp. 6 and 7). Jeris, Johnson and Anthony analyze to what extent the development of human resources is relevant to a merger or acquisition in the initial decision-making. Relative weight of human resource development was fairly low at the initial decision (See Jeris, Johnson et al. 2002, p. 9)

936 See Aguilera and Dencker 2004, p. 1363

937 See Child, Faulkner et al. 2001, p. xx

938 See Bower 2001, pp. 98 and 99

with clear communication and information flow, streamlining systems and procedures, leads to success[939].

After going-public, management will not have to deal with the conflicts arising when merging two organizations. Still, empirical evidence assigns importance to the management of human resources for the survival. Since the going-public will prompt a significant cash-out by the employees, the post-exit owners will consider to install new compensation schemes to ensure sustained incentivization. IPOs that place more value on employees and human resource management show higher survival rates. Examples are the extent of training programs, the presence and size of human resource staff, the proportion of lifelong and full-time contracts and mission statements, to name but a few. Second, those IPOs that apply progressive compensation programs are also more likely to survive. Compensation programs cover stock options, profit-sharing plans, as well as group-based incentives and performance-related pay[940]. Among the options to implement pay-for-performance programs, direct profit-sharing programs have the highest correlation to financial performance[941]. Furthermore, the employees may feel honored to work for a listed company and enjoy the heightened publicity.

To conclude, the focus on human resources seems to increase when entering into an LBO. At the exit is seems unlikely that, particularly during a trade sale, human resource management receives the attention required for a smooth transition. Some strategies directed to growth may compensate this and continue to emphasize human resources. Other strategies may impose severe conflicts and weaken motivation and productivity of the workforce. For a going-public, the cash-out will most likely lead to a reduction in the motivation of employees, if management does not substitute it with other equivalent compensation schemes. Unlike other activities, emphasis for human resource management seems to be less dependent on debt and on underinvestment. Much more, the investment objectives of the new owners and the individual motivation of the management group members determine the attention towards human resources. Following hypotheses are exclusively formulated for the activity level of governance and managerial shareholdings:

---

939 See Tetenbaum 1999, p. 34, Horwitz, Anderssen et al. 2002, p. 3

940 See Welbourne and Andrews 1996, pp. 906 et seqq.

941 Zwaan, Eije and Witte analyze incentive systems after going-public. They hypothesize that a public company, as opposed to a private one, encourages profit sharing and employee ownership. The survey indicates that motivation of employees is of minor interest. Among 70 IPOs, only 12 state that the issue is to some degree related to having employees feeling incentivized and challenged by the stock market. They report that higher profit-sharing, as opposed to options or shares, directly spurs the financial performance (See Zwaan, Eije et al. 2002, p. 132).

Hypothesis 25a: Emphasis on human resources will decrease with a reduced activity level of governance after the exit from the buyout.

Hypothesis 25b: Emphasis on human resources will decrease with reduced managerial shareholdings after the exit from the buyout.

4.5.2 Top Management Resources

During the restructuring of the buyout, industry-specific and generic managerial skills will be of advanced importance[942]. Top managers are required to service debt payments by tight cost control, while adjusting strategy to a changing market and business environment[943]. Investors will seek to install a management board with such a profile and consider appointing suitable executives to the board if necessary.

If the buyout company is sold in a trade sale, the new owner will consider placing trusted managers on the board. They will seek to secure the implementation of their intended strategy and business plan. Appointed managers will have a significant experience and skill set related to the company. In a going-public, the top management will have to fulfill the growth expectations of the stock market. Most likely, industry-specific knowledge will be widespread among the management.

4.5.2.1 Quality and Composition of Team

Without doubt, quality and right composition of top management is one of the most essential success factors during the LBO and after the exit[944]. Skill set and requirements of a management trusted with the restructuring of a buyout are in some aspects different from management in a normal running situation[945]. Senior managers responsible for the restructuring in a buyout situation will need a detailed understanding of the industry to be able to develop a new strategy and acquire new customers, even while encountering potential competitors[946]. They will have to be experienced in running a company with some degree of autonomy[947] and be willing

942 The skills and abilities can be distinguished into generic resources, industry-specific resources, and firm-specific resources. They are embedded in a hierarchy from most to least transferable between different firms (see Castanias and Helfat 1991, p. 156).

943 Castanias and Helfat argue that in industries with discontinuities leading to retrenchment and cost-cutting, generic skills, e.g., in cost containment, will be valued most (See Castanias and Helfat 2001, p. 671)

944 See Luippold 1991, p. 61, Vest 1995, p. 184, Sharp 2003, p. 19, Achleitner and Müller 2004, p. 10

945 Sharp lists mulitple factors required for the management of an LBO: experience and competence, motivation, commitment and drive, range of functional skills, trust and reliability, and vision and judgment (See Sharp 2003, pp. 19 et seqq.). Many are part of the skill set required for the management of any firm of comparable size. The author will focus on the specific aspects of competencies required for managing an LBO.

946 See Vest 1995, p. 186

947 See Baker and Smith 1998, p. 98, Sharp 2003, p. 19

to work under increased risk exposure to external markets[948]. The senior managers will encounter a significant increase in leadership and hence have to possess a high level of self-confidence and self-discipline. The incumbent management of a former division, in particular, will have in a spin-off to compensate for the loss of former parent resources and experienced senior managers[949]. They will have to take responsibility for corporate reporting, treasury and tax functions, and general control systems, which prior to an LBO are in most cases located at the corporate[950]. In addition, they have to overcome massive organizational reluctance, e.g., streamlining administrative processes leading to increased productivity and potential layoffs. Such turnaround change agents often come from outside the company and are familiar with crisis management[951]. Besides the necessity for turnaround skills, the role of the CFO and finance director, respectively, is crucial for the LBO success[952]. He has to anchor the emphasis on cash flow throughout the entire organization.

Hence, buyout investors closely assess the executives' track record of comparable leadership challenges and of adequate functional skills. They seek to establish a close relationship to the management. The management board will serve as key interface between the investors and the company activities[953]. However, the German two-board system does not tend to have non-executive members on the management board. Instead, the investors may designate a representative either as an active board manager, e.g., an interim or full-time senior manager, or to a position on the supervisory board. The representatives may be executives and partners of the private equity partnership or may be experienced professionals trusted by the investors and selected due to their specific expertise. Some buyout investors, e.g., Clayton, Dubelier and Rice, have partners with strong operational skills, and are experienced to step in as operating managers. Other specialists, e.g., KKR, focus on financial and strategic control, and appoint trusted executives from their advisor network[954]. A further consideration related to the composition of the management team may be to reduce the board size, therefore, increasing efficiency in decision-making and general agenda alignment. The turnover rate of top management may be higher at the entry during the buyout. The buyout investors will change management if they consider it insufficiently experienced or inefficient. From a manager's perspective, it would be

948 See Hoffmann and Ranke 1990, p. 43

949 See Sharp 2003, pp. 21 and 22

950 See Baker and Smith 1998, p. 98

951 See Khandwalla 1983, p. 20

952 See Baker and Smith 1998, p. 101, Sharp 2003, p. 99

953 In US and UK buyouts, buyout investors appoint representatives as external, non-executive board members to the management board (Refer for instance to Sharp 2003, pp. 99 et seqq.).

954 See Baker and Smith 1998, p. 100

irrational to leave the company, without investing in the LBO, if they anticipate that the company is undervalued.

Evidence of changes in quality and composition of management is fragmented, yet reveals considerable modifications. First, surveys confirm the importance of the management team for the success of the buyout[955]. In a survey by Birley, Muzyka, and Hay, the quality and expertise of management is reported to be valued even above the business opportunity itself[956]. Data indicates that premiums paid are linked to the quality of the management team[957]. Second, the hypothesis that smaller management boards are more efficient finds sound evidence[958]. However, the size apparently depends on the prior management level. In the case of spin-off buyouts, investors trust the former management and appoint it as a complete team to the board[959]. Surprisingly, the observations contradict the third conjecture of significant turnover and restructuring of the board[960]. Only a small proportion of LBOs change the top management, with turnover rates at or slightly above industry average. It is much more likely that the buyout investors seek to install an improved compensation

---

955 A survey on the criteria in evaluating potential buyout investments confirms the importance of quality of management. The authors argue that the results are similar to criteria applied by venture capitalists without considering that, in an established business like a buyout, skills are much more embedded in the actual organization than in the leadership itself. In contrast to early stage investments, investors value leadership capability as a team more than the team leader himself (See Birley, Muzyka et al. 1999, pp. 112 et seqq.). Other research confirms the necessity to improve quality of management in LBOs (See Robbie and Wright 1995, p. 544).

956 Birley, Muzyka and Hay report that investors assess the quality of the team higher than the actual business opportunity. Among the 7 most highly ranked criteria, 6 were related to management: leadership quality of management (Rank 1), track record (Rank 2), track record of the team leader (Rank 4), completeness and balance of the team (Rank 5) and leadership capability of the team leader (Rank 6) (Birley, Muzyka et al. 1999, pp. 113 et seqq.)

957 Easterwood et al. find the relationship, however, to be statistically not significant (See Easterwood, Hsieh et al. 1988). A later survey by Harlow and Howe observes a significant, slightly higher premium for LBO with third-party as opposed to incumbent management (See Harlow and Howe 1993, pp. 118 et seqq.).

958 Jakoby investigates the relationship of board size and finds that successful buyouts have a smaller team size (on average 2.4 vs. 3.2 board members (See Jakoby 2000, p.,196). Vest reports that turnaround-buyouts typically have very small management teams, in many cases only led by a single senior manager (See Vest 1995, p. 197). Forst also measures smaller, average team sizes for family-control and succession buyouts, with over 70% of buyout teams having only one senior executive (See Forst 1992, p. 69).

959 For spinoff-buyouts, both Vest and Forst allude that the teams are composed of the former middle management and, not surprisingly, have more board members (See Forst 1992, p. 69, Vest 1995, p. 197). The team have worked together and possess an efficient share of responsibilities, with clearly marked decision rights (See Forst 1992, p. 69).

960 Muscarella and Vetsuypens report a modest share of 6.9% of LBOs where a new team is installed. In 80% of LBOs observed, management remained in the same company in the same position prior and during the LBO. During the following 3 years, turnover rate was about 20%. This rate is comparable to an overall 11.5% annual rate reported by a general survey on turnover. Hence, turnover occurring during private ownership is most likely not related to the elimination of inefficient executives (See Muscarella and Vetsuypens 1990, p. 1396). In an additional survey, an even lower share of LBOs (4.2%) is measured where management is reorganized (See Muscarella and Vetsuypens 1990, p. 1397).

scheme and motivate management than to appoint new, external managers[961]. Instead of the management board, buyout investors in Germany change the composition of the supervisory board[962]. However, there is some evidence that management members do not join the buyout board if they lack the necessary motivation[963]. Further, Kaplan rejects the assumption that managers abuse their information asymmetry when going-private[964]. The right synthesis may be to understand buyout investors as facilitators of interest alignment. They serve as 'watchdogs' and do not hesitate to exchange managers if they do not follow their interests[965].

The departure of senior managers however has a negative relationship to the company's performance. Canella and Hambrick report a detrimental effect from the departure of the highest ranking executives. The performance decrease is related to the loss of substantive experience. The seniority of the departing executives had the strongest moderating effect on the negative turnover-performance relationship[966]. A study by Kaplan shows that the likelihood of top management turnover is significantly higher in Germany with poor stock performance and earning losses but is, however, unrelated to sales and earnings growth[967]. Hence, owners penalize top management for poor current performance. The study measures a higher turnover in the supervisory board with low stock returns, indicating that investors are concerned with the company's prospects and increase their attention, e.g., with experienced professionals on the board[968]. Interestingly, turnover is not higher for concentrated

---

961 Baker and Smith report that KKR rarely replaces the managers of companies they invest in. KKR prefers to change the governance structure and compensation, while avoiding a change in management (See Baker and Smith 2000, p. 101). Peck agrees that inverstors seek to restructure poorly designed incentives rather than replace poorly performing CEOs. The likelihood of a CEO change remains nearly equal, with a share of 15.3% in the year prior and a share of 16.9% in the first year after the LBO (See Peck 2004, p. 5).

962 A recent German survey reports that in most cases (68%), the existing supervisory board is reorganized. Buyout investors bring in executives experienced in both the industry and a buyout situation (See Schmalenbach-Gesellschaft 2006, p. 254).

963 Jakoby shows that an LBO is more successful if a part of the management does not participate in the LBO, as opposed to if the entire management enters the new board. Jacoby details that the most frequent reasons mentioned by managers not participating were lack of motivation and too high risk (See Jakoby 2000, pp. 189 et seqq.).

964 Kaplan measures that in 25% of cases observed, either the Chairman or the CEO do not join the new management board team. Kaplan interprets the high turnover as information asymmetry to the advantage of management not being fairly high during the entry into the LBO (See Kaplan 1989a, p. 249).

965 Baker and Smith elucidate that the buyout specialist is more concerned with rapid and beneficial replacements after departures during the holding period, e.g., if a senior manager chooses to leave the firm, than with massive dismissals at the beginning. Further, the specialists intervene if the appointed board members do not follow the agree-upon value-creation plan (See Baker and Smith 1998, pp. 102 and 103)

966 See Cannella and Hambrick 1993, pp. 148 et seqq.)

967 See Kaplan 1995, p. 25

968 See Kaplan 1995, p. 31

shareholdings. Kaplan argues that banks typically control through their voting rights much more actively when a large blockholder is absent[969]. In contrast, Denis, Denis and Sarin report an increased likelihood of turnover if an outside blockholder is present. Higher managerial shareholdings prohibit turnover and insulate top management from internal monitoring[970]. Holdnerness and Sheehan detail that significant changes in ownership, in particular those leading to majority shareholders, yield an increased turnover of management[971]. Weisbach finds that turnover is much more sensitive to performance with a higher level of outside directors[972]. In addition, Perry elucidates that CEO turnover is higher with outside directors' remuneration closely tied with financial incentives[973].

Research on changes in the top management team by different exit channels from LBOs is fragmented. Empirical evidence on changes following acquisitions, whereof a part will be the purchase of LBOs through a trade sale, reports above average rates of turnover. In particular, senior managers are most likely to depart. For instance, Walsh reports that top management turnover is significantly higher than normal turnover rates. The rate increased from 25% (in year 1) to 59% (in year 5). Top and more senior managers in comparison to middle managers are most likely to depart. The rate does not depend on the type of acquisition, in particular whether the business is related or unrelated[974]. The rate is higher for the case of cross-border acquisition, where cultural differences are more prominent[975]. Such voluntary turnover is dependent on the perception by the executives of the growth perspectives of the company[976]. Further, the greater the degree to which the autonomy and self-determination of the acquired former buyout is removed, the greater the propensity to depart is[977]. Existing senior managers will be appointed as trusted members to the

969 See Kaplan 1995, p. 33

970 See Denis, Denis et al. 1997b, p. 195

971 See Holderness and Sheehan 1988, p. 331

972 See Weisbach 1988

973 See Perry 2000

974 See Walsh 1988, pp. 177 et seqq.).

975 Krug and Hegarty argue that top management turnover is higher for cross-borders acquisitions. Individual differences become more important when people of different nationalities interact. Further, uncertainty related to a post-acquisition situation is worsened if the acquirer has a different cultural background. The likelihood for turnover is significantly higher starting around three years following the acquisition. It is plausible to consider that cross-national differences are offset until around three year after the acquisition. Further, turnover depends on the nationality of the acquirer. (See Krug and Hegarty 1997, pp. 670 et seqq.)

976 The authors Krug and Hegarty detail the reasons behind the turnover of top management. They report that executives with a positive perception of the merger announcement will stay. Further, they find a higher likelihood for turnover if the managers had less favorable perceptions of the long-term effects of the acquisition (See Krug and Hegarty 2001, pp. 188 et seqq.).

977 See Hambrick and Cannella 1993, p. 752

management and supervisory board. They will influence the decision-making in their interest. However, a survey by Govindarajan on the profile of business unit managers reports that general managers arising from the business unit organization itself are most likely to succeed[978]. A survey by Singh and Zollo elucidates that the higher the rate of replacement is, the lower the performance of the acquired company is. The authors argue that the frictions and disruptions occur by the management replacement offset the improvements by the new management team[979].

The arguments furnish the finding that the dynamics of turnover have to be differentiated in a short-term and long-term effect in a trade sale. From empirical evidence and a control viewpoint of the acquiring company, the short-term turnover after the acquisition will be higher. However, the supervisory board will have a lower level of outside representatives and be less independent. It is likely that the reduced independence will lead to a reduced sensitivity toward manager performance. Further, the most likely reduced power by the incumbent management after having returned their shares will weaken their position in any negotiations on strategy and, in the corollary, on their own position. Furthermore, the composition of the management board will tend to be more industry- and company-specific, since the requirements of tight cost control and debt service are less important.

Hypothesis 26a: Turnover of top management will increase in the short term (but remain constant in the long term) with reduced activity level of governance after the exit through a trade sale.

Hypothesis 26c: Turnover of top management will increase in the short term (but remain constant in the long term) with reduced managerial shareholdings after the exit through a trade sale.

Hypothesis 26e: Top management will have a higher share of industry-specific and company-specific skills with a reduced activity level of governance after the exit through a trade sale.

For LBOs going public, one may derive from the abovementioned empiricism that a dispersion of shareholders does not at first imply a decrease in the likelihood of turnover[980]. However, if new blockholders acquire significant stock, higher turnover is likely[981]. In addition to the internal market for corporate control, sharpened external markets place additional surveillance on senior management. A closer

978 See Govindarajan 1988, p. 844
979 See Singh and Zollo 1998b, p. 4
980 See Kaplan 1995, p. 31
981 See Holderness and Sheehan 1988, p. 331

analysis of the post-exit period reports that CEO turnover is inversely related to stock returns[982]. However, on average it remains at the level of industrial counterparts. In general, board composition is seen as the outcome of the bargaining between the senior managers and outside shareholders. Data showed that the stronger the bargaining position of a CEO is - either related to his tenure, age, status, or shareholdings - the more he can install a board favorable to his policy[983]. Furthermore, roles and skills obligatory to top management will shift after the LBO exit. Even more challenging than in a trade sale, new management will have to permanently satisfy stock market desire for growth prospects - which is of minor or, in best case, of average interest during the LBO. Hence, stock market will demand managers experienced with the industry dynamics and business environment.

Concisely, turnover will most likely stay constant in the long-term, but may increase shortly after going-public to accommodate for new ownership. One should not expect turnover in the long-term to decrease, as capital markets will ensure a frequent review of performance, even though the general activity level may be reduced. Board composition will be dependent on the bargaining power between internal and external shareholders. With a weak management, turnover will continue to be high in the long-term, ceteris paribus. Notwithstanding, the profile of the management board may most likely alter towards a higher share of managers with industry-specific background. Hence, the following hypotheses are to be tested:

Hypothesis 26b: Turnover of top management will increase in the short term (but remain constant in the long term) with reduced activity level of governance after the exit through a going-public.

Hypothesis 26d: Turnover of top management will increase in the short term (and decrease in the long term) with reduced managerial shareholdings after the exit through a going-public.

Hypothesis 26f: Top management will have a higher share of industry-specific skills with a reduced activity level of governance after the exit through a going public.

4.5.2.2 Incentive System and Compensation

The compensation scheme can be modified in various dimensions to achieve the intended top management behavior[984]. Three objectives have to be fulfilled: (i) to

---

982 See Engel, Gordon et al. 2002, p. 512

983 See Baker and Gompers 2003, p. 584

984 The incentive system and the related compensation scheme can be designed with a higher or lower level sensitivity for payments by performance. The compensation can be linked to the share price and options if available, to a specific accounting position, or to other success-related indicators, e.g., customer

maximize the personal effort from every individual manager, (ii) to avoid any investments in non-value adding projects, e.g., for empire-building or fringe benefits, and (iii) to align the risk attitude of both managers and owners.

Investment behavior and risk attitude will supposedly alter over the buyout cycle. High debt leverage will reduce the likelihood of investments, even if every single investment may be performance enhancing for the company. Further, debt leverage will lead to higher likelihood of bankruptcy, therefore increasing the risk of failure. The exit from the LBO will presumably allow higher spending on investments at higher risk. In general, LBOs take place in low-risk businesses with a certain predictability of cash flows. In a situation with higher debt and increased risk during the LBO holding period, managers may shift their risk propensity to the disadvantage of the debt holders. An equity position has a convex payoff structure, where shareholders gain additional value by investing in higher risk projects, even when the incremental NPV is presumably negative, following the argumentation of Jensen and Meckling[985]. Management compensation should therefore also reward the stability of future cash flows. Since equity shareholders are residual claimholders, they will also benefit from reduced agency costs of debt.

From a control and incentive standpoint, strong pay-for-performance is beneficial. However, a too strong link of managers' compensation to company performance may lead to risk-avoiding behavior, since managers are less effective in diversifying their risk when investing their entire human capital in the company[986]. Managers will prefer a given value of cash at the same level in stock or options as they can diversify their risk by buying bonds and common stocks. Compensation-based penalization and pay-for-performance programs can however be substituted by direct monitoring. If a manager does not accept a level of compensation risk tied to the company performance, more intense monitoring by the supervisory board will be required[987]. From an efficiency perspective, a buyout investor may substitute a sophisticated compensation scheme if he can provide effective monitoring at a favorable cost level.

Empirical evidence of the change in the top management compensation scheme at the entry into a buyout reports a significant increase in the absolute compensation level[988], in pay-for-performance[989], and an enlargement of the group of managers

---

satisfaction. The payment may be in cash, via shares or stock options.

985 See Jensen and Meckling 1976

986 See Fama 1991, Scholes 1991

987 See Fama and Jensen 1983, Beatty and Zajac 1994

988 EVCA measure for European LBOs that in 70% of buyouts responding, total compensation for top management rose significantly. Similar shares of over 70% are reported for middle management, and 60% for other employees (See EVCA 2001, p. 14).

eligible for share and stock options programs[990]. In total, buyout investors introduce more sophisticated compensation programs[991]. However, active monitoring by investors[992] and tighter debt terms[993] substitute for progressive compensation programs. Surveys on German LBOs show similar activities by investors. For 92% of LBOs investigated, a recent survey measures a significant change in the management compensation scheme[994]. From the buyout investors interviewed, 60% report a variable share of the total compensation of over 50%. However, buyout investors argue that wealth growth through management shareholding is much larger than through compensation. Therefore, equity is much more important to the motivation and alignment of management. For Germany, stock option schemes are less attractive since they are taxed as bonus schemes and hence subject to full taxation. In contrast, capital gains are tax-free after a holding period of at least 1 month if the owner (manager) holds less than 1% of the nominal capital. For family-controlled partnerships, the 1% threshold applies separately for each family member with an interest in the partnership. Hohaus and Braunschweig conclude that in Germany management equity programs are therefore designed to achieve capital gains treatment[995].

As hypothesized for the post-exit period, companies with a weaker governance structure have higher average top management remuneration. Berle and Means hypothesize that CEOs and top managers translate their power to their personal benefit, e.g., in higher, excessive salaries and low risk compensation schemes.

---

989 Peck analyzes the change in the different components of compensation at the entry and during the LBO. The author reports that the percentage of stock options awarded (from 0.2% to 3.4%) and total cash compensation as percentage of assets (from 0.17 to 0.20) are significantly higher in year 1 after compared to last year before the buyout. Bonus as percentage of salary increases from 73.8% to 94.6% (See Peck 2004, p. 5).

990 Baker and Wruck report that significant parts of shareholdings (18%) are distributed to management and key employees. Buyout investors increased basic salary to adjust for increased responsibility of a free-standing corporation. They further enlarged bonus range, from a mean of 10.3% in 1985 to 65.8% in 1987. Bonuses were linked to overall company, divisional and individual performance (See Baker and Wruck 1989)

991 Muscarella and Vetsuypens investigate in detail the managerial incentive compensation plan during the restructuring period of multiple reverse buyout. Based on the information of the IPO prospectus, they report that 96% (74%) have at least one (two) program in place. The most popular plan is based on stock option prices, indicating that a subsequent return to public was already planned during the buyout.

992 Peck reports that tight debt structures may also be substituted by additional outside directors and smaller board sizes. However, the author concludes that internal, e.g., compensation schemes, disciplinary forces are more efficient and preferable rather than external, e.g., tight debt terms (See Peck 2004, p. 2).

993 Peck argues that managerial shareholdings and stock option programs are negatively correlated to the use of tighter debt terms. He claims that debt and compensation are substitute for each other. In addition, the author measures a decrease in the likelihood of bankruptcy during the buyout restructuring with increase usage of incentive compensation, in particular common stock option (See Peck 2004, p. 2).

994 See Schmalenbach-Gesellschaft 2006, p. 254

995 See Hohaus and Braunschweig 2006, p. 2

Empirical evidence confirms this conjecture[996], however, allows the interpretation that a successful CEO may bargain for less active governance and higher compensation[997]. From an agency theory perspective, the greater the owners' relative shareholdings the greater their influence should be to design top management compensation contracts aligned with their interests[998]. Eisenhardt argues that large shareholders will implement less outcome-based but more behavior-based compensation[999]. Other determinants are the extent of outside directors and existing managerial shareholdings. Outside directors, comparable to the external representatives on the supervisory board in the German two-tiered system, act more independently and increase the sensitivity to pay-for-performance, e.g., by raising the level of equity-based compensation[1000]. Empirical research on German executive compensation reveals, in addition, that greater ownership dispersion is related to higher compensation levels[1001]. Large block ownership and strong presence of banks can reduce compensation. The board will use less equity-based compensation scheme if managers already have large equity holdings. Additional empirical research has questioned potential links between the compensation scheme and the debt structure. A high level of cash compensation correlates negatively with the existence and restrictiveness of covenants, whereas it correlates positively with the CEO stock wealth and the relative share of ownership of the company[1002]. If a company is in severe financial distress, top managers incur significant personal losses of up to 35% in compensation[1003]. A reduced likelihood of financial distress will allow the usage of equity-related compensation instruments to be increased.

In the corollary, a trade sale should lead to an increase in total compensation. Supervisory and management board will have a significant lower share of outside representatives and executives. Further, activity level of governance should decrease with a less independent board. Therefore, top managers will be more successful in negotiating beneficial compensation schemes with higher average salary. Empirical

---

996 Core, Holthausen, and Larcker report that compensation levels are higher for firms with a weaker governance and with a larger board. They find evidence that organizations with a low level of inside directors have agency problems and are less effective in controlling what compensation the CEO receives in excess of the level implied by the economic determinants (See Core, Holthausen et al. 1999, pp. 403 et seqq.).

997 See Hermalin and Weisbach 2003, p. 16

998 See for instance empirical evidence from Khan, Dharwadkar et al. 2005, p. 1082.

999 See Eisenhardt 1989a, pp. 65 et seqq.

1000 See Mehran 1995, p. 173

1001 See FitzRoy and Schwalbach 1990, Schmid 1997, Elston and Goldberg 2003

1002 See Begley and Feltham 1999, pp. 242 et seqq.

1003 See Gilson and Vetsuypens 1993, pp. 429 et seqq.

research confirms that total compensation increases after an acquisition[1004]. Since improvements in company performance do not coincide with a compensation augment, research cast doubts on whether the managerial motivation is to maximize shareholder value. In addition, the sheer increase in company size leads to higher top management compensation, not least reflecting the sales-based compensation schemes[1005]. Empirical evidence argues that only in the case of tight monitoring and governance will the increase be dependent on the actual returns achieved by the acquisition[1006]. From the pay-for-performance perspective, three arguments have to be considered. First, the top managers will seek to decrease the pay-for-performance share to maximize the expectation value of total compensation. Second, reduced risk and likelihood of financial distress will grant equity-based share to be augmented. John and John argue that a top management scheme is dependent on the capital structure, e.g., the level of risky debt. Following the discussion of risk-shifting from managers in situations of high risk, the researchers measure a low pay-for-performance sensitivity for companies in financial distress[1007]. Third, monitoring will decrease. The compensation schemes should compensate for reduced direct control and increase the sensitivity of the contract. Since the level of pay-for-performance during the LBO is exceptional high, regardless of financial distress, the sensitivity will decrease. Hence, changes in the incentive structure are hypothesized as:

Hypothesis 27a: Level of total compensation for top management will increase with the reduced activity level of governance after the exit through a trade sale.

Hypothesis 27c: Extent of pay-for-performance for top management will increase with reduced activity level of governance after the exit through a trade sale.

The entry to the stock market through a going-public will lessen the business risk, since proceeds in most cases reduce the likelihood of bankruptcy. To reduce the exposure of personal wealth, the demand for additional share-based compensation of management will stagnate, as long as the top management does not cash out. Management will prefer, therefore, a cash compensation[1008]. The level of pay-for-performance through stock options, equity and non-cash equivalents should increase. The cash infusion will lead, at least in the beginning, to a decrease in total compensation. Zwaan, Eije and Witte find different empirical evidence from

1004 See Schmidt and Fowler 1990, p. 566

1005 See Baker, Jensen et al. 1988, Schmidt and Fowler 1990

1006 See Wright, Kroll et al. 2002, p. 605 et seqq., Wright, Kroll et al. 2002

1007 John and John stress the importance of mitigating conflicts between debt and equity holders at management level. Strip financing allows to reduce agency costs of both debt and equity (See John and John 1993, p. 968).

1008 See Bryan, Hwang et al. 2000, p. 668

companies going-public. The first group is primarily motivated by the cash proceeds, while the second follows a more profound strategy and regards the going-public as final step of a long development[1009]. In the latter strategy, shareholders tend to reward top management more by options and less by shares. Further, restraining top management from taking options is positively associated with efficiency. Noteworthy is that those IPOs who distribute shares to many employees are more successful than those who give options to a few top managers. Beatty and Zajac substantiate the relationship of pay-for-performance to company risk at going-public. The proportion of compensation subject to incentive-based, variable compensation is negatively related to company risk[1010]. The authors conclude that companies strive to address the problem by structuring their boards with stronger monitoring instruments: percentage of outside directors and outside directors with significant shareholdings is higher; and likelihood of larger blockholders and continued private equity backing increases. To conclude, the level of total compensation directly after going-public will decrease, however, it will in the long-term increase. Stock-market listed companies in general pay higher top management salaries. Scrutiny of the stock market will likely lead to a more diligent modification of the pay-for-performance as opposed to an exit through a trade sale. Since pay-for-performance is rather high during the LBO, the author would not expect any significant changes, except as a substitution for instruments chosen.

Hypothesis 27b: Level of total compensation for top management will increase with a reduced activity level of governance after the exit through a going-public.

A final comment should be placed on managerial shareholdings and costs of debt. Higher levels of both equity ownership and stock options lead to higher borrowing costs[1011]. With enlarged managerial ownership, the risk attitude converges between principal (owner) and agent (manager), therefore motivating management to undertake more risky projects.

1009 See Zwaan, Eije et al. 2002, p. 134

1010 See Beatty and Zajac 1994, pp. 320 et seqq.

1011 See Parrino, Poteshman et al. 2005, Ortiz-Molina 2006

5 Performance Development during the Buyout Cycle

5.1 Introductory Remarks

Since the emergence of LBOs as a new form of organization with enhanced incentives and monitoring, researchers have questioned how sustainable any performance improvement is and whether any improvement is purely a wealth transfer to the disadvantage of some other parties involved. Hence, research has quite extensively analyzed the change in performance indicators, in particular operating income and cash flow.

For studies on performance development during the LBO holding period, the source of the data characterizes the categories of research. Publicly available financial statements, supplemented by specific buyout related databases, e.g., the database of the CMBOR, are the base for the majority of studies. Additional studies refer to stock markets, where return to shareholders is correlated to data from financial statement. To deepen the understanding of the underlying factors and independent variables determining performance during the buyout, researchers conduct extensive surveys. In Germany, dedicated surveys are the exclusive base, since public data is sparse.

The author sets his focus on the performance development for a period of three years and longer. Capital market-based studies, in particular, analyze the effect of an announcement of entering into a buyout on a very narrow time base. Further, studies are precluded if they do not explicitly relate to quantitative measures of performance development, e.g., cash flow or operating income.

5.2 Performance Development during Buyout Restructuring

The majority of studies, either based on data from financial statements, stock market, or surveys indicate an upswing in operating income and cash flow during the buyout restructuring. The magnitude of improvement, however, and the underlying explanatory factors differ significantly throughout the studies (see Table 10 and Table 11 for an overview of the reviewed surveys).

Performance Enhancement on Basis of Operational Improvements

A number of studies find evidence that financial performance improvements are associated with improvements in operational efficiency, specially related to cost control, and reject any conjectures of single-sided wealth transfer. Kaplan reports an increase in operating margin and in net cash flow to sales for LBOs completed during 1980 and 1986[1012]. After adjusting for the industry average, sales decrease in average by 8% while operating margins increase slightly by 1.5%[1013]. Kaplan also observes that the LBOs did not outperform their announced projections in the buyout statement. He concludes that the operating improvements induce the performance enhancements, and rejects any wealth transfer from employees or hidden information of managers. Smith reinforces Kaplan's results and finds even stronger evidence for a positive performance development in a review of 58 MBOs between 1977 and 1986. The author documents a significant increase in operating returns as well as operating-cash-flow-to-book value of operating assets, both before and after adjustment for industry trends[1014]. The companies reviewed sustained the improvement throughout year 1 and 2. Smith also analyzes the potential wealth transfer hypothesis and rejects a transfer to the disadvantage of the workforce. The author relates the performance improvements rather to reduced inefficiencies, resulting from incentive effects of change in ownership structure. Muscarella and Vetsuypens examine the entire period between buyout and going-public[1015]. For a sample of reverse IPOs, they find evidence for a significant increase in gross and operating margin. Divisional reverse LBOs seem more successful in efficiency gains than full reverse LBOs. Due to strong bargaining power of sellers in divisional buyouts, the exceptional performance increase reflects operating improvements rather than wealth transfer from pre-buyout bondholders. Performance improvements are mainly due to cost reductions rather than revenue generation or asset productivity. The authors disclose that the revenues grow, however, are not signifycantly higher than the random sample. The study by Opler finds performance improvement results comparable to those of Kaplan and Smith. Both operating margin and operating-cash-flow-to-sales increase from year 1 to year 2. The magni-tude of change from post- to pre-buyout is impressive, in particular with net-cash-flow-to-sales soaring by 58.1% after industry adjustment. The sample, however, differs in its focus on large LBOs and in the time period observed (second half of 1980s)[1016]. Opler hypothesizes

---

1012 The impact of the buyout on the operating margin is greatest in year 3 post-buyout, the last year observed. The financial performance indicators net-cash-flow-to-sales and net-cash-flow-to assets are greatest in year 2 post-buyout. See Kaplan 1989a

1013 Kaplan further analyzes the relationship between the performance changes observed and ths stock market-adjusted returns. Although the sample is small, the author finds strong evidence for a high correlation of net cash flow and less correlation of operating income with market-adjusted returns.

1014 To single out the effect of performance improvement based solely on divesting underperforming operations, two groups with and without major asset disposals are formed. For both, considerable performance accretions can be observed.

1015 See Muscarella and Vetsuypens 1990

1016 The median value of sales for Opler 1992 is USD 870 Million versus USD 370 Million in Smith's sample

that expenses such as R&D are cut to the disadvantage of long-term performance. However, he does not provide any data series to prove his hypothesis.

Performance Enhancement on Basis of Non-Operational Improvements[1017]

A second series of studies finds a broader explanation for performance enhancement, and argues that changes in non-operations contribute notably. Again, they reject any wealth transfer hypothesis. Bull reports performance improvements in operations similar to Smith and Kaplan[1018]. Operating-income-to-assets as well as net-cash-flow-to-sales significantly outperform their industry counterparts from year 2 pre to the year post-buyout. The LBOs reduce their asset base substantially and increase sales at a lower level than industry average. Bull further conducts extensive interviews with buyout CEOs and buyout investors on changes in managerial practice through the buyout. The common theme is a reduction of administration, e.g., internal discussions and excessive documentation, anecdotally described as 'internal politics'. Moreover, management acquires a quicker and more decisive response to market environment. Bull, beyond approving reduced agency cost and inefficiencies, proposes entrepreneurial management as key for owner-managers. The author exemplifies the increase in entrepreneurial orientation with new opportunities and managerial freedom for the owner-managers. Wright, Thompson and Robbie report a high share of performance improvement for a sample of UK-based buyouts[1019]. Of the respondents, 61.1% claim that revenues aresubstantially or slightly better than before the MBO. Further, 68.7% elucidate that operating profit has increased. The authors further question the influence of different factors on performance, and find that the most impact was related to overhead reduction and improved R&D. Productivity improvements are less important. However, a growth focus had an adverse, negative effect on performance for a minority group of buyouts.

Longevity of Performance Enhancement

Researchers further questioned the longevity of the apparently significant performance improvement. Some evidence indicates a long-term, sustainable shift of performance to a superior level, other evidence indicates a temporary limitation of the shift. Long and Ravenscraft enlarge the time observed to a 5 year post-transaction period. First, they confirm the aforementioned enhancement of operational performance, although not significant and at a lower level. Second, they observe a

---

(See Smith 1990b).

1017 The listed studies in the following paragraph do not exclusively relate the performance enhancement to non-operational improvements.

1018 See Bull 1989a

1019 See Wright, Thompson et al. 1992, p. 65

decline in the performance enhancement after year 3 post-buyout. Both operating margins and cash flow-to-sales-ratios return to insignificance in year 4 and 5. The authors conclude that an LBO has a limited effect in producing above-industry average returns. They claim that in the long-term, competition levels out any competitive advantage.

A second source of detrimental performance might be the decline of the buyout market in the second half of the 1980s[1020]. Zahra also reports a significant increase in both productivity and profitability. Buyouts have higher gains than the average company in their industry has. The author, however, limits the results to a short-term period and argues that the long-term effect, in particular after five years and longer, is still unclear. Cotter and Peck report a positive increase of both EBITDA-to-sales and EBITDA-to-assets at entry into the buyout[1021]. The advanced performance continues throughout the five years observed during the buyout restructuring. Buyouts backed by a buyout specialist perform better than non-backed. The management-controlled buyouts, in the long term, significantly drop in the EBITDA-to-sales ratio. The authors argue that buyout investors are superior in selecting appropriate buyout candidates, are better in monitoring the management, and choose targets with a higher share of dispensable assets. A survey by Wright, Wilson and Robbie even reports a significant lag of three years until the up-shift in performance occurs. The lengthy disposal of underperforming assets supposedly causes the time lag. Average-profit-per-employee also becomes significant in year 3 and holds up to the last observed year 6 post-buyout.[1022] The authors, in addition, analyze productivity improvements and find evidence for above-industry performance from year 2 to 6 post-buyout[1023].

Wright, Wilson and Robbie consolidate that successful buyouts restructure their cost base and undergo innovations to succeed in the longer term alike[1024]. Indeed, the long holding period imposes high diligence on financiers and buyout investors. Without additional sales growth, the buyouts are not able to maintain the above average cash flow generation in the long term. The buyout governance structure is, therefore, appropriate for growth as well as for restructuring.

1020 Various bankruptcies resulted in stronger anti-trust legislation and a crisis in the high yield bond market brought a halt to the vivid public-to-private market (See Shleifer and Vishny 1991).

1021 See Cotter and Peck 2001, pp. 120 et seqq.

1022 In year 4, profit per employee is not significant, however it returns to a significance level of 5% in year 5 post-buyout. See Wright 1997, p. 564.

1023 A more detailed analysis on the impact of labor and asset productivity is presented in chapter B3.2.

1024 For the latter assumption, no distinctive empirical evidence beyond the longevity analysis is to the knowledge of the author available.

									Average (adjusted) changes in cash flow-based indicators				Average (adjusted) changes in operating income-based indicators			
Author	Year	Sample	Investigation period	Geo-graphi-cal focus	Observed time period [in years][1]	Source	Result overall	Total sales	Net cash flow/ sales[2]	Net cash flow/ assets[2]	Opera-ting cash flow/ sales[2]	Opera-ting cash flow/ assets[2]	Operating income	Operating margin (opera-ting income/ sales)[2]	Opera-ting income/ assets[2]	Net margin (net income/ sales)[2]
Bull[4]	1989	25 LBOs	1971 to 1983	US	t-2 to t+2	FinStat	Positive	Slight increase[ns]	+48.9%[b]					+13.5%[c]	+37.7%[c]	
Kaplan	1989	48 MBOs	1978 to 1985	US	t-1 to t+3	FinStat	Neutral	+2.7%[ns]	+28.3%[c]	+64.3%[c]			+24.1%[c]	+34.8%[a]	+21.3%[b]	
Kitching	1989	110 LBOs	1980 to 1987	US	t to t+3	FinStat	Positive	Slight increase[ns]			+55.0%[ni]					
Jensen, Kaplan, Stiglin	1989	48 LBOs	1979 to 1985	US	t-2 to t+2	FinStat	Positive	N/ a					+25.0%[ni]			
Smith	1990	58 MBOs	1977 to 1986	US	t-1 to t+2	FinStat	Positive	N/ a				+24.7%[b]				
Muscarella, Vetsuypens	1990	72 LBOs	1981 to 1986	US	t+1 to x-1	FinStat	Neutral	Slight increase[ns]						+23,5%		-31.5%[3]
Singh	1990	65 LBOs	1980 to 1987	US	t-1 to x-1	FinStat	Positive	+17.5%[b]					+14.2%			
Opler	1992	44 LBOs	1985 to 1989	US	t-1 to t+2	FinStat	Positive	N/ a	+49.6%[a]		+11.6%[b]			+11.6%[6]		
Long, Ravenscraft	1993	209 LBOs	1978 to 1989	US	t to t+5	FinStat	Positive	N/ a						+7,7%		-94,4%
Kaplan, Stein	1993	124 MBOs	1980 to 1989	US	t-1 to t+2	FinStat	Positive	N/ a	+41.8%[c]					+12.1%[ns]		
Verma	1993	16 LBOs	1982 to 1986	US	t-1 to t+1	FinStat	Neutral	N/ a			+0.71%[ns]					
Wiersema, Liebeskind	1995	64 LBOs	1980 to 1989	US	t-1 to t+3	FinStat	Neutral	Slight increase[ns]								
Walsh	1999	32 MBOs	1982 to 1989	US	t-1 to t+3	FinStat	Negative	N/ a							-10.9%[a]	
Cotter, Peck	2001	64 LBOs	1984 to 1989	US	t to t+5	FinStat	Positive	N/ a	+16.1%[ns]	+31.8%[ns]						
Desbrieres, Schatt	2002	132 MBOs	1989 to 1994	France	t-2 to t+2	FinStat	Neutral	N/ a	-11.7%[c]					-12.3%[c]		-9.9%
Hanney	1986	120 MBOs	1983 to 1984	UK	n/ a	Survey	Positive	Strong increase[ni]						+[ni]		
Forst	1992	14 MBOs	1976 to 1991	Germany	t-2 to t+2	Survey	Positive	N/ a						+[ns]		
Wright, Thompson, Robbie	1992	159 LBOs	1983 to 1986	UK	n/ a	Survey	Positive	Strong increase[ni]						+[ni]		
Gräper	1993	37 MBOs	1981 to 1989	Germany	n/ a	Survey	Positive	+14,8%[c]					+24,8%[c]	+[ns]		
Vest	1994	29 MBOs	1985 to 1991	Germany	n/ a	Survey	Positive	N/ a						+[ns]		
Zahra	1995	47 LBOs	1992	US	t to t+3	Survey	Positive	N/ a						+[a]		
Wright, Wilson, Robbie	1997	155 MBOs	1983 to 1985	UK	t to t+6	Survey	Positive	N/ a						+[ns]		
Jacoby	2000	62 MBOs	1976 to 1996	Germany	n/ a	Survey	Positive	N/ a						+2,93%[7]		
EVCA	2001	300 LBOs	1992 to 1997	Europe	t-1 to t+3	Survey	Positive	Strong increase[ni]						+[ni]		
Wegner	2003	31 MBOs	1990 to 1999	Germany	n/ a	Survey	Positive	N/ a						+[b]		
FAZ/DBAG/3i	2004	49 MBOs	1998 to 2003	Germany	n/ a	Survey	Positive	Strong increase[ni]						+[ns]		
Kitzmann	2005	21 MBOs	1988 to 2001	Germany	t-2 to t+3	Survey	Positive	+10.8%[ns]	+48.6%[b]					+30.3%[ns]	+210.4%[c]	

[1] Longest time span in the survey conducted
[2] Adjusted for industry/ market effect
3 Not adjusted for industry/ market effect
4 Bull reports mean and medians, however significance reported only for means; changes therefore calculated as change of
5 Desbrieres does not report median; all changes are changes of mean
6 Opler only reports operating profit to sales
7 Changes are reported in %-points

[a] Change significant at the 1% level
[b] Change significant at the 5% level
[c] Change significant at the 10% level
[ns] Not significant at at least the 10% level
[ni] No information about significance
[na] Not industry adjusted

Table 10: Performance studies for restructuring during buyout based on data from financial statements and surveys[1025]

1025 See also Kitzmann 2005, pp. 69-118

To summarize, the surveys conducted by Bull, Kaplan, Kitching, Smith, Long Ravenscraft and Opler report quite consistently significant LBO performance improvements. It may be important to mention that the studies partly cover the same transactions and analyze similar periods of the emerging LBO phenomenon in the early 1980s. Long and Ravenscraft report the exceptional performance of buyouts to the mid 1980s. However, only very little research exists covering the first half of the 1990s and no substantial publication for the late 1990s. The latter absence of research is partky due to the necessary time lag of at least 3 to 5 years to cover the long-term effect of an LBO.

Author	Year	Sample	Investi-gation period	Geo-graphi-cal focus	Event free time [in days]	Observed period [in days]	Data source/type	Result overall	CAR	Premium	Compa-rison days
Lowenstein	1985	28	1979 to 1984	US	*n/a*	*n/a*	Going private	Neutral	*n/a*	56,0%	*30*
Wu	1997	87	1980 to 1987	US	[-600; -401]	[-400; -10]	Going private	Negative	-7,2%	*n/a*	*n/a*
Lee	1992	114	1973 to 1989	US	[-200; 70]	[-69; 250]	Divestment	Positive	14,8%	*n/a*	*n/a*
Easterwood, Seth, Singer	1998	32	1980 to 1990	US	*n/a*	*n/a*	Other	Positive	*n/a*	51,0%	*n/a*

Table 11: Overview of performance studies for restructuring during buyout based on data from capital markets[1026]

Neutral and Negative Performance Development

Finally, some studies indicate a neutral effect or even contradict the positive effect of an LBO on performance. Furthermore, finance researchers provide evidence that confirms some wealth transfer to the disadvantage of other parties involved. Verma investigates in more detail the changes in operating performance during the LBO. The increases are insignificantly different from zero, therefore, indicating no change in performance although a sample part resembles the group of the study of Kaplan. The authors relate the insignificant change to the weaker performance of the non-manufacturing companies in the sample. The latter group is able to respond more quickly to changes in their business environment and implement efficiency programs. A study by Walsh seeks to understand the post-buyout changes in the light of the impact of tax revenues. Walsh finds a slight increase in operating income to assets, however, after adjusting for industry effect, this ratio decreases by 10.9% (at the 1% significance level) until year 3 after the buyout. A potential explanation may be the subsample of very large buyouts (assets of at least over USD 500 million), further, the decline in performance in the outcome of the 1980s, as for instance also

1026 See also Kitzmann 2005, pp. 69-118

reported by Kaplan and Stein. Lowenstein seeks to unearth the sources for performance improvement after the announcement of an LBO. He finds evidence that the premiums paid correlate to the expected tax gain. The tax gains are, therefore, the major source of welfare increase. Lowenstein also reports that management leverages its advantage from information asymmetry during negotiations to achieve a higher sales price. Lowenstein argues that an upturn in the number of open auctions will help to increase transparency and sales price, leading to a more well-formulated and efficiency-based investment plan. Easterwood, Seth and Singer report similar premiums. Wu investigates whether top managers manipulate earnings prior to entering the buyout. The data favors the hypothesis that management actively manipulates earnings downwards to reduce the price for equity.

Empirical Evidence for the European and German Market

In general, the performance implications of buyouts are similar in the European market. The EVCA conducted an extensive survey on the economic and social impact of buyouts and buyins[1027]. From 300 responses to their questionnaire, 22 came from Germany. From the buyouts observed (total sample), 45% are former corporate spinoffs, additional 23% name succession problems or retirement of the owner as the trigger to enter into a buyout. For 10%, performance weaknesses are the reason for the sale. Profitability measured by EBIT margin increases from 4.2% pre-buyout to 7.5% in year 1 post-buyout and remains around 7% for the next 2 years reported. The growth of annual turnover also shifts from 9.1% in year 1 before the buyout to 16.7% in the third year after the buyout[1028]. The majority of buyouts (65%) consider their post-buyout EBIT margin to be higher than their industry competitors, while a majority (67%) also considers to have raised their turnover above industry average. On operational changes during the buyout restructuring, the focus lies on expansion of the product range (70%), growth in new markets (63%), and investment in new locations (54%). Increased control on financial controls (4.2), improved customer service (4.2), improved business efficiency (4.2) and reduced costs (3.8) also triggered considerable performance enhancements[1029].

Finance researchers have also analyzed the performance of German buyouts. Surveys on German buyouts by Forst, Gräper, Wegner and Kitzmann cover transactions from the 1980s and 1990s. In one of the first study on management buyouts and buyins in

---

1027 See EVCA 2001

1028 For growth of both turnover and EBIT margins no adjustment for industry trend is noted.

1029 Ratings where obtained from a 5 point scale from 1 (very low importance) to 5 (very high importance). See EVCA 2001, p. 9.

Germany, Forst examines how buyouts solve the succession of mid-sized companies, since 79% of the companies were sold mainly due to the lack of a successor[1030]. Performance improvements from pre- to post-buyout cannot be exactly quantified since only the post-buyout situation is analyzed. During this period, Forst reports an increase in operating margin for 50% of the buyins and 86% of the buyouts. Further, 54% of the buyouts observed achieve an annual growth over 5% and 50% an operating margin over 5%. Forst reasons that the buyouts return to sustainable growth and profitability. The author does not provide further testing of significance or a comparison to industry average. Gräper analyzes the implication of LBOs as an instrument for spinoffs from former conglomerates and for succession-related buyouts. He reports that buyouts outperform the growth of their industry both in sales and in operating income. Among the different group of LBOs, spinoffs demonstrate a much slower growth in the pre- and post-buyout period than buyout arising from succession. Gräper argues that these buyouts are typically turnaround or even restructuring cases, therefore, require significant time to revitalize product portfolio and customer structure for new growth. In contrast, operating income increases two years prior to the spinoff and indicates that the parent seeks to qualify the company for a buyout and to motivate management. After the buyout, spinoffs outperform both their industry peers and the succession-related buyouts. Wegner analyzes the characteristics of growth buyouts as opposed to non-growth buyouts in Germany. He report that growth buyouts excel with an average of 15.5% annual sales growth, while non-growth buyouts only achieve 1.8%. Among the growth buyouts, 82% of managers claim that the buyout regime is the main cause for accelerated growth. The EBIT margin, however, remains nearly unchanged for the growth-buyouts with 10.0% at the beginning and 9.8% at the end of the restructuring period. For non-growth buyouts, Wegner measures an increase from 1.7% at start to 4.7% at the end of the buyout[1031]. Managers state as sources for performance improvement: (1) unexploited growth potential, (2) excessive bureaucracy, (3) suboptimal capital structure and (4) operational inefficiencies[1032]. A recent survey on the long-term performance of German buyouts by Kitzmann reports an above-average development of growth and profitability during the restructuring period. The sample

---

1030 The buyouts analyzed are relatively small, with 82% achieving annual sales less than EUR 50 Million and only 16% employing more than 500 people. See Forst 1992

1031 For sales growth as well as margin development, no adjustment for industry effects above qualitative assessment of managers of industry competitiveness and growth perspectives are provided.

1032 Growth buyouts rate acquisition and innovation as the most important main drivers for value creation. For non-growth buyouts, an increase in operational efficiency is the key value driver. Financial reengineering is reported from growth and non-growth buyouts to be a primary benefit during the restructuring.

of LBOs observed shows above industry profitability already prior to the buyout. During the holding period, they enlarge their profitability gap to their peers. Relative difference of EBITDA margin increases from 67.0% (average prior-buyout) to 99.6% (average post-buyout). Kitzmann measures similar results for the EBIT margin (from 95.8% to 124.8%). Even sales growth accelerates after entering into the buyout (from 24.8% to 69.0%). Others surveys on German buyouts referring to positive value creation, e.g., Vest, Jacoby and DBAG, do not further detail the performance development, but rather focus in the changes to capital structure, corporate strategy, and operations. More broader market studies without separate surveys confirm that the performance of buyouts in Germany has improved. McKinsey & Company reports an average IRR of 31% between 1984 and 2001 for buyouts in Germany[1033]. In comparison to other European markets, German buyouts achieve rather low returns and at a relatively high risk level. In turn, relative risk and IRR has slightly improved for the period from 1994 to 2001. A survey of the Deutsche Beteiligungsgesellschaft on the German mid-market indicates higher sales and employee growth for PE versus non-PE funded companies[1034]. Strong upswing in sales (7.4% versus 3.9% for a five-year average), especially in 2003, is partly attributed to the smaller average size and higher volatility. The researchers also report a stronger growth in employees (4.5% versus 2.2% for a five-year average) and find some evidence for lower cutbacks in the economic decline in 2001 and 2002. However, productivity development of the buyout was not significantly higher, which the authors link to the high share of service versus manufacturing companies.

German buyouts significantly increase their performance when entering into the holding period. During the last years, the German buyout market has increased its attractiveness. However, the individual performance development scheme differs and depends on the specific pre-buyout governance the buyout was subject to. Although the increase in debt is much smaller than in comparable US and UK transactions, the refinement of capital structure and financial engineering is still a major value driver, even for the latest sample. Not surprisingly, the backing by a professional private equity company is seen as crucial to the buyout success.

Impact of Individual Constituents of Corporate Governance

Besides measuring the long-term development of performance of buyouts, selected studies have sought to elicit the relationship of the individual constituents of the buyout governance to performance.

1033 See McKinsey 2004

1034 See FINANCE-Studies 2005, pp.15 et seqq.

The free cash flow theory by Jensen emphasizes the role of debt to bond management. Surveys and empirical research endorse broadly Jensen's theory[1035]. For non-leveraging, going-private transactions, Long and Ravenscraft measure a significantly lower operational improvement than high-leveraged buyouts. The researchers do not find evidence for the importance of management participation. Furthermore, the authors observe that active monitoring partly compensates management bonding. Cotter and Peck compare the performance development of management-controlled as opposed to investor-controlled buyouts. In the former group, debt leverage has a significant positive influence on performance. The authors further reason the performance to be caused by efficient governance, where buyout investors compensate for reduced alignment and bonding of management through close and active monitoring. The authors argue that beyond mere debt payments, debt covenants and terms serve as effective instrument to discipline management and enhance performance. However, not all empirical evidence examining the relationship of debt to performance during the buyout period confirms the crucial role of debt. Phan and Hill disentangle the relationship of debt and management shareholdings to management's agenda and, indirectly, to performance[1036]. Whereas management equity seemingly directs management's agenda to both growth and efficiency, increases in debt only affect the focus on efficiency. In addition, Phan and Hill decompose the variance in performance by change in debt and in management shareholdings into a direct and indirect effect. A change (increase) in management shareholdings accounts for up to 69.5% of the explained variance (increase) in productivity and 74.3% of profitability. Debt, however, is much less important. Thompson, Wright and Robbie do not find evidence that the debt-to-equity ratio contributes to explain improvement in the return. The authors reject the free cash flow theory, at the limitations of a small sample of 21 buyouts[1037]. For German buyouts, Jacoby examines whether a higher debt-to-equity-ratio spurs performance[1038]. The author argues that the risk aversion of German managers and the high gearing through the prevalent 'house bank' lead to a lessened likelihood of (higher) leveraged buyouts. The data does not reveal any significant differences in the debt-to-equity ratio and a low average of debt to total capital of 55% in general.

1035 See the detailed summary of changes in debt from the pre- to post-buyout period in B2.1.1.
1036 See Phan and Hill 1995 p. 733
1037 See Thompson, Wright et al. 1992, pp. 415 et seqq.
1038 See Jakoby 2000, p. 260

Author	Year	Sample	Investigation period	Geo-graphi-cal focus	Correlation to performance development: Debt	Mgmt. share-holdings	Owner-ship concentr.	Activity level
Cotter, Peck	2001	64 LBOs	1984 to 1989	US	+/-[1]		+	
Thompson, Wright, Robbie	1992	31 LBOs	1982 to 1989	UK	(+)	+		
Long, Ravenscraft	1993	209 LBOs	1978 to 1989	US	+	-		-
Kaplan, Stein	1993a	124 MBOs	1980 to 1989	US		+		
Phan, Hill	1995	214 LBOs	1986 to 1989	US	+	+		
Gräper	1993	37 MBOs	1981 to 1989	Germany		+		
Vest	1994	29 MBOs	1985 to 1991	Germany		+		
Zahra	1995	47 LBOs	1992	US	(+)			
Jacoby	2000	62 MBOs	1976 to 1996	Germany	0	+		
EVCA	2001	300 LBOs	1992 to 1997	Europe				+

[1] Increased debt positive related to performance (EBITDA/ sales) for buyout specialist-controlled, negative for management-controlled buyouts

Table 12: Impact of changes in governance structure on performance development

Empirical evidence draws a consistent, positive picture of the relationship of management shareholdings to performance. Kaplan and Stein measure a significant increase in the probability of default for buyouts with low post-buyout equity owned by management[1039]. Wright, Thompson, and Robbie examine the excess return to investors in the time from entry to exit of a buyout through an IPO[1040]. In a regression analysis, the researchers find the management equity variable to be positive and statistically significant. Easterwood, Hsieh, and Singer formulate a hypothesis that higher pre-buyout management shareholdings imply lower agency costs, and, therefore, offer limited improvement potential during the buyout restructuring.

The authors test their hypothesis against premiums paid at buyouts and find the expected negative correlation[1041]. Jacoby investigates in detail the changes in and implications of management shareholdings for German buyouts[1042]. First, Jacoby questions whether the risk related to the level of personal wealth invested correlates to the success, measured by the operating margin and growth. Since Jacoby does not find a significance, he argues that personal wealth invested may function both as a motivating and as a paralyzing force. Second, the author examines whether managerial shareholdings before entering the buyout reduce the potential for interest alignment and associated efficiency improvement, similar to the study conducted by Easterwood, Hsieh and Singer. As expected, buyouts with pre-entry shareholdings demonstrate a smaller relative enhancement of performance, albeit a small sample. Third, Jacoby elucidates whether higher management shareholdings to total equity at

1039 See Kaplan and Stein 1993, p. 354

1040 See Wright, Thompson et al. 1992, pp. 425 et seqq.

1041 See Easterwood, Hsieh et al. 1988

1042 See Jakoby 2000, pp. 206 – 213, pp. 275 . 276, pp. 339 - 340

the entry into the buyout achieve higher performance increases. As expected from agency theory, higher relative shareholdings to total equity correlate with success. The significance increases for the equity share of managers three years after the entry into the buyout. Fourth, Jacoby tests whether an increase in variable compensation, beside shareholdings, spurs performance. He does not find any significant differences between successful and less successful buyouts.

Although finance and strategy researchers have examined the concentration of ownership in detail, a closer analysis of the effect on the performance development during a LBO restructuring has not been conducted yet. However, what has been questioned is the correlation of the identity of owner to performance. In general, buyouts backed by professionals from private equity companies are more successful[1043]. In Germany, the share of companies in ownership of a majority shareholder is comparably high. Therefore, the reduction of agency costs of equity may, as detailed in chapter 2.1.2, be less beneficial than in other non-German companies. Further research does not perform direct tests on statistical significance. Many surveys have further elucidated the importance of the monitoring and support by an active investor, as detailed in chapter A3.4. For instance, the EVCA survey on buyout performance reports that the majority of buyout managers highly value the contribution of the buyout specialists[1044]. About 39% admit that without the contribution of the specialists, the company would no longer exist and a further 45% claim that the buyout would have grown at a much slower pace without the backing. Other research, e.g. by Wegner, Wright, Thompson and Robbie, confirm the beneficial role of active ownership during the buyout to performance, however, they do not perform direct tests on statistical correlation.

In summary, the changes of governance affect the performance development in different intensities. The increase of management shareholdings seems to be the strongest motivational factor that leads to actual performance enhancements. Further, debt also seems to bond management. However, within Germany, the effect of debt is apparently weaker as the companies have a higher pre-buyout leverage. Much more, the companies benefit from reduced average capital cost related to a refined structure of debt instruments and improved financial engineering. Sparse empirical evidence on the implication of ownership concentration and active governance exacerbates a concrete prediction. For the post-exit period, as described in the following chapter, the decrease of management shareholdings bears the

1043 See Cotter and Peck 2001, pp. 120 et seqq.

1044 See EVCA 2001, p. 15

highest risk for increasing agency costs. Further, a strong decrease in debt, in particular during a going-public, will enhance management discretion and endanger buyout profitability levels.

5.3 Post-Exit Performance Development

As aforementioned, post-exit performance depends on the new governance structure of the former LBO. The empirical research of buyouts exiting through anIPO is ample, since public data is accessible from stock market reporting. On the contrary, empiricists have not analyzed the acquisition by a strategic buyer in detail. The interesting question will be if performance changes can be exclusively linked to changes in the governance structure, independently of the exit channel chosen and new owners engaged.

Which exit the former owners and investors of the buyout choose will affect not only the short-term valuation but also the long-term survival and success of the company. Much more than maximizing sales price, the exit has to consider several long-term, strategic factors[1045]. Technology disruptions and new regulation in an industry may require considerable capital to continue profitable growth, and prevent to return fully the proceeds to the buyout investors. The exit decision will depend on the progress of the buyout restructuring, of debt repayment and of solving governance issues the company may have faced. Investors will question whether the company is already prepared to be divested not only in terms of attractive returns but also in terms of future corporate governance.

5.3.1 Exit Market Development in Germany

In general, companies may exit the buyout structure via five distinctive exit channels: through (i) a (reverse) going-public, (ii) a trade sale, (iii) a secondary buyout, (iv) a share buyback, and (v) receivership. The data on the buyout volume differentiated by exit channel is for the German market sparse and incomplete[1046]. Studies on

---

1045 See Liang and Florence 2003

1046 The BVK reports the total volume per exit channel over all private equity asset classes, hence, including seed and early stage divestments, etc. The association has started to separately report the buyout volume since 2003. Two factors make a comparison of the existing three years difficult: first, only members of the association are reported and, second, the large Anglo-Saxon buyout investors are underrepresented (See BVK 2004a, BVK 2004a; BVK 2004b; BVK 2005; BVK 2006b, BVK 2007, BVK 2007). In contrast, CMBOR reports number and volume of deals over the past years by channel, with the limitation that it differentiates the exits by trade sale, IPO, and MBO/MBI with no further specification about receivership and secondaries. Not all exits included have a deal volume reported. Further, CMBOR focuses on large buyouts (See CMBOR 2006). In the following discussion, the author will refer to the data series of the BVK for the total German Private Equity market.

German buyouts have relied on data on the changes in the volume of all Private Equity asset classes as reported by BVK[1047]. The two main sources, the German BVK and CMBOR, report diverging total volume (see also Figure 10 and Figure 11). At least the relative growth numbers of the exit channels are of similar order[1048]. Although the most discussions arise about the (reverse) going-public, the majority of exit volume is shouldered by receivership (average 1998 to 2005 of 26.8%) and trade sale (25.1%)[1049]. However, exit activity has moved towards secondaries (27.0% in 2005) and going-public (21.5%)[1050].

Exits through going-public are dependent on the general stock market disposition and liquidity available. In the years 2002 to 2004 volume dropped significantly, but recovered in 2005 and achieved an average growth of 28% since 1998. Since the IRRs are in most cases highest for going-public, most investors seek to place their investments in the public equity market. However, the requirements are also the highest in respect to market and competitive position, product quality, and quality of management[1051].

Since 2004, Deutsche Börse offers three levels of transparency: the entry standard, the general standard, and the prime standard[1052]. Only companies fulfilling the requirements of the prime standard can be included in tailored indices focusing on specific investor objectives. Amongst the various indices, SDAX[1053] and MDAX[1054] are of particular interest for an LBO exit. For companies with a sizable stake remaining in the hands of the founders or owners, Deutsche Börse introduced the GEX. GEX is an index for companies with a listing history of below 10 years to

---

1047 See Leschke 2003, pp.252-253, Kitzmann 2005, pp. 242-245

1048 BVK reports a relative growth in order of secondary (85%) to IPOs (28%) and trade sale (18%), identical to the CMBOR order (secondary (93%) to IPOs (56%) and trade sale (36%)). See BVK 2006a, BVK 2007 and CMBOR 2006.

1049 Share of exit volume over all Private Equity asset classes (See BVK 2006a, BVK 2007)

1050 See the separated statistics on German buyout exit volume (See BVK 2006b, BVK 2007)

1051 See Leschke 2003, p. 250

1052 The entry standard offers the lowest entry barriers to the German capital market. The transparency requirements are based on the general open market rules. Further, it demands the publication of audited consolidated financial statements and management reports, the publication of a brief, up-to-date company profile, a calendar of company events, the publication of a interim report and an immediate publication of important price-sensititve news or facts about the company. The general standard covers general statutory requirements of German securities law, such as annual and interim reports and ad-hoc disclosures in German. The prime standard in addition requires quarterly reporting, application of international accounting standards (IFRS/IAS or US-GAAP), publication of a financial calendar, staging of at least one analyst conference per year, and ad-hoc disclosure also in English. See www.boerse-frankfurt.com

1053 The SDAX is the selection index of the Deutsche Börse for smaller companies from traditional sectors. It starts directly below the MDAX and has 50 constituents. See www.boerse-frankfurt.com

1054 The MDAX is the selection index of the Deutsche Börse for mid-sized companies from traditional industry sectors and covers 50 constituents. The smallest market cap currently represented accounts to EUR 690 Million (June 2007). See www.boerse-frankfurt.com

intensify investor awareness and liquidity for medium-sized companies[1055]. To bear the costs of the requirements of the German stock market, Leitinger calculated that companies should at least have an emission volume of EUR 40 Million[1056].

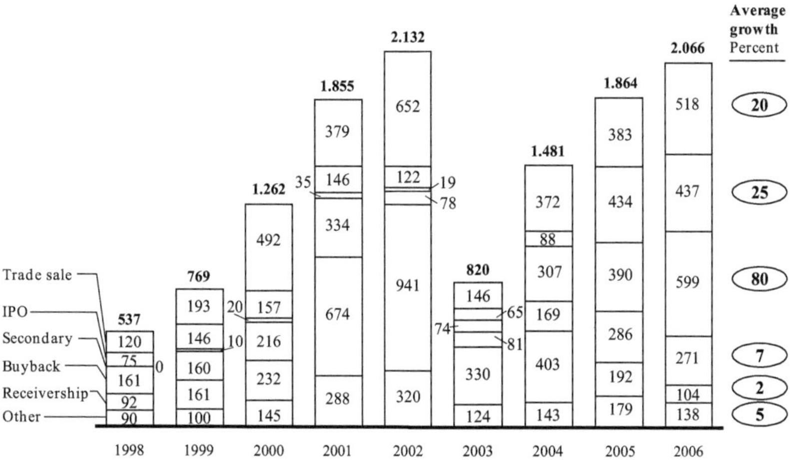

Figure 10: Development of exit volume of German Private Equity[1057]

As a result, several going-publics prefer a flotation in a foreign, more customized stock market segment. Notwithstanding, the upraise in the economy vitalized the going-public as an exit option for LBOs in 2004. A survey by Paffenholz for the German IPO market underlines the necessity of very strong growth prospects and operational excellence as a prerequisite for a public sale, combined with the right market timing[1058].

Exits through a trade sale have grown at a steadier pace, even though the growth rate of 18% (since 1998) is lower than for IPOs. A trade sale does not have to meet the strict legal requirements of an IPO and does not require convincing a wide group of investors. In the situation of a distressed stock market, the exit through a trade sale will often be the most preferable option[1059]. The strong industry base with several

1055 The GEX has the objective of combining the "entrepreneurial firms" in an index, therefore, covering only young shares (less than 10 years on the stock market) with a majority shareholder (at least 25%). The company has to be located in Germany and listed on the prime standard of the Frankfurt stock exchange. It serves as a benchmark for family-owned companies and seeks to increase investor awareness. One year after the introduction, the trading volumes of the companies covered have increased by 101% (vs. 68% of the SDAX). See Kaserer, Achleitner et al. 2006, p. 14. See further Achleitner 2005

1056 See Leitinger 2000, pp. 308 et seqq.

1057 See BVK 2006a, BVK 2007

1058 See Paffenholz 2004, p. 166

1059 See Becker 2000, p. 108

internationally successful companies and comparably low penetration with PE partnerships will keep the exit through a trade sale to a strategic buyer in Germany an attractive option. Nevertheless, the liquidity of the market for corporate control will also be dependent on the general economic situation, as buyers have to provide funds for the acquisition[1060]. Surveys disclose that the exit via a trade sale is the most successful one if the LBO excels in operations[1061]. Despite growth prospects being still esteemed vital, they are much lower than in the other exit channels. Preference for trade sales reflects buyers' intention to leverage the LBO for his own business.

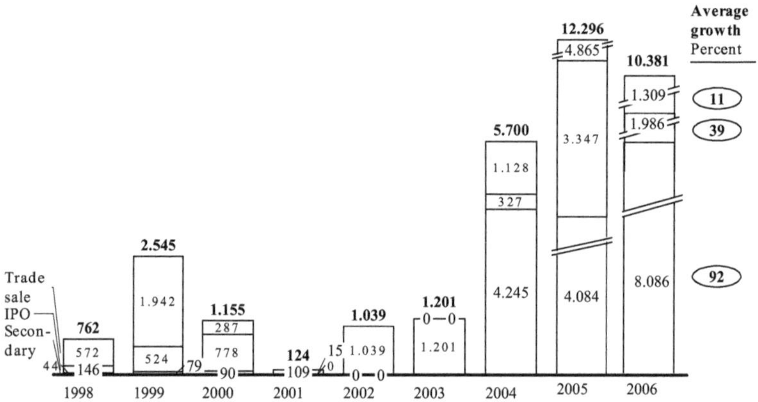

Figure 11: Number of exits and share of exit volume for buyout in Germany[1062]

Among other exit channels, secondary buyouts have demonstrated strongest growth with average yearly rates of 85% (since 1998). The exit channel substituted the weak public equity market, reaching a peak share of 56% of exit volume in 2004[1063]. Since the flipover of an LBO to a second buyout investor was uncommon for the German market, a part of the growth can be attributed to the closure of the backlog, when comparing the penetration to more established market like the UK[1064]. Although investors expect high IRRs and put pressure on the sales price[1065], several exits have resulted in prices at or beyond the level of trade sales[1066]. Therefore, buyout investors

1060 See Paffenholz 2004, p. 121

1061 See Paffenholz 2004, p. 166

1062 The data is based on different sources than in Figure 10. For instance, the total exit volume in 2005 exceeds the total exit volume for German Private Equity as reported by the BVK. See CMBOR 2006, BVK (2006a)

1063 See BVK 2006b. The relative market share as reported by CMBOR equals 74%, however, excluding buy-backs and receivership (See CMBOR 2006).

1064 In the UK, exits by secondary buyouts reached a volume of GBP 2.585 million in 2005 and was, after trade sales, the second largest exit channel ((See BVK 2006a, p. 28). See also Paffenholz 2004, p. 126

1065 See Daniels 2004, p. 50

1066 See CMBOR 2002

in Germany have started to consider a secondary buyout as an viable exit option besides a trade sale or a going-public.

The fourth exit channel, buy-backs, is still a viable option, but has halved its share from 30% in 1998 to 15% of exit volume in 2005. Buy-backs cover the sale of (dormant) equity and repayment of principal loans by management and (former) investors. In many cases, a buy-back is the confession that the buyout is not attractive enough for a going-public or a trade sale, but attractive enough to continue its business. Information asymmetry between buyout investors and management as well as restrictive covenants from the initial purchase agreement lead to a low sales price. Requirements for such an exit are lower than for the three aforementioned exit options. Investors give the highest priority to the condition of the buyer's markets and growth prospects, closely followed by operational success[1067]. Latter prioritization points to the necessity of financing the deal with the buy-back.

To summarize, the positive general economic and stock market situation in Germany has given rise to the activity level of the IPO market since 2004. As result of the maturation of the German LBO market, the flexibility towards different exit channels in Germany has incremented. Buyout investors respect a secondary buyout as a viable option. The secondaries have thereby reached a penetration in the Germany comparable to other markets. In many cases, buyouts prepare themselves for two or three different exit options during the divestment period[1068]. Private equity has return-adjusted outperformed equity[1069], however, suffers from illiquidity[1070], in particular if equity market valuation is low. Exit volume is nevertheless expected to increase.

5.3.2 Determining Concerns for the Choice of Exit Channel

When selecting the exit channel, any vendor will consider more aspects than the sheer sales price. On an abstract level, the vendor will assess the information costs he will have to bear to dissolve the information asymmetry between him and any acquirers. He will further outweigh any costs against the achievable sales price. Further considerations are the liquidity in the exit channel and the proposed capital structure.

Vendors have to contend with buyers' valuation difficulties stemming from information asymmetry. They may have to bear high costs to demonstrate status and

1067 See Paffenholz 2004, pp. 166-168
1068 See Ernst and Young 2005
1069 See Kaserer and Diller 2004
1070 See Kaserer and Diller 2004

value of the company in a credible and efficient way. In the corollary, they may not always be able to obtain a selling price reflecting the true value of the business. In particular, companies with a higher degree of growth opportunities are more difficult to value[1071]. A going-public can more easily ameliorate ex-ante transaction costs related to search costs and information asymmetries in the market for corporate control[1072]. Several researchers argue that a public offering may be used to reduce information asymmetry and achieve the desired ownership structure of the company before undergoing a trade sale. However, a going-public requires a strenuous process with onerous disclosure and due diligence requirements[1073]. Companies with higher level of uncertainty, for instance from technology discontinuities or governmental regulation, will imply higher costs to inform potential investors and will be more difficult to value[1074]. Further, the degree of consolidation within an industry determines the likelihood of a takeover. More fragmented industry structures simplify an acquisition. Brau, Francis and Kohers find evidence for higher IPO activities in relation to the level of industry consolidation[1075]. Any vendor will require participating from the considerable strategic and operational synergies of the businesses. Hence, the vendor will favor a direct sale to gain the control premium.

One may further ponder some general considerations on where to achieve the maximum sales price. The likelihood of achieving a control premium will depend wheter the vendor is willing to sell the control rights. The investor might not be able to seize the potential value from control rights (premium) if no major blockholder engages during the book-building period. To seize the willingness to pay, the seller may use dual class shares to optimize the sell-out of both cash flow and control rights. Dependent on the premium related to the control rights, a direct trade sale to

---

1071 With increased information asymmetry about future growth prospects and risk, they will face higher costs of external financing. On the flipside, a firm, after going-public, has higher discretion to allocate capital to the most promising projects. Poulsen and Stegemoeller measure that IPOs have higher pre-IPO growth rates (44.6%) as opposed to firms that are sold privately (26.2%) (See Poulsen and Stegemoller 2006, p. 15). A study by Helwege and Packer, however, shows that IPO candidates possess less growth opportunities than comparable public companies (See Helwege and Packer 2003).

1072 Reuer and Shen show empirics suggesting that a two-stage divestments - first going-public, than trade sale - are more likely in industries with fragmented ownership and in firms with a noteworthy share of intangibles (See Reuer and Shen 2004, pp. 262 et seqq.). Zingales reports that the two-stage process allows the proceeds from cash flow and control rights to be maximized. In the model by Zingales, the cash flow rights are preferably sold to a dispersed shareholder base than to a single bidder (See Zingales 1995, pp. 442 et seqq.)

1073 See Sharp 2003, p. 114

1074 In a review of the two-stage process, Mantecon and Thistle report that a higher level of uncertainty results in a higher likelihood of firms completing their IPO before selling the company (See Mantecon and Thistle 2004, pp. 3 et seqq.). For cross-sectional variations in the share of public versus private firms, see also Chemmanur and Fulghieri 1999, p. 271

1075 See Brau, Francis et al. 2003, pp. 598 et seqq.

a strategic buyer may be the more feasible exit to incorporate a control premium[1076]. To compensate for the seemingly lower liquidity and investor sentiment during a trade sale, the vendor may further choose an auction process, with multiple interested investors bidding for the target company. Finally, an exit channel may be chosen upon the likelihood of a cash consideration, e.g., a trade sale.

Beyond information asymmetry and price, liquidity for new stock determines the choice of exit. Stock markets are highly sensitive and often not receptive to flotations. Even if capital can be raised, the feasibility may be diminished by unattractive trading levels[1077]. In a depressed market, the IPO track is unviable, even for the most promising businesses[1078]. Hence, the likelihood of a successful exit bears a higher risk when seeking a going-public. Even if the buyout investors decide an IPO, they may have to abort at short notice due to unfavorable market conditions. When liquidity for a going-public is low, a trade sale may be the only option to exit from the buyout. In addition, vendors may accomplish a trade sale in a much shorter time[1079]. In contrast, a certain size of a company may not be digestible for potential industrial buyers and will only find sufficient investor demand from the general stock market. Hence, liquidity will correlate to some degree with the size and therefore with the likelihood of an IPO[1080].

Concerning the capital structure, the dispersion of ownership as well as the ratio of insider versus outsider ownership implies different levels of monitoring and control over the company. The first differential spurring the likelihood of an IPO is the debt leverage. The company can expect to achieve a cash inflow through the primary offerings. In a trade sale, the purchase price will entirely flow to the former owners, whereby the acquisition financing may impose a debt pushdown on the acquired company and even weaken available funds. The empirical evidence confirms that a high leverage is more likely to lead to an IPO than to a trade sale[1081]. Paulsen and

---

1076 See Sharp 2003, p. 111

1077 See Ritter 1991

1078 Wall and Smith report that 70% of venture capitalists admit having faced substantial difficulties around exiting through a going-public. The main reasons were stock market sentiment, lack of institutional buyers, lack of trade buyers for a specific investment, uncooperative management, bad due diligence, and poor performance by the business (See Wall 1997, pp. 6-7).

1079 See Wall 1997, p.9

1080 In addition, a certain size is necessary to bear the costs of listing and justify the costs for analyst coverage. Research by Busaba, Benevneste and Guo as well as by Mantecon and Thistle does not confirm a difference in size, whereas Brau, Francis and Kohers find evidence that larger firms prefer to choose a stock market listing (See Busaba, Benveniste et al. 2001, pp. 88 et seqq., Mantecon and Thistle 2004, p. 15, Brau, Francis et al. 2003, p. 600).

1081 See Busaba, Benveniste et al. 2001, pp. 86 et seqq., Brau, Francis et al. 2003, p. 604 et seqq., Poulsen and Stegemoller 2006, p. 29

Stegemoeller review the SEC filings for a matched sample and find in 50.8% of IPOs the debt reduction as the reason mentioned, as opposed to 0% of the sellouts. Further, the authors find evidence that the IPOs are more constrained in their capital, which can be alleviated by access to public equity. The buyout vendor will also have to balance the upside from flotation as opposed to a required share retention. New investors often demand a lockup period to ensure risk sharing and to bind in the buyout investors for some time to the company. However, industrial buyers may also limit their risk by imposing a conditional vendor note. The second differential, the distribution of ownership, has three important considerations. First, the shareholders of a public company with a capital base dispersed among a large number of investors will be much better diversified than in a private company. Second, a more dispersed shareholder base will have a considerably smaller degree of bargaining power against managers in the absence of a large blockholder. Third, free ridership from monitoring is much higher, implying that the level of monitoring will be lower and efficiency potentially diminished[1082]. The level of insider as opposed to outsider ownership and the willingness of the managing team to sell or to maintain their shares determine the third differential. In the case the insiders carry a high share and seek to sell their stake for whatever reasons, a trade sale is much more likely. A trade sale or sellout will in most cases demand from the managing team to render their shares. In the case of an IPO, the capital markets will interpret a large sale by insiders as a signal of overpricing and of limited value creation potential[1083]. However, if the insiders wish to maintain control over the company, it is more likely that they will choose to follow an IPO. Especially, if the going-public follows a successful restructuring with additional future growth perspectives, the management will seek to continue participating in any value creation[1084]. Through the separation of cash flow and control rights, they may maintain effective ownership and control while raising capital through new shareholders. In some cases, they openly oppose a trade sale. In contrast, one may argue that the level of insider shareholders is less important to the exit decision. Brau, Francis and Koher confirm the different degree of insider ownership and the expected liquidity effect. During an IPO, only 11% of the deal value is paid in cash, as opposed to 60.4% in the case of an acquisition. For buyout investors exiting their investment, retained shares

---

1082 See Chemmanur and Fulghieri 1999, pp. 250-251

1083 The price will be depressed, hence, the total amount raised will be reduced and the probability of full subscription diminished. See Leland 1977, Brau, Francis et al. 2003

1084 See Wall 1997, p.9

and continuous ownership may be an attractive means of sharing in value creation from future growth[1085].

To conclude, various reasons exist to favor either a going-public or a trade sale. The process of information disclosure in preparation to the going-public mitigates the information asymmetry. Further, liquidity is ample and, therefore, the realizable valuation of the company high. Cash restricted buyouts however will further prefer the disposition of the proceeds from a going-public. Strong insider ownership may also fear the loss of control in a trade sale. However, control premiums by potential industrial buyers may favor a trade sale, in particular if the vendors choose an auction. In a tense market environment, the considerations, however, narrow down to the simple question: where are relevant buyers?

5.3.3 Costs and Benefits

Costs related to a going-public and continued listing are remarkable. Ritter measures that registration and underwriting costs alone represent up to 14% of the proceeds raised[1086]. After going-public, management has to invest considerable time into investor communi-cation. Detailed information on company strategy and profitability will leak into the market. Further, quality and extent of new monitoring is unclear and depends on the new shareholders. The stock market will require permanent earnings reports and increase management's short-term focus.

On the other side, the takeover threat will form a beneficial disciplinary force on management. Further, former owners and management can easily partake in supplementary performance improvement by rise of share price.

Concerning costs and benefits of going-public, the German market has some specific characteristics[1087]. The equity capital market is less developed than in the US and still operates at a relatively low IPO level[1088]. On the other hand, the introduction of the entry standard with simplified regulations has lowered listing costs. A recent survey by Kaserer and Schiereck measures that flotation costs are lowest for both small and large cap companies among international stock markets[1089]. Further, prevailing private control benefits derogate a stronger growth of IPO activity given the comparatively weak protection of minority shareholders[1090]. For German IPOs,

---

1085 See Wall 1997, p.8
1086 See Ritter 1987
1087 See Böhmer and Ljungqvist 2005, p.4
1088 See BVK 2006b, p. 3
1089 See Kaserer and Schiereck 2007
1090 Dyck and Zingales report that private benefit controls are up to ten times more important in Germany than in the US (See Dyck and Zingales 2002)

Boehmer and Ljungqvist confirm that the likelihood for going-public is closely linked with the level of relative marlet valuations, which have been comparatively low. Criteria for a former LBO to exit via going-public are presented in Table 13.

Criteria	Effects on the probability of going-public of former buyouts (versus other exit channels)	Potential consequences after the going-public for former buyouts
1. Costs of going-public		
Fixed costs and scrutiny from listing	High burden from listing; larger buyouts more likely to go public	Management distracted by investor communication, strong growth focus
Loss of confidentiality, product market competition	Disclosure of confidential information; companies operating in low-margin industries less likely to go public	Higher R&D spillover to competitors, tighter contracts with suppliers and customers
Loss of control of shareholder base	Established buyouts typically with limited private benefits for the owner, therefore, increased likelihood of an IPO	Quality and extent of new monitoring unclear; potential loss of private benefits
Reliance on market conditions	IPO valuation and success dependent on market conditions; long-term investors, e.g., family-owners, less likely	Stronger short-term focus
2. Benefits of going-public		
Overcome borrowing constraints, liquidity	Crucial for high-debt companies/leveraged buyouts	Deleveraging, increase in capital expenditure
Diversification	Riskier buyouts, e.g., high growth industries, more likely to go public	Former blockholder or majority shareholder decreases his stake
Stock market monitoring	Less relevant, since monitoring is typically at a high level during the buyout	Beneficial disciplinary force from takeover threat
Access to new investors	Mature buyouts in most cases with good access to investors; however, access to risk-neutral investors	Change of risk versus reward trade-off
Increase bargaining power with banks	Backing by buyout specialists with strong expertise; less beneficial for capital costs	Risk reduction of bondholders after going-public will enable to re-negotiating debt terms
Flexibility in transfer of control	Stepwise reduction of ownership; attractive for both management and buyout specialists	Smooth transfer from pre- to post-exit governance structure

Table 13: Overview of costs and benefits of a going-public for a LBO (author)

A trade sale incurs less direct costs as a stock market listing. Much more, the former LBO faces inefficiencies from misalignment of interests and indirect costs. In particular, management renders control over the company since, in most cases, they have to sell their shareholdings to the acquirer and are limited in their entrepreneurial freedom.

The management of the acquiring company will have to find the right balance between offering the former buyout management enough area for independent decision-making on the one hand and focus on joint resource allocation and synergy realization on the other hand. Oftentimes, the monitoring the former buyout will overstrain the corporate management, since they have limited experience in the business and market environment of the target. The German market is known for the high level of industry cross-holdings[1091]. Hence, holding companies should have at least some modest experience in acquiring, managing and divesting businesses. Observations indicate that the market for independent, professional adviser may still

1091 See the detailed discussion on the different ownership structures in Germany in chapter B2.1.2. See also Goergen, Manjon et al. 2004, p. 45

have to develop, in particular in respect to the smaller to medium-sized companies[1092]. Criteria for a former LBO to exit via trade sale are presented in Table 14.

Criteria	Effects on the probability of a trade sale of former buyouts (versus other exit channels)	Potential consequences after the trade sale for former buyouts
1. Costs of trade sale		
Restricted monitoring	Head office of parent company with less time and commitment for monitoring; effect stronger for smaller companies with lack of good governance/ lack of management expertise	Higher level of management entrenchement, potential decrease in profitability
Job losses due to expected synergies	Synergies, justifying the control premium and related to increased operational efficiency, will put pressure to cut back and downsize in overlapping activities; in most cases incurs resistance from the workforce	Loss of motivation and commitment, decline in productivity
Loss of control by management	Incumbent management fears loss of control of business (and potential private benefits); for cases with management majority trade sale less likely	Discontent of management board members, departure of managers
Reduction of shareholdings	Reduction in both management and employee shareholding (potential delisting); less attractive	Reduced interest alignment, increase in management entrenchment
Cross-subsidies	Potential subsidies to other, less successful and less cash flow-generating business units; in all cases hindrance to trade sale	Underinvestment in former buyout
2. Benefits of trade sale		
Access to resources	Access to valuable resources, e.g., employees, sales channels, customer base; highly attractive	Potential facilitator for additional growth and higher profitability
Liquidity	Buyouts benefit from enlarged financing capabilities of parent; increases likelihood	Additional capital investments and M&A activity

Table 14: Overview of costs and benefits of a trade sale for a LBO (author)

5.3.4 Performance Development of a LBO exiting via Going-Public

5.3.4.1 General Empirical Evidence Related to a Going-Public

Surveys of the performance development of companies after a going-public show contradictory implications. Different motives of managers determine post-exit performance.

First, managers will seek to maximize their proceeds from going-public and choose a favorable time of market overvaluation, leading to underperformance in the first years after listing. Reduction of information asymmetry und correct assessment of fair company value requires substantial time, in which the company may develop below market average. Ritter reports that IPOs significantly underperform their industry in the first three years. The major reason for underperformance lies in the timing of the going-public, as stock market overvalues the company's share price[1093]. Loughran and Ritter, with an extended sample, confirm the results and conclude

1092 See Bassen, Kleinschmidt et al. 2004
1093 See Ritter 1991, p. 23

"investing in companies issuing stock as hazardous to your wealth"[1094]. However, to weaken the reproaches against management, smaller companies are typically subject to fads and investor sentiment[1095].

Second, moral hazard of managers may lead to creative accounting prior to the IPO. Companies have the incentive to show superior earnings and increase current accruals, e.g., advancing the recognition of revenues and postponing the recognition of expenses. Hence, (financial) performance will peak in the pre-IPO period, and decrease in the years following. Pagano, Panetta, and Zingales measure a decline of cash flow to assets[1096]. The decline increases gradually in the post-IPO period. The main argument by the authors is adverse selection (a going-public timed when profitability is about to decline permanently) and moral hazard (where blockholders extract private benefit from minority shareholders). Researchers expect that the occurrence of both adverse selection and moral hazard is to be larger when managers are observed to sell extensively equity[1097]. It is shown that the relationship between performance decline and the post-IPO incumbent's stake is negative, confirming reproaches of moral hazard by management.

Third, vendors may time the going-public to facilitate the expansion of the business at a crucial point[1098]. The entrepreneur may wait until the productivity increase related to the going-public is sufficient to outweigh the costs by the benefits of stock market listing. The performance will not decline, therefore, significantly. Much more, the business will reach its optimal scale after the IPO and after some time slow down its growth. Chemmanur, He and Nandy detail this hypothesis and find a pattern of increasing productivity, measured by the total factor productivity, starting five years prior to the IPO, culminating in the peak in the year of going-public, and declining in a modest way in the years following[1099]. The authors translate the decrease (increase) of TFP post (prior) to the buyout into a decrease (increase) in profits of 16% (23%).

The researchers can not relate the inverted U-shape to the manipulation of accounting numbers. Instead, the researchers argue the increase is the result of a company expanding its scale of operations around the IPO, hereby using external financing. The sales development additionally shows an inverted U-shape.

1094 See Loughran and Ritter 1995, p. 46
1095 See Brav and Gompers 1997, p. 1820
1096 See Pagano, Panetta et al. 1998, pp. 50 - 51
1097 See Leland 1977 hypothesizing that lower equity retention is a signal of bad quality and heightens agency problems (see Jensen Meckling 1976).
1098 See Clementi 2002
1099 See Chemmanur, He et al. 2005, pp. 26 et seqq.

Author	Year	Sample	Investigation period	Geographical focus	Observed time period [in years][1]	Data source	Total sales (adjusted)	Capital expenditure/ assets	Average (adjusted) changes in cash flow-based indicators: Operating cash flow/ assets[1]	Operating cash flow/ total capital	Average (adjusted) changes in operating income-based indicators: Operating margin (Operating income/ sales)[2]	Operating income/ assets[2]	Net margin (net income/ sales)	Cumulative returns	Buy and hold returns[3]
1. Exit of buyouts															
Mohan	1990	83 LBOs	n/a	US	x to x+2	FS	*N/a*	-2.9%[ns]			+1,6%[5]	-49,2%[6]			
Degeorge, Zeckhauser	1993	62 LBOs	1983 to 1987	US	x to x+2	FS, SM	*N/a*					+6,9%[a],			+ 15,2%
Mian, Rosenfeld	1993	85 LBOs	1983 to 1988	US	x to x+3	FS, SM	Slight decrease, ns							+ 21,1%[a]	
Holthausen, Larcker	1996	90 LBOs	1983 to 1988	US	x-1 to x+4	FS, SM	*N/a*		-15,9%[a]			-10,4%[c]			+ 11.0%[ns]
Jalilvand, Switzer	2002	200 LBOs	1981 to 1992	US	x-1 to x+4	FS	*N/a*		+19,2%[c]			-22,8%[a]			
Bruton, Keels, Scifres	2002	39 LBOs	1980 to 1988	US	t-1 to x+3	FS	+37.6%[c]						-20,7%[a, 7]		
Jelic, Saadouni, Wright	2005	167 MBOs	1964 to 1997	US	x to x+3	SM	*N/a*							-2,4%[ns]	- 0,3%[b]
2. Exit through IPOs (excerpts)															
Jain, Kini	1994	682	1976 to 1988	US	x-1 to x+3	FS	+80.7%[a]	+111.0%[a]	-4.7%[a]			-6.8%[a, y]			
Mikkelson, Partch, Shah	1995	238	1980 to 1983	US	x-1 to x+1	FS	*N/a*				-2%[a, y]	-9%[a, y]			
McConaughy, Dhatt, Kim	1996	99	1985	US	x to x+7	FS	+20%[c, 2]		+13.3%[ni, 3]		+0.08%[ni]				
Brav, Gompers	1997	934[8]	1972 to 1992	US	x to x+5	SM	*N/a*								-3%[ns]
		3407[9]	1972 to 1992	US	x to x+5	SM	*N/a*								-21%[ns]
Pagano, Panetta, Zingales	1998	69	1982 to 1992	Italy	x to x+3	FS	Slight increase, ns	-15%[a]	-3%[a]						
Gompers, Lerner	2003	3661	1935 to 1972	US	x to x+5	SM	*N/a*							-0.1%[ns]	-33.4%[a]
Chemmanur, He, Nandy	2006	2578	1972 to 2000	US	x to x+4	FS,	Decrease, ns	Decrease[b]			-10%[a]				
3. Exit of German IPOs															
Uhlir	1989	70	1977 to 1986	Germany	x to x+15[in m]	SM	*N/a*								-0.5%[ns]
Hannson, Ljungqvist	1992	141	1978 to 1991	Germany	x to x+2	SM	*N/a*							-1.9%[ns]	
Wasserfallen, Wittleder	1994	92	1961 to 1987	Germany	x to x+1	SM	*N/a*							+15%[ns]	
Ljungqvist	1994	145	1970 to 1990	Germany	x to x+3	SM	*N/a*							-8.3%[ns]	
Kaserer	1996	165	1983 to 1993	Germany	x to x+3	SM	*N/a*								-8.0%xx
Georgen	1997	62[7]	1981 to 1988	Germany	x to x+6	FS	*N/a*			-1.7%[ns]				-6.2%[ns]	
Ljungqvist	1997	180	1970 to 1993	Germany	x to x+3	SM	*N/a*								-12.1%[b]
Ehrhardt	1997	195	1960 to 1993	Germany	x to x+3	SM	*N/a*								-5.2%[ns]
Stehle, Ehrhardt	1999	187	1960 to 1995	Germany	x to x+3	SM	*N/a*								-5.0%[ns, 4]
Stehle, Erhardt, Przyborowsky	2000	187	1960 to 1992	Germany	x to x+3	SM	*N/a*								-6.6%[ns, 6]
Ehrhardt, Nowak	2003	105	1970 to 1990	Germany	x to x+3	SM	*N/a*								-8.1%[ns]
Jaskiewicz, Gonzalez, Menendez, Schiereck	2005	153	1990 to 2001	Germany	x to x+3	SM	*N/a*								-32.8%[a]

[a] Change significant at the 1% level
[b] Change significant at the 5% level
[c] Change significant at the 10% level

[y] Operating income adjusted to operating return

[ns] Not significant at at least the 10% level
[ni] No information about significance
[na] Not industry adjusted

[1] Operating cash flow in some cases approximated by EBITDA
[2] Not adjusted for industry
[3] Cash flow margin reported as cash flow to sales
[4] Equally weighted market portfolio
[5] Value weighted market portfolio; in percentage points
[6] Adjusted by size portfolio
[7] Only family controlled firms
[8] Venture backed
[9] Non-venture backed
[10] Measured as change in absolute capital expenditure

FS = financial statement
SM = stock market

Table 15: Overview of long-term performance studies for going-public, buyout and non-buyout (excerpts)

Studies on European IPOs contradict the hypothesis of US-based research that IPOs finance subsequent investment and growth. Companies in Europe rather rebalance their accounts for further, continuous growth, whereas more mature companies in the US seek to pay down their debt[1100]. A potential explanation is the maturity and higher age of IPOs in Europe. In particular, German IPOs are on average older than comparable listings in the US[1101]. Boehner and Lindqvist stress that German IPOs are much less start-ups than in the US [1102]. Hence, any research will have to consider that the companies are in a later stage in their life cycle, and, therefore, comparable to the average buyout company seeking an exit.

Some research has sought to disentangle the development of German IPOs after stock market listing, with evidence indicating some differences to the US-based studies. German IPOs seem to be less subject to long-term underperformance. The question of remaining ownership, however, seems to be more important. For instance, German IPOs more often use dual class shares to retain control while raising capital. This is not surprising, since a large share of IPOs comes from the sample of established family-controlled companies. Still, evidence on potential causes for performance development is sparse. A potential cause for underperformance may be linked to higher maturity and diminished information asymmetry, since underwriters and stock market have access to richer information. In contrast, the traditionally high gearing of German companies and monitoring of Hausbanks may not be substituted by monitoring from the stock market.

In one of the first extensive analyses of the German IPO market, Uhlir reports evidence of underperformance for going-public between 1977 and 1987 against the market value-weighted All Share Index after 15 months[1103]. Ljungqvist also measures a modest underperformance against a value weighted market portfolio[1104]. Kaserer and Kempf, in contrast, find no significant underperformance of the CAR for a 250-day period [1105]. In a later paper by Kaserer, a buy-and-hold return of -8% (benchmark against DAX) for a 36-month period is measured. However, Kaserer

---

1100 See Rydqvist and Högholm 1995, Pagano, Panetta et al. 1998, Mikkelson, Partch et al. 1997

1101 Ehrhardt and Nowak report that the average age in Germany for a firm going-public is 63.6 years (See Ehrhardt and Nowak 2003, p. 225). The Euopean average as elucidated by Rydqvist and Högholm at around 40 years (See Rydqvist and Högholm 1995) . The firms heading for stock market listings in the US are with an average 5 to 18 years considerably younger (See Gompers 1996).

1102 See Böhmer and Ljungqvist 2005, p. 15.. Stehle, Ehrhardt and Przyborowsky, for instance, name Hacker Pschorr, VW, Veba abd VEW, all well-known German companies, and all founded before 1940, as examples of established firms going public at a later stage (See Stehle, Ehrhardt et al. 2000, pp. 177 -178)

1103 The index is the former index of the Federal Statistical Office. See Uhlir 1989, p. 13

1104 See Ljungqvist 1997

1105 See Kaserer and Kempf 1995, p. 52

includes the IPOs underwritten by the Portfolio Management GmbH, which similarly to the results of Lingqvist negatively biases the results[1106]. In a review of Wasserfallen and Wittleder, a sample of IPOs between 1961 and 1987 does not outperform the book-weighted FAZ-index of 100 leading shares within the first year after stock market listing. Only ex-ante uncertainty spurs underperformance, otherwise the secondary market is reported not to compensate for the initial high returns. An extension of the investigation period by Ljungqvist to 36 months post-IPO confirms the aforementioned results of a neutral relative performance for the first 12 months, measuring an insignificant 1.8% loss. The additional cohort of 88 IPOs between 1988 and 1990, however, brings the total sample to a loss of 12.1%. Ljungqvist concludes that in the longer term, German IPOs share the US characteristic of underperformance, where the characteristic seems to be time-dependent, rather than the result of an equilibrium. Later research refined the sample by the size dependency of performance for the German stock market. For a sample of IPOs between 1960 and 1992, Stehle and Eckhardt measure an underperformance for a 36-month period. The same sample shows a neutral performance if measured against a market-value weighted portfolio. Hence, the larger IPOs seem to perform significantly better. Further, Stehle finds that the average annual return of the larger stocks (non-IPOs) is significantly lower than the smaller stocks in the period between 1954 and 1990[1107]. Stehle, Erhardt and Przyborowsky extend the analysis by building size portfolios as a benchmark. After comparing market-value adjusted benchmarks, size portfolios, and control stocks, the authors suggest using size portfolios, since German IPOs have small to medium market capitalization[1108]. Similar results are measured by Drobetz, Kammermann and Wälchli for a sample of Swiss IPO from 1983 to 2000. They find evidence for underperformance, in particular in the very long run[1109]. However, after comparing the sample to a small capitalization index, the differences turn to insignificance, similar to the conclusions of Brav and Gompers. Boehmer and Lingqvist investigate a large sample of German IPO on basis of their financial statements. The companies seem to time their IPO announcement to the climax of their sales growth cycle. Further, industry-adjusted earnings increase in the years after the announcement. However, only two thirds of the companies actually enter the public equity market after the announcement.

1106 In a separate analysis of 9 cases of the Portfolio Management GmbH, Ljungqvist measures an underperformance of -144.6% (See Ljungqvist 1997, p. 1312).

1107 See Stehle 1997, pp. 241 et seqq.

1108 See Stehle, Ehrhardt et al. 2000, p. 190

1109 See Drobetz, Kammernmann et al. 2005, pp. 261 et seqq.

Ehrhardt and Nowak examine the post-IPO performance of family-owned businesses. In total, the companies underperform the industry. However, underperformance is exclusively linked to the performance of non-voting shares issued. Further, the level of post-offering ownership determines performance. A comparatively small stake (less than 25% of voting rights) or a comparatively large stake (over 75% of voting rights) leads to a negative abnormal return[1110] . The most promising governance correlates with 25% to 50% of voting rights in the hands of the family. The data shows that the separation of cash flow versus control rights is applied in conjunction with a controlling shareholder structure, but not with a dispersed ownership structure. Georgen also measures the performance of a sample of German, family-controlled companies versus a sample of UK widely-held companies to find potential post-IPO differences related to ownership[1111]. Both cash flow and CAR decrease, however, not significantly against the matched industry sample[1112]. Furthermore, Georgen explicitly analyses time trends, but does not find, however, any time-related characteristics. Jaskiewicz, Gonzales, Menendez and Schiereck also investigate the performance of family-controlled going-publics. They find that the subsample underperforms significantly (-40.7%) against non-family controlled going-publics (-19.9%)[1113]. A significant part of the difference is related to size, since smaller companies have a stronger underperformance. Further, the authors find evidence favorable to business age and family influence as explaining the long-run underperformance. Kraus and Burghof examine whether IPOs with backing by VC outperform their competitors. The VC(non-VC)-backed IPOs sell a smaller (larger) part of insider shareholdings, however, a larger (smaller) share from outside shareholdings. In the longer run, both groups of IPOs underperform the benchmark. At the beginning, the VC-backed companies outperformed the non-VC backed group in the medium term. Later (after 20 weeks), the performance differences vanish[1114]. Within the sample, the larger and VC-backed companies perform significantly better[1115]. However, the exit of the VC, especially after the ending of the lock-up period, has a much less severe impact on the share price than expected.

The going-public of a German company seems also not to be immune against underperformance in the first months after the stock market listing. The cumulative

---

1110 See Ehrhardt and Nowak 2003, pp. 229 et seqq.

1111 See the results from changes in ownership on performance development in the following chapter.

1112 See Goergen, Manjon et al. 2004, pp. 13 et seqq.

1113 See Jaskiewicz, Gonzalez et al. 2005, pp. 191 et seqq.

1114 See Kraus and Burghof 2003, pp. 22 - 24

1115 See Kraus and Burghof 2003, p. 26

abnormal return, however, becomes more or less insignificant if adjusted for size. Further, a major blockholder with a share of 25% to 50% throughout the going-public seems to mitigate potential information asymmetry. No surveys have analyzed the long-term development of operating performance based on actual financial data. The stronger focus on proceeds to foster future growth may indicate that sales growth will accelerate, while asset turnover and productivity will at best remain constant, if not decrease in the first years post-IPO. Since the requirements for a going-public are relatively high for the German stock market, the company will most likely operate before the going-public above industry average. Although a decline of the operating performance in the first years after stock market listing is indicated by the stock price-based underperformance, the performance will presumably remain above industry average, corresponding to the US-based surveys.

5.3.4.2 Changes in Corporate Governance and Performance at Going-Public

The basic model of Jensen and Meckling proposes that any significant reduction of insider ownership, in particular by management, will be detrimental to performance. Empirical evidence has revealed that the degree of managerial shareholdings is even more prevailing and of higher causality to the success of the LBO than debt leverage. Is this effect as prevailing for a going-public as for the LBO? How vital is the existence of a major shareholder as an active investor in the first years in the public equity market?

The post-offering occurrence of a major shareholder will be dependent on expected control premia and benefits from monitoring achievable from the new shareholders. Large shareholders and active investors are crucial for high level monitoring activity. Hereby, underpricing plays an important role in attracting potential large shareholders[1116]. Research confirms a positive relationship between underpricing and occurrence of large shareholders[1117]. Empirics show that a public offering can be used to fine-tune the ownership structure as intended[1118]. New outside investors are aware of private benefits and potential corporate actions, which are not in their best interests under private ownership. Any residual losses as deviations from the optimal corporate policy and actions that cannot be compensated by monitoring will be accounted for in the share price.

1116 Pricing in the run-up to the listing allows to steer the type of investors. Pricing is determined by balancing demand for a wide ownership distribution (higher price), high institutional ownership (lower price), and a liquid secondary market (lower price). Any investors have to produce costly, initial information about the firm and its growth prospects. In an equilibrium, underpricing price level should compensate for information costs and equal later total market value of the firm (See Booth and Chua 1996, pp. 291 et seqq.)

1117 See Brennan and Franks 1997, Pagano and Roell 1998, Stoughton and Zechner 1998, Booth and Chua 1996

1118 See Zingales 1995, Brennan and Franks 1997, Mello and Parons 1998, and Stoughton and Zechner 1998

Evidence can be found for both a continuation and dis-continuation of the former ownership concentration. Mikkelson, Partch, and Shah report that the average share of equity of officers and directors as a group declines significantly from 67.9% prior, to 43.7% in the year of, to 28.6% five years, and finally 17.9% ten years after the offering. However, the share of venture capitalists (20.0% prior and 16.8% ten years after) as well as of financial companies (12.5% prior and 12.3% ten years after) remain constant. In total, ownership becomes considerably less concentrated. McConaughy, Dhatt, and Kim, in contrast, report that holdings of directors and officers remain constant, from year one (31%) to year seven (25%) after the stock market listing[1119]. Brennan and Franks show a similar continuity in ownership by active managers. In their sample of IPOs, the active directors from the pre-IPO period continue to hold their shares years after going public[1120].

As previously outlined[1121], the relationship between ownership, performance and company value may most likely not be positive across all potential values of insider ownership. High levels of ownership will shield management from the market for corporate control and beneficial disciplinary forces. For stock market listed companies, Stulz, reports that an increase in the fraction of voting rights in the hands of the management equals an effective takeover defense and reduces the probability of successful takeover bids[1122]. Roosenboom and van der Goot measure that for companies going-public, ownership entrenchment at a high level starts to outweigh the incentive effects[1123]. Similar results are reported by Mantecon and Thistle. They find a non-linear relationship between ownership structure and company value[1124]. Shareholdings of corporate insiders with an equity share of up to 45% spur company value. Beyond 45%, the evidence implies the relationship to performance turns negative[1125]. However, the majority of surveys report a positive relationship of ownership to performance for the post-offering period. Brennan and Franks report that in the case of essential reductions of shareholdings, agency costs increase due to

---

1119 See McConaughy, Dhatt et al. 1996, pp. 47-48

1120 In contrast, shareholdings from non-directors are virtually all sold. Two thirds of the shares offered are sold to outside shareholders, leaving 31% in the hands of active management and relatives. See Brennan and Franks 1997, pp. 406 et seqq.

1121 See the discussion of the relationship between ownership concentrations, in particular by management, and performance in chapter B2.1.2.

1122 See Stulz 1988

1123 Further, certificates that shield the autonomy of management and allow consuming at a higher level of private benefits are penalized, however at a non-significant level. The researchers further find that both independent supervisory directors and non-management shareholders reduce agency costs and enhance firm value. See Roosenboom and Van der Goot 2005, pp. 53-55

1124 See Mantecon and Thistle 2004

1125 See Morck 1988, McConnell and Servaes 1990

an advancing separation of ownership and control. Jain and Kini examine the relationship of managerial shareholdings and performance in the post-IPO period. For the group with higher shareholdings after the IPO, the decreases in operating return and cash flow to assets are less severe, significant in most cases at 1%[1126]. Further, sales growth and growth in capital expenditure is higher. Jain and Kini conclude that the results confirm the implications from agency theory and signaling models on the changes in insider ownership.

An analysis by Mikkelson, Partch and Shah reveals quite the contrary: that neither level nor changes in managerial shareholdings explain the level or change in operating performance[1127]. Only companies of higher age, indicating longer survival, show higher median operating performance for higher post-IPO insider ownership. However, the researchers find for the group of companies where prior investors sold at least 50% of the shares after the IPO operating performance to drop significantly. They conclude that secondary sales are timed to follow a peak in performance, which is not sustainable after the going-public[1128]. Further, they argue that, although their sample has a similar pre-offering and post-offering ownership structure than to the sample of reverse buyout by Holthausen and Larcker,

> "... the changes in ownership and incentive effects are more important for firms that have previously converted from public to private ownership [the former buyouts] than for firms that are going public for the first time "[1129].

Following the authors, the interest alignment remains high after the going-public, since additional disciplinary forces from stock-based compensation and takeover threat substitute for the incentive benefits from stock ownership. They further report the backing of a venture capitalist and outside ownership does not to relate to post-offering performance.

For German family-controlled IPOs, Goergen rejects a negative relationship between decrease in ownership and performance[1130]. Goergen argues that ownership finds the right way to maximize company value. Ehrhardt and Nowak examine the ownership changes for the sample of German IPOs under former family-control. Ten

---

1126 From year 1 prior to year 3 post IPO, the operating cash flow to assets ratio declines for the high (low) ownership group by 4.9% (7.7%). See Jain and Kini 1994, pp. 1709 - 1714

1127 Although the sample is similar to Jain and Kiri, they come to different results due to a more precise measurement of the ownership changes. Jain and Kiri refer to estimates on stakes retained by pre-offering stockholders. Mikkelson, Partch, and Shah, in contrast, directly measure the changes in ownership (See Mikkelson, Partch et al. 1997, pp. 297 et seqq.).

1128 Earnings may be succumbing to earnings manipulation (See Mikkelson, Partch et al. 1997, p. 305)

1129 See Mikkelson, Partch et al. 1997, p. 306

1130 See Goergen 1997, pp. 16 et seqq.

years after the going-public, the families still own on average 40.4% of voting rights[1131]. In those cases where the family-owners exit after the going-public, the companies underperform in the three year period observed[1132]. In those 60% of companies where the family is still involved, they maintain a controlling stake of on average even 63.1%. Further, they introduce dual-class shares to maintain control and gain private benefits. The mean proportion of voting rights 10 years after the going-public is still at 51.8%, in contrast to an average share of 31.7% when only ordinary shares are offered. Hence, families continue to have a considerable influence on the corporate. It may be noteworthy, that tax regulation in Germany favors holding privately held stakes as opposed to selling.

In summary, not all going-public companies seem to suffer from the decrease in insider shareholdings. For more mature and older companies, however, the changes in ownership seem to have a significant detrimental effect on performance. It seems that for family-owned business, a change in ownership is less likely in the case of a stock market listing. Further, private control benefits seem still to be high in Germany.

5.3.4.3 Performance of LBOs Going Public

Several studies have examined the degree of (short-term) underpricing and (long-term) underperformance of LBOs going public.

(Short-term) underpricing is dependent on the uncertainty and risk about the value of the issuer, and based on information asymmetry between managers and existing investors versus new investors. Inasmuch former LBOs have been public, they should have a reduced information asymmetry to public equity markets. For former non-public companies, the LBOs at least have proven that they possess a sustainable business model. They have already shown a track record in terms of product and service quality, quality of management, etc., and hence simplify any assessment and valuation[1133]. Data confirms a reduction of information asymmetry and underpricing[1134]. Muscarella and Vetsuypens and Nornonha and Yung report that reverse LBO that went through a full reverse are to some degree less underpriced than former divisional spinoff[1135]. A more detailed survey by Ang and Brau tests whether the costs related to the going-public are truly less for reverse LBOs than for

1131 See Ehrhardt and Nowak 2003, pp. 225 - 228
1132 See Ehrhardt and Nowak 2003, pp. 229 et seqq.
1133 See Muscarella and Vetsuypens 1989, p. 185.
1134 See Muscarella and Vetsuypens 1989, Ainina and Mohan 1991, Jalilvand, Stewart et al. 1996
1135 See Muscarella and Vetsuypens 1989, Noronha and Yung ,

normal IPO[1136]. Ang and Brau find the evidence that former LBOs pay, as expected, less to enter the public markets. Ang and Brau reports high levels of underpricing, similar to ordinary IPOs. Further, the group of non-acquired IPOs shows significantly lower levels of underpricing, similar to the (short-term) results reported by Ritter[1137].

Information asymmetry may by further reduced by the backing of prestigious underwriters[1138]. A recent study also confirmed the significance of underwriters for German IPOs[1139]. Overall, the empirical evidence suggests a weak relationship of prestige to the level of underpricing for LBOs. Coefficients have the expected negative sign, but are not statistical significant[1140]. What researchers do find is that companies with higher post-offering performance have underwriters with higher prestige. Hence, the underwriters sponsor higher-quality companies to maintain their own reputation[1141].

Further, investors may fear that manager-owners and buyout investors abuse their information advantage to maximize proceeds in a period of market overvaluation and manipulate earnings to maximize share price. Degeorge and Zeckhauser find evidence that the going-public coincides with a peak in the operating performance, indicating that managers actively time the return public ownership. In the year before the offering, operating income to assets increases by 7% points. In the first year of public trading, however, the reverse LBOs underperform their industry. Managers might have deferred expenses and borrowed future sales. The incentive to cash out will endorse managerial efforts to improve at least reported accounting performance. Yet after exceptional performance during going-public, the performance level will return to the long-term mean. Although Degeorge and

---

1136 The authors compare former LBOs going public against (See Ang and Brau 2002, pp. 9-12, and also Muscarella and Vetsuypens 1989, pp. 189-191). The higher transparency is hypothesized to affect the costs in several ways: (i) costs of issuance are reduced; (ii) risk of undersubscription is reduced due to more information about the issuing company; (iii) administration fees related to auditing and legal services are reduced since the companies is known; and (iv) extent of overallotment option reduced/avoided. First, the initial mispricing is significantly less for the former LBO sample (5.5%) as opposed to the sample group (8.0%). Second, total flotation costs, comprising the cost positions from (i) to (iii), are significant higher for non-former LBOs (18.6% to 14.9% total costs of flotation to closing price). Third, transparency differs by the former degree of exposure to public equity markets. The former public LBOs have the least costs (13.8%), followed by former subsidiaries (15.6%) and finally the LBOs that went private (17.8%). In addition, the initial mispricing has the some indication (See Ang and Brau 2002, pp. 13-16)

1137 See Ritter 1991

1138 See Beatty and Ritter 1986, Chemmanur and Fulghieri 1994

1139 See Neuhaus and Schremper 2003, pp. 461 et seqq.

1140 The researchers contend that the buyouts are, as expected, less subject to asymmetric information problems than average IPOs. See Jalilvand, Stewart et al. 1996, pp. 49 et seqq., Jalilvand and Switzer 2002, pp. 10 and 11

1141 See Jalilvand and Switzer 2002, pp. 10 and 11

Zeckhauser hypothesize 'hidden information' or 'performance manipulation' as reason for the disappointing year 1 share price development, neither explanation is subjected to detailed empirical testing. Holthausen and Larcker, on the flipside, interpret their findings as providing no evidence that managers exploit information asymmetries in reverse LBOs at the expense of new shareholders in the offering. They conclude that reverse LBOs appear to be priced rationally at the offering, particularly relative to typical first-time IPOs.

In summary, the underpricing is significantly lower and indicates that new investors have truly richer information on going-public LBOs. The next question therefore is, whether the LBOs achieve long-term (operating) outperformance after going-public. Studies indicate that LBOs after going-public perform superior to their industry peers, however, decline in relative performance with advancing distance to their going-public (see the overview in Table 15).

Mohan measures a continued productive allocation of resources and efficient management[1142]. Operating profit to sales remains in both years after going-public above industry average. Employee productivity, measured by sales per employee, even increases. Operating profit to total capital decreases, however, mainly due to higher market valuation and, therefore, a greater nominator. Since some LBO go public to private again, Mohan argues that LBOs in the long-term lose their achieved efficiency gains while being public. However, no further testing for the latter hypothesis over a long-term period is provided.

Holthausen and Larker report an advancing relative decline, albeit the performance of the former buyouts continues to remain superior in absolute numbers. Accounting performance in year 1 prior to the offering is significantly better than the performance of industry peers, and remains superior the after going-public. Even in year 4, both cash flow to assets and operating income to assets remain above industry level, but with a decline in relative performance to the fiscal year before and of going-public.

The study by Bruton, Keels and Scifres, although analyzing a similar time frame than the former two studies, shows a more clearer picture on the accelerating decline in post-offering performance. The authors measure the performance over the buyout cycle. First, they observe a significant net margin increase from going-private by 28% to an average of 13.3%. Second, after the public offering, margin remain constant with 13.0% for the first two years. In year 3 after going-public, net margin decreases

---

1142 See Mohan 1990

substantially to 10.5%, remaining only 0.1% above the pre-buyout level. The decline in year 3 is significant when industry and matched-companies covariates are introduced. The authors note that, despite the decrease, the observed changes were not significantly different from the percentage changes experienced by the industry from year 2 to 3. The researchers concluded that it takes time until inefficiencies enter back into the company's operations. The time lapse indicates, that inefficiencies are not managers' purposeful intent, but much more the result of various small choices not made in the best interest of the company. Otherwise, the decline would occur at the rate and magnitude seen in the efficiency gain when going private.

Jalilvand and Switzer find evidence for strong financial performance after adjustment for industry effects. First, the authors report that performance peaks in the year prior to going-public. Hence, managers may time going-public to performance and benefit from their private information advantage. Second, in the five years following, both operating income to assets and cash flow to assets remain above industry average. However, the distance to the industry average declines. Similar to the survey before, Jalilvand and Switzer interpret the decline as a gradual reappearance of agency problems.

Both studies cover a sample of buyouts where management shareholdings remain significant in the post-buyout period. Holthausen and Larcker characterize for their sample that the ownership structure is a hybrid between a buyout and a typical corporation.

		Independent variables				
Dependent variable	**Medium level in year -1**	**Change in debt/ capital**	**Change in mgmt.** Percent equity	**Change in non-mgmt. insider** Percent equity	**Change in industry performance**	**Adj.R²** Percent
• Change in firm OPINC/ assets from						
– Year -1 to +1	0.193	0.0221 (0.647)	0.0014 (0.034)	0.0018 (0.024)	0.7943 (0.111)	10.2
– Year -1 to the average of years +1 to + 4		0.0044 (0.948)	0.0021 (0.028)	0.0023 (0.030)	1.0766 (0.162)	14.7
• Change in firm OCF/ assets from						
– Year -1 to +1	0.195	-0.0754 (0.315)	0.0037 (0.001)	0.0038 (0.003)	1.1552 (0.210)	25.3
– Year -1 to the average of years +1 to + 4		-0.0380 (0.623)	0.0044 (0.000)	0.0036 (0.006)	0.3249 (0.685)	31.7

Table 16: Cross-sectional regression analysis of changes (industry-adjusted) in company performance[1143]

Of particular interest are the results from Holthausen and Larcker on the importance of the different constituents of corporate governance on the post-IPO performance

1143 See Holthausen and Larcker 1996, p. 317

(see Table 16). Both management and insider, non-management shareholdings have a significant influence on the operating cash flow and operating income. The coefficient on management shareholdings is, for instance, for the four year post-IPO effect 0.0044. Hence, when a company bears a decline of management shareholdings of 10%, it resembles in a decline of 4.4% percentage points of the quota of operating cash flow to assets. In the consequence, cash flow-related profitability decreases by 23%. Similar order is calculated for non-management insider ownership. On the flipside, the decrease of debt has the expected sign, however, is not significant for both cash flow and operating income. The authors conclude, that

> "... the positive incentive effects associated with more concentrated ownership by managers and active investors who monitor management, and that the organizational changes are conducive to superior performance... The economic interpretation that ownership, but not leverage, affects performance is critically dependent on the assumption that the change in organizational structure is exogenous"[1144].

Similar results on the importance of managerial shareholdings as opposed to debt are also reported from a sample of buyouts in the UK that returned to public[1145].

In contrast, Jalivand and Switzer do find a strong relationship between leverage and performance, measured by operating income. However, similar to Holthausen and Larcker, the coefficient on cash flow to assets is not significant. Since the operating income is more subject to accounting accruals than operating cash flow, the results have to be interpreted with caution[1146].

To conclude, post-LBO performance after going-public is not granted to be negative. Much more, it is highly dependent on the post-LBO governance structure implemented. In particular, the continuation of a close alignment of managers' with owners' interests through significant post-offering shareholdings is crucial. Further, active investors are important to maintain the quality and intensity of monitoring which is apparently beneficial to performance. Without close monitoring, performance is likely to decrease significantly and return to pre-buyout levels. High level of private control benefits in Germany make interest alignment and monitoring even more important. In addition, high level of family ownership in Germany has to be closely balanced with owners that are more objective in decision-making and participate less in private benefits. Further, post-LBO investors have to expect a high sensitivity of governance structure for former LBOs to performance than for normal IPOs. Finance researchers have disclosed that debt is less effective disciplining

1144 See Holthausen and Larcker 1996, pp. 328 - 329
1145 See Lloyd, Hand et al. 1987 and Parker 1988as quoted in Wright 1995, p. 464
1146 See Jalilvand and Switzer 2002, p. 7

management after exiting from the LBO. Still, debt will determine to a certain level the emphasis on efficiency. In the corollary, one would expect for the post-buyout performance of a going-public:

Hypothesis 28a: Company performance will decrease with a reduced debt leverage after the exit through a going-public.

Hypothesis 28c: Company performance will decrease with a reduced level of ownership concentration after the exit through a going-public.

Hypothesis 28d: Company performance will decrease with a reduced activity level of governance after the exit through a going-public.

Hypothesis 28f: Company performance will decrease with a reduced level of management shareholdings after the exit through a going-public.

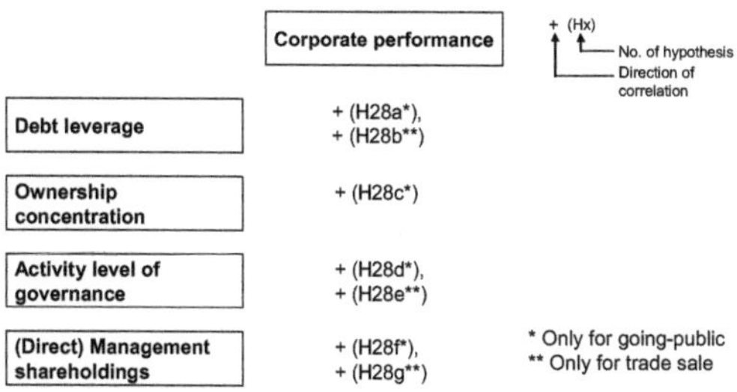

Figure 12: Changes in post-exit performance

5.3.5 Performance Development of a Buyout Exiting via Trade Sale

5.3.5.1 General Empirical Evidence related to a Trade Sale

Empirical research has much more been conducted for the performance development after acquisitions of former public companies, and, with some limitations, also after mergers[1147], than for former LBO. In a recent review of the surveys of the return to the target and acquirer company shareholders, Bruner concludes, from analyzing 130 publications, a short-term, material positive return[1148]. The short-term increase can be interpreted as the materialization of any control premiums the acquirer is willing

1147 In general, data related to the performance after mergers and acquisitions is rich. Nevertheless, empirical evidence corresponding to the performance development in a trade sale after an LBO that is long-term (at least 3 years), comparable (identical legal entity before and after the exit) and based on accountant information (financial statement as opposed to stock market) is very sparse, in particular with explanatory power for the German market. Bruner, for instance, reviews in 2001 130 studies related to M&A, Deepak et al. 41 studies in 1992, Murray et al. 10 studies in 1987, and Jensen and Ruback 16 studies in 1983.

1148 See Bruner 2001, p. 17. Representative studies on the return to target shareholders are Bradley, Desai et al. 1983, Lang, Stulz et al. 1989, Franks, Harris et al. 1991, Healy, Palepu et al. 1992, Kaplan and Weisbach 1992, and Loughran and Vijh 1997.

to pay that leads to wealth gains for the target shareholders. However, the question remains whether observed gains will correspond to future performance increases or result from information inefficiencies and wealth transfer to the disadvantage of the bidders.

Target shareholders seem to benefit from an acquisition. Bradley, Desai and Kim, for instance, report that in those cases where the bid fails and no subsequent transaction materializes, any excess returns to the target stock around the announcement disappear within five years[1149]. In the corollary, a tender offer seems to have a beneficial effect as operational synergies are raised and management disciplined. In addition, the return to former stock prices indicates that the acquisition does not reveal any superior information about the true value of the target. Loughran and Vijh test the cumulative abnormal return over five years for target shareholders who roll over their proceeds by investing in the acquirer stock. For the total sample, a positive and significant CAR is measured. In particular, cash based acquisitions gain the most value. Amongst acquisitions, tender offers generated higher returns than mergers. Although mergers gains are observed for the first two years, average return is not significant different from zero[1150]. Further, the relative size of acquirer to target is significant and serves as a proxy for anticipated efficiency gains. The larger the target is in relation to the acquirer, the smaller the returns are.

The majority of surveys investigate the performance development purely from the bidder's perspective, since nearly all targets are delisted. As such, the findings are of minor value to anticipate post-LBO performance. Studies conclude that aggregate, abnormal returns for bidder shareholders are essentially zero, indicating that M&A are neither creating nor destructing value[1151]. Jensen and Ruback, for instance, report insignificant positive returns following tender offers and significant underperformance after mergers[1152]. However, a number of researchers do not confirm a significant underperformance in the years after the acquisition[1153]. It should be not surprising that bidders apparently benefit less than the target. In most cases, the target is considerably smaller than the bidder, hence, the share of joint profit, e.g., by synergies, is much smaller and less significant.

1149 See Bradley, Desai et al. 1988, pp. 21 et seqq.

1150 Loughran and Vijh report some significant characteristics for the type of acquisition. Tender offers suggest higher returns than mergers (+97.3% in year 5), further, cash acquisitions are more successful than stock-based ones (+75.6%) (See Loughran and Vijh 1997, p. 1785)

1151 See the review by Bruner 2001, pp. 6 et seqq.

1152 See Jensen and Ruback 1983; further significant underperformance after the acquisition is reported by Asquith 1983, Agrawal, Jaffe et al. 1992, Loderer and Martin 1992, Rau and Vermaelen 1998 and Megginson, Morgan et al. 2002

1153 See Bradley and Jarrell 1988, Franks, Harris et al. 1991

Further, the relatedness of business positively drives performance. Montgomery and Singh examine the relative suitability of target and bidder. They report that acquisitions of related companies in term of product, market and technology achieve higher returns than unrelated[1154]. In addition, the gains are more likely to accrue to the target than to bidder shareholders. Some inconsistency on the evidence of relatedness can be dissolved when examining the relatedness of the underlying resources. Theory and evidence suggests that differences in resource allocation patterns offer valuable synergies. Complementary resources are argued to create unique and private synergy than similar resource base[1155].

An interesting hypothesis regarding the acquisition of strong cash flow companies is proposed by Smith and Kim. They argue that the acquisition of cash flow-generating former buyouts by slack-poor companies will provide required financial means to the acquirer[1156]. Data confirms the return of slack-poor bidders and high free-cash flow targets to be the highest (+16.9% versus +8.9% for total sample).

Limitations of stock price-based empirics for bidders' related performance improvements are challenged by research on actual accounting measures. Evidence on performance is inconclusive, with signs for both negative[1157] and positive[1158] performance development. However, some success factors can be extracted. The exchange of a weak performing management team significantly increases the likelihood of success. In the contrary, even a bad-performing management is powerful enough to withhold the best propositions from new owners[1159]. Further, if companies are successful after the acquisitions, the performance improvements are truly related to productivity increases, as opposed to cutbacks of expenses[1160]. An

---

1154 See Singh and Montgomery 1987, pp. 383 et seqq.; see also Shelton 1986, Lubatkin 1987

1155 See Harrison, Hitt et al. 1991, p. 187

1156 Smith and Kim refer to the underinvestment adressed by Myers and Majluf. Information asymmetry tends to lead to a lack of financial resources and an underinvestment (See Smith and Kim 1994, pp. 281 et seqq.)

1157 Ravenscraft and Scherer measure in the pre-acquisition period a target profit slightly inferior to industry (-0,97 percentage points in operating income to assets). After the acquisition, authors report a significant decrease of performance (-3.10 percentage points for tender offers). A significant part of the decrease, however, stems from the asset value writeups. See Ravenscraft and Scherer 1987, pp. 150 et seqq.

1158 Healy, Palepu and Ruback also seek to reveal the sources of any merger-related gains. They report, in contrast, significant post-merger improvements in operating cash flow of 3.2% for a five-year post-acquisition average. The increase is industry-adjusted and significant at the 5% (See Healy, Palepu et al. 1992, pp. 150 et seqq.). Parrino and Harris, covering acquisitions from the 1980s, report an increase of post-acquisition cash-flow-to-assets of 2.1%See Parrino and Harris 1999, pp. 92 et seqq.

1159 Ghosh tests whether weak performance prompts higher turnover of senior management. Managers with poor performance retain their jobs, indicating a weak effectiveness of the governance in place (See Ghosh 2001, p. 176). Parrino and Harris measure in the cases where a new management is appointed the highest gains. The authors explicitly accentuate the importance of the changes in corporate governance of monitoring the management (See Parrino and Harris 1999, p. 95)

1160 Healy, Palepu and Ruback test whether the performance increase observed are related to cutbacks of

overlap of businesses is also beneficial to the performance development[1161]. Furthermore, stock markets seem to anticipate correctly the actual performance changes reflected in the financial statement, as indicated by high correlations[1162]. Finally, acquired companies who are high performers contribute to performance of the acquirer[1163]. The intention to buy low profit or weak performing companies, in the light of their attractive price, and achieve a turnaround does apparently not succeed[1164]. In summary, some factors seem to be exogenous to the success of an acquisition, in particular the relatedness of business and the relative size. On the other hand, others factors are related to the caliber of management and management of the joint company. In line to the evidence of going-public, a qualified and aligned management is crucial to the performance development.

Again, data for the performance development of acquisitions in Germany is sparse. Surveys indicate a positive increase in share price for target shareholders[1165]. For bidders, post-acquisition performance differs, but in average indicates a slight decrease in performance[1166].

Management again plays a pivotal role to performance. Among the different owner identities, management-controlled companies achieve the highest returns in the post-acquisition period. Relatedness of businesses, in particular horizontal expansion, drives positive post-acquisition performance. However, there is no profound research on the development on basis of accounting performance. Considering the success factors for performance development, there are further characteristics for German companies. High cash flow does not prevent the acquirers to buy successfully underperforming companies and to achieve high returns. They outperform companies which are more restricted in their financial means and most

---

capital expenditure and R&D, but undoubtedly reject expense adjustments at the expense of the long-term viability (See Healy, Palepu et al. 1992, pp. 150 et seqq.). See also Ghosh 2001, pp. 162 et seqq.

1161 Healy, Palepu and Ruback report that performance improvements are significantly higher for companies with a high overlap of the line of businesses. (See Healy, Palepu et al. 1992, pp. 150 et seqq.).

1162 Healy, Palepu and Ruback correlate the changes in share price to the actual changes in accounting performance. They report a significant correlation, rejecting propositions of capital market inefficiencies in the pre-acquisition period (See Healy, Palepu et al. 1992, pp. 150 et seqq.)

1163 See Kusewitt 1985, p. 160-161

1164 See Kusewitt 1985, p. 160-161

1165 Buehner examines acquisitions that have taken place in Germany in the 1970s and 1980s. For the target shareholders, Buehner reports a positive development, with an increase of CAR of +12.7% 24 months after the announcement (See Bühner 1990, pp. 43 et seqq.). Gerke, Graz and Oerk also document positive and significant CARs for the target shareholders.

1166 Buehner measures a negative, average cumulative abnormal return of - 6.9% in the time period of 24 months after filing (See Bühner 1990, pp. 43 et seqq.). Boehmer and Loeffler report a positive, significant increase of the CAR of 1.44% for the bidder. However, the positive development can be referred to acquisition in period of strengthness of economic activity, whereas in periods of weaknesses, no significant increase can be found. See Böhmer and Löffler 1999, pp. 322-323

likely may be more diligent in the selection of their targets. Target companies benefit from banks as second or third largest shareholder at the acquirer. However, a bank as largest, influential shareholder produces the weakest post-acquisition performance[1167]. Further, research indicates a bias for weak-performing companies to pursue acquisitions[1168]. In addition, cross-borders acquisitions achieve higher cumulative abnormal returns than national acquisitions[1169]. Among cross-border acquisitions, those with strategic intent of horizontal expansion, e.g., in terms of products and technologies, achieve the highest CAR, while vertical and non-related acquisitions show negative CARs[1170]. In many cases, management conducts non-value creating acquisitions in fields not core to the business, what is penalized by the stock market.

Author	Year	Sample	Investigation period	Geo-graphical focus	Observed time period in days [d] or months [m]	Cumulative abnormal returns
1. Return for target firms						
Bühner	1990	9	1973 to 1985	Germany	t-24m to t+24m	+27.1%[a]
Gerke, Garz, Oerke	1995	105	1987 to 1992	Germany	t-40d to t+40d	Positive[c]
2. Return for bidding firms, German studies						
Bühner	1990	95	1973 to 1985	Germany	t-24m to t+24m	-9.4%[a]
Bühner	1992	39	1973 to 1987	Germany	t-24m to t+24m	+4.1%[ns]
Gerke, Garz, Oerke	1995	105	1987 to 1992	Germany	t-40d to t+40d	Neutral[ns]
Boehmer	1998	715	1984 to 1995	Germany	t-10d to t+2d	+0.5%[b]
Boehmer, Loefller	1999	672	1980 to 1993	Germany	t-30d to t+10d	+0.6%[ns]

[a] Change significant at the 1% level
[b] Change significant at the 5% level
[c] Change significant at the 10% level
[ns] Not significant at at least the 10% level
[ni] No information about significance

Table 17: Overview of (long-term) performance studies related to trade sales in Germany

5.3.5.2 Changes in Corporate Governance and Performance after a Trade Sale

Until now, no surveys at knowledge to the author have analyzed the implications of the ownership structure, in particular the identity of the owner and the level of

1167 Boehmer examines the event-related effect of an acquisition on the holdings that are widerspread in Germany. In particular, he tests the effect of bidders' ownership structures and bank control to assess the effect of external monitoring. In general, acquisitions are beneficial to the bidding company, but not to the surrounding business group. Banks as a second or third largest stakeholder increase decision quality and spur performance of share price. As largest shareholder their ownership correlates with the weakest post-acquisition performance. See Böhmer 1998, pp. 23 et seqq.

1168 In contrast to the US-based studies, returns are negative in the two years period preceeding the acquisition. To proof whether the decrease correlates with actual performance, Buehner reviews the development of accounting figures of the bidder. The EBT-to-total-equity decreases slighty, but not significantly. The EBIT-to-total-capital, however, declines significantly in the six years period after the filing. See Bühner 1990, pp. 53 et seqq.. Different to Healy, Palepu and Ruback, the CAR does not correlate significantly with the EBT-to-total-equity or EBIT-to-total-capital, respectively (See Bühner 1990, p. 61)

1169 Amongst the cross-borders acquistions, those with other European companies are higher valued than acquisitions with US based companies. See Bühner 1992, pp. 445 et seqq.

1170 Gerke, Graz and Oerk measure that only horizontal acquisitions achieve a positive CAR, while vertical acquisitions and non-related acquisitions (towards a conglomerate) are penalized by the stock market (See Gerke 1995). See also Bühner 1992, pp. 454 et seqq.

concentration, for the performance development exiting a LBO structure through a trade sale. General evidence related to changes in ownership structure are: (i) concentration of ownership is beneficial, different owner identities will (ii) display varying level of monitoring and will (iii) seek to incorporate different levels of private control benefit. Not all empirical evidence has reasoned that ownership concentration is beneficial to the company[1171]. In particular, ownership by a single institution will restrict liquidity and potential sources of capital[1172]. However, the larger the company is, the less is the likelihood of capital restrictions.

Buehner questions for German transactions whether post-acquisition performance is determined by ownership concentration. He differentiates owner-controlled (>50% of shareholdings), limited owner-controlled (between 25% and 50%) and management-controlled companies (<25%). From a capital market perspective, owner-controlled show the weakest performance (with a CAR of -18.3%), whereas limited owner-controlled companies suffer from a less severe decline (CAR of -5.2%) and the management-controlled companies even gain returns (CAR of +3.5%). However, owner-controlled companies have the highest relative profitability based on actual accounting numbers. From pre- to post-acquisition, both EBT-to-total-equity and EBIT-to-total-capital decline significantly. The limited owner-controlled companies bear similar losses, however, not statistical significant. The third group, the manager-controlled companies, performs best with a significant increase of EBT-to-total-equity. Buehner does not find a systematic acquisition strategy, e.g., focusing on horizontal or vertical acquisitions, that allows to explain the differences in the performance. One of the reasons, however, for the weak stock price performance may lie in the limited interest by the owner-controlled companies in an increasing share price. They may want to participate in any capital increase necessary for the acquisitions and, therefore, seek to keep the share price down.

Post-exit performance will also depend on the identity of the owner, regardless of exit chosen. In other words, the location of control rights can be a more important determinant of the degree of control exerted than ownership concentration.

One would expect that family founders and individuals holding large shares demonstrate an high interest in the success of the company than investors for which the company is just one investment in their portfolio. As detailed in the introductory chapters, family-ownership in Germany is common, and in general not more or less successful than other types of ownership. The most successful companies are

---

1171 See the detailed review in chapter B2.1.2

1172 See Pagano and Roell 1998

reported to limit the ownership of family to 25 to 50% of shareholdings. Further, the ownership structure for successful companies includes a second strong blockholder, for instance a financial institution, who provides monitoring and restricts the majority owner from private benefits. However, it is unclear whether these results also hold for the significant change of ownership. In many cases, the family investor is related to or identical to the family founder, and steps into management. It is though not unlikely that the change into the LBO structure is the ultimate lever to reduce agency costs and remove organizational slack tolerated by the former owner. Whether the re-installation of the family is beneficial depends on the general monitoring mechanisms in place.

For industrial buyers a prediction of performance development is even more complex. First, any strategic or operational changes to the target will depend on the ultimate ownership structure of the industrial buyer, what may be any owner, e.g., a family, a bank or a dispersed shareholder based. Second, the high level of cross-holdings makes a direct identification of the true source of control difficult. Third, the high levels of voting rights make it difficult to measure the real strength of the owner. Empirical evidence, for instance for large US corporates, indicates that business units may underperform to the degree that the internal capital markets do not function[1173].

In this respect, investors without a personal interest may be better for corporate performance. Banks can be such unbiased investors. If monitoring turns more inexpensive, the company performance should advance. However, the positive role of hausbanks in Germany is largely related to the historic weakness of the German equity market. It is though doubtful that a bank will step in as an acquirer of a former buyout, since they are not used to act as an active owner with significant monitoring.

To conclude, a trade sale will yield significant changes to the ownership structure. First, management shareholdings will in most case decrease significantly and, in the corollary, increase the agency costs[1174]. On basis of the general evidence, the management again plays a pivotal role to performance, whereas management-controlled companies achieve the highest returns. Second, ownership will presumably remain concentrated, hence offering enough incentive for an intense monitoring. However, performance will depend on the specific utility function of the

1173 See Lang and Stulz 1994, Shin and Stulz 1998

1174 Kaplan reports that for purchased buyouts, the avaerga insider shareholdings account up to 6.6%, whereas management keeps 39.0% of shareholdings when the former buyout remain public (See Kaplan 1991, p. 305.

owner. In the case of a private person or a family, the level of private control benefits will increase. For a larger corporation, performance development will depend on the overall corporate policy followed by the acquirer's senior management and supervisory board. Third, debt has been reported to be less effective in the post-buyout period for a going-public. This is to some degree related to the presence of the proceeds of the offering. In the context of a trade sale, the continuation of a debt service will most probably bond more effectively management, even more as surveys indicate that leverage remains high. Debt will substitute for the likely lack of managerial shareholdings, and, hence, will reduce agency costs. Further, post-exit performance will depend on the relatedness of businesses, with a positive bias to horizontal expansion as opposed to vertical and to unrelated expansion. In summary, the post-LBO performance is expected to develop as:

Hypothesis 28b: Company performance will decrease with a reduced level of debt leverage after the exit through a trade sale.

Hypothesis 28e: Company performance will decrease with a reduced activity level of governance after the exit through a trade sale.

Hypothesis 28g: Company performance will decrease with a reduced level of management shareholdings after the exit through a trade sale.

C Empirical Part

1 Research Methodology

1.1 Identification of Case Studies

Criteria for identifying target companies

The initial sample consisted of all LBOs in Germany where buyout investors had exited as (dominant) owner before 2004. This ensured a post-exit investigation period of at least three complete fiscal years in respect to the data consolidation at the end of 2007. Since the LBO governance structure is required to be decisive on management's objectives and corporate policy-making, a minimum holding period of three years by the buyout investors was demanded. Hence, the companies at the earliest entered into the buyout in 2001. As a precautionary measure, the author also cuts the sample to an earliest exit in 1999, since one would expect that the quality and consistency of data, in particular the self-assessment by management, deteriorates with increasing time. In the next step, the sample was adjusted to those buyouts that exited either through a trade sale or through a going-public. Finally, those cases where the buyout investors continued to hold a significant share of equity were deleted.

Sample building

The primary sources for identifying potential private equity-sponsored buyouts formed the transaction databases of Initiative Europe[1175]. For reasons of comparability, only LBOs in industry sectors with significant performance improvement in operations were selected (see Figure 13)[1176]. Further, very small buyouts in terms of revenue size where excluded, as they face different restructuring challenges during an LBO and only apply a subset of the levers in strategy and operations as introduced in chapter B1[1177].

Unfortunately, the sample were not complete in respect to the occurrence of an exit. Consequently, all relevant LBOs as identified in the databases were screened on their status of ownership by public information and direct contact to ensure that no exit

---

1175 In the available database of Initiative Europe, the documentation of German, private equity-sponsored buyout transactions starts in 1988.

1176 Financial services, pharma and health care, real estate, software& computer services, and general retailers were excluded.

1177 Threshold for excluding LBOs was a revenue size of EUR 25 Million.

was overlooked[1178]. Various reasons factored out potential candidates for the investigation: (i) unbroken ownership by buyout investors; (ii) pass-over to another buyout investor in a secondary buyout; (iv) reestablishment of ownership by management through a buy-back[1179]; (v) merger of the former legally independent LBO with the acquiring company; (vi) dissolution of the former LBO through massive divestments and asset sales. The author found that not all LBOs were recorded in the reviewed transaction databases[1180]. Hence, further sources were consulted to find supplementary candidates, e.g., published lists of exits by buyout investors[1181].

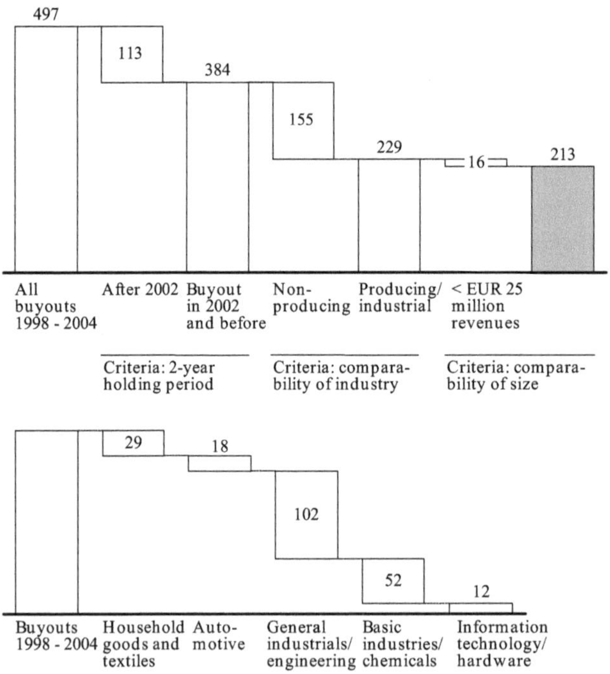

Figure 13: Derivation target sample group by Initiative Europe

1178 Admittedly, not all firms were willing to inform about their current ownership status. In the case of ambiguous data on their ownership, the author left the buyouts in the sample of potential candidates.

1179 For a general overview of the development of exit channels of buyouts refer to the overview in chapter B5.3.1.

1180 On the one hand, a significant number of buyout are private-to-private and therefore not known to the public. On the other hand, there is no regulatory requirement to report a leveraged buyout transaction to public authorities. In the corollary, both smaller and private transactions are likely to be left out by the databases.

1181 The author reviewed the published investment portfolios of all associated members of the BVK.

The consolidated list of candidates was the basis to find participants for a detailed case study. After establishing a first contact, the companies were reviewed on the initial criteria of changes in governance structure at the exit. Not surprisingly, willingness to participate in the investigation was low due to required disclosure of confidential information and to the controversial public debate on the role of buyout investors[1182]. Nevertheless, the author is grateful that three companies, Wincor Nixdorf, Techem and Trevira, representing two going-public and one trade sale, were willing to take part.

1.2 Measures for Analyses

The review of the companies surpassing the buyout cycle will require to record the corresponding level of analysis, of which four have been delineated in the basic model: (1) post-exit changes in governance structure; (2) the effect of a new governance structure on management objectives; (3) the effect of a new governance structure on managerial activities and applied levers, both strategic and operational; and finally, (4) the effect of a new governance (post-exit) structure on corporate performance[1183] . Hence, measures have to be defined that allow a longitudinal test. Further, the case study analysis will be judgmental since no statistical tests can be applied. The author presents all implications with the full evidence to allow independent assessment of the findings.

During the case study analysis, the author will refer to three time periods: (i) before the LBO, the period prior to the transition into a LBO structure; (ii) during the LBO, the period between the company's buyout and exit (t to x); (iii) post-exit, the period after the exit (x, x+1, x+2, x+3, x+4[1184]).

1.2.1 Measures for Corporate Governance

The governance structure is decomposed into four determining factors as outlined in the introductory part: debt leverage, ownership concentration, activity level of governance, and management shareholdings. These factors are measured throughout the buyout cycle, and will grant capturing the transaction in the governance structure at the exit.

To quantify debt leverage, all existing bank debt facilities are tracked, both by amount, by residual term, and by any specific covenants. Cash items are

---

1182 See the introductory discussion in chapter A1.1.

1183 A detailed illustration of the basis model is provided in the introductory chapter B1.

1184 In the case of Trevira, data is only available up to year three (x+3) post-exit.

supplemented to derive the net bank debt of the company. The leverage indicators net debt to EBIDTA and equity to total capital are supplemented for a relative comparison of the level of indebtedness. The indicators concede analyzing the actual leverage and financial distress the company is currently facing.

Ownership concentration is measured by shareholdings of buyout investors and other co-investors. For the post-exit period, all notable (non free-float) shareholders (above 5% share) are listed to extract the level of ownership concentration. Further, the author notes the identity and related type of investor, in particular to differ between long-term value investor as opposed to short-term hedge fund investor.

To estimate the activity level of governance of the respective investors, parameters covering both the supervisory board, the frequency of monitoring, as well as the involvement level are measured as listed in Table 18. Further, the author measures the relative shareholdings as percentage of stock held by the CEO, other board members, non-board level management, as well as other employees of the company. In addition, any share related to stock option scheme and other stock-based compensation programs are revised.

Constituents of governance	Measures
Debt leverage	Bank debt: total Bank debt: residual term up to 1 year Bank debt: residual term between 1 and 5 years Bank debt: residual term more than 5 years Cash items Net debt to EBITDA Equity to total capital
Onwershp concentration, equity shareholdings	Shareholdings of buyout investors Shareholdings of other investors Shareholdings of institutional investors
Activity level of governance	Composition of supervisory board Skill profile of supervisory board Number of supervisory board meetings Extent strategic control/ financial control Usage of performance indicators Involvement in management board appointment Involvement in operational issues
(Direct) management shareholdings, employee shareholdings	Shareholdings of management Shareholdings of employees Shares related to stock option schemes

Table 18: Measures for the corporate governance constituents

1.2.2 Measures for Management Objectives

Emphasis on efficiency is operationalized by the extent of cost control, measured by the emphasis on (gross) profit margin, profit, and cash flow generation. Further, existence and importance of improvement programs and unpopular measures such as asset disposals, layoffs or decisive changes of core business processes are recorded. The author further separately measures the contribution in monitoring and advising by the owner for efficiency-related issues.

The emphasis on entrepreneurial growth is measured by the ambition for sales growth, by the importance of market share and by the risk affinity altered over the buyout cycle. The author further reviewes whether the decision criteria to investments change. Observations on the activity level of encouragement of the investors towards entering into new markets and bringing new products to market are also recorded.

1.2.3 Measures for Value Creation Levers

Operations and Production

For the operational productivity, the first indicators reviewed is the development of the number of employees and the corresponding total personnel costs including social benefits plan and other supplementary costs. The core indicators of financial performance (see subsequent chapter) are then divided by the number of employees, hence, enabling the track the productivity development over the buyout cycle. The preliminary analysis indicates that the operating cash flow has to be eliminated by any net working capital movements. Otherwise, the non-operations related changes in working capital would considerably dilute the explanatory power of this indicator. Additional qualitative assessments will cover any considerable improvement measures and initiatives conducted. Asset productivity is measured by relating the core indicators of financial performance to the operating assets. Operating assets are calculated as sum of operating working capital and fixed assets[1185]. In addition, the development of the asset base, differentiated by fixed assets (PP&E) and intangibles assets in general is tracked. Qualitative assessments elucidating improvement measures and initiatives will be recorded. For outsourcing and offshoring, the major indicator is the share of COGS (costs of purchased goods and services) to sales. Further indicators to be reviewed are the share of raw material and direct labor to sales. In addition, the change in the production footprint and sourcing network, in particular the number of locations and volume of production outside of Germany, is revised. The efficiency with which working capital is managed is reviewed by measuring the share of inventory and trade payable to COGS as well as the share of trade receivables to sales. The resulting net working capital is reviewed in comparison to sales over the entire buyout cycle. Companies will in addition be asked about changes in the policy of receivable management, e.g., the existence of

---

1185 See Koller 2004, p. 165 et seqq.

dunning blocks, and in any measures to minimize inventory, e.g., by reducing lead times.

Administration and Overhead

Overhead productivity will be measured by the share of expenses related to administration, in particular SG&A to total sales, and by company-specific productivity indicators adjusted to the individual business setup, e.g., new contracts per sales employee or the quality index of customer service. The author will also document what kind of best-practices may have been introduced. For hierarchical complexity, the case analysis will record any changes to the number of hierarchy levels. Furthermore, complexity will be measured by the extent of delegation and level of autonomy the company concedes its managers and employees. The complexity has to be adjusted by growth of the business. In addition, management control systems will be closely reviewed. First, the type of reports used over the buyout cycle will be recorded. Second, the related frequency of reporting will be documented. In particular, it will be of interest to understand to what degree reports measure any cash flow-related items after the exit. Third, it will be of interest to understand how risk in the different business functions is reported and how it is dealt with as part of the management controlling.

Strategy

To capture changes in strategy positioning, three measures are recorded: (1) relative importance in the core strategy dimensions; (2) the width of positioning; and (3) the resource base with its respective fit to the market environment. The core dimensions picture the choice between market leadership, cost leadership, and innovation leadership, to name a few. The width captures any choices between the poles of a niche as opposed to a mass-market position. Finally, an important dimension is to measure the strategic fit as defined as the suitability of resource bases with the company's competitive environment. For a trade sale, it will be necessary to compare further the strategic fit between acquirer and target company in terms of the mutual resource base. The process of strategy formulation is likewise expected to alter after the exit, and, hence, will also be recorded. The process will be measured in terms of the existence and nature of a formalized planning process and in terms of the extent to which employees below the senior management level are involved. Beyond the strategy position, the level of diversification is of particular interest. The basic measure will be the number of businesses and segments, respectively, whereby the author will differentiate between the number of core businesses, of related and of unrelated businesses.

Innovation

With regards to the R&D spending and efficiency, the indicators reviewed are R&D budget and the raio of budget to (respective) sales. Additional indicators to capture the R&D output, e.g., the number of patent applications and awards, will round the analysis and be compared with budget invested. Further qualitative observations, e.g., on improvements in the development processes and cross-functional cooperation, will be supplemented. It will be of further interest to understand any changes in the focus of the R&D program.

Market Development

The materialization of the growth strategy will be measured in the dimensions growth of domestic and growth o non-domestic markets. Besides growth rates in the respective markets and business segments, the development of market share and implied position will be recorded. It will be also of interest to understand the number of markets served, the number of international subsidiaries installed, and extent of resources (in particular number of employees) placed. Analysis will seek to understand how the customer service is organized both in the domestic and in the non-domestic markets, and to what extent the company relies upon partnerships.

Human Resources

Change in the emphasis of the development of human resources will be recorded by different indicators. Firstly, the number and extent of programs installed will be tracked. Further, the extent of appraisals and of individual coaching will be reviewed. The analysis will include the review of agreements between the company and its workforce, e.g., part-time programs and pension arrangements. Composition of board and mgmt. turnover will be closely tracked. Of particular interest is the skill profile represented on the managing board and the board size itself. Finally, the compensation scheme beyond the managerial co-ownership is documented.

It will be intriguing to depict any changes in basic salary and in variable compensation. In particular, the analysis will seek to understand any modifications to the variable component and respective underlying measurables, e.g., sales growth EBIT, ROIC and others.

Levers of value creation	Measures	Availability
Operational productivity	Number of employees	Te, TR, W
	Total wages &. Salaries,	Te, TR, W
	Average wage &. salaries per employee	Te, TR, W
	Sales per employee	Te, TR, W
	EBIT per employee	Te, TR, W
	Operating cash flow per employee	Te, TR, W
	Free cash flow per employee	Te, TR, W
	Operating cash flow pre working capital per	Te, TR, W
Asset productivity	PP&E	Te, TR, W
	Intangible assets	Te, TR, W
	Total operating assets	Te, TR, W
	Sales to operating assets	Te, TR, W
	Operating profit to operating assets	Te, TR, W
	Operating cash flow to operating assets	Te, TR, W
	Free cash flow to operating assets	Te, TR, W
	Operating cash flow pre working capital to operating assets	Te, TR, W
	Return on invested capital (ROIC)	Te, TR, W
Outsourcing and offshoring	Raw material to sales	Te, TR, W
	Costs of purchased goods and services to	Te, TR, W
	Direct labor costs to sales	Te, TR, W
Working capital	Inventories (absolute, as % of COGS)	Te, TR, W
	Trade payables (absolute, % of COGS)	Te, TR, W
	Trade receivables (absolute, as% of sales)	Te, TR, W
	Total working capital (absolute, % of sales)	Te, TR, W
	Collection period	Te, TR, W
	Credit period	Te, TR, W
Overhead productivity	Sales productivity	Te, W

Levers of value creation	Measures	Availability
Hierarchical complexity	Number of hierarchical levels	Te, TR, W
Management control systems	Number of reports	Te, TR, W
	Number of cash flow-based reports	Te, TR, W
Strategy position	Dimensions: market, innovation, cost, etc.	Te, TR, W
	Width: standard/ mass market, niche, etc.	Te, TR, W
	Fit: resource base, market environment	Te, TR, W
Strategy formulation	Formalized process yes/ no	Te, TR, W
	Level of involvement	Te, TR, W
Diversification and scope	Number of core business	Te, TR, W
	Number of related businesses	Te, TR, W
	Number of unrelated businesses	Te, TR, W
R&D spending and efficiency	R&D expenses	Te, TR, W
	R&D expenses to total sales	Te, TR, W
	R&D expenses per patent	W
Market development	Growth domestic markets	Te, TR, W
	Growth international markets	Te, TR, W
	Number of international subsidiaries	Te, W
	Employees located in international markets	Te, W
Human resources	Number of programs installed	Te, TR, W
	Differentiation of programs	Te, TR, W
Top-management turnover	Number of changes in management board	Te, TR, W
	Skill profile of management board	Te, TR, W
	Size of board	Te, TR, W
Pay-for-performance	Base salary level	Te, TR, W
	Extent of pay-for-performance	Te, W

Te: available for case study Techem
TR: available for case study Trevira
W: available for case study Wincor

Table 19: Measures for levers of value creation

1.2.4 Measures for Performance Development

Due to periods of private ownership, the author refers to accounting-based measures, even though share price development for the two IPO cases is in addition analyzed. Due to the differentiated analysis sought for, the author assembles a series of measures, similar to the leading previous post-LBO research[1186]. The analysis of performance has thereby two objectives. First, the case study examines the post-exit performance against the company itself, and in particular against the performance during buyout period. Second, the analysis seeks to relate the performance against its industry to measure whether the company under- or outperformed its peer group.

Annual revenue growth indicates to what degree the company is able to increase its revenue base. Growth development will have to be differentiated between growth nurtured by acquisition, by organic growth or belittled by divestments. Further, growth momentum will be revised against general economic development and specific industry environment the observed company is operating in. In comparison with margin and cash flow development, growth per se yields less information about performance development given is exposure to management discretion.

Gross profit is the difference between revenues and all costs directly related to the production of products and provision of services, respectively. These costs include manufacturing expenses such as raw material, labor, costs of bought-in services, and direct attributable selling costs. However, the costs not directly related and variable to making the product, such as SG&A costs, as well as R&D, are excluded. The exact definition depends upon the industry the company is operating in. A comparison within the industry peer group indicates the efficiency with which the company its manufacturing. The operating profit is the difference between revenues and all costs directly and indirectly related to making the products or providing the service, respectively. It includes depreciation and amortization, though excludes income and expenditure from non-recurring or discontinued activities. It further excludes interest payments and taxes. On an industry base, the profit allows to compare both the operational performance as well as the depreciation policy, which may alter if the company follows a different investment cycle or has a higher asset intensity.

Cash flow from operations is regarded as cash generated from operations. Any costs related to investments on capital items or investments in securities are excluded. This indicator facilitates the comparison of cash generation with the the peer group. Further, any accounting accruals can be eliminated. The author will in some

1186 See Holthausen and Larcker 1996, Bruton, Keels et al. 2002 occasions review the cash flow from operations pre any net working capital movements to eliminate the effect of changes in working capital management. In the second step, cash flow from investment is measured. Besides payments for long-term assets a company needs in order to make and sell its products, this cash flow will also include any investments related to the purchase or disposal of assets and companies. Even though this indicator may be studied on an industry base, it is in particular of interest to analyze whether a company on a stand alone base increases or decreases its investment intensity over time. Free cash flow is derived as sum of cash flow from operations and from investments, equaling the remaining cash to serve the claims of both debt and equity holders. As previously outlined, free cash flow indicates to what degree management is bounded by pre-determined cash flow for the operation of the business, for (regular) investments and for interest payments.

Category of performance development	Measures
Sales	In % annual growth Industry-adj. annual growth Annual growth adj. to buyout average Sales development indexed to last FY prior exit Industry-adj. sales dev. indexed to last FY prior exit
Gross margin	In % of total sales Industry-adj. gross margin Gross margin adj. to buyout average Gross profit indexed to last FY prior exit Industry-adj.gross profit indexed to last FY prior exit
Net operating profit	In % of total sales Industry-adj. net operating profit to sales Net operating profit adj. to buyout average Indexed to last year prior exit Industry-adj. net operating profit to last FY prior exit
Operating cash flow	In % of total sales Industry adj. operating cash flow to sales Operating cash flow adj. to buyout average Indexed to last year prior exit Industry-adj. operating cash flow to last FY prior exit
Free cash flow	In % of total sales Industry adj. free cash flow to sales Free cash flow to sales to buyout average Indexed to last year prior exit Industry-adj. free cash flow to last FY prior exit

Table 20: Overview of performance indicators

In terms of productivity of the underlying asset base, the author further analyzes the invested capital and implied return on invested capital (ROIC). Invested capital equals the operating assets, consisting of operating working capital, fixed assets, intangible assets, and net other long-term operating assets, minus the operating liabilities[1187]. Out of the invested capital, an operating profit is generated defined as

1187 See Koller 2004, p. 165 et seqq.

net operating profit less adjusted taxes (NOPLAT)[1188]. NOPLAT equals the total income generated from the aforementioned capital base (accounting for the liabilities) available to all investors. As indicated, the author will assess the performance of the case study companies using a series of measurables. First, the unadjusted measure of the performance of the observed company is examined. Further, industry-adjusted performance is measured, which controls for time and industry-adjusted effects by subtracting the contemporaneous mean performance of the companies[1189]. To account for different company size, both gross profit, operating profit and outlined cash flow items will be reviewed on a ratio to sales[1190]. Further, the metrics will be in selected cases referred against size-related indicators such as number of employees. The industry sample group was constructed on basis of comparable companies with the same four digit SIC code and consisted between 6 and 8 companies.

For the post-exit period, analysis is complemented by an comparison with the buyout average. The author introduces an indexed performance development, which allows accommodating for any cumulative effects and potential time lags. An industry-adjusted indicator is added to alleviate for any exogenous factors.

1.3 Data Collection

Multiple sources of information were addressed and consolidated in a cumulative, iterative manner. In the first step, all publicly available information were reviewed, including financial reports and statements, investor reviews and analysts' reports, press releases and articles, industry reports and information from competitors. The company was approached and asked to provide additional important documents such as articles of association, auditor reports, bylaws for management and supervisory board protocols, as well as internal studies and presentations. The information was consolidated into a draft of the descriptive part and preliminary hypotheses formulated. In the following, multiple interviews were conducted with

---

1188 See Koller 2004, p. 174 et seqq.

1189 The measures of the industry sample are calendarized to the fiscal year end of the case study company.

1190 The author has chosen to omit asset base as deflator and instead refer to total sale. During the LBO, assets are often written up since the buyout price exceeded the book value of assets at the time of the entry into the LBO. If write-up of assets and creation of goodwill exceeds the extent of that activity of the industry, performance is biased toward poorer performance by the LBO. Further, the industry sample span various countries and accounting regimes, and therefore may value congenerous assets differently. Holthausen and Larcker argue that the deflation by sales removes the effects of efficiencies from the performance measure that management might have derived frombeing able to increase sales without a corresponding increase in assets. However, they report that their results on basis of a deflation by assets are qualitatively similar. See Holthausen and Larcker 1996, p.305

the company's management and selected employees. Management often contributed only limited insight beyond the post-LBO period given the turnover in the composition of the managing board. Additional interviews with selected employees, in particular from the strategy, planning and marketing departments broadened the information base and closed any hiatuses. Finally, former buyout investors were interviewed. The observations were discussed and observation of governance and monitoring refined. In two of three case studies, buyout investors stayed for a longer time on the supervisory board, and, therefore, provided additional observations to the post-LBO period. The case study was presented to the company and top management. The triangulation from multiple data source allowed refining the substantiation of the constructs and hypotheses.

2 Case Study: Wincor Nixdorf

2.1 Case Description

2.1.1 Company Development before the Buyout

Computer pioneer Heinz Nixdorf founded in 1952 Paderborn-based Nixdorf Computer AG, which later became Wincor Nixdorf. Nixdorf manufactured in the 1960s and 1970s computer hardware. By the mid-1980s, Nixdorf had made his company Europe's fourth-largest computer group, a pioneer of IT solutions for the banking and retail industry. The company was sold in 1990 in the wake of Nixdorf's death to Siemens which de-listed it and renamed it Siemens Nixdorf Informationssysteme AG. But by the early 1990s, Siemens Nixdorf's banking and retail business units were booking losses. The banking unit could not compete with competitors like Diebold and NCR on pricing for its automated teller machines (ATMs) despite stable customer demand. Similarly, the retail unit could not compete on cost but its competitors too were loosing money. To address the problems and return the company to profitability, Siemens in 1991 appointed a new management team headed by Karl-Heinz Stiller and Eckard Heidloff[1191]. The new management's restructuring turned Siemens Nixdorf around after two more years of annual losses of DM 300 million in 1992 and 1993[1192]. This success focused top management on the need for tight cost controls across the spectrum from product design to production and distribution. The company continued to grow until 1997 by expanding into development of software solutions for banking and retail hardware. Siemens in 1998 formed as an independent subsidiary Siemens Nixdorf Retail and Banking Systems GmbH focused exclusively on the banking and retail sector.

By 1999, the Siemens-Nixdorf Retail and Banking Systems GmbH was up for sale. Siemens' expansion into several new businesses had overburdened management's capacity and led to deteriorating performance. Poor financial results in 1998 prompted Siemens CEO Heinrich von Pierer to draft a ten-point-restructuring program aimed at enhancing profitability and restoring strategic focus. The company began divesting itself of non-core businesses, including Siemens Nixdorf Retail and

---

1191 New CEO Karl-Heinz Stiller had been Siemens Nixdorf's senior vice president of production while new CFO Eckard Heidloff, was the unit's head of group accounting.

1192 The new management changed attitudes towards the development of Nixdorf products. Instead of designing machines based on the company's best engineering skills, target costs were defined to achieve market prices. This set the frame for allowable costs for single modules and components. It also reduced the product portfolio to serve profitably only the core markets of banking and retail. These steps led to leaner, more market-oriented products able to earn profit despite competition from NCR and Diebold.

Banking Systems. Nixdorf's top management sought for independence and entrepreneurial freedom and warned that it would leave if the unit were sold to a strategic investor. The entry of buyout investors, however, was a welcomed instrument to ensure entrepreneurship.

Siemens Nixdorf's growth prospects prompted KKR and Goldman Sachs to initiate discussions with senior management. The company had doubled its turnover to EUR 1.3 billion between 1993 and 1998. It had more than 3,400 employees in 21 subsidiaries across the globe. Nixdorf ranked third in the market for electronic point of sale systems (ePOS) and fourth in the market for ATMs. Nonetheless, it lacked a strong market footprint outside of Germany because it had failed to capitalize on its growth potential in high-margin solutions and services business. Management under Karl-Heinz Stiller and Eckhard Heidloff continued however to meet its financial targets. This coupled with its growth potential made Nixdorf a highly attractive LBO target. KKR Managing Director Ned Gilhuly said Nixdorf represented the opportunity "to acquire an established business with excellent management and attractive growth prospects. We are very impressed with the current management's achievements, and we look forward to working with them to grow this business on an international scale". KKR London Managing Director Johannes Huth later added that "the decisive factor in considering this investment was the know-how and the strong reputation that the company has developed in information systems and solutions for the retail and banking industries". Frankfurt-based Goldman Sachs Managing Director Alexander Dibelius, who was the investment bank's point man on the deal, commented: "It is our objective to become the leading systems and solutions provider in the retail and banking industries by growing the company, both organically and through acquisitions." Value creation expected to result from growing revenue growth with a stronger international presence. The buyout investors expected additional, profitable growth from the entry into services industry. They further intended to achieve efficiency improvements in operations and administration after the carve-out from Siemens.

CEO Stiller shared KKR and Goldman Sachs's vision of untapped potential for global expansion and market share expansion: "Given the fact that we have grown much faster than the market, our desire to be the world's number 1 player in the field of information systems for the retail and banking industry is achievable," Stiller said. KKR European Fund and Goldman Sach's GS Capital Partners III, Limited Partner agreed to acquire together with management 100% of Siemens Nixdorf Retail and

Banking Systems GmbH (see Table 31), as of October 1, 1999 for EUR 736 million on a debt and cash-free basis[1193]. KKR acted as lead investor. The new company was incorporated as Wincor Nixdorf, Wincor standing for "winning" and "core competence".

2.1.2 Company Development during the Buyout Period

2.1.2.1 Efficiency-Focused Management Activities

Although management returned the company to profitability, room for additional improved efficiency remained. To reduce operations and administration costs, management introduced its 'ProImprove' cost saving program while the buyout investors continued to expect value creation to come largely from entrepreneurial growth. .

Management reconfigured manufacturing and assembly processes at the Paderborn according to the principles of lean manufacturing. Workflow production flow replaced lot production. Standardization of work tasks was increased, which enabled better labor utilization. The transition to workflow production spanned the second half of the LBO and continued in the post-exit period. Designers and product engineers redesigned the product architectures of the main product groups to broaden the usage of standardized modules. Engineers and designers reviewed all components in terms of their functional benefit to cost-ratio and by best of benchmark. Management also closely reviewed the value stream and increased the share of bought-in-material. For some lower value components, combined cost of material and labor was higher than external purchase[1194]. However, during the 2003 upswing, the share of external purchases increased to overcome capacity bottlenecks. The introduction of a 'strategic purchasing' department highlighted the increasing importance of optimized purchasing. Purchasing terms were reviewed and partly re-negotiated. Moreover, coordination of the supply chain between different production facilities, for instance in Singapore, was improved and allowed more smooth production.

Operation managers and engineers considerably reduced complexity in production and development processes. The improvement program covered over 50 projects.

1193 The purchase price of EUR 736 Million included net assets (179), product expertise (206.7), goodwill (351.6), negative goodwill (1.3) and other assets (41.1). The amount of 41.1million was written-off in full in fiscal year 1999/2000. The remaining amounts were amortized over a period of two to ten years for product expertise and 20 years for goodwill. In the case of product know-how, the costs of amortization were recorded under cost of sales, while goodwill fell under other operating expenses.

1194 As a result, the share of bought in services increased between 2000 and 2004 (see Table 22).

The 'kaizen' program served to institutionalize continuous improvement. Operational productivity in terms of operating profit per employee improved considerably (see Table 23). Management in 2003 expanded production capacity based on higher productivity and introduction of a two-shift production in hardware assembly. Nonetheless, the share of employees in production related to total employees decreased from 40.3% in 2000 to 29.1% in 2003 (see Table 21). Plastic replaced expensive, non-crucial steel parts to lower raw material costs. Productivity of the fixed asset base also benefited from re-arrangements of production equipment and modest investments in modernization (see Table 24). Management did not embark on major asset disposals or write-offs during the buyout. The productivity improvements in operations and administration notwithstanding, the number of total employees nearly doubled from 3.400 in 1999 to over 6.000 at the exit in 2004 because of the sales and business growth.

Management established Wincor Nixdorf Logistics GmbH to focus on supply management. It bought all former spare parts from Siemens and created an international logistic system consisting of warehouses, depots and short-and long haul transport with the support of Siemens Business Services. Management further reduced operating working capital through tight receivables management and optimized inventory management (see Table 25). It hired a treasurer responsible for cash management and cash flow-based forecasts. The introduction of just-in-time delivery and optimized work-in-progress levels enabled the reduction of stock levels. Tighter credit management and simplified dunning also yielded lower receivables. Collection was brought back to less than 60 days and the average life of payables was extended.

As a stand-alone organization, Wincor Nixdorf had to build new overhead resources. Staff functions at group level such as legal, finance, tax and patents had to be established. The company created a risk management group and an internal revision department. At the business level, Wincor Nixdorf invested in an international sales force and the creation of an independent service network. As a result, employment in sales and administration increased significantly, prompting an increase of SG&A cost from 17.0 % of sales in 1999 to 18.3% in 2003. Management countered the increase with a cost reduction program in corporate headquarters and domestic sales in the banking segment. Nevertheless, additional personnel were hired for new services such as the in-house customer call center. In addition, Wincor Nixdorf improved coordination between sales, local product engineering and production with standard configuration software introduced in all sales subsidiaries.

To improve management control systems, the buyout investors advocated moving from accounting-based reporting to reporting of actual key performance indicators. Wincor Nixdorf's management also introduced new reports more closely monitoring cash flow generation and enabling cash flow forecasts. To derive Wincor Nixdorf group results, reporting of results of more than 20 companies and subsidiaries had to be consolidated.

2.1.2.2 Entrepreneurial Growth-Focused Management Activities

Manager-owners and investors opted for an aggressive growth plan despite high debt. They expected to create value by increasing profit growth from an enhanced revenue base rather than by repaying debt and reducing leverage. Management and buyout investors had a common understanding of that growth would come from: (i) entering into the high-margin solution and services business; (ii) enhancing international market presence and entering into new markets; and (iii) advancing into adjacent businesses such as lotteries and hospitality.

In terms of strategic positioning at the start of the LBO, Wincor Nixdorf targeted growing its solutions and services business to a meaningful size by establishing a robust customer base and benefiting from potential economies of scale. The key to this expansion was the decision to rebuild a proprietary service network. Siemens had negotiated as part of the sale that Siemens Business Services and its subsidiary Sinitech would support Wincor Nixdorf in servicing of hardware. This was challenged however by the transformation of the businesses. A countrywide service network had to be established. Standards had to be refined to ensure the intended service level. Several service products, particularly value-added services, were still in their infancy. New customer contracts gave confidence to the expansion plans and led to the creation of Wincor Nixdorf Services GmbH in 2002. As a result, the workforce increased from 234 in 2000 to 996 in 2003 largely by hiring service technicians[1195]. To ensure an area-wide service network. Nixdorf Wincor entered into supplementary cooperation arrangements with local providers.

In the banking segment, Wincor Nixdorf captured market share from competitors and grew faster than the market. Management revitalized business by winning new customers for ATMs in post offices and in saving banks. The strengthened service network was key to acquiring new customers. In advanced West European markets, management focused on offering high-order products and software such as the Pro-

1195 As elucidated in the section of the post-exit period, the growth continued and resulted in a staff level of around 2,700 by beginning of 2007.

Classic Enterprise systems; in developing markets in Eastern Europe and Asia it supplied mono-functional machines. In the retail segment, management shifted the portfolio to higher margin products and services to compensate for falling prices. This alo included related software solutions and consulting that allowed for enhanced efficiency and increased customer retention. Weak profit in the retail business prompted the buyout investors to wonder whether the business should not be downsized or closed. Nixdorf's senior management was convinced, however, that the business offered attractive returns and promised to improve profitability.

Internationalization produced a second major improvement. Wincor Nixdorf increased its international presence between 1999 and 2003 from 34 to over 90 countries, a massive increase in sales power. This was achieved by opening subsidiaries or entering into strategic partnerships with local distributors. Wincor Nixdorf established itself as a reliable partner for a number of internationally recognized banks and retailers. As a result, non-German increased from 47 % of total sales in 1999 to 62% in 2004[1196]. Wincor Nixdorf outpaced IBM in 2003 and became not only Germany's largest supplier with a 40% market share but also in Europe's[1197]. By 2004, Wincor Nixdorf serviced 22 of Europe's 25 largest banks and 19 of its 25 largest retailers[1198]. Wincor Nixdorf benefited from a constant replacement cycle for ATMs and ePOS. Changes in technology upgrades occurred at a constant rate and flattened the demand curve. The company, however, profited from the one-time year 2000 conversion and the introduction of the Euro in 2002. The subsequent decline in 2002 in banking resulted largely from advanced investments in 2001.

Finally, Wincor Nixdorf's move into adjacent businesses by organic growth contributed significantly to the improvement. It leveraged existing self-service and checkout system technologies and developed its own machines for gastronomy and service stations. The few acquisitions that were not material helped to broaden the distribution platforms in new markets, and acquire add-on businesses in related service industries[1199].

1196 The sales increase was accompanied by an increase of international workforce from 29% in 1999 to 47% of total employees in 2004 (see Table 21).

1197 Both estimated are based on the number of delivered EPOS systems.

1198 The ranking of the banks is based on their market capitalization. For the retail companies, the base was their annual sales.

1199 End of 2002, EUR 3.0 Million was used to acquire SID Societa Italiana Distrobutione. In 2003, EUR 3.2 million was invested in the acquisition of the banking service business of Banksys S.A. in Belgium. EUR 2.5 Million were invested in March 2004 in the assets and warranty business of Prokent, a firm operating in image recognition and automation of receiving and returns processes. Later in 2004, Wincor Nixdorf

The strategic decision to expand into the solutions and services industry forced Wincor Nixdorf to acquire new technological expertise. Management aimed to become the industry's innovation leader given its position in the hardware segment. Management and buyout investors were convinced to increase company's R&D budget and employee level substantially (see Table 27). R&D efficiency improved in terms of the number of patents, average costs per patent application, and sales from new revenues. In the banking segment, ATMs and cash dispensers were upgraded with new functionalities. Wincor Nixdorf also developed automated cash recycling systems. For retail, the R&D program refocused on promoting ePOS systems and introducing new product groups such as self-checkout systems in supermarkets and reverse vending machines. Management further introduced innovative systems that enabled system-wide cash management as well as maintenance service throughout the entire product life cycle. Services were also offered in project management and advanced consulting in the core business.

Wincor Nixdorf recognized the beneficial effect of variable compensation and sharing risk and success with the workforce. Management introduced a profit participation rights program for all German employees in 2001. It also introduced a pay-for-performance program for non-managerial positions by converting parts of tariff-fixed salaries into variable compensation. Employees further benefited from the introduction of a company pension scheme.

With these steps, the company relied on the high caliber of its workforce. The vocational training program continued to be the most important incentive for new personnel. On average, Wincor Nixdorf trained over 140 young apprentices a year in technical and administrative functions. The board also recognized the necessity of standardized training seminars for international management. A three-year program was launched in Germany to prepare young candidates for management positions. Management had to integrate not only apprentices and young graduates but also personnel inherited as part of the acquisition from of Banksys S.A. and Prokents.

2.1.3 Company Development after The Exit

2.1.3.1 Market and Competitive Environment

The market environment for Wincor Nixdorf's development remained favorable after the exit. Retail banks re-discovered the private client business as a stable source of profits. They raised their investments to modernize their branch and filial operations.

---

purchased the remaining shares of the French subsidiary Thales Nixdorf. Datalect, a service company, was acquired to increase national service delivery.

This involved purchasing new hardware and software. Retail banks also decided to improve their service offerings by integrating different sales channels. Branches installed multifunctional service stations and modern ATMs to enhance customer convenience. To establish full functionality in internet and telephone banking, retail banks needed higher levels of IT-integration. Advanced software solutions were introduced that consolidated customer data to strengthen customer loyalty. Nonetheless, traditional bank branches remained the most attractive platform for direct customer contact. Wincor Nixdorf moved into a new business with the outsourcing of ATM networks. Outsourcing as well as cash management service was part of efforts by retail banks to reduce fixed costs of operation and benefit from scales of economy by moving out of non-core businesses in their value chain. A market study in 2007 reported annual 7% investment growth rate for automation of branches 7% and 6% for ATMs including networks.

The retail sector posed a greater challenge in terms of growth and profitability. Low margins in the discount retail industry kept prices low. Continued industry consolidation increased competition, particularly in Germany. However, the need to reduce costs through modernization and improve customer service quality kept demand for Wincor Nixdorf products alive. Retailers continued to upgrade their ePOS systems to integrate them into their IT infrastructure. Growth was further nurtured by regulatory change. The 2003 compulsory return law in Germany sparked extraordinary growth of sales of reverse-vending machines for cans and bottles. Other EU countries passed similar laws. The second phase of the return law came into force in 2006, requiring retailers to take back not only their own but also used items of other providers. This increased demand for reverse-vending machines[1200]. A market study in 2007 reported annual investment growth rates for hardware sales accounting of over 5% and for software of over 7%.

2.1.3.2 Efficiency-Focused Management Activities

2.1.3.2.1 Operations and Manufacturing

The "ProImprove" program constituted a core element of management's efforts to enhance efficiency and reduce material, labor and overhead costs. Intended as a tool for long-term efficiency improvement, it became a tool to control cost management in daily business. It targeted an annual 10% cost reduction to compensate for price declines and ensure competitiveness.

1200 The sales related to reverse vending machines totaled in 2006 EUR 80 million.

Operational Productivity and Employment

High labor costs in Germany and increased attractiveness of production facilities in low-cost countries intensified pressure to reduce unit costs in German production facilities. The supervisory board and management repeatedly discussed ways to ensure competitiveness of the German labor force in production. Management negotiated by mid-2005 more market-oriented conditions of employment production, sales and administration in German subsidiaries. This led to increasing flexibility in working hours and lower reduced average wages per employee[1201]. Productivity also benefited from increasing global market share and offshoring of production. Still, overall growth spurred a growth of workforce of over 40% after the exit.

	PostLBO								LBO							
	x+4		x+3		x+2		x+1		t+4		t+3		t+2		t+1	
	2007 (Sept 30)	Share of total	2006 (Sept 30)	Share of total	2005 (Sept 30)	Share of total	2004 (Sept 30)	Share of total	2003 (Sept 30)	Share of total	2002 (Sept 30)	Share of total	2001 (Sept 30)	Share of total	2000 (Sept 30)	Share of total
Total employee, end of year	**8.379**		**7.787**		**6.937**		**6.114**		**4.983**		**4.618**		**4.433**		**3.694**	
By region, end of year																
Germany	3.810	*45%*	3.685	*47%*	3.395	*49%*	3.248	*53%*	3.032	*61%*	2.936	*64%*	2.926	*66%*	2.563	*69%*
Europe	2.534	*30%*	2.404	*31%*	2.076	*30%*	1.707	*28%*	1.009	*20%*	794	*17%*	710	*16%*	506	*14%*
Asia-Pacific & Africa	1.661	*20%*	1.456	*19%*	1.291	*19%*	1.009	*17%*	816	*16%*	766	*17%*	675	*15%*	529	*14%*
America	374	*4%*	242	*3%*	175	*3%*	150	*2%*	126	*3%*	122	*3%*	122	*3%*	96	*3%*
Total employee, year average	**8.121**		**7.444**		**6.590**		**5.575**		**4.798**		**4.547**		**4.176**		**3.530**	
By function, year average																
Production	1.829	*23%*	1.790	*24%*	1.665	*25%*	1.499	*27%*	1.398	*29%*	1.444	*32%*	1.479	*35%*	1.422	*40%*
Sales	5.172	*64%*	4.621	*62%*	3977	*60%*	3205	*57%*	2633	*55%*	2.383	*52%*	2.039	*49%*	1.493	*42%*
R&D	829	*10%*	762	*10%*	689	*10%*	630	*11%*	569	*12%*	537	*12%*	502	*12%*	469	*13%*
Administration	291	*4%*	271	*4%*	259	*4%*	241	*4%*	198	*4%*	183	*4%*	156	*4%*	146	*4%*

Table 21: Change in employee mix (Wincor Nixdorf)

	PostLBO								LBO							
	x+4		x+3		x+2		x+1		t+4		t+3		t+2		t+1	
In TEUR	2007 (Sept 30)	as % of sales	2006 (Sept 30)	as % of sales	2005 (Sept 30)	as % of sales	2004 (Sept 30)	as % of sales	2003 (Sept 30)	as % of sales	2002 (Sept 30)	as % of sales	2001 (Sept 30)	as % of sales	2000 (Sept 30)	as % of sales
Net Sales	**2.144.563**		**1.947.569**		**1.743.732**		**1.575.947**		**1.439.960**		**1.344.611**		**1.462.000**		**1.336.669**	
Raw material, supplies & bought in goods	(788.456)	*37%*	(793.349)	*41%*	(625.454)	*36%*	(685.979)	*44%*	(613.337)	*43%*	(568.166)	*42%*	(699.922)	*48%*	(663.020)	*50%*
Bought in services	(407.742)	*19%*	(342.400)	*18%*	(339.636)	*19%*	(343.080)	*22%*	(281.149)	*20%*	(264.409)	*20%*	(259.912)	*18%*	(253.915)	*19%*
Costs of material	(1.196.198)	*56%*	(1.135.749)	*58%*	(965.090)	*55%*	(1.029.059)	*65%*	(894.486)	*62%*	(832.575)	*62%*	(959.834)	*66%*	(916.935)	*69%*
Wages and salaries	(424.551)	*20%*	(382.827)	*20%*	(353.564)	*20%*	(296.639)	*19%*	(250.704)	*17%*	(242.462)	*18%*	(223.032)	*15%*	(180.592)	*14%*
Social security payments &	(67.799)	*3%*	(56.200)	*3%*	(56.200)	*3%*	(48.641)	*3%*	(40.924)	*3%*	(38.090)	*3%*	(34.109)	*2%*	(28.562)	*2%*
Pension costs	(13.748)	*1%*	(27.464)	*1%*	(7.664)	*0%*	(6.887)	*0%*	(8.186)	*1%*	(8.219)	*1%*	(7.701)	*1%*	(4.680)	*0%*
Costs of personnel	(492.350)	*23%*	(439.027)	*23%*	(409.764)	*23%*	(345.280)	*22%*	(299.814)	*21%*	(288.771)	*21%*	(264.842)	*18%*	(213.834)	*16%*

Table 22: Changes in operations-related cost positions (Wincor Nixdorf)

Average operating profit per employee increased year by year. But generated sales stagnated. Only in 2007, the last year observed, did operating and free cash flow surpass the exit level. A closer look at the underlying movements of cash flow generation indicates that particularly funds for working capital in the post-exit

1201 The average salary and wage per employee of EUR 53.652 in 2005 decreased by 4.1% to EUR 51.428 in 2006.

period recouped for any productivity gains. A pre-working capital movement comparison (see last line in Table 23) shows that operational productivity continued to grow. Stagnating sales productivity was related to the build-up of the service network that resulted in lower sales but higher profit.

Operational productivity	PostLBO								LBO						
	x+4		x+3		x+2		x+1		t+4		t+3		t+2		t+1
	2007		**2006**		**2005**		**2004**		**2003**		**2002**		**2001**		**2000**
	(Sept 30)	YoY	(Sept 30)	YoY	(Sept 30)	YoY	(Sept 30)	YoY	(Sept 30)	YoY	(Sept 30)	YoY	(Sept 30)	YoY	(Sept 30)
In EUR															
Total wages & salaries [In TEUR]	424.551	11%	382.827	8%	353.564	19%	296.639	18%	250.704	3%	242.462	9%	223.032	24%	180.592
As part of total sales	19,8%		19,7%		20,3%		18,8%		17,4%		18,0%		15,3%		13,5%
Aver. wage/ salary per employee	52.278	2%	51.428	-4%	53.652	1%	53.209	2%	52.252	-2%	53.324	6%	50.312	3%	48.888
Sales per employee	264.076	1%	261.629	-1%	264.603	-6%	282.681	-6%	300.117	1%	295.714	-16%	350.096	-8%	378.660
EBIT per employee	21.062	11%	18.913	13%	16.751	10%	15.255	28%	11.904	21%	9.810	-1%	9.903	-54%	21.707
Operating cash flow per employee	22.209	7%	20.775	3%	20.127	-8%	21.932	-2%	22.491	0%	22.572	72%	13.120	-59%	31.944
Free cash flow per employee	16.861	10%	15.390	-3%	15.809	-7%	17.038	-5%	17.876	-4%	18.716	139%	7.847	-70%	26.512
Operating cas ow *pre-working capital movement* per employee	27.109	-4%	28.094	30%	21.678	-12%	24.561	21%	20.301	15%	17.700	16%	15.304	10%	13.861

Table 23: Changes in operational productivity (Wincor Nixdorf)

Asset Productivity

The value chain was optimized to meet the needs of the business during the LBO restructuring. Wincor Nixdorf invested extensively to create group functions it did not have as a Siemens subsidiary. There was no need for considerable disposals to shift asset productivity. Some minor asset disposals were linked to the need to consolidate the customer retail business portfolio as part of the ProImprove program.

Investments in tangible assets involved new production facilities, general machinery and technical equipment in existing plants. Funds were also dedicated to the purchase of specialized tools for new products and data processing systems. Management further invested in fixed assets used for outsourcing deals. Capital expenditure in fixed assets increased from EUR 22.1 Million in 2003 to EUR 43.3 Million in 2007[1202]. Capital expenditures for intangible assets included acquisition of commercials patents and licenses for new technologies. They remained at LBO level[1203].

1202 Cash flow from investments reached a (negative) total of EUR 22 to 30 Million in the second half of the LBO and significantly increased to EUR 66 Million in 2007. From 1999 to 2001, the ratio of cash flow from investments to sales was 3.3% to 4.5%. In 2002 it decreased to 1.8% and in 2003 to 2.2%. In 2004 and 2005, the average ratio returned to an average of 3.1%. In 2006, after adjustment for the endowment of the pension trust the normalized cash flow reached EUR 49 Million (2.5% of total sales). In 2007, we measured a ratio of 3.1%.

1203 Continuous reduction of the intangible asset base was due to high amortization of product expertise incurred by the carve-out from Siemens (annual amortization of product expertise of EUR 20 (2005) to 26 (2006) million). The observed increase of productivity of the intangible asset base, therefore, should not be attributed to specific managerial efforts.

Post-exit asset base productivity developed similar to operational productivity. Operating profit to (operating) asset base improved year by year. In terms of cash flow, however, productivity stagnated and was diluted by movement in working capital. The corrected pre-working capital indicator and return on invested capital illustrate management's success in permanently increasing asset productivity. Cash flow-based indicators improved notably in the last year observed. Because underperforming assets had already been disposed of during the LBO, improvements stemmed largely from investments in the expansion of production facilities. The author found that ROIC improved annually, surpassing by far the WACC of 7.5 to 8%.

Outsourcing, Offshoring and Partnering

To compensate for productivity increases at the Paderborn manufacturing facility and avoid layoffs, management re-integrated previously outsourced activities. The share of wages and salaries as a function of total sales increased by about 1.7% from 2003 to 2007, while the share of bought-in-goods and bought-in-services decreased by 6.3% (see Table 22). Wincor Nixdorf nonetheless continued to outsource production, enabling it to pass on price declines and adjust capacity as needed. The share rose modestly as indicated by the slight increase of costs for bought-in-services (see Table 22).

Asset base	PostLBO								LBO						
	x+4		x+3		x+2		x+1		t+4		t+3		t+2		t+1
	2007		**2006**		**2005**		**2004**		**2003**		**2002**		**2001**		**2000**
	(Sept 30)	YoY	(Sept 30)	YoY	(Sept 30)	YoY	(Sept 30)	YoY	(Sept 30)	YoY	(Sept 30)	YoY	(Sept 30)	YoY	(Sept 30)
In TEUR															
PP&E	115.011	11%	104.066	-2%	106.338	6%	100.389	5%	95.774	2%	94.092	-1%	95.467	8,5%	87.982
Intangible assets	367.275	-4%	383.646	-4%	400.800	-4%	418.694	1%	414.835	-9%	458.258	-8%	498.800	2,8%	485.089
Operating assets	782.420	7%	733.663	19%	615.004	3%	598.467	19%	502.799	-10%	556.109	4%	533.606	3%	519.837
Asset productivity															
Sales to operating assets	2,7409	3%	2,6546	-6%	2,8353	8%	2,6333	-8%	2,8639	18%	2,4179	-12%	2,7398	7%	2,5713
Operating profit to operating assets	0,0058	15%	0,0051	17%	0,0044	16%	0,0038	8%	0,0035	18%	0,0029	0%	0,0029	6%	0,0028
Operating cash flow to oper. assets	0,2305	9%	0,2108	-2%	0,2157	6%	0,2043	-5%	0,2146	16%	0,1846	80%	0,1027	-53%	0,2169
Free cash flow to oper. assets	0,1750	12%	0,1561	-8%	0,1694	7%	0,1587	-7%	0,1706	11%	0,1530	149%	0,0614	-66%	0,1800
Oper. cash flow *pre-working capital movement* to operating assets	0,2814	-1%	0,2850	23%	0,2323	2%	0,2288	18%	0,1937	34%	0,1447	21%	0,1198	27%	0,0941
ROIC (excl.goodwill)	25,5%		22,4%		19,5%		17,6%		15,2%		3,2%		12,8%		10,3%

Table 24: Changes in asset base and asset productivity (Wincor Nixdorf)

Wincor Nixdorf's share of global production was enlarged despite a decision by management and the supervisory board to keep core parts of production in Germany. Selected final assembly steps were offshored to production facilities in local markets. While Paderborn continued to concentrate on hardware for banking, Singapore, established in 2005, produced hardware for retail. Capacity in the

Shanghai facility was expanded to serve local demand and produce more simple cash dispenser ATMs[1204]. A plant was erected in Brazil to serve the local market. In 2007, production capacity in China was tripled to accommodate immense regional growth. Wincor Nixdorf opened a new facility in Illmenau, Germany, that produced reverse vending systems for the retail industry. Standardization based on uniform components and modules simplified the relocation of production facilities and ensured German quality standards The German facilities continued to be the technology supplier for mechatronic components as well as recycling and deposit systems. Paderborn also provided logistics support for the European market.

A central purchasing department coordinated all purchasing activity. Coordination ensured that the group activity met strategic considerations, production and enhanced customer service. The strategy was to internationalize the supplier base further with a focus on low-cost manufacturers. Management sought long-term relationships with local low-cost suppliers and to adjust processes in line with demands for group quality. These demands were laid out in a Supplier Code of Conduct, which enabled to control outsourcing of components and protect its technological prowess, particularly with regard to electro-mechanical dispensing. Management feared that Asian low cost producers would enter the 'second tier' market by copying simple cash dispensers. The enlargement of the Shanghai production site in 2007 added new suppliers to Wincor Nixdorf's procurement network.

The lean manufacturing system continued to put pressure on suppliers to reduce lead times and lower component prices. Having said this, the enlarged international diversification of suppliers increased the likelihood of disruptions of deliveries. The production sites in Shanghai and Singapore shortened transportation as well as local delivery times and balanced fluctuations in product prices.

Working Capital Management

Reduction of working capital constituted an essential tool in raising funds to reduce the debt during the LBO period. The ratio of working capital to sales in the period between 1999 and 2003 decreased by 6.8% or EUR 78 Million (see Table 25). Reduction of working capital after the exit remained a management priority. The lean management system in manufacturing, purchasing and material logistics continued to reduce throughput time between order entry and delivery. But complex deadline-compliance and order flexibility challenged production logistics.

1204 See also the following subchapter on outsourcing, offshoring and partnering.

	PostLBO				LBO			
	x+4	x+3	x+2	x+1	t+4	t+3	t+2	t+1
In TEUR	**2007** (Sept 30)	**2006** (Sept 30)	**2005** (Sept 30)	**2004** (Sept 30)	**2003** (Sept 30)	**2002** (Sept 30)	**2001** (Sept 30)	**2000** (Sept 30)
Net working capital								
In tsd EURs								
Inventories	294.309	312.756	223.861	234.958	155.853	152.097	162.048	114.707
Trade receivables	317.367	262.572	241.595	232.840	227.884	256.054	248.190	280.035
Trade payables	234.610	213.410	194.529	197.975	150.726	173.845	176.176	199.987
Advances received on orders	54213	76368	26.571	39.503	20.955	18.609	9.471	0
Deferred income	72.234	74.936	57.116	47.041	39.392	36.568	29.374	39.562
Total	**250.619**	**210.614**	**187.240**	**183.279**	**172.664**	**179.129**	**195.217**	**161.500**
Sales growth implied change	21.303	21.888	19.513	16.306	12.702	(15.675)	15.143	163
Other change	18.702	1.486	(15.552)	(5.691)	(19.167)	(413)	18.574	(89.455)
Total annual change	40.005	23.374	3.961	10.615	(6.465)	(16.088)	33.717	(89.292)
Relative								
Inventories (% of COGS)	18,9%	22,1%	17,8%	21,0%	15,4%	16,3%	15,5%	12,1%
Trade payables (% of COGS)	15,1%	15,1%	15,5%	17,7%	14,9%	18,6%	16,8%	21,0%
Trade receivables (% of sales)	14,8%	13,5%	13,9%	14,8%	15,8%	19,0%	17,0%	21,0%
Advances received on orders (% of sales)	2,5%	3,9%	1,5%	2,5%	1,5%	1,4%	0,6%	0,0%
Deferred income (% of sales)	3,4%	3,8%	3,3%	3,0%	2,7%	2,7%	2,0%	3,0%
Total (as % of sales)	**11,7%**	**10,8%**	**10,7%**	**11,6%**	**12,0%**	**13,3%**	**13,4%**	**12,1%**
Collection period	**54,0**	**49,2**	**50,6**	**53,9**	**57,8**	**69,5**	**62,0**	**76,5**
Credit period	**55,1**	**55,2**	**56,5**	**64,6**	**54,5**	**67,9**	**61,4**	**76,7**

Table 25: Changes in working capital (Wincor Nixdorf)

The need for inventory control grew with the increased international material and parts flow. Management reduced the average collection period despite operations' need for additional inventory. Strong growth in 2007 took its toll with an increase in trade receivables making a EUR 40 Million cash injection necessary. In summary, working capital in the post-exit period remained at a lower level in terms of a percentage of sales.

2.1.3.2.2 Administration and Organization

Overhead Productivity

The domestic sales force continued to grow after the exit, but at a slower than average growth rate[1205]. To maintain high sales efficiency and smooth coordination between regional sales and account management, Wincor Nixdorf introduced a strict account policy that made key account managers responsible for the entire product range. The build-up of services staff was a core focus of the company and led to the largest relative increase in the number of employees. Services employees accounted for 19% of the total workforce in 2003 and 36% in 2007.

The renegotiation of employment conditions in German subsidiaries also covered contracts of sales and general administration personnel. Similar to labor costs in

---

1205 Wincor Nixdorf relied on their sales force as the company reached some 90% of its customers through direct sales channels and its own sales force.

manufacturing, revised contracts increased flexibility in working hours and reduced overtime and overhead costs. Numerous steps to improve efficiency continued to optimize overhead processes. The ratio of SG&A to net sales fell as a result back to 14.4% of total sales in 2007 from 18.3% in 2003. The administration benefited particularly from significant growth in production volume and economies of scale.

Hierarchical Complexity

The exit from the LBO did not substantially change the number of hierarchical levels, departments, or stages of decision-making. Continuous revenue growth did prompt changes in the organization. Additional management positions and responsibilities were introduced to match the growing number of subsidiaries. At the top management level, two new members joined the supervisory board in September 2004.

Senior management gave employees a large degree of independence. The board had good experiences during the turnaround with granting significant autonomy to local business units and responsible country managers.

Management Control Systems

Senior management reporting did not change significantly after the IPO. The CEO and CFO focused on cash-related implications of company operations since the 1990s liquidity crisis and turnaround. The reporting structure during the LBO did not call for substantial adjustment. As a listed company, reporting met the requirements of a capital market. Stock market indicators such as EPS and P/E ratio were added tot the management reporting. The close focus on cash flow-related indicators remained. Reporting involved financial and non-financial indicators that fed into a central KPI control system at group level. It was further refined after the LBO. The indicators measured success on the level of regional entities, associated companies, business and market segments including hardware. Indicators were split down to the department level. For the general performance review, management relied primarily on growth in net sales, profit, operating margin and cash flow per reporting unit[1206]. Senior management also tracked the group's net income and earnings per share. The

1206 For the solution business, for instance, performance was measured by growth in the sub-segments comprising software, consultancy, and services. For production and development department, performance was measured by a series of KPI elucidating productivity gains and resource utilization. Non-financial indicators were also measured for quality, supplier reliability and stock turn. Working capital including collection period and inventory as days of sales, was closely tracked. Non-operating departments were controlled on a value-base, with a particular focus on the financial result and the Group's effective tax rate.

global production and development network was managed based on quality, supplier reliability, and stock turn indicators.

The detail in risk analysis changed following the exit. Operational planning was enhanced with a review and assessment of business risks and opportunities. This led to the introduction of a reward system and risk-based evaluations. Together with the monthly rolling forecasts, management was able to respond to deviations from agreed targets at an early stage and take prompt measures if needed.

2.1.3.3 Entrepreneurial Growth Focused-Management Activities

2.1.3.3.1 Strategy

Wincor Nixdorf's management restated in 2004 its strategic objectives in preparation of the IPO and as part of its investor communications. Management reiterated its intention to continue expansion of the core banking and retail businesses as well as it goal to expand overall business[1207]. It also reasserted its interest in capitalizing on growth potential in neighbouring business areas.

Strategic objectives were changed only marginally because contextual exogenous factors remained practically unchanged. The core business continued to be attractive given ample growth opportunities resulting from underpenetration of hardware and software in established West European and North American markets. The industry remained dominated by the top 3 producers, Diebold, NCR and Wincor Nixdorf, who together accounted for up to 70% market share. This was balanced by a highly diversified customer base with no customer exceeding a 10% revenue share. The required economies of scale and R&D constituted a barrier for the entry of new competitors. If changes in strategy were expected they would have to be found in changes in governance after the exit from the LBO. Increasing saturation in the domestic market, however, made an extension of strategic focus on growth in new businesses all the more necessary. The need to re-define sources of further profitable growth was apparent in 2007. Having achieved a dominant market position in Germany during the LBO and in Europe during the first years after the exit, management now targeted achieving a leading market position in the core banking and retail business banking and retail in non-European markets of Europe. The focus on R&D as a key growth driver and differentiator to achieve attractive margin was strengthened. Additional growth was expected from increasing Wincor Nixdorf's share in the value chain towards the customer. This included increased outsourcing

1207 The expansion within the core business and the targeting of new growth will be addressed in this chapter. The worldwide business expansion is discussed as part of the market development in chapter C2.1.3.3.3.

and professional services such as network-supported monitoring and inventory management. Management believed it could achieve growth in adjacent market segments.

1. **Expansion of the core business and core competencies**	2. **Worldwide business expansion**	3. **Tapping new growth potential**
i. *For products:* • Use and expansion of expertise in the areas of self-service, cash and non-cash systems, automation and point-of-sale sytems i. *For solutions and services:* • Maximize business potential with existing customers • Address new service customers • Focus on higher quality solutions and services	• Strengthening and expanding leading position in Europe • Continuing global expansion	• New business areas in core retail and banking markets, such as outsourcing • Transferring core competencies to businesses with strong branch outlet and structures similar to retail and banking, such as post offices, lotteries, hospitality and service stations

Figure 14: Post-exit corporate strategy objectives in 2004 (Wincor Nixdorf)

Business segment products

For banking, the strategy focused on further developing existing ATMs and expanding advanced cash and check deposit modules. Although the basic hardware appeared to be commoditised, continued growth proved that it remained an attractive specialized market for a selected group of producers able to permanently increase quality and reliability because customers increasingly attributed importance to accuracy and low error rates. To avoid a technology spill-over to potential low-cost competitors, manufacturers kept manufacturing to a large extent in-house. However, increasing cost pressure prompted the outsourcing of manufacturing of NCR to Flextronics, including high-end products. Wincor Nixdorf management positioned the company as the most advanced and innovative leader in a bid to achieve above average market growth.

A similar strategy was applied to retail. Existing ePOS systems ensured a steady and recurring revenue stream from replacement and upgrades. However, retail required ePOS systems to be less accuracy than ATMs and the market was less regulated. A strategy aimed at differentiation by innovation was moreover less feasible because retailers such as Metro and Wal-Mart, did not require additional functionalities for their systems. Competition was more intense and largely based on price. PC-based technology increased competitive pricing with manufacturers such as Dell and Hewlett Packard entering the market. Wincor Nixdorf continuously extended the product spectrum to incorporate additional in-store processes of retailers in a bid to tap new growth potential. By 2006, the portfolio included machines for electronic checkout systems, payment terminals and machines for reverse vending of bottles and cans. Supporting automation technologies were expanded to serve the entire cash-handling process chain. But low profitability remained the core weakness of the retail business. The "ProImprove" program defined various measures to advance with restructuring. Senior management narrowed the business scope to profitable software systems. Non-value creating partner offerings were cancelled. Business was limited to traditional retailers. With the help of investments in new products, particularly for in cash check deposit modules, reverse vending systems and net-centric software, earnings growth accelerated, producing a 5.6% return on sales in 2007.

1. Growth through global expansion	2. Growth through innovation	3. Growth through high-end services	3. Growth from operations in related industries
• Strengthen market position in Germany • Within Europe, aim to take over No 1 in Banking segment, having already achieved this in Retail • Become Top 3 provider in both segments in Asia/ Pacific/ Africa • Strengthen market position in America	• Maintain high level of spending on R&D • Expanding activities in the field of R&D	• Expand activities in the fields of managed services and outsourcing • Expand activities in the fields of professional services	• Leverage the expertise gained in the branch operations to other industries with similar customer processes or a distinct branch network • Attractive prospects expected in the postal industry, gas station operators, restaurant chains

Figure 15: Post-exit corporate strategy objectives in 2007 (Wincor Nixdorf)

Business Segment Solutions and Services

Wincor Nixdorf's closest competitors Diebold and NCR had achieved by 2003 a 50% sales share of the solutions and service-related business. Wincor Nixdorf management decided to increase its share to a comparable level because margins in that business were significantly higher and demand more stable. The service area was planned to include software for branch and store applications, integration software, implementation-related consulting services as well as hardware maintenance services. Wincor Nixdorf wanted to be the technology leader and outperform its competitors in service and quality.

For banking, the services offerings were based on management and control of ATM networks and complex software. Management extended the product portfolio by integrating multiple sales channels into standardized, server-based software architecture. For retail, management leveraged its position as market leader in ePOS systems. Add-on services concentrated on administration of the existing network.

The product spectrum was widened to offer maintenance service for both ePOS systems and hardware in related sectors such as lotteries[1208].

	Banking	Retail
Products	▪ Cash solutions ▪ Non-cash solutions ▪ Banking terminals ▪ Printers	▪ EPOS ▪ Self-checkout systems ▪ Reverse-vending machines
Software & services	▪ Multichannel solutions ▪ Banking-specific process solutions (eg cash management)	▪ Integrated in-store solutions ▪ Integrated supply& demand chains ▪ Retail solutions ▪ SAP consulting
	▪ Product-related services (eg multivendor) ▪ Outsourcing	▪ Operational enterprise services ▪ Systems integration

Table 26: Product portfolio at exit from buyout (Wincor Nixdorf)

Diversification and Scope

Besides banking and traditional trade retail customers, Wincor Nixdorf increasingly targeted neighbouring sectors. New payment and checkout machines were successfully introduced for lottery shops, kiosks, large supermarkets, service stations and hospitalities. The resulting growth was encouraging, however, remained at a comparatively low level. The company also started to offer facility and IT-based estate management as a new business segment, assuming the responsibility of the operation of self-service systems and the management of data centres and networks. One example was the pioneering contract with Barclays Bank in the UK. Wincor Nixdorf signed in 2004 a five-year agreement for running and maintaining 3,900 ATMs. The outsourcing contract allowed Barclays to increase availability of self-service terminals and in optimize its cost structure. This strategic partnership between Barclays and Wincor enabled Barclays to focus on its core competence, banking[1209]. It also allowed Barclays to control costs more flexibly and keep up with major technological developments more efficiently. Expansion into the outsourcing business involved an increased business risk for Wincor Nixdorf because it was

1208 One example was the "Store vision"-application, software that supports the migration of customers and related technology upgrades. The front solutions were TP.net and TPLinux, running on the different hardware systems. These solutions formed the foundation for retail customers expanding their international branch operations. The software was applicable for single-lane systems and hypermarkets with over 200 checkouts. In summary, Wincor Nixdorf's objective was to develop a neutral, open-standard interface.

1209 A similar contract was closed with the Bank of Ireland (servicing 600 ATMs) and with ABN Amro (servicing 2,000 ATMs).

entrusted with highly sensitive operations requiring significant capital investments. In Germany, Wincor Nixdorf succeeded to service savings banks, which traditionally have a large share of German retail banking. Portavis, owned 51% by Wincor and 49% by the savings banks, was created in 2005. Portavis offered complete maintenance and management of non-core IT services[1210]. Wincor Nixdorf also extended its value chain to additional services such as on-site consulting, implementation and training, and support for the running of operations. The expansion into outsourcing and managed services constituted Wincor Nixdorf's biggest strategy change in the post-exit period. These new businesses should be seen as natural steps following the transition of the business as such, and did not considerably change Wincor Nixdorf's degree of diversification. Instead, it extended, market share of existing businesses and expanded service to additional niches.

Management noted in 2004 that acquisitions to achieve strategic goals "...targeted smaller corporate acquisitions, which complement and round out our areas of operation." The company sought organic growth by capitalizing on business opportunities related to the core business. Wincor Nixdorf's acquisitions were small compared to its size. The international subsidiary network was strengthened[1211] and the service business endorsed through strategic acquisitions[1212]. Expertise in new technologies was enhanced, particularly with the acquisition of Swiss BEB Industrie Elektronik in 2005; a company specialized in image recognition. In the years after the LBO, investments in acquisition amounted to EUR 39 Million[1213]. Wincor Nixdorf Retail Services GmbH was created to provide maintenance and other services to retail customers. No significant assets were disposed of to fund the investments. The

---

1210 Of the capital investments of EUR 61 (56) Million in 2007 (2006), EUR 16 (15) million were related to the setting up of the outsourcing business. As a joint-venture company that specializes in outsourcing services, Wincor Nixdorf Portavis was established together with savings banks Hamburger Sparkasse and Sparkasse Bremen; Wincor Nixdorf had a majority interest. HSH Nordbank outsourced the operation of their PCs, networks, telecommunications systems, servers and databases to Wincor Nixdorf Portavis. In addition to the operations of the national sites of HSH Nordbank, operating processes also for foreign subsidiaries of HSH Nordbank were to be outsourced. As part of the outsourcing agreement, 35 HSH Nordbank employees were transferred to Wincor Nixdorf Portavis.

1211 Here fore, remaining shares of the French and Finnish sales franchises were acquired. New subsidiaries were opened in China, Thailand and Russia. Intense efforts related to substantial investments were also made in recruiting personnel, particularly in Indonesia, and expanding a new company in Hong Kong. The remaining shares of affiliated sales and services companies like those in Finland and Belgium were acquired.

1212 Wincor Nixdorf acquired 100% shares of the Datalect Group to enhance growth in the services business in United Kingdom, one of the fastest growing markets. The services business in Netherlands, Heros Security, was acquired in 2006 and allowed to complement the process chain for the Dutch outsourcing business.

1213 Thereof EUR 20 million in 2004, 8,4 Million in 2005, 0,8 Million in 2006, and 10,0 Million in 2007. Investments exclude funds for the expansion of existing or new own subsidiaries.

last divestment was shortly before the exit in May 2004[1214]. To conclude, all acquisitions focused on the existing core businesses and sought to further the strategic transition.

2.1.3.3.2 Innovation

Technology leadership remained crucial to the strategy and success of Wincor Nixdorf. The company continued to benefit from an increasing share of technology and substitution of manual routines by IT systems. New software and network systems broadened its technology base. Still, most activities aimed to refine the existing basic products platform of ATMs and ePOS.

R&D Spending and Efficiency

Management continued to commit resources to R&D and even slightly increased funding to achieve its goal of continued technology leadership. New R&D facilities were opened in Singapore, Shanghai, and Boston. Wincor Nixdorf had by 2006 seven development centres in place[1215]. Between 2003 and 2007, employment (Table 21) and total R&D spending increased each by 46%. In relative terms, the percentage of the R&D workforce in terms of the total workforce decreased slightly as a result of the build-up of the new services businesses.

Since the service and solution business did not require R&D, expenses have to be compared with revenues of the products business only. The ratio of R&D expenses to adjusted sales remained stable. Required spending per awarded patent declined, indicating a more efficient development process and more diligent spending pattern.

In EUR Million	PostLBO								LBO						
	x+4		x+3		x+2		x+1		t+4		t+3		t+2		t+1
	2007 (Sept 30)	YoY	**2006** (Sept 30)	YoY	**2005** (Sept 30)	YoY	**2004** (Sept 30)	YoY	**2003** (Sept 30)	YoY	**2002** (Sept 30)	YoY	**2001** (Sept 30)	YoY	**2000** (Sept 30)
Number of patents applications	na		na		na		60		55		52		72		95
Number of patents awarded	75	39%	54	-2%	55	22%	45	41%	32	0%	32		na		na
Total number of patents	1028	12%	920	6%	866	5%	822	1%	812		na		na		na
In EUR															
R&D expenses per employee R&D	116.489	2%	114.747	1%	113.218	-2%	115.727	0%	116.225	-1%	117.101	12%	104.398	-2%	106.371
R&D expenses per patent application	972	52%	639	-47%	1.202	-14%	1.397	16%	1.202	-5%	1.272	38%	919	32%	696
R&D expenses per patent awarded	838	-28%	1.165	2%	1.143	-18%	1.397	-32%	2.067	0%	2.067		na		na
Total R&D expenses to total sales	4,5%		4,5%		4,5%		4,6%		4,6%		4,7%		3,6%		3,7%
Total R&D expenses to product busines	7,7%		7,6%		7,6%		7,6%		7,5%		7,7%		5,2%		5,5%

Table 27: Changes in R&D input, output and efficiency (Wincor Nixdorf)

The R&D department was divided into the banking and retail segments to ensure sufficient vertical industry focus. The R&D department was gradually decentralized

1214 In December 2003, the former affiliated company Wincor Nixdorf Engineering was disposed.

1215 The other development centres already existing before the going-public were located at various sites in Germany, in Burgdorf (Switzerland), and in Jakarta (Indonesia).

to deepen knowledge of local customer demand. The banking and retail sector were however increasingly converging in terms of the basic technology they applied. Wincor's management endorsed collaboration between the two R&D departments to accelerate cross-industry application development. Management pooled R&D resources and introduced frequent benchmarking with best-practice standards. Continued benchmarking and enhanced transparency facilitated tighter cost control of the suppliers and produced substantial savings.

R&D Focus and Cooperation

The R&D focus did not change considerably after the IPO. New technologies such as image recognition played an increasing role in the business processes of customers, and required additional expertise in basic research in the related field. Competences regarding software and integrated platforms such as Java and net centric architectures became increasingly important. But basic competences related to mechatronics and security systems including encryption and fraud detection remained the fundament of Wincor Nixdorf's technology expertise. As before, the company aimed to maintain its innovation leadership through combining hardware and software with latest, far-reaching technologies.

For banking, R&D focused on widening the product spectrum of self-service systems. This included traditional ATMs, information and transaction terminals, as well as voucher printers[1216]. A further key area was the development of intelligent deposit systems with automation of the entire account-entry process and elimination of further manual processing of cash or checksFor retail, Wincor Nixdorf promoted hard and software systems. In hardware, new reverse-vending systems for bottles and crates were finalized and added to the product portfolio. In software, new offerings were developed to integrate retail stores into the corporate IT infrastructure. For services, current products based on hardware and software were extended to more customer-specific offerings. A new cash management system was developed that streamlined all processes from the outset to the ATM. The banking and retail industry were customers and benefited from the system that pinpointed the ideal replenishment interval. Wincor Nixdorf also introduced an „eServices Platform" to simplify procedures and interfaces for customers and partners. For outsourcing, capacities were expanded for project administration, operational planning and risk management across all stages of an outsourcing project. An

1216 For instance, a new product family of ATMs called "extended edition (xe)" was finished in 2004 and offered a wider range of services.

international infrastructure was introduced with local specialist data centres, helpdesks, and a network of partners for services not provided in-house such as the supply of cash stocks to ATM. R&D also focused on monitoring of customer systems via highly advanced diagnostic functions for network-based systems.

In selected product areas, basic research was supported by partnerships with some 50 technology leaders worldwide, including Microsoft, Sun, Oracle and SAP. Collaboration with public-sector research institutes enabled Wincor Nixdorf to integrate the newest developments into product design and participate in latest research. For instance, the collaboration with the Fraunhofer Institute helped advance security technology and prevent system manipulations. Another example was joint research with the Ilmenau University of Applied Sciences, where detection methodologies and algorithms for image recognition were developed. Management also continued to undertake key strategic developments with tier one customers.

The core technological competences of Wincor Nixdorf, particularly mechatronics, remained the focus of the R&D program. Management expanded the focus to basic technology research in image recognition and embedded software. In these fields, Wincor Nixdorf became one of the industry's technology leaders[1217]. Wincor Nixdorf also directed R&D to promote integrated hardware, software, and services solutions covering the customers' entire process chains.

2.1.3.3.3 Market Development

After the LBO, management sought to continue market expansion by joining Wincor Nixdorf's customers in their international growth. A "road to the top" program concentrated sales and marketing resources on key countries with enhanced strategic importance. Management sought a leading market position in these countries supported by a detailed business plan. The top five customers per country had to be served. A minimum gross margin needed to be achieved. Products had to be tailored to local needs to avoid a hawker's tray offering. The program resulted in tailored sales and margin objectives per country and was anchored in the compensation scheme for regional managers.

Wincor was especially successful in Eastern Europe based on its multiple local sales partners and subsidiaries. In North America, the company joined with IBM as a

---

1217 In 2004, Wincor Nixdorf was the first producer of recycling technology in self-service application to be certified by the Deutsche Bundesbank. It was twice awarded the"Banker's much-respected Banker Technology Award" and received the "new channel innovation" award for the introduction of 500 new kiosk systems at Barclays

distribution partner, besides providing its own in-house resources to the local market. To accompany international expansion with the targeted service level, management recognized the need for improved local service. Subsidiaries introduced regional solution centers for banking customers[1218]. The service network was expanded with local customer care centers operating in three different time zones. Additional employees were hired, with non-domestic staff increasing by 234% in the post-exit period[1219]. By the end of 2007, Wincor Nixdorf provided services in more than 90 countries, 36 of which hosted its own subsidiaries.

Additional managerial resources had to be invested in international coordination and development of the customer base of local subsidiaries. The increasing size of the sales organization required stronger integration and a formalized exchange of information, internally and externally. Management created a series of platforms to share knowledge and experiences internally and with key customers. In 2007, management introduced a central project management system to create a standardized and professional approach across the entire group.

	PostLBO								LBO							
	x+4		x+3		x+2		x+1		t+4		t+3		t+2		t+1	
In EUR Million	2007 (Sept 30)	Share of total	2006 (Sept 30)	Share of total	2005 (Sept 30)	Share of total	2004 (Sept 30)	Share of total	2003 (Sept 30)	Share of total	2002 (Sept 30)	Share of total	2001 (Sept 30)	Share of total	2000 (Sept 30)	Share of total
Total sales (markets)	2.145		1.948		1.744		1.576		1.440		1.345		1.462		1.338	
Total by region																
Germany	572	27%	569	29%	513	29%	515	33%	542	38%	535	40%	693	47%	682	51%
Europe	1.129	65%	992	51%	902	52%	764	48%	648	45%	579	43%	571	39%	508	38%
Asia-Pacific & Africa	277	16%	232	12%	196	11%	184	12%	172	12%	159	12%	134	9%	98	7%
America	167	8%	155	8%	133	8%	113	7%	78	5%	72	5%	64	4%	50	4%
Growth (relative)																
Germany	1%		11%		0%		-5%		1%		-23%		2%		na	
Europe	14%		10%		18%		18%		12%		1%		12%		na	
Asia-Pacific & Africa	19%		18%		7%		7%		8%		19%		37%		na	
America	8%		17%		18%		45%		8%		13%		28%		na	

Table 28: Market growth by regions during and after the buyout (Wincor Nixdorf)

By the end of 2004, Wincor had become market leader in ePOS terminals in Europe and continued to be the No. 2 in the market for ATMs. Worldwide, Wincor Nixdorf was the No. 3 manufacturer of ATMs and programmable ePOS systems.

Germany remained its largest single market. The company suffered until 2005 as a result of the weak German market. By end of 2005, however, renewed domestic demand fuelled growth. The compulsory return law prompted massive sales growth

1218 The centers allowed for accommodating product offerings tailored to local requirements and simplifying integration into the customers' IT environment. They also produced greater in-depth knowledge of local customer processes.

1219 The number of employees working outside of Germany increased from 1.951 in 2003 to 4.569 in 2007.

in 2005 and 2006 of reverse vending machines, where Wincor gained a 30% market share.

Wincor Nixdorf's revenue growth in other parts of Europe was healthy since 2003, and in many cases exceeded the market. In Western Europe, retail banks rationalized their branch operations. Strong growth was for instance achieved in the United Kingdom, where traditional product offerings and new outsourcing services were successfully brought to market. In Eastern Europe, banks profited from underpenetration. They began to install for the first time self-service and automation solutions in their branches. In North America, Wincor Nixdorf seeked to stepwise gain 5% market share by 2006. In Asia, strong competition among financial institutions nurtured growth. By 2006, Wincor Nixdorf was able to establish a meaningful market position in China. Outsourcing enhanced the growth of the solutions and services business.

2.1.3.3.4 Human Resource Management

General Human Resources

The need for excellent human resources increased considerably with Wincor Nixdorf's enhanced international exposure and the more complex coordination between its different business units. As a result, the company established a number of different career development and coaching programs for its talents. A new program entitled"people with spirit" offered standardized career training and continuous professional development with early hands-on responsibility. An "eTraining" program was implemented in 2005 to improve efficiency of the training curriculum. Candidates with training needs from all countries and subsidiaries were invited to join a virtual group and participate in online training courses and conferences. A "peer group" program was introduced, where employees in the same entering time frame were offered opportunities to develop knowledge and capabilities as a group and build informal networks with their colleagues in other parts of the company and other countries. Wincor Nixdorf also established an international management seminar to increase the exchange and sharing of knowledge between different subsidiaries. Finally, the personnel department introduced a development program specifically designed for talented young staff to enhance their training, motivation and retention. The "young professional program" prepared new employees hired directly from university over a period of three years for management positions in the group. Participants in the program were offered enhanced performance-related pay to increase their performance and strengthen identification with the company. The program was popular because Wincor Nixdorf preferred to fill management positions with skilled personnel from within its own ranks. To ensure a high level of personnel management across the entire group, management drafted a "Code of Conduct" that was binding for all employees.

Employees benefit from Wincor Nixdorf's success in terms of income. Right at the exit, the company significantly increased the share of profit- and performance-related pay. The workforce was offered variable compensation of 20% in sales and production, and 50% in distribution. New employment contracts[1220] enhanced labour flexibility and sought to facilitate balancing seasonal and cyclical demand fluctuation. The introduction of flexible working programs and part-time contracts was expanded to accommodate the increased number of female staff. Employee pension obligations were safeguarded in 2006 with direct asset allocations. This contractual trust arrangement was valued at EUR 100 Million and covered pension obligations of some 3,000 past and present employees[1221]. Wincor Nixdorf signed in 2007 a new framework salary agreement with IG Metall and the workers' representatives. A significant number of employees continued to benefit from the LBO participation program. Some 220 managers and employees had equity at the time of the IPO worth about EUR 60 Million, which increased to 210 Million by March 2007.

In summary, the importance of diligent development and management of human resources remained constant and in some respects, particularly in terms of career development even increased. Employees continued to be rewarded at an attractive level through an increasing share of variable compensation.

Top Management Resources

The executive board included 7 senior managers with the CEO and CFO forming the board of directors at the exit in March 2004. Continuous growth of revenue and international presence increased managerial tasks at director level. A supervisory board meeting in September 2005 decided to add three members to the board of directors. CEO Karl-Heinz Stiller resigned in January 2007 when reach retirement age of 65. Former CFO Eckard Heidloff became the new president and Stiller joined the supervisory board and was elected Chairman at the following annual general shareholder meeting. The open CFO position was filled by Jürgen Wunram, a former management consultant. The management team remained more or less stable after the IPO. Enlargement of the board of directors was prompted, according to the CEO,

1220 See chapter C2.1.3.2.1.

1221 Wincor Nixdorf transferred EUR 100 Million out of its pension provisions into an off-balance trust. The funding was provided by cash (EUR 56 Million), trade receivables (EUR 30 Million) and real estate (EUR 14 Million).

by the company's strong growth. With Philip Mantle and Lim Khoon Hong, two senior managers from regional subsidiaries joined the executive board.

The new compensation scheme introduced after the LBO had three components. A fixed basic salary including fringe benefits and pension commitments. A performance-based, variable compensation complemented the fixed salary and depended on achieving specific targets defined in the employment contracts. Targets were based on sales, incoming orders, EBITA, and operating cash flow[1222]. Variable compensation was capped at a maximum of 200% of the fixed annual salary. These two components were the basis for the annual target remuneration, which was specified for the entire life of the contract. The third component was a share option program[1223].

		Until Sept. 30th, 2005		After Oct. 1st, 2005		After Jan. 29th, 2007		After March 1st, 2007		After Oct., 2007	
Name	Function	Board of director	Board of executives	Board of director	Board of executives	Board of director	Board of executives	Board of director	Board of executives	Board of director	Board of executives
Karl-Heinz Stiller	President and CEO	x	x	x	x						
Eckard Heidloff	CEO (former CFO)	x	x	x	x	x	x	x	x	x	x
Stefan Auerbach	Executive VP Banking (former Senior VP)		x	x	x	x	x	x	x	x	x
Javier Lopez Bartolomé	Senior Vice President America		x		x		x		x		x
Martin Löser	Senior Vice President Research and Development, CTO		x								
Rainer Pfeil	Senior Vice President Human Resources		x		x		x		x		x
Jürgen Wilde	Executive Vice President (former Senior VP)		x	x	x	x	x	x	x	x	x
Philip Mantle	Executive Vice President Banking			x	x						
Khoon Hong Lim	Senior Vice President Asia				x		x		x		x
Reinhard Rabenstein	Senior Vice President Research and Development, CTO				x		x		x		x
Jürgen Wunram	CFO							x	x	x	x
Jens Bohlen	Senior Vice President, Services						x		x		x
Herbert Machill	Senior Vice President, Retail										x

Table 29: Changes in composition of top-management board (Wincor-Nixdorf)

Wincor introduced a specific training program for the development of its own management personnel. The program was introduced in Germany and expanded to the international organization shortly after the IPO. Part of the program involved an

1222 In relationship to the achievement of the agreed target, the board member received a bonus ranging between 25% (80% of agreed target) and 175% (120% of agreed target). If the achievement of the target was below 80% of one of the two targets, an employee was not entitled to a bonus payment. If the employed achieved 120% of the target, his or her bonus rose to 175% of the applicable fixed basic salary of the board member in question. In accordance with contractual requirements, variable compensation was capped at a maximum of 200% of the respective fixed annual basic salary. All targets were focused on increasing enterprise value.

1223 See chapter C2.2.1.4.

individual development curriculum including different functional stations. The strong growth of international operations demanded expansion of the management development program. Wincor Nixdorf's IPO helped attract top-caliber management talent and experienced senior management.

2.2 Case Analysis

2.2.1 Changes in Governance over the Buyout Cycle and in the Post-Exit Period

At the entry into the LBO structure in 1999, KKR and Goldman Sachs changed the governance structure in three of its four introduced constituents: reducing debt leverage, introducing a management participation program, and intensifying the activity level of monitoring.

After five years in the LBO structure, the private limited company Wincor Nixdorf Holding GmbH was converted into a stock company on May 5, 2004 through a merger with its parent company, Wincor Nixdorf AG. Two weeks later, on May 19, 2004, Wincor Nixdorf' was listed on the Frankfurt Stock Exchange in the prime standard segment[1224]. At the exit, governance changed accordingly. Proceeds of IPO repayed debt. Debt leverage had been reduced to an entry-like level through a special dividend for shareholders shortly before the exit. In the following years, debt was further lowered to a level comparable to the industry average because of robust cash generation. The buyout investors sold their shares in Wincor Nixdorf's secondary offering. Shares were distributed among institutional investors and retail shareholders. The managers sold part of their participation, but regained shares because of the share option program and became the company's largest shareholder. The activity level of monitoring was adjusted to the standard of a German listed company, even though two former buyout representatives remained members of the supervisory board.

2.2.1.1 Debt Leverage

Indebtedness at the beginning of the LBO balanced by expected cash generation and growth. The buyout investors decided to withhold generated cash to repay debt and finance growth investments.

Initial debt in 1999 consisted of a EUR 290 Million senior debt credit facility with a seven-year maturity, a EUR 110 Million senior debt facility with an eight-year

---

1224 The buyout investors stressed that Wincor Nixdorf was the "icebreaker" IPO that re-opened the market for IPOs after a longer period during which equity capital markets had been closed.

maturity and a revolving credit facility of EUR 75 Million[1225]. A syndicate of banks led by Goldman Sachs and the Bayerische Hypo- und Vereinsbank arranged the loan agreement. Goldman Sachs was, as such both a debt and equity shareholder. The debt was syndicated without high yield bonds because the business generated such unexpected strong cash flow. The buyout professionals said that the debt's disciplinary force of debt was balanced by the fact that Wincor Nixdorf returned cash at a rate higher than initially expected. Alone the reduction of working capital generated over EUR 90 Million in cash in 1999 and 2000.

The owner-managers and buyout investors decided at the end of 2003 to pay out a significant amount of cash because the prospects for an IPO were unclear and funds had not been returned to shareholders since the entry in 1999. Wincor Nixdorf used EUR 160 Million of paid-in-capital and borrowed EUR 140 million under the senior credit facility to repay capital to shareholders. As a result, total interest-bearing liabilities increased to EUR 412 Million by March 31, 2004 against EUR 77 Million in equity. The ratio of net debt (EUR 307 Million) to EBITDA to total capital and debt to book equity increased considerably, but stayed below the buyout entry level.

Karl-Heinz Stiller said he had not expected to go public within the 6 months after the repayment. Nonetheless, stock market prospects improved for IPOs and the company decided to offer 2.44 Million new shares as primary to the public. The offer increased its number of shares by 17%. The EUR 102 million in proceeds from the placement of shares in May 2004 were used to pay down loans (EUR 85 Million) and the cost of the stock issue (EUR 16 Million).

Rising operating and free cash flow allowed Wincor Nixdorf to reduce debt continuously. Wincor Nixdorf paid back in August 2005 the syndicated loans with a new credit arrangement involving an unrestricted credit of up to EUR 350 Million (7 year multi-currency facility) and a revolving credit facility of EUR 75 Million. Caylon, Dresdner Kleinwort Wasserstein, Natexis and WestLB led the syndicate. Bank liabilities were at the end of 2005 EUR 227 Million, of which EUR 223 Million had a residual term of 1 year or less. The maturity of debt decreased significantly from more than 5 years at the exit to less than 1 year after the exit. Debt repayment in 2006 slowed down with the introduction of a pension trust for employees, but picked up in 2007 with payment of EUR 21 Million. Wincor Nixdorf nonetheless continued to operate with high leverage while paying considerable dividends to shareholders. Besides high dividends, Wincor's shareholders also benefited from share buybacks.

1225 To note, Wincor Nixdorf never drew any amount under the revolving credit facility.

	PostLBO				LBO			
	x+4	x+3	x+2	x+1	t+4	t+3	t+2	t+1
In TEUR	**2007** (Sept 30)	**2006** (Sept 30)	**2005** (Sept 30)	**2004** (Sept 30)	**2003** (Sept 30)	**2002** (Sept 30)	**2001** (Sept 30)	**2000** (Sept 30)
Net debt								
Bank liabilities	206.546	209.350	226.694	325.082	296.950	377.836	451.371 0	444.645
Residual term up to 1 year	*36.415*	*16.873*	*222.589*	*40.382*	*56.266*	*47.574*	*87.690*	*60.248*
Residual term between 1 and 5 years	*169.591*	*6.298*	*3.204*	*163.200*	*107.434*	*152.439*	*168.843*	*147.237*
Residual term more than 5 years	*540*	*186.179*	*901*	*121.500*	*133.250*	*177.823*	*194.838*	*237.160*
Cash (and equivalents)	24.469	9.536	50.859	64.788	34.408	48.655	44.870	34.306
Marketable securities	0	68	69	26.674	439	292	271	246
Total net debt (cash)	**182.077**	**199.746**	**175.766**	**233.620**	**262.103**	**328.889**	**406.230**	**410.093**
Annual change	(17.669)	23.980	(57.854)	(73.822)	(66.786)	(77.341)	(3.863)	na
Net debt to EBITDA	**0,78x**	**0,98x**	**1,05x**	**1,64x**	**2,08x**	**3,03x**	**3,88x**	**4,22x**
Net debt to total capital	**39,8%**	**42,5%**	**43,6%**	**54,6%**	**54,8%**	**61,1%**	**63,8%**	**70,9%**
Equity	**275.623**	**269.819**	**227.633**	**194.015**	**216.265**	**208.951**	**230.926**	**168.687**
Equity to total capital	**22,5%**	**23,2%**	**20,5%**	**17,0%**	**21,4%**	**18,8%**	**20,0%**	**15,6%**
Debt to book equity	**74,9%**	**77,6%**	**99,6%**	**167,6%**	**137,3%**	**180,8%**	**195,5%**	**263,6%**

Table 30: Changes in debt leverage over the buyout cycle (Wincor Nixdorf)

Wincor Nixdorf had a high debt propensity despite its leverage. The strong growth outlook because of underpenetration in new markets and an excellent cost position ensured continuous revenue growth and cash generation. Management's track record in terms of achieving financials targets inspired confidence of the financial community. The IPO further simplified access to potential additional capital. This was highlighted by Wincor Nixdorf's inclusion in the MDAX index in September 2004. At an industry level, the company specific risk was at the lower end. Although management did not mind operating with high financial leverage, it opted to repay debt instead of investing into questionable acquisitions or returning excessive debt-financed dividends to shareholders.

2.2.1.2 Ownership Concentration

No significant changes in ownership concentration occurred at the buyout entry[1226]. What did change over the cycle was the identity of the owner and their investment objectives[1227]. KKR and Goldman Sachs investment objectives involved divestment within a foreseeable period while achieving an internal return rate comparable on employed equity to the industry average of more than 20%. The two buyout

1226 For the change in ownership, see Table 31.

1227 At the level of Wincor Nixdorf, the agency costs of equity were low before the buyout. The managers of Siemens entrusted with Wincor Nixdorf did not have private control benefits, which limited the potential wealth loss. Throughout the ownership by Siemens, corporate management supported the senior management of Wincor Nixdorf in the turnaround of the business. Given Siemens' size, they were no constraints on providing sufficient funds to ensure the survival of the firm. The management of Wincor Nixdorf felt obliged to succeed in the turnaround and invested significant personal effort, requiring limited monitoring.

investors together held 89% of the company and cooperated closely based on previous joint deals and mutual trust. Wincor Nixdorf's management as the third shareholder acted cohesively because it believed in it its own strength after the successful turnaround.

Ownership concentration significantly decreased after the IPO in a number of steps. KKR and Goldman Sachs sold part of their stake in the listing in May 2004. They sold the remaining shares seven months later, in January 2005. Institutional investors entered and by the end of fiscal year 2006, Threadneedle Asset Management, Fidelity, DWS, Schroders and Lazard Asset Management reported holdings of at least 5% each. In total, some 80% of the shares were in the hands of institutional investors. Only Threadneedle and Fidelity kept more than a five percent stake long-term. CEO Karl-Heinz Stiller reported that the work related to investor relations increased substantially[1228]. None of the new investors was represented on the supervisory board. The CEO had to keep two groups informed on the progress of the company: the supervisory board composed of industry experts and shareholders including institutional investors. In FY2006/2007, Wincor Nixdorf reported that the board of directors and investor relations team conducted more than 200 meetings with institutional investors. Senior management presented itself at some 25 industry investor conferences in 2007 to court potential investors.

The two different governing groups, supervisory board members and fund managers of institutional investors, required different levels of information. The board demanded a detailed discussion of strategy, finance and operations, and wanted to be informed on any major decision to be taken. The fund managers were elusively interested in whether growth and earnings targets were being met. Neither CEO nor the CFO had experience in managing a listed company and needed to adjust to the requirements of a listed entity.

Management had the largest equity stake, which simplified monitoring in many respects. Interviews and discussions with the board show that management was motivated by the desire to benefit from the value creation potential. There was no indication that management sought to abuse its position for private control benefits.

1228 Whereas during the buyout only two principal investors, KKR and Goldman Sachs, had to be informed about the progress of the firm, as public company around 45 investment funds had to be updated on a regular basis after the going-public.

	Pre-IPO		Post-IPO					
	March 2004		FY2004 (+6 months) (Sept 30 2004)		FY2005 (Sept 30, 2005)		FY2006 (Sept 30, 2006)	
Equity shareholders	Number of shares	In %	Number of shares	In %	Number of shares	In %	Number of shares	In %
1. Buyout specialists								
KKR	10.021.760	71,3%	5.038.002	30,5%	0	0,0%	0	0,0%
GS Capital Partners	2.505.460	17,8%	1.259.510	7,6%	0	0,0%	0	0,0%
Total	12.527.220	89,1%	6.297.512	38,1%	0	0,0%	0	0,0%
2. Management and employees								
Management participation program	1.532.882	10,9%	1.410.963	8,5%	1.518.634	9,2%	1.678.624	10,1%
Changes due to director's dealing					-67.579	-0,4%	-6.900	0,0%
Share options granted			212.500		175.250	1,1%	166.890	1,0%
Trust	1.918	0,0%	1.018	0,0%	0	0,0%	0	0,0%
Total	1.534.800	10,9%	1.624.481	9,8%	1.518.634	9,2%	1.678.624	10,1%
3. Institutional investors								
Threadneedle Asset Management Ltd.			1.257.192	7,6%	1.499.743	9,1%	833.080	5,0%
Fidelity International Limited			987.557	6,0%	990.099	6,0%	841.988	5,1%
DWS Investment GmbH			864.700	5,2%	838.700	5,1%		< 5%
Schroder Investment Management Ltd.					1.004.805	6,1%		< 5%
Lazard Asset Management					1.052.103	6,4%		< 5%
Fidelity Management & Research							903.193	5,5%
Total			3.109.449	18,8%	5.385.449	32,6%	2.578.261	15,6%
4. Free float								
Total	0	0,0%	5.511.052	33,3%	9.[illegible]	58,3%	12.285.609	74,3%
Total shares	14.062.020	100,0%	16.542.494	100,0%	16.542.494	100,0%	16.542.494	100,0%

Table 31: Changes of ownership in the post-exit period (Wincor Nixdorf)

2.2.1.3 Activity Level of Investors

In the initial months following the LBO entry, KKR and GS closely tracked performance of Wincor Nixdorf. KKR's Johannes Huth, Ned Gilhuly, and Silke Scheiber and Alexander Dibelius of Goldman Sachs were entrusted with operational monitoring of performance progress. At the entry, the buyout investors reviewed the management team. Management's successful turnaround of the business in the 1990s and its expertise during due diligence convinced the buyout investors that it had the skills to run the company through the LBO.

As part of due diligence and purchase price consideration, the buyout investors developed a business plan for the holding period, including a schedule for debt repayment based on the assumption of a five-year holding period. CEO Stiller saw the business plan as ambitious, but relied upon his team's proven track record and caliber. The managing board had the challenge of meeting agreed financial targets and referred to the business plan as the "bible". KKR and GS introduced multiple ways of monitoring. They appointed their own investment professionals to the supervisory board. The board met every three months in accordance with the requirements of the German AG law, and discussed major strategic and financial decisions Wincor Nixdorf faced. The buyout investors did not appoint industry experts to the board. But KKR had broad experience in retail and in financial services, and relied on experts in its network who provided valuable insight into how internationalization could be accelerated and how to enter the services and solutions business. The investors introduced a smaller advisory board that included the CEO, CFO and core representatives of the buyout investors. This board convened monthly monitored in detail performance and general progress in line with the business plan. Finally, weekly informal face-to face or telephone meetings complemented the monitoring. The buyout investors trust increased in Wincor Nixdorf's senior management during the initial months as it continuously outperformed agreed targets. As a result, KKR and Goldman Sachs significantly reduced the frequency and intensity of monitoring. The buyout investors interviewed said management was highly independent throughout the holding period witnessed by the fact that investors refrained from engaging external consultants.

Board composition after the IPO changed in accordance with the new ownership structure. The board's profile shifted from private equity and corporate finance practioners to senior managers with industry experience[1229]. According to the company's articles of association, the supervisory board consisted of 12 members, six representing shareholders and six the employees. Before the IPO, the board included four KKR representatives, two GS representatives. two German Metal Workers Union representatives and four representatives of Wincor Nixdorf employees. Following the first post-IPO annual general meeting, two KKR representatives including the chair, and one GS representative from Goldman Sachs remained on the board while two industry experts and an academic joined it[1230]. The managing directors of the buyout investors remained on the supervisory board, with KKR's Johannes Huth as Chairman for nearly three years after the sale of their stakes. The continuity on the board signaled to capital markets that the buyout investors believed in further upside potential. It eased of the transition of Wincor Nixdorf to a publicly listed company vulnerable to the demands of the stock market. The presence of the investment professionals compensated in part for the absence of representation

---

1229 By May 31 2004, two weeks after the stock market listing, Silke Scheiber and Neil Richardson of KKR and Stephen Trevor of Goldman Sachs resigned from the supervisory board. First, Hero Brahms, an experienced senior manager and former CEO of the German Treuhandanstalt, joined by June 1 2004 and brought general industry experience as well as a strong network with the German business community to the board. Second, Prof. Dr. Walter Kröll, president of the research center association Hermann von Helmholtz-Gemeinschaft Deutcher Forschungszentren, was appointed to the board to provide expertise to the technology and innovation strategy of Wincor Nixdorf. Third, Walter Gunz, a trusted consultant to the senior management, joined the board.

1230 The latter three board members were chosen to support the managing board in development of the company. Walter Gunz was familiar with retail and was asked to support restructuring of the retail business segment. Hero Brahms, an experienced German general manager, was appointed to second the CFO in handling capital markets communications. Finally, Volker Kröll had excellent relations with the German R&D community and helped the company advance with emerging technologies, such as image recognition and biometry.

of the institutional investors. The activity level remained high following the exit until January 2005 when GS and KKR divested their remaining stakes in the company. Johannes Huth left the board in February 2007 but his GS counterpart Alexander Dibelius continued to serve on the board[1231]. Former CEO Karl-Heinz Stiller succeeded Huth as Chairman.

		Skill				Membership			
Name	Role	Finance	Industry	Operations	Turnaround	Prior exit	FY 2004/2005	FY 2005/2006	FY 2006/2007
Hero Brahms	Consultant advisor		(x)	(x)			x	x	x
Alexander Dibeilius	MD, Goldman Sachs	x			(x)	x	x	x	x
Manfred Feierabend (Dep. Chairman)	Technician, Wincor		x	x		x	x	x	x
Edward A. Gilhuly	MD, KKR	x			(x)	x	x	x	
Walter Gunz	MD, Axel Springer eCommerce		(x)	(x)			x	x	x
Johannes P. Huth (Chairman)	MD, KKR	x			(x)	x	x	x	
Volker Kotnig	German Metalworkers Union					x	x	x	x
Prof. Dr. Volker Kröll	Consultant advisor		(x)	x			x	x	x
Thomas Meilwes	Promoter, Wincor		x	x		x	x	x	x
Bernard Motzko	Head of Logistics, Wincor		x	x					x
Edmund Schaefer	Financial dept, Wincor	x	x	(x)		x	x	x	
Michael Schild	Programmer, Wincor		x	x		x	x	x	x
Helga Schwarz-Schumann	German Metalworkers Union					x	x	x	
Silke Scheiber	KKR	x				x			
Karl-Heinz Stiller (Chairman)	Former Chairman	(x)	x	x	x				x
Neil Richardson	Former MD, KKR	x			(x)	x			
Franz Tölle	German Metalworkers Union								x
Stephen Trevor	MD, Goldman Sachs	x			(x)	x			
Prof. Dr. Harald Wiedmann	MD, KPMG	x	(x)						x

Table 32: Membership structure of the supervisory board (Wincor Nixdorf)

Institutional investors together with managers-owners determined governance in the post-exit period. The investors were new to Wincor Nixdorf and presumably had to invest significantly bridge the information gap with management. As stated before, only two investors, Threadneedle and Fidelity, kept their stake of about 5% for a longer period. As a result, institutional investors' industry expertise and company-specific knowledge needed to control and to challenge management was limited. Because no investor representative joined the supervisory board, their influence on corporate policy-making was restricted to informal means. The quality of information required was significantly different as explained in the previous chapter. The supervisory board held five scheduled meetings with the board of directors in fiscal year 2003/2004 and 2004/2005, six in 2005/2006, and seven in 2006/2007 of

1231 The remaining shares of KKR and Goldman Sachs were sold on January 27, 2005.

which two were extraordinary meetings[1232]. The board, in accordance with German corporate determination law, created three committees: a liaison committee, a personnel committee dealing with personnel issues pertaining to the board of directors, and an audit committee. In summary, the activity level resembled the general standard for stock market listed companies in Germany[1233].

The intensity of governance decreased slightly in the post-exit period compared to the frequency and interactions in the buyout. Supervisory board meetings focused on continued refinement of strategy (8 counts), changes in capital structure and share distribution after the exit (7 counts), budgeting (4 nominations) and repayment of loans (2 counts). Less prominence was given to discussions related to operations (1 count)[1234]. The supervisory board became more and more sophisticated in assessing business trends and risks. This became increasingly important as the company became larger and increased the number of its businesses and regional units.

FY 2003/2004	FY 2004/2005	FY 2005/2006	FY 2006/2007
(1) Release of part of the free additional paid-in-capital and repayment thereof to shareholders	(1) Entry of the company into outsourcing contracts	(1) Increasing development to an integrated solutions provider	(1) Resolution of capital increase
(2) Business performance in the Americas and Eastern Europe	(2) Replacement of the syndicated loan agreement	(2) Outsourcing	(2) Execution of stock buy-backs
(3) Acquisition strategies and decisions	(3) Refinancing of Wincor Nixdorf on improved terms	(3) Implementation of contractual trust arrangement	(3) Optimizationof group financing
(4) Conversion of the holding company into a public limited (joint stock) company	(4) Improvement of competiveness of jobs in Germany by menas of changes in conditions	(4) Budget proposal for following fiscal year	(4) Implementation of German corporate governance code
(5) The company's IPO and new issues of stock	(5) Budget proposal for following fiscal year	(5) Medium-term strategic business development	(5) Budget proposal for following fiscal year
(6) New shareholder-appointed members of the supervisory board	(6) Medium-term strategic business development	*Six scheduled meetings*	(6) Medium-term strategic business development
(7) Issues of share options to employees.	*Five scheduled meetings*		(7) Appointment of new CEO
(8) Budget proposal for following fiscal year			(8) Appointment of new CFO
(9) Medium-term strategic business development			*Five scheduled and two extraordinary meetings*
Five scheduled meetings			

Table 33: Topics of supervisory board meetings (Wincor Nixdorf)

To conclude, the activity intensity of governance was at a level comparable to other listed companies, but at a lower level compared to the LBO period.

1232 Two meetings were due to the election of the former CEO as Chairman of the supervisory board and the appointment of the new CFO.

1233 A quarterly meeting is standard to review firm's current performance development and to discuss legal required issues. In total, surveys, e.g. Heidruck and Struggles (2005), p.5, measure an average of five board meetings in Germany.

1234 The discussion around implementing a contractual trust arrangement in FY2005/2006 was not accounted for, since it was a non-recurring issue.

2.2.1.4 Managerial Shareholdings

The buyout investors were a welcome facilitator for senior management's bid to get entrepreneurial freedom following the period of CEO Karl-Heiz Stiller. Board members and senior employees were offered in August 2000 to join the equity participation program. A leveraged management participation program similar to leveraged equity purchase plans was introduced to ensure significant management stakes[1235]. Shortly before the IPO, 222 employees, including the two board members, purchased shares under the program accounting for 10.9% of equity[1236]. This significant management stake confirms the results of Forst for spin-off companies where the management equity is higher because the teams are larger and former ownership structures such as in the case of family-succession buyouts do not have to be prolonged[1237].

After the IPO, board members, managers and employee were allowed to sell their stakes for the same, relative price as the buyout investors did[1238]. Immediately after the listing, equity held by managers and employees decreased to 8.5%. With the final sale of KKR and GS's stake in January 2005, employees were free to sell their remaining shares. However, management chose to keep its stake, indicating that it believed in a long-term upside potential not reflected in Wincor Nixdorf's share price. This observation is in line with Holthausen and Larcker's results[1239].

Management itself became the biggest shareholder of the company after the exit in terms of voting rights (see Table 31). The CEO and CFO held about 1.2% of equity. Managers benefited from being manager-owners and had an interest in long-term value creation of the company. CEO Karl-Heinz Stiller viewed the entrepreneurial freedom stemming from significant management ownership as the key motivator and most efficient tool to ensure interest. In his view, it was crucial to have management and employees share risk and success in a balanced way. Moreover, the continuation of management's participation in performance development at the group level facilitated increasing coordination with business units, regions, and

---

1235 The buyout investors offered to finance 80% of the purchase price of shares through a loan from Wincor Nixdorf Management Participation Trust. The remaining 20% had to be raised in personal funds. The acquired shares were not freely tradable and had to be sold back in case of departure of the board member or manager. Employees hired after 2000 were also offered to participate in the program. Stakes beyond specific thresholds had to be financed entirely with personal funds. See also {Stewart, 1990 #1019}, p.127

1236 Some 176 managers joined when the participation program was launched. In the buyout period, more managers and key employees were allowed to enter the program.

1237 See Forst 1992, p. 72

1238 Both KKR and Goldman Sachs reduced their shareholding by 42.93%.

1239 See Holthausen Larcker 1996, p. 302

functions. To motivate management after the IPO, the general shareholders' meeting adopted a share option program for board members and key employees.

Over a five-year period, 1.406.112 share options were distributed, of which 100.000 were reserved for board members and the remaining shares for selected employees[1240]. In the four years after the IPO, management and senior employees obtained more than 10.1% of equity[1241]. As a result, it could be argued that Wincor Nixdorf moved from a 'governed' to a 'managed' corporation.

Supervisory board members were not tied to the company by direct returns. Monitoring efforts were not distorted by significant free-ridership. The board discussed the plans as presented by management, with limited time to develop an independent view.

Contrary to when the buyout investors entered, the board did not in the first meetings after the exit review or renew corporate strategy. Strategy was instead reviewed as a part of standard discussions between the supervisory and management boards.

A moderating factor and determinant of the modest monitoring level at Wincor Nixdorf was the low business risk and the comparatively low company specific risk given senior management's experience. The company also quickly returned to a leverage level in line with industry averages and was vulnerable to the threat of a secondary takeover by financial sponsors. As a result, senior management was interested in maintaining a relatively high share price as a defensive measure. However, it was unlikely that the company would be acquired if management with more than 10% of equity was perceived to be opposed to the move.

1240 The vesting period of the share options was two years. The holder of the option had to remain in the company's employment until the end of the vesting period. The purchase of share options has to be accompanied by an investment into stock at a ratio of 1:10 share-to-share options.

1241 In December 2006, the Board of Directors of Wincor Nixdorf AG passed a resolution for the repurchase of up to 166,390 of the company's shares constituting up to 1.01% of the current capital stock via the stock exchange. The repurchased shares were used for settling obligations, arising either from share options already issued or to be issued to members of the Board of Directors, other managers or general staff.

Explanatory variables	Hypo-thesis	Expected change after exit		Key observations
Debt leverage	1	(-)	CF	Proceeds of IPO (primary offering) fully dedicated to repay debt
			CF	Rapid debt repayment given strong cash flow, return to industry average by post-exit year 3
			NCF	Special dividend paid out shortly before IPO, returning leverage to LBO entry level
			NCF	Simplified access to debt after IPO, high debt propensity
Ownership concentration	2a	(-)	CF	Complete exit of buyout investors within 7 months after the exit
			CF	No new investor with more than 10% shares
			CF	(Current) investors not represented on the supervisory board (partly to avoid insider status)
			NEU	Management became largest shareholder group with around 10% equity stake; hence, reduced takeover threat from capital market
Activity level	3a	(-)	CF	Reduced interaction frequency on board level; reduced scope of topics discussed and decreased independent efforts in information gathering
			CF	No independently developed strategy nor business plan
			NEU	Low business risk and decreasing firm specific risk
			NCF	However, experienced board members (former buyout investors)
Mgmt. shareholdings	4a	(-)	NCF	Management continued to hold significant shareholdings

CF: Observations confirm hypothesis
NCF: Observations do not to confirm hypothesis
NEU: Observations neither confirm nor reject hypothesis

Table 34: Synthesis of changes in governance (Wincor Nixdorf)

2.2.2 Changes in Management Objectives

Emphasis on Efficiency

Given continued debt repayments, management was likely to remain focused on efficiency for at least five years after the IPO. Long-term efficiency improvement measures, particularly the ProImprove program, were still being implemented. Many tasks like portfolio restructuring of the retail business had not been completed. Executives who had drafted the efficiency programs and developed specific measures were still in their management positions. The ProImprove program was continuously extended and remained key to ensuring permanent cost improvements.

Senior managers benefited moreover directly from continued high efficiency because of their stakes in the company. They only partially cashed out in the IPO and still risked significant personal wealth. They also had the organizational power to introduce unpopular measures.

Their focus was therefore unlikely to change after the flotation. But the focus on efficiency was likely to weaken when leverage returned to a pre-buyout level and after improvement programs were realized. Wincor Nixdorf's senior management was still influenced in their planning and budgeting by the 1990s crisis and maintained a strong focus on cost structure and associated cash generation.

The alignment of interests through management secured the focus on efficiency. Restructuring of employment contracts crystallized management's two objectives: keeping costs at a comparably low level and not compromising on unpopular measures because of a sense of responsibility towards the workforce and the need to prevent the loss of potentially valuable employees.

Emphasis on Entrepreneurial Growth

Entrepreneurship remained at the top of management's agenda. In its first annual report as a listed company, CEO Karl-Heinz Stiller, claimed that Wincor Nixdorf, „ (...) must operate quickly and entrepreneurially at all levels, and give as much decision-making freedom as possible. We cultivate a company culture characterized by flat hierarchies, flexibility and autonomous responsibility". Wincor Nixdorf benefited from the independence and managerial freedom after the carve-out from Siemens. Senior management introduced a long-term strategy with a clear entrepreneurial growth path including expansion of the solutions and services business and into new markets. Investments in capabilities and R&D were significantly increased, while measurable growth rate during the LBO remained low.

Management objective	Hypothesis	Explanatory variables: Debt leverage	Explanatory variables: Ownership concentration	Explanatory variables: Activity level	Explanatory variables: Mgmt. Shareholdings		Key observations
Efficiency improvement	5	(+)				NCF	Continued restructuring of the retail business with rigid adjustments to businesss scope
						NCF	Management became used to operate under high financial leverage
	6		(+)			CF	Effiicency focus maintained by high managerial share-holdings, compensated for lack of supervisory board monitoring
						CF	In particular, strong engagement of management for restructuring of German workforce
	7			(+)		CF	Limited number of discussions in supervisory board on efficiency-related issues
	8				(+)		*Not applicable; to note: high personal effort to ensure cost efficiency while preserving German facilities*
Corporate entrepreneurship	9	(-)				CF	Acceleration of international sales growth and build-up of outsourcing business
	10		(+)			CF	Dispersed ownership structure with fluctuating investors demanding (short-term) earnings growth
	11			(+)		CF	Limited number of discussions in supervisory board on entrepreneurial growth-related issues
						CF	Change from 'strategic' to 'financial' control, (limited) focus on delivery on growth targets
	12				(+)		*Not applicable; to note: mgmt. shareholdings helped to withstand short-term demand for growth by institutional investors*
		Direction of expected correlation					

CF: Observations confirm hypothesis
NCF: Observations do not to confirm hypothesis
NEU: Observations neither confirm nor reject hypothesis

Table 35: Synthesis of changes in management objectives (Wincor Nixdorf)

As described, Wincor's management stayed aligned with the principal's interest because of its significant equity stake. It pursued a long-term growth plan and voted to continue comparatively high investments. With a 10% share after the exit and the new stock option program, management was likely to retain significant organizational power.

The massive entry of institutional investors after the exit meant that non-management shareholders may question the level of investments and favor an increase of short- to medium-term earnings and sales growth. Pension funds with a stake were interested in medium-term share price growth The fluctuation of funds indicates that some of the larger investors had holding periods of less than two years (see Table 31). However, the author did not note a shift towards short-term cash flow increases at the expense of investments.

The intention of debt holders constituted a further caveat with respect to entrepreneurial orientation. With Wincor Nixdorf burdened with EUR 410 Million in debt at the exit in May 2004, it was unclear whether the interaction and resulting narrow information gap could be maintained. The loan arrangement was luckily renegotiated shortly before the IPO and offered a clear strategic framework in which management could operate.

In fact, sales and earnings growth increased significantly after the exit[1242]. The growth momentum did not reflect a short-term increase in focus on corporate entrepreneurship. Instead, it reflected the deferred acceleration of growth due to the time lag between corporate entrepreneurship and performance as management had stepped up the level of entrepreneurship in the second half of the LBO. Management continued after the exit growth-related investments in sales expansion and new products. Funds were allocated to the building of the outsourcing business. The company pursued a strategy of organic growth and made only selected acquisitions. Management continued the growth plan to the same extent and at the same speed as during the LBO, and slightly increased the risk level with its investments in outsourcing despite the fact that it had significant personal wealth at stake.

2.2.3 Changes in Efficiency-Focused Management Activities

Mnagement constantly improved operational productivity. Admittedly, the company was in a comfortable situation in the first four post-exit years with sales growth remaining strong. It could rely on optimized workforce capacity and high

1242 After Wincor Nixdorf was carved out from Siemens, expenses for R&D, product commercialization and market expansion rose in relation to total sales and other costs.

productivity established during the LBO. Debt leverage was therefore not the determining factor but remained high. Instead, management itself was the driving force. Managers committed personal wealth with equity stakes facilitating necessary restructuring. They were eager to maintain the competitiveness achieved during the LBO. Significant management equity stake simplified decision-making across business units, regions, and functions, particularly with regard to renegotiation of employment contracts and division of labor between production facilities. Supervisory board members as part of governance discussed the cost situation at German production facilities, for instance at a board meeting in fiscal year 2005 (See Table 33), and contributed to maintaining operational productivity.

Management was also diligent with investments in the asset base. Expansion of the global production network required significant investments but the asset base was only modestly increased. Although debt and cash flow facilitated considerable funding at the latest at the end of 2005, managers followed adopted a conservative investment policy towards sales growth. Management in 2006 increased investments in tangible fixed assets. One can reject the hypothesis of underinvestment because revenue growth between 2004 and 2006 showed no lack of resources or growth capacity. With regard to the level of outsourcing and offshoring, the author noted a slight increase in the share of wages and salaries as a percentage of total sales and costs, indicating a potential increase in the level of in-house production. This could be interpreted in two ways: management's risk aversion decreased and allowed after the exit increased fixed cost or management was less keen to adopt unpopular closures of German facilities and relocation to low-cost countries. The initial observations gain importance as new personnel was hired in international subsidiaries on average salaries lower than those in Germany. Discussions with senior management produced no indications of a deliberate change in outsourcing policy. The increased share of wages and salaries was partly related to the expansion of the service network, which incurred less material costs than other businesses.

The LBO structure served as a catalyst for a one-time improvement in working capital, which had a positive effect that extended into the post-exit period[1243]. Despite significant sales growth, management continued to track development of receivables and inventories successfully reduced the collection period by 4.7 days. Above-average growth of the less-WC intensive solutions and service business

---

1243 Parts variety was significantly decreased as part of the ProImprove program and significantly reduced inventory. As Wincor Nixdorf accomplished these measures, it was increasingly challenge to reduce working capital.

helped maintain low working capital. The outcome in terms of relevance to the corporate governance is primarily due to the ProImprove program and related operational measures. The cash infusion from the proceeds from the IPO did not affect the level of working capital. There was no indication that the new owners discussed this objective in any detail. Instead, management focus remained on sustaining operational efficiency for the post-exit years observed, confirming previous detailed empirical evidence of a positive lingering effect of the LBO.

As shown in earlier empirical research, changes in overhead staff and productivity are often the most direct indicator of changes in the way management governs the company. It is not unusual for management to increase slack resources in overhead departments less comparable in terms of productivity to enhance their status and organizational power.

In Wincor Nixdorf's case, the share of overhead costs decreased significantly after freeing management from the strict LBO regime[1244]. One would have expected a modest increase due to the enhanced international sales presence and coordination between subsidiaries. On the contrary, management continued to restructure and reorganize the sales department by introducing for example clear account responsibilities to serve customers in more efficiently. One should take, however, into account that the impact of the LBO reorganization had its full effect in the first post-exit years. A further explanation may be that during the LBO, a lean resource base and efficient processes were created that enabled departments to benefit from idle capacity and scales efficiency. Significant management stakes in the post-exit period also continued focus on this.

The hierarchical complexity did not change because of the governance structure. The complexity was a function of accelerating growth in domestic and non-domestic markets and confirmed the results by Phan and Hill from a post-exit perspective. The degree of delegation of decision-making remained high as a result of the management equity stakes. The degree of detail of management control systems improved with senior management's interest in tracking business development and being able to respond preemptively given its significant personal wealth commitment.

1244 The SG&A to sales-ratio decreased by 3.8% percentage points from 18.7% in March 2004 to 14.9% for September 2006.

	Hypothesis	Explanatory variables: Debt leverage	Ownership concentration	Activity level	Mgmt. Shareholdings		Key observations
Operational productivity	13a	(+)				NCF	Continued restructuring of labor-intensive processes, even though debt leverage was initially fairly high
	13b		(+)			NEU	Supervisory board discussion on means to increase labor unit costs at German production facilities
	13c				(+)		*not applicable; to note: high personnal commitment in renegotiation of employment contracts and balance of work*
Asset productivity	14a	(+)				NCF	Further increase of asset productivity, selected margin-increasing investments despite initial high debt leverage; no indications of underinvestment hypothesis
	14b				(+)		*not applicable*
Outsouring and offshoring	15a	(+)				CF	Slight tendency of increased insourcing; investments into global production to endorse adaptation to local
	15c		(+)			NEU	No observation made, reduced interest in operational issues to advantage of earnings growth
	15d			(+)		CF	Limited discussion in supervisory board on core and non-core activities around the value chain
	15e				(+)		*not applicable; to note: high care to balance necessity for cost savings from offshoring and job security at headquarter*
Working capital management	16a	(+)				NCF	Ongoing focus on restrictive working capital management, no proceeds dedicated to working capital
	16b			(+)		CF	Limited / no discussion in supervisory board around working capital management
	16c				(+)		*not applicable; to note: high management attention to keep working capital small*
Overhead productivity	17a	(+)				NEU	Low level of SG&A, productivity increase alleviated by strong operational leverage and restructuring efforts during the LBO coming to full benefit in the post-exit period
	17b				(+)	CF	not applicable; to note: mgmt. shareholdings ensured high personal involvement, e.g., reorganization and renegotiation of employments contracts
		Direction of expected correlation					

CF: Observations confirm hypothesis
NCF: Observations do not to confirm hypothesis
NEU: Observations neither confirm nor reject hypothesis

Table 36: Synthesis of changes in efficiency-focused activities (Wincor Nixdorf)

2.2.4 Changes in Entrepreneurship-Focused Management Activities

With debt remaining high in the first two years, all business segments were obliged to achieve strong operating cash flow. Management continued to pay attention to consolidation of the product portfolio and closure of unprofitable market niches in the retail segment. Institutional investors were satisfied with current operating profit, but urged management to develop performance based on enhanced growth, for example, through intensified M&A. Management acquiesced in this interest with the entry into neighboring sectors such as lottery kiosks and service stations that amounted to an expansion of the business scope. Two considerations should be noted: machines were in terms of technology and components similar to the existing portfolio and the entry was in response to saturation in core markets and a necessary way to maintain above-market growth. The creation of an independent global services network was decided in the LBO period, and cannot be attributed to post-exit governance changes. The entry into outsourcing constituted the most important expansion of corporate strategy. To some degree, it was a natural response given that Wincor Nixdorf produced ATMs and software relevant to a market that hardly existed before. What may be related to governance changes is the degree of funds made available, of which investments of EUR 15 million in 2005 were low compared to total average cash flow from investments. To summarize, the number of businesses Wincor Nixdorf engaged in did not significantly change in the initial four post-exit years. Management opted for organic growth rather than growth by acquisition. Wincor Nixdorf did not face significant obstacles in terms of market entry barriers that would have made an acquisition impossible. As management outlined in interviews, funds would probably have been available even during the LBO if an attractive deal would have presented itself.

At the entry into the post-exit period, investors reviewed the strategy as part of their pre-IPO due diligence. They approved Wincor Nixdorf's strategy to benefit from the inherent growth potential of the industry while achieving high earnings from cost-optimized operations. In board meetings after the IPO, strategy was discussed but not as explicitly as during the LBO. Rigid adherence to the business plan agreed between management and owners was significantly less than in the LBO period. Strategy formulation in the supervisory board was function of accrued issue-driven discussions of business opportunities and threats such as the entry into the outsourcing business.

One determinant for the level of funding of R&D funding was decision to grow organically rather than through acquisition. Management expected the same R&D output in terms of the ratio of new sales to total sales from innovation as during the buyout. Leverage was already not restricting during the LBO. One could argue that the company and its related department were already used to operate with limited funds. Although debt decreased significantly by the end of year two, funding did not change.

It was unclear how R&D productivity would evolve. The growing international presence and need to adapt products to local technological requirements potentially reduced productivity. Potential private control benefits for management could have prompted it to follow personal interests in certain R&D projects that significant risked productivity. Increased R&D productivity in the post-exit years observed, however, indicated that management remained focused on value creation. They restructured R&D and permanently adjusted it to the changing market environment. One may finally note that the supervisory board did not demonstrate an activity level higher than during the LBO with regard to R&D expenditure. The potential shift to financial control and reduced activity was partially balanced by discussions in the management board.

In terms of commitment to and spending on R&D, one can discuss the thesis of a potential use of R&D expenditure to influence the IPO offer price given that it peaked in the year of the IPO. This can be interpreted in a way that investors appreciated the long-term growth potential and were not averse to a short-term earnings generating R&D policy. The continued significant management equity stake argued against the notion that manager-owners manipulated the stock market to their own advantage. One may also discuss the fact that Wincor Nixdorf initially witnessed an information gap between investors and management, even though this was continuously narrowed after the exit. Because the information gap is particular true for R&D intensive companies, one may have expected the new disperse shareholder base, involved additional monitoring costs to have urged management to reduce R&D funding. This did not happen and R&D expenditure decreased only slightly.

The focus of R&D did not change significantly. The company continued to engage in basic, applied and developmental R&D. The degree of cooperation with other companies remained moreover high. The IPO simplified access to complementary companies as Wincor Nixdorf was more known and more inclined to share information.

Management succeeded in market development by ensuring a sales presence in a number of new markets. Post-exit market development strategy shifted to expanding local operations by adding service operations, developmental R&D and in some countries production facilities. Relief from predetermined cash flow allowed for the allocation of additional funds to international expansion. This was particularly noticeable in the significant increase of sales staff in the general and non-domestic workforce.

The proposed inverted 'u-form' relationship between internationalization and performance, positioned Wincor Nixdorf on the rising left side as it benefited from increased scale of operations and cross-country learning. Management increased the degree of formalization and systematization by introducing a "road to the top" program. This signaled the need for coordination between the group and the regions. It also reflected senior management's continued 'control'-interest. This was partially triggered by the significant management equity stake. One could suggest that this stake and exposure of personal wealth exposure would have persuaded management to refrain from risky ventures in new markets.

Domestic and non-domestic market development gained importance as management focused on organic growth. The observed pattern of expansion in core markets while maintaining business diversification was in line with patterns observed previously by Bruton, Keels and Scifres[1245]. The increase of R&D resources and international growth both benefited because the large customer base justified significant R&D investment and the competitive advantage derived from innovative products helped increase customer awareness and build a strong brand. In line with this school of thought, R&D, was arguably in the interest of growth-seeking investors to accelerate international sales growth.

A key observation is that the continued focus on human resources management at the same level as during the LBO and the fact that it even partially increased. Various measures as detailed in the descriptive part were implemented to further train, develop and retain the workforce. The supervisory board was concerned with the development of the German workforce as part of the negotiation of employment contracts. It is unclear however to what degree the focus was related to management or to owners given that the success of numerous initiatives depended on individual engagement at the manager level.

With respect to composition and skill profile, one should note that management as the biggest shareholder had significant influence on composition of the board. The external market for corporate control was without a major block holder. CEO Karl-Heinz Stiller moreover had a strong bargaining position due to tenure, age, track record, and last but not least, personal equity stake.

1245 See Bruton Keels Scifres 2002, pp. 717 and 718..

	Hypothesis	Debt leverage	Ownership concentration	Activity level	Mgmt. Shareholdings		Key observations
		Explanatory variables: Direction of expected correlation					
Strategy position	20b	(+)				NEU	No broadening of strategic focus in core markets; able to organically grow in existing markets
Strategy formulation	21a		(+)			NEU	Product and market positioning kept constant
						CF	Entry into neighboring market segments endorsed by institutional investors
	21c			(+)		CF	Frequency of strategy discussion at supervisory board level reduced to average comparable with listed
	21e				(+)		*not applicable*
Diversification and scope	22b			(-)		NEU	Diversification slightly increased: (i) selected extensions along value chain, e.g. build-up of service network, and (ii) advanced entry into neighboring markets
	22d				(-)		*not applicable; to note: mgmt. shares prevented entry into uncertain businesses as proposed by institutional investors*
R&D efficiency	23b	(+)				CF	Share of r&d to sales remained constant given continued focus on organic growth by technological
						NEU	R&d expenses per patent increased; high initial debt leverage to be considered
	23c		(+)			CF	Significant information asymmetry related to R&D due to low industry knowledge by institutional
						NCF	Peak of R&D budget at going-public,however, indicates investors' favor of long-term growth
	23e			(+)		CF	R&D not discussed explicitly at supervisory board level
						NCF	Manager-owners ensured ongoing efficiency improvement initiatives, e.g., benchmarking
	23g				(+)		*not applicable*
Market development	24b	(-)				NEU	High resource commitment and growth momentum already during the LBO
						CF	Additional allocation of resources in the post-exit period; initially constrained by debt leverage
	24d			(+)		NEU	Supervisory board review market strategy on a regular base
						NCF	High share of growth investors expecting Wincor to deliver on the initial growth plans
	24f				(+)		*not applicable*
Human resources	25a			(+)		NCF	Supervisory remained concerned about human resource management, eg training and career development
	25b				(+)	NEU	Senior managers endorse the development of human resources to comply with the advancing competitive
Top mgmt.: turnover	26b			(+)		NCF	New shareholders welcome continuity in the top management having succeed in the LBO
						NCF	No change in top management team after exit
	26d				(+)	CF	Constant high mgmt. stake provided the board with a strong bargaining power with regards to the board
Top mgmt.: skill profile	26e			(+)		NEU	Given company size, managers during LBO have exclusively been industry experts; after exit, no change in
						CF	New board members stemming from business unit/ country manager cadre; exception with new CFO
Top mgmt.: compensation	27b			(+)		CF	Pay-for performance increased to maintain the level of alignment and motivation; total compensation modestly increased

CF: Observations confirm hypothesis
NCF: Observations do not to confirm hypothesis
NEU: Observations neither confirm nor reject hypothesis

Table 37: Synthesis of changes in entrepreneurial growth-focused activities (Wincor Nixdorf)

It is likely that board appointments favored incumbent management and involved candidates within the company. New appointments to the board in 2005 came from within the company; the new CFO appointed in 2006 was a management consultant who had previously served on the board. The notion of increased industry-specific skills may not be rejected but was also not confirmed because all management board members and, with some exceptions, almost all sub-board senior managers served during the buyout as industry experts.

The expansion of the ownership structure and the strengthening of the managers' position suggest that increased compensation was likely. The observation concluded the opposite contrary as total compensation remained constant for the entire post-exit period and involved a high degree of variable pay. The average salary level increased with the growing number of senior managers and the pace of sales growth.

2.2.5 Changes in Performance Development

Performance development was reviewed for the LBO holding and the post-IPO period. Performance is compared relative to its own LBO average and that of a selected group of competitors[1246].

Wincor Nixdorf enjoyed during the LBO strong revenue growth, with the exception of a sales decline in 2002. The decline was mainly due to recession in the Germany banking market and led to a growth rate considerably below the international industry sample. However, Wincor was able to improve continuously its gross margin, even in the aforementioned weak year. Gross margin peaked at 28% in the fiscal year ending before IPO. This was even more apparent in the net profit margin where Wincor Nixdorf achieved industry level at the exit. The generated operating cash flow dropped below industry level in 2001 and outpaced the industry for the first time again after the IPO in 2005. A similar pattern was observed for free cash flow that also declined in 2001. A closer look shows that cash in 2001 was burdened by the interest expense of the first full year in a high debt LBO structure[1247].

Wincor Nixdorf was able in the post-exit period to strengthen its performance against its own LBO average and its industry peers. In terms of cumulative sales growth, it outpaced its competitors in the first four post-exit years. While competitors outperformed Wincor Nixdorf during the LBO, their sales growth stagnated after

1246 The sample group of competitors comprises De La Rue, Diebold, Ingenico, NCR, Optimal, Pitney Bowes, Radiant Systems, and Tomra.

1247 The interest expense of EUR 47.9 Million was considerably higher than in the previous fiscal year 1999/2000 of EUR 26.2 Million and following year 2001/2002 with EUR 30.1 Million.

Wincor's IPO. Adjusted for industry, revenues rose in total by 49%. The company moreover managed to surpass its own growth rate during the LBO. But revenue growth slowed in comparison to the industry and was below average in post-LBO years three and four. Industry growth was nurtured by the surge in sales of reverse vending machines, which benefited smaller competitors rather than established producers such as Wincor Nixdorf and Tomra.

In terms of gross margin, the company underperformed the industry, particularly in the first post-exit year. But because Wincor Nixdorf achieved a higher sales growth rate, its absolute gross profit growth exceeded industry profit growth. One explanation for the lower margins despite strong growth is the rising share of revenues from outsourcing contracts particularly in 2005 and 2006 that brought with it higher than average costs. Another explanation is declining product prices because of heightened competition with Diebold and NCR, which pressured margins. A third explanation may be that Asian competitors entered the low-end market with substantial price discounts despite having similar input costs for components. Finally, the business itself had a low operating leverage because 25% of its existing cost base was fixed. Strong revenue growth therefore did not translate into substantial increase of gross margin. Only the service business network had a high operating leverage and benefited from the increase of service contracts. In terms of net operating profit, Wincor Nixdorf outperformed its former LBO performance level and industry average. Efficiency improvement stemming from the cost reduction program enabled it to maintain its current profit margin. Sales growth did impact margins even though operating leverage was low.

In line with the margin development, cash generation from operating activities remained strong and at the level of the last two years of the LBO period. Interest expenses declined as debt was reduced; taxes on income increased. Stronger cash flow growth was limited by increasing accruals for pensions and warranties, particularly in 2006. Sales growth took its toll on working capital. However, Wincor Nixdorf surpassed the average of the LBO in the last year (t+4) observed. In comparison to its industry, cash flow generation continued to be depressed and at a significantly lower level.

Cash flow for investment activities increased related to the financing of acquisitive growth in the years following the exit. Average payments for investments amounted on average to EUR 25 Million during the LBO, but required funds doubled after the exit to an average of EUR 55 Million between 2004 and 2007. Investments related to the expansion of the outsourcing businesses contributed to growth. In total, increased cash demand from investments remained below the growth of cash from operations. Still, the capex requirement of 2 to 3% of total sales was comparatively low, and, together with robust top-line growth, enabled generation of considerable funds for deleveraging.

	PostLBO				LBO			
	x+4	x+3	x+2	x+1	t+4	t+3	t+2	t+1
	2007 (Sept 30)	**2006** (Sept 30)	**2005** (Sept 30)	**2004** (Sept 30)	**2003** (Sept 30)	**2002** (Sept 30)	**2001** (Sept 30)	**2000** (Sept 30)
Sales growth								
In % annual growth	10,1%	11,7%	10,6%	9,4%	7,1%	-8,0%	9,4%	0,1%
Industry-adj. annual growth	-4,3%	-5,0%	6,6%	12,3%	16,2%	-13,4%	-9,2%	-26,4%
Annual growth adj. to LBO average	8,2%	9,8%	8,8%	7,5%				
Sales development indexed to last LBO FY	149	135	121	109	100			
Ind.-adj. sales dev. indexed to last LBO FY	110	115	120	113	100			
Gross margin								
In % of total sales	26,9%	26,5%	26,4%	27,3%	28,0%	28,7%	26,7%	26,5%
Industry-adj. gross margin	-7,1%	-7,7%	-7,6%	-10,0%	-2,3%	-2,4%	-4,8%	-5,5%
Gross margin adj. to LBO average	-0,6%	-1,0%	-1,1%	-0,2%				
Gross profit indexed to last LBO FY	143	128	114	107	100			
Ind.-adj.gross profit indexed to last LBO FY	95	96	101	89	100			
Net operating profit								
In % of total sales	8,0%	7,2%	6,3%	5,4%	4,0%	3,3%	2,8%	5,7%
Industry-adj. net operating profit to sales	1,3%	1,5%	3,4%	1,0%	2,0%	0,2%	-1,9%	-1,4%
Net operating profit adj. to LBO average	4,0%	3,3%	2,4%	1,4%				
Indexed to last year of LBO	299	246	193	149	100			
Ind.-adj. net operating profit to last LBO FY	64	70	126	66	100			
Operating cash flow								
In % of total sales	8,4%	7,9%	7,6%	7,8%	7,5%	7,6%	3,7%	8,4%
Industry adj. operating cash flow to sales	-1,8%	-1,6%	-0,4%	-2,3%	-1,7%	-2,7%	-5,1%	1,7%
Operating cash flow adj. to LBO average	1,6%	1,1%	0,8%	0,9%				
Indexed to last year of LBO	167	143	123	113	100			
Ind.-adj. operating cash flow to last LBO FY	112	118	140	107	100			
Free cash flow								
In % of total sales	6,4%	5,9%	6,0%	6,0%	6,0%	6,3%	2,2%	7,0%
Industry adj. free cash flow to sales	-0,8%	-0,5%	1,9%	0,0%	0,4%	0,3%	0,9%	6,2%
Free cash flow to sales to LBO average	1,0%	0,5%	0,6%	0,6%				
Indexed to last year of LBO	160	134	121	111	100			
Ind.-adj. free cash flow to last LBO FY	91	98	162	105	100			

Table 38: Change in overall performance, stand-alone and industry adjusted (Wincor Nixdorf)

Free cash flow remained constant at 6% of operating sales. In comparison to its LBO average, Wincor Nixdorf improved its performance, even though the average was distorted by the weak result in 2002. Without 2002, the company operated slightly below the LBO average of 6.4%.

Cash flow from financing activities in the first post-exit year was determined by the primary placement. In fiscal year 2005, the loan was repaid and substituted by a new syndicated loan[1248]. The balance of EUR 115 Million was financed with cash flow from operations and available cash at hand. In terms of payments to its shareholders, Wincor Nixdorf consistently returned a net profit to its shareholders. The company in 2004 repaid EUR 160.0 Million to shareholders KKR, Goldman Sachs Capital Partner and management, from additional paid-in before the IPO. In the remaining six months of 2004, Wincor Nixdorf returned another EUR 20.0 Million to shareholders. In the years after the LBO, the company continued to pay dividend to

1248 See the elucidation on changes in debt leverage in chapter xxx.

its shareholders with an increasing distribution share. In 2007, more than EUR 88.1 Million of distributable net profit of EUR 88.2 Million was paid to shareholders[1249].

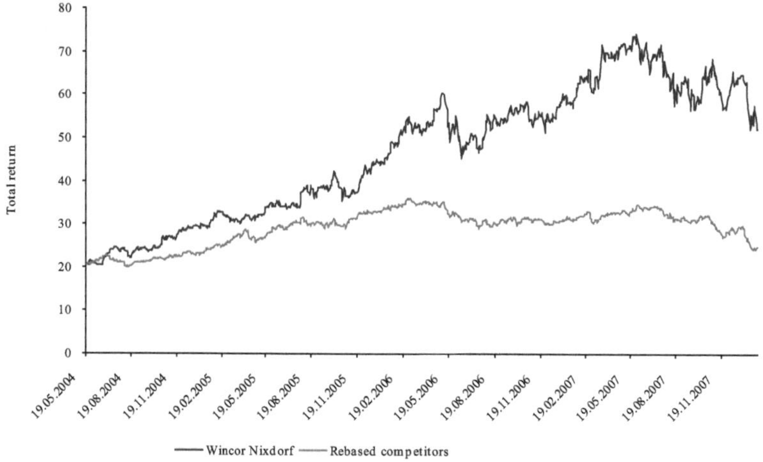

Figure 16: Development of total return since IPO (Wincor Nixdorf)

The author noted that the company outperformed its industry in sales and margin development, but slightly underperformed in cash flow generation. The author did not note a considerable decline in performance in the post-exit period. Instead, he saw a notable upswing, related partly to a more positive market environment. A longer observation throughout year four would reveal to what degree the company will continue to be governed as diligently and cohesively as in the first post-exit period.

As outlined, management's equity was decisive for Wincor Nixdorf's post-exit period success given its focus on efficiency and entrepreneurship-related activities. This ensured alignment of owners and management's interests. The equity stake compensated for the decrease in ownership concentration and lack of one large shareholder. The observations confirm that management always had long-term development in mind and avoided surrendering t0 individual vanity or internal politics. The supervisory board succeeded in averting the risk of myopic, short-term

1249 The dividend in 2007 included an extra dividend representing the full distribution of funds held within the tax reserve account which was made available for shareholders. In 2006 (2005), the sum of EUR 46.3 (34.7) Million of distributable net profit of EUR 55.2 (46.1) Million were paid to the shareholders, increasing the distribution share to 83,9% (75,4%).

cash flow maximization demanded by some institutional investors. Instead, it targeted balanced, long-term performance improvement leading to sustainable value creation. The results reinforce the conclusions of Holthausen and Larcker who noted the strongest relation in post-exit performance to the level of management stakes.

To a degree not explicitly measurable, equity in the hands of management constituted a 'shield' against emergence of organizational slack and inefficiency. In terms of control, significant management equity stakes also served as an effective defense against takeovers[1250]. The stakes were not beyond the inflection point assumed to be between 25 and 40%[1251] where the cost of concentrated ownership would outweigh the benefit of interest alignment. The high degree of variable compensation despite senior top management obtaining significant wealth in the IPO, offered sufficient incentive to maintain a high level of personal effort. Debt leverage ensured that management continued cost-optimizing measures and initiatives, an attitude rooted in the 1990s turnaround. Wincor Nixdorf was to a certain degree managed independent of the debt to equity ratio as cash flow generation was sufficient to provide needed growth capital.

The author suggests consideration of some mitigating factors in the analysis of the post-exit performance. In terms of the information gap and the suggested under pricing Wincor Nixdorf was not new to stock markets. Its predecessor, Nixdorf Computer AG, was listed until 1990. The previous owner Siemens was listed and reported Siemens Nixdorf Informationssysteme AG as well as its successor, Siemens Nixdorf Retail and Banking Systems GmbH, as a business segment. Moreover, the lock-up of buyout investors as a major shareholder mitigated the potential information gap. This was highlighted by the fact that the KKR representative remained chair on the supervisory board. The, moral hazard from managers can be ruled out because they only moderately sold shares and over the time returned to their pre-IPO ownership level. The results confirm the conclusions of Holthausen and Larcker with regard to rationale pricing and contradict suggestions by Degeorge and Zeckhauser who measure a performance peak in the year prior to the offering[1252]. However, there is an indication that the industry-adjusted performance declined in the second year after the exit.

1250 In Germany, a squeeze-out requires 90% of shares. Since management and leading employees possessed above 10%, it was unlikely that a potential unfriendly takeover would succeed. We may also note that the average AGM presence was around 60% A takeover seems unlikely if the manager with their shareholdings would esteem an approach as hostile.

1251 See chapter B2.1.2

1252 See chapter B5.3.4.3

	Hypothesis	Explanatory variables: Debt leverage	Explanatory variables: Ownership concentration	Explanatory variables: Activity level	Explanatory variables: Mgmt. Shareholdings		Key observations
Company performance (after the exit)	28a	(+)				CF	Reduced debt allowed investments in outsourcing business that in turn unlocked additional growth
						CF	Sufficient funds to finance international market expansion, hence continue growth trajectory
						CF	Further, sufficient funds to modernize asset base and install global production network
						NEU	Management group with high cash flow focus given turnaround experience; debt leverage not necessary to ensure efficiency emphasis
	28c		(+)			NCF	Substitution of lack of ownership concentration through cohesive managers-owner group holding 10% equity stake; high diligence and cohesiveness of governance by managers-owners
						NCF	Risk of myopic, short-term maximizing cash flow investor objectives mitigated by supervisory board members and by senior management
	28d			(+)		CF	Reduced activity level, selected discussion of core strategic and operational issues, e.g., entry into outsourcing business and costs at German production sites
						NCF	Continuation of buyout investors on supervisory board simplified interaction with capital market and ensured high quality of monitoring given comfort with Wincor Nixdorf business environment
						NEU	Strong performance gave limited reason for high activity level
	28f				(+)	NEU	*Not applicable; note 1: continuation of mgmt. shareholdings substituted for decrease of activity level and more dispersed ownership structure*
						NEU	*Note 2: committed personal wealth ensured that management remained aligned; high level of variable compensation ensured sufficient appetite of risk to seize upon growth opportunities*
		Direction of expected correlation					

CF: Observations confirm hypothesis
NCF: Observations do not to confirm hypothesis
NEU: Observations neither confirm nor reject hypothesis

Table 39: Change in performance (Wincor Nixdorf)

3 Case Study: Techem

3.1 Case Description

3.1.1 Company Development before the Buyout

Friedrich Ott founded Techem in Frankfurt in 1952. He started with three people and a license of a Danish company to mount simple evaporator metering devices. With the help of metering devices, the heating costs could be for the first time fairly distributed in apartment blocks. Over time, the company expanded across all regional German markets through organic growth and growth by acquisition. In 1981, the Federal parliament promulgated the German Heating Cost Decree. The decree made it mandatory to disclose the costs separately for buildings with two or more apartments. By this time, Techem had already installed 11 million serviced heat allocators. In 1985, Techem passed the DM 100 Million revenue threshold. After Germany's reunification, Techem invested in East Germany and established in 1990 Techem Messdienst GmbH to repeat its success in West Germany. In 1993, Techem decided to enter into the energy contracting business by acquiring a 30% stake in Heitech, a company located near Frankfurt that was active in the power supply market. That same year, Techem changed its legal structure to an AG to strengthen its capital base and accelerate growth. Throughout the 1990s, Techem enjoyed continuous growth because of its entry into East Germany and into selected countries in Western Europe, particularly Austria. Techem also moved into Eastern Europe, establishing local representations.

This strong growth required considerable funds, particularly because of the rising share of the rental business, which could not be entirely financed out of operating cash flow. As a result, the equity to total capital ratio decreased to 13% at the end of 1994. The family owners assessed several options, one of which was a stock market flotation. However, they were not satisfied with the company valuation at the time. The shift from selling equipment to renting was new and the company lacked the track record to be successful. In summary, the time was not yet ripe to go public. A first step to strengthen the capital base was the arrangement of a shareholder loan by the founding Ott family and the entry of Allianz AG with a minority stake. By 1996, growth had taken its toll and required additional capital. With limited options left, the founding family considered divesting their shares.

At the same time, buyout investor BC Partners considered investing in Techem and approached the founding family. Both management and owners saw an LBO as an attractive option. The owners did not want the company to be swallowed by a large conglomerate and loose its identity. They welcomed the involvement of an independent financial investor.

At the time, Techem's business model lent itself for a LBO structure. The core energy services business covering the installation and maintenance of metering devices for both private and commercial clients provided a steady cash flow secured by long-term contracts. Energy contracting, moreover, offered tailor-made energy services from owned and leased plants to the property industry. The increasing professionalism of this industry and its focus on core business guaranteed constant growth.

On December 20, 1996, the family owners sold 56.7% of their equity, equaling 201.852 shares, to BC Partners and their funds for EUR 113 Million. In May 1997, the family owners sold an additional 97.188 shares of Techem for EUR 54.4 Million (see Table 49). The remaining 56.970 shares of the old Techem AG were introduced as a contribution in kind into the new Techem AG.

3.1.2 Company Development during Buyout

3.1.2.1 Efficiency-Focused Management Activities

Techem's operations were based on three pillars. The first was measuring, maintenance and billing of the metering devices. To ensure area-wide coverage, Techem entrusted partly own service personnel and partly third parties with the support of the servicing and with the installation of new metering devices. The second pillar included the billing of the services and the management of the energy supply contracts in the back-office. The third was the purchase of gas, oil, heating and rental equipment. Techem could rely on a large regional organization that consisted of regional, branch and field offices. The interaction and coordination of resources and tasks between these offices determined how well Techem performed against its peers.

In general, the efficiency of Techem's operations benefited from economies of scale, particularly in the back-office and administrative processes. Since Techem was the market leader in Germany, it possessed a natural cost advantage. BC Partners expected efficiency improvements from process innovations due to improved IT support and the ongoing optimization of the service network. In addition, the level of working capital offered room for improvement.

At the start of the LBO, task coordination between the regional and branch offices offered significant cost savings potential in terms of centralization and modernization. Every regional office was responsible for its own billing, although the process was highly standardized. Numerous activities were still processed manually in the branch and field offices, instead of being centralized and automated where feasible. Furthermore, each regional office had its own warehouse with large inventories.

As its initial core task, management started to consolidate the number of regional and branch offices. By end of the LBO, the number of branch office was reduced from 116 in 1997 to 98 in 2000, but still offered room for improvement. In terms of coordination, networking of the IT systems of the field service organization and the central office achieved a significant reduction in throughput times. The measuring processes were simplified by introducing mobile data collection (MDE)[1253], reducing the amount of paper printouts and allowing comparing measured and historic data to reduce the failure rate. Also, new radio-controlled devices decreased the expenses for maintenance and servicing. Furthermore, various meters were installed that allowed contactless measuring. As a result, operational productivity improved considerably in terms of operating cash flow per employee (see Table 40)[1254]. On the other hand, the acquisitions of less productive companies in 1999 and 2000 (see Figure 17) distorted growth and counterweigthed the improvement of profit and cash flow.

The asset base reflected the elaborated operations. At the entry into the LBO, some 50% of the fixed assets consisted of rental equipment in the form of metering devices Techem had purchased for its customers. The remaining intangibles were largely goodwill (EUR 96 Million) related to the merger of Techem Meßdienst GmbH with Techem AG, and the subsequent change of corporate structure to the Techem AG & Co[1255] in 1996. Of the current assets, around 70% were trade receivables. With other words, the majority of annual investments were dedicated to the purchase of devices[1256]. Techem's management initiated investments to fund subsidiaries in new markets[1257], enter into new businesses[1258] and undergo selected acquisitions related

1253 MDE is the German abbreviation for mobile data collection ('mobile Datenerfassung').

1254 Decline in operating cash flow per employee in 2000 was related to higher depreciation due to investments in new business and due to enlarged deferred taxes.

1255 As a result, the balance sheet of FY1996/1997 and 1995/1996 are of limited comparability (see the balance sheet in the appendix).

1256 Between 1997 and 2000, the share of investments into metering devices accounted between 69% (1998/1999) and 87% (1997/1998) of total capital expenditure. Further, considerable investments were made for the thermal supply facilities that were related to the energy contracting business segment.

1257 In 1999/2000, the Calortherm AG, a Swiss company engaged in the measuring and billing service for energy and water, was acquired for EUR 5.0 Million.

1258 In 1998, Techem founded the EnyMore GmbH with EUR 0.6 Million to enter in the market for power supply. In addition, management allocated significant funds (EUR 0.8 Million in 1998, EUR 3.4 Million in 1999) to the expansion of the house-automation business segment.

to the core business[1259]. In summary, management succeeded in enhancing asset productivity, both in terms of sales, of operating profit and of cash flow (see Table 41). Although Techem executed numerous acquisitions, the related risk was low as these were in the core business of metering and strengthened Techem's cost advantage from increased volume. The reorganization and modernization also involved the sales processes. New IT systems were installed in the services division that optimized the workflow and eliminated numerous sources of processing errors. Furthermore, Techem reintegrated a considerable part of the business that was previously managed by independent sales representatives[1260]. As a result, total share of selling to total costs decreased from 25.1% in 1997 to 22.2% in 1999. By contrast, the share of general and administrative costs increased as they had to bear costs from the higher share of business. Further, Techem had to bear the cost of improved IT systems and an integrated data warehouse in the regional and branch offices, as well as ongoing depreciation from goodwill and rented facilities.

In terms of working capital, several measures were implemented. The central warehouse was modernized to reduce the share of local inventory by offering just-in-time delivery. Furthermore, Techem closed a contract with Best Accounts Receivable Inc. to factor receivables from rental contracts in cash[1261]. In total, the share of working capital to sales was reduced from 54.7% in 1996 to 21.2% by end of 2000 (see Table 44).

3.1.2.2 Entrepreneurial Growth-Focused Management Activities

Although the LBO structure implied a high level of pre-determined cash flow and restricted funds, management was confident it could finance growth and related investments in devices. The buyout investors expected the value creation to originate from the usage of untapped market potential that would outlast the LBO and enable an attractive exit.

Strategically, the pattern of Techem's success remained intact. Long-term contracts with attractive conditions continued to secure revenues. More and more countries

---

1259 Techem acquired in FY1997/1998 the thermo data GmbH for EUR 7.7 Million, a local provider of metering services. In the next year, Techem purchased the Tec-Systems for EUR 2.0 Million as an expansion for the energy contracting business.

1260 New business was managed by a central sales and distribution system ('VIS', zentrales Vertriebsinformationssystem) that monitored all major construction projects in Germany by the local sales employees in the offices. For energy contracting, separate regional sales offices were in places that were former branches from Heitech.

1261 The contract allowed factoring up to the amount of EUR 204 (DM 400) Million and was signed to allow financing of the purchase of the devices. By end of FY1999/1999, the amount was fully used and was reflected on the one side in the inflow of cash, and on the other side in long-term deferred items.

made the introduction of energy metering mandatory. The scale advantages of the business served effectively as barrier for market entry, while the churn rate of customers remained low. Within the different business segments, traditional billing services remained the biggest revenue pool, whereby the share of revenues from equipment rental and maintenance increased. The most promising growth momentum came from the energy contracting business with a CAGR of 45% between 1997 and 2001. House automation was still in its infancy and did not contribute significantly to sales. With regard to achieved sales per sold unit, the average prices increased from 1996 to 1998 (see Table 45). However, revenues could not keep up with volume growth in 1999 and 2000, partially due to stable low oil and gas prices.

To move the revenue base beyond market growth within the energy service segment, three options existed: (1) upgrading the devices installed to generate more revenues per device; (2) acquiring a competitor with an attractive customer base; (3) or entering into new markets. Upgrading meant modernizing older measuring equipment by substituting evaporators with electronic heating and radio controlled systems (see Figure 18)[1262]. Beside modernization, Techem pursued selected acquisitions at a modest pace to increase market share[1263]. Further, Techem also actively pursued oranic growth options in international, non-domestic markets. Implementation of CO_2 emissions restrictions in Western Europe accelerated the introduction of consumption-based billing. Techem expanded the number of its subsidiaries and national offices to participate in additional growth. In particular, Techem focused on Austria and Switzerland, achieving a market share of 64% in Austria in 1999. Further, Techem invested in local subsidiaries in Italy, the Netherlands, and Sweden. Techem International GmbH, a 100% subsidiary of Techem AG, managed all international operations. During the LBO, management also focused on emerging Eastern European markets[1264]. By end of 1999, local sales subsidiaries were in place in the Czech Republic, Hungary, Poland, and Slovakia. The board realized nonetheless that it would take time until individual markets were ready for Techem's advanced billing and calibrated carefully the timing of its investments. During the LBO, Techem also accomplished its targeted market

1262 Management introduced newer devices in 1996, and grew sales from 61,000 devices sold in 1997 to 465,000 in 2000. In most cases, Techem passed the installation and purchase costs by the property owners to the tenants, what relieved the property owners from cash investments and simplified the modernization decision.

1263 In 1998, Techem acquired thermo data that enlarged its installed base by 400.000 devices, of which 200.000 were located in Poland.

1264 The penetration of households with measuring devices for energy consumption in emerging countries was low. In the 1990s, consumption-based energy billing was gradually made mandatory for households. Given high energy prices, tenants were strong proponents of installing modern metering devices.

penetration in Eastern Germany, reaching a market share equal to that in Western Germany.

Techem also conducted selected acquisitions in the energy contracting business. In 1999, Techem's subsidiary Heitech acquired all shares of TEC Systems AG. Heitech's customers had signed contracts for energy supply for on average 15 years. Large commercial real estate and housing companies increasingly recognized the advantage of outsourcing the entire management and control of their energy supply. Techem's management enforced the entry and development of this business field through a series of small investments. From 1996 to 1998, revenues in energy contracting doubled[1265]. One of the most promising growth drivers was the liberalization of the German energy market. In 1999, Techem decided to found Enymore GmbH to position itself as an independent supplier of power supply-related services. With Enymore, Techem produced energy power to Techem's core customer accounts (general current for the building) and their tenants (individual current for apartments and residences). As a result, Techem sought to acquire new contracts based on its close relationships to real estate companies. Techem further targeted the market for domestic automation. In particular, the sales force targeted wealthier customers with state-of-the-art communication technology that combined reading meters with an automated climate control system.

Technology leadership remained a core strategy objective to differentiate Techem from its competitors. To achieve this, Techem adopted a two-pronged strategy. It sought to advance its service as well as quality related to measuring and billing energy through process innovation. Mobile data collection was bolstered by upgrading the service division's IT infrastructure. On the spot metering was uncomplicated and trouble free, and simplified the data processing significantly. Furthermore, Techem introduced a new data transfer system that allowed a customer to directly link to Techem's billing system. Techem also aimed to develop new devices and instruments that optimized the metering itself and allowed it to enter into new markets because of its product innovation. Radio-controlled systems were cheaper and easier to install, and could be connected to security systems. The spread of wireless communication and processing technology encouraged thinking about home automation systems. This would connect all metering and heating devices to a

1265 Techem continuously augmented its service offering in this business segment, by expanding into the planning, financing and installing of the energy production facility with related services and maintenance.

central system where the settings where automatically controlled on the basis of a programmed protocol[1266].

Ensuring Techem's high quality of services and remarkable growth rested largely on the shoulders of the workforce. To ensure a high caliber of human resources, Techem continued to invest in its employees with formal training, individual coaching and development programs[1267]. However, Techem refused to offer an equity participation program to its employees with the exception of management and supervisory board members (see Table 49).

The composition of the management board did not change significantly during the LBO. At the entry, the investors established a relationship of trust with the management and left the team unchanged. In April 1999, CEO Hans-Ludwig Grüschow resigned because of age and became Chairman of the supervisory board. The former CFO Dieter Dannheimer was appointed as new CEO. Walter Schmidt, who had been with Techem since 1986, was promoted to new CFO.

3.1.3 Company Development after the Exit

3.1.3.1 Market and Competitive Environment

Techem continued to benefit from the market and technology environment. Greater environmental awareness and political support resulted in legislative enforcement of sub-metering in an increasing number of countries in Western and particularly Eastern Europe. This was underpinned by increasing demand from tenants for a fair and detailed allocation of heating and water costs according to consumption, irrespective of legislative enforcement. Liberalisation and privatization of public utilities enhanced competition among suppliers and entailed the separation of the value chain. Formerly integrated utilities became specialized providers of either power generation, network services or sales distributors. With the coverage of energy services, energy contracting and IT services, Techem had a unique selling proposition compared to its direct competitors.

1266 Techem had developed in previous years, jointly with its partner Dr. Riedel Automatisierungstechnik, the 'comfort-tech' house automation system that was wire-based but had been, due to its high costs and complexity, not as successful as planned.

1267 Target group specific development programs were offered that allowed employees to qualify as retail specialists and as project leaders. Further, employees gained project-related qualifications (mobile data collection, SAP) at numerous events. The individual qualification requirements were identified by means of systematic employee reviews and personal goal agreement meetings. Further, staff fluctuations, in particular in 1997/1998, were offset by a systematic expansion of the dual company-specific vocational training program. Techem also introduced an executive development program for prospective managers. In terms of compensation, average wage increased modestly during the buyout (see Table 40).

However, the continued weak domestic market that still accounted for over 90% of revenues and mounting competition increased the pressure on margins. The German market was dominated by the three leading providers, Techem, Viterra (renamed as Ista in 2005) and Brunata, an association of eight companies ("Arbeitsgemeinschaft Heiz- und Wasserkostenverteilung e.V."), accounting in total for 75% of the market[1268]. As growth slowed down in 2001, the market became increasingly cost competitive. Furthermore, recession in the German real estate market brought an end to various innovative business ideas. Techem's direct competitor Ista entered into an LBO and optimized its cost position with a clean balance sheet and sufficient capital.

In the later post-exit period starting 2004, market prospects improved, especially in Germany. The energy contracting industry remained the motor of Techem's growth. Legislative enforcements such as the energy pass for house sellers accelerated market growth. Large market players continued to benefit from a highly fragmented industry where smaller providers were willing to hand over their contracts because of their small size and market positioning.

3.1.3.2 Efficiency-Focused Management Activities

3.1.3.2.1 Operations and Manufacturing

In terms of management of the operations and related productivity, one can identify two periods. In the first period, 2000 to end of 2002, operational productivity declined significantly. As a reaction to the deteriorating profit base, the (new) management[1269] installed a cost improvement program entitled "Fokus" that heralded the second period. The program included measures in all functional areas to enhance operational productivity and lasted throughout the remaining years observed[1270]. Recovered customer demand and implied volume growth accelerated the recovery of operational productivity.

Operational Productivity and Employment

At the time of the IPO, management founded a series of new businesses. Resources were invested into innovative products in IT services and home automation, including new personnel and equipment. These investments, however, did not yield in corresponding revenues. Further, coordination between Techem's regional offices

1268 The remaining market was divided up among approximately 150 mainly regional providers. As technology became more and more important, smaller providers found it difficult to finance the requisite high investment in the technical know-how and pre-finance the rental equipment.

1269 The change in management team is elaborated in chapter C3.1.3.3.1.

1270 The Fokus program resulted in annual savings in operations and administration of EUR 12 Million. One-time expenses, in particular for severance payment, accounted up to EUR 15 Million.

remained difficult and absorbed significant resources, despite restructuring efforts during the LBO. As a result, total productivity declined. A closer look shows that productivity deteriorated in particular in sales organization as opposed to productivity in the service operations with gross profit declining slower than operating profit (see Table 40). Although one may argue that the decline was an outcome of the weak general market environment, continuously growing sales productivity indicated that the profit decline was largely linked to the cost increase in sales and administration (see Table 45)[1271].

The new management implemented restructuring efforts in sales, administration and field operations to return the company to its previous profit level. Management reduced the temporary workforce to increase utilization. The personnel department offered the possibility of pre-retirement part time work, which a large number of selected employees took advantage of. Weekly working hours were raised from 38 to 40 hours and a flexible annual working model was introduced to reduce an overtime supplementary. As compensation, Techem introduced a variable bonus and salary system for various groups of employees. Management also succeeded in integrating the regional network organization of Heimer's concept in 2005[1272]. Increased usage of low-maintenance metering devices, in particular radio-controlled meters, further supported cost improvement. In 2004, a second generation of radio-controlled meter was brought to market with lowered sourcing and production costs. The devices were a combination of electronic and radio-controlled meters with the option for the house owner to switch from manual to radio-controlled or wireless reading while reducing reading costs for Techem. As expected, operational productivity returned to previous levels, both in terms of sales, operating profit, and cash flow per employee[1273].

By end of 2004, employment in the German offices and particularly the headquarters was reduced by some 150 people. In 2006, Techem again reinforced its focus on cost leadership with a concentrated optimization program[1274].

1271 The opposite increase in operating (free) cash flow basis was due to non-operating items. In 2002, Techem benefited from the release from tax accruals and from reduced investments in working capital.

1272 Techem integrated nine Heimer branches into the existing Techem network. At other acquisitions, management chose to integrate the operations if related to the core business, but kept the operations independent if they where an addition to the existing resource base.

1273 The decrease on a cash flow base in 2006 was related to significant provisions made for tax and other items of EUR 23.2 Million as opposed to a release of provisions of EUR 22.1 Million in 2005 (see Appendix cash flow statement)

1274 Based on extensive benchmarking with best-practice in the industry, management formulated ambitious targets with an annual net cost reduction of around EUR 10 to 15 Million by FY2009/2010, amounting to a

Asset Productivity

The asset base consisted of rental equipment, trade receivables and goodwill from acquisitions. Even though the business had to be regarded as asset intensive, the required asset base continued to be a competitive advantage as it shielded Techem against new market entrants. The higher level of rental business (and assets), moreover, positively effected profit as long-term contracts earned in general higher margins. Management continued to invest at a comparable level to the LBO period. Without acquisitions, the basic needs for investments in fixed assets accounted for 12 to 15% of total sales[1275]. Further, capital expenditures were dedicated to growth acquisitions and to new software. In the first half of the post-exit period (2000 to end of 2002), these investments increased considerably to EUR 30 to 50 Million per year, with a peak in 2002. Asset productivity declined in the first two years of the post-exit period at the same rate as operational productivity. Further, ROIC declined to 7.6% in 2002 due to the growth of goodwill from acquisitions. The divestment of non-core businesses such as the sale of Techem's stake in HausPerfekt in 2003 was initiated by the "Fokus" program and returned asset productivity to the level of the IPO. In 2005, the acquisition of Heimer Concept reduced the ROIC and decelerated the growth of operating profit from operating assets.

Outsourcing, Offshoring and Partnering

Techem owned only a small share of its value chain. All relevant devices, both traditional evaporators and modern electronic units, were purchased from market leaders in the metering equipment industry. As a result, secured long-term supply agreements and stable procurement in terms of volume and price were crucial for Techem's business[1276]. To reduce dependency of the core suppliers, Techem established a series a 'second tier' supply sources in 2003. These 'second tier' suppliers were equipped with a set of appropriate production tools. The shareholders acknowledged the importance of the suppliers with the appointment of Horst Ziegler, Chairman of Hydrometer and one of the most important suppliers to Techem, to the supervisory board.

In addition, a comprehensive quality assurance system was introduced that covered the manufacturing processes at the suppliers and significantly reduced the failure

---

relative improvement of 4 to 6%.

1275 Investments in fixed assets were directed to rental and technical devices and office equipment in field offices. In 2006, for instance, the purchase of fixed assets totaled to EUR 64.4 Million, resembling 12.3% of total revenues of EUR 523.0 Million (see also Appendix on income and cash flow statement).

1276 The EL-ME GmbH and Elcoteq were the main suppliers for supply electronic and radio-controlled heat cost allocators. Techem purchased water meters mainly from Hydrometer.

rate of devices. Nonetheless, management claimed continuous cost savings from its suppliers as their contribution to the "Fokus" cost improvement program. Management also introduced an internal procurement price index, and identified potential savings in supplies and materials. As a result, expenses related to procurement fell significantly after 2002.

Working Capital Management

Like with operational productivity, the post-exit quality of working capital management declined. The collection period for receivables dropped to over 55 days in 2001. As a result, working capital increased as a share of sales (see Table 44). However, significant improvements in the collection period were measured again in 2002. The new management continued with the improvement measures, in particular abolishing the policy of dunning blocks. In summary, the collection period declined to 32 days by end of 2004. Further decrease of inventory stemmed from improved production planning and optimized supply chain processes due to the closure of small part storages and the centralisation of warehousing. Inventory could, therefore, be reduced from 26.2% of total sales in 2000 to 6.7% in 2005.

3.1.3.2.2 Administration and Organization

Overhead Productivity

Reduced attention for overhead efficiency and investments into new businesses increased overhead expenses rapidly. In the two years after the IPO, total expenses for overhead grew at a rate way above revenue growth. In particular, the share of overhead personnel surged dramatically from 14.6% of total sales in 1999 to 18.0% in 2002, constituting an absolute increase of EUR 25 Million. This was even more remarkable as numerous activities were largely fixed in nature and independent of the revenue level. Starting in 2002, management worked on increasing efficiency of the sales network, including the external independent representatives. 50% of the sales team were still independent representatives who held valuable customer relationships and absorbed a significant share of profit margin. The restructuring gained significant momentum after the management team change and the introduction of the 'Fokus' program. Part of the program was a further consolidation of the regional offices[1277].

1277 The network density of the branch offices was reduced, since they represented high one-time expenses. Techem had a sales network of regional offices (in 2001: 8, in 2002: 7, in 2003: 5, in 2006: 4), branch offices (in 2001: 93, in 2002: 88, in 2003: 84, in 2004: 78, in 2006: 68) and field offices (in 2001: 19, in 2003: 24, in 2004: 22, in 2006: 31) that it continuously downscaled.

Operational productivity: total	PostLBO												LBO								
	x+6		x+5		x+4		x+3		x+2		x+1		t+4		t+3		t+2		t+1		t
	2006 (Sept 30)	YoY	2005 (Sept 30)	YoY	2004 (Sept 30)	YoY	2003 (Sept 30)	YoY	2002 (Sept 30)	YoY	2001 (Sept 30)	YoY	2000 (Sept 30)	YoY	1999 (Sept 30)	YoY	1998 (Sept 30)	YoY	1997 (Sept 30)	YoY	1996 (Sept 30)
In EUR																					
Total wages & salaries [In TEUR]	130.106	3%	126.214	7%	117.993	-6%	125.239	12%	111.399	19%	93.398	12%	83.275	19%	70.088	5%	66.572		na		na
As part of total sales	24,9%		27,0%		27,3%		30,7%		29,4%		26,3%		25,8%		23,7%		24,2%		0,0%		0,0%
Aver. wage/ salary per employee	52.621	-5%	55.357	6%	52.163	-1%	52.832	8%	48.924	6%	46.191	1%	45.618	11%	41.180	-4%	42.702		na		na
Sales per employee	211.520	3%	204.733	7%	190.988	11%	172.317	3%	166.559	-5%	175.603	-1%	176.771	2%	173.761	-1%	176.140	4%	168.918		na
Gross profit per employee	93.518	1%	92.580	7%	86.618	20%	72.105	-27%	98.993	-9%	109.281	-3%	112.741	11%	101.269	2%	99.526	5%	95.096		na
Operating profit per employee	43.030	16%	37.016	-3%	37.972	102%	18.800	10%	17.015	-35%	26.249	12%	23.538	5%	22.461	24%	18.176	20%	15.145		na
Operating cash flow per employee	28.745	-43%	50.445	5%	47.995	11%	43.099	7%	40.113	38%	29.129	0%	29.103	-7%	31.352	1%	31.122	48%	20.987		na
Free cash flow per employee	2.706	-89%	24.448	4%	23.615	16%	20.301	310%	4.953	nm	-6.145	nm	70	-98%	2.847	135%	1.213	-94%	20.987		na
Operating cash flow *pre-working capital movement* per employee	41.029	-29%	57.436	13%	50.938	38%	36.920	-10%	40.952	2%	40.215	2%	39.271	-7%	42.039	2%	41.300	39%	29.775		

Table 40: Changes in operational productivity (Techem)

Asset base	PostLBO												LBO								
	x+6		x+5		x+4		x+3		x+2		x+1		t+4		t+3		t+2		t+1		t
In TEUR	2006 (Sept 30)	YoY	2005 (Sept 30)	YoY	2004 (Sept 30)	YoY	2003 (Sept 30)	YoY	2002 (Sept 30)	YoY	2001 (Sept 30)	YoY	2000 (Sept 30)	YoY	1999 (Sept 30)	YoY	1998 (Sept 30)	YoY	1997 (Sept 30)	YoY	1996 (Sept 30)
Tangible assets	210.442	7%	196.524	3%	190.846	0%	191.427	2%	187.837	12%	168.326	11%	152.072	-2%	155.783	4%	149.562	4%	144.319	49%	96.663
Intangible assets	232.599	22%	190.200	52%	125.297	3%	121.497	-10%	134.629	42%	94.854	7%	89.054	3%	86.826	0%	86.443	3%	83.720	1403%	5.570
Operating assets	440.312	11%	397.017	6%	374.687	0%	373.287	0%	375.049	27%	294.211	14%	258.555	2%	253.775	5%	240.922	2%	236.312	9%	216.030
Operating current assets	229.870		200.493		183.841		181.860		192.625		127.162		112.342		109.751		106.757		111.029		119.367
Inventories	21.678		17.056		17.611		21.247		29.776		34.281		30.615		29.420		28.188		27.721		29.066
Trade accounts receivable	200.022		175.852		159.129		154.159		156.934		87.389		76.795		75.809		74.857		79.916		77.678
Working cash @2% sales	8.170		7.585		7.101		6.454		5.915		5.492		4.932		4.522		3.712		3.392		12.623
Tangible assets	210.442		196.524		190.846		191.427		182.424		167.049		146.213		144.024		134.165		125.283		96.663
Property, plant and equipment	69.071		57.164		55.847		53.321		46.223		39.192		36.608		45.725		40.932		40.818		22.730
Rental equipment	141.371		139.360		134.999		138.106		136.201		127.857		109.605		98.299		93.233		84.465		73.933
Asset productivity																					
In EUR																					
Sales to operating assets	1,188	1%	1,176	2%	1,153	5%	1,094	8%	1,011	-16%	1,207	-3%	1,248	7%	1,165	2%	1,140	9%	1,044	0%	1,047
Operating profit to operating assets	0,242	14%	0,213	-7%	0,229	92%	0,119	16%	0,103	-43%	0,180	9%	0,166	10%	0,151	28%	0,118	26%	0,094	9%	0,086
Operating cash flow to oper. assets	0,161	-44%	0,290	0%	0,290	6%	0,274	12%	0,244	22%	0,200	-3%	0,205	-2%	0,210	4%	0,201	55%	0,130		na
Free cash flow to oper. assets	0,015	-89%	0,140	-2%	0,143	11%	0,129	nm	0,030	nm	-0,042	nm	0,000	-97%	0,019	143%	0,008	-94%	0,130		na
Oper. cash flow *pre-working capital movement* to operating assets	0,230	-30%	0,330	7%	0,308	31%	0,234	-6%	0,249	-10%	0,276	0%	0,277	-2%	0,282	5%	0,267	45%	0,184		na
ROIC (incl. goodwill)	12,2%		11,8%		14,3%		9,1%		7,6%		11,9%		12,6%		12,4%		22,5%		14,0%		na

Table 41: Changes in asset productivity (Techem)

Therefore, management sought to reintegrate these agents. In addition, the sales and distribution concept of home automation was restructured. The direct sales channel Techem had established to reach out to private customers was expensive and inefficient in terms of attracting new customers. With the stronger emphasis on cost control, management chose to promote the business through key account managers that received additional training tailored to the market launch of the home automation system.

Another challenge in terms of overhead was the integration of Heimer Concept. As the acquisition was justified by the volume increase in the German market, it was clear that significant savings in operations, in particular in overhead, could be realized. The central functions of Heimer at its headquarters in Gütersloh were discontinued. Also, management introduced a new IT infrastructure at Techem in 2004 and 2005 as part of the 'Fokus' program, including new CRM and billing software. These seamless processes allowed enhancement of sales productivity per employee by roughly 15%. By 2006, management had established a key account management system, accompanied by a separate complaints management and an enhanced quality management system in the branch offices.

Hierarchical Complexity

As part of the 'Fokus' restructuring program, the hierarchical structure applicable to the directors who were responsible for coordination between the major regional hubs was completely disbanded. To compensate the loss of managerial competence, the scope of responsibility at the regional head level was significantly expanded. Dismissing of a full layer of management helped to achieve the reduction of the workforce.

Management Control Systems

The basic report formats and frequency remained unchanged after the exit from the LBO. The interviewees noted that management added selected reports as part of the introduction of the key account reporting. The reports allowed monitoring of the customer development at a new aggregate level of transparency and responsibility. There were no other obvious changes in the management control systems in the post-exit period.

3.1.3.3 Entrepreneurial Growth Focused-Management Activities

3.1.3.3.1 Strategy

During the IPO preparation, Techem's management restated its strategic objectives (see Table 42). Innovation leadership continued to be the fundament of its strong market position and above market sales growth. Management confirmed its interest in seizing new growth potential in energy contracting and its interest in the home automation market previously not served. To further expand the revenues, management stated to continue with the internationalization with focus on East European markets. Further, Techem's management was willing to couple organic growth with active growth by acquisition.

Changes in strategy objectives in 2000 were modest. The growth targets were ambitious even in the considerably improved context. The strategy reflected management's diminishing risk aversion. It should be noted that although leverage still amounted to a multiple above the average of listed companies, debt repayment was apparently not on management's 'top agenda'. Management instead was willing to fund additional growth investments and accept increased debt. However, the downturn in the domestic market in 2001 and 2002 required a change in strategy. Profit warnings in 2002 caught investors off guard, especially as the business had always been seen as robust. The long-term contracts and stable growth certainly contributed to senior management's low attention to costs[1278].

As a result, management had to reconsider Techem's corporate strategy. In general, the industry remained attractive: strong customer lock-in through long-term contracts, regulation requiring continuous upgrade of the devices installed, and high barriers for market entry. Further, Techem continued to hold a unique position within the industry: the highest service quality due to its national distribution network and efficient IT infrastructure, the highest purchasing power for metering devices, and access to state-of-the-art technology.

Nonetheless, management had to initiate significant improvements in its growth, its market strategy and operational efforts. The costly sales and marketing initiative in the home automation business segment was halted and organized in a more inexpensive manner through key accounts. Add-on acquisitions in related business segments, in particular IT services, were stopped. The focus on technology leadership as a core competence of Techem was reinforced, although R&D spending did not significantly increase in the following years.

By 2006, the management under leadership of Horst Enzelmüller had returned the company to its previous level of profit. The strategic objectives communicated to the stock market concentrated on maintaining technological leadership in the energy services business, while achieving cost leadership through modern IT systems and

1278 For a detailed discussion on the underlying causes for the changes of objectives of management see chapter C3.2.2

optimized operations and sales processes. Management further targeted selective acquisitions to increase domestic market share and enter into new markets.

Strategy in Business Segment Energy Services

Techem's core business remained energy services accounts. Techem positioned itself as leading service provider to the residential property industry. In Europe, each customer of Techem had in average some 20 apartments and around 890 metering units installed. After the IPO, growth of equipment sales was hampered by the rising saturation in Techem's home market, Germany. New construction projects accounted for less than one percent of the total number of devices in operation.

After going-public in 2000	In 2003	In 2006
(1) Innovation • Further development to ensure high quality and reliability • Expand into new business fields *(2) For energy contracting* • Tailor-made service offerings • Focus on large residential blocks and commercial buildings *(3) For home automation* • Participate from growing market • Expand into segment of individual family houses *(4) Internalization* • Broad expansion into Eastern Europe *(5) Acquisitions* • Supplement to organic growth	*(1) Germany* • Market leadership through organic growth in energy services • Stronger interaction of business units *(2) Internationalization* • Growth through taking account of national characteristics *(3) Quality* • Industry leader in quality • Service-oriented structure and customer proximity *(4) Costs* • Reduction cost base • IT based processes *(5) Innovation* • Leader in fully-automated taking of automated readings	*(1) For energy services* • Improvement of service quality • Cost leadership • International expansion *(2) For energy contracting* • Individual solutions for energy management • Investigating the usage of renewable energies (biomass) *(3) For IT services* • Exploit cross-selling opportunities

Table 42: Post-exit corporate strategy objectives (Techem)

Hence, revenue growth was increasingly dependent on the transition from evaporation-based to radio-controlled technology. The key success factors for Techem remained technology and innovation leadership. This was accompanied by an unrivalled quality in delivery and service. The lasting outperformance of its peers proved that Techem was following the right strategy and illustrated the market's readiness for technical innovations. By the end of 2004, Techem had gained a market share of over 80% of all radio-controlled devices used in Germany. Techem could further secure its strategic position as economies of scale in purchasing and distribution of metering enhanced the barriers to market entry.

Furthermore, the rental business was expanding, particularly in radio-controlled devices. Although their purchase price exceeded the price of traditional evaporators by far, the devices where highly attractive for landlords as they ensured precise measuring and did not required the presence of tenants when metering was due[1279]. For Techem, the margins were higher due to the underlying long-term contracts and to the cost advantage of electronic data transfer. Even though the business required significant investments in the purchase of equipment, the emphasis was maintained after the change in management.

On the basis of the existing systems and network of devices installed, Techem's management intensified in 2000 their focus on home automation. Techem's technology strength enabled it to pioneer this market. The first generation of radio systems were introduced to the market after the IPO and continuously updated. The strategic intent was again market leadership on the basis of distinctive skills in technology and customer service. The economic downturn in Germany in 2002 eroded the profitability of the home automation business segment and required a strategy change. The business segment was reintegrated into the energy services business unit. The independent sales and marketing setup was consolidated, focusing on indirect rather than expensive direct sales channels and distribution partners.

Strategy in Business Segment Energy Contracting

The strategic concept had been developed around the energy supply to larger residential blocks and commercial buildings[1280]. The contracting services included providing energy[1281] from Techem's own or from leased energy generating plants. In the market, Techem positioned itself as the most professional asset manager with innovative products designed to lower operating costs and to raise yields. In terms of customer segments, management targeted the housing industry and the commercial sector, with a focus on acquiring large-scale projects. The contracting business however required new expertise in plant planning, installation, financing, maintenance, and consumption billing[1282].

1279 Between 2000 and 2006, their share from new devices rose from 15% to 46%, and surpassed 50% by begin of 2007.

1280 The revenues for the contracting business arose from three revenue pools: (i) a fixed handling fee for energy delivery, (ii) the price for the underlying delivered energy, and (iii) the billing fee.

1281 Such services covered a building's central heating system or the supplying of heat and electric power.

1282 In 2005, a "NutzEnergieContracting" product offering was launched that encompassed the servicing of real estate with energy for heating, air condition, light and ventilation. The contracts included the energy procurement and operational management. The extended offerings were targeted in particular to hotels,

The growth was nurtured by industry consolidation and increasing outsourcing by customers. On the one hand, the industry structure consisted of small, local utilities that where only allowed to operate in their local area. On the other hand, larger traditional energy service suppliers such as Vattenfall, Harpen, and Steag, entered into the market. The ongoing liberalization of the energy market enabled customers to choose between various energy sources, to whom access had been difficult. To conclude, the industry offered significant growth potential from consolidation. Techem as one of the market leaders had a mere 3% market share. On the customer side, Techem benefited from accelerating competition within this industry, as established international investors, including real estate funds like Lone Star, entered the German market. Such investors regarded energy as a pure cost position and opted to outsource it to specialized providers.

In contrast to the energy service business, this segment provided a lower margin while requiring higher capital expenditure[1283]. Although this was to some degree conflicting, management continued to invest into the business after the strategy adjustments in 2003. This was rewarded by exceptional growth in 2005 and 2006, partially related to the enormous cost pressure from increasing energy factor costs.

Strategy in Business Segment IT Service

After the IPO, this new business segment was established by merging the IT-related services with the eServices product offerings, with a clear focus on residential property customers. The business encompassed energy and facility management as well as general management of the residential property. The market was dominated by Aareon that held a market share of around 70%, with Techem the No. 2 with a 5% share. Several competitors ceased their operations, leaving market niches behind. Techem reasoned that the existing relationship to its customers and its common product ranges would not suffice to advance growth. Despite its cross-selling potential, Techem decided that organic growth had to be supplemented by a partner, partially because the company lacked appropriate skills and know how. In 2006, management entered into discussion with its direct competitor, Aareon, and agreed on a strategic partnership[1284] in which the companies would provide a

---

schools, hospitals, production facilities and logistic centres

1283 Average EBIT margin for energy contracting amounted to an average of 9.0% (2002 to 2006), in comparison to the average of 19.1% (2002 to 2006) for the energy services business.

1284 Techem planned to exchange the IT services business unit for Aareon Energy management. The rationale was to enhance the offer by Aareon's ERP system on SAP base and open Techem's products to Aareon's customers. Thereby, Techem paid a cash compensation of EUR 6.5 Million to Aareon.

comprehensive service to landlords in the areas of tenant administration, meter reading and billing services.

In terms of profitability, the IT business was burdened by continuous ramp-up investments and remained unprofitable throughout the entire post-exit period. This was partially due to the high development and maintenance costs of the software and expensive sales network. After 2002, management decided to concentrate on core applications and, as a result, was able to significantly reduce losses[1285]. In the long-term, the market for property management software was seen as attractive due to the high market entry barriers. The development of special software for this relatively small market presupposed a readiness to incur high investment outlays. By 2005, the investment backlog gradually disappeared and helped stabilize the business.

Diversification and Scope

The long-term customer contracts made acquisitions highly attractive and the only way to grow significantly above the market average. Acquisition targets were compared to Techem relatively small and operated in niche markets. Against its strategic interest, Techem was prevented by cartel rules from takeovers larger than EUR 10 Million in the energy services market in Germany. Techem also targeted acquisitions that would expand its know-how base and resources, particularly with regard to specific R&D and technologies[1286]. Techem also sought to obtain the majority stake in subsidiaries initially founded as joint ventures with local partners.

In the initial post-exit period, management diversified into new business areas, in particular IT-related services. For instance, the acquisition of the Haus Perfekt GmbH in 2001 opened the market for property management software. The software covered simple bookkeeping procedures as well as the general management of the residential property, and formed the nucleus for the IT business segment. Techem's intention was to penetrate the market of property management. With the additional acquisition of WODIS in 2002 Techem became the No. 2 market leader in providing software and communication services to the housing property market[1287].

1285 In 2002, IT services accrued a negative operating profit of EUR 11.1 Million at a sales level of EUR 8.4 Million. In 2006, the business was still loss making with a negative operating profit of EUR 4.2 Million at a sales level of EUR 10.4 Million.

1286 For instance, Techem acquired Veridis Software-Systeme GmbH, a developer of billing systems for measuring services companies and energy suppliers. The company had gained significant expertise through diverse large-scale R&D projects.

1287 WODIS targeted companies managing at least 1,000 units. WODIS offered broad consultancy services to the housing industry. The acquisitions enabled Techem to become a full-service provider for outsourcing complete business processes. However, the acquisition of WODIS came at a high price, since the firm

After the strategic adjustments, selected non-core businesses were sold in 2003 and 2004 (see Figure 17). Having refocused the business, Techem decided to acquire a direct competitor, Heimer Concept, who was the number six player in the German metering market with approximately 40.000 customers and 2.5 Million installed devices, for EUR 48 Million. The acquisition was a one-off opportunity to acquire market share. Heimer was a pure energy service player with no activities in energy contracting and in IT services. As a result, the acquisition involved no change in business scope and allowed Techem to realize significant savings from scale effects. One should note that Techem undertook acquisitions with serious diligence. For instance, it retreated from the takeover battle for the French CIS group when management concluded that the prices offered were too expensive.

	2000	2001	2002	2003
Acquisition	Techem Wassertechnik, *Austria* Calortherm, *Switzerland* Meßtech AG, *Switzerland*	Veridis Softwaresysteme, *Germany* Haus Perfekt, *Germany* NCCC Calorlux, *Luxemburg*	Caloribel, *Belgium* WODIS wohnungswirts. Software, *Germany* Niersberger, *Germany*	*No substantial acquisitions*
Divestment	*No substantial divestments*	*No substantial divestments*	*No substantial divestments*	Haus Perfekt, *Germany*
	2004	**2005**	**2006**	
Acquisition	Techem Messtechnik (remaining 12%), *Austria*	heimer Concept, *Germany*	Mesa GmbH, *Germany* Daniel S.A., *Greece* CMS/ DMS, *Denmark* Servito, *Rumania*	
Divestment	EL-ME AG, *Germany* Techem Drecount Utility Service GmbH, *Germany*	*No substantial divestments*	*No substantial divestments*	

Figure 17: List of substantial acquisitions and divestments in the post-exit period (Techem)[1288]

3.1.3.3.2 Innovation

R&D Spending and Efficiency

Technology leadership and high product quality remained the key success factors in Techem's strategy. In the year of the IPO, the R&D budget leaped by 54%. The volatility of R&D expenses between 2001 and 2006 (see Table 43) was largely related to the project nature of R&D, including the introduction of the home automation system in 2001 and the development of Ecotech in 2005. In some cases, management mandated external engineer centres to ensure sufficient resources while remaining flexible on costs.

---

suffered a negative EBIT EUR 3.4 Million at revenue of EUR 6.8 million.

1288 Only acquisitions and divestments above a value of EUR 0.5 Million are listed. Further, the purchase of remaining shares of subsidiaries is not listed, as they are not material for the change in diversification.

	PostLBO												LBO								
	x+6		x+5		x+4		x+3		x+2		x+1		t+5	t+4		t+3		t+2		t+1
	2006 (Sept 30)	YoY	2005 (Sept 30)	YoY	2004 (Sept 30)	YoY	2003 (Sept 30)	YoY	2002 (Sept 30)	YoY	2001 (Sept 30)	YoY	2000 (Sept 30)	1999 (Sept 30)	YoY	1998 (Sept30)	YoY	1997 (Sept 30)	YoY	1996 (Sept 30)
R&D relatred performance indicators																				
Total R&D expenses to total sales	0,9%		1,5%		1,6%		1,3%		0,9%		1,3%		1,3%	0,9%		na		na		na
Three year rolling average	1,3%		1,4%		1,3%		1,2%		1,2%		1,1%		1,1%	0,9%		na		na		na

Table 43: Changes in R&D input, output and efficiency (Techem)

R&D Focus and Cooperation

After the IPO, Techem enhanced the scope of its R&D projects, while keeping the general focus unchanged. In energy services and devices, work focused on product innovation. New generations of metering equipment were introduced that led to considerable cost and process optimization (see the product evolution in Figure 18). In particular, permanent product improvement and adaptations were introduced for radio-controlled systems. Their capacity to gradually upgrade through remote metering resulted in an increase in the rate at which the conventional metering devices were replaced with radio-controlled technology. Field data collection was simplified to such an extent that readings could be taken from all electronic measuring devices without any contact and with minimized errors. In October 2005, a new series of radio-controlled devices called "Ecotech" was launched that allowed remote reading of over 5 Million installed devices. The remote measuring was automatically linked to the central Techem computing and billing centre, allowing real-time consumption and billing management by the customers. For home automation, the strategic intent was to bring the first system to market and to subsequently continuously update the technology. The systems were built as expandable modules to permit increasing customer demand. In 2001, the first home automation system called "Assisto" was successfully launched. The system offered control of under floor heating. Additional components for remote control were developed, for instance individual room temperature control, consumption measurement, temperature-based security surveillance, and boiler control. Management also pursued product innovation for IT-related services. The usage of an electronic data exchange via Internet was promoted, in particular covering internet-based billing management and archiving.

After the strategy adjustments in 2002 however, a series of unpromising R&D projects were ceased. With the acquisition of WODIS, the focus was expanded to the development of full service software management systems. In 2005, a new release of the software was launched, leading to additional customers. For the energy contracting business, management probed different energy technologies. A new type of power plant built to prove the profitability of renewable energies, however, did not fulfil the expectations.

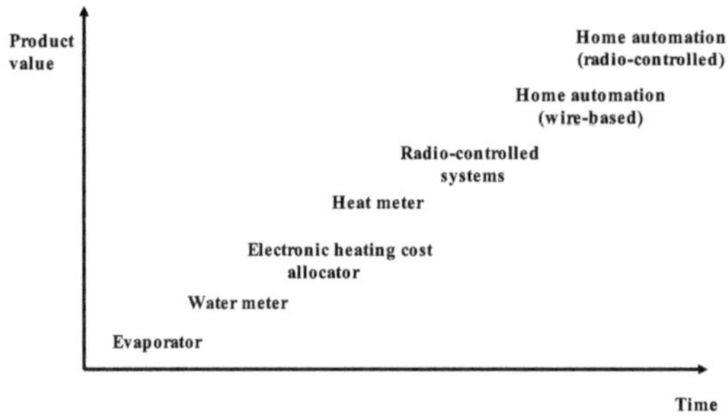

Figure 18: Product evolution (Techem)

Techem's management continued with the joint R&D projects with its industrial partners that were crucial for Techem because it did not produce its own water and heat meters and radio-controlled devices. Techem maintained its close cooperation with partners like EL-ME, Diehl, and Hydrometer, each the most important supplier for their individual business segment. All corporation was based on binding contracts. The joint development teams were responsible for the technical development, the concept of the service related to the new device, and had to organize the market entry. Alongside Techem's own staff of technicians and engineers, management initiated cooperation with scientists from universities and colleges, including Paderborn, Dresden and Stuttgart.

In summary, the R&D competences of Techem in the metering business were continuously strengthened. The focus was on updating devices in remote control measuring. Fluctuating expenses in the post-exit period reflected the project nature of R&D, whereby the share to total sales on a rolling average modestly increased. As a result, Techem remained the technology leader in the German market in its business.

3.1.3.3.3 Market Development

International market expansion was one of the top three objectives of the strategy agenda formulated in 2000. To accompany the international expansion, management harnessed significant resources to establish subsidiaries in the new markets and secure local service networks.

Cooperation and Resource Development

In the year of the IPO, subsidiaries were founded in Sweden and Bulgaria. Between 2001 and 2006, further representations were established in Belgium, Brazil, China, Czech Republic, Kazakhstan, Norway, Romania, Slovakia, and Turkey. The workforce outside Germany increased by 22%, while the domestic workforce declined by 7%. By 2006, 25% of Techem's employees were non-domestic. The share of employees was much higher than their 15% share of total sales. On the one hand, this reflected Techem's lower stake in the value stream in Germany, including, sales representatives and third parties for servicing the network. On the other hand, the efficiency with which the service was conducted in non-domestic markets was much lower. Techem relied on local sales partners in many countries. Over time, Techem, however, sought to own the subsidiaries and brand them with its own company name.

The strategy adjustments in 2003 did not lead to a slowdown of international expansion. Non-domestic revenue declined in 2004 and the workforce was slightly reduced. The revived sales momentum in 2005 led to an increase in employment.

Market Development for Energy Services

In Germany, growth in energy services flattened in 2002 as a result of the recession in the construction industry. By the end of 2004, the market for new constructions started to turn, however, at a comparatively low level. The East German residential market suffered from high vacancy rates and a government demolition program. Not surprisingly was hence the price decline in 2005 on a sales per unit base (see Table 45), after the peak in 2004. The decline was related to enhanced price competition among the large metering providers. Efficiency gains in the purchase, installation and maintenance of the meters, which increasingly consisted of radio-controlled devices, sparked reduced sales prices. This was in particularly noticeable in decreasing sales per rental contract and rented meters. Techem experienced a significant slowdown in growth in maintenance services due to market saturation. Maintenance contracts were offered only in Germany[1289] and to a considerably smaller extent in Austria and Switzerland. The maturity of these markets indicated only moderate growth potential. The sales of home automation were to be triggered by intensive direct sales. The introduction of key accounts only partly stimulated new growth, since the market suffered from a low level of new construction projects and a slowdown in modernization and renovation.

In Eastern Europe, the market was especially attractive due to energy liberalization and interest in consumer-oriented billing. Even though funding for new housing and renovation work was not available, heat cost allocations developed as a favourable means of cost savings. Techem closely monitored the progress of the local markets and seized growth opportunities as soon as a consumption-based measuring system

1289 Around 15% of installed device in Germany were covered with such contracts.

became mandatory[1290]. Few markets were quickly developed and reached a maturity where further growth was reliant on upgrading the metering devices to radio-control and on taking market share from competitors and undergoing selected acquisitions[1291], similar to the strategy in Germany. Extensive market saturation caused equipment sales in Eastern Europe to decline temporarily and resulted in a tangible decrease in sales revenue in 2003. Some Western European markets offered growth outlooks similar to some of the emerging Eastern European markets[1292]. In pioneering markets for Techem - Brazil[1293], China, Russia, and Ukraine - there were large urban populations living in apartment blocks not yet subject to consumption-based billing. In these markets, legislation was moving to consumption-based billing to control growing demand for energy. Techem intensified their lobbying efforts, while acting as market maker and offering advice on pilot projects. These countries represented a new quality of challenge due to size and investment Techem's management had to master.

Market Development for Energy Contracting

For the energy contracting industry in Germany, growth was invigorated by the entry of foreign investors acquiring formerly unseen portfolios of residential property. With such professional investors adopting a clear yield-orientation, this meant a paradigm shift for the management of residential property in Germany. Techem benefited from the market dynamics with an annual growth of 30% and brought an integrated, real-time billing package in 2005 to market that was accompanied by a concentrated marketing and sales offensive[1294]. The introduction of the 'Nutz Energie contracting' stimulated further customer demand. By the end of 2006, Techem had reached the No. 4 market position in Germany, operating behind RWE, Urbana and Getec. In the sub-market related to residential housing, Techem was already the No. 2. In terms of total sales, the contracting business grew from 6% in 2000 to 18% in 2006.

1290 The strong position of Techem with over 80% market share in 2007 in Bulgaria, for instance, was a result of the enactment of the 2001 energy law and the immediate market entry.

1291 In Eastern Europe, Techem reached a certain market maturity in Bulgaria and the Czech Republic. A similar market position was taken in Western countries directly neighboring to Germany, in particular in Austria, in Benelux, Denmark (by acquisition), and in Switzerland.

1292 Techem aggressively targeted France, Italy, Sweden, Norway, and Turkey. In theses markets, management enhanced their sales activities and actively offered radio controlled devices.

1293 In Brazil, Techem targeted to benefit from the growth opportunities in the water metering market.

1294 The market volume was estimated at EUR 2 to 3 billion and growing rapidly.

Net working capital	PostLBO						LBO				
	x+6	x+5	x+4	x+3	x+2	x+1	t+4	t+3	t+2	t+1	t
In TEUR	2006 (Sept 30)	2005 (Sept 30)	2004 (Sept 30)	2003 (Sept 30)	2002 (Sept 30)	2001 (Sept 30)	2000 (Sept 30)	1999 (Sept 30)	1998 (Sept 30)	1997 (Sept 30)	1996 (Sept 30)
Inventories	21.678	17.056	17.611	21.247	29.776	34.281	30.615	29.420	28.188	27.721	29.066
Trade receivables	59.140	52.356	38.341	38.170	52.927	53.893	46.032	84.850	74.857	79.916	77.678
Trade payables	31.878	22.051	16.409	11.085	12.371	9.840	8.371	10.937	9.011	7.154	5.259
Total	**48.940**	**47.361**	**39.543**	**48.332**	**70.332**	**78.334**	**68.276**	**103.333**	**94.034**	**100.483**	**101.486**
Sales growth implied change	5.701	3.183	2.785	5.420	5.335	6.850	9.418	7.239	11.401	33.366	na
Other change	(4.122)	4.635	(11.574)	(27.420)	(13.337)	3.208	(44.475)	2.060	(17.850)	(34.370)	na
Total annual change	1.579	7.818	(8.789)	(22.000)	(8.002)	10.058	(35.057)	9.299	(6.449)	(1.003)	na
Relative											
Inventories (% of COGS)	7,4%	6,7%	7,5%	8,9%	19,4%	25,6%	26,2%	23,8%	23,6%	25,7%	na
Trade payables (% of COGS)	20,3%	20,5%	16,2%	16,1%	34,4%	40,2%	39,4%	68,8%	62,7%	74,1%	na
Trade receivables (% of sales)	11,3%	11,2%	8,9%	9,3%	14,0%	15,2%	14,3%	28,7%	27,3%	32,4%	41,9%
Total (as % of sales)	**9,4%**	**10,1%**	**9,2%**	**11,8%**	**18,5%**	**22,1%**	**21,2%**	**34,9%**	**34,2%**	**40,7%**	**54,7%**
Collection period	**41,3**	**40,9**	**32,4**	**34,1**	**50,9**	**55,4**	**52,1**	**104,7**	**99,5**	**118,3**	**152,8**
Credit period	**74,0**	**74,7**	**59,3**	**58,6**	**125,6**	**146,7**	**143,7**	**251,0**	**228,8**	**270,6**	**na**

Table 44: Changes in working capital (Techem)

Sales productivity	PostLBO												LBO								
	x+6		x+5		x+4		x+3		x+2		x+1		t+4		t+3		t+2		t+1		t
In EUR	2006 (Sept 30)	YoY	2005 (Sept 30)	YoY	2004 (Sept 30)	YoY	2003 (Sept 30)	YoY	2002 (Sept 30)	YoY	2001 (Sept 30)	YoY	2000 (Sept 30)	YoY	1999 (Sept 30)	YoY	1998 (Sept 30)	YoY	1997 (Sept 30)	YoY	1996 (Sept 30)
Energy services sales per meter	10,46	2%	10,22	-9%	11,26	-5%	11,90	1%	11,76	8%	10,85	14%	9,52	-5%	10,03	-8%	10,89	3%	10,57	13%	9,39
Energy services sales per househol	56,68	2%	55,70	-1%	56,05	5%	53,51	0%	53,28	-3%	54,82	4%	52,51	-6%	55,67	-10%	61,79	3%	59,76	13%	52,87
Billing sales per meter	5,33	4%	5,14	-10%	5,68	-5%	5,98	2%	5,85	7%	5,46	16%	4,70	-3%	4,85	-7%	5,20	0%	5,21	10%	4,72
Equipment sales per sold meter	12,58	-14%	14,63	5%	13,91	12%	12,44	13%	11,02	2%	10,85	-10%	12,00	-19%	14,76	-26%	20,04	15%	17,49		na
Sales per rental contract	289	-3%	297	-7%	318	3%	309	-5%	324	-5%	340	-1%	343	-3%	353	-3%	364	-3%	374	-2%	383
Sales per rented meter	8,50	-1%	8,61	-4%	9,01	5%	8,58	-2%	8,72	-2%	8,90	0%	8,87	5%	8,46	5%	8,09	0%	8,12	0%	8,16
Sales per maintenance contract	144	0%	145	-7%	155	2%	151	13%	134	-1%	135	-4%	140	-8%	153	2%	149	-12%	169		na
Sales per maintenained meter	5,58	2%	5,47	-3%	5,66	3%	5,52	9%	5,06	-7%	5,46	-6%	5,80	-6%	6,18	6%	5,83	-10%	6,50		na
Sales per energy contract	94,6	28%	74,1	19%	62,1	2%	60,6		na		na		na		na		na		na		na
Sales per sold megawatt	138,0	29%	107,1	14%	93,8	0%	93,4	4%	90,2	-9%	98,9	4%	95,5	36%	70,2		na		na		na

Table 45: Changes in sales productivity (Techem)

Market Development for IT Services

IT benefited after the IPO from the strong economy and excitement surrounding the Internet. Techem was one of the full service providers for business application solutions for the real estate industry. The company focused its applications on the IT-support of billing and discontinued non-core activities, such as online Hausing and Hausperfekt. Although the relative position of Techem improved, it could not elude the declining sales trend. However, the market recovered and by 2006 Techem had gained the No. 2 position in the market in Germany. The synergy between the measuring service and the IT environment of the customer and the resultant process advantages for real estate persuaded Techem to sign a strategic partnership with Aareon in June 2006. As a preferred Aareon partner, Techem served the majority of installed ERP systems in the real estate industry. Techem's implied leverage effect was with the partnership much higher than as an ERP provider. As a result, Techem sold its IT services to Aareon and received in return Bautec Energiemanagement GmbH, the former billing services division of Aareon

Techem's pace of international expansion accelerated after the IPO, but remained largely unaffected by strategy adjustments after the profit warning in 2002.

3.1.3.3.4 Human Resource Management

General Human Resources

Techem attempted through professional development and career training to cope with the increasing complexity of the product offering and international nature of the business. Given the entry into a series of new business fields, such as, home automation and energy contracting, Techem invested considerably both in the training of the existing workforce and in hiring external experienced managers and employees. In 2006 (2000), 56% (60%) of all employees attended a training. Techem also provided specific programs for short-term required competencies like cross-selling after the restructuring of the sales department[1295].

For the advancement of its own management personnel, Techem established a specific training program[1296]. In addition, Techem maintained the high level of

1295 In 2001 and 2002, Techem recognized the need for enhanced project management skills and implemented a one-year modular program for qualifying employees. In 2004, 236 employees were trained in cross-selling as part of the restructuring of the sales department. In 2006, key account managers obtained specific additional qualifications.

1296 Selected employees passed a two year modular program to advance their career and acquire management skills. Further, Techem offered a 'junior staff career advancement'-program to simplify thee integration of new personnel and to enhance the attractiveness of a job position at Techem.

vocational training, since this was the core source for new employees. In 2005, Techem introduced a profit-sharing scheme replacing the former static payment system[1297]. However, only a limited number of employees in the sales division and in management were paid this scheme.

As mentioned, the workforce in field services, sales, and general administration was reduced as result of the 'Fokus' program. Working hours were changed and flexible working models were introduced. The restructuring, in addition to the personnel adjustments, slowed down yearly salary growth. Average growth during the buyout of 3.4% jumped to 3.6% annual growth from 2000 to 2002. After 2002, however, growth decreased to 1.8% (from 2002 to 2006).

Top Management Resources

After the exit from the IPO, management initially remained constant, but changed in the medium-term (see Table 46). At the time of the IPO, the management board consisted of three of the initial four members at the entry into the LBO. Structurally, the only change at the time was the CEO being appointed Chairman of the supervisory board. Throughout the LBO, senior managers had the trust of the buyout investors.

Herbert Böhm, responsible for service, development and technology, retired in September 2001. The profit warnings in 2002 prompted the owners and supervisory board members to loose, confidence in the CEO. Taking effect on August 31, 2002, Dieter Dannheimer, chairman of the board of directors, tendered his resignation in a mutually agreed move. On January 1, 2003, Horst Enzelmüller joined the board as chairman and surrounded himself with a team of loyal executives. According to employees at Techem, Horst Enzelmüller managed to quickly win the confidence of the workforce through numerous open discussion forums and direct communication. CFO Peter Wunderlich and the board member responsible for IT, Stefan Pattberg, followed Enzelmuller from his former employer, Colt Telecom. After differences on corporate strategy with the new CEO, the Chairman of the supervisory board and former CEO, Hans-Ludwig Grüschow, resigned. By that point, Enzelmüller had obtained the full support of the supervisory board to follow his strategy and support his strict cost-cutting strategy.

1297 The scheme intended to recognize special achievements. Profit-sharing up to 3% was granted, depending on the result generated by the company. The model was negotiated with the works council, and targeted to increase the variable profit-linked income by up to 8% during the years 2005 to 2008.

Name	Responsibility	As of Oct.1st, 1999	After Jan. 1st, 2001	After Sept. 30, 2001	After Jan. 1, 2003	After August, 2003	After October, 2005	After December, 2006
Dieter Dannheimer	*Chairman;* Human Resources, law and public	x	x	x				
Walter Schmidt	Accounting, finance, commerce, controlling and IR	x	x	x	x			
Herbert Böhm	Service, development and technology	x	x					
Rainer Schamoni	*Deputy chairman;* marketing, sales services, development, international business andsubsidiaries From August 2003: sales Germany, energy contracting, technology, services		x	x	x	x		
Horst Enzelmüller	*Chairman* ; Foreign sales, marketing, business development, legal affairs, M&A, personnel, IR				x	x	x	x
Stefan Pattberg	*CIO* ; IT business					x	x	
Peter Wunderlich	*CFO* ; Finance, accounting, receivables manag., logistics & infrastructure, controlling, audit					x	x	x
Hans-Lothar Schäfer	Technology, international markets						x	x
Bernd Süllberg	Sales Germany						x	x
Markus Toporowski	Services							x

Table 46: Changes in the management board (Techem)

The last remaining member of the former management team, Rainer Schamoni, left the board in October 2005. In May 2006, Stefan Pattberg left the board.

To ensure motivation and a common interest within the management group in the post exit period, a stock option program was introduced in 2000[1298]. Management continued to enjoy a fixed and variable compensation scheme (see Table 47). By fiscal year 2003/2004, compensation of the management board was modified. The stock option program was stopped and partially substituted by a stock appreciation rights program.

	For fiscal 2000 to 2003			Fiscal year 2004			Fiscal year 2005 and following		
	Parameter	Varia-bility	Proportion upon target	Parameter	Varia-bility	Proportion upon target	Parameter	Varia-bility	Proportion upon target
Fixed emoluments (basic salary, benefits)	Function, area of responsibilty	Fixed	n/ a	Function, area of responsibility	Fixed	52% (46-58%)	Function, area of responsibility	Fixed	40% (37-43%)
Variable emoluments	Techem Group EBIT, individual performance	n/ a	n/ a	Techem Group EBIT and ROCE	0-200%	38,5% (29-50%)	(a) Techem Group EBIT and ROCE (b) Outperformance in relation to the M-DAX	0-200% 0-200%	33% (30-38%) 19% (17-23%)
Support benefits (pensions, etc.)				Length of service		9,5% (0-13%)	Length of service		8% (0-11%)

Table 47: Changes in compensation scheme (Techem)

The variable compensation was moreover linked to the group's EBIT and ROCE performance. In total, the variable part accounted for up to 47% in 2005 and 39% in 2006. Between 2000 and 2002, average remuneration per board member grew by 16%,

1298 The author will discuss the implications of the stock option scheme in the course of the evolvement of managerial shareholdings in the exit period in chapter C3.2.1.4.

from 2002 to 2006 by 21%. Share-linked bonus plans were also set-up for non-board, senior executives of the German and international subsidiaries. Remuneration was linked to the performance of the Techem share on the MDAX.

3.2 Case Analysis

3.2.1 Changes in Governance over the Buyout Cycle and in the Post-Exit Period

At the entry into the LBO structure in 1996, the new shareholders under the leadership of BC Partners changed the governance structure in all four constituents: debt leverage, ownership concentration, monitoring, and management participation.

After 4 years as LBO, Techem AG was listed on the Frankfurt Stock exchange on February 24, 2000. The constituents of governance changed accordingly. The proceeds of the IPO were largely used to repay debt. Although the company exclusively dedicated the proceeds of the primary offering to deleveraging, the debt level remained above that of comparable competitors. The buyout investors sold their shares in Techem in a first tranche as a secondary at the IPO and in a second tranche 12 months later. The shares were distributed among institutional investors and retail shareholders. From the manager group, only selected persons were entitled to participate in the equity management program. Shortly after the exit, the total management board held roughly 1% of all shares. Monitoring was adjusted to meet the standard of a German listed company, even tough a representative of BC Partners remained on the supervisory board for one year and the former CEO joined as Chairman.

3.2.1.1 Debt Leverage

BC Partners as the new majority shareholder of Techem were approved with the expectation that the new structure would enable funding of the company's strong growth. The buyout investors together with other shareholders were to create a debt structure that would provide enough flexibility for management's growth plans.

Several loan agreements between Techem AG and Dresdner Bank in December 1996 financed the entry of BC Partners and the co-investors. The bank arranged two acquisition loan agreements of EUR 74 Million (four year maturity) and EUR 15 Million (five year maturity) to finance the share purchase from the family owners. An additional facility of EUR 184 Million was agreed to restructure existing debt (at the time EUR 131 Million, four-year maturity) and provide sufficient funds for new growth investments. The three loan agreements were closely tied by cross-default covenants and by additional covenants with respect to the information requirements of management. In total, debt increased to EUR 246 Million by the end of 1997, equaling a net debt to EBITDA-ratio of 5.4x.

During the preparation of the IPO at the end of 1999, Techem's capital structure was still characterized by a small equity base and high debt leverage (see Table 48)[1299]. Techem nonetheless paid out EUR 23 Million of its retained earnings as special dividend to its shareholders. As a result, the debt to equity-ratio declined to 2.3%. To cushion the enhanced likelihood of bankruptcy, a personal loan was given by family founders, Ursula Felten and Martin Ott, of EUR 53 Million for the acquisition of Techem Service AG & Co.

After the successful IPO, the proceeds of EUR 56 Million were as planned used to reduce debt, finance capital leases, and increase working capital. By the end of the fiscal year 2000, debt leverage had declined to net debt to EBITDA-ratio of 3.3x. In 2002, Techem set up a special purpose entity to sell a large amount of trade receivables. This allowed management to exchange the former factoring of deferred items and accounts receivables for a (current) bank liability over EUR 204.5 Million. In 2003, Techem renegotiated its loan agreements to convert the short term-heavy financing structure (90% of debt was financed with a run time of below 1 year) into a medium- to long-term one. A bank consortium led by Dresdner Kleinwort Wasserstein arranged a new financing contract of EUR 350 Million[1300]. The basis for the improved covenants was the commitment of the new management team to repay at least EUR 20 Million per annum to a target amount below EUR 150 Million. As a result, management was able to lower annual financing costs by around EUR 1.5 Million. The reduction of debt remained challenging. Management's appetite for acquisitions again increased debt leverage in 2002 to a 3.1x net debt to EBITDA-ratio.

Techem's propensity to carry debt was high due to its low-risk business model. Long-term contracts with attractive margins ensured revenues and cash flow for periods often longer than the loan agreements. Techem's market position made fierce price competition unlikely and kept market entry barriers intact. This was illustrated by the ease with which Techem was able to optimize constantly its financing arrangements, even during the change in management team, including its CFO, in 2003. Management refused to pay dividends to shareholders until 2004, as it

1299 In the meantime, the loans had been refinanced. By end of 1999, the loan structure had had been shifted to a short-term structure due to the low interest rates and in expectance of the proceeds.

1300 The financing contract consisted of three tranches. An amortizable loan of EUR 150 Million with payments of EUR 15 Million scheduled every half year was concluded. A bullet term loan of EUR 70 Million was arranged and a revolving facility of EUR 90 Million was provided, of which EUR 40 Million was used by Techem at end of fiscal year 2003.

preferred to repay debt instead of debt-financed dividend to their shareholders[1301]. Due to successful cost management, the company was able to repay EUR 48 Million of debt in 2004. The debt burden was reduced to a net debt to EBITDA-ratio of 1.6x, equaling industry-standard capital structures. By 2005, Techem again refinanced the exiting loan and closed a new contract for EUR 300 Million with a 7-year facility[1302]. At the end of 2005, CEO Horst Enzelmüller announced that debt repayment was not anymore a top management priority and, revised the initial debt target of EUR 150 Million[1303]. The acquisition of Heimer Concept and capital expenditure for rental equipment due to strong revenue growth prevented Techem from a similar decrease of leverage in 2005 and 2006.

The high debt propensity mitigated the relationship of debt leverage and risk attitude by management. Even though the buyout investors imposed high debt on Techem, management may have reacted less sensitive than in other companies. The repeated approach by buyout investors and hedge funds underpinned the debt propensity and attractiveness of Techem's business for an LBO-like structure[1304].

3.2.1.2 Ownership Concentration

The LBO resulted in a distribution of ownership among three investor groups with different investment objectives[1305]. The largest group, the buyout investors with BC Partners as their leader and the largest equity share in relative and absolute terms, intended to divest with in a foreseeable time after maximizing their return rate on their employed equity. The background of the investors in this group differed according to the origin of their funds, since the two smaller members were largely financed by German investors while BC Partners has an international investor base. The second group constituted the two representatives of the family founder. Their intention was to develop the business to a point where they could take it public at a fair price after initial discussions with potential investors in 1995 had not produced an attractive valuation. The third and smallest group was the senior managers who held minor stake.

During the LBO, no major conflicts were observed. All groups mutual benefited from the complementary expertise, e.g., family's industry expertise and buyout investors'

1301 For details, see the discussion of the cash flow from financing to debt- and shareholders in chapter 0.

1302 Of the total funds, EUR 150 Million were an amortizable loan with payments of EUR 10 Million every half-year and a revolving facility of EUR 150 Million. Techem used the latter revolver in the amount of EUR 59 Million at end of fiscal year 2005.

1303 In particular, the CEO feared a too high attractiveness for financial sponsor and buyout investors.

1304 See chapter C3.2.1.2 for the details of the takeover bids.

1305 For the change in ownership see Table 49.

corporate finance expertise. A shareholder agreement set forth the exit preconditions eliminated potential conflicts[1306].

After the IPO, the ownership concentration decreased considerably. The two smaller buyout investors divested their shareholdings; BC Partners reduced their share to 33% of equity (see Table 49). The family owners also reduced their shareholdings to 25%, but stayed above an important threshold in terms of voting rights. Management, as elaborated in the previous chapter, retained their shares. After the look-up period of one year, BC Partners sold their remaining shares in February 2001.

The founding family compensated partly for the exit of the buyout investors by maintaining their 25% stake. Nonetheless, new investors entered the picture. Different investors reported shareholdings beyond 5%, however, with none holding a stake above 10%. All in all, institutional investors accounted for some 65% of total shares, or 86% of the free float. Since none of the new investors were represented on the supervisory board, management had to intensify their informal discussions with the investor community. The CEO had to inform two groups about the progress of the company: the supervisory board, including the family owners (25% of equity) and industry experts, and the actual shareholders composed of a group of institutional investors (65% of equity). He admitted that about 25% of his time was dedicated to communicating with the investor community. In addition, Techem carried out regular surveys in order to measure the way in which the company was perceived by the stock market.

In February 2006, the Felten and Ott families sold their 25% stake to the open market. Techem, as a result, lacked a long-term investor base with a large controlling stake. However, the stability of cash flows and the attractive low indebtedness made Techem an attractive target for a financial investor or a strategic investor wanting to enter into the German and European metering market. As a defense against a hostile takeover, the supervisory board extended all agreements with the board members to include a change-of-control clause, which would only become effective if a change of control took place, and both supervisory and management board would vote against the acceptance of a takeover bid.

1306 The observations reflect the findings on a survey on the cooperation of family owners and buyout investors. See Achleitner, Schraml et al. 2008

Net debt	PostLBO						LBO				
	x+6	x+5	x+4	x+3	x+2	x+1	t+4	t+3	t+2	t+1	t
In TEUR	**2006** (Sept 30)	**2005** (Sept 30)	**2004** (Sept 30)	**2003** (Sept 30)	**2002** (Sept 30)	**2001** (Sept 30)	**2000** (Sept 30)	**1999** (Sept 30)	**1998** (Sept 30)	**1997** (Sept 30)	**1996** (Sept 30)
Bank liabilities	287.814	212.921	221.274	268.345	322.589	100.464	83.629	129.624	61.282	245.931	135.259
Residual term smaller 1 year	28.143	22.954	34.420	35.004	283.857	65.374	25.782	99.415	15.143	10.146	118.894
Residual term between 1 and 5 years	229.671	139.809	185.904	231.889	31.775	32.357	51.693	21.113	35.908	235.786	14.517
Residual term more than 5 years	30.000	50.158	950	1.452	6.957	2.733	6.154	9.096	10.231	0	1.848
Shareholder's loan (total)	0	0	0	0	0	0	0	0	53.174	0	0
Long-term capital lease	5.938	2.888	3.783	6.062	3.439	0	388	3.063	8.213	13.361	0
Current capital lease	1.646	1.843	2.516	2.945	2.054	388	2.675	5.151	5.148	4.750	0
Financing provided by factoring	0	0	0	0	0	204.517	204.517	204.517	196.183	0	0
Cash (and equivalents)	20.966	9.720	14.439	16.038	13.756	9.225	5.260	6.717	4.933	12.117	7.408
Total net debt (cash)	**274.432**	**207.932**	**213.134**	**261.314**	**314.326**	**296.144**	**285.949**	**335.637**	**319.067**	**251.925**	**127.852**
Annual change	66.500	(5.202)	(48.180)	(53.012)	18.182	10.195	(49.688)	16.571	67.141	124.074	na
Net debt to EBITDA	**1,69x**	**1,54x**	**1,56x**	**2,76x**	**3,14x**	**2,89x**	**3,28x**	**4,28x**	**4,91x**	**5,40x**	**0,69x**
Equity	**227.157**	**206.565**	**166.072**	**122.340**	**111.548**	**98.383**	**86.065**	**9.412**	**26.901**	**24.392**	**14.003**
Equity to total capital	**31,0%**	**33,6%**	**30,9%**	**23,0%**	**20,0%**	**21,7%**	**20,0%**	**2,3%**	**6,5%**	**5,9%**	**6,4%**
Debt to book equity	**126,7%**	**103,1%**	**133,2%**	**219,3%**	**289,2%**	**102,1%**	**97,2%**	**1377,2%**	**227,8%**	**1008,2%**	**965,9%**

Table 48: Change in debt leverage over the buyout cycle (Techem)

FY 1999/2000	FY 2000/2001	FY 2001/2002	FY 2002/2003	FY 2003/2004	FY 2004/2005	FY 2005/2006
(1) Corporate planning and budget (2) Long-term strategic orientation (3) Preparation of transformation into new millennium (4) Planned secondary offering (5) Allocation of business duties at the management level *Three scheduled meetings*	(1) Corporate planning and budget (2) Future development of the economic position of the group as well as individual subsidaries (3) Strategic direction *Four scheduled meetings*	(1) Corporate planning and budget (2) Transactions on part of company and affiliates (3) Deviations from business plan (4) Risk management and risks that have come apparent (5) Future development of the economic position of the group as well as individual subsidiaries (6) Strategic direction *Six scheduled meetings*	(1) Corporate planning and budget (2) Future development of the economic position of the group as well as individual subsidiaries (3) Strategic direction (4) Progress on „Fokus" cost-cutting program (5) Downsizing of workforce in Germany and related costs *Seven scheduled meetings*	(1) Corporate planning and budget (2) Future development of the economic position of the group as well as individual subsidiaries (3) Strategic direction (4) Growth opportunities outside Germany (5) Future EDP concept (6) Updating bylaws binding board of directors (7) Implementation of German Corporate Governance Code (8) Efficiency of reporting to supervisory board *Four scheduled meetings*	(1) Corporate planning and budget (2) Future development of the economic position of the group as well as individual subsidiaries (3) Strategic direction (4) Improvement of service quality (5) Strategy and organization of international activities (6) Optimization of legal structure (7) Financing and dividend policy (8) Remote measuring through radio technology *Five scheduled meetings*	(1) Corporate planning and budget (2) Future development of the economic position of the group as well as individual subsidiaries (3) Strategic direction (4) Potential acquisitions Optimisation of marketing structure (5) Status of improvement in service quality (6) Integration of heimer concept (7) Development of international activities and potential in individual countries (8) Compensation of board of directors *Five scheduled meetings*

Figure 19: Topics of supervisory board meetings (Techem)

In October 2006, the infrastructure fund Macquarie announced a takeover bid, which was rejected by both management and supervisory. In November 2006, the former buyout investor BC Partners countered the offer and was welcomed by the management board. One month later, Macquarie increased its voluntary public tender offer to a 45% premium to the three months share price average. However, Macquarie's improved bid did not win the necessary acceptance, even after both board recommended accepting the offer. The shareholders, particularly the hedge funds, seemed to expect a sweetened offer and were not willing to sell. The offer failed even after Macquarie lined up with BC Partners.

	Pre-IPO				Post-IPO					
	Sept 30, 1999		Jan 20, 2000		Sept 30, 2000		Sept 30, 2001		Nov 30, 2006	
Equity shareholders	Share capital	In %	Share capital	In %	Share capital	In %	Share capital	In %	Share capital	In %
1. Buyout specialists										
BC Partners	1.374.250	51,5%	11.019.980	51,3%	8.147.834	33,2%				
Belfinance Participaties	133.958	5,0%	1.075.020	5,0%						
Bd W	66.468	2,5%	533.000	2,5%						
2. Management and employees										
Herbert Böhm	9.715	0,4%	77.900	0,4%	77.900	0,3%	77.650	0,3%		
Dieter Dannheimer	14.572	0,5%	116.850	0,5%	116.850	0,5%	92.500	0,4%		
Horst Einzelmüller									12.000	0,0%
Hans-Ludwig Grüschow	19.480	0,7% S	156.210	0,7%				0,0%		
Rainer Schamoni	0	0,0%	77.900	0,4%	77.900	0,3%	59.900	0,2%		
Hans-Lothar Schäfer									1.984	0,0%
Walter Schmidt					0	0,0%	0	0,0%		
Bernd Sülberg									3.700	0,0%
Markus Toporowski										
Total	43.767	1,6%	428.860	2,0%	272.650	1,1%	230.050	0,9%	17.684	0,1%
3. Institutional investors										
Capital Group Companies									1.273.168	5,2%
Jupiter Asset Management									3.452.470	14,0%
Total										
4. Family founders										
Total	1.048.148	39,3%	8.405.000	39,2%	6.170.286	25,2%	6.170.286	25,1%	6.566	0,0%
5. Free float										
Total	0	0,0%	0	0,0%	9. .	40,5%	18.176.	74,0%	19. .688	80,7%
	2.666.592	100,0%	21.461.860	100,0%	24.524.929	100,0%	24.576.999	100,0%	24.690.260	100,0%

Table 49: Changes in ownership structure (Techem)

Although no bidding party was able to acquire Techem, two financial investors, Macquarie Bank and Elliott International Capital Advisors, dominated the shareholder base. In the first weeks after the takeover battle, management increased the dividend payout ratio to approximately 80% (see the discussion on cash flow to shareholders in chapter 0). Management backed away from initial plans to conduct a 50% capital increase and issue a convertible. As a result, earnings per share increased.

The early divestment by the family meant that the private control benefits were of minor interest. In addition, any benefit-seeking behavior was limited to 25% of voting rights. Several empirical surveys confirm that family control is most beneficial for an ownership concentration under 50% and for companies that are publicly quoted[1307]. The free float was furthermore large enough to ensure sufficient liquidity. Due to its small equity share, management played a minor role beyond its role as manager in the governance structure.

Despite the entry of hedge funds, the shareholder base continued to lack investors who pursued long-term investment objectives. The management had only limited means to balance these objectives. The hedge funds did not announce how long they would hold their shares. Management said it would seek investors who would have a long-term investment horizon.

3.2.1.3 Activity Level of Investors

The board composition changed modestly after the IPO. Jens Reidel, the former Chairman of the supervisory board, left shortly after the divestiture of BC Partners and was replaced by a representative of the family owner. Former CEO Hans-Ludwig Grüschow was elected as new Chairman. The remaining five shareholder representatives included three industry experts, including the former chairman of management board; one representative of BC Partners; and a lawyer and tax advisor affiliated to the company. The changes in the following years gradually included external stakeholders of Techem. With Prof. Horst Ziegler an industry expert of a supplier joined the board. Ziegler was a member of the advisory board of Hydrometer GmbH, a partner in R&D and market development, and had been a board member prior to the LBO. Volker Riebel, CEO of a property management company and customer of Techem, joined the board in 1995.

		Skill				Membership								
Name	Role	Finance	Industry	Operations	Turnaround	Prior exit	FY 1999/2000	FY 2000/2001	FY 2001/2002	FY 2002/2003	FY 2003/2004	FY 2004/2005	FY 2005/2006	FY 2006/2007
Hans-Ludwig Güschow	Chairman		x	x			x	x	x	x				
Jens Reidel	MD, BC Partners	x			(x)	x	x	x						
Prof. Horst Ziegler, Ph.D.	Chairman (of FY 2002/ 2003), Industry expert		x	x					x	x	x	x	x	x
Martin Ott	Family owner representative		x			x	x	x	x	x	x	x	x	x
Harald C. Bieler	Consultant		x	x		x	x	x	x	x	x	x	x	
Stefan Zuschke	BC Partners					x	x	x	x	x	x	x	x	
Hans-Jochen Otto	Lawyer and tax advisor	x	(x)			x	x	x	x	(x)				
Wilhelm Bender	Industry expert		x	x						(x)	x	(x)		
Ursula Felten	Family owner representative		x								(x)	x	x	x
Volker Riebel	Industry expert		x	x								(x)	x	x
Martin Stanley	MD, Macquarie	x			(x)									x
Robert Hock	MD, Elliott	x			(x)									x

Table 50: Membership structure of the supervisory board

1307 See Lehmann and Weigland 2000, pp.185

In the first two years, the activity level met the average of listed companies in Germany. For those, a quarterly meeting is standard to review company's current performance development and discuss legally required issues. Topics covered development of the company in terms of financial controls such as reviewing the annual budget (see Figure 19). The exception to this was former CEO and new Chairman Hans-Ludwig Grüschow, who continued to actively participate in managerial meetings and intervened in daily operations to the dislike of new CEO Horst Enzelmüller. The new corporate governance structure faced a litmus test with the profit warning in 2002, when it became apparent that profit was declining and debt repayment had to be halted. An intense discussion evolved between the CEO and the Chairman about the implementation of the right strategy. The supervisory board seemed to respond to this crisis in governance reactively rather than proactively[1308]. In 2002 and 2003, the activity level of the supervisory board peaked at six and seven meetings, respectively. In the following two years, 2004 and 2005, the agenda of the supervisory board meetings concentrated on implementation of the cost improvement program as well as progress on international growth and service quality. In 2006, the board needed to stabilize the new ownership situation and handle the takeover battle together with the management board. Because of the ownership structure, two representatives of the financial investors, Martin Stanley and Robert Hock, joined the supervisory board.

Overall, Techem went through three periods of activity level. In the first period between 2000 and 2002, the activity level was on par with the average of listed companies. Of the supervisory board members, only the two family representatives were bound to the company's success with direct returns. The board appeared to discuss plans as presented by the management, with little inclination to take an independent view. No conflicts of interest between family representatives and other shareholders were observed. A moderating factor for the average monitoring level was certainly the low business risk and high mutual trust between the Chairman and CEO. Similar to Wincor Nixdorf, the existence of the founding families as blockholder shareholder made a takeover of Techem unlikely. In addition, no substituting disciplinary effect could be expected from a takeover threat. The second period started with the crisis in 2002 and forced the supervisory board to reshuffle the board and actively enter into decision making with regard to refining the corporate strategy and developing the cost cutting initiative. The board relied on the

1308 For instance, significant investments had been approved at the beginning of 2002, even though net income was already stagnating.

new team under the leadership of Horst Enzelmüller. Since the supervisory board had actively set-up the new corporate strategy, the activity level again declined. The third period was heralded by the exit of the family investors in March 2006. Changes in the supervisory board with a shift to financial engineers who were focused on maximizing shareholder returns occurred shortly after the takeover.

3.2.1.4 Managerial Shareholdings

The entry of BC Partners and minority buyout investors Belfinance and BdW made it possible to put in place an exit strategy for the family founders while ensuring Techem's independence. Senior management became true entrepreneurs and received around 2% of total equity at the entry into the LBO.

At the IPO, the management board members retained their shares[1309]. To reward the employees for their efforts during the LBO and ensure continuous alignment of interests, the investors offered all employees and sales representatives the possibility to sign up for shares of up to 7.500 EUR per person, as their total did not exceed 10% of equity. Although the senior management group held shareholdings directly after the exit, their ownership stake decreased rapidly due to the departure of board members and their continuous shares sales (see Table 49)[1310]. By 2006, the shares held by active management board members accounted for 0.1%.

Initially, Techem had adopted an initial stock option plan entitling management to accumulate stock options directly after the IPO. The program allowed granting up to 1,609,624 shares of common stock to senior managers and employees of Techem[1311]. A second stock option plan was introduced in March 2001, with the granting of up to 436,716 shares. The difference was a shorter vesting period (two years), a longer life time (seven years), and a shorter option plan (seven years). The subscription rights for both option programs of each 50% were exercised only when one or both of the following two performance targets were achieved: (a) the market price of the shares of the Techem rose by a cumulative annual average of at least 7% within the period between the grant and the exercise of the subscription rights; (b) the market price of the shares of Techem performed at least equal to the M-DAX, or out-perform the M-

1309 This observation of the management refusing to sell their shareholdings again resembles the results from Holthausen and Larcker (See Holthausen and Larcker 1996, p. 302)

1310 During the change in management in 2002 and 2003, former CEO Dieter Dannheiemer and two other board members left the company. Rainer Schamoni, the last board member of the pre-IPO team, also left the board in 2005. In total, this equaled 1.8% of total equity. The subsequent board members, however, did not acquire significant shareholdings of the company.

1311 Under the option plan, options granted approximate market value of the shares at the date of the grant. Such options vested at the end of a three-year period commencing at the date of grant. Further, the life of the option was a maximum of three years. The term of the option plan was for eight years.

DAX. Since the performance targets were neither achieved during the fiscal years 2000 to 2003 nor at the balance sheet date, no compensation expense was recognized between 2000 and 2003.

Because the stock option program did not materialize given that the performance of the company failed to fulfill the prerequisites for three years in a row, the entire top management compensation scheme was altered[1312]. The supervisory board's personnel committee linked the compensation tighter to actual accounting performance and less to share performance. The committee also introduced a voluntary program for the conversion of stock options into stock appreciation rights in 2004[1313]. In terms of alignment of interests, stock appreciations rights do not make the participating employee a true owner of the company, since he does not provide personal wealth upfront.

The options may motivate management to myopic behavior by fulfilling short- to medium-term expectations of stock market. By the end of 2005, the lock-up period for a part of the rights had ended and finally yielded payment to management that was exercised in cash as opposed to shares, and, as a result, did not increase managerial stakes. It was understandable that management strived to cash-out a substantial part of their compensation and reduce financial exposure of their personal wealth, since the previous years had not resulted in a cash-out with respect to the stock option programs[1314].

By comparison with Wincor Nixdorf, differences in corporate strategy between owners and managers were not obvious. On the one hand, senior management held only a comparatively small stake and was less dependent on share price development. On the other hand, they also had limited influence on decision-making in the supervisory board.

1312 See the overview of changes in management compensation scheme in Table 47.

1313 This program resembled a 'virtual stock option' program. The basis of the computation for the new stock appreciation rights program was the number of stock options granted under the first stock option plan converted at a ratio of 1:1.2. The investor granted selected key employees with additional stock appreciation rights. As a result, the number of options outstanding decreased significantly. With the stock appreciation rights, employees received variable compensation based on an amount that depended on the performance of the share price without the employees becoming shareholders. Those eligible to the program had the right within the exercise period to a payment of cash of the difference between the agreed subscription price and the minimum share price at that given point in time. A condition that had been met was that the share price exceeded the exercise price, plus a cumulative 5% for each completed financial year starting from the end of the minimum holding period.

1314 See Bruton, Keels et al. 1999, p. 403

Explanatory variables	Hypo-thesis	Expected change after exit		Key observations
Debt leverage	1	(-)	CF	Proceeds of IPO are fully dedicated to debt repayment
			NCF	In post-exit year 1 and 2, various acquisitions and massive investments in oper. asset base
			NCF	Special dividend shortly before IPO increasing leverage to LBO entry level
			CF	After statefy change, debt repayment returned on top agenda and reached industry average in post-exit year 4
Ownership concentration	2a	(-)	CF	Complete exit of buyout specialists within 12 months post-exit
			CF	New investors only partly represented on the supervisory board
			NCF	Founding family continued to hold 25% of equity in first years
			CF	However, family investor divest after share price recovers from turnaround
Activity level	3a	(-)	CF	Reduced activity level in post-exit year 1 and 2, focus on delivery on growth targets; however low business risk and decreasing company risk make reduced activity economically reasonable
			NEU	Due to the minority stake of the founding family, not takeover threat; however, activity level not fully substituted by founder family
			NCF	"Managed corporation":: activity (only) after company crisis in 2002; increased activity however issue-driven and may have been prevented by proactive cutbacks to business expansion
Mgmt. shareholdings	4a	(-)	CF	After change of management team new managers without substantial shareholdings
			NEU	Unfavorable market development hinder acquisition of shares based on stock option program; further high turnover dilute existing management shares

CF: Observations confirm hypothesis
NCF: Observations do not to confirm hypothesis
NEU: Observations neither confirm nor reject hypothesis

Table 51: Synthesis of changes in governance (Techem)

3.2.2 Changes in Management Objectives

Emphasis on Efficiency

Continued high debt leverage after the IPO imposed massive pressure on cash flow generation. Management favored a growth strategy designed to strengthen cash flow by growth, particularly given the positive market outlook at the IPO. Throughout the previous years, each year saw an increase in growth and earnings. The supervisory board and the new institutional investors shared management's beliefs and welcomed an offensive growth strategy. The long-term contracts and stable growth outlook underpinned management's position. As a result, management's attention to costs unintentionally declined. A further explanation for the low focus on cost was management's relatively high level of fixed salaries and low shareholdings.

Given the enhanced risk appetite and growth ambitions, the recession in the domestic market hit Techem even more. Two profit warnings in 2002 caught investors off guard, especially as the business model had always been deemed to be stable. As a result, the supervisory board changed management. The new team under the leadership of Enzelmüller refocused corporate efforts on cost efficiency and introduced the 'Fokus' program. The strong cost focus continued in the following four years observed, even though Techem made large acquisitions in 2005 and management still did not have a significant stake.

Emphasis on Entrepreneurial Growth

Throughout Techem's corporate history, management and owners jointly followed a strategy based on organic growth complemented by selected acquisitions and entry into new markets. Not surprisingly, management maintained this strategy at the time of the IPO despite the small equity base with the introduction of a long-term entrepreneurial strategy.

The IPO prospectus claimed revenue growth, both through iinternationalization and selected acquisitions, next to the build-up of innovative service and system packages as cornerstones of corporate strategy. This was underpinned by the reorganization of the legal structure resulting in a strategic holding company in 2002[1315]. The question, however, was whether management would be diligent enough in their choice of growth projects and whether it would avoid non-value creating diversification and empire-building.

1315 Techem dissolved former strong functional units and transformed them into independent operational units, offering a high level of entrepreneurship to the responsible managers.

Management objectives	Hypothesis	Explanatory variables: Debt leverage	Explanatory variables: Ownership concentration	Explanatory variables: Activity level	Explanatory variables: Mgmt. Shareholdings		Key observations
Efficiency improvement	5	(+)				NCF	Despite high debt leverage reduced attentiveness to cost position
	6		(+)			CF	Effiicency focus reduced despite strong family founder shareholder position
						CF	Initially limited interest to adjust workforce and conduct layoffs
	7			(+)		CF	Initially limited number of discussions in supervisory board on efficiency-related issues
	8				(+)	NEU	Despite unchanged managerial shareholdings decreased emphasis on efficiency
						CF	However, relationship diluted by very small managerial shareholdings
						CF	New management team with high efficiency focus despite low shareholdings
Corporate entrepreneurship	9	(-)				CF	True for the interest in non-core busines entrepreneurship
						NCF	To be rejected for the interest in core business entrepreneurship
	10		(+)			CF	Dispersed ownership structure with fluctuating investors demanding short-term earnings growth
	11			(+)		NEU	Frequent discussions in supervisory board on growth related issues, e.g., acquistions and progress on interntional subsidiaries
	12				(+)	CF	Higher risk affinity given low exposure to personal wealth and considerably high fixed salary
						CF	Stock option program with comparatively high threshold partly spurred growth appetite even in high-risk, uncertain business fields
						CF	New management team with high entrepreneurship focus despite (low) none shareholdings
		Direction of expected correlation					

CF: Observations confirm hypothesis
NCF: Observations do not to confirm hypothesis
NEU: Observations neither confirm nor reject hypothesis

Table 52: Synthesis of changes in management objectives (Techem)

As mentioned, the alignment of interests suffered because management only had a minor stake. Shareholdings were held only by a highly select group of senior managers.

Investors further implemented alternative instruments to align interests and increased the threat of myopic investment behavior with the stock option and appreciation rights program. Given their high fixed salaries, management was less risk averse and more willing to invest in uncertain business areas unfamiliar to Techem. The entry into new businesses, however, did not produce appropriate profits for Techem within a reasonable period. At the strategy review in 2002, the supervisory board did not question the ambitions for growth in the core business. Instead, they curbed the extent of diversification and investments in non-core businesses. As a result, the current and former CEOs left the boards given that they were identified with the earlier diversification strategy.

The return to previous profit levels revitalized management's appetite for growth, as indicated by the acquisition of Heimer Concept in 2005. The strategy resembled the former balance of organic and selected growth by acquisitions. The focus on entrepreneurial activities remained unchanged at least for the core business despite the crisis. It appeared that this focus was largely independent of the emphasis on efficiency. The challenge of any monitoring and governance structure was, to ensure sufficient focus on efficiency.

3.2.3 Changes in Efficiency-Focused Management Activities

The optimization of operations in the service network and in the offices had continuously been a priority of management. The most important decision had been the consolidation of the network, which lasted beyond the LBO into the post-exit period. New technology development triggered a series of process improvements such as the introduction of mobile data collection. During the LBO, no layoffs or divestments were needed to meet the debt repayment schedule. Therefore, debt leverage was not the determining factor for improvement of operational productivity, as long as operations generated the intended cash flow. Furthermore, the owners and supervisory board had not shown serious interest in detailed measures. However, after unrest in the management board, the activity level of investors did considerably increase. They discussed the cost structure and quickly introduced the 'Fokus' program, and participated in the restructuring. The board also closely tracked the development of service and delivery quality.

	Hypothesis	Explanatory variables: Debt leverage	Explanatory variables: Ownership concentration	Explanatory variables: Activity level	Explanatory variables: Mgmt. Shareholdings		Key observations
Operational productivity	13a	(+)				CF	With stronger capital base, management comfortable with productivity levelsand left setup of operations
						CF	After return to high debt level, return to operational improvements, e.g., lean coordination between field offices, that in turn prompted high productivity levels not formerly achieved
	13b		(+)			CF	Majority of shareholders interested in short-to medium growth of revenue base
						NCF	Ongoing tracking of service quality and delivery
	13c				(+)	CF	Focus even further weakened after reduced managerial shareholdings
Asset productivity	14a	(+)				CF	After management change in 2002 strong emphasis, e.g., divestment of non-core IT businesses
						NEU	In principal, strong demand for capital expenditure demanded from business model (in particular rental
	14b				(+)	CF	Management primarily focussed on long-term revenue increase, neglecting short- to medium return on
Outsouring and offshoring	15a	(+)				NEU	Given high debt payments, management passed on cost reductions to the suppliers and increased the
						CF	Increased capital made helped to equip second tier supplier with production equipment
	15c		(+)				*No observations*
	15d			(+)			*No observations*
	15e				(+)	CF	In first two years, decreased shareholdings yielded in less willingness to increase level of partnering
Working capital management	16a	(+)				CF	Cash proceeds supported lax management of working capital in first post-exit years
						CF	After return to high debt level, strong emphasis, e.g., abolishment of dunning blocks and centralization of warehouses to reduce inventory
	16b			(+)		CF	Limited discussion in supervisory board around working capital management
	16c				(+)	CF	In first two years with comfortable capital structure, lax attention towards working capital
						CF	Management actively steered against working capital increase after debt increase in 2002
Overhead productivity	17a	(+)				CF	Decrease in debt yielded growth ambitions, inducing additional sales and back-office resources
						CF	After return to high debt, management downscaled overhead functions, e.g., expensive key account management and high share of independent sales representatives
	17b				(+)	CF	Reduced managerial shareholding resutled in high risk appetite and investments in growth-enhancing overhead functions
						NCF	Despite ongoing low managerial shareholdings, new team continuously seeked to improve overhead
		Direction of expected correlation					

CF: Observations confirm hypothesis NCF: Observations do not to confirm hypothesis NEU: Observations neither confirm nor reject hypothesis

Table 53: Synthesis of changes in operations (Techem)

A large part of the investment in assets was predetermined by rental equipment purchases and other investments related to new customer contracts and upgrades. After the IPO, these investments measured as a share of total sales to remaind unchanged, denying a potential underinvestment hypothesis. Management enlarged the asset base by acquiring new IT-related equipment and making acquisitions in new business areas.

After the introduction of the restructuring program end of 2002, both management and shareholders actively demarcated the extent of necessary assets. As a result, management divested non-core assets to fund debt repayment. However, excluded from any adjustments to the asset assets were funds for the operations of the core business, for which management continuously ensured sufficient financing[1316].

In terms of in- or outsourcing activities in the value chain, Techem was less subject to such trade-offs as its business setup relied entirely on the purchasing of all components. To some degree, Techem was in the hands of a small number of suppliers. In the first two years after the exit, management did not alter contracts with suppliers. After the change in management, the new managers decreased the level of dependency and increased considerably the number of qualified suppliers.

The increased capital base helped to equip the 'second tier' suppliers with a set of appropriate production tools. On the other hand, the need to serve debt payments yielded a notable pressure on suppliers to reduce cost.

With respect to working capital management, the exit from the LBO reduced management's efficiency focus. The cash infusion from the proceeds to some degree led to lax receivables management and a significant increase in the collection period. Like with operations, management's attention weakened considerably, even though debt leverage was high. However, the inflection point for refocusing back on efficiency was reached in 2001 and resulted in first improvements of both receivables and inventory at the end of 2002. The new board managed to generate further cash flow from the reduction. In this case, the role of the owners and supervisory was less active than in the previous two cases.

This said, the influence on the level of administration, sales and other overhead staff was much more significant. The growth strategy resulted in massive investments in sales and marketing resources to develop new business segments. At first glance, this can be attributed to the fact that overhead departments are traditionally less

1316 Only limited observations were able about the level of outsourcing and offshoring across the buyout life cycle. Management claimed a contribution of the suppliers to the restructuring program.

comparable in terms of productivity and lack managerial attention. At second glance, the cost increase can also be attributed to the intentional buildup of new resources to establish the new business segments and sales channels. The increased costs reflected the higher risk and start-up characteristics. Management can be credited with the decisiveness with which adjustments were made after the recession of the German market in 2001. The new management team believed that the overhead functions left significant room for improvement. Various measures were implemented to optimize back-office processes. Techem rapidly integrated the acquired companies into its network. Even after reducing debt in 2006, management continued to impose cost improvement targets with a focus on sales and back-office.

For Techem, the hierarchical complexity changed in two dimensions in the post-exit period. First, because of network consolidation and the restructuring program, a complete managerial layer was abolished. Second, business units were given a much greater degree of independence, as central functions were dissolved. The first measure directly resulted from the cost improvement initiative. The second resulted from the enhanced entrepreneurial focus of management.

3.2.4 Changes in Entrepreneurship-Focused Management Activities

Robust historic growth and a positive outlook at the time of the IPO to some degree resulted in a decoupling of corporate strategy from debt. Management believed that operating cash flow would be enough to meet the debt repayment schedule irrespective of the growth strategy. Not until the profit warnings in 2002 did management consider a change in strategy. Management realized that refocusing on the core business of energy services and energy contracting was necessary and that the IT business needed to be gradually shut down and home automation downscaled. After having returned to an industry average debt level in 2004, management avoided acquisitions in non-core businesses. On the contrary, the only substantial acquisition of Heimer Concept strengthened the core business of metering in the domestic market. A more risky acquisition in related markets, the acquisition of CIS in France, was not pursued. With the unrest in 2003, the new management also reestablished cost leadership at the top of its agenda.

At the entry into the post-exit period, investors closely reviewed the corporate strategy as part of their pre-IPO due diligence. They appraised the business model with its secured long-term contracts and robust cash flow. They agreed with management's assessment that the characteristics of this business could be transferred to related industries such as property industry management. In addition, they shared the ambition of international growth. In supervisory board meetings after the IPO, the strategy was discussed, but not as explicitly as during the LBO.In the first two years after the exit, however, the level of stringency and rigidity of the business plan between management and owners was considerably less than in the LBO. Strategy formulation in the supervisory board occurred in a series of issue-driven discussions of opportunities and threats. The crisis in 2002 led to a higher activity level of the supervisory board, as differences on strategy emerged. The 'Fokus' restructuring program reflected the binding strategy plan the supervisory board advised the management to follow.

Management itself could rely at least in the first period on the proven strategic frame in which it had previously operated. Commitment to an intense and open strategy discussion was therefore limited. The long time the board had been in place produced a high degree of consent among board members, as well as in the supervisory board after departing CEO Hans-Ludwig Grüschow became Chairman. To some degree, they felt uncomfortable discussing decisive changes in strategy. By the end of 2002, this discussion, however, became inevitable. The new strategy was decided jointly by the supervisory and management board. After 2003, management could gradually recover control of the company to the extent trust of the supervisory board was reestablished.

For the level of R&D funding, two determinants were identified. First, Techem continued to have the ambition to be regarded as a technology leader in its industry. Second, management had decided to enter into businesses not served yet where new resources and know how had to be acquired. Debt leverage did not constitute a constraint during the LBO. With the decision to enter into new IT-businesses, funding increased significantly around the exit year and remained high until post-exit year 2. Further, various projects, for which the outcome was unclear such as home automation and internet-related services, were funded. The new investors supported management's growth plans and apparently increased R&D expenses. The project nature and time lag made it difficult to measure R&D efficiency over time. However, it seems that management and owners were in the post-exit year 2 dissatisfied with the funding level and reduced the funds by 30%. In particular, management targeted reduction of external work in non-core business.

After the management change in 2003, the focus of R&D did not change significantly. Techem continued to engage in both applied and developmental R&D. Management maintained to rely on R&D, since acquisition targets became sparse and Techem had to differentiate itself in the domestic market to an increasing degree through technology leadership. Funding levels returned to previous levels at the same time as debt returned to industry levels. Process innovation, including the introduction of

MDE, resulted in significant costs savings and was actively pursued. The level of cooperation with other companies remained high.

The proceeds and partial relief from predetermined cash flow permitted dedicating additional funds to international expansion. Management continued to establish subsidiaries in numerous markets dependent on progress in consumption-based billing. It seemed that funding and therefore debt was not a limitation, since Techem had already followed an active international growth strategy during the buyout[1317]. Again, the supervisory backed management's growth plan as it was arguably in the interest of the growth-seeking investors to accelerate the international sales growth..

The strategy adjustments in 2003 did not affect the commitment to market development in the core businesses, energy services and energy contracting. However, the growth rate of total non-domestic markets dropped to that in the domestic market. One explanation may be that management did not have a sophisticated growth program in place to expand their local operations. An alternative explanation is the risk aversion of the management team after 2003 that had to become familiar with the dynamics of international business. The increase in staff levels, to some degree an indicator of future growth potential, did not increase in step with expected international growth potential.

The fact that Techem entered into a strategic partnership with Aareon with limited financial exposure, as opposed to a takeover, also underpinned the conjecture of risk aversion. This would deny the thesis that low shareholdings and limited personal wealth exposure would not restrain management from undertaking risky ventures. For the domestic market, the degree of freedom was only limited. Long-term customer contracts drove growth, while the ability to acquire was restricted by anti-cartel rules. Additional resources for sales would have not adequately implied additional growth.

Human resource management remained a key topic on the management agenda, perhaps even with an increased focus. Management was aware of the importance of well-trained personnel and implemented various measures to further train, develop and retain the workforce. The entry into the new businesses implied investments in new know how and competencies.

1317 The international growth was not as funds intensive as in other industries. At the beginning, Techem could rely on the provision of metering devices from its domestic production network, while testing the readiness of the market with pilots in urban regions. With increasing growth and success, Techem gradually enlarged its operations and acquired local distribution partners to establish area-wide coverage. Further, the operator was not obliged to provide the complete country.

	Hypo-thesis	Explanatory variables: Debt leverage	Owner-ship concen-tration	Activity level	Mgmt. Share-holdings		Key observations
Strategy position	20b	(+)				CF	Cash proceeds gave management comfort to expand already broad strategy approach
						CF	After return to high debt (2002), refocussing of strategy and enhanced cost leadership
						NCF	Despite reduced debt leverage since post-exit year 4 (2004), continuous focussed strategy with limited diversification appetite
Strategy formulation	21a		(+)			CF	Institutional investors interest limited to fulfillment of growth targets. No detailed discussion of strategy, much more, general support of organic growth and growth by acquisitions, supposing robust basic cash flow that was likely given historic reliable performance.
	21c			(+)		CF	Frequency of strategy discussion at supervisory board level reduced to average comparable with stock market listed companies
						NCF	Active role during transition with engagement in strategy making
	21e				(+)	CF	Trust and lack of mgmt. shareholdings prompted low activity level concerning strategic decisions beyond the chosen growth strategy
Diversification and scope	22b			(-)		CF	Entry into new business segments, e.g. property planning software
	22d				(-)	CF	Low business risk and limited personal wealth exposure resulted in high risk growth strategy until post-
						NCF	New management team actively supported strategy refocussing and sell/ closure of non-core business
R&D efficiency	23b	(+)				NCF	Despite high debt leverage, R&D expenses peaked in going-public and the two following years
						CF	R&D expenses were considerably reduced in post-exit year 3 due to low R&D efficiency
						CF	After debt repayment, R&D funding returned to previous levels in post-exit year 4 and following years
	23c		(+)			NCF	Continuous high R&D level in first two post-exit year indicates investors' favor of long-term growth
	23e			(+)		CF	R&D not discussed explicitly at supervisory board level
						NCF	R&D funding cut as part of cost improvement initiative accompanied by intense board involvement
	23g				(+)	CF	(Initial) growth focus and risk appetite also affected willingness to undergo R&D project with more
		Direction of expected correlation					

CF: Observations confirm hypothesis NCF: Observations do not to confirm hypothesis NEU: Observations neither confirm nor reject hypothesis

Table 54: Synthesis of changes in entrepreneurial growth-focused activities (Techem)

	Hypothesis	Debt leverage	Ownership concentration	Activity level	Mgmt. Shareholdings		Key observations
Market development	24b	(-)				NEU	High focus on domestic market development and international expansion, including partnerships, in first two post-exit years
						CF	After strategy refocussing to core business segments, debt repayment resulted in slowed market
	24d			(+)		NCF	Supervisory board members continuously welcomed market development throughout entire post-exit
						NCF	High share of growth investors expecting Techem to deliver on the initial growth plans
	24f				(+)	NEU	In first two post-exit years, no changes in intensity and direction of market development (at constant mgmt. shareholdings)
						CF	New management team apparently was more careful in terms of international market expansion. Further, it had to become familiar with the risk and return profile of the local markets.
Human resources	25a			(+)		NCF	Supervisory board remained concerned about human resource management
	25b				(+)	NCF	Management remained concerned about human resource management, in particular for build-up of new
Top mgmt.: turnover	26b			(+)		NCF	New shareholders welcome continuity in the top management having succeed in the LBO
						NCF	No change in top management team after exit
	26d				(+)	NCF	Initial management team with considerable bargaining power
						NEU	New management team was able to develop a high trust of the supervisory board given their successful restructuring track record
Top mgmt.: skill profile	26e			(+)		NEU	No change in top management team directly after exit
						CF	New board members appointed from a company in a comparable industry (communication service
Top mgmt.: compensation	27b			(+)		CF	Total compensation increased significantly after management team change
						CF	Pay-for performance increased to maintain the level of alignment and motivation

Explanatory variables: Direction of expected correlation

CF: Observations confirm hypothesis NCF: Observations do not to confirm hypothesis NEU: Observations neither confirm nor reject hypothesis

Table 55: Synthesis of changes in entrepreneurial growth-focused activities (Techem, continued)

The supervisory board was directly concerned with the development of the German workforce and discussed the severe incisions as result of the restructuring program at various times in the board in 2002 and 2003 (see Figure 19).

In terms of managerial resources, the composition and skill profile of the board remained unchanged. The thesis of increased industry-specific skills cannot be rejected (but also not confirmed) since all management board members in place during the LBO were industry experts. This was also true for change in the management board at the end of 2002 and in 2003. Three of the new board members came from Colt Telecom, a company that although not directly the same industry resembled in many respects the business Techem was in. Management as stakeholder was in no position to influence appointments and the skill profile of new board members. Since Techem's challenge was to refine strategy and return operations to previous levels, it was likely that managers with industry skills would be favored.

Managers, given their tenure and track record, were in a strong bargaining position with the owners at the beginning of the post-exit period. They agreed on a compensation scheme with a high share of pay-for-performance. On the one hand, this was counterintuitive to the findings that companies with high debt favor a higher cash component[1318]. On the other hand, this was comprehensible as the business risk remained low and the supervisory board sought to provide management with shares. After the change in management in 2002, the stock option program was refined. Variable compensation was tied to actual accounting measures, indicating that management may have overestimated share price development. Management's increasing confidence and trust of the supervisory board also supported the above average growth of total compensation.

3.2.5 Changes in Performance Development

Performance development was reviewed for the holding period and for the post-IPO episode and compared relative to its own LBO average and to a selected group of competitors[1319].

During the LBO, Techem enjoyed strong revenue growth. In particular, the establishment of the rental equipment and the energy contracting business powered the sales increase. The volume increase in the energy services businesses resulted in significant scales of economy. The company was able to improve the gross and

1318 See Begley and Feltham 1999, pp.242 et seqq.

1319 The sample group of competitors comprises Aggreko, Davis service, Intertek, Homeserve, Neopost, and Rentokill.

operating margin, and convert improved margins into increased operating and free cash flow. The free cash flow in 1999 and 2000 was nonetheless burdened by investments into rental equipment. After the LBO, Techem was able to continue its strong growth despite the troublesome restructuring in 2002 and 2003. However, the growth lost momentum to the LBO average. Techem underperformed its competitors, particularly during the restructuring. In those two years, industry competitors mostly benefited from growth enhancing acquisitions. In 2004 and 2005, the acquisitive growth took its toll and resulted in some substantial refocusing. One may interpret this in the way that Techem passed through the restructuring period in advance of its competitors and returned to strong (organic) growth one year ahead of the industry. As a result, Techem was not able to regain its lost growth momentum ending 12% points lower on an industry-adjusted index in relation to fiscal year 1999/2000 (see Table 56).

In comparison to the constant sales increase, the development of the margins was not as robust. Until end of 2001, Techem continued to enhance its profitability, both in terms of gross and operating profit, while slightly outpacing its sales growth. In 2002 and 2003, margins decreased significantly because of the elaborated investments for establishing businesses that did not materialize as intended. Until post-exit year 4, Techem under-performed its industry peers with regard to operating profit[1320]. The new management team's efforts have to be acknowledged as they managed to lift profitability to previously not reached levels and outperform industry peers in 2004 and 2006. The strong revenue growth in 2006 resulted in an extraordinary strong profit due to the operating leverage of a 20% fixed costs base. One should admit that the positive development from post-LBO year four onwards can only partly be related to the exit from the LBO and is much more the outcome of the newly installed governance structure, particularly the quality of management and the enhanced monitoring level.

In addition to the observations made for the operating profit, the development of cash flow from operations was subject to changes in working capital. In contrast to weak profit in 2002 and 2003, renewed management focus on a stricter receivables management resulted in cash generation that outpaced its industry peers. After 2003, the performance was further endorsed by the recovery of profitability.

1320 The gross margin should be studied with a caveat, as Techem reported until 2003 under German HGB and was, therefore, only comparable on an operating profit base.

	PostLBO						LBO				
	x+6	x+5	x+4	x+3	x+2	x+1	t+5	t+4	t+3	t+2	t+1
	2006 (Sept 30)	**2005** (Sept 30)	**2004** (Sept 30)	**2003** (Sept 30)	**2002** (Sept 30)	**2001** (Sept 30)	**2000** (Sept 30)	**1999** (Sept 30)	**1998** (Sept 30)	**1997** (Sept 30)	**1996** (Sept 30)
Sales growth											
In % annual growth	12,0%	8,1%	5,8%	7,7%	6,8%	10,0%	9,1%	7,7%	11,3%	9,1%	21,8%
Industry-adj. annual growth	-0,8%	0,8%	6,0%	-6,7%	-15,0%	0,5%	-2,8%	-8,3%	-3,9%	na	na
Annual growth adj. to buyout average	2,7%	-1,2%	-3,5%	-1,6%	-2,5%	0,7%	-0,2%				
Sales development indexed to last FY prior exit	162	145	134	127	118	110	100				
Industry-adj. sales dev. indexed to last FY prior exit	88	89	88	83	88	100	100				
Gross margin											
In % of total sales	44,2%	45,2%	45,4%	41,8%	59,4%	62,2%	63,8%	58,3%	56,5%	56,3%	47,8%
Industry-adj. gross margin	0,9%	-3,6%	2,2%	-1,9%	15,6%	15,5%	16,5%	10,3%	12,8%	15,4%	na
Gross margin adj. to buyout average	-12,3%	-11,3%	-11,2%	-14,7%	2,9%	5,7%	7,3%				
Gross profit indexed to last FY prior exit	112	103	95	83	110	107	100				
Industry-adj.gross profit indexed to last FY prior buyout	67	61	68	59	88	99	100				
Net operating profit											
In % of total sales	18,2%	15,2%	16,4%	6,3%	6,5%	9,8%	8,2%	6,4%	2,4%	2,4%	3,6%
Industry-adj. net operating profit to sales	2,3%	-0,1%	2,1%	-8,2%	-9,4%	-8,8%	-10,9%	-13,7%	-16,7%	-10,5%	na
Net operating profit adj. to buyout average	13,6%	10,6%	11,8%	1,7%	1,9%	5,2%	3,5%				
Indexed to last year of buyout	362	270	269	98	94	132	100				
Industry-adj. net operating profit to last FY prior buyout	235	206	236	84	85	124	100				
Operating cash flow											
In % of total sales	13,6%	24,6%	25,1%	25,0%	24,1%	16,6%	16,5%	18,0%	17,7%	12,4%	na
Industry adj. operating cash flow to sales	-5,8%	6,2%	3,8%	5,6%	3,8%	-5,7%	-4,2%	-0,2%	11,5%	na	na
Operating cash flow adj. to buyout average	-2,6%	8,5%	9,0%	8,9%	7,9%	0,4%	0,3%				
Indexed to last year of buyout	134	216	204	192	172	111	100				
Industry-adj. operating cash flow to last FY prior buyout	77	149	130	134	131	94	100				
Free cash flow											
In % of total sales	1,3%	11,9%	12,4%	11,8%	3,0%	-3,5%	0,0%	1,6%	0,7%	na	na
Industry adj. free cash flow to sales	-5,2%	5,4%	2,8%	4,8%	-3,2%	-8,1%	-4,4%	-2,3%	-1,3%	na	na
Free cash flow to sales to buyout average	0,5%	11,2%	11,6%	11,0%	2,2%	-4,3%	-0,7%				
Indexed to last year of buyout	nm	nm	nm	nm	nm	nm	100				
Industry-adj. free cash flow to last FY prior buyout	nm	nm	nm	nm	nm	nm	100				

Table 56: Change in overall performance, stand-alone and industry-adjusted (Techem)

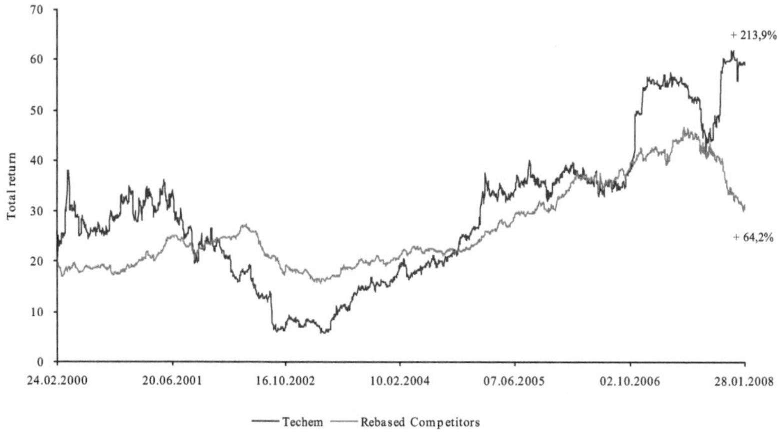

Figure 20: Development share price (Techem)

In 2006, cash flow was limited by increasing accruals for tax, pensions and other balance sheet items. In terms of investment activity, funds for rental, technical and office equipment determined the cash flow[1321]. Investments were considerable, and absorbed for instance in 2000 the entire operating cash flow.

In 2001 and 2002, the company conducted several acquisitions. As discussed before, management decided to divest a significant part of these businesses that produced proceeds in 2004, 2005 and 2006. In terms of free cash flow, Techem underperformed its industry sample from 2000 to 2002. The operating cash flow that already started to recover in 2002 was not able to compensate for the acquisition strategy. After the restructuring measures in 2003, Techem continuously generated free cash flow ratios above industry level. The extensive provisions in 2006 accordingly affected the free cash flow.

In the first post-exit year, the proceeds from the IPO determined the cash flow from financing activities. The high level of investment activity and comparatively modest increases in cash flow from operations slowed down the repayment of debt. In fiscal year 2003, a new syndicated loan replaced the former loan. Steps taken by the new management team refocused the company on debt repayment. In 2004, Techem repaid EUR 47.9 Million of debt. On the flipside, investments in tangible assets in both 2005 and 2006 again reduced the speed of repayment.

1321 As discussed in chapter C3.1.3.2.1, this growth capex was constant to total sales and were related to the purchase of rental devices.

	Hypothesis	Explanatory variables: Debt leverage	Ownership concentration	Activity level	Mgmt. Shareholdings		Key observations
Company performance (after the exit)	28a	(+)				CF	Reduced attentiveness to margin development in first two post-exit years (x+1, x+2), eg, sales and administration expenses
						CF	Increased risk appetite and investments with higher uncertainty yielded in unprofitable/ low margin
						CF	After return to LBO-like debt level, return of efficiency emphasis and readjustment of strategic focus by new management team
	28c		(+)			NEU	(Formal) ownership concentration remained notably high due to 25% stake of founding family; however, no/ limited observations that famly exerted control in accordance to the voting rights
						CF	Founding family now in joint ownership with institutional investors. Latter group eager to achieve short-term performance development based on visible growth.
	28d			(+)		CF	Appointment of former CEO to Chairman position reduced likelihood for instantaneous strategic turnaround. Initially, no active counterpart to challenge growth ambitions of management
						NCF	Frequent discussions on growth realted issues, e.g., progress on international expansion and acquisitions.
	28f				(+)	CF	After the exit, low shareholdings resulted in a decrease of interest alignment and motivation of management
						NEU	New management team showed despite lack of shareholdings high motivation and interest alignment
		Direction of expected correlation					

CF: Observations confirm hypothesis
NCF: Observations do not to confirm hypothesis
NEU: Observations neither confirm nor reject hypothesis

Table 57: Change in performance (Techem)

With respect to cash flow to its shareholders, Techem returned EUR 23 Million in 1999 prior to the IPO. During the IPO, Techem stated a dividend payout ratio of about 30%.

However, the strong growth in 2000 and 2001 as well as the profit slump in 2002 and 2003 prevented the company from paying any dividend. After the recovery of profits, Techem returned EUR 12.3 Million in 2005 to its shareholders, in line with the initially planned 30% payout ratio. In 2006, the dividend payout ratio was increased to 82% to appease new investors.

The author observes that Techem performed well after the LBO, but remained below its industry peers in terms of sales, gross margin and operating cash flow. The author found that company performance peaked in the year of the IPO. Even though gross margin slumped dramatically in 2002, the company was able to maintain its strong cash flow generation. After 2003, Techem was able to close the performance gap to its peers, and returned to above-industry performance in terms of operating profit and adjusted operating cash flow (before provisions) in the last year (x+6) observed.

The change in debt leverage influenced the performance of Techem in different ways. The reduction of leverage after the exit in 2001 resulted in a reduced management focus on cost development. The risk appetite of Techem's management increased considerably, supported by the reduced exposure of management's personal wealth given lower shareholdings. The return to LBO-like debt leverage at the end of 2002 meant that the supervisory board and management focused on a strategic turnaround of Techem, even though the company was not facing immediate financial distress. The decline of margin and cash flow can be therefore at least partly attributed to the change in debt.

Despite the 25% minority stake of the founding family, concentration in ownership decreased, as the family did not exert the control they could have with their voting rights. The family did not demonstrate the level of monitoring as could have been expected given their stake. The Felten and Ott families had gotten used to fact that buyout investor BC Partners engaged in reviewing monthly and yearly results and challenging Techem's s management. Even though the founding families did not alter their shareholdings, they had to return to their role as sole major shareholder given that institutional investors were eager to achieve short-term performance improvement.

The former management team was closely aligned with the owner's agenda and acted to maximize the value of the company. After the LBO, the level of alignment and underlying motivation decreased. Senior management realized a large amount of their value creation during the LBO by selling the majority of their shares. As a result, management was less inclined to show the same level of personal effort. Techem's management moreover enjoyed a relatively high fixed salary. Both low shareholdings, reduced debt payments, high fixed salary and a stock option program spurred management's risk appetite given that their own was considerably reduced. Even though growth investments were related to businesses adjacent to Techem's core business, it was highly uncertain whether they would yield similar returns. The appointment of the CEO to the supervisory board made a rapid change in strategy more difficult. In strategy reviews, the supervisory board did not question the ambitions for growth. Instead, they curbed the extent of diversification and investments in non-core businesses. With the former CEO turned Chairman, it took time to admit potential mistakes in terms of acquisitions, and initiate restructuring. After the crisis, the new management group succeeded in outperforming the industry. The return to LBO-like performance levels confirmed that the decline in performance was not the result of organizational slack and inefficiency. Instead, the decline was the outcome of strategic diversification initiated shortly before the exit. It was reversed as part of the restructuring in 2003.

4 Case Study: Trevira

4.1 Case Description

4.1.1 Company Development before the Buyout

Trevira's success story begins in 1956. An invention by English chemists John R. Whinfield and James T. Dickson prompted Hoechst in Bobingen, Bavaria, to produce the first polyester filaments under the Trevira brand. Trevira stemmed from the development of a synthetic chemical, polyester-based fibre. Fabrics made of these fibres could easily be taken care of, were universally applicable, and available at a fair price. Their colours were resistant and did not fade. Trevira extended its products with the introduction in 1980 of Trevira CS. CS stood for "comfort" and "security" because the fabric was flame retardant.

The fibre succeeded from its introduction with demand for it increasing because it could be employed for multiple uses. Trevira initially serviced the clothing industry with its new fibre. Over time, Trevira introduced applications for home textiles, furniture, hygienic textiles, and automotive interiors. The fibre's elasticity and flame retardance were enhanced. Trevira owes its success to the high quality of the material, its sense for fashion trends, and excellent service throughout the value chain. This gave it a broad and diversified customer base.

Hoechst spun off its fibre brand as Trevira GmbH & Co KG in 1998[1322] as part of a major reorganization. Shares in the company were later that year transferred to European Fiber Industries B.V., a joint venture between Indonesia's Multikarsa Group (60%) and Hoechst (40%). Hoechst sold its remaining 40% stake to Multikarsa, a holding company owned by Texmaco Group and active in polyester and polyester raw materials, textile technology and textiles, after a transition period. Texmaco operated across a variety of businesses, including financial services, iron and steel casting, plant engineering construction, machine tools and automotive components. Hoechst transferred only the European part of its textile polyester business to the JV[1323]. Its non-European, global business of fibres for industrial applications, polyester intermediates and PET resins was sold to another industry consortium.

1322 After a dramatic profit collapse, Hoechst's board opted for a radical divestment and break-up of the company. All non-core businesses were to be put in a partnership or sold.

1323 This business covered the former company Ernst Michalke, Frankfurt along with its site in Guben, the plant in Eastern Germany, the company Kaj Neckelmann in Silkeborg, Denmark, the Portalegre site of Hoechst Fibras in Portugal and parts of the Bobingen site of Hoechst Trevira in Germany.

Hoechst's European textile's fibre business accounted at the time of the spin-off for some DM 800 million in sales and a workforce of 2,400 (1996 figures). Texmaco and Hoechst expected their JV to produce synergies and embark on an active investment policy to improve cost structures and win market share for the textile polyester fibre business in European markets.

The JV did not live up to the partners' expectations. The gradual elimination of import prompted by the ATC[1324] led to increased competition in the European textile market. Asian manufacturers in the 1990s established new production facilities with cost-efficient machinery and inexpensive personnel. The market for standard products (commodities) was particularly hard hit by the entry of low-cost textile polyester producers. The JV also suffered because Texmaco had no experience with Trevira's high-end business. Aggravating issues was the fact that Texmaco encountered financial problems and was forced shortly after its acquisition of Trevira to relinquish management and look for a buyer.

Deutsche Bank Investor (DBI), Deutsche Bank's private equity arm[1325], bought 100% of Trevira GmbH's shares on October 13, 2000 from European Fiber Industries BV for an undisclosed amount[1326]. DBI expected continuously improved profitability and growth to create value. DBI believed that introducing innovative products and enhancing Trevira's already respected brand would grow. DB Investor Chairman Axel Pfeil said:

> "We see Trevira as a high-value company that has proven its profit-making capability in the economic cycle by its focus on specialty products. In collaboration with the management, DB Investor will, as finance investor, continue to push forward the strategy of Trevira and substantially increase company profitability in the coming three to five years."

Pfeil, a buyout specialist, was convinced that with competitive pressures Trevira should strategically move into more profitable market niches: "Trevira was probably the only European fiber producer in 1999 to be profitable. [...] We performed significantly better than any of our competitors". He intended to transform the existing management into entrepreneurs by giving them significant equity stakes. DBI planned to maintain its investment for three to five years and to then sell the company to a strategic buyer or take it public. Even though the acquisition was made

---

1324 World Trade Organization signed an Agreement on Textile and Clothing (ATC) that called for the elimination of all restrictions over a ten-year transition period starting in 1996.

1325 Deutsche Bank's private equity holding company comprised the various investment activities and industrial holdings of Deutsche Bank, totaling approx. DM 45 Billion in 2000.

1326 The exact value of the acquisition was not disclosed. It is, however, known that the Texmaco demanded a purchase price in the range of what the DM 400 million plus bonus that it paid in 1997.

at the time of an industry consolidation, DBI viewed it as attractive because it had paid an exclusively negotiated fair price and had not bought the company in an auction.

4.1.2 Company Development during the Buyout Period

4.1.2.1 Efficiency-Focused Management Activities

DBI believed its return on investment would come from rapid repayment of the purchase price that had been largely financed through increasing Trevira's debt. This was challenging given intense competition and continued price pressure. It meant Trevira would have to improve its productivity in operations as well as develop new revenue sources.

While Trevira increased revenue in this challenging market environment, accelerating raw material costs severely depressed its gross margin, particularly in the standard products market for filaments. Incumbent manufacturers and new market players created considerable overcapacity in the European market. Trevira's management, prompted by DBI, launched its 'Topas'[1327] efficiency program in June 2001. Topas aimed to optimize operational and non-operational processes. Trevira operations managers reviewed and reconfigured manufacturing workflows in the Bobingen, Guben, Quevaucamps, and Silkeborg plants. Management increased machine availability with improved task standardization and optimized operations scheduling. Despite the improvement efforts, the filament segment suffered severely from fierce competition. Management laid off some 380 of the 2,600 employees, 320 of which in the filament business to save approximately EUR 22 Million in annual operating costs no later than by the end of 2003[1328]. The competition forced management in 2003 to introduce another filaments efficiency improvement program named 'Profil'[1329].

Introduction of a new employment agreement in 2000 that enabled flexible working times and eliminated payments of premium for overtime constituted a cornerstone of operational improvement. This allowed Trevira to fine-tune its labour capacity more closely with the production demand and reduce the number of contract workers who caused quality problems because they were not accustomed to the complex manufacturing process. Total personnel expenses were reduced by some 10%. The workforce contributed significantly to the restructuring by renouncing its year-end

1327 TOPAS was an abbreviation for "Trevira Optimierungsprogramm für alle Standorte", translated with "Trevira optimization program for all sites".

1328 In 2001, restructuring costs of EUR 13 Million occurred as result of the personnel adjustments.

1329 PROFIL was an abbreviation for "Profit in filaments".

bonus in 2002 as part of a transition agreement between management and the workers council.

DBI intended to improve asset productivity without significantly investing in modernization and capacity expansion. The rate at which low cost manufacturers gained market share however forced Trevira to invest in more high-tech textile production facilities far earlier than expected. To concentrate on specialized high-tech fibres and filament products required the ability to produce small lot sizes at competitive costs. However, Trevira's manufacturing facilities were designed for large, highly automated, efficient lot sizes. Trevira's management, supported by DBI, decided in 2002 to purchase an entire new generation of machinery for fibre production and to introduce new high-margin bi-component production at a total cost of EUR 20 Million. Installation of the new polycondensation production in Bobingen site was completed in 2004. The new machinery was able to produce two different polymer types at the same time. Modernization saved considerable transport costs between the two manufacturing sites and enabled stripping out polluted process water. Trevira invested further in modernization and quality improvement of filament production in Bobingen and Guben. Trevira Neckelmann, the Danish subsidiary that produced textile yarns from German preliminary products, purchased additional air texturizing facilities. Falling demand in 2002 and 2003, however, reduced cash flow generation and led to a considerable reduction of original capital expenditure plans for 2003 and 2004. Lagging sales growth in the specialized products market led to considerable overcapacity that was short-term compensated for with the production of commodity products. Accepting reduced profitability for a while, management in 2003 decided to reduce gradually the company's filament production capacity.

Increasing oil prices continued to drive up the prices of raw materials. Purified therephtalic acid (PTA) and mono ethylene glycol (MEG) constituted Trevira's core input materials. Prices stagnated in 2001 because of general economic weakness. However, from 2002 on, raw material prices driven by surging oil prices and increased global demand rose rapidly, at times. Management sought to recover price volatility from customers but had only limited success in the commodity segment. MEG prices, for example, increased more than 70% between 2000 and 2004, with management unable to compensate for much of that cost.

Trevira's sales network knew the company's product portfolio over a long period. The company services selected markets through its own subsidiaries as well as through representatives and agents. The new owners largely did not change the organization. The company's headquarters were kept in Frankfurt, Germany, where central sales, marketing and finance were located. Manufacturing sites in Denmark and Portugal maintained their own sales personnel.

DBI closely monitored development of working capital and urged management to reduce inventory and trade receivables. Working capital decreased by the end of 2002 by 2.7%, leading to a cash inflow of EUR 27 million. But tougher conditions from suppliers reduced the credit period, which cut into the savings (see Table 61). The reduction in 2004 of payables produced a net increase in working capital.

To conclude, Trevira continued to be disadvantaged by the distribution of labour over different manufacturing sites despite operational and productivity improvements. Contrary to its, Trevira had to move a considerable number of products between its various sites at high cost. Trevira did not have the resources to concentrate all production activity in one site because of its lack of sufficient free cash flow and DBI's refusal to provide additional capital no later than in 2003. DBI gradually extended its management control system to service its reporting needs. However, DBI was less experienced than other buyout investors because Deutsche Bank had only created it in 1998. As a result, DBI's reporting system was not as advanced as that of others. This became evident when DBI did not anticipate the covenants breach, according to those interviewed. External consultants introduced in 2002 additional measure-based controls to track in detail progress of in restructuring. Alvarez & Marsal introduced in 2004 a cash flow-based reporting that allowed for a detailed cash flow forecast.

4.1.2.2 Entrepreneurial Growth-Focused Management Activities

DBI expected Trevira's growth strategy to be successful from the beginning of the LBO because it had produced considerable growth in the standard market for polyester yarns and fibres with high-quality products in previous years. However, the entry of low-cost producers into the filaments market in the 1990s significantly slowed down the growth momentum. DBI could see that at the time of its acquisition of Trevira in 2000[1330]. Trevira needed to find new sources of growth, but high debt leverage did not allow it to invest significantly in new products and markets.

Western Europe production continued to slack after 2000. A number of companies with a long tradition in the industry could not match the low cost positions of new players in the market, particularly those in the commodity product markets[1331].

1330 Between 1997 and 2000, imports for filaments in Western Europe increased by approx. 70,000 tons, while Western Europe production decreased by 60,000 tons.

1331 Some of manufacturers moved into profitable market niches, but numerous companies went into receivership. To alleviate the pressure from competition, the EU introduced in 2000 an anti-dumping toll

Staple fibres proved to be more robust because they offered higher basic growth. The growth of non-woven specialty fibre products partly compensated for losses in the commodity market. Trevira repositioned itself with a sharpened focus on profitable market niches in specialized, high-tech products. At the same time, management closed its commodity filaments business in 2001. The share of non-standard products increased as a result from 70% at the buyout entry in 2000 to around 85% at the buyout exit in 2004. Management further focused on active diversification into sectors related to Trevira's furnishing and automotive core businesses[1332] such as its more systematic move into textile equipment for hospitals and nursing homes and becoming the sector standard as it already was in its core markets[1333]. Trevira CS developed a new area with its application for commercial airplanes and in the maritime shipping. This expansion was coupled with Trevira's divestment of the Portuguese fibres and PET plant, Trevira Fibras[1334].

DBI and Trevira's management expected in 2000 to put the difficult period behind them with the slow recovery of growth in the flame retardant textile market. Instead, things worsened with weak performance in 2000 and 2001 in core industries such as automotive[1335], home textiles, technical textiles and clothing that were crucial for Trevira. As a result, Trevira did not have the funds to make additional growth investments in new markets were. Trevira's CEO formed in 1999 a joint venture in Brazil with a polyester yarn producer who serviced the local automotive industry. Trevira also entered the US. Trevira based its Brazilian and US expansion plans on its close relationships with German automotive manufacturers who were expanding their global presence with local manufacturing. The Brazilian joint venture nonetheless proved to be loss making and was shut down in 2002 because funds were drying up.

---

on imports from Asian countries and in 2006 again raised tolls, leading to a temporary reduction of price pressure.

1332 At the entry of DBI, apparel was the core business, accounting for 29% of turnover, followed by polyester chips (26%), home textiles (19%). The younger sectors in which Trevira was operating were automotive (17%) and hygiene/semi-technical (9%), both with above average growth rates.

1333 The technical guidelines on textile use in European hospitals, established jointly by the Association of Hospital Directors and the Hohensteiner Textile Research Institute, recommended for instance Trevira CS for drapes, curtains, and bedding.

1334 Due to soaring demand in the Iberian market, local business had grown considerably, but moved away from Trevira's core business in terms of customer base and technology. Because profitability was under pressure and debt repayments were impending, management decided in 2001 to divest the production of chips for the PET bottle business in Portalegre, Portugal.

1335 Demand from the automotive industry decreased due to declining car sales in Western Europe and reduced usage of textiles in the interior.

In its core European market, Trevira had insulated itself to some degree from market growth in the late 1990s because its main Trevira CS trademark increasingly was replacing other flame retardant textiles, even though the basic product was more than 20 years old[1336]. Trevira was in 2000 the No. 3 market leader for staple fibres in Europe. It was however market leader in the sub-segment for flame-retardant fibres and filaments. Management consolidated in 2000 its existing brand portfolio and introduced an umbrella brand with a modernized logo and a series of sub-labels serving different market needs to strengthen its product portfolio and market projection. The company launched in 2002 its 'Profil' program, which sought to identify news market segments and customers as well as potentially new applications in the flagging filament segment. The market for texturized yarns came under particular pressure, leading European manufacturers to close several production facilities. The market for specialized, high-margin fibres demonstrated stable growth despite a significant setback in 2002. Management countered low utilization with commodity sales. As outlined in the previous chapter, management decided to reduce production capacity accordingly because profitability did not recover. Continuous new product introductions led to additional market share. Increasing demand from Eastern Europe and North America fuelled production of stable fibres such as non-wovens, clothing and home textiles, prompting tonnage in 2003 alone to grow by more than 35%.

Basic R&D enabled Trevira to unveil continuously new applications to market based on its proven technologies. Trevira introduced, for example, its bioactive fibre offering antimicrobial fibre attributes for all textiles[1337] and its elastic textured polyester yarn. With this yarn, Trevira designed stretchable textiles with optimized rebound force for the sports and leisure clothing market. Trevira also introduced various tailor-made textiles in the corporate wear market segment. It continuously brought to market new fibres with superior flame retardance attributes[1338]. Designers

---

1336 Trevira CS owed its superior attributes to the usage of polyester, which was itself to some degree flame retardant and the addition of phosphorous-organic components. Flame retardance was reduced neither by washout nor by dissolution. It did not require chemicals. Competitor's produces had the disadvantage that their flame retardant agents weighted up to 25% of the textile. Trevira had the further advantage that its products did not need replacement of the flame retardant after washing. However, Trevira CS's price was higher.

1337 The fibre incorporated anti-microbial fibre attributes directly into the textile, instead of treating the fibre with chemical additives. A further important source for growth was the development of a series of bi-component fibres with health-non harming finishes that were admitted by the American FDA. The fibre was designed for clothing and other textile-based equipment in the health sector.

1338 During the buyout, the Trevira NSK (NSK was an abbreviation for „niedrig schmelzende Komponente"or low-melting component) yarn was introduced that incorporated the attributes of both flame retardance and strengthened material. The product could be dyed, printed, pleated, or crushed.

developed new products for the automotive industry, particularly for car headliners, such as "Stratos" and "Aramis" for large European and North American OEMs. Trevira's R&D department also developed technologies for the production process. The change in 2002 from LOY (low oriented textile filament yarn) commercial applications to more textured titers permitted longer machine runtimes. Complementary innovations enabled enhancement of color equability. Advanced technology also facilitated a reduction of sleeve failures. The 'Topas' program envisioned a series of improvements of R&D, including measures to enhance customer service support and product quality. The R&D budget remained as a result unchanged, and constituted with stagnating revenues a constant cost as a percentage of sales.

Trevira's management also introduced an internal training program in 2001 to develop workforce skills compensate for layoffs. The program offered tailor-made training and coaching programs to help employees improve their know how-profile. DBI appointed Bernd Sassenrath as Trevira's CEO to ensure that its investment strategy was implemented. Sassenrath took over from Ulrich Huwe, who left the company. He had previously worked in Hoechst's fibre division before it was sold to Multikarsa in 1998. Hartmut Last was entrusted with the staple fibres business unit and was responsible for production and technology at Trevira. Gerd Hochapfel was appointed as head of the filaments business unit and all Trevira sales and marketing activities. A new supervisory board was established, under chair of Dr. Karl-Gerhard Seifert, a former member of Hoechst AG board. Dr. Seifert was also a former head of Morgan Grenfell Private Equity Ltd, DBI's predecessor.

4.1.3 Company Development after the Exit

With hindsight, it seems that Trevira's acquisition by DBI and its transfer into an LBO structure was an inappropriate solution given market consolidation. When DBI acquired Trevira, it was already evident that the company would need considerable restructuring and support of an industrial partner. Funding was a challenge and demanded considerable support and guarantees by the owners. When Deutsche Bank changed strategy in 2003 and decided to reduce its exposure to private equity, DBI under the supervision of the corporate investments division initiated the sale of Trevira.

With the breach of the debt covenants, DBI mandated Alvarez & Marsal, specialists in financial restructuring and interim management, to look at different exit options. Planned restructuring excluded an exit via an IPO. A sale to a strategic buyer seemed the most viable option, and better than liquidation. From DBI's perspective, the

Reliance Group was the right strategic partner to take Trevira through industry consolidation. Trevira CEO Bernd Sassenrath said:

> "The combination of Reliance and Trevira creates a global leader in polyester fibres and will significantly strengthen Trevira's competitive position going forward. We envisage that this transaction will enable Trevira not only to benefit from the access to new markets and raw materials sources but also to leverage the Trevira brand and contribute our marketing skills and technology in specialty polyester fibres."

Elaborating on the acquisition of Trevira, Mukesh Ambani, Chairman and Managing Director of Reliance, argued that

> "Trevira gives Reliance a well-timed entry into Europe to capture the growth potential in Eastern Europe. It also gives us the opportunity to bring many of its valuable specialty polyester products to the Asian textile industry."

On the company's future course of action in the textile sector, Mr. Ambani added:

> "Over the next ten years, Reliance will be investing significant amounts of money in polyester research and development to sustain global leadership, by building an intellectual property portfolio and developing new products."

Subodh Sapra, the President of the Polyester Sector of Reliance, commented:

> "We are delighted that Trevira is our first overseas polyester acquisition. We expect that the strong commitment of Reliance to the growth of polyester and our integration into polyester raw materials will help both Trevira and Reliance to serve all our customers in Europe and other world markets with superior polyester products and even better supply chain services".

The industry viewed the acquisition as a major step that would make Reliance the world's largest polyester manufacturer. Trevira, the leading manufacturer in Europe, presented an excellent platform in the market, offering unmatched know how in textiles. For its part, Reliance offered access to new markets and capital to shield the company from industry restructuring.

Reliance had a short, impressive history in the polyester business[1339]. It commissioned in 1982 a 10,000 ton per year plant in Patalganga, India. Capacity was gradually organically as well as through acquisitions of smaller polyester facilities India. The polyester business reported by 2004 some EUR 1 billion in sales. The acquisition was subject to EU regulatory approval, which was granted by the European Commission in August 2004.

1339 The Reliance Group was founded by Dhirubhai Ambani and was India's largest business house with total revenues of over US$ 22.6 billion (2004). The Group's activities included exploration and production (E&P) of oil and gas, refining and marketing, petrochemicals (polyester, polymers, and intermediates), textiles, financial services and insurance, power, telecom and infocom initiatives.

4.1.3.1 Market and Competitive Environment

Market fundamentals and the competitive environment had not changed since DBI decided to invest in Trevira. Market demand for textile filaments and staple fibres increased at a stable but modest rate. Demand picked up as European economies recovered, particularly in industries most crucial to Trevira's success such as automotive, home textiles and apparels.

Imports to Europe from low cost manufacturers continued to rise despite the increased demand and put strong pressure on traditional European producers. The growth of specialized products enabled producers such as Trevira to compensate partially for revenue losses and margin decreases. Trevira's customers, particularly fabric producers, finishers and converters, needed to move into more specialized, high tech products, with attributes such as antimicrobial yarn and high elasticity.

Trevira's sale to Reliance reflected in some reflects the changes in the industry. High-end European textile fibres producers were not able to match the cost base of emerging low cost producers and withdrew from the standard mass markets. They lost market share, and were forced to refocus on new revenue in market niches.

4.1.3.2 Efficiency-Focused Management Activities

4.1.3.2.1 Operations and Manufacturing

Competition from low cost manufacturers continued to pressure Trevira. The company's new owner, management and employees realized that the company would have to reduce further cost, particularly in the filament business, to ensure Trevira's survival. As further restructuring was inevitable, Reliance sought to put a positive spin on the efforts by announcing in early 2005 "The New Trevira" program.

Reliance was an integrated conglomerate with operations in oil and gas exploration, olefins and aromatics production, polymers and fiber intermediates production and textiles manufacturing. It was positioned in the value chain in mass markets and highly efficient in dealing with standard products on a large scale. For its part, Trevira was by the time of the 2004 acquisition a niche player offering specialized high-tech fibre. Despite their different market positioning, Reliance offered Trevira's operations a broad set of business opportunities and potential synergies.

Operational Productivity

At the exit in 2004, Trevira had a total manufacturing capacity of 130,000 tons per year of polyester staple fibres, filament yarns and chips. It had production facilities in Bobingen and Guben (Germany), Silkeborg (Denmark), and Quevaucamps (Belgium). Reliance's total polyester fibre and filament yarn production capacity exceeded 1.8 Million tons with its production in India and Trevira acquisition, making it the world's largest polyester fibre and yarns producer. Reliance's strength in integration and management of large-scale manufacturing facilities was expected to provide Trevira an operational advantage. Reliance initially appointed a new head of production from its India business division.

The new owners continued with earlier efficiency improvement efforts. The texturising department was moved in November 2004 from Danish subsidiary, Trevira Neckelmann A/S in Silkeborg, to Germany. The subsidiary specialized in production of high-quality textured and dyed yarn, primarily for the European automotive and home textile industry. The move led to the layoff of 100 employees and annual savings of EUR 3 Million. It created 114 new jobs at Guben. A training program was created to qualify the new Guben Trevira employees. The Guben production capacity was underpinned by strong demand for synthetic yarns and for specialized fibres. Further restructuring was accompanied by a social plan that was extended for a period of two years until the end of 2007. Trevira moved other production units in Silkeborg in June 2006 to a new manufacturing site in Zielona Gora, Poland, to produce KDK and chenille (high-end texturized yarns) for the automotive and home textiles industry. Under pressure from labor, management faced a choice between removing the product group from the market, which would have been painful because major filaments customers demanded these specialized products, or moving production to a low-cost manufacturing site. Restructuring also involved reducing manufacturing and logistics costs in German production sites, particularly related to production administration.

As Reliance replaced Trevira's standard partially oriented yarn (POY), polyester texturized yarn (PTY), and polyester staple fibres (PSF) with its own products, Trevira needed better trained personnel to produce its remaining high tech products. Guben was by 2006 the only fully integrated site in Europe manufacturing polyester filament specialties for the textile industry. Bobingen remained the parent plant where new product ideas were developed, including manufacturing of staple fibres and filament yarns, and the company's textile technology centre. Silkeborg in Denmark continued to produce texturized and dyed polyester filament for the automotive, home textiles and apparel sectors.

Critics of Reliance's acquisition feared that Reliance was only interested in the Trevira brand and would gradually close down the company's costly European plants and transfer production to India and other low cost countries. Reliance would benefit from the higher value of one of the industry's most prestigious trademarks. This strategy however involved the risk of redundancy costs at the German sites, political opposition to asset stripping, and loss of the reputation of the Trevira brands. Any potential price premium at the time of the Reliance acquisition could have been jeopardized by a move to a low cost production country.

Operational productivity	PostLBO						LBO						
	x+3		x+2		x+1		t+4		t+3		t+2		t+1
	2006 (Dec 31)	YoY	**2005** (Dec 31)	YoY	**2004** (Dec 31)	YoY	**2003** (Dec 31)	YoY	**2002** (Dec 31)	YoY	**2001** (Dec 31)	YoY	**2000** (Dec 31)
In EUR													
Total wages & salaries [In TEUR]	65.134	2%	63.900	2%	62.645	-1%	63.584	1%	62.748	-4%	65.391	-7%	70.325
As part of total sales	22,7%		24,3%		23,8%		24,6%		23,7%		23,1%		24,5%
Aver. wage/ salary per employee	40,009	0%	40,063	-1%	40,521	2%	39,765	1%	39,514	2%	38,556	-5%	40,674
Sales per employee	176,149	7%	164,549	-3%	169,923	5%	161,624	-3%	166,785	0%	166,568	0%	166,211
EBIT per employee	1,298	nm	(3,395)	nm	(0,024)	nm	0,616	-84%	3,934	-58%	9,427	27%	7,440
Operating cash flow per employee	1,510	-78%	6,770	-21%	8,610	-225%	(6,876)	-120%	34,081	18%	28,958	82%	15,943
Free cash flow per employee	(0,813)	-201%	0,802	-73%	2,991	-123%	(12,740)	-147%	27,014	39%	19,463	22%	15,943
EBIT pre material costs per employee	110,225	17%	94,558	-3%	97,546	8%	90,634	-3%	93,066	-7%	100,018	0%	100,1249
Operating cash flow *pre-working capital movement* per employee	2,173	76%	1,234	-87%	9,334	nm	(1,356)	nm	27,359	9%	25,203	58%	15,943

Table 58: Changes in operational productivity (Trevira)

The restructuring efforts and cost reduction programs paid off. Sales and operating profit per employee increased over the three year period. Share of wages and salaries to total costs was further reduced. A closer look shows that productivity recovered after a severe decline in 2005. The reduction in profitability and cash flow were due to increasing raw material costs. A comparison of operating profit pre material costs, however, showed only a modest decrease. Operating cash flow pre working capital moreover reveals that the potential to generate cash flow from working capital decreased after DBI had minimized the level working capital during the buyout. However, cash flow was diluted in 2004 from one-time effects. Operational productivity was further diluted because the reported number of employees included those already being laid off.

Asset Productivity

The installation of new bi-component machinery was completed in 2005. Investments in capacity expansion for spun-dyed filament yarns at the Guben manufacturing site were also made. Capacity was added in Bobingen for fibre bicomponent production.

High debt repayment forced management to backtrack on further investments in fixed assets in 2004 and 2005. The 2005 liquidity report showed lower than expected operating cash flow, persuading management to reduce capital expenditure in tangible assets. Some of technical equipment was moved to the new plant in Zielona Gora, Poland.

The asset base continued to shrink after the exit in 2004. Capital expenditure for tangible goods dropped from a peak of EUR 16.1 Million in 2001 during the LBO to EUR 8.7 Million in 2004. Investments in 2004 and 2005 in the new plant and German facilities led to a higher investment of EUR 9.5 Million in 2005, but were massively reduced to EUR 3.8 Million in 2006. In the main plant in Bobingen fire damage in

December 2006 made additional investments in modern fibre spinning equipment necessary.

	PostLBO						LBO						
	x+3		x+2		x+1		t+4		t+3		t+2		t+1
	2006		2005		2004		2003		2002		2001		2000
Asset base	(Dec 31)	YoY	(Dec 31)	YoY	(Dec 31)	YoY	(Dec 31)	YoY	(Dec 31)	YoY	(Dec 31)	YoY	(Dec 31)
In TEUR													
PP&E	43.238	-15%	50.684	-5%	53.486	-8%	58.025	-10%	64.465	-6%	68.931	-2%	70.169
Intangible assets	6.607	-25%	8.811	-20%	11.038	-17%	13.255	-15%	15.567	-12%	17.760	-11%	19.845
Operating assets	125.487	0%	125.343	-3%	128.762	-6%	136.662	-8%	148.592	-4%	155.393	0%	155.475
Asset productivity													
Sales to operating assets	2,285	9%	2,094	3%	2,040	8%	1,891	6%	1,782	-2%	1,818	-2%	1,848
Operating profit to operating assets	0,017	nm	(0,043)	nm	(0,000)	-104%	0,007	-83%	0,042	-59%	0,103	24%	0,083
Operating cash flow to oper. assets	0,024	-77%	0,106	-20%	0,132	-264%	(0,080)	-122%	0,364	15%	0,316	78%	0,177
Free cash flow to oper. assets	(0,011)	-203%	0,010	-72%	0,036	-124%	(0,149)	-152%	0,289	36%	0,212	20%	0,177
EBIT pre material costs to oper. assets	1,430	19%	1,203	3%	1,171	10%	1,060	7%	0,995	-9%	1,092	-2%	1,113
Oper. cash flow *pre-working capital movement* to operating assets	0,028	80%	0,016	-86%	0,112	nm	(0,016)	-105%	0,292	6%	0,275	55%	0,177
ROIC (excl.goodwill)	5,83%		1,41%		-0,01%		-8,49%		2,58%		6,48%		8,16%

Table 59: Changes in asset base and asset productivity (Trevira)

Post-exit productivity of the asset base developed in a pattern similar to operational productivity. Operating profit and cash flow to asset base increased over the three post-LBO years significantly, with a drop in 2005. Adjusted operating profit pre material costs and ROIC show that management was successful in downscaling the asset base under the new ownership and increasing productivity - at least partially because on an adjusted cash flow base productivity declined.

During the LBO management sought to retire underperforming assets and relocate others to more cost efficient locations in terms of competitive operating costs. In the post-exit period it needed to maintain productivity at existing sites despite stagnating sales. Asset-intense, automated production was exchanged against more flexible, small-lot manufacturing.

Outsourcing, Offshoring and Partnering

The raw material markets continued to experience price volatility and high oil prices. The drop in value of the USD against the Euro to some degree mitigated the increase in oil prices. However, prices for two major raw materials, purified therephtalic acid (PTA) and mono ethylene glycol (MEG) increased 20% and 22% in 2004. The new owner made clear that increasing raw material costs were not an excuse. Trevira faced in 2004 price increases of a total of EUR 30 Million that were mitigated by price and volume increases and changes in the product mix. Management decided as part of the restructuring at Silkeborg to relocate labor-intensive manufacturing activity to Eastern Europe. It also decided in the wake of its 2005 strategy review to start sourcing partially oriented yarns from Reliance.

In summary, the costs of goods sold continued to increase as part of total sales even though there were no changes in the share of the value chain. Between 2003 and 2006, the share increased 6.1% points, indicating management's need to compensate for this cost acceleration.

	PostLBO						LBO						
	x+3		x+2		x+1		t+4		t+3		t+2		t+1
	2006		2005		2004		2003		2002		2001		2000
Direct costs structure	(Dec 31)	YoY	(Dec 31)	YoY	(Dec 31)	YoY	(Dec 31)	YoY	(Dec 31)	YoY	(Dec 31)	YoY	(Dec 31)
Total costs of goods sold	**61,8%**	2%	**59,5%**	2%	**57,4%**	2%	**55,7%**	2%	**53,4%**	-1%	**54,4%**	-1%	**55,8%**
Raw materials and consumables used	52,7%	1%	51,5%	1%	50,9%	2%	49,3%	2%	47,7%	-1%	48,7%	-2%	50,3%
Costs of purchased goods and services	9,1%	2%	8,0%	2%	6,5%	0%	6,4%	1%	5,8%	0%	5,7%	0%	5,5%
Total personnel	**22,7%**	1%	**24,4%**	1%	**23,8%**	-1%	**24,6%**	1%	**23,7%**	-1%	**24,9%**	2%	**22,8%**
Wages	17,7%	1%	19,2%	1%	18,6%	-1%	19,4%	0%	19,0%	0%	19,3%	1%	18,0%
Costs of employee benefits	5,0%	0%	5,2%	0%	5,3%	0%	5,2%	1%	4,7%	-1%	5,6%	1%	4,7%

Table 60: Change in material costs as part of total sales (Trevira)

Working Capital Management

Management was able to reduce inventory due to improved planning quality and supply chain management. Raw material and finished goods warehouses were reconfigured to balance capital commitment and the ability to deliver. Management also focused on the development of trade receivables. Senior management tracked the development of outstanding trade receivables in its daily business management report. Management introduced a daily stock report designed to control the daily stock of raw material, work-in-progress and finished goods. Stock levels were reported alongside manufacturing processes and warehouse positions. This enabled management to track changes of the inventory in the entire supply chain and in sales channels on a daily base. Management also introduced in 2005 SAP's material requirement program module to further optimize production planning and ensure availability of supply to its customers.

Management controlled changes in working capital with a weekly receivables and payables aging report. Trade receivables were listed per business segment as well as in terms of payable accounts with their maturity. Customer credit terms were further tightened in 2005. To mitigate risk of outfalls, Trevira adopted a receivables outfall policy that covered 85% of the underlying value. To generate cash, management started factoring in 2006 some EUR 25 Million of outstanding receivables.

Reduction of working capital during the LBO was an essential tool for raising funds to repay debt. After the exit, these steps enhanced the ability to track constituents and made tighter capital management possible. This led to a further reduction of working capital of EUR 2.5 Million in 2004, EUR 11.3 Million in 2005, and EUR 16.1 Million in 2006 (see Table 61). After adjusting for sales effects, Trevira reduced working capital in the post-IPO period by by EUR 33.1 Million.

Net working capital	2006	2005 PostLBO	2004	2003	2002 LBO	2001	2000
	x+3	x+2	x+1	t+4	t+3	t+2	t+1
In TEUR	**2006** (Dec 31)	**2005** (Dec 31)	**2004** (Dec 31)	**2003** (Dec 31)	**2002** (Dec 31)	**2001** (Dec 31)	**2000** (Dec 31)
Inventories	38.257	34.705	35.011	36.734	39.415	40.406	39.779
Trade receivables	11.525	25.337	33.632	33.783	36.360	35.545	46.351
Trade payables	36.805	30.993	28.308	27.640	41.723	31.225	35.037
Total	**12.977**	**29.049**	**40.335**	**42.877**	**34.052**	**44.726**	**51.093**
Sales growth implied change	2.867	(237)	537	(656)	(3.306)	(751)	na
Other change	(18.939)	(11.049)	(3.079)	9.481	(7.368)	(5.616)	na
Total annual change	(16.072)	(11.286)	(2.542)	8.825	(10.674)	(6.367)	na
Relative							
Inventories (% of COGS)	21,6%	22,2%	23,2%	25,5%	27,8%	26,3%	24,8%
Trade receivables (% of sales)	3,8%	9,2%	12,1%	12,3%	13,0%	11,7%	15,1%
Trade payables (% of COGS)	20,8%	19,8%	18,8%	19,2%	29,5%	20,3%	21,9%
Total (as % of sales)	**4,3%**	**10,5%**	**14,5%**	**15,6%**	**12,1%**	**14,8%**	**16,6%**
Collection period	**14**	**33**	**44**	**45**	**47**	**43**	**55**
Credit period	**76**	**72**	**68**	**70**	**108**	**74**	**80**

Table 61: Changes in working capital (Trevira)

4.1.3.2.2 Administration and Organization

Overhead Productivity

One of the most crucial steps following the acquisition was the smooth alignment and partial integration of the global sales network with that of its new owner. Traditionally, Trevira concentrated on European markets and had small representations in specific markets outside of Europe. Reliance's access to Trevira's well-developed sales network allowed it to strengthen its local presence in European markets and approach Trevira's customer base. Trevira benefited from Reliance's international sales network, whose size and resources offered it a rapid and efficient entry into new markets. Trevira reached out only indirectly to end customers. Its customers processed fibres and forwarded textiles to textile producers and retailers.

To reach out more efficiently to customers and provide a higher level of service to those operating in specialized market segments, Trevira created a business development team that operated on a regional and a market segment level. Individual teams serviced hospitality customers, cruise ships, healthcare, office and public spaces, aircrafts, and railways.

The introduction of Reliance's SAP system to Trevira's production planning and administration processes contributed to integration between the two. Selected back office operations were offshored to Reliance's headquarters in Mumbai. Terms with service and IT providers where re-negotiated and cheaper partners chosen. To increase sales force productivity Trevira's management introduced a daily business management report showing gaps between planned and actual sales volume, revenues, and gross profit. Reliance bolstered the closer tracking with steps as part of the 2005 restructuring that led to a reduction of the workforce in general administration. At the same time, human resources were added to create the customer business development team.

Hierarchical Complexity

Trevira's legal structured was streamlined at the exit from the LBO in 2004. The three former holdings companies were merged into Trevira Holding GmbH. To ensure full control of the company, Reliance made Trevira a subsidiary of Reliance Industries Limited. Reliance created a shareholder committee headed by Reliance senior management of the polyester business unit. A Reliance representative, Hemant Sharma, became a Trevira executive board member. No other management changes were made.

Although the new investor had clear investment objectives, it granted management significant independence. The new management imposed on all business units and manufacturing facilities tight and immediate reporting and interfered on various occasions. To smoothen coordination within the company, management transferred the headquarters of the former sales and marketing departments at Hattersheim near Frankfurt to the Bobingen production and development facility. CEO Jörg Hellwig argued that the move would put them in closer contact with product development and manufacturing, and enable them to present brands and quality directly to customers.

Management Control Systems

The new owners continued to monitor closely progress of Trevira's performance improvement and restructuring. The new Head of Finance came from Reliance and made sure that controls were clear and met Reliance's reporting needs.

A daily performance report summarized business development according to sales, revenues, raw materials, gross profit, variable manufacturing costs, and gross profit per business segment: filaments, fibres and PET-chips[1340]. The report closed with an indicative calculation of EBIT and EBITDA. Management tracked on a monthly basis progress in performance with a pro forma balance sheet, a profit and loss, and cash flow statement. It tracked manufacturing costs in terms of the main cost categories and on a cost per volume unit basis. The manufacturing report accompanied by a quality report that consolidated by-products, complaints, return shipments, depreciation and inferior products. These reports were partially introduced as a part of reporting during the LBO. Trevira also continued to track liquidity development

1340 The main costs - personnel, other fixed costs, depreciation and interest - were reported on the level of Trevira GmbH.

under Reliance's ownership. Liquidity reporting was part of the weekly report that included a detailed overview of incoming and outgoing cash payments by category such as revenue, raw material, energy, freight, personnel, insurance, interest and tax. The report also offered a forecast of the liquidity development over a three-month period.

Introduction of detailed risk reports constituted a more far-reaching professionalisation. Management began in 2005 to monitor systematically risks divided into market risk, strategy risk, cost risk, financial risk, and environmental risk[1341].

4.1.3.3 Entrepreneurial Growth Focused-Management Activities

4.1.3.3.1 Strategy

Reliance became with the acquisition of Trevira the world's largest polyester fibre and yarn player. It gained access to the European market and selected industries such as the automotive sector. The new owner enabled Trevira to strengthen its resource base, to expand its home textiles segment, and to establish globally the Trevira brand. Reliance's international sales organization allowed Trevira to more actively develop markets outside of Europe (see details in chapter 4.1.3.3.3).

The entry of low cost producers made clear that Trevira could only remain profitable if it stopped being a mass-market producer and focused on specialized products. Under DBI's ownership, Trevira's management did not fully execute the needed change in focus because debt repayment limited its ability to make the necessary capital investments. Incorporation into the Reliance consortium helped Trevira accelerate the change in focus. Trevira was able to use Reliance's low cost production facilities so that it could offer standard products at significantly reduced cost. Management was also able to move to a more focused sales and customer approach. In the DBI period, Trevira started to reorganize its sales department to achieve a higher degree of customization. In return, Trevira gave Reliance a strong footprint in Europe and put it in a position to cater globally to all market segments of polyester fibres and

---

1341 Market risk assessment was reflected in the three months report and the full year forecast. Both reports included a detailed comparison of planned and actual volume and price development, which helped identify market-related risks early on. In 2005, the reporting allowed to anticipate a lower than expected development of market demand and to adjust capacity accordingly. Strategy risk was assessed in an annual strategy review by management in close association with the owner. In 2005, management recognized that market demand did not increase as expected and took a series of steps (see the later chapter on changes in strategy). The manufacturing report enabled management to assess the risk related to cost development. Management relied on the monthly performance and liquidity report for risk assessment, and imposed severe measures in 2005 to ensure sufficient financial flexibility as outlined in the previous paragraph on tighter working capital management.

filament yarns[1342]. Trevira was further able to complete its strategic shift by increasing production flexibility for smaller lot sizes. Management realized that its growth options in existing markets and segments were exhausted. Additional revenues could be achieved by addressing new customer segments, entering into new markets and bringing new products to market. As a first step, management expanded its global presence by combining its resources with those of Reliance. Nonetheless, 85% of total sales still originated in 2005 in the European Union.

The focus in the market segments served by remained on the automotive and home textiles segment. These segments each accounted in 2006 for 30% of sales, followed by technical/hygiene (including hospital) with a share of 24%, apparel market with 13%, and polyester chips 4%. The segment for corporate wear became increasingly unattractive because of the high level of standard products and competition from low-cost manufacturers. As a result, management decided to restructure this segment and shift capacity to other more high-margin markets.

Under Reliance's supervision, management created distinct business development teams designed to support customers in defining and refining intended product configurations and advise them on streamlining their supply chain. By providing services and information to fabric producers, finishers, converters, interior decorators, and end customers (See Figure 21), Trevira developed downstream activities in the value chain by. Trevira, for example, published a brochure with applications of its fibres for interior designers and architects. It also made sure it was present at interior and home textile fairs rather than at filaments fairs.

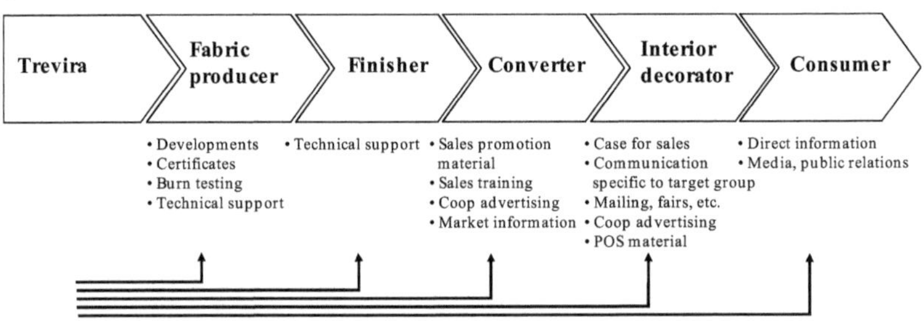

Figure 21: Trevira marketing concept (Trevira)

Trevira increased close cooperation between product developers and customers. Management sought to enhance its creative design capability. This move was clear in

1342 In USD 20 Billion revenues, Reliance's export share was only USD 7.3 Billion (in 2006). This underscored the strategic need to increase the revenue base outside of India.

Trevira CS's gaining of market share in the contract sector. Reliance's annual strategy review constituted the basis for the change in strategy. Based on the review management reorganized operations and strategy, starting with serious cost restructuring, to expand market share in the US and Asia, and source from Reliance in India.

4.1.3.3.2 Innovation

Trevira was at the exit in 2004 a highly specialized manufacturer of polyester products. The company had more than 150 valuable patents and technologies as well as an exceptional R&D setup that has accumulated considerable knowledge in the development, testing and production of polyester fibres and filament yarns. Trevira's knowledge base, as Reliance Industries President Subodh Sapra believed, would complement Reliance's own research and development given its limited experience in 1the high performance fibres market that Trevira serviced. He argued that at the exit, "the synergy will provide comprehensive and innovative solutions for apparel and non-apparel applications of polyester to customers worldwide." Trevira's knowledge base complemented Reliance's R&D facility, the Reliance Technology Center in Bombay. The Bombay, Bobingen, and Silkeborg centers together had more than 200 experts working on mono- and co-polymer polyester fibres, filaments and resins.

Management continued to refine the company's premium textile fibres for different fashion markets and corporate wear with brands such as Trevira Perform, Trevira Classixx, Trevira Xpand and Trevira Bioactive. Trevira Fitness was for sports clothing and Trevira Fill for mattresses. Trevira brought to market a series of additional products for health care and the medical segment. Various modifications were introduced to Trevira Bioactive designed as a medical textile for hospital staff work wear of hospital staff and for highly-strained towels. Trevira polyester filament yarns also used high-elasticity texture in elastic bandages and trans-dermal therapeutic systems. In a bid to speed up the move from R&D to production, Reliance created a global competence center with a centralized development team and global responsibility to advance a new application to a 0-series and transfer it to a commercial production in the most appropriate manufacturing facility. The development team was based in Silkeborg and Bobingen, the transfer team at the relevant manufacturing facility.

To innovate production, Trevira simplified manufacturing of spun-dyed filament yarns and installed a new generation of spun and air-texturizing machines. It also more closely involved customers in the product development process. Cost pressure led to core customer's loss of technical know how. Trevira's focus on technology leadership compensated for their lack of knowledge and strengthened its customer relationships.

The new management focused to increase Reliance's R&D productivity but still cut back on personnel in 2005 and 2006 despite the fact that Trevira had an exceptional know how base. The cutbacks did not affect the Bobingen Textile Technology Centre's reputation as the most modern establishment for new products and applications in the field of high-tech polyester. R&D rejuvenated the product spectrum and contributed newly developed fibres being less than 5 years old constituting 65% of sales of fibre products younger than 5 years old.

4.1.3.3.3 Market Development

Trevira's brand gained access through Reliance's sales network to India, one of the fastest growing textiles markets in the world. In return, Trevira offered Reliance a strong footprint in Europe and positioned it to cater globally to the polyester fibres and filament yarns markets.

Emerging markets in Eastern Europe and Asia offered Trevira ample growth opportunities. Increasing purchasing power and a growing middle class demand own homes fuelled the growth momentum. New representations opened in China and in Japan in 2006. A regional sales and marketing office was opened in 2007 in Dubai. Trevira was able to supply the majority of Dubai's new hotels and commercial buildings with flame retardant, premium textiles. All in all, the number of offices abroad rose to seven in 2006, in addition to the company's more than 30 representatives worldwide. In Germany, sales suffered from low domestic demand, declining by 11% alone in 2004, despite Trevira gaining market share. By 2006, Trevira managed to decouple its revenue development from the total market, with sales jumping by 13% alone in Germany (see Table 62).

Management increased customer service in regions served and implemented a customer information system. This system supplied customers and interested parties with constantly updated data and information buttressed by Trevira's internet homepage, which had an online showcase for flame retardant fabrics. Trevira also stepped up its customer service by granting clients direct access to experts on trends and developments, particularly related to fire and other textile tests. Sales material was improved and distributed more actively to core decision makers such as architects and interior designers.

In TEUR	PostLBO						LBO							
	x+3		x+2		x+1		t+4		t+3		t+2		t+1	
	2006 (Dec 31)	Share of total	2005 (Dec 31)	Share of total	2004 (Dec 31)	Share of total	2003 (Dec 31)	Share of total	2002 (Dec 31)	Share of total	2001 (Dec 31)	Share of total	2000 (Dec 31)	Share of total
By regions														
Inland	90.346	32%	79.909	30%	89.655	34%	85.331	33%	91.657	35%	101.058	36%	97.162	34%
Other EU countries	154.363	54%	148.162	56%	144.437	55%	142.650	55%	145.957	55%	150.643	53%	162.454	57%
Other European countries	11.771	4%	9.354	4%	11.230	4%	15.649	6%	15.289	6%	17.483	6%	18.595	6%
North and South America	18.841	7%	14.936	6%	9.381	4%	7.088	3%	5.194	2%	7.320	3%	4.768	2%
Africa, Asia, Oceania	11.449	4%	10.095	4%	7.998	3%	7.718	3%	6.757	3%	5.995	2%	4.399	2%
Total	286.770		262.456		262.701		258.436		264.854		282.499		287.378	
Growth by regions														
Inland	13%		-11%		5%		-7%		-9%		4%			
Other EU countries	4%		3%		1%		-2%		-3%		-7%			
Other European countries	26%		-17%		-28%		2%		-13%		-6%			
North and South America	26%		59%		32%		36%		-29%		54%			
Africa, Asia, Oceania	13%		26%		4%		14%		13%		36%			
Total	9%		0%		2%		-2%		-6%		-2%			

Table 62: Market growth by regions during and after the buyout (Trevira)

As outlined in the previous chapter on efficiency-related measures, market development was strengthened with the creation of segment specific customer business development teams. Trevira focused its efforts on understanding the customer's supply chain and providing specific customer solutions. The polyester segment remained depressed by market demand and rising raw material costs. Like in previous years, producers were unable to pass on the cost increases. Management continued to reduce capacity in commodity filament products. Trevira was able to increase gradually its market share, 4% in 2005 alone, despite the closure of its European production facilities.

Preliminary products dropped in 2005 because of the product's move to Reliance. Competition in smooth threads from low cost producers continued to push back European manufacturers and produced a negative growth tend. The staple fibres segment however showed positive growth. Growth was boosted by fibres for non-woven textiles and low-pill fibres. Trevira expanded its market share by 2% in 2005 alone. Revenues in textured threads benefited from new production capacity and increased considerably. In 2006, revenues surged in both staple fibres and textured threads. By 2007, Trevira had insufficient capacity to meet demand for Trevira CS.

In TEUR	PostLBO						LBO							
	x+3		x+2		x+1		t+4		t+3		t+2		t+1	
	2006 (Dec 31)	Share of total	2005 (Dec 31)	Share of total	2004 (Dec 31)	Share of total	2003 (Dec 31)	Share of total	2002 (Dec 31)	Share of total	2001 (Dec 31)	Share of total	2000 (Dec 31)	Share of total
By product groups														
Intermediates	14.637	5%	10.197	4%	20.459	8%	21.677	8%	24.946	9%	24.842	9%	15.778	5%
Flat yarns	63.370	22%	67.911	26%	79.120	30%	80.412	31%	84.331	32%	85.420	30%	98.689	34%
Textured threads	76.501	27%	62.015	24%	45.070	17%	42.298	16%	48.143	18%	47.533	17%	50.922	18%
Staple fibre	132.262	46%	122.333	47%	118.052	45%	114.049	44%	107.434	41%	124.670	44%	121.800	42%
Finished goods	0	0%	0	0%	0	0%	0	0%	0	0%	34	0%	189	0%
Total	286.770		262.456		262.701		258.436		264.854		282.499		287.378	
Growth by product groups														
Intermediates	44%		-50%		-6%		-13%		0%		57%			
Flat yarns	-7%		-14%		-2%		-5%		-1%		-13%			
Textured threads	23%		38%		7%		-12%		1%		-7%			
Staple fibre	8%		4%		4%		6%		-14%		2%			
Finished goods	nm		nm		nm		nm		nm		-82%			
Total	9%		0%		2%		-2%		-6%		-2%			

Table 63: Change in sales by business segment during and after the buyout (Trevira)

The strongest growth in terms of sales by industry segment came from the technical textile industry. Sales for the automotive industry recovered slowly and offered modest growth opportunities. By 2006, Trevira was the leading textile supplier to this important industry. Home textiles, Trevira's traditional market in which it started its business, stagnated in the post-LBO period. Reliance Industries Limited access to Trevira's sales and customer base was highly beneficial and significantly increased its revenues through new customers.

4.1.3.3.4 Human Resource Management

General Human Resources

The human resources department had two missions: ensuring the workforce's qualifications in an increasingly competitive market environment and efficiently adjusting the workforce to the relocation of two major manufacturing sites.

With Trevira's new strategic focus, management sought to offer more complex, tailor-made services to its customers. This required well-trained and experienced employees able to integrate technical and commercial aspects. The business development teams needed top caliber personnel. The relocation of the texturiser departments from Danish subsidiary Trevira Neckelmann A/S in Silkeborg to Germany made it necessary to train more than 100 new workers. At the same time, productivity improvements and capacity adjustments meant that a smaller workforce was needed. The HR department implemented a management-approved social plan as part of the restructuring measures. The life of the plan was extended by two years until the end of 2007.

Trevira's management maintained the evaluation and personnel development process introduced during the LBO. The acquisition by Reliance offered opportunities to enhance personnel skills in international marketing, sales, and product development. Shortly after the trade sale, Trevira began sending employees to key departments in Reliance such as R&D and purchasing to ensure transfer of best practice know how. After the recovery in 2006 and 2007, Trevira started again to hire new personnel at the level of apprentices as well as in terms of experienced professionals in sales, marketing, engineering and research.

Top Management Resources

The new owners realized that former management structures had to be removed. Reliance first reduced the number of board members from from five to two members. Jörg Hellwig, a former manager within the fibre business of Bayer, replaced Bernd Sassenrath as new CEO in 2005. Board members Jürgen Muth and Jürgen Idzko resigned in the middle of 2005. Reliance stopped relying on external consultants brought in to support various improvement programs. The second member on the management board, Hemant Sharma, a senior manager of Reliance's polyester business unit, was appointed Head of Marketing and Sales. Jörg Hellwig resigned for personal reasons in November 2007 and was replaced by Uwe Wöhner. The post-LBO management did not receive stakes in Trevira[1343]. To motivate management and ensure a common interest, management received an increased fixed salary and greater variable compensation. Because management met the agreed objectives, total compensation was higher than that of the previous top management.

		Prior exit			Post exit		
Name	Responsibility	As of January, 2001	As of Octover, 2001	As of July, 2003	As of September, 2004	As of September, 2005	As of November, 2007
Bernd Sassenrath	*Chairman*	x	x	x	x	x	
Hartmut Last	Business unit leader staple fibres; Technology and Production	x	x				
Gerd Hochapfel	Business unit filaments; Marketing and Sales	x					
Jürgen Muth	Finance & Controlling, IT and Personnel	x	x	x	x		
Jürgen Idzko	Production, Technology, Research & Development, Environment, Health and Safety			x	x		
Hemant Sharma	Marketing, sales, supply chain management, *Chairman*				x	x	x
Jörg Hellwig	*CEO*					x	
Uwe Wöhner	*CEO*						x

Table 64: Changes in composition of top-management board (Trevira)

4.2 Case Analysis

4.2.1 Changes in Governance over the Buyout Cycle and in the Post-Exit Period

At the entry into the buyout in 1999, DBI changed the governance structure in three of the four categorized constituents: increased debt leverage, introduction of management participation, and enhanced activity level of monitoring. Concentration in ownership remained unchanged.

After four years in an LBO structure, DBI sold Trevira GmbH on August 11, 2004, to Reliance Industries Limited. The deal was an outright purchase for EUR 80 Million in cash. Given that that Trevira had EUR 80 Million in net debt at the time, there was little to no equity exit value left for DBI, which had invested some EUR 70 Million in equity at the entry in 2001.

1343 See the subsequent chapter on managerial shareholdings.

At the exit, the constituents of governance changed. From day one, Reliance monitored closely on the basis of its industry experience and strategic objective to make Trevira the fundament of its European strategy for its polyester business. Management had to surrender its stakes to the new owner, which demanded 100% equity. Another governance change was the (modest) de-leverage as a result of Reliance giving Trevira additional equity in the form of some of its retained earnings while handing guarantees to banks for Trevira's bank debt.

4.2.1.1 Debt Leverage

At the entry into the buyout in 2000, DBI renegotiated debt terms and facilitated a new debt arrangement with Chase Manhattan with a EUR 136 Million consortium credit that was fully pushed down on Trevira. Additional interest was charged to service the EUR 90 million shareholder loan. DBI sources interviewed said the LBO financing was challenging already at the entry, and showed Trevira's limited ability to repay debt. Nonetheless, DBI believed Trevira would be able to repay.

In the first two years, Trevira serviced interest and repaid debt on schedule. The proceeds of the EUR 27 million sale of Trevira Fibras were passed on. In 2004, total interest-bearing liabilities included EUR 80 Million in bank debt and a EUR 111 Million shareholder loan. During the LBO, Trevira partly repaid debt through annual principal payments and divestment proceeds. However, weak cash flow from operations forced Trevira to breach the covenant terms in January 2003 and renegotiate credit terms. Chase agreed to reduce debt payments for 2003 to 2005 to ensure that the company had sufficient liquidity to maintain operations following a due diligence report by JP Morgan. The revolving EUR 18 Million credit facility was extended to give Trevira short-term flexibility. In return, the bank demanded that shareholders provide an additional loan over EUR 11 Million. It also wanted shareholders to write off EUR 20 Million of cumulated interest. This amounted to an additional EUR 30 Million in equity[1344].

The LBO financing put pressure on Trevira's restructuring. Although Trevira had a high debt propensity, dropping profits and weak cash flow prevented it from making substantial changes in production facilities to accommodate smaller lot sizes and facilitate higher efficiency. At the exit of the LBO, Trevira's bank debt facility was refinanced under Citicorp's leadership. It amounted to EUR 60 Million in senior debt and a revolver of EUR 20 Million drawn in the amount of EUR 10 Million.

1344 One may argue that the interest of 10% on the shareholder loan was rather high with respect to an average interest rate of 6.5% to 7.0% on bank debt. Further, the EUR 30 Million in equity equaled an actual cash-out of EUR 11 Million, since the interest on shareholder loan had been cumulated within Trevira.

Trevira GmbH, the holding company, was the only entity with a bank liability against a third party. The shareholder loan of EUR 112 Million was transferred from Trevira Holding GmbH to operating company Trevira GmbH. The operating company received a receivable for the corresponding amount. The shareholder loan was later passed on to Reliance Investments s.a.r.l., a subsidiary of Reliance Netherlands BV. The new owners provided additional equity by increasing retained earnings in the amount of EUR 14 Million. Bank debt was reduced even though the capital structure remained leveraged. Pre-exit annual debt redemption amounted to EUR 13 Million, interest to EUR 7 Million. Post-exit redemption payments slightly increased to EUR 15 Million and interest to EUR 2 Million. Weak operating profit brought the financial stability down to a 7.1x net debt to EBITDA ratio. Still, management succeeded in downpaying debt as scheduled in 2004, 2005 and 2006.

	PostLBO			LBO			
	x+3	x+2	x+1	t+4	t+3	t+2	t+1
In TEUR	**2006** (Dec 31)	**2005** (Dec 31)	**2004** (Dec 31)	**2003** (Dec 31)	**2002** (Dec 31)	**2001** (Dec 31)	**2000** (Dec 31)
Net debt							
Bank liabilities	56.798	67.345	70.215	46.420	48.576	70.186	76.169
Residual term smaller 1 year	41.798	37.345	25.215	18.631	9.193	8.086	5.983
Residual term more than 1 year	15.000	30.000	45.000	27.789	39.383	62.100	70.186
Cash (and equivalents)	1.685	1.841	954	1.014	6.512	9.565	2.013
Total net debt (cash)	**55.113**	**65.504**	**69.261**	**45.406**	**42.064**	**60.621**	**74.156**
Annual change		(3.757)	23.855	3.342	(18.557)	(13.535)	
Net debt to EBITDA	**3,66x**	**7,10x**	**4,55x**	**2,43x**	**2,01x**	**1,98x**	**2,38x**
Equity							
Susribed capital and profit	15.519	15.519	15.519	15.519	15.519	15.519	14.545
Consolidation	7.001	3.430	5.686	9.158	14.129	18.724	32.092
Capital reserve	89.531	89.531	89.531	75.907	75.907	75.907	76.881
Total equity	**112.051**	**108.480**	**110.736**	**100.584**	**105.555**	**110.150**	**123.518**
Equity to total capital	**67,0%**	**62,4%**	**61,5%**	**68,9%**	**71,5%**	**64,5%**	**62,5%**
Debt to book equity	**49,2%**	**60,4%**	**62,5%**	**45,1%**	**39,9%**	**55,0%**	**60,0%**
Debt to adj. equity	**366,0%**	**434,0%**	**452,4%**	**299,1%**	**313,0%**	**452,3%**	**523,7%**

Table 65: Changes in debt leverage over the buyout cycle on holding level (Trevira)

Reliance ensured that management was forced to run the company independent of its parent company. Management could not expect additional loans to compensate for incurring losses. However, Reliance guaranteed to mitigate the default risk. On a stand-alone base, Trevira had a low debt propensity. Business was highly cyclical and the necessary restructuring involved risks on an industry and company level. Management relied on cash flow generation from operations to successfully restructure and make Trevira a profitable niche player. One of the first steps to accelerate principal repayments was factoring of EUR 27 million (2006) in receivables.

4.2.1.2 Ownership Concentration

Ownership concentration remained largely unchanged throughout the buyout cycle. What did change over the cycle was the identity of the individual owner and related investment objectives[1345]. The new ownership under the LBO included two investor groups: the buyout experts with 90% of the shares and management with 10%. DBI 's investment objective was to hold a company for three to five years, in which the company would achieve an IRR in line with the industry average. DBI wanted to develop the business to a point where it be taken public or sold to strategic buyer at a fair price. Although DBI was a subsidiary of Germany's largest bank, it adopted the investment strategy of an independent LBO fund.

Ownership concentration changed only slightly with the move of Trevira and its management from DBI to Reliance. Reliance's investment objectives differed however significantly from those of DBI. Reliance had no plans to divest Trevira in a foreseeable time. It stated that the acquisition was a strategic investment with no time restriction. However, Reliance expected Trevira to earn cost of capital and be run as an independent, stand-alone business. Reliance realized that the operational cost synergies were limited. It justified the investment with the mutual benefit of complementary geographical footprints that were all the more important. Trevira allowed Reliance to achieve its strategic objective of entering into the European market as Reliance wanted to become the world's largest manufacturer of Polyester.

			Post trade sale			
	Pre trade sale		August 11, 2005		January 1, 2007	
Equity shareholders	Share capital	In %	Share capital	In %	Share capital	In %
1. Buyout specialists						
DB Industrials Holding		45,0%				
MEFIS Beteiligung		45,0%				
2. Management and employees						
Dres. Bischoff Wirtschaftstreuhand		10,0%				
3. Industrial buyer						
Reliance Netherlands B.V.			23.500.000	94,0%	12.500.000	50,0%
Silvassa Industries Private ltd.			1.500.000	6,0%		
Motech Software B.V.					11.000.000	44,0%
Varun Mercantile Ltd.					1.500.000	6,0%
Total	0	100,0%	25.000.000	100,0%	25.000.000	100,0%

Table 66: Change of ownership in the post-exit period on holding level (Trevira)

1345 The investment objectives of Multikarsa had been to raise significant synergies between its basic polyester business and Trevira's high-end textile business, despite the differences in business and market focus.

However, ownership of Reliance itself changed. The founding Ambani family controlled Reliance Industries and its parent, Reliance Group. They had an in-depth understanding of the polyester business and held several senior management positions. For its part, DBI had been monitored by the managing board of Deutsche Bank, Germany's largest corporate bank. Deutsche Bank had a number of institutional investors but no single, dominating shareholder. The implied activity level will be explained in detail in the following chapter.

4.2.1.3 Activity Level of Investors

Pre-buyout owner Multikarsa had to supervise a diverse portfolio of participations in different industries. Senior management had to invest significantly in understanding a company's underlying market conditions and to supervise the subsidiaries. The parent was likely to be less efficient in monitoring because it had to cover a number of different industries. Observations are limited but the whole management team was changed in September 1999 by Multikarsa and the creditors. When Multikarsa went bankrupt, the pre-buyout investor focused on introducing a sales process.

DBI as the buyout investor implemented an intense monitoring process. DBI appointed an operating partner and an investment manager from its management team to supervise the company on a monthly basis, reviewing progress on the initial business plan. It also appointed the former head of the private equity subsidiary of Deutsche Bank, Karl-Gerhard Seifert, as Chairman of Trevira's supervisory board. After the decline in profitability in the beginning of 2001, DBI intensified their monitoring activity and urged Trevira management to launch a restructuring program. They hired several industry experts to support the CEO in his restructuring efforts. DBI hired external consultants to implement improvement measures aimed at returning the filament business to profitability. Another major decision was the divestment of Fibras.

Based on interview quotes, DBI underestimated the speed of the industry consolidation. Those interviewed said that management and DBI should have perhaps responded more firmly. Trevira succeeded with DBI's help to cut costs, but this did not compensate for the decline in sales and increased raw material costs. Those interviewed also said that the buyout investor underestimated Trevira's degree of exposure to standard products at the entry into the LBO. The structure of a LBO inhibited the making of the necessary investments. For instance, DBI did not approve investments into more flexible production equipment to accommodate smaller lot sizes and more customer-specific products because this would have required significant cash that could not be financed by Trevira's operating cash flow. At the same time, DBI was unwilling to provide further cash to Trevira, particularly (and understandable) after the strategic decision to sell the business. With the divestment decision, DBI shifted focus from actual monitoring to the divestment process.

		Skill				Membership			
Name	**Role**	**Finance**	**Industry**	**Operations**	**Turnaround**	**Prior exit**	**As of March, 2004**	**As of September, 2004**	**Until 2007**
Karl-Gerhard Seifert	*Chairman*		x	x		x			
Christian Krupp	Consultant	(x)	x	(x)		x	x		
Günter Gunzenheimer	Workers' representative		x			x			
Klaus Seeger	*Chairman*						x		
Subodh Sapra	*Chairman*; President of the polyester sector at Reliance Industry		x	x	(x)			x	x
Ganther Gunzenheimer	Workers' representative		x				x	x	x
Hans-Joachim Becker	Industry expert							x	x

Table 67: Membership structure of the supervisory board (Trevira)

With the trade sale to Reliance, the activity level of governance was intensified as first-hand industry expertise was brought to Trevira. Reliance followed clearly defined strategic objectives as outlined in the previous chapter. Reliance expected Trevira to earn its cost of capital. To ensure that Trevira adhered to these targets, Reliance employed various instruments of monitoring. A trusted representative was appointed to Trevira's board. The leadership of Reliance's polyester unit business engaged in frequent discussions with senior management. Matters discussed included strategic and operational issues. Reliance was a sparring partner for the senior management and offered support given its resources and business network. Reliance also offered low cost production facilities and attractive purchasing terms. Finally, Reliance offered various experts to Trevira who, for example introduced a new SAP system. This was previously done by hiring expensive external consultants. Reliance's experts understood the functional challenge and the textile industry.

Those interviewed said that Trevira was strategically controlled by Reliance. One can assume that the supervision of Trevira amounted to a 'governed' corporation. The new owner relied on its in-depth industry knowledge and associated Trevira's strategic outlook with that of the parent company and its polyester business unit. Subodh Sapra, president of Reliance's Polyester Sector, said in July 2004:

> "Polyester manufacturers understand something about polyester, bankers understand something about banking".

Businesses where not integrated even though Reliance selectively consolidated operations such as purchasing and back-office, where cost savings where apparent.

Control was exerted through intense discussions with management on the correct strategy and operational setup. Discussions facilitated a strong alignment between Reliance's position as principal and Trevira's role as agent.

Another instrument to align interests was the debt burden that Reliance imposed on Trevira. It ensured that management invested diligently and raised growth opportunities with company's own resources. Given industry consolidation, the industrial ownership seemed more appropriate than ownership by a of buyout expert.

4.2.1.4 Managerial Shareholdings

Senior management received 10% of equity at the entry into the LBO in 2000, which was held by a trust. Financing of the participation to the tune of EUR 7 Million was arranged as an equity participation program and structured as direct shareholder equity. Management also participated pro rata in a EUR 90 million shareholder loan. Because of the liquidity shortage at the end of 2003, renegotiation of debt obliged shareholders to raise new funds in an additional shareholder loan of EUR 11 Million and to wave cumulative interest of EUR 20 Million.

Over time, managers (and the buyout investors) realized that their equity would be of little or no value in a foreseeable DBI exit because debt remained high and the company was unable to increase debt repayment. As long as Trevira did not achieve considerable profit, shareholdings could not motivate management. Management' shares were sold to Reliance and its equity holding subsidiaries as part of the trade sale in 2004[1346]. The new owner insisted on acquiring 100% of the company. All former senior management team members left within the first year post-exit the company. None of the new senior managers received equity shareholdings. In order to provide sufficient motivation and ensure interest alignment, the supervisory board increased fixed salaries for the two board members.

One member was a trusted senior manager from the acquirer's polyester business unit and represented the new owner in ensuring smooth coordination with the international sales network. Reliance was confident that he would act in the interest of their strategic intention. The new CEO was the former business unit head of Bayer Fibre and this was the first time he managed a stand-alone business. One may assume that he was highly incentivized to demonstrate his senior management skills.

1346 Due to the weak performance, the required restructuring, and the high debt burden, the management could achieve only limited returns on their employed equity. The exact amount has not been disclosed.

Explanatory variables	Hypo-thesis	Expected change after exit		Key observations
Debt leverage	1b	(-)	NEU	Reliance provided additional equity over EUR 13.6 Millions. Capital structure and cover ratios change however only modestly, remaining leveraged relative to industry
			CF	Total debt repayment (interest and redemption) in the corollary were reduced
			CF	Further, Reliance signed a guarantee to Trevira's bank debt
Ownership concentration	2b	(constant)	CF	Ownership passed over from DBI and to Reliance. Minority stake of senior management (10%) acquired by Reliance.
Activity level	3b	(-)	NCF	Intensified strategic control by new parent. Hereby, in-depth discussion on both strategy, e.g., international growth, and operations, e.g., manufacturing workflow and purchasing in basis of industry expertise of Reliance.
			NCF	Reliance appointed trusted representative to Trevira's management board and general management
			NCF	Reliance supported restructuring with own industry experts,e.g., for SAP introduction.
Mgmt. shareholdings	4b	(-)	CF	Reliance acquired outstanding managerial shareholdings.

CF: Observations confirm hypothesis
NCF: Observations do not to confirm hypothesis
NEU: Observations neither confirm nor reject hypothesis

Table 68: Synthesis of changes in governance (Trevira

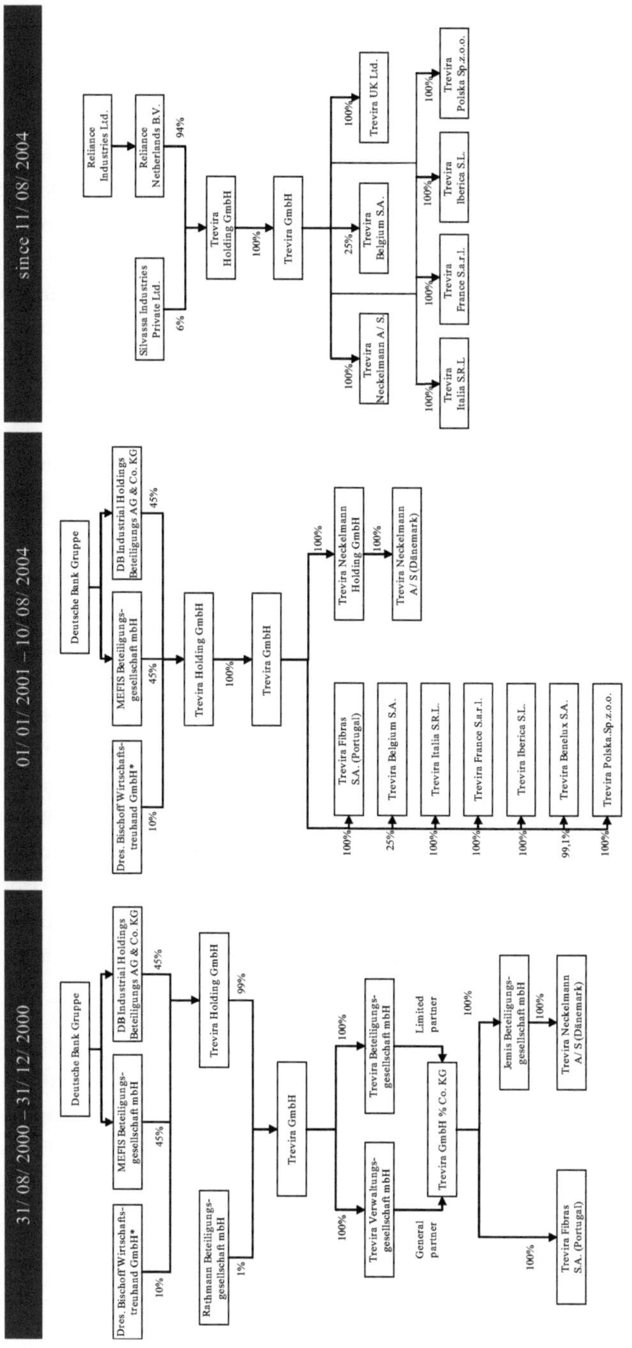

Figure 22: Change in legal structure of Trevira and its subsidiaries (Trevira)

.

4.2.2 Changes in Management Objectives

Focus on Efficiency

Although new equity reduced debt, the post-exit capital structure remained leveraged and fueled the need to generate cash to service debt payments. The previous management had recognized the need for restructuring. The cost cutting 'Topas' program was launched in 2001 and aggressively aimed to reduce the cost base and return the company to profitability. When the filament market continued to stagnate, management immediately launched project 'Profil' to seize additional market potential and extend the profit focus of the Topas program. Earlier restructuring limited new management to generate short-term cash flow, for example, by improving working capital or disposing of underperforming non-core assets. In 2005 and 2006, management severely reduced investments and maximized factoring of receivables to pay the debt tranches. Further, it focused on ongoing operational improvement to generate cash flow from operations.

With respect to the activity level, the new owners engaged intensively in decision-making because of their industry expertise and outlined integration plan. This was evident in the gradual relocation of the production of standard products to India and the ramp-up of the business development teams. Relocation took two years because of quality requirements that would benefit both Trevira and Reliance even though Trevira could have obtained commodities elsewhere. Reliance was able to efficiently monitor the board in terms of management objectives and implied activity. The new owners could not rely on the effect of management stakes to motivate management and ensure that it saw its interest inline with their own ones. Management nevertheless agreed to the unpopular relocation of production from Silkeborg to Poland despite criticism by the employees' union representatives. In summary, management maintained a strong focus on efficiency-oriented measures.

Focus on Entrepreneurial Growth

Entrepreneurship to enter into new markets and launch new products was at the top management's agenda but was inhibited by the need to return to profitability. New capital provided by Reliance was largely used to modernize machinery in German facilities. As a result, management had limited capital to invest in resources in new markets and depended on utilizing the existing network.

Reliance also had an entrepreneurial interest because Trevira gave it access to its reputable customer base. Reliance sought to complement its own offerings with specialty products carrying Trevira's well-known, prestigious brand. Although management did not have a stake, it demonstrated considerable entrepreneurship in terms of market and product strategy. Entrepreneurial freedom continued to the degree that management succeeded in achieving cost of capital and running the company without additional financing from the parent.

The supervisory board and the representative of Reliance in the management board supported Trevira's strategy and decided most business issues in accordance with local management. Because the German management recognized that restructuring required growth from new markets, it sought to leverage the existing Reliance network and open new representations within the capital restrictions. The new owner supported Trevira in entering new markets.

The high monitoring level and debt leverage forced management to focus on efficiency. This compensated at least partly for the lack of a management stake. Growth-related value creation from shareholdings was of less importance because the core challenge was to lead the company to profitability and complete the transition to a specialized market player according to a road map.

4.2.3 Changes in Efficiency-Focused Management Activities

The new management team continued restructuring and implemented measures not taken by the previous owner to improve operational productivity. It relocated parts of production from Denmark to a low cost manufacturing facility in Poland and continued to downscale production of standard products and to source commodities from Reliance. It relaunched an efficiency program at the German facilities and cut back on production administration. This required high personal commitment to convince employees and counter union criticism of these radical steps. Determining factors for these steps affected corporate governance in different ways. Debt leverage demanded continuous cash flow and constituted a limited buffer against major defaults. The new owner however understood the industry disruption and urged management to accelerate change of strategy and restructuring of operations. Finally, management itself was convinced of the need to restructure the business.

The limited capital base and stagnating cash flow impacted the level of capital investments. A large part of investment in the initial post-exit months was predetermined by the introduction of bi-component machinery and ongoing modernization at the two German facilities. Following completion of these major investments, management reduced capital investment plans to a minimum. Smaller investments were allowed for efficient production of small lot sizes.

Management objectives	Hypo-thesis	Explanatory variables: Debt leverage	Ownership concen-tration	Activity level	Mgmt. Share-holdings		Key observations
Efficiency improvement	5	(+)				NEU	Still operating under a leveraged financing structure
						NEU	Continuous restructuring to increase operational productivity
	6		(+)			NEU	No change in concentration
	7			(+)		NEU	Continuous high level of active monitoring by industrial owner, eg management board representative
	8				(+)	NCF	Albeit lack of shareholdings, management willing to undergo unpopular measures, eg relocation of production
						NCF	Rigid reorganization of overhead, introduction of detailed planning and controlling system
						CF	Other disciplinary forces, eg debt and active monitoring, substituted for lack of managerial shareholdings
Corporate entrepreneurship	9	(-)				CF	True when considering that Trevira remained leveraged and level of corporate entepreneurship did not change significantly
						NCF	Enhanced growth focus yet under the premise of limtied investments and usage of Reliance international sales network
	10		(+)			NEU	No change in concentration
	11			(+)		NCF	Continuous high level of active monitoring; mutual consent of supervisory and management for growth to secure position as global specialized high-tech manufacturer
						NCF	Reliance granted access to own international sales network (and vice versa)
	12				(+)	NCF	Management actively pursued growth opportunities and was willing to invest despite limited financial means
						NCF	Other disciplinary forces, eg debt and active monitoring, substituted for lack of managerial shareholdings
		Direction of expected correlation					

CF: Observations confirm hypothesis
NCF: Observations do not to confirm hypothesis
NEU: Observations neither confirm nor reject hypothesis

Table 69: Synthesis of changes in management objectives (Trevira)

The integrated production network enabled Trevira to service all markets and regions with a sufficiently modern production capacity[1347]. No further divestments were expected, since former management had demarcated the level of core assets during the LBO. One may conclude that available funds did not increase notably after the exit. However, Reliance provided low-cost operations and attractive sourcing conditions at little or no cost that were for Trevira of high value and yielded direct cost savings. The new management was willing to streamline the operational setup evident with the decision to team-up with Reliance in terms of sourcing counter increasing raw material prices by capitalizing on higher purchase power. It was also clear from the enhanced level of control of working capital management. Although management succeeded in generating cash during the buyout by reducing receivables and inventory, it also decreased stock and outstanding days. Reliance encouraged Trevira to introduce their SAP system and track operational productivity with daily reports. Management's focus on operational efficiency was already high during the buyout but was enhanced by Reliance's industrial expertise and greater transparency because the new reporting system allowed an even higher level of operational control.

Like the operational changes, administrative changes in selling and general administration functions were encouraged by Reliance, which offered industry best practice and attractive low cost capacity for selected Trevira activity.

The introduction of new business development teams reflected the change in the way Trevira intended to service its customers. The new sales approach stemmed from Trevira management's understanding of the changing market environment and its response. A second observation on administration was that Trevira retained a constant staff level in its non-domestic sales force even though management sought to enhance its international presence. Management was again concerned about major changes in cost and related reduction of cash flow. However, to increase the sales presence, Reliance urged Trevira to integrate sales forces where appropriate. The head of finance, a former Reliance manager, introduced in Trevira a number of reports to increase comparability in operational and non-operational tasks. Finally, Reliance urged management to offshore selected back office activities to its headquarters to save costs.

1347 For instance, new customers outside of Europe could be serviced by Trevira's production sites in Europe or Reliance's in India. However, production at Reliance was geared to smaller, customized offerings like those of Trevira.

	Hypothesis	Explanatory variables: Debt leverage	Ownership concentration	Activity level	Mgmt. Shareholdings		Key observations
Operational productivity	13a	(+)				CF	Given high debt, ongoing mgmt. attention to increase cash generation from operations, in particular by additional reorganization and by downsizing of production administration
	13b		(+)			NEU	Reliance with strong focus on operational improvements given the strong industry expertise, in particular in low-cost manufacturing.
	13c				(+)	NCF	Despite no shareholdings, management conducted a series of unpopular measures to advance operational productivity, eg production relocation to Poland and India
						CF	Owner Reliance and board representative closely monitored management and may have partly substituted for lack of managerial shareholdings
Asset productivity	14a	(+)				NEU	Increase of asset productivity partly related to new machinery decided upon already in LBO.
						CF	Given high debt, reduced investments in asset base, however, operations not underinvested after major new machinery (e.g., bi-component). Minimum investments to facilitate transition to small-lct production
	14b				(+)	NCF	Persistent efforts of management to enhance asset productivity, eg by refined reporting and relocation of production parts to India and to Poland
Outsouring and offshoring	15a	(+)				CF	Advancing competition and small capital base initiated relocation of production to Poland and India as well as tranfer of sourcing in India.
	15b		(+)			NEU	Senior management of Reliance actively supported relocation to domestic facilities in India
	15c			(+)		NEU	Active discussion in supervisory board on core and non-core activities around the value chain of Trevira
	15d				(+)	NCF	Management decides for offshoring and global sourcing even though they do not hold any shares in the
Working capital management	16a	(+)				CF	Given high debt, necessity to generate cash. Trevira managers succeed to further decrease working capital even after significant reductions during LBO
	16b			(+)		CF	High activity level of Reliance in monitoring; suggest to introduce their advanced SAP system to allow higher sophistication in working capital management
	16c				(+)	NCF	Management engaged in reducing stock and receivables even though they do not hold any shares in the
		Direction of expected correlation					

CF: Observations confirm hypothesis
NCF: Observations do not to confirm hypothesis
NEU: Observations neither confirm nor reject hypothesis

Table 70: Synthesis of changes in efficiency-focused management activities (Trevira)

	Hypothesis	Explanatory variables: Debt leverage	Ownership concentration	Activity level	Mgmt. Shareholdings		Key observations
Overhead productivity	17a	(+)				CF	Given high debt, welcomed cost savings from co-location of departments to production site and offshoring of selected back-office activities to India.
	17b				(+)	CF	Despite no co-ownership, management willing to support the improvement measures, e.g., offshoring to
						NCF	Further, management implemented a new sales approach that resulted in considerable doubts and resistance amongst the salesforce
Hierarchical complexity	18a	(-)				CF	Continued high debt. No change in number of management levels and related overhead staff
						CF	Higher level of centralized decision-making to ensure progress in restructuring and in cash generation
	18b				(-)	NCF	Despite no co-ownership, senior managers concerned with keeping decision-making as efficient as possible
						NCF	Move of corporate headquarters to the production site Bobingen to smoothen internal coordination
Efficiency of mgmt. control systems	19a	(+)				CF	Permanent high focus on cash flow-based reporting.
	19b			(+)		CF	Enhanced activity level of new owners.Reliance facilitates introduction of more sophisticated controlling systems with focus on operational indicators for daily and weekly performance review
						CF	No need to apply to parent reporting standards. However, reporting formats served as guidance and 'best
	19c				(+)	NCF	Management fully supported introduction of enhanced management reports; ensured high fit between contextual factors and necessary reporting formats
		Direction of expected correlation					

CF: Observations confirm hypothesis
NCF: Observations do not to confirm hypothesis
NEU: Observations neither confirm nor reject hypothesis

Table 71: Synthesis of changes in efficiency-focused management activities (Trevira, continued)

Having said this, the lack of management stakes in the post-exit period did not prevent management from focusing on efficiency in this area too. Hierarchical complexity did not change after the LBO exit. The holding structure was simplified with Reliance continuing to exert control through the shareholder's committee created by previous owner DBI.

Management kept strong ties to operational units and demanded intense reporting. This amounted to a higher degree of centralization. Management sought to safeguard the progress of restructuring and ensure sufficient cash generation for debt repayment. Those interviewed said that communication between departments and business units increased considerably with the entry of Reliance.

The new management significantly enhanced the level of detail and completeness in management control system following Reliance's acquisition. Although Trevira was becoming a niche player, it still operated in markets where control based on standard performance indicators was appropriate. As previously outlined, reports were introduced to facilitate daily and weekly control of core parameters of the business. The author recorded that the level of sophistication of control systems during the LBO period was not as high as in the other two case studies. There was significant room for improvement, which Reliance and the new management recognized. One could not not see Trevira being forced to conform by requiring it to introduce Reliance's reporting systems. However, reporting formats adopted in various dimensions to Reliance's controlling measures even though they were amended to accommodate the specifics of Trevira's accounting regime and IT systems.

4.2.4 Changes in Entrepreneurship-Focused Management Activities

To the degree that funds were restricted because of high debt servicing and necessary machinery modernization, limited means were available for entrepreneurial activity. Reliance encouraged management to be entrepreneurial in terms of market development and innovation.

Funding restrictions prompted the transition to a specialized high tech fibre manufacturer. Reliance supported this strategic change in various ways. Firstly, Trevira could continue offering standard products as part of a larger corporate family and at the same produce products at a profitable cost level. Secondly, Trevira's management could also concentrate on its core competences: providing leading technology in fibre production and servicing customer needs with the highest quality. These objectives led to the introduction of the business development teams, expansion of the creative design department, and strengthening of joint development teams. The forward-integration towards end-customers in terms of know how and market position constituted an unpretentious strategy refinement because none of the competitors had Trevira's market recognition. Reliance's senior management supported Trevira's strategic refinements. Even though Reliance had plans for Trevira's future development, Trevira staff acted as agents of the transition given their respective know how.

Under DBI, Trevira, given the limited capital base, had been unable to fully focus on specialties the way it could with its internal operations and resources under Reliance. According to those interviewed, DBI had underestimated the exposure to standard products, which Trevira had at the entry into the LBO. Reliance finalized this strategic transition.

Reliance encouraged Trevira to introduce a stringent, systematic strategy formulation process. As previously outlined (see chapter 4.1.3.2.2), Trevira introduced an annual strategy review for group and senior managers to discuss changes in market environment and decide upon necessary strategy adjustments. The 2005 strategy review was the initial spark for various changes, not only in market strategy, but also for the operating cost base.

To determine how the R&D funding level changed in the post-exit period, several factors must be considered. Management continued to rely on new products as a primary source of new growth (beside international expansion) as opposed to acquisitions. Reliance actively sought to strengthen its R&D and technology base, and, therefore, urged Trevira to maintain its high caliber know how base. The R&D base was also key to the strategic transition to a specialized high tech fibre manufacturer. Trevira's new management and Reliance's leadership supported this transition. A countervailing factor to the enhanced focus was the limited funds because of debt payments.

Initially it was unclear whether synergetic motives might lead to a significant decrease of funds and relocation of valuable resources to the parent. Reliance relied on a strategy to buy external growth, implying that internal growth driven by R&D might be less important. Trevira's advantage was that their R&D department focused on markets and products different from those of Reliance. Synergies in this context could be refined in terms of complementary resource bases that reinforced each other and avoided overlapping work on similar topics. Finally, Reliance followed an investment strategy that allowed Trevira to operate as an independent entity, leaving in place all resources crucial for Trevira's success. In sum, R&D funding remained unchanged, while its productivity increased considerably with an enhanced share of new products.

Trevira expanded the focus of its R&D in two directions. Management recognized the need to add more design competence to its development team to reach out more actively to customers. Trevira also extended its R&D know how base to include bioactive and antimicrobial filament yarns. This involved more basic R&D while the design competence was more application-oriented. In summary, the R&D focus increased, while maintaining a high productivity level.

Actual steps taken after the exit more than strategic intentions affected the changes in governance to market development. The enhanced sales resource base enabled Trevira to access new markets in a highly efficient manner. The new owner supported the strategy of international growth and provided Trevira's management with the confidence to follow an aggressive growth plan. The former management under the buyout regime had already focused on international growth, but was not supported by the buyout investors and could not secure the funds needed to open new sales representations.

Under Reliance, non-domestic market development gained significant importance. Together with the new owner, management relied on organic growth and regarded Trevira's superior products and brands of Trevira as essential to gaining market share. The appointment of Hemant Sharma as head of marketing and sales demonstrated Reliance's sincerity in realizing international growth. In terms of the proposed inverted 'u-form' relationship of internationalization to performance, Trevira was positioned on the rising left side, benefiting from increased scale of operations and cross-country learning. The new offices indicate that Trevira may have underutilized its growth options.

A remark to the risk awareness of Trevira's management again elucidates the previous observation that the governance instruments in place substituted for the lack of shareholdings. Although management only partially benefited from new international operations while increasing the business risk, it did not hesitate to exploit growth options. The intense discussion with Reliance as well as the appointment of Hemant Sharma ensured an alignment with the management group. Management realized that an enhanced revenue base in the targeted market niches was the only way to ensure survival of Trevira after having streamlined the cost base to the optimum. The alternative of risk-averse restructuring of operations and maintaining the existing customer base in captive markets was not a viable option.

In general, Trevira employees welcomed the Reliance acquisition. After DBI had mandated Alvarez & Marsal, employees feared that the company would be broken up and put into receivership.

	Hypo-thesis	Explanatory variables: Debt leverage	Owner-ship concen-tration	Activity level	Mgmt. Share-holdings		Key observations
Strategy position	20a	(+)				NEU	Management pursued with strategic transition into profitable market niches and withdrawing from mass-
						CF	Reliance actively tracked the transition to a specialized high tech manufacturer and endorsed cost-savings
Strategy formulation	21a			(+)		NCF	Active participation in strategy discussion and formulation on basis of close strategic dialigue with the management, on basis of providing expertise (e.g. operations), and of appointing a senior manager to
						NCF	Reliance encouraged a systematic and formal annual strategy review at Trevira
	21d				(+)	NCF	Management introduced intense strategy formulation process despite lack of shareholdings
						NCF	Relocation of production to Poland and to India reflected management's willingness to undergo unpopular
Diversifi-cation and scope	22b			(-)		NEU	High activity level of Reliance who fully supported Trevira's downstrean strategic diversification towards
						CF	In particular, Reliance benefited from earnings diversificatio by bringing Trevira to their home markets
	22d				(-)	NCF	Management disciplined by ongoing high debt services and close monitoring by Reliance
R&D efficiency	23b	(+)				NEU	Limited available funding. Still, R&D know how-base regarded as crucial for both strategic transition and
						NEU	Share of r&d to sales remained at buyout level
	23d			(+)		NEU	Ongoing high monitoring level of new owner driven by strategic importance of R&D for acquiror and for
						NEU	New owners interested in high productivity and efficient cooperation between parent R&D and R&D of
						NCF	Partly increase for deveplopment / application engineering by the parent to ensure technological
	23f				(+)	NEU	Management actively fostered strengthening of productivity and efficient cooperation between parent
						NEU	Management disciplined by ongoing debt service, intrinsic motivation, and close monitoring
Market development	24a	(-)				CF	Given debt leverage, management hindered to invest significantly in new international sales resources
	24c			(+)		NEU	Continuous high monitoring level; Reliance demonstrated high interest in growth plans of Trevira and appointed senior manager as Head of marketing and sales to Trevira board to enhance international sales
						NEU	Albeit limited funds, Reliance urged management to open new representations and to leverage their sales
	24e				(+)	NEU	Despite lack of shareholdings, management recognized necessity for external growth to succeed in
Human resources	25a			(+)		NEU	Ongoing active monitoring. Reliance as new owner was highly concerned to retain key employees
						NEU	Mutual transfer of personnel to exchange best practice endorsed by management
	25b				(+)	NCF	Management recognized the necessity to retain key employees and ensure sufficient training for the increasingly challenging competitive environment
Top mgmt.: turnover	26a			(+)		CF	Reliance installed entire new management team; albeit, two of the board members resigned age-wise; since
						NCF	Reliance, however, observed to track individual performance much more intensely than the previous
	26c				(+)	NCF	Long-term (limited to three year post-exit observation period) highly stable management team
TM: skill profile	26e			(+)		NEU	New board members highly experienced pracitioneers with indepth industry and functional as well as
Top mgmt.: compensation	27a			(+)		CF	New owners intensively supervised selection and compensation agreement of new management
						NEU	Higher salary to compensate for lack of managerial shareholdings
	27c			(+)		NEU	Ongoing active monitoring. Managers equipped with a higher level of fixed compensation to compensate for lack of shareholdings while recognizing the inability to short-term raise profitability

Direction of expected correlation

CF: Observations confirm hypothesis NCF: Observations do not to confirm hypothesis NEU: Observations neither confirm nor reject hypothesis

Table 72: Changes in entrepreneurial growth-focused management activities (Trevira)

As outlined in the discussion on R&D, Trevira's advantage for Trevira was that the acquirer and target operated in different markets and products. Synergies could be refined in terms of complementary resource bases that reinforced one another and did not involve eliminating overlapping resources. Reliance as the new owner facilitated mutual learning by frequent exchange of personnel. The new owners left the existing organization in place with its implicit roles and hierarchies but did not compromise on labor productivity and streamlining of selected activities in Trevira's advantage. As a result, new employees felt respected by Reliance and focused again on the restructuring challenge Trevira was facing. Because Reliance intended to expand Trevira's product and market scope, management sought to retain key employees and partially increase variable compensation. Although debt servicing also burdened the budget for personnel costs, Trevira's management diligently allocated available funds to maximize retention. To summarize, the focus on human resources remained high and was in terms of personnel development and pay-for-performance, even extended.

Given change in strategy, it was not surprising that Reliance changed the management team. A five-member board was too large for a company this size. Two of the existing board members had reached retirement age. Increased turnover cannot therefore be associated with dissatisfaction with previous management. Changes in turnover and compensation were not a result of change in risk attitude or internal organizational standing. Those interviewed said that in terms of long-term Reliance was concerned with the personal effort of managers. They expected that the parent would not hesitate to change management if dissatisfied with its performance. The main reason for this was the parent's stringent management the fact that a family held Reliance.

The increase in compensation intended to attract a higher management caliber. Increases in manager salaries applied to all senior German management. The new owners realized that it would take time to succeed with restructuring, and that management could not capitalize on value creation without having a stake. That is why they gave management an increased fixed compensation. The level of industry-specific knowledge did not change with the exit of DBI. Reliance carefully selected senior managers familiar with the textile industry and corporate restructuring.

4.2.5 Changes in Performance Development

Performance is compared relative to its own LBO average and to a selected group of competitors[1348]. During the LBO period, Trevira faced a challenging environment with the entry of low cost competitors and demand from its core customers stagnating. Total sales decreased at a rate similar to the industry sample. The strategic shift in 2003 to move into more stable market niches started to pay off, as Trevira was able to shield itself modestly from the industry downturn, with a decrease of only 1.9%. The industry group lost 7.0% of revenues in 2002 and 5.8% in 2003. In terms of gross profit, Trevira managed to earn a higher margin than its direct peers did and increased its margin during the buyout period. However, on an operating profit and cash flow base, Trevira was less successful. In the first two years under DBI ownership, Trevira was more profitable and enjoyed stronger cash flow-generation. From 2002 onwards, the relative outperformance, however, decreased significantly. One explanation may be the higher level of non-direct costs such as general expenses for sales, marketing, administration and R&D, that Trevira encountered and the fact that management was unable to reduce the rate of direct costs. Another explanation was the high restructuring costs and provisions Trevira had to make, which were potentially higher in Germany than in the other European countries in which Trevira's competitors were operating.

Prospects for the post-exit performance were promising. As outlined, Trevira had a resource base to complimentary to that of Reliance. As indicated by Harrison[1349], complementary resource bases between bidder and acquirer can create unique and private synergies. The target was moreover relatively small in comparison to the acquirer, avoiding ambiguous discussions on who had actual power in the combined entity; this was beneficial for both parties. Synergies were expected from additional sales and productivity increase as opposed to cutbacks in expenses.

The textile industry benefited in terms of sales growth from recovering demand for textile fibres and filaments. In 2004, European producers on average grew by 1.9%, slightly above Trevira's growth of 1.3%. The European textile industry in 2005 lost again 5.1% of its revenue base. Trevira's revenue base, however, appeared to be more robust and declined in 2005 only 0.6% because of its focused market position. General market development in 2006 was even more promising for Trevira with a

1348 The sample group of competitors comprises Advansa, Unifi, Eybl, Sabanci, Safety, Ten Cate, Suominen, and DMC.

1349 See Harrison, Hitt et al. 1991

revenue growth of around 9.9%, significantly outperforming the industry. The increase was mainly due to the excellent market position and increasing international presence.

Gross margin continued to lie above the industry average, although the entire industry group, including Trevira, still suffered intense competition. The margin in 2005 came under significant pressure and dropped to the industry average by 6.6%. Trevira suffered from the intense competition and achieved 20.4%, a margin 2.9% below the previous year. Part of this incisive retracement was the positive prospects of 2004 that led to the assumption that 2005 would also witness growth. Manufacturers failed to adjust their cost base in line with the unexpected decrease in sales. In terms of net operating profit, Trevira continued to underperform the industry average. Trevira delayed in 2005 and 2006 restructuring provisions for the workforce, at the Silkeborg, Guben and Bobingen facilities. Continued high material costs kept in 2006 despite revenue growth gross margin low, while operating profit regained 2.7% points to sales.

The implied cash flow from operations fluctuated significantly in the observed post-exit period. High restructuring costs and provisions in 2004 totaling EUR 9.4 Million depressed profit. Interest expenses started to decline modestly in 2005 because of the enhanced equity base and reduced principal payments. On basis of the industry group, competitors were able to limit weak operating performance in 2005 and hold their level of operating cash flow. Industry-wide cash flow generation gained momentum in 2006 and increased to 6.7% of sales as opposed to 4.8% in 2005 and 5.0% in 2004. Trevira was not fully able to seize upon improving sales in 2006 and had to invest significantly in working capital. In summary, cash flow Trevira achieved from operations remained below the industry average.

As a result, management acted with discipline regarding cash flow for investment. Total investments in 2004 dropped to EUR 8.8 million. Management in 2005 allocated additional funds because of a fire in a German facility. In general, management did not consider additional investments necessary to achieve the strategic transition and international revenue growth. However, the reduction of capex plans of Trevira mirrored the industry trend. Average cash flow for investments in 2004 decreased by 5.4% of sales to 3.4%. The industry in 2005 and 2006 was more confident and invested around 4.9% of sales in 2005 and 5.2% in 2006. Given the debt payments, investments in 2006 reached a low of 1.3% of sales.

Although the investments were dramatically curtailed, the level of free cash flow to sales further decreased in the post-exit period. Trevira generated a free cash flow of over 10% to sales in 2001, but this ratio decreased to 0.5% in 2005. In 2005, Trevira outperformed its industry group, which had a negative ratio of 0.1%. Revitalized market demand materialized in 2006 in a higher free cash flow to sales ratio of 1.5%. However, Trevira, given the weak cash flowfrom operations, underperformed the industry.

	PostLBO			LBO			
	x+3	x+2	x+1	t+4	t+3	t+2	t+1
	2006 (Dec 31)	**2005** (Dec 31)	**2004** (Dec 31)	**2003** (Dec 31)	**2002** (Dec 31)	**2001** (Dec 31)	**2000** (Dec 31)
Sales growth							
In % annual growth	9,9%	-0,6%	1,3%	-1,9%	-7,4%	-1,5%	
Industry-adj. annual growth	10,9%	4,5%	-0,7%	9,2%	-1,7%	1,2%	
Annual growth adj. to buyout average	13,3%	2,9%	4,7%				
Sales development indexed to last FY prior exit	111	101	101	100			
Industry-adj. sales dev. indexed to last FY prior exit	116	104	99	100			
Gross margin							
In % of total sales	20,2%	20,4%	23,3%	24,5%	27,1%	26,0%	26,6%
Industry-adj. gross margin	15,3%	14,8%	17,6%	18,2%	13,1%	7,2%	9,9%
Gross margin adj. to buyout average	-5,8%	-5,6%	-2,7%				
Gross profit indexed to last FY prior exit	109	87	96	100			
Industry-adj.gross profit indexed to last FY prior buyout	143	100	104	100			
Net operating profit							
In % of total sales	0,7%	-2,0%	0,0%	0,4%	2,2%	5,3%	4,2%
Industry-adj. net operating profit to sales	-1,8%	-5,6%	-4,1%	-5,5%	-6,3%	0,0%	-1,2%
Net operating profit adj. to buyout average	-2,3%	-5,0%	-3,0%				
Indexed to last year of buyout	215	(550)	(4)	100			
Industry-adj. net operating profit to last FY prior buyout	518	(917)	(5)	100			
Operating cash flow							
In % of total sales	0,8%	3,9%	4,8%	-4,0%	19,3%	16,2%	9,0%
Industry adj. operating cash flow to sales	0,5%	0,1%	2,9%	-12,8%	6,0%	12,4%	6,4%
Operating cash flow adj. to buyout average	-9,3%	-6,2%	-5,3%				
Indexed to last year of buyout	-28	-121	-154	100			
Industry-adj. operating cash flow to last FY prior buyout	-786	-291	-715	100			
Free cash flow							
In % of total sales	-0,4%	0,5%	1,7%	-7,4%	15,3%	10,9%	9,0%
Industry adj. free cash flow to sales	-1,6%	1,0%	4,8%	-8,2%	5,1%	9,8%	10,5%
Free cash flow to sales to buyout average	-7,4%	-6,5%	-5,3%				
Indexed to last year of buyout	6	(6)	(23)	100			
Industry-adj. free cash flow to last FY prior buyout	5	10	6	100			

Table 73: Change in overall performance, stand-alone and industry adjusted (Trevira)

Trevira was able to finance operations because Reliance restructured its debt facilities and consolidated all obligations in Trevira GmbH. As a result, operating company Trevira GmbH was burdened with an additional EUR 38 Million in bank debt. In summary, bank debt totaled to EUR 83 Million at the beginning of 2004. However, the provision of retained earnings and renegotiation of the debt contracts led to a decrease of total cash for repayment and interest from EUR 20 Million to EUR 17 Million[1350]. Although the payments decreased, Trevira in 2005 was unable to generate cash from operations and drew funds from its working capital facility of EUR 12 Million.

Evidence of the acquirer governance so far indicates that ownership concentration was not as decisive for the performance development for the post-exit development of the target in terms of the general arguments for acquisitions outlined for the buyout cycle.

1350 See the outline of change in debt leverage in chapter C4.2.1.1.

	Hypothesis	Explanatory variables: Debt leverage	Ownership concentration	Activity level	Mgmt. Shareholdings		Key observations
Company performance (after the exit)	28b	(+)				NCF	Given Trevira's necessary restructuring und underinvestment during the LBO, the disciplinary force of debt was outweighted by additional capacity and modernization from new investments.
						NEU	Reliance choose to keep Trevira with a leverage capital structure, though provided additional equity to facilitate strategic transition to a specialised manufacturer. Debt does not seem to have withholded performance improvements, in particular because of provided resources by Reliance.
	28e			(+)		NEU	Intensity and quality of monitoring increased. Reliance clearly expected from Trevira to run business independently and earn cost of capital
						CF	Strategic advise, management resources and operational expertise (e.g., sourcing) clearly contributed to performance improvement.
	28g				(+)	NCF	Despite no co-ownership, high mangerial concern on performance development, in particular with respect to operating profit and cash flow generation.
						NEU	Notwithstanding, debt leverage, activity level and ownership concentrated substituted for lack of managerial shareholdings
		Direction of expected correlation					

CF: Observations confirm hypothesis
NCF: Observations do not to confirm hypothesis
NEU: Observations neither confirm nor reject hypothesis

Table 74: Change in performance development (Trevira)

Reliance was held by a series of institutional investors, with none of the shareholders holding more than 8%. The founder, Dhirubhai Ambani, gradually divested his shareholdings. One may therefore classify the acquirer as a management-controlled company. As such, the studies so far performed, including that of Buehner[1351], indicate that they perform best, with the caveat that they show a higher interest in stock performance than family-owned controlled companies do. Another factor to be considered is management discretion and the potential cost of free cash flow. Researchers have concluded that available cash flow has a positive impact, allowing the acquirer to choose the most suitable target as opposed to leading to non-value adding overpayment for an unattractive asset. Reliance and its subsidiary Reliance Industries had sufficient funds to pursue even larger acquisitions than Trevira. Various European manufacturers of similar size were in a similar stressed situation and most likely for sale. As outlined throughout the discussion on efficiency and entrepreneurship-related activity, active monitoring by Reliance was decisive for the post-exit success of Trevira. Discussions on strategic and operational matters in which Reliance participated and support provided in production and purchasing enabled completion of the transition to a specialized high tech fibres manufacturer. The discussions kept Trevira's management aligned with Reliance's agenda. Ownership concentration in the hands of Reliance guaranteed that it would invest heavily in the monitoring of Trevira.

Debt leverage ensured Trevira management's cost discipline as well as related measures and initiatives. Trevira learned as an institution to operate with high debt despite the strategic transition. The owners matched the need for sufficient capital to maintain technological leadership and the highest quality while ensuring continuous debt repayment. In this case, the slight decrease in debt was beneficial as Trevira had suffered from underinvestment.

In summary, the previously presented governance instruments compensated for the lack of management stakes. Nevertheless, general human resources and valuable management resources came at a price for Reliance. Because management stakes had to be returned to the acquirer, they were not decisive for the post-exit success of Trevira.

In addition to the outlined changes in governance, one may assess to what degree further explanatory power outside the governance regime may be related to factors identified in the discussion on determinants for the performance development after a

1351 See Bühner 1990, pp.171-172

trade sale[1352]. The author stresses the fact that the businesses of Reliance and Trevira were related in terms of product and technology. As observed by Healy, Palepu and Ruback, this carries a high explanatory power for post-trade sale performance[1353]. Efficiency gains from the combined entity accrued to the target rather than to the bidder[1354]. As outlined, Trevira benefited (beside the high activity level of monitoring) from the various resources Reliance provided. For a cross-border transaction, a horizontal expansion as in the Reliance-Trevira case resulted in higher returns than would have been the case in a vertical expansion. Because both companies had limited to no operational overlap, no disputes emerged regarding reduction of resources and allowing management to focus on Trevira's growth development. Parrion and Harris[1355] noted that the change of management contributed to the likelihood of success. Although the change in management was only partially because of underperformance, the new team brought the correct industry and restructuring mindset to the company. If the acquisition was intended to achieve synergies from productivity increases and enhanced revenues as opposed to cost savings, they resulted in higher performance.

One may further comment on indicators of the transaction structure and terms for post-exit performance. Ghosh[1356] argued that the payment form was an indicator of the relative valuation of the acquirer and the confidence of the acquiring management. In the case of a cash-based compensation as in this case, Reliance managers saw their stock as undervalued[1357]. One may further argue that they anticipated positive marginal performance improvement from the acquisition with their own performance. The reaction of capital markets to an acquisition proves to be an excellent indicator for post-exit development. In this case, the 2.9% share price increase at the announcement reflected the stock market's appreciation of the deal rationale and value creation.

One saw that Trevira outperformed its industry peers in terms of maintaining sales levels, but underperformed in terms of operating profit. The author measured a free cash flow level slightly above industry average, accomplished on the basis of a reduced investment policy. A longer-term observation throughout year four would allow detailing to what degree the company will continue to be governed as diligently and cohesively as in the first post-exit period.

1352 See chapter 'general empirical evidence related to a trade sale'
1353 See Healy, Palepu et al. 1992,pp.150 et seqq.
1354 See Singh and Montgomery 1987, Shelton 1988
1355 See Parrino and Harris 1999,pp. 92 et seqq.
1356 See Ghosh 2001, pp.162 et seqq.
1357 This observation resembles to asymmetric information hypothesis as outlined by Myers and Majluf 1984.

5 Comparative Case Study Analysis

5.1 Changes in Governance Structure

5.1.1 Debt Leverage

The comparison of change in debt indicates that in two of the three cases leverage decreased considerably after the exit. To understand how change influenced performance of the companies observed, the author will elaborate on the origin of the funds for the de-leveraging, on what determined the level of post-exit leverage and on whether disciplinary force altered given changes in governance.

Reduction of leverage at the exit can come from different sources. In a going-public, a buyout investor may share some of the equity value and allow the company to offer primary shares and so that it can repay debt from primary proceeds. This was indeed the case in the LBOs that went public. The buyout investors cushioned their returns with a special dividend received shortly before the exit. In a trade sale, a new investor may be willing to repay debt facilities after having acquired the company's equity. In Trevira's case, the new owner Reliance provided equity to the former LBO, but left debt financing unchanged and at the disposition of Trevira. Management decided to reduce bank debt modestly. For both exit channels, leverage remained at the upper end of comparable companies in the industry and confirmed findings of Holthausen and Larcker as well as Jalilvand and Sweitzer that former LBOs continue to operate under a higher leverage level than their competitors[1358]. Debt leverage continued throughout the post-exit period to remain above comparable industry levels. Wincor Nixdorf, for example, paid a large percentage of its distributable profit to its shareholders, offering an attractive dividend yield that resembled the capital structure of an LBO.

The interesting question is who actually determines post-exit debt leverage. Understandably, LBO investors will seek to maximize their proceeds. In the case of both Wincor Nixdorf and Techem, the lead institutional investors indicated in pre-IPO discussions their goals for target capital structure and conceded leverage. In the case of a trade sale, the new owner determines the capital structure. Even though Trevira retained high leverage, Reliance as 100% parent and co-debtor assumed responsibility in case of a financial default. One may argue, therefore, that the default risk was in fact alleviated.

1358 See Holthausen and Larcker 1996, Jalilvand and Switzer 2002

A further determinant of the debt level is the company-specific risk as increased default probability reduces debt capacity[1359]. Analyzing the context of the LBOs investigated, the author found an increase in the level of risk propensity only in one of the three cases. For Trevira, the enforced competitive environment produced a stop to debt repayments shortly before exiting the LBO. At that time, Trevira was in the middle of a corporate restructuring and witnessed changes in its senior management team. The default risk from the perspective of the debt providers had therefore increased. As a result, the company was less likely to increase its leverage and exit as it intended to exit through an IPO or a secondary LBO. Management of Wincor Nixdorf and Techem, on the contrary, felt comfortable operating with higher leverage than the industry average. Strong cash flow generation mitigated potential concerns of enhanced financial distress.

This confirms the thesis that debt leverage is reduced. The presence and takeover threat by buyout investors encourages senior managers of companies attractive for an LBO structure to keep their capital structure leveraged after the exit. Contrary to previous research that has argued that the return to the public equity markets is nurtured by the need to access new risk bearing equity and to reduce financial inflexibility (the 'under-investment hypothesis'), the LBOs of the size observed exited after having achieved the expected internal rate of return for investors. Even under the LBO, they maintained access to both equity and debt markets and could continue operating with considerably high, yet lower leverage than during the buyout. For the trade sale, the hypothesis of a reduction of debt has to be rejected. In a more detailed analysis, one can divide the impact of the leverage into the bonding agent for cash flow maximization and the disciplinary threat of financial distress. At Trevira, cash flow maximization remained intact, while the threat of financial distress was cushioned by the industrial owner. Moreover, no specific changes in debt structure and maturity were observed.

5.1.2 Ownership Concentration

In all three cases, ownership structure changed as anticipated. At Wincor Nixdorf and Techem, equity shareholdings were distributed on the stock market. At Trevira, the strategic buyer acquired 100% of all shareholdings.

In both IPOs, the buyout investors divested their entire shareholdings after a lock-up period. At Wincor Nixdorf, the employees together with senior management became the largest investor group with around 9% of shares. This share of ownership by

---

1359 See Johnson 1997, p. 54

insiders is considerable compared to other companies listed in Germany, and confirms previous research. In the case of Techem, the family owners remained block holders with 25% of equity. The remaining shares were sold to institutional and retail investors, with institutionals holding the majority of shares. The companies reported that most investors sought to achieve long-term value creation. None of Techem's investors acquired a stake of more than 10%. Only after the family owners sold their 25% stake, did institutional investors start acquiring more than 10% of the shares and initiate a takeover battle, as attractiveness of control premium and of re-entry into LBO was high. The strong position of Wincor Nixdorf's senior management and excellent performance development in an LBO-like structure prevented investors from pursuing a takeover. In both cases, dilution of ownership concentration led to a replacement of supervisory board members. None of the new institutional investors was represented on the supervisory board. Notwithstanding the lack of direct, formal voting power in the board, investors demanded continuous discussions with senior management[1360].

In the Trevira trade sale, the new industrial owner insisted on acquiring 100% of the shares and buying out the former management. This was eased by the fact that the former management left the board and ended its relationship with the company. Legal requirements did not make an appointment of a supervisory board necessary. Nonetheless, Reliance appointed an advisory counsel that consisted of two representatives from its senior management. Reliance also appointed the management team and delegated a former manager of the parent company to the board as its representative. Attractiveness for partnersip with a buyout investor was low given the restructuring challenge and limited financial engineering ability.

5.1.3 Activity Level of Investors

At Wincor Nixdorf and Techem, activity level of monitoring was at times above the average of German listed companies. Still, the activity level was below that of a company operating under an LBO structure.

As previously argued, there are substituting factors that compensate for the reduction in intensity and quality of monitoring. For one, overall business risk of both companies was at the exit from the LBO comparatively low. Techem operated in an environment with long-term customer contracts that secured ongoing cash flows. Wincor Nixdorf benefited from its advanced technology and the need for continuous

1360 One could observe in these cases a professionalism of monitoring of German companies as investors appoint independent industry experts to oversee the managing board. The concurrence of ownership and representation is to some degree diluted to the advantage of the quality of monitoring.

replacement of its ATMs. The fact that the companies succeeded in going public underpinned the stability of the external environment. The threat of a potential takeover served further as a disciplinary force, with Techem to some degree being protected by its 25% family stake and Wincor Nixdorf by its management stake. The continuation of the former buyout investor's representatives on the board ensured that the companies stuck to their strategy plans. The reduction of the activity level of monitoring was partly possible because of the success of the restructuring during the buyout.

In addition to the activity level, one saw changes in the type and quality of monitoring particularly at Techem. Supervisory board members discussed strategic and operational initiatives as presented by management, while reducing their time investment to form an independent view. In most cases, management plans were approved by the supervisory board. The author previously referred to such management-dominated governance as the 'managed corporation'. In the crisis at Techem in 2002, the board was to some degree reactive, rather than proactive. After some time, the board retook strategic control, and was able to steer the company through a change in the management and key divestments. The former CEO, who approved the activities of management, dominated the monitoring perhaps for a too long period. Compared to the powerful position of the Chairman, the founding family played a minor role, despite their 25% stake. At Wincor Nixdorf, one did not observe the same type and quality of monitoring as at Techem. The manager-owners as largest shareholder maintained a high interest in active monitoring and controlled the board to a certain degree. Continuity in the management team shielded the company from considerable changes in strategy. The author did not observe abuse of controlling rights for private benefits.

At Trevira, the activity level was high during the buyout, but lacked the industry expertise needed to master the challenges of the advancing industry consolidation. The new owner, Reliance, provided various monitoring resources. In contrast to Techem and Wincor Nixdorf, Trevira faced low-cost competitors and was forced to withdraw from various markets and invest heavily in technology to justify premium prices Only few investors would have been able to provide the support Trevira needed and Reliance was one of the few. A further difference between the two IPOs was that the exit had not been chosen as result of the investor having achieved his investment returns. Instead, the buyout investor realized that he was no longer the 'best owner' of the business and needed an industrial investor to ensure the survival of the company. In summary, the way Trevira was supervised in the post-LBO period was according to the pattern of a 'governed' corporation.

These IPOs support the thesis of a reduction of governance activity levels. The decrease was to some degree economically reasonable, since the companies operated in a low risk- environment. However, the 'managed corporation' risked overlooking a potential crisis. The activity level in a trade sale, challenges if not denies the hypothesis. The new owner clearly demonstrated more active monitoring than the buyout investor did. The company was acquired in an environment and context of comparably high risk. This was evident with the entry of the industrial owner and determined the monitoring level from the beginning. Risk and specific company distress are overlaying moderating factors to be considered in further research.

5.1.4 Managerial Shareholdings

The (relative) shareholdings of the management group decreased in the exit from the LBOs of both Techem and Trevira.

Wincor Nixdorf's management maintained its stake. Senior management 's belief in the long-term upside potential offset motives of cash-out and diversification. Markets not served and untapped business fields offered significant room for growth and value creation. Management remained the same, and was therefore interested in retaining shares. The stock option program provided additional shares and compensated for the modest sales at the time of the IPO. The difference to Techem was that no member of the management team left and that the former CEO joined the supervisory board. The replacement of management in 2002 at Teche, further decreased the likelihood of management having a significant stake. In addition, the stock option program did not materialize since the performance targets were not achieved until 2003. Trevira's financial distress persuaded the new management not to demand a stake. None of the managers was willing to invest for fear of further distress.

Furthermore, the industrial owner demanded 100% ownership of the company. Therefore, profit-based compensation and other instruments of governance such as active monitoring and high debt leverage motivated management instead. This will be discussed in detail in the analysis below of changes in managerial focus and activity. In the corollary, the hypothesis of a reduction in managerial shareholdings can not be confirmed for both group of companies, neglecting the continuity in management and upside potential in the Wincor Nixdorf as moderating factor. The cancellation of shareholdings in the trade sale was facilitated by substituting governance instruments. The owner may not have anticipated active monitoring and debt leverage and may have facilitated a management participation program.

	Hypo-thesis	Review of observations	Key findings
Debt leverage	1	(-) CF	Debt leverage decreased for going-public exit track, however, remains at upper end to keep management disciplined and prevent takeover. Underinvestment hypothesis as reason for de-leverage rejected given broad access to both equity and debt markets. High leverage seen as optimal and accompanied by high payout ratio. In the trade sale case debt was slightly decreased but used to control management and hence remained considerably high. Threat of financial distress cushioned by a bank guarantee of the parent company.
Ownership concentration	2a, b	(-) CF* / (constant) CF**	In both IPOs concentration of ownership decreased, with largest shareholder holding 9% and 25% equity share, respectively. Attractiveness of high ownership in one case macerated by excellent management operating in LBO-like environment. In the other case, sale of 25% stake initiated a new takeover battle indicating control premium and attractiveness of re-entry in LBO. Ownership in trade sale to 100% handed over to industrial owner. No attractivenes for partnership with buyout investor given restructuring challenge and limited financial engineering.
Activity level	3a,b	(-) CF* / (-) NCF**	In both IPOs activity level of investors for monitoring decreased, however, has to be adjsuted for the reduction of business risk and success of restructuring during the buyout. One may conclude that the reduction was to some degree economically reasonable. In one of the IPOs, the supervisory board oversaw a crisis and left the control of the company to management ('managed corporation'). This in turn required a lengthy turnaround. In the trade sale, activity level remained constant and increased in quality given the strong industrial expertise.
Mgmt. shareholdings	4a	(-) NCF	Hypothesis of reduction of management shareholdings can not be confirmed given that in one case stake remained constant. However, continuation of high management stake supported by continuity in management team and considerbale upside potential in the stock. In the other case, decrease of shareholdings hindered by high management turnover and drop out of stock option program. In trade sale, management had to sell shares to acquirer as expected.

(+), (-): Direction of expected relationship
CF: Observations sufficient to confirm hypothesis
NCF: Observations not sufficient to confirm hypothesis
* Only for trade sale
** Only for going-public

Table 75: Review of hypotheses for change in corporate governance constituents (H1 to H4)

5.2 Changes in Management Objectives

Differences in the patterns of changes in governance structure were likely to reflect themselves in changes in management objectives. In all three cases, focus on efficiency-focused activities decreased with different cause and effect-relationships and with differing intensity. The cases of Wincor and Techem confirm notion that IPOs promise significant growth potential and increased focus in strategy as part of corporat entrepreneurship[1361]. However, Trevira's post-exit development shows that the growth focus was hampered by limited investments.

Wincor Nixdorf's debt was not the prevailing issue in the mind of management, even though repayments were comparatively high. Instead, management shareholders were the driving force for the continued focus on efficiency. Supervisory board played a minor role, and did not dwell on operational aspects of the business or provide a critical independent view. Ongoing restructuring programs facilitated continued focus on efficiency-related activities. The role of Techem's supervisory board was similar, though one noted that it was more interested in growth-related matters than in efficiency. Techem's management believed that the stable cash flow of the core business would underwrite debt repayments. The supervisory board's lack of an own stake resulted in the anticipated decline of emphasis on efficiency. Management instead directed its effort toward revenue growth and new business fields. Trevira's change in focus was overtaken by the appointment of a new management team. The influence of change in governance was mitigated as the principal imposed his own agenda by appointing appropriate managers. The high activity level of the new industrial owners and the continued high debt influenced the intrinsic bias of the new management in favor of efficiency and ensured sufficient cash flow generation.

One cannot reject the thesis of influence of debt, even though its effect was less apparent than expected. Techem's management did decrease its emphasis as predicted. Trevira's debt leverage remained largely unchanged (at higher risk) and contributed to focus on efficiency. Wincor Nixdorf continued restructuring and optimization of its operations despite the reduced leverage and with management shareholdings serving partly as a substitute.

One further can confirm the importance of ownership concentration and implied activity level for the focus on efficiency. In the cases of Wincor Nixdorf and Techem,

1361 See Leschke 2003, p. 250

where ownership was less concentrated, the supervisory board was less keen on detailed discussions on efficiency improvements and increased productivity. Trevira's ownership remained in the hands of Reliance, which pursued a restructuring plan.

For the management shareholders, one finds evidence that weakens the hypothesis. While Techem's management did reduce their focus on efficiency after having returned their shares at the exit, senior Trevira managers withstood the temptation of inefficiencies. Instead, management continued its restructuring despite not sharing in the upside. The support from industrial owner Reliance empowered management to take unpopular measures and compensated for a potential lack of bargaining power.

One can confirm the hypothesis that reduced debt unleashs entrepreneurial growth. Wincor Nixdorf, for instance, committed significant funds to outsourcing that they had not identified as a core growth sector before relinquishing the LBO structure. Yet, neither Techem nor Wincor missed considerable growth options during the LBO. After the exit, Trevira's management pursued selected growth investments despite high debt. Finally, one may note that debt leverage did not as expected prevent Techem's management from continuing investments in non-core businesses despite the high debt repayments.

The author saw the focus on entrepreneurship weaken in those companies where ownership was diversified. Wincor Nixdorf saw a substantial part of its investor base striving to enhance short-term cash flows at the expense of investments in long-term value creation[1362]. Significant management ownership prevented such myopic investment behavior and confirmed previous empirical evidence[1363]. Among shareholders of Techem, some investors also demanded enhanced short term cash flows. One should note that Techem's debt repayment and growth investments prevented it from paying a dividend in the first five years after its IPO. Since the company had been presented as a stable and cash generating business, investors had expected an attractive dividend yield rather than efforts to preserve cash flows to fund growth.

One may further confirm that the implied activity level with respect to a focus on entrepreneurial growth decreased. In board meetings at both Techem and Wincor Nixdorf, monitoring shifted from strategic to more financial control. The board discussed major growth-related investments in far less detail than in the LBO period.

1362 See Jensen and Meckling 1976, p. 244
1363 See Wright 2001, p. 114; Westhead and Wright 1998, p. 175

Management objectives	Hypothesis	Explanatory variables: Debt leverage	Ownership concentration	Activity level	Mgmt. Shareholdings	Key findings
Efficiency improvement	5	(+) CF				Effect and influence of debt was lower than orginally expected. To some degree, companies have learnt during the LBO to operate under limited funds. Decrease of debt leverage did not yield decrease of management attention.
	6		(+) CF			In the two IPO cases, shareholders with lower individual shareholdings were as expected less keen on detailed discussions on efficiency improvements and operational details
	7			(+) CF		High activity level in the case of the trade sale to direct the interest of management to further efficiency improvement measures.
	8				(+) NCF	Management shareholdings driving forrce behind continued efficiency focus. In one of the IPOs, management after having returned their shares withstood the temptation to allow the return of inefficiencies. However, less focus on efficiency in acquisitions. In the trade sale, the support from industrial parent empowered management to take unpopular measures and compensate for a potential lack of bargaining power.
Corporate entrepreneurship	9	(-) CF				Reduced debt unleashed entrepreneurial growth. In the IPOs, fundings of growth opportunities outside core business were increased. Yet, no IPO missed considerable growth options in the core business during the LBO. Further, still high debt leverage did partly not hinder management from pursuing
	10		(+) CF			Lower ownership concentration resulted in short-term growth focus from the institutional investors at the IPOs due to the disadvantage of the efficiency and efficacy of CE.
	11			(+) CF		Activity level with respect to CE decreased. Monitoring shifted from strategic to more financial control. The board discussed major growth-related investments in far less detail than in the LBO period. LBO exiting via trade sale benefited from the resource base enabling CE activities in new markets.
	12				(+) CF	Co-ownership by managers positively influenced the focus as anticipated. In one case, the sale of shares led to enhanced growth investments in the initial post-exit period. At the other trade sale, management shareholdings remained unchanged. The company exiting via trade sale did not experience a decrease in the level of entrepreneurship. This was to the advantage of a successful restructuring.

(+), (-): Direction of expected relationship

CF: Observations sufficient to confirm hypothesis
NCF: Observations not sufficient to confirm hypothesis

Table 76: Review of hypotheses for change in management objectives (H5 to H12)

As outlined by Baysinger and Harrison as well as Wright[1364], control of corporate entrepreneurship is far more strenuous and requires significant effort to understand the context and likelihood of realizing growth options. Again, Trevira benefited from the concentration of ownership in the hands of Reliance and its monitoring.

Management shareholders did influence the focus as anticipated at Techem, where the sale of shares led to enhanced growth investments in the initial post-exit period. Trevira experienced no decrease in the level of entrepreneurship. This was to the advantage of a successful restructuring. At Wincor Nixdorf, management shareholdings remained unchanged.

In summary, constituent elements of governance partly substituted each other at the exit from the LBO but did not change as presumably had been intended. Trevira's activity level and choice of management compensated for the lack of management shareholders. Manager-owners in Wincor Nixdorf compensated for lacking monitoring activity and debt leverage. At least one of the constituents has to work at a high level to be able to compensate the lack of another constituent. As a result, governance should be measured as the sum of the individual governance constituents identified at a consolidated level.

5.3 Changes in Efficiency-Focused Management

Operational Productivity

In general, operational productivity was high in the LBO and improved further although all case studies operated alredy at a high level. In all three cases, management relied on improvements with a strong focus on operations that had been partly initiated during the LBO and partly after the LBO. Wincor Nixdorf's total number of employees dedicated to operations could be increased. Productivity increases were gladly overcompensated by revenue growth. Techem's rising unit costs and lagging productivity was, however, not compensated by revenue growth. The restructuring after appointment of the new management team led to a recovery in operational productivity to LBO levels and above. Trevira's management relocated parts of the workforce in German sites to low-cost countries. Against the conjectures, the companies did not return to previous process setups. Instead, they benefited in the long-term from 'best practices' implemented during the LBO.

Even though the reduction of debt modest, one should support the thesis of a potential decrease in productivity. The return of Techem's debt leverage to LBO

1364 See Baysinger and Hoskisson 1989, p. 327, Wright 2001, p. 112

levels only two years after the exit was the catalyst for redirecting management focus toward operational productivity. Productivity decreased in sales that were less subject to performance measurement given limited standardization. Continued management focus was therefore crucial to ensure appropriate performance. Wincor Nixdorf's leverage initially remained high and, in combination with sales growth, yielded a permanent increase in productivity. In the case of Trevira, the company's debt burden also positively effected productivity.

The supervisory board demonstrated concern for the well-being of the workforce in all three cases. At Wincor Nixdorf supervisory board members demanded a detailed briefing on measures to re-establish competitiveness of the German production facilities. Despite this concern, detailed tracking of operational productivity decreased with the concentration of ownership. Techem's supervisory board was laid back with respect to efficiency of operations, until debt servicing started to stutter. In the two IPOs, the board remained in control of the company's financial indicators, and did not attempt to understand in detail operational productivity, acknowledging that this was to some degree economically reasonable. In the case of Reliance the board jointly with management decided on operational issues and provided active support, for example by sending their own manufacturing experts.

Besides the two previous parties to corporate governance, management itself was the most important key to increased operational performance. Trevira's lack of managerial shareholdings did not prevent management from engaging in ongoing improvement of operational productivity. Nonetheless, one can believe that a reduced number of shareholders does likely lead to a decrease in operational productivity. Techem's management trusted the measures implemented during the LBO, but neglected to continue close monitoring. Management relied on the growth trajectory and was motivated by the stock option program, as opposed to the previous equity participation program. Management of Wincor Nixdorf, even though their equity stake remained unchanged, took a number of tough decisions, including layoffs, after exiting the LBO.

Asset Productivity

In all three cases, one can not confirm the 'underinvestment' thesis as the motivation for a return to public equity markets or to seek ownership by a liquid parent company. Capital expenditure remained at or slightly above LBO level. Techem and Wincor Nixdorf witnessed a considerable increase in investment in related businesses rather than their core business. Trevira's capital expenditure partly dropped to a level below the LBO.

Productivity of asset base was in line with operational productivity outlined above. Techem's restructuring raised productivity of its operating assets. However, achieved productivity in terms of adjusted operating cash flow ratio to assets and ROIC did not match the levels recorded during the LBO. Wincor Nixdorf, nonetheless, surpassed its LBO average in the three post-LBO years observed. At Trevira, management reduced the asset base to significantly increase productivity.

One could witness modest changes in post-LBO funding levels as a result of the influence of debt to capital expenditure, particularly in non-core business. Investments in core businesses remained however constant. Management reported that they were satisfied with their pursuit of growth plans despite the restrictions of an LBO because they had sufficient access to funds. It comes therefore as no surprise that the level of investment level in core businesses did not change in the post-LBO period. In fact, managers reported that funds for more risky investments in non-core businesses were available. Investments yielded for Wincor returns comparable to those in its core business. This observation however should be treated with caution given that time lags may render the observed period of three years too short Techem's investments were less successful and showed low-margin asset profitability. Trevira's new owner provided some new equity to enable management to pursue restructuring and grow the core business, but did not allow the company to expand into new business fields.

Shareholdings of management involving their personal wealth appear to affect positively asset productivity. Techem, for example invested in non-core business with a management that did not have a personal stake. Management was less risk averse and decided on investments that were less likely to succeed. At Wincor Nixdorf, investors urged management to invest actively in non-core businesses. Management, however, assessed each investment opportunity on its implied long-term value creation. Both Trevira's management and new owner agreed to restrict investments to the core business. Other corporate governance constituents substituted for lack of management equity.

Outsourcing and Offshoring

Outsourcing and offshoring was observed to gradually increase after the exit. Wincor Nixdorf's senior management relocated parts of the assembly to local markets. The offshoring of assembly was in line with a strategic plan delineating future roles of the different locations within the production process despite a potential preference for opportunistic offshoring. Provision of sufficient capital may have prevented management from taking more radical steps, such as relocating the entire production. Techem took a similar strategic approach geared towards expanding its supplier base. Techem depended on close relationships to its suppliers because of its much smaller stake in the value chain. In the post-LBO period, senior management broadened the supplier base and qualified a group of 'second tier' suppliers. As a result, the number and breadth of business partners increased significantly. Trevira's supply chain involved largely raw material rather than components or pre-assembled modules. Success related to outsourcing and offshoring depended more on Trevira's ability to access the cheapest resources rather than on managing a series of qualified suppliers. Supported by its new owner, Trevira further relocated significant parts of its sourcing to low-cost countries like Poland, and capitalized on attractive purchasing agreements of its parent company.

One can note that the level of outsourcing and offshoring was in part negatively affected by debt relief. Wincor Nixdorf slightly increased while continuous repaying debt its share of in-house production even though this increased its fixed cost basis. Unlike Wincor, Trevira's continued high debt leverage coupled with increased price competition forced management to relocate lower value activities to low cost facilities. Senior managers at Techem did also not have the leverage to insource.

Techem and Wincor Nixdorf's supervisory boards demonstrated interest in offshoring and outsourcing given their impact on the workforce in German facilities. The involvement of Wincor Nixdorf's board led to the decision to increase the local share in production to compensate for assembly lines that were offshored. To evaluate the board's interest, one has to take into account the co-determination in the supervisory boards of German AGs. Trevira's industrial owner consulted management on steps needed to regain competitiveness through significantly lowering costs. These discussions on core vs. non-core activities of the company were crucial to the success of the post-LBO turnaround. In summary, owner involvement in offshoring and outsourcing was significant while owners were less engaged in other activities.

There was mixed evidence on the degree to which ownership or management determined the willingness to outsource and offshore. Risk aversion of Wincor Nixdorf's management decreased. To some degree, management was less willing to take unpopular measures such as layoffs at German manufacturing sites despite having sufficient bargaining power and having committed significant personal wealth. One should note that management operated in close proximity to workers at the Paderborn headquarters. Given that profits were sufficient to sustain expected capital costs, it would have posed a challenge for management to argue in favor of relocating additional parts of production to further reduce debt payments. As previously outlined, Trevira's management pursued the relocation of production to low-cost countries despite not having a stake in the business.

Working Capital Management

Results of the development of working capital were inconclusive. The proceeds from the IPO at Techem prompted a more lax attitude toward management of working capital. After the replacement of management, Techem reduced working capital to a level far below the LBO average. The decrease related largely to operational improvements in inventory levels. Wincor Nixdorf's and Trevira's management succeeded in further reducing working capital throughout the observed period. One should note that all three companies were fundamentally reorganized during the LBO in terms of lead times for purchasing, production, and distribution. Shifts in working capital were likely to be to some degree robust against changes in governance, as argued by Gräper[1365].

It is difficult to clearly determine a cause and affect relationship between debt and working capital. All companies enjoyed robust growth in the post-exit that naturally required working capital. Since growth was mostly above industry level, debt does not appear to have limited growth. A senior manager of Wincor Nixdorf noted that despite significant management stake in the company, gradual debt reduction did not undermine attention to working capital. At Techem. the increase of working capital was not significant, although later reductions of more than 40% indicate that the previous management did not fully utilize its potential. Considerable parts of the proceeds were invested in working capital related to new customer accounts. In this case, there is evidence denying the results of Holthausen and Larcker who claimed that proceeds do not yield less focus on working capital[1366]. Trevira's management emphasized the need for working capital, presumably because of intensive monitoring. In conclusion, on an isolated, ceteris paribus base, decrease in debt produced a decrease of working capital.

Same arguments confirms the positive effect of management shareholdings on working capital. Management of working capital was for Wincor Nixdorf increasingly challenging as international sales advanced. Nevertheless, senior management continued with detailed tracking of collection and credit periods, and continuously decreased the relative level of working capital. Cash restrictions in the 1990s coupled with management's personal stake led to discipline on the part of management. Since working capital is generated and dealt with by a number of managers covering various business units and regions, involvement of senior and middle managers as well as group leaders in the equity participation program produced an alignment of interests also in this regard. Cash restriction also

1365 See Gräper 1993, p. 142
1366 See the discussion in chapter B3.2.4.

encouraged Trevira's management to maintain focus. By contrast, Techem did not benefit from management shareholdings. The conclusion therefore confirms previous evidence of a positive correlation between insider ownership and limited investment in working capital[1367].

All interviewees reported that working capital was a key performance indicator reviewed with difference levels of rigidity by all owners. This was natural since the new monitoring relied increasingly on financial indicators. However, controlling without a discussion of underlying causes and necessary counter-measures was viewed as insufficient. In sum, reduced activity levels decreased interest in and rigidity towards working capital management. The observations therefore confirm the previous empirics that the level of insider ownership exceeds the importance of ownership concentration and that governance activity affects most importantly the level of working capital.

Overhead Productivity

Previous empirical research has shown that changes in level of overhead staff and related resources are often the most reliable indicator for changes in management approaches. The author measured differing results for overhead productivity in the post-LBO period.

Wincor Nixdorf experienced a significant increase. The company benefited from high operational leverage in overhead functions. Further, management continued with an intense refinement of underlying functions and processes. Improvements in overhead processes were also found at Trevira. A series of measures, partly related to decisive changes in operational setup, resulted in productivity increase of of sales and administration. Since Trevira was managed as a separate entity with limited operational cooperation with its parent, no additional resources were required for coordination. The opposite was true for Techem. The intended strategy change towards increased business scope required resources in particular with regards to sales and marketing. As a result, overhead expenses jumped significantly in the first two post-LBO years. This demonstrates that the productivity decline was not the result of a lax attitude. Had this been the case, one would have observed a lagging effect on cost increase stemming from self-serving management choices over time, as argued by Bruton, Keels and Scifres.

1367 See Holthausen and Larcker 1996, pp.320 and 321

	Hypothesis	Explanatory variables: Debt leverage	Ownership concentration	Activity level	Mgmt. Shareholdings	Key findings
Operational productivity	13a to 13c	(+) CF	(+) CF		(+) CF	High interest by non-management shareholders, partly due to co-determination. Employment increased in two of three cases in post-exit period. Operational productivity benefits from robustness of measures implemented during LBO. Reduced debt leverage, ownership and manag. shareholdings yield in less management attention as expected. Mutual substitution of governance constituents.
Asset productivity	14a, 14b	(+) CF			(+) CF	Asset productivity benefits similar to operational from robustness of measures implemented. "Underinvestment" hypothesis can be rejected. Funding levels particularly in non-core businesses increased with lower debt leverage. Reduced incentive from low managerial shareholdings measured but compensated from substituting governance constituents.
Outsouring and offshoring	15a to 15d	(+) CF	(+) NCF* / (+) NCF**	(+) CF	(+) NCF	High interest and activity level by non-management shareholders in both trade sale (based on expertise of parent) and in going-public (given co-determination). Continuous high debt prevented from insourcing, however, insourcing coincided with lower debt levels. Despite high shareholdings, management not willing to confront relocation even though economically potentially reasonable.
Working capital management	16a to 16c	(+) CF		(+) CF	(+) CF	High activity level by management and non-management shareholders. Working capital remained key parameter of post-exit monitoring. On a isolated, ceteris paribus base, increased funds weakened focus on working capital. Any measures during the buyout period are less robust as underlying efforts are only partly standardized and partly subject to management's discretion.
Overhead productivity	17a, 17b	(+) CF			(+) CF	Overhead productivity harmed by by enhanced growth focus and increased strategic focus, in particular related to decrease debt leverage enabling the broadening of the strategy position and focus. Management equity stakes shielded from further decrease. Activity level by parent in trade sale substituted for lack of management shareholdings.
Hierarchical complexity	18a*, 18b*	(+) CF			+ (NCF)	Cost emphasis from debt service also positively correlates with hierarchical complexity in the post-exit period. Need for cash generation kept management seeking for an efficient organization. Managerial shareholdings were not observed to be decisive to the complexity vs. efficiency of the organization.
Management control systems	19a* to 19c*	(+) CF	(+) CF		+ (NCF)	Need for constant cash flow kept management focused on efficient and fast-reacting control systems. Industry expertise from parent company in trade sale helped to improved the management control system. However, "conformity effect" was not observed. Management shareholdings with less importance than activity by owners and cash generation necessity.

(+), (-): Direction of expected relationship

CF: Observations sufficient to confirm hypothesis
NCF: Observations not sufficient to confirm hypothesis

*Only for trade sale
**Only for going-public

Table 77: Review of hypotheses for change in efficiency-focussed management (H13 to H20)

Observations confirm that overhead productivity is significantly influenced by debt, confirming previous empirical results. On an isolated, ceteris paribus base, reduction in debt leverage yields decreased overhead productivity.

Management shareholdings played an important role, in particular at Wincor Nixdorf. Improvements stemmed from in-depth reorganization and renegotiation of employment contracts that required a high degree of personnel commitment on the part of senior management. Again, the wide distribution of shares among managers and non-managers facilitated a convergence of interests. Techem's lack of share participations did not prevent increased administrative costs. Trevira's careful selection of management ensured a focus on restructuring of overhead functions. Overhead productivity appears as a result to be negatively related to the level of management shareholdings.

Hierarchical Complexity

Changes in corporate governance and capital structure led to changes in hierarchical complexity. Wincor Nixdorf's hierarchy was changed to accommodate increasingly complex external factors such as strong international growth and intensified coordination. New positions were created to ensure efficient collaboration between subsidiaries and head office. By contrast, Techem's senior management slimmed down the organization by abandoning the level of regional managers. Trevira simplified its holding structure. It saw a higher degree of centralization with senior management seeking to safeguard progress in restructuring and ensure that there was sufficient cash generation for debt repayment.

The need for cash generation for debt repayment kept Trevira's management focused on maintaining an efficient organization. Senior management centralized decision-making. Techem consolidated its corporate structure immediately after the exit because of initiated cost savings programs. This can be attributed to the beneficial influence of debt leverage. Despite limited empirics, one can confirm the thesis that debt leverage hinders greater hierarchical complexity.

In line with previous observations regarding the compensation of the lack of management stakes, Trevira's new management engineered a positive effect on the hierarchy because of its personal commitment. A number of corporate functions were relocated to the Bobingen manufacturing site. Techem and Wincor Nixdorf illustrate the expected positive influence of management co-ownership on the way hierarchy was dealt with. One cannot therefore confirm that management shareholdings alone decide upon the degree of hierarchy. Further analysis is required to assess whether that degree would have decreased without substituting factors. As expected, no observations were found that the new owners intervened and advised management on the organizational setup.

Management Control Systems

Sophistication of management control systems remained constant and increased in one of the three cases, whereas the other two cases stayed at the LBO level.

Wincor Nixdorf did not witness changes in detailed reporting in terms of frequency, cash-flow orientation, or adaptations to the business environment. Minor amendments to control were reported to accommodate the higher level of international business. Similar adaptations were witnessed at Techem, where control systems remained unchanged given the increasing importance of key account management. Further, both Wincor Nixdorf and Techem complemented their reporting with stock market indicators such as earnings per share. Trevira's level of sophistication of control systems during the LBO was not as high as in the other two case studies. The new management significantly enhanced the level of detail and completeness of management control systems after the acquisition by Reliance. Reports were introduced that facilitated daily and weekly control of the core parameters of the business. The author did not observe a 'conformity effect' with Trevira being forced to introduce Reliance's reporting systems. However, reporting formats resembled in various dimensions the control measures of Reliance and can be regarded as a transfer of 'best practice'.

The need for constant cash flow kept Trevira's management focused on highly efficient and fast-reacting control systems. For instance, reports on a decreasing order book enabled management to reduce capacity and production in a timely fashion in 2005. Further reporting revealed the operational productivity of various manufacturing sites and allowed management to optimize the production network in terms of resource allocation. As a result, initial high debt leverage kept management's focus on efficiency of the management control system. There was a brief period in which debt leverage decreased, but this did note effect the usefulness of the management control system. It should be added that in the case of Techem, efficiency of the management control system was limited by the fact that it did not enable the supervisory board to correct excessive growth plans and decrease cash flow in a timely fashion. Instead, the board responded once inefficiencies had already produced considerable negative free cash flow.

In the case of Trevira, governing elements encouraged focus on efficiency of management control systems despite the lack of management shareholdings. Reports recommended a significant time effort to scan different risk dimensions, including strategy, risk, cost, financial, and environmental factors. However, as mentioned, reports contributed considerably to the quality of planning, with management willing to put in the necessary personal effort. As in the case of the observations on hierarchical complexity, one cannot confirm that management shareholdings alone determine the efficiency of management control systems. Substituting factors compensated for the lack of such shareholdings.

5.4 Changes in Entrepreneurial Growth-Focused Management

Strategy Position and Diversification

Observations on strategy, both in terms of relative positioning and diversification, indicate that debt leverage was much less decisive than expected. Rather, it seems that management shareholdings are pivotal to corporate strategy. One can confirm that monitoring influences the strategy chosen, but to a comparatively lesser degree. All three former LBOs were market leaders in their respective industries prior to their exit. Wincor Nixdorf advanced its strategic position by entering into sectors related to its core business after exiting the LBO, while maintaining its basic strategic position. Techem expanded its strategic focus in multiple dimensions. Management ultimately regained its strategic focus following a decline in performance. Trevira sharpened its focus as a niche player for specialities.

Wincor Nixdorf benefited from a highly concentrated market where only few companies were able to compete successfully in terms of technology leadership and international presence. With customers demanding high-quality products, there was no reason to adjust its position as premium producer, particularly as it was able to compete on a cost base against it direct rivals. New opportunities for growth were explored in adjacent businesses, e.g., in postal office and hospitals. Techem benefited from a quasi-oligopoly structure in the German metering market. In non-domestic markets, Techem succeeded on the basis of technological advanced products, such as radio-controlled meters. After the exit, management board expanded the strategic focus horizontally in terms of new customer segments and products, and vertically in terms of downstream products. After a considerable performance decline and return to LBO debt level, management regained strategic focus and concentrated on the company's metering and energy services businesses. Trevira's management perfected the transition to a specialized high-tech manufacturer. Given low-cost operations of its parent Reliance, Trevira could maintain a broad product offering while concentrating on high-margin specialized fibers. After the exit, Trevira was able to reconfigure its production to improve competitiveness and to accommodate change to smaller lot sizes. The international sales network of its parent Reliance moreover allowed Trevira to efficiently step up its entry into new markets.

In terms of strategy evolvement, the findings correspond with established patterns found by previous research. Both Techem and Wincor Nixdorf achieved the size needed to compete on the basis of market leadership and relative cost position. They could access a resource base and invest in both innovative technology and cost-competitive production. The pattern resembles propositions of Desset al., Zahra et al., and Murray who all argued for dominant strategies that pursue high quality and cost efficiency[1368]. The observations are further in line with the findings of the survey of German companies by Meffert et al, where the 'competence leader' incorporates the strengths of an innovation leader and cost-efficient production. Strategic expansions into adjacent businesses, such as Wincor Nixdorf's hospitals and postal offices, were chosen based on joint resources and competencies. Trevira's relatively small size made it impossible for it to compete on a cost base. Management therefore continued to pursue a strategy based on differentiation from its competitors in line with Porter's findings.

Continued high leverage imposed a level of discipline on strategy, even though companies learnt to operate with limited funding. Trevira's leveraging remained high and prevented management from entering aggressively into new market segments. However, the company had sufficient funds to successfully transit into specialized high-tech fiber manufacturing. This denies the assumption that a trade sale of a former LBO enhances its strategic position. Given the related-supplementary strategic fit between Reliance and Trevira, it is more appropriate to assume that the post-exit level of specialization and international division of labor benefits higher utilization and productivity. Wincor Nixdorf's senior management continued to be under pressure to restructure the retail business by closing unprofitable market niches. Furthermore, management remained cautions with strategic additions to segments served. Techem's robust historic growth and positive outlook at the IPO stage decoupled to some degree debt from corporate strategy. Management believed that operating cash flow would enable it to service debt independent of the growth strategy. With debt returning to LBO levels, the new management refocused on the core business of energy services and energy contracting. Although management underestimated the debt to industry average, no acquisitions in unrelated businesses were conducted. The new management maintained cost leadership at the top of its agenda. Therefore, the thesis that the level at which former LBOs pursue cost strategies decreases after the going-public has to be rejected. Observations on strategy, both in terms of relative positioning and diversification, indicate that debt

---

1368 See Dess, Lumpkin et al. 1999,Zahra and Covin 1993, Murray 1988

leverage was a far less decisive factor than had been assumed. Instead, it seems that management only changes strategy when leverage exceeds a certain threshold.

Wincor Nixdorf's management shareholdings played a key role in preventing the company from backing the interest of institutional investors to create short- -term value from enhanced though unprofitable growth. The management opted instead for organic growth. Admittedly, the company did not face significant obstacles such as market entry barriers that would have made an acquisition unavoidable. Techem's new shareholders supported management's assessment that the characteristics of the business could be applied to related industries such as industrial property management. They also did not inhibit growth aspirations with detailed discussions with management of underlying business models and potential risks. Trevira's new owners actively entered into discussions on strategy and market position. They supported the strategic goal of extending the focus to active management of the downstream process, involving investment in a creative design department and joint development teams. To conclude, the decline of ownership concentration did lead to a broadening of the market approach in the case of Techem. Senior management's strong position in Wincor Nixdorf shielded it from the wishes of the company's investor base that had a short-term perspective.

In terms of strategy formulation, Techem's management relied at least initially on its proven strategy which had previously produced success. The need for an intense and open strategy discussion after the exit was therefore limited. Lack of awareness of market changes in 2002 led to greater involvement of the supervisory board, in which differences regarding the correct strategy emerged. The 'Fokus' restructuring program reflected the mandatory strategy plan suggested to management by the supervisory board. At Trevira, Reliance encouraged management to pursue a stringent, systematic strategy formulation process. The established strategy process at the parent company served as a model. As a result, various processes were introduced that ensured a systematic approach towards assessing market potential and seizing growth opportunities. Wincor Nixdorf's strategy was discussed at board meetings after the IPO, but these discussions were not as explicit as during the LBO. The mandate and rigidity of the business plan agreed between management and owners was considerably less than in the LBO period. Still, strategy formulation in Techem's supervisory board appeared more balanced and was more apparent in, for example, the company's entry into the outsourcing business. In sum, reduced activity particularly affected negatively the intensity with which strategy was discussed and developed. Reduced monitoring loosens financial control and increases the probability that a company will pursue opportunistic growth options.

The stakes of management seem to constitute the most crucial constituent element of corporate governance in post-LBO strategy development. Wincor Nixdorf's continuity of management and equity meant that no significant change in strategic position occured. With no disruptions in the competitive environment, the need for such changes was limited. Management concentrated on achieving market position in countries targeted and decided, after having achieved a certain level of saturation, to enter gradually into adjacent markets. Techem's divestment of the management shareholdings resulted in higher risk affinity on the part of the management board. With high salaries fixed, management sought attractive opportunities to accelerate the growth trajectory and comply with demands from institutional investors. Following changes in the board, new management pursued a much more focused strategy despite the fact that it had no shareholdings in the business. Similarly, Trevira's management remained disciplined because of Reliance's involvement and ongoing debt servicing. Hence, one can support the thesis that reduced management shareholdings lead to an increase in diversification. The absence of management shareholdings is balanced by other positive effects of governance. This is also valid for management's commitment to discuss and, if needed, revise strategy.

R&D Focus and Efficiencies

In the post-LBO period, one could witness an increase in R&D spending at Techem, but not at Wincor Nixdorf or Trevira. One could further notice that Wincor Nixdorf and Trevira enhanced their R&D efficiency, while Techem experienced reduced efficiency in the initial post-LBO years. This confirms previous findings that the level of R&D is largely independent of cash infusions from the IPO proceeds and subject to long-term strategic considerations[1369]. One further did not observe the level of R&D to influence IPO pricing by signaling growth potential to investors.

Irrespective of management considerations, one noted that company strategy determined R&D levels. Techem's management strived to become the technology leader in its industry and decided to enter into businesses not served yet. Hence, they invested heavily in new resources and know how. Wincor Nixdorf's opting for organic growth rather than growth by acquisition led to a constant R&D budget. Management expected the same R&D efficiency in the post-LBO period as during the buyout, and therefore left funding unchanged. The same arguments in terms of organic growth and international expansion were valid for Trevira. R&D was a key success factor in its strategic transition to specialized high-tech fiber manufacturing. In terms of synergistic motives, Trevira's advantage was that its R&D operated in

1369 See Holthausen and Larcker 1996, pp. 311 et seqq., Bruton and Scifres 1992, p. 16

different fields than that of Reliance. Synergies in this context could be refined with regard to complementary resource bases. Reliance allowed Trevira to operate as an independent entity, leaving in place all resources crucial to Trevira's success. One, therefore, can confirm the rationale of former researchers that acquisition motives related to accessing a highly exclusive resource base retain the focus on R&D[1370].

For the senior management of Wincor Nixdorf, debt was not a constraint during the buyout. One may argue that the company was used to operating with limited funds, as outlined by Long and Ravenscraft who argue that debt produced a beneficial cutback of less productive R&D[1371]. While debt decreased significantly by end of year two, funding did not. Similar observations were made at Techem. With the decision to enter into new IT-businesses, funding increased significantly around the exit year and remained high until the second year after the LBO exit. Moreover, a number of projects with an unclear outcome such as home automation and internet-related services were funded in the first two years after the exit. As a result, one could observe that management was less sensitive to higher uncertainty of returns on considerable investment in R&D. The strategic considerations for Trevira outweighed any concern for cash flow generation. It is, therefore, difficult to establish precisely the relationship between debt and R&D spending. In summary, one should deny that debt leverage determines the level of R&D spending in the short-term. However, one could observe an increase in funding of R&D projects with higher uncertainty that were not directly related to the core business.

Following the lead of Wincor Nixdorf's senior management, investors appreciated the long-term growth potential and were not fixated on an R&D policy that would generate short-term earnings. Even though their monitoring was hampered by an information gap, R&D spending remained unchanged. Techem's new investors supported management's growth plans and augmented R&D expenses. The project nature and time lag made it difficult to measure the R&D efficiency over time. Management and owners were in the second year after the LBO exit dissatisfied and reduced funding by 30%. The reductions targeted external work in non-core business. Therefore, the notion that a more disperse shareholder base must result in reduced R&D can be rejected. One could find that institutional investors did not exhibit short-term investment behavior and valued capital investments in long-term R&D projects[1372], despite the information gap, particularly in the case of Techem.

1370 See Ahuja and Katila 2001, pp. 209 et seqq.
1371 See Long and Ravenscraft 1993a, p . 131 - 132
1372 The results resemble the findings of Baysinger, Kosnik and Turk (See Baysinger, Kosnik et al. 1991, pp. 210

However, one can confirm the thesis that the activity level of the shareholders was not decisive in determining R&D efficiency. Managers' personal effort was vital in terms of bridging the information gap with investors and ensuring a high quality in selecting appropriate R&D projects. Equity was a core motivating factor for management, and in the case of Wincor Nixdorf, prevented it from pursuing non value-creating R&D projects.

Market Development

All three former LBOs could witness continued focus on development in domestic and non-domestic markets. Besides revenues from new products, the sales increase from acquiring new market share constituted the most essential revneu driver. All three companies had the advantage of benefiting above average from an enlarged scale of operations and cross-country leverage. They also benefited from the positive relationship between internationalization and performance as they were operating on the rising left side of the 'u-form' . All companies further benefited from the mutually positive relationship between innovation and international growth. They were able to rely on their strong brand and customer awareness to lower significantly the cost of new market entries[1373].

Wincor Nixdorf displayed a pattern of expansion in core markets at the same pace as in the LBO period with business diversification remaining unchanged, as argued by Bruton, Keels and Scifres[1374]. The expansion was accompanied by significant investments in resources. Techem's development of new markets was linked to the acceptance and maturity of consumption-based billing. Growth in the domestic market was limited by long-term contracts and the ruling out of acquisitions because of cartel considerations. Trevira benefited from Reliance's international sales network and established representation in selected new markets. The pace of international growth highlighted a growth plan that was more aggressive than in the LBO period. The evidence therefore contradicts the results of Anand, Capron, and Mitchell who argued that advantages of market expansion typically accrue to the acquirer (Reliance), while the acquired company (Trevira) benefits from the product extension[1375].

---

et seqq.). One can rule out the observations of Bushee as the investors were typically value investors, willing to engage long-term (See Bushee 1998, pp. 318 et seqq.).

1373 See Porter 1985, p. 15, Kotabe, Srinivasan et al. 2002, pp. 82 et seqq.

1374 See Bruton, Keels et al. 2002, pp. 717 and 718, as well as the detailed discussion in chapter B4.4.

1375 See Anand 2005

	Hypothesis	Explanatory variables: Debt leverage	Ownership concentration	Activity level	Mgmt. Shareholdings	Key findings
Strategy position	20a*, 20b**	(+) NCF*/ (+) NCF*				Observations on strategy position indicate that debt leverage was much less decisive than expected. It seems that the strategy as an outcome of leverage (re-positioning into a niche) is only changed if leverage exceeds a certain threshold (too high). Much more, management shareholdings are pivotal to the positioning. One can confirm that monitoring influences the strategy chosen, but to a comparatively lesser degree. For the trade sale, the new ownership did not lead to an broadening, but rather to a further specialisation of the strategic positioning (niche), benefiting from the corporate-wide division of labor. The decrease in ownership concentration at IPOs increases the likelihood of a broader market positioning. Cost leadership is less than expected influenced by the decrease of leverage. For the IPOs, a proven strategy and less active investors resulted in a less open discussion on strategy. In the trade sale, the new parent installed an intense, systematic process, taking considerable ownership on the strategy formulation.
Strategy formulation	21a to 21e		(+) CF	(+) NCF*/ (+) CF**	(+) NCF*/ (+) CF**	
Diversification and scope	22a to 22d			(-) NCF*/ (-) CF**	(-) NCF*/ (-) CF**	
R&D efficiency	23a to 23g	(+) NCF*/ (+) CF**	(+) NCF**	(+) CF*/ (+) CF**	(+) NCF*/ (+) CF**	Spending and efficiency of R&D remained constant in those cases where strategy position and level of diversification was unchanged. In the case where strategy position and scope was broadened, R&D budget increased and efficiency decreased. The "underinvestment" hypothesis can not be confirmed. No short-term myopic investment to the disadvantage of long-term R&D. Management shareholdings shielded against pursuing non value-creating R&D projects in the case of the going-public. In the case of trade sale lack of management co-ownership was substitutedby higher activity level.
Market development	24a to 24f	(+) CF*/ (+) CF**		(+) CF*/ (+) CF**	(+) NCF*/ (+) CF**	Continued focus on market development in domestic and non-domestic markets, most essential value driver in case studies. All case studies benefited from the positive relationship betw.internationalization and performance. Relief from debt payments yielded higher investments in resources. Investors with high interest in company's growth and, hence, market development.
Human resources	25a, 25b	(+) CF			(+) CF	Human resources viewed as crucial to strengthening competitive advantage and achieving growth plans. Compensation schemes changed to facilitate higher pay-for-performance. Continuous high interest by non-management shareholders and by management independent of their stake in all cases observed.
Top mgmt.: turnover	26a to 26d			(+) CF*/ (+) NCF**	(+) CF*/ (+) CF**	No evidence for short-term increase in turnover in going-public, since management succeeded in LBO and will be replaced if required by new investors already during IPO preparation. In trade sale, turnover less due to performance than to management approach. Strong bargaining reduces likelihood of replacement.
Top mgmt.: skill profile	26e/ f			(+) NCF*/ (+) NCF**		High level of industry-specific knowledge already during the LBO. Presumably less balanced skill set in smaller LBOs. No intervention by the supervisory board.
Top mgmt.: compensation	27a to 27e			(+) CF*/ (+) CF**		Total compensation increased, with higher fixum but even higher share of pay for performance (alleviated by reduced business risk). At both IPOs, activity level did decrease. At trade sale, higher total compensation to attract better management.

(+), (-): Direction of expected relationship

CF: Observations sufficient to confirm hypothesis
NCF: Observations not sufficient to confirm hypothesis

* Only for trade sale
** Only for going-public

Table 78: Review of hypotheses for change in entrepreneurial growth-focussed management (H20 to 27)

One observed that the gradual reduction in debt servicing released funds for growth. Wincor Nixdorf's funding increased for sales employees in general and its non-domestic workforce in international expansion in particular. Techem's goal of capturing market share in international markets was underwritten with additional resources, partly to enter into partnerships. Funds were invested in the immature energy contracting market to establish a leading position in the domestic market, before reaching out to non-domestic markets. The crisis in 2002 and 2003 produced a slight adjustment of the workforce. When comparing Wincor Nixdorf and Techem, Wincor's substantial increase in new sales per employee can be related to the company's continued strategic focus. By contrast, Techem expanded its focus and partly overstretched its managerial capability. Higher returns on investments in the core business are in line with the findings of Bruton, Keels and Scifres[1376]. High debt servicing restricted Trevira's growth. The new owner, however, favored capitalizing on growth opportunities. He believed that low investment activity during the LBO was one of the reasons that growth stagnated. As a result, the level of committed resources increased considerably, but remained at a comparatively low level. In summary, the emphasis on market development increase was fueled by reduced debt leverage.

The involvement of the new owner, Reliance, was crucial to the willingness of Trevira's management to become far more engaged than in the LBO period. The growth-seeking investors in Wincor Nixdorf arguably saw it as their interest to accelerate international sales growth. Techem witnessed a similar pattern, with the supervisory board backing management's plan to accelerate international sales growth. However, that was based less on a thorough understanding of the business plan and growth prospects or independent monitoring, and constituted more a reflection of the investors' interest in the company's growth. One has to reject the thesis that the emphasis on market development decreased with a lesser involvement in management decisions.

Senior management demonstrated considerable personal interest. Wincor Nixdorf's group managers imposed more formal operating procedures on subsidiaries. In line with its desire to control, management viewed market entries to some degree as risky ventures and was eager to minimize manageable risks given the exposure of their own personal wealth. Previous empirics of buyouts[1377] corroborate these findings, namely that higher insider ownership focuses on the core business and carefully

1376 See Bruton, Keels et al. 2002, pp. 717 and 718

1377 See Bruning and Verwaal 2005, pp. 21 and 22)

balances growth against cash flow limitations. One did not observe that desire to control and to formalize undermined the entrepreneurial focus as asserted in earlier studies[1378]. Techem's new management moreover displayed a certain level of risk aversion after 2003, as it became familiar with the dynamics of international business. This observation is supported by the strategic partnership with Aareon involving limited financial exposure. This is surprising as it contradicts the notion that minor shareholdings and limited risk of personal wealth does not stop management from undertaking risky ventures. Trevira's management reported that they were initially averse to committing resources to market development, but gained confidence with Reliance's encouragement. To some degree, one could argue that the previous management felt insecure entering into markets not related to those Trevira was already serving and therefore did not fully exploit the company's market potential. In summary, the notion that management shareholdings alone are crucial to the emphasis on market development can be ruled out. Other management factors can compensate for a decrease in such incentives.

Human Resources

The focus on human resources increased in all three former LBO companies. Managers viewed this as crucial to strengthen their competitive advantage and achieve their growth plans. Furthermore, all former LBO companies changed their compensation schemes to facilitate higher pay-for-performance, albeit with different specifications.

Wincor Nixdorf's senior management recognized the need for well-trained and experienced employees to enhance coordination between the international subsidiaries. Programs were introduced to improve managerial and functional skills. To maintain the level of motivation nurtured by the equity participation program during the LBO, Wincor Nixdorf introduced pay-for-performance compensation varying from 20% (production, sales) to 50% (distribution). By contrast, Techem's human resource development was troubled by restructuring following the 2002 crisis. The increased diversity of products and cross-selling potential involved an enhancement of the skill level similar and partly above what one recorded at Wincor Nixdorf. However, management had to increase considerably labor productivity while reducing unit costs. The company continued its slightly lower level of career training opportunities. The compensation scheme was expanded with a profit-sharing component, but limited the number of employees paid on a pay-for-performance scheme. The restructuring in 2002 slowed down annual salary growth

1378 See Covin and Slevin 1990, Zahra 1993b, Altinay and Altinay 2004 in the second half of the post-LBO period. Trevira's requirements for the workforce also rose after the exit. Senior management sought a stronger focus on integrated customer service that demanded well-trained and experienced employees able to integrate both technical and commercial aspects. The company also had to manage the relocation of two major manufacturing sites and ongoing workforce adjustments. To develop systematically talent, Trevira continued its intense personnel appraisal process. The acquisition by the new parent offered employees opportunities to expand skills in international marketing, sales, and product development and the possibility of being sent to key departments at the parent.

Even though the supervisory board's overall involvement decreased in the two IPO cases, one could note continued interest in human resource-related issues. Techem's supervisory board discussed details of the restructuring with management in 2002 and 2003. A similar level of interest was evident at Wincor Nixdorf, with debates on new employment contracts, training and career development. To evaluate the interest correctly, one has to note that equal worker representation on the supervisory board of a German AG encourages such interest. Reliance was concerned about retaining key employees and ensuring a mutual transfer of best talents. One, therefore, can support previous findings that acquisitions intended to access valuable resources produce retention measures[1379]. Clear and upfront communication encouraged a sense of security among employees and prevented a decrease in productivity. In summary, one may notice that the level of involvement of owners did not decrease with regards to human resource development, even if overall activity in the cases of Wincor Nixdorf and Techem declined.

One could note that senior management shared the supervisory board's interest in human resource development. Managers of Wincor Nixdorf spended significant personnel effort in mentoring and developing non-management employees. They recognized the advantages of variable compensation and were willing to invest in the employees. Techem's management was less involved in modifying compensation schemes for non-managerial workers. Management displayed interest in accommodating the numerous layoffs at manufacturing sites. One could not see any conflict over control or responsibilities in Techem's integration with Reliance. Reliance consolidated selected activities while respecting Trevira's procedures and systems. Where Reliance expected the highest synergies, it jointly with management articulated expectations and changed processes in a timely fashion. In all three cases, one did not see a risk of management loosing control over resources as previously

---

1379 See Child, Faulkner et al. 2001

discussed. Having said this, the strategic control over resources was indeed strongest in the case of Wincor Nixdorf, and confirms the importance of management shareholdings as argued by previous research[1380]. To some degree, the correlation of wider pay-for-performance and profit sharing schemes may have contributed to the efficiency decline at Techem in the first two post-LBO years. Zwaan, Eije and Witte elaborated on the correlation between higher profit sharing and financial performance for post-IPO performance[1381]. To conclude, one can reiterate that management shareholdings alone are not key for an emphasis on human resources. Other governance factors can successfully compensate for a decrease in such shareholdings. Lack of substitutes however enhances the possibility of reduced emphasis on human resources.

Top-Management Resources

Analysis indicates that management stayed more or less the same after the exit from the LBO. The level of industry-specific skills was already high prior to the exit and was sustained. The IPO companies' top managers were experienced both in restructuring and their respective industries and did not need to be replaced.

Given that Wincor Nixdorf's management is its biggest shareholder, management obviously exerted considerable influence on appointing a board consisting of internal candidates. The CEO had in this a strong bargaining position[1382]. Overall, continuity marked the board's composition. The CEO's successor in year 3 after the exit was the former CFO who already had been for more than 15 years with the company and enjoyed the trust of the supervisory board and capital markets[1383]. The composition and skill profile of Techem's board remained unchanged at the exit. All management board members during the LBO were industry experts, and remained on the board after the IPO. The board changed because of the crisis in 2002 with three of the new board members coming from Colt Telecom, a company operating in businesses similar to those of Techem. In contrast to Wincor Nixdorf, Techem's management was in no position to influence board appointments or the skill profile of new board members. At the same time, Techem's family founders, minority shareholders with 25%, did not exert notably more pressure on the board than other remaining institutional shareholders. Trevira witnessed a replacement of the entire board.

1380 See Phan and Hill 1995, Bacon, Wright et al. 2004, p. 327

1381 See Zwaan, Eije et al. 2002, p. 132

1382 The observations reinforce previous findings on the bargaining power of the board and particularly the CEO (See Baker and Gompers 2003, p. 584).

1383 One should comment that the new CFO appointed in the second half of the post-exit period came from outside and was a former management consultant.

Given that two of the five board members had reached retirement age, the board turnover reflected only in part dissatisfaction with the previous management's performance.

Based on the limited observations, one cannot find any evidence to support the thesis that the turnover of senior management increases considerably immediately after the exit. If a change of management had been viewed as necessary, interested investors would have demanded this in the pre-IPO phase. Capital markets moreover appreciated the fact that Wincor Nixdorf and Techem executives succeeded during the LBO and had established a trust relationship with challenging buyout investors. These observations confirm previous findings of the existence of a negative relationship between the departure of senior managers and the company's performance[1384]. A change of management may have been demanded if new investors had not seen the development of a different company strategy. One can reject the assumption that a blockholder shareholder, as Techem's founding family, enhances the likelihood of a management turnover. However one can confirm that the turnover remains constant when the exit involves an IPO. In the case of Trevira's trade sale, one could observe that the new owner reviewed management and appointed a completely new team as part of the acquisition. This was largely because Reliance was dissatisfied with the restructuring and wanted a different strategic approach. One should not conclude that a trade sale generally results in a change of management given that if management succeeded in the LBO a new owner could welcome it. Reliance worried about Techem management's personal effort given Reliance's stringent management approach and given that it was family owned. Consequently, one should recognize the notion that management change is a long-term given in an exit via a trade sale. Interviewees said the concentration of ownership with Reliance played an important role in its approach. One should also confirm that management's shareholdings and bargaining power reduce the likelihood of a replacement of management.

With respect to the profile and composition of the managing board, one cannot confirm that the share of industry-specific (and company-specific) skills increases because of the exit. All the more so, given that management was already staffed with senior industry experts during the LBO. The majority of Wincor Nixdorf's board and, with some exceptions, nearly all sub-board senior managers during the LBO were industry experts with a long tenure with the company. The same continuity was evident at Techem. The level of industry-specific knowledge in Trevira did not

1384 See Cannella and Hambrick 1993, pp. 148 et seqq.)

change with the exit of DBI. Reliance carefully selected senior managers that understood the textile industry and corporate restructuring. The thesis of increased industry-specific skills may not be rejected (but also not confirmed) since all management board members during the LBO were industry experts. The size of the LBOs studied may have diluted this relationship, because it implies that high caliber managers have a set of skills not typical for smaller buyouts. One did observe a higher level of industry-specific knowledge in the supervisory boards. Wincor Nixdorf and Techem replaced representatives of the buyout investors with industry experts. Only their chairs remained on the board.

In terms of the compensation scheme, the notion of an increase in total compensation can be confirmed. Techem's incumbent managers negotiated an increased fixed base and a higher share of pay-for-performance. This contradicted findings that companies with a high indebtedness favor a higher cash component[1385] but was comprehensible as the business risk itself was low and the supervisory board sought to provide management with shares. After the crisis of Techem in 2002, variable compensation was tied closer to actual accounting measures, indicating that management may have over-emphasized the share price development. One did note attempts by the family owners to block the increase in compensation, as previously outlined for German executive compensation[1386]. Given the dispersion of ownership and the strengthening of the managers' position at Wincor Nixdorf, an increase of compensation levels was likely. Total compensation however increased only modestly increased as did the high level of variable pay. At Trevira, the level of monitoring of management performance increased in contradiction to earlier findings. The new owner introduced a higher level of fixed and variable compensation. The increase was intended to attract better management and compensate for the lack of management shareholdings. Although compensation also increased in Trevira, it was not due to reduced activity as argued by Schmidt[1387]. Trevira's reduced risk because of the parent's guarantee of the bank debt highlighted the sensitivity of management contracts[1388]. Management was willing to accept proportionally higher variable compensation with its fixed salary also increasing. Overall, the level of total compensation did increase in the post-LBO period. One can also confirm the notion that pay-for-performance increases proportionally as part of the overall benefits package.

1385 See Begley and Feltham 1999, pp.242 et seqq.
1386 See FitzRoy and Schwalbach 1990, Schmid 1997, Elston and Goldberg 2003
1387 See Schmidt and Fowler 1990, p. 566
1388 See John and John 1993, p. 968

5.5 Changes in Performance Development

5.5.1 During the LBO

All companies where able to improve productivity in operations and administration, but showed different patterns of performance development (see overview in Figure 23 and details in the performance overview in the case studies). Wincor Nixdorf and Techem were fortunate to translate productivity gains into enhanced financial performance, while Trevira, facing industry consolidation, failed to improve margin and cash flow even though it largely outperformed its industry. Wincor Nixdorf and Techem's operating cash flow was sufficient to finance debt repayment and necessary growth investments. By contrast, Trevira suffered a lack of funds to seize upon growth opportunities and to conduct necessary productivity improvements.

At the entry into the LBO regime, Wincor Nixdorf enjoyed a robust demand for new products and replacement. Some of its competitors opted to enhance growth through acquisitions. They achieved higher growth rates, but lower margins. Wincor Nixdorf managed to improve its gross and operating margin as well as strengthen its cash flow from operations. Since the company had undergone a severe restructuring prior the LBOs, it was unlikely that it would significantly shift in performance. Improvements were the outcome of steady change including the gradual withdrawal from unprofitable segments of the retail business, and organic growth, from, for example, entry into the high-margin services business.

Unlike Wincor, one could observed a shift in productivity and gross margin at Techem in the first fiscal year and in the fourth year after the entry into the LBO. The majority of these improvements were the result of the consolidation of the service network and investments into the efficiency of the service personnel. Constant sales growth coupled with the productivity upswing. Even though margins increased, in particular in year four and five in the LBO, profitability was still far below industry average, both in terms of gross margin and operating profit. In terms of cash flow, Techem continuously increased its relative operating cash flow generation and reached its strongest performance in the last year of the LBO.

Trevira encountered a challenging environment with the entry of low-cost competitors. Notwithstanding stagnating sales, Trevira was able to stave off a downturn by moving into profitable niches. As a result, Trevira outpaced the industry in terms of sales growth and improved its gross margin. Furthermore, Trevira achieved significant productivity improvements in the first two LBO years transforming itself to a stand-alone organization. The improvements were most visible in cash flow generation, as the company learned to be more diligent in investing in working capital and with expenditure for fixed assets. Independent of management's efforts, the industry consolidation overhauled these improvements. In the third and fourth year of the LBO, Trevira did not succeed to accelerate the cost adjustments accordingly, and underperformed the industry with respect to cash flow generation. The company did not have sufficient funds for necessary investments in machinery that is more efficient.

The partial decline of free cash flow in the second half of the LBO regime at both Wincor Nixdorf and Techem (despite strong operating cash flow) indicates that the buyout investors were willing to allow higher investments to secure future growth necessary to succeed in the exit. At Trevira, the operating cash flow deteriorated in the third year of the LBO and did not allow for investment into new machinery. The buyout investor was not willing to provide additional equity. The finding is in line with Gräper who measures a much slower growth of former German spinoff LBOs and who relates this underperformance to the necessity of revitalizing the product portfolio and customer structure to facilitate new growth[1389]. The findings do not correspond with Kitzmann's observations. Kitzmann argues that German LBOs demonstrated superior profitability already prior to the buyout and widened the performance advantage during the buyout[1390]. Finally, the findings also do not correspond to the distinction of growth buyouts as opposed to non-growth buyouts identified by Wegner. All three LBOs sought to improve in parallel operating margin and growth during the buyout[1391].

5.5.2 Post-LBO

5.5.2.1 Revenue Growth

Changes in corporate governance seems to alter the growth pattern. The emphasis on growth may produce a bigger appetite for external growth. The pace of pursuing new market entries may increase notably. Competitiveness in terms of product attractiveness, however, will presumably not change on a short- to medium-term base and should not lead to sudden changes in the post-LBO growth pattern.

Wincor Nixdorf was able to strengthen its sales performance compared to both its own LBO average and its industry peers. In terms of cumulative sales growth, it outpaced its competitors in all post-exit years observed. The highest annual growth was recorded in the third post-LBO year. However, the relative revenue growth slowed down in comparison to the industry and was below average in post-LBO year three and four. The industry growth was nurtured by the surge in the sales of

1389 See Gräper 1993
1390 See Kitzmann 2005
1391 See Wegner 2003

vending machines, particularly for smaller competitors, while larger competitors performed at the level of Wincor Nixdorf. The sales growth at Techem peaked in the first post-LBO year at industry average. However, the growth lost momentum in post-LBO years two and three. In these two years, industry competitors benefited from growth-enhancing acquisitions, while Techem's previous growth emphasis took its toll and resulted in substantial refocusing. After 2003, Techem regained some of its lost sales momentum, but remained behind the industry average throughout the observed post-LBO years. The industry average mirrored an offensive growth strategy of both new market entries and acquisitions.

Techem, however, given its former over-emphasis, refused to pursue acquisitions of considerable size and relied on organic growth. This limitation produced a notable margin improvement (see subsequent discussion). Trevira enjoyed a modest increase in relative sales. In the first post-LBO year, it was not able to benefit from the recovering demand for textile fibers and filaments. However, in post-LBO year two and three, Trevira succeeded in seizing growth opportunities, especially from internationalization, and outperformed both its LBO and industry average. In particular, the management increased sales productivity and took advantage from joint sales resources with its parent company.

In conclusion, it seems that the post-LBO governance generated a positive sales development at Wincor Nixdorf and Trevira. In both cases, the exit resulted in balanced growth objectives, whereby Wincor Nixdorf's performance declined in post-LBO year three and four. Techem, by contrast, only returned to balanced growth objectives with the strategy adjustment in 2002. Its debt burden and understandable risk aversion fostered after 2002 a more cautious growth pattern preventing the company from overtaking the general industry growth, at least on a short- to medium-term base.

5.5.2.2 Margin Development

The margin level is also subject to changes in corporate governance, though, at a reaction rate slower than that of the sales development. As outlined in previous research, the reappearance of inefficiencies in operations and administration takes its time and is likely to occur earliest in post-LBO year three[1392]. However, a highly aggressive emphasis on growth resulting in the opening of new businesses and acquisitions can produce a short-term margin decline, despite profitability robustness of the core business.

1392 See Holthausen and Larcker 1996, Jalilvand, Stewart et al. 1996, Bruton, Keels et al. 2002

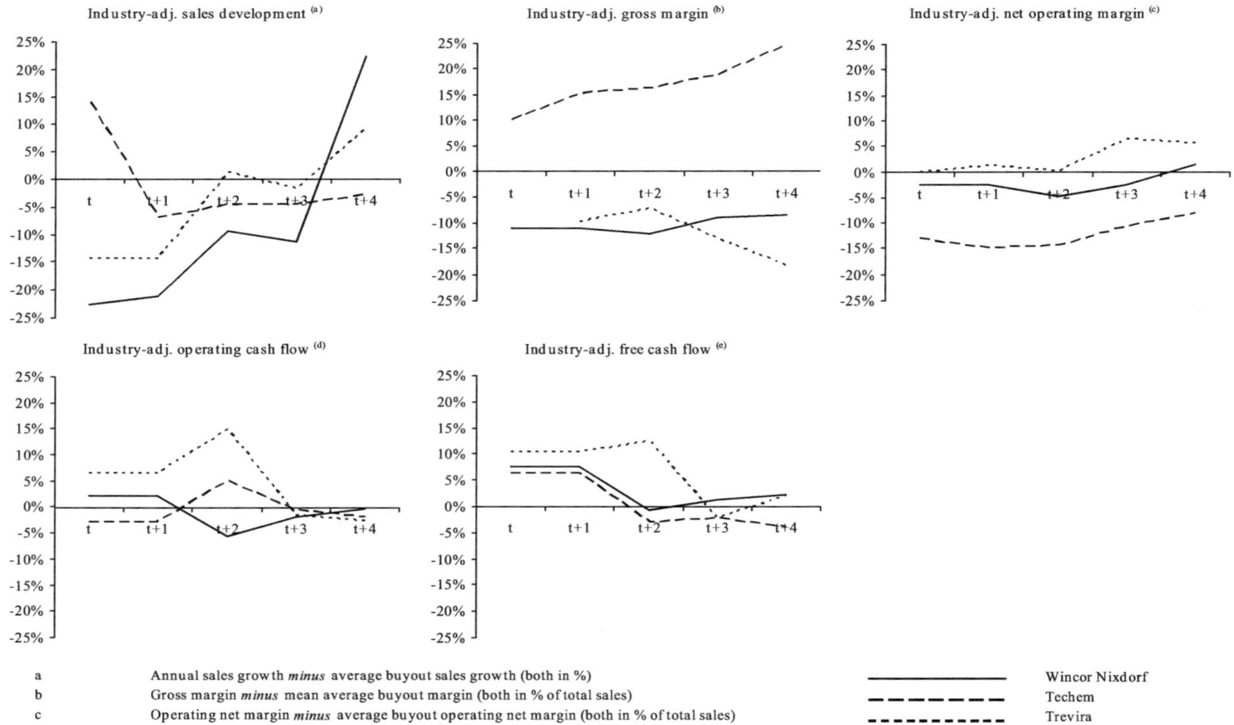

a Annual sales growth *minus* average buyout sales growth (both in %)
b Gross margin *minus* mean average buyout margin (both in % of total sales)
c Operating net margin *minus* average buyout operating net margin (both in % of total sales)
d Operating cash flow *minus* average buyout operating cash flow (both in % of total sales)
e Free cash flow *minus* average buyout free cash flow (both in % of total sales)

Figure 23: LBO performance adjusted to industry average

The cost structure and the ratio of fixed to variable costs will determine margin sensitivity to sales development.

Wincor Nixdorf succeeded in continuously improving its net operating profit and peaked margin levels in the last post-LBO year observed, year four[1393]. The industry in general, however, seems also to have strengthened its profitability, leaving the relative performance of Wincor Nixdorf despite the increase unchanged. Its management continued its expansion into service-oriented business fields in the post-LBO period, which significantly contributed to margin improvement. The core 'hardware' business, however, continued to offer only modest margins. Wincor Nixdorf was able to benefit from operational leverage given strong revenue growth, as the share of SG&A perpetually declined. Techem's margin development was much more volatile and reflected the changes in strategy, despite the stability of the core metering business. Until post-LBO year four, Techem underperformed its industry peers, but outperformed its own LBO average. In post-LBO years two and three, margins decreased significantly because of elaborate investments in establishing businesses that did not materialize as intended. Interviews indicated that besides the diluted business focus, inefficiencies in administration functions increased as an outcome of growth projects and a certain rebound on the previous strict cost management under the LBO. The new management lifted profitability to previously not reached levels after ceasing operations in non-core businesses and returning the cost focus to the top of management's agenda. As a result, Techem outperformed its industry peers in post-LBO year four and six on basis of a 20% fixed cost base. The positive development from starting with post-LBO year four can only partly be related to the exit from the LBO and is more the outcome of the newly installed management structure, in particular the quality of management and enhanced monitoring. At Trevira, management was not able to accomplish an operating profit at industry level, but reduced relative underperformance up to the third post-LBO year observed. In post-LBO year two, margins came under significant pressure. In this year, Trevira was hit by intense competition and was caught by surprise by weak demand with positive results in 2004 persuading it that 2005 would also witness growth. In this year, despite productivity improvements, Trevira failed to adjust the cost base in line with the unexpected decrease in sales. By contrast, Trevira succeeded to increase considerably its relative performance in the third post-LBO based on improved operations and a higher revenue base.

1393 Comparability of gross margin for Wincor Nixdorf is diluted from different cost structure and allocations of cost position between gross and operating profit.

The emphasis on growth, particularly with the entry into new businesses led to considerable volatility in margin development in the post-LBO period. Despite the stability of the core business, Techem's margins declined dramatically in the first two years after the exit. Yet, management was able to regain former profit generation in a short time period and even outperform the former LBO average. This indicates that agency costs have to be considered on different levels, in particularly in terms of inefficiencies in operations and administration as opposed to strategy focus and diversification. Trevira's decline was subject to external demand weakness, and it benefited in the medium to long-term from the LBO exit. At Wincor, the exit did not yield any profound changes in the profitability of the business.

5.5.2.3 Cash Flow from Operations

Cash flow from operations is to far more than sales and operating profit at management's discretion. Beyond dependence on margin development, the metric is subject to management's diligence in investing in and divesting of current assets and liabilities, particularly operating working capital. Interest and tax payments affect cash flow from operations. As a result, changes in corporate governance will more directly impact the cash flow metric.

Wincor Nixdorf's cash flow from operations stabilized at the level of the last two years of the LBO, but underperformed compared to the industry average. Interest expenses declined due to decreasing debt, while taxes on income increased. Additional cash flow growth was limited by increased accruals for pensions and warranties. Investment in working capital remained high given the sales growth. Still, operating cash flow fuelled by sales peaked in the last year observed (post-LBO year four). Techem's development of cash flow from operations was affected by significant changes in working capital management. Management's heightened attention to stricter receivables management resulted in cash generation that outpaced its industry peers in the crisis year 2002.

After the management change in post-LBO year three, cash flow generation further benefited from improved profit generation. Trevira's cash flow from operations was highly volatile. In the first post-LBO year, high restructuring costs and provisions depressed cash flow. In the second year, weak profit generation did not allow attractive cash flow generation. In third post-LBO year, the strong sales growth required considerable cash for the working capital. Trevira however outperformed the industry in all three post-exit years, however will declining distance.

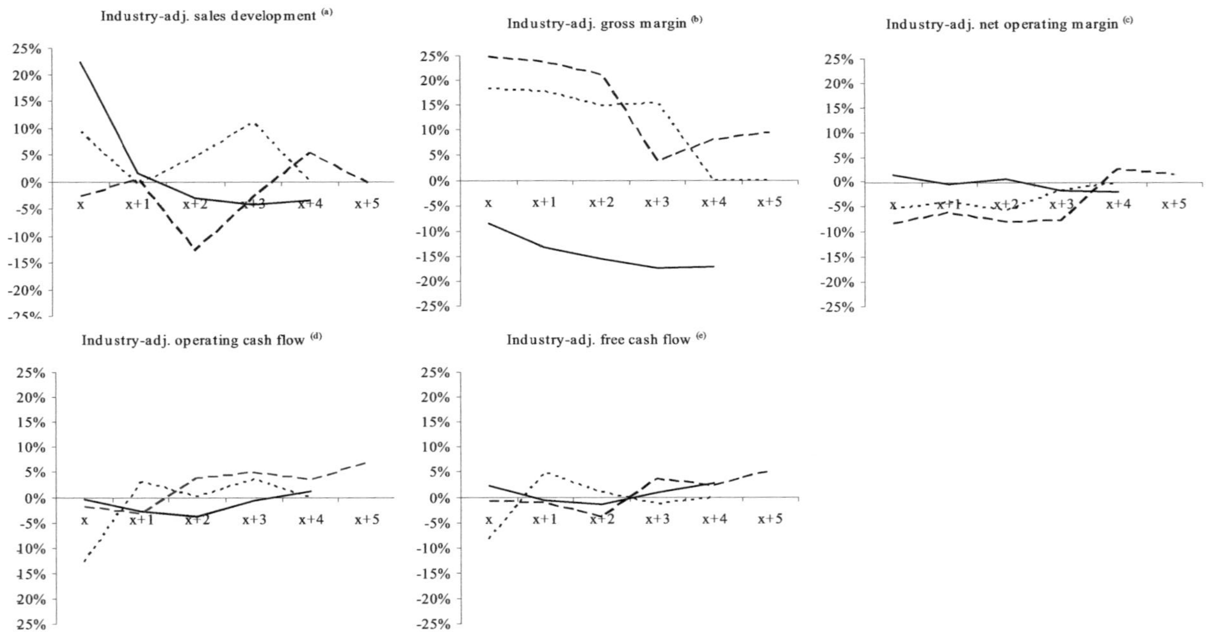

a Annual sales growth *minus* mean industry annual sales growth (both in %)
b Gross margin *minus* mean industry gross margin (both in % of total sales)
c Operating net margin *minus* mean industry operating net margin (both in % of total sales)
d Operating cash flow *minus* mean industry Operating cash flow (both in % of total sales)
e Free cash flow *minus* mean industry free cash flow (both in % of total sales)

Note: The measures of the industry sample are calendarized to the fiscal year end of the case study company.

Figure 24: Post-LBO performance adjusted to industry average

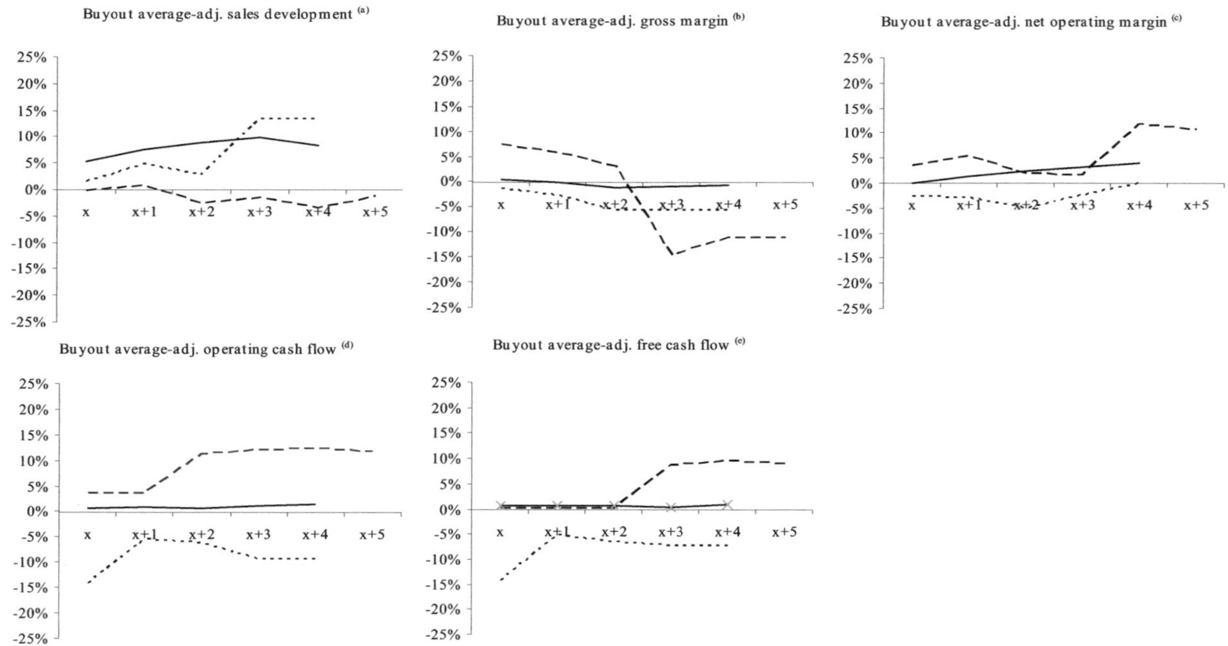

a Annual sales growth *minus* average buyout sales growth (both in %)
b Gross margin *minus* mean average buyout margin (both in % of total sales)
c Operating net margin *minus* average buyout operating net margin (both in % of total sales)
d Operating cash flow *minus* average buyout operating cash flow (both in % of total sales)
e Free cash flow *minus* average buyout free cash flow (both in % of total sales)

Wincor Nixdorf
Techem
Trevira

Figure 25: Post-LBO performance adjusted to buyout average

In summary, all three former LBOs gradually increased their cash flow from operations in the post-exit period, even though in one case slightly underperformed its industry. The main source for improvement (beyond factors outlined for the margin development) was working capital management. One could further argue that cash flow from operations appears to be partly independent of margin development. An example for this is the increase in operating cash flow despite a decrease in margin development at Techem in post-LBO year three. This again indicates that agency costs have to be considered at different levels. On the one hand, management is optimizing basic operations of the company that require considerable time to generate tangible improvement. On the other hand, management is optimizing planning and administrative processes that may yield short-term cash flow improvements[1394]. Despite the same setup of corporate governance, management discretion's varies significantly among the different optimization levers.

5.5.2.4 Cash Flow from Investments and Resulting Free Cash Flow

Free cash flow is the residual of cash flow from operations and investments. It will mirror all abovementioned effects of management change. One would expect cash flow for investments to remain at least constant, if not to increase given potential underinvestment during the LBO. Volatility will be high due to the discretionary aspect of investments and working capital development. A strong free cash flow will enhance debt repayment and generate an attractive income for equity shareholders.

Wincor Nixdorf generated a constant level of positive free cash flow throughout the entire post-LBO period. Cash flow for investment activities rose considerably due to the entry into the service businesses and the expansion of outsourcing businesses. Increased funds needed for investments remained, however, below growth of cash from operations. Since management also diligently invested in working capital, Wincor Nixdorf was able to improve its free cash flow and achieved the industry average in the third post-LBO year. The company was able to pay dividends throughout the entire post-LBO period and increase the payout ratio on an annual basis. Techem underperformed its industry sample in the first and second year after the LBO in terms of free cash flow. Investment in rental, technical and office equipment absorbed the majority of the operating cash flow. In post-LBO year one

1394 A weak profit generation and resulting low net income will thus enhance the necessity to avoid any expenditure for working capital. Such a capital constraint could be observed at Trevira in the second post-LBO year and should be considered as a moderating factor when assessing the emphasis on working capital.

and two, the company completed several acquisitions that required external financing. After restructuring, Techem enhanced its free cash flow and outperformed the industry level from year three onwards. Extensive provisions in the last year observed affected the free cash flow. The relatively high free cash flow was used to repay debt. Not until the fifth post-LBO year did management back away from paying dividends despite the company's promise at the time of the IPO of a dividend payout ratio of about 30%. Trevira's level of free cash flow to sales further decreased, even though management cut severely back on investment. Management was very disciplined with respect to cash flows for investment keeping funds to the absolute minimum. One also saw reduced investment at Trevira's competitors. Despite declining free cash flow, Trevira outperformed its industry group in all three post-LBO years reviewed.

Overall, one could see that the volatility of free cash flow in the first post-LBO years increased as result of changes in general operational performance and investment policy. Management has to balance correctly cash flow for investments, particularly acquisitions, with cash flow deriving from corresponding operations, and required cash flow for financing. Against the backdrop of a long-term exit, volatility decreased and new corporate management achieved a more balanced, industry-equivalent free cash flow generation.

5.6 Discussion

Debt Leverage

One can observe that despite the gradual reduction of leverage after the exit, debt continued to impose cost discipline and push financial performance. Wincor Nixdorf and Trevira's discipline did not stem from covenants or coverage ratios with which the companies had to comply. Instead, the LBO had anchored a strong emphasis on cost in the minds of managers and sparked improvements and initiatives that outlasted the LBO.

The seeds for Wincor Nixdorf's strong focus on cost were planted during the turnaround in the 1990s. Cost improvement programs continued after the LBO exit and ensured that the company retained its strong focus on cost. On the other hand, Wincor Nixdorf despite high debt leverage in the first post-IPO months had sufficient funds to finance necessary growth investments. As detailed below, management shareholdings stopped the board from excessively pursuing growth opportunities. At Techem, IPO proceeds and reduced debt burden significantly fuelled management's focus on growth and appetite for risk. The return to LBO-like debt leverage at the end of 2002 heralded Techem's strategic turnaround. Declining margin and cash flow can at least partly be attributed to decreased debt. Even after returning to the debt to industry-average, Techem retained its focus on cost emphasis. Trevira's continued debt leverage underpinned management's cost discipline reinforced by the new owner. Unlike Techem and Wincor Nixdorf, Trevira's debt repayments were significant and forced the company to keep investments down. Trevira learnt to with significant debt despite its strategic transition.

To conclude, debt burden itself is insufficient to secure management's focus on efficiency. A combination of different disciplinary forces, particularly intense, strategic control-oriented monitoring and of management co-ownership, produce the sought focus. Companies and their management are forced to focus on costs during an LBO. A decrease in debt does not automatically result in reduced focus on cost emphasis. However, on a stand-alone basis, it is likely that management with reduced debt leverage will try to trade profitability for growth and pursue higher risk acquisitions. The underlying cause-and-effect relationships observed indicate that company performance will decrease.

Ownership Concentration

As expected, the decrease in ownership concentration reduced the former owners' interest. Short-term investors urged management to focus on strong growth while supervisory board members authorized management to pursue a more balanced growth strategy.

The entry into Wincor Nixdorf of a number of institutional investors fuelled its appetite for growth. The supervisory board however, mitigated the risk of myopic, short-term cash flow maximization, targeting instead balanced, long-term performance improvement that would lead to sustainable value creation. Management group as the largest shareholder compensated for reduced ownership concentration and lack of one major shareholder. The supervisory board focused on long-term development refused to concessions to individual vanity or internal politics. Management shareholdings also protected the company against takeover attempts[1395]. Shareholdings did not exceed the inflection point assumed to be between 25 and 40%[1396] where cost of concentrated ownership outweighs the

---

1395 In Germany, a squeeze-out requires 90% of shares. Since management and leading employees possessed above 10%, it was unlikely that a potential unfriendly takeover would succeed. One may also note that the average AGM presence was around 35% and a 10% share therefore would surpass the 25% voting rights threshold. Finally, a takeover seems unlikely if the manager with their shareholdings would esteem an approach as hostile.

1396 See chapter A3.4.2

benefits of interest alignment. Concentration of ownership at Techem decreased with the family not exerting control in line with their voting rights. The Felten and Ott families were comfortable with buyout investor BC Partners's review and monitoring of Techem's management. Even though the founding family did not change its shareholding, it was forced to retake its role as the major shareholder among institutional investors who were seeking short-term value creation. The founding family was however less objective in its decision-making and beholden to management.

In summary, the decrease in ownership concentration resulted in a lower company performance. Even though Techem's founding family reinstated itself as the major blockholder, this did not improve monitoring. If anything, the ownership concentration, identity of the owners, their investment objectives and their monitoring have to be reviewed closely. Wincor Nixdorf management's strong position as shareholders counterbalanced the risks of growth. Such a high share of shareholdings can however also produce private control benefits and a focus on pursuit of short-term growth to maximize the share price.

Activity Level

The intensity and quality of monitoring alongside management shareholdings was one a key determinant of post-LBO performance. The activity level appeared to be less contingent on ownership concentration than had been expected.

At Wincor Nixdorf, monitoring decreased to a standard comparable to other listed companies, but at a less intense level than during the LBO period. Continuity in the board and the high level of industry expertise ensured that the board remained aware of the market environment and of strategy challenges management was facing. The board counseled management on the direction and pace of internationalization as well as the entry into related, downstream businesses. Techem's monitoring did not provide independent opinion needed to prevented excessive diversification. The supervisory board's strategy reviews did not question ambitions for growth. Instead, they curbed diversification and investment in non-core business. The former CEO who became Chairman was less able to admit potential own mistakes, e.g., in terms of acquisitions, and to commence with the required strategic restructuring. The return to LBO-like performance levels confirmed that the decline in performance did not result from organizational slack and inefficiency. The decline stemmed from strategic diversification that began shortly before the exit and was reduced as part of the restructuring. Reliance's monitoring of Trevira bore the characteristics of a 'governed corporation' and was crucial for post-LBO performance. Discussions on both strategic and operational matters to which Reliance was party and its resources provided enabled Trevira's successful strategic transition to a high-tech fibers manufacturer.

To conclude, quality and intensity of monitoring was crucial to post-LBO performance of Techem and Trevira. Wincor Nixdorf's decline in intensity was offset by the quality of monitoring and interest alignment with management. Monitoring and active ownership exercised by Reliance in case of Trevira offset the lack of co-ownership by management. The thesis that company performance decreases with reduced monitoring after exit from an LBO seems valid.

Management Shareholdings

The fourth constituent of corporate governance, management shareholdings, has proven to be one of the most, if not the most pivotal factor in post-LBO performance. Analysis showed that other important factors are inclusion of share-based option schemes and pay-for-performance instruments as incentives.

Although the decrease in shareholdings in Wincor Nixdorf did not occur, one could observe the positive of influence of management continuing to have a significant stake. These shareholdings ensured that the interests of management and owners were aligned. They also ensured that manager-owners adopted a sustainable strategy balancing growth and profitability despite efforts by institutional investors to achieve a short-term share price increase.

This supports the findings of Holthausen and Larcker who described the strong relationship in post-exit performance to the level of management shareholdings[1397]. To a degree not explicitly measurable, equity in hands of management was a 'shield' against organizational slack and inefficiency.

One may conclude that high variable compensation, even if top management gained considerable wealth in the IPO, created sufficient incentive for it to sustain its high level of personal effort. Techem's former management proved to be closely aligned with the owner's agenda and acted to maximize the value of the company.

After the LBO, the degree of alignment and underlying motivation decreased in part because of the divestment of management shares. Techem's management was given a relatively high fixed salary. Low shareholdings, reduced debt payments, high fixed salaries and a stock option program fuelled management's risk appetite as their own risk had decreased considerably. To amplify the interest divergence, monitoring was relatively weak.

1397 The regression analysis identified the managerial shareholdings to be the most decisive on post-LBO performance measured by operating income and operating cash flow to assets. See chapter B5.3.4.3.

		Explanatory variables				
	Hypo-thesis	Debt leverage	Owner-ship concen-tration	Activity level	Mgmt. Share-holdings	Key findings
Company performance	29a, 29b	(-) CF* / (-) CF**				Debt continued to impose cost discipline and push financial performance.However, debt burden itself is insufficient to secure management's focus on efficiency. Combination of different disciplinary foces, particularly strategic control and management co-ownership prompt the sought focus.With reduced debt, management is likely to trade profitability for (lower margin) growth.
	29c		(-) CF*			Decrease in ownership concentration results in lower company performance. Entry of institutional investors fuelled the appetite for growth. However, beyond ownership concentration, identity of owners and their investment objectives have to be reviewed closely. In one of the IPOs, 25% stakeholder did not show the activity level in monitoring as expected. Independent supervisory board can mitigate the risk of myopic short-term cash flow maximization.
	29d, 29e			(-) CF* / (-) CF**		Intensity and quality of monitoring was key to post-LBO performance, being less contingent on ownership concentration as expected. Activity level in the trade sale in the sense of a 'governed corporation' heavily supported the successful strategic transition. In one of the IPO cases, reduced monitoring was compensated by management. In the other IPO case, the supervisory returned to higher level after crisis and was then highly supportive to the successful turnaround.
	29f, 29g				(-) CF* / (-) CF**	Management shareholdings proven to be one of the most if not the most privotal to post-LBO performance. In one of the IPO cases, mgmt. Shareholdings ensure sustainable strategy balancing growth and profitability against short-term profits. Further, it served as "shield" against organizational slack. Equity was successfully combined with high variable compensation. In the othe IPO case, low mgmt. equity, a stock option program and high fixed salary prompted a high risk strategy. In the trade sale, absence of shareholdings were cushioned by strong monitoring by the parent company.

(+), (-): Direction of expected relationship

CF: Observations sufficient to confirm hypothesis
NCF: Observations not sufficient to confirm hypothesis

* Only for trade sale
** Only for going-public

Table 79: Review of hypotheses for change in company performance (H29)

The absence of management shareholdings in Trevira may have accelerated the divergence in interests. Reliance's monitoring however ensured that management, some of whose members came from Reliance, decided in its favour.

In summary, the thesis of a negative relationship between management shareholdings and post-LBO company performance can be confirmed. Additional components of the executive compensation scheme ensure an alignment of interest between management and owners.

5.7 Closing Remarks

In addition to the outlined changes in management, one may assess the degree to which further explanatory power outside of management can be related to factors identified in the discussion on determinants for the performance development after the exit.

For the exit via going-pulic, information gap and underpricing may have influenced post-LBO performance. The gap at Wincor Nixdorf was to some degree alleviated by the fact that the company was not new to stock markets. Its predecessor, Nixdorf Computer AG, had been listed until 1990, as well as its successor, Siemens Nixdorf Retail and Banking Systems GmbH, as a business segment of Siemens AG. The lock-up of the buyout investors as major shareholders mitigated the potential information gap. The fact that representatives of the buyout investors at both Wincor Nixdorf and Techem stayed as Chairman of the supervisory board supports this observation. A slip in morale among managers could not occur, at least for Wincor Nixdorf, as they sold only few shares in the period that the company returned to its pre-IPO ownership level. This confirms Holthausen and Larcker's results on rationale pricing and contradicts the thesis of DeGeorge and Zeckhauser who measure a performance peak in the year prior to the offering[1398]. However, there is an indication that the industry-adjusted performance declined in the second year after the exit.

For the exit through a trade sale, one again should stress the fact that the businesses of Reliance and Trevira were related in terms of product and technology. As observed by Healy, Palepu and Ruback, this carries explanatory power to the post-trade sale performance[1399]. Efficiency gains from the combined entity accrued to the target company rather than the buyer[1400]. As outlined, Trevira benefited from various resources that Reliance provided in addition to its monitoring. Horizontal

---

1398 See chapter B5.3.4.1
1399 See Healy, Palepu et al. 1992, pp.150 et seqq.
1400 See Singh and Montgomery 1987, Shelton 1988

expansion as in the Reliance-Trevira case produces higher returns in general compared to a vertical expansion. Since both companies had at best limited operational overlap, there were no disputes over where to reduce resources, allowing management to focus on development of Trevira's growth. Parrion and Harris[1401] indicate that the change of the management team contribute to the likelihood of success. If the acquisition is intended to achieve synergies from productivity increases and revenues as opposed to cost savings, it yields higher performance. The new team brought the right industry and restructuring mindset to the company. Finally, capital markets reaction to an acquisition has proven to be an excellent indicator of post-exit development. In this case, the share price increase of 2.9% at the time of the announcement reflected the appreciation of the deal's rationale and value creation by the stock market.

1401 See Parrino and Harris 1999, pp. 92 et seqq.

D Synthesis and Outlook

1 Research Synthesis and Conclusion

Since the emergence of leveraged buyouts as a new form of organization with enhanced incentives and monitoring, researchers have questioned how sustainable any performance improvement is and whether any increase in value purely is a wealth transfer to the disadvantage of other parties involved. Post-exit performance depends on the new management structure of the former buyout. The motives and efforts of parties involved - managers, employees, and owners – depends on their share of benefits related to the company and the individual utility function. The interesting question, therefore, was whether changes at the exit are a return to the pre-LBO structure or the birth of a significantly different governance structure allowing post-LBO superior performance. The author has investigated the changes in governance, strategy, operations and performance after the exit from a leveraged buyout structure based on three case studies in Germany. This concluding chapter summarizes the insights that can be drawn from the preceding analysis.

The first objective of this thesis was to review how the corporate governance of a former LBO changes after the exit (H1 to H4).

With the different patterns of corporate governance observed, it seems that a performance-enhancing environment can be accomplished by a series of governance instruments, of which one instrument may substitute for the lack of an other. Not all post-LBO situations allow installing the governance instruments as intended. Furthermore, some instruments may not exert disciplinary force as expected. Therefore, corporate governance should be seen as the sum of instruments that influence the decision-makers (the agents) in the interest of the key external stakeholder, in particular the equity shareholders (the principals).

The debt leverage decreased considerably after the exit, though, remained at a level significantly higher than the industry peer group. In the case of the companies going-public, the LBOs are often re-leveraged by a special dividend before they are sold and further receive only limited primary proceeds. In addition, many companies imitate the former debt leverage and pursue a high payout policy, minimizing excessive free cash. During the LBO, managers got used to operating under enhanced risk of financial distress. For both exit channels, the leverage remained at the upper end of comparable companies in the industry and confirmed the findings of Holthausen and Larcker as well as Jalilvand and Sweitzer that former LBOs continue to operate under higher leverage than their competitors[1402] In light of the observation that the risk propensity increased, the higher than average debt appears to be of minor significance. Thereby, debt has proven to be an efficient instrument to control management in terms of cash flow maximization. However, it only works on an alone-standing base if the leverage is extremely high and if alternative access to capital is limited. Hence, they are to a certain degree more familiar with operating under higher leverage.

The concentration of ownership changed as anticipated. In both IPOs , one shareholder gained a considerable share. However, the relative share size does not per se determine the level of monitoring, as even blockholding shareholders may not invest in the respective supervisory work and not provide independence in decision-making as predicted. It seems more adequate to look at the investment objectives and the effort in monitoring which the individual investor pursues. In the case of an IPO exit, monitoring was divided between supervisory board members, fund managers and representatives of institutional investors. The latter group did not participate in strategic discussions and decision-making. Professional industry experts appointed to the supervisory board provided the level of 'strategic control' required. Investors, however, seem to limit their monitoring to 'financial control'. In the cases reviewed, buyout investors were interested in ensuring a smooth transition and establishing stable and efficient post-LBO governance. They encouraged the appointment of professional supervisory board members and sought to assemble a group of experts most suitable in terms of industry expertise and management support in dealing with capital markets. In the case of a trade sale, monitoring equal the 'governed corporation' model. The acquirer relied on his profound industry knowledge and operational expertise. Monitoring was divided between the advisory board, dealing with strategic decision-making and other corporate-level decisions, and delegated managers, ensuring as members of the management team that day-to-day decisions were in the interest of the parent.

Management shareholdings and complementary performance-linked compensation instruments have proven to be pivotal for post-LBO corporate performance. Shares seem to incorporate the right balance between risk awareness and entrepreneurship, both linked to exposure of personal wealth and participation in performance improvement. Shareholdings nurture a long-term investment horizon and provide

1402 See Holthausen and Larcker 1996, Jalilvand and Switzer 2002 manager-owners with the needed bargaining power. Option-based schemes may foster short-term price maximization and nurture higher risk strategies given low personal wealth exposure. Owner-managers have proven to be good shepherds of the company as long as their shareholdings do not pass a certain inflection point where costs from private control benefits outweigh the benefits. However, managers in Germany do not hold the same relative share in the companies they are responsible for as in other comparable countries.

The second objective of this thesis was to review how the changes of corporate governance affect management objectives (H5 to H12).

The management did, as predicted, over-emphasize growth and under-emphasize efficiency in the post-LBO period. At a closer look, the difference in the post-LBO governance structure produced different patterns of objectives.

The emphasis on efficiency is safeguarded in the post-LBO period by intense monitoring, management co-ownership, and debt, with debt continuing to be comparatively high. In addition to the measured governance constituents, management itself appears to be pivotal to the focus, as, even without disciplinary shareholdings and active monitoring, managers are wiling to invest heavily in cost saving initiatives. Past improvement initiatives and programs may have facilitated the focus on efficiency. However, they are dependent on the 'agent' who has to sustain the focus on a daily base.

For entrepreneurial growth, all prospects for an enhanced focus seem to be confirmed. Debt is far less decisive for the change in focus than the change in investor objectives and the increase in management's risk affinity. To be clear, buyout investors also pursue a focus on growth. The environment for growth is though more attractive after exiting from the LBO. Companies are able to rely on optimized, cash-maximizing operations. The marginal utility of creating additional cash from operations is considerably higher than from new products, markets and acquisitions. From a monitoring perspective, investors and supervisory boards are likely to prefer discussion of potential external growth options rather than of supplemental cost improvement, given sparse company-specific knowledge and their limitation to 'financial control'.

The third objective of this thesis was to review how previously outlined changes of corporate governance affect the company's strategy and operations (H13 to H28).

Improvements of performance at a micro-level of operations have proven to be robust and able to withstand weakening of governance for a considerable time. Improvements in the manufacturing processes, production logistics, and the overall value chain outlast the exit and continue to generate high returns. This also applies to standardized administrative tasks like customer order processing. New planning processes as well as reporting and controlling formats survive in the post-LBO period and continue to be used by management to control the company. Despite the robustness, risk increases the further away an exit is while looser monitoring is likely to produce relative declines in productivity. 'Best practice' competitors will increase their productivity and after some time establish considerable advantage, which can only be compensated by continuous efforts extending into the post-LBO period. In addition, less standardized and more project-based operations will be more subject to changes after the exit from an LBO because they require continuous efforts by employees and managers on a task-by-task basis. Institutional investors in companies exiting via an IPO typically do not deal in detail with operational issues. Monitoring is delegated to the industry experts on the supervisory board. Given the co-determination in a German AG board, the supervisory board maintains a particularly high interest in worker-related issues. The board is also interested in changes to the value chain and the degree of offshoring and outsourcing. Dependent on the strategy of the acquirer in the case of a trade sale (or a blockholder shareholder with an industry background in the case of an IPO), the interest in operational productivity may rise depending on the shareholder's industry expertise.

The productivity of the asset base also demonstrates robustness at first glance after the LBO exit. In terms of the asset base itself, LBO investors typically raise all possible improvement during the holding period. Improvements may occur from underinvestment as one could observe in one of three cases. Other observations indicate that the majority of performance-enhancing investments were initiated during the LBO and not subject to limited funds. Projects with long-term growth potential are not subject to short-term investment considerations. But the investment intensity in the core business does not significantly change in the post-LBO period. Investment activities in higher risk projects and non-core business rose considerably. In most cases, they did not yield the same return as the basic investment activity, and indicate a potential 'positive crowding out' effect during the LBO. The sensitivity to performance decrease in the post-LBO period of asset productivity is high[1403].

For any activities that are to a larger degree subject to management's discretion, the risk of performance decline increases. This is particular true for investment policies, management of working capital, and control of less-standardized overhead functions. The complex management of working capital requires daily, personal effort to discipline different business units. Excluded from this is inventory, which in

1403 See also the subsequent comments on diversification

line with the robustness of the operational improvements is largely immune to changes in the governance structure. On the other hand, management of receivables and payables appears to fluctuate considerably. A broad distribution of shares among management and employees eases control significantly while debt leverage and active monitoring prove less detrimental. This is also true for overhead functions because focus on growth and changes in strategy sparks greater volatility in productivity. The limited ability to measure performance means that functions are increasingly subject to a lax attitude of management.

Management control systems did not change after the LBO in a way that may have affected the performance development positively or negatively. As predicted, control systems were adjusted to accommodate the new owner, in terms of, for example, stock market indicators for companies going public and corporate-wide established indicators for companies being acquired in a trade sale. However, control systems do not appear to have contributed to the financial performance of the companies in one way or another.

With all levers revised, it appears that corporate strategy is at best subject to management's discretion. The breadth of a position and the level of diversification may be threatened by management's growth- and risk appetite. Management shareholdings appear to be the most efficient mechanism to ensure the right balance between growth and profitability. Since LBOs occur mostly in mature, low-growth industries, additional sources of growth have to be identified. Typically, these sources are found in adjacent businesses, either directly neighbouring existing segments or covering downstream services. The cash flow strength of the core business may lead management to exaggerate growth and invest in high-risk or low-return new business fields. With the absence of management shareholdings, other instruments, in particular an intense 'strategic control' can mitigate this shortcoming. The case of Techem leads to the notion that a new, post-LBO governance structure needs time to find the right balance between growth and profitability, if this cannot be determined in the transition after the exit. Above all, there is one important difference between the LBO and the post-LBO period. The LBO investor develops a detailed, independent strategic plan for the forthcoming investment horizon. At the exit through an IPO, management provides a strategy plan for potential investors based on which they make an investment decision. Typically, the plan will be a continuation of existing strategy, complemented by selected growth opportunities. To far greater extent, the strategy will be at management's discretion during the buyout.

The two core sources for entrepreneurial growth, market development and R&D, benefit from the enhanced focus on growth of management and investors.

Management will decide to rely on above-average growth either through acquisitions or organically. In the latter case, both market development and R&D will profit even more. Trevira could also rely on the strategic interest of its acquirer. Since the resource bases of target and acquirer had no overlaps, the growth focus was also valid for this exit track. Similar to the observations on asset productivity, resources available for higher risk and for non-core R&D projects increase considerably after the exit. This is also true for the entry into new markets and partnerships designed to access new growth sources. Investors show a greater interest in market development than in other performance enhancing levers. As stated earlier, investors and the supervisory board prefer to discuss potential external growth options instead of supplemental cost improvement, given sparse company-specific knowledge and their limitation to 'financial control'.

The focus on growth ensured that human resources remained a management focus and were often given additional attention. Employees were seen as crucial to strengthening the company's competitive advantage and achieving formulated growth plans. New owners and investors were interested in ensuring high retention and providing sufficient development opportunities.

Management resources were pivotal to the company's success. Turnover at the exit was low, since those who were in office at the end of the LBO had succeeded under the ownership of the buyout investors. It was therefore unlikely that they would be replaced immediately. Strategic intent and alignment of this intent with the incumbent management are far more decisive for the likelihood of turnover than ownership concentration and level of monitoring. High turnover in the case of Trevira was a result of strategy changes made by the new owner as well as the incumbent management's wish to leave. As expected, the compensation scheme reflected reduced business risk and offered stable fixed salaries, while at the same time significantly increasing variable compensation.

The fourth objective of this thesis was to review how these changes in strategy and operations influence corporate performance development of the company (H29 and H30).

The most important observation is the fact that performance in terms of revenue growth, margin development, and cash flow generation does not weaken after the exit. On the contrary, it remains partly above industry average and in most case continues to outperform the company's own LBO average for an investigated period of four (five) post-LBO years. If the hypothesis of a value transfer to the disadvantage of the company would be true, a considerable decrease in performance would have become visible in that period given that for instance cutbacks of R&D budgets have a time lag at the companies observed of two to four years. As result, the notion that short-term cash flows are replaced by long-term growth potential is incorrect.

Not all companies strike immediately after the exit the right balance between growth appetite and profitability. The gradual decrease of the debt burden yields higher revenue growth at the expense of lower margins. As previously outlined, improvements in operations and partly in administration are robust and generate high margins, but changes in strategy focus and diversification can harm margin development even in the short-term. While revenue growth and margin development remain to some degree stable, the volatility of cash flow generation from operations increases considerably. Management has to find the right balance between cash flow for investments, particularly for acquisitions, cash flow deriving from corresponding operations, and needed cash flow for financing. With increasing distance in time to the exit, volatility decreases and the new corporate governance produces a more balanced, industry-equivalent free cash flow generation.

A further caveat has to be placed on the weakening of the corporate governance. Even though the observed case studies did not display a significant performance decrease, less rigid monitoring and a divergence of interests between managers and owners does bear considerable risk. For all constituents of management, one founded evidence that they negatively affect corporate performance albeit with differing intensity and in different cause and effect relationships.

In two of the three cases reviewed, disciplinary control exerted by the corporate supervisor remained constant. A combination of different disciplinary forces, particularly of intense, strategic control-oriented monitoring and of co-ownership by management produced the aspired balance between efficiency and entrepreneurial growth. To put the observations in the right context, one should recall that post-LBO performance deteriorated for the majority of companies because of less-effective corporate monitoring. The level of monitoring in many cases decreases, while private control benefits from non-financial investors come into play. Management moreover is not properly incentivized towards a common long-term objective and seeks instead to achieve short-term revenue growth and profit. Management shareholdings are most appropriate and one of the most efficient ways to ensure interest alignment. A dispersed ownership structure without a dominant shareholder leads to less aligned interests by the shareholders. For their part, industrial owners are less sensitive to performance development and will demand less aggressive return rates than buyout investors. The quality of the monitoring will decrease, particularly, if the supervisory board does not include experienced senior managers and industry experts.

2 Contributions to Research and to Practice

2.1 Contributions to Agency Theory

Preliminary research illustrates that a return to a governance system similar to the pre-buyout regime will increase agency and weaken organizational performance[1404]. Nonetheless, it is not automatic that performance of a former buyout will deteriorate. The new principals may be able to introduce a new governance system with reasonable agency costs.

Firstly, the agency costs is expected to increase by the higher amount of free cash flow the former LBOs carry after the exit, even though their debt leverage remained above the industry average. The three case studies indicate that the agency costs of free cash flow based on gradual reduction of debt varies depending on the governance pattern. In the first case (Wincor Nixdorf) reviewed, the amount of free cash flow rose due to strong cash flow from operations and IPO proceeds. To the advantage of the principal, other disciplinary forces filled the void left by the absence of debt. Management opted for a continuous high dividend payments to avoid the impression of the funds being under their managerial discretion[1405]. Significant co-ownership aligned management with the principal's interest and limited its interest in excessive private control benefits. In the second case analyzed (Techem), the amount of free cash flow also rose due to strong cash flow from operations and IPO proceeds. Even though the company had initially promised to return a high dividend to its shareholders, it withheld any net income. Free cash under management's discretion increased and was in the first two years not fully dedicated to debt repayment. Management conformed to its own utility function and increased the revenue on basis of managerial empire building[1406]. After replacement of management, the company reduced the free cash flow under their discretion and started to distribute a large part of the net income. In the third case (Trevira) investigated, the company nearly sank into financial distress as the free cash flow was too low. During the LBO, cash flow became sparse with industry consolidation depressing the cash flow from operations while debt repayments remained high. After the exit, the industrial owner provided equity to continue operations of the

---

1404 For a detailed discussion of the performance implications in the post-exit period please refer to chapter B5.3. See also Muscarella and Vetsuypens 1990, Holthausen and Larcker 1996, as well as Bruton, Keels et al. 2002.

1405 See Jensen 1986, p. 324

1406 See Hoskisson and Turk 1990, p.463

company. In the subsequent post-exit years, free cash flow remained comparatively low since various investments in machinery and growth had to be made. The observations show that a strict dividend policy with a high pay-out ratio can reduce the costs of free cash flow in the post-exit period, as well as the interest alignment by management co-ownership.

Secondly, the agency costs of equity will increase given the lower concentration of ownership[1407]. Additional costs for monitoring and bonding after exiting the LBO will occur[1408]. The case studies displayed efficient post-LBO monitoring, even though the intensity and quality of supervision did decline. In the two IPOs, monitoring was handed over by the former LBO professionals to supervisory board members, funds managers and representatives of the institutional investors. The former group consisted of professional industry experts appointed to the supervisory board. They provided the level of 'strategic control' required. The latter group did not participate in strategic discussions and decision-making and limited their monitoring to 'financial control'. In one of the cases (Wincor Nixdorf), the management group became the largest shareholder. Their shares served as a defense against takeovers but weakened the potential beneficial market disciplinary effect on corporate control[1409]. They simplified monitoring because they gave the needed expertise to the supervisory board without being entitled to board seats. In the other IPO case (Techem), the largest shareholder and therefore natural prime source of independent advice was the founding family. The family was, however, satisfied with the monitoring of the buyout investor. In the post-exit years, the family shareholder did not provide the board with the objectivity in decision-making to the board other investors may have contributed. In the case of the trade sale (Trevira), ownership concentration remained high at equal, relative monitoring cost to the respective new owner. The supervisor relied on his profound industry knowledge and operational expertise. Monitoring was divided between the advisory board, which dealt with strategic decision-making and other corporate decisions, and delegated manager, who as members of management took day-to-day decisions in the interest of the

---

1407 See Admati, Pfleiderer et al. 1994, pp. 1124 et seqq., Hoskisson and Turk 1990, p. 464

1408 A dispersed shareholder structure in a post-IPO company imposes free-ridership on monitoring of the management board. Hence, shareholders will underinvest in monitoring. On the other hand, the return to the stock market imposes market discipline on corporate control. See Grossman and Hart 1983, p. 107, Jensen and Ruback 1983, pp. 29 et seqq., Morck 1988, pp. 101 et seqq., Rappaport 1978, p. 84

1409 In Germany, a squeeze-out requires 90% of shares. Since management and leading employees possessed above 10%, it was unlikely that a potential unfriendly takeover would succeed. One may also note that the average AGM presence was around 35% and a 10% share therefore would surpass the 25% voting rights threshold. Finally, a takeover seems unlikely if the manager with their shareholdings would esteem an approach as hostile.

parent. To conclude, the agency costs of equity on the one hand remain low as industry experts are appointed to the board. On the other hand, the unity of ownership and monitoring is separated and produces higher agency costs as none of the new investors is represented on the supervisory board.

Thirdly, agency costs of equity are also threatened by the reduction of managerial shareholdings. Decreased co-ownership will potentially make management less willing to invest significant personal effort[1410]. Observation of these three case studies validates the notion that co-ownership by management and complementary performance-linked compensation instruments are pivotal to post-LBO corporate performance. In particular, they compensate for decreased monitoring. In one of the cases (Wincor Nixdorf), management continued to hold a considerable stake. This ensured that owners saw common interest. It also ensured that the manager-owners adopted a sustainable strategy, balancing growth and profitability, despite the fact that institutional investors sought short-term share price increases. To a degree that is not explicitly measurable, equity in hands of management shielded the company from organizational slack and inefficiency. In the second case (Techem), alignment and underlying motivation decreased due to the divestment of management shares. Smaller shareholdings, reduced debt payments, high fixed salary and a stock option program encouraged management's risk appetite given that their own risk had been significantly reduced. This divergence in interests was amplified by relatively weak monitoring. In the third case (Trevira), the trade sale, the lack of management shareholdings may also have lead to a divergence of interests. However, monitoring by the acquirer ensured that management acted in his favour. All the more so because a number of managers were transferred from the parent company. The observations confirm the previous conjecture that management shareholdings are the most efficient instrument to align interests. In the two cases with decreased co-ownership, the agency costs of equity increased due to additional monitoring and the necessity to exchange the management team.

2.2 Contributions to Corporate Governance Theory

From a corporate governance perspective, it was of interest to analyze how the interactions of the different stakeholders – equity shareholders, supervisory boad members, debt holders, and employees, to name the most important - change in the post-exit period.

1410 See Hoskisson and Turk 1990, Holthausen and Larcker 1996

Three groups of investors were investigated: institutional investors, family owners, and industrial owners. In the two cases of ownership by institutional investors, the respective utility function exclusively focused on maximizing shareholder value. As predicted, they invested little time and left the companies to a certain degree unmonitored[1411]. They also limited their monitoring to financial results and avoided investing in specific industry and market knowledge. In both cases, they largely pursued a short-term, myopic investment objective. However, they understood that the company would be best served if the supervisory board had experienced senior managers and industry experts. In one case (Techem), a family owner held a minority stake and took two seats on the supervisory board. The family owner did not seek to achieve private gains and was no more risk-averse than other investors. He broadly supported the growth strategy of management and were not, as initially expected, afraid of losing control or demanding a focus on a niche strategy that would minimize risk[1412]. However, after successfully mastering the strategic turnaround, the family owner decided to sell its stake to diversify their personal wealth. In the case of the trade sale (Trevira), ownership by the industrial buyer indeed produced better division of labor. Despite initial predictions, the buyer kept the acquired company's funding intact. The buyer provided limited investment for new products but put the parent's resources at the disposal of the acquired company to achieve growth.

Beside the identity and investment objective, the exit from the LBO also changed the actual monitoring work by the equity shareholders. In the two IPOs, the monitoring was divided between industry experts and representatives of the institutional investors. The former group did not benefit from co-ownership in shareholdings and was paid with a fixed compensation. Hence, they had limited incentive to invest into independent information gathering and opinion-making, and relied on their industry expertise. Monitoring by a supervisory board and by representatives of institutional investors replaced the former unseparated supervision by the buyout investor. The institutional investors trusted in the strategic control by the supervisory board members, and merely applied a financial control. They urged management to follow an offensive growth plan. In one the two cases (Techem), the former LBO was subject to a public tender offer that produced a significant control premium. Jensen saw such a premium as evidence for the low level of corporate control[1413]. The trade sale (Trevira), in the contrary, involved close monitoring by a highly motivated new

1411 See Short, Keasey et al. 1999, p. 343
1412 See Shleifer and Vishny 1997, p. 758
1413 See Jensen 1989c, p. 37

owner. The active monitoring by the new industrial owner displayed the characteristics of a 'governed corporation' and was decisive for post-LBO performance. However, the governance of one of the IPOs, Wincor Nixdorf, produced superior performance throughout the entire post-exit period. Even though the direct control was dissolved, the new governance by the incumbent management was beneficial to the company. The findings make it necessary to consider the quality and intensity of the corporate governance including the acting management and the instruments with which the managers are motivated.

The employees contributed to the success of all three LBO companies. In the case of the trade sale, their efforts were pivotal for the successful turnaround and improvement in operational productivity. In the cases of the IPO, the productivity of the workforce was enhanced in a similar manner. In all companies, the requirements and hence necessary skills of the employees increased significantly. The companies provided the required training and hired additional employees. The employees were willing to invest into company-specific training and participated accordingly from the success with increasing salaries. In one of the IPOs (Wincor Nixdorf), the employees benefited beside the salary development from an equity participatation program that continued into the post-exit period. No conflicts were observed that weakened the performance of the companies investigated. Through the change to an AG, the employees in the two IPO cases could partly extend their influence taking in seats on the supervisory board. In the trade sale (Trevira), the formal influence exercised by the employees remained unchanged. However, given their highly specialized knowledge, they were of particular value to the acquirer, and could avoid any relocations to low-cost countires and despite the distressed situation negotiate higher salaries[1414]. In sum, employees did not loose or gain influence on the decision-making.

The debt holders did not play a crucial role. In the case of the trade sale (Trevira), the breach of covenants during the LBO resulted in the engagement of restructuring consultants, though it did not severely change the strategy or operations of the company.

The results open additional research fields for the corporate governance theory. The governance of a company should be modeled including both the equity shareholders

1414 The findings are in line with the observations of Blair. He suggests a governance model where all parties contributing to company-specific investments participate and negotiate in the distribution of the economic surplus See Blair 1995, p. 14

and management. The theoretical discourse of the studies have further derived a set of hypotheses that can be refined in statistical tests.

2.3 Contributions to Operations Management, Strategy, and Corporate Entrepreneurship Research

The present study has analyzed the changes in strategy and operations at the exit of the LBO, assuming changes of similar magnitude as when entering into the LBO regime.

The starting point for the operations was the observation that the entry into the LBO significantly encourages productivity and is sometimes referred to as 'shock therapy'. In the exit, the weakening of corporate governance was expected to result in a considerable decrease in performance, mirroring the observed decrease in financial performance. The case studies show that improvements of performance on the micro-level of operations are robust and withstand weakening of governance for a considerable period. Improvements in the manufacturing processes, production logistics, and overall value chain outlast the exit and continue to generate high returns. This observation further applies to standardized administrative tasks. Despite the robustness, risk increases with the distance to the exit that weaker monitoring leads to relative productivity decreases. At the same time, less standardized, project-based operations are more sensitive to changes after the exit because they involve continued attention from employees and managers on a task-by-task base. This is particularly true for investment policies, management of working capital, and control of overhead functions. Furthermore, development of productivity in operations demonstrates a higher variance and reflects the different governance structure the companies adopt as opposed to the uniform control under a LBO. The thesis shows a close relationship between changes in the governance of a company and the management of the operations. In the next step, the findings should be verified with a larger empirical survey. The findings can be applied to similar changes in corporate governance, for example for a recapitalization or a spin-off.

For strategy research, the thesis details the relationships between the constituents of corporate governance and the different dimensions related to strategy. The case studies show that corporate strategy in the post-exit period is at best at management's discretion. In particular, the level of differentiation (vs. mass-market) and the level of diversification are threatened by management's growth- and risk-appetite. Since LBOs occur in most cases in mature, low-growth industries, additional sources of growth have to be identified and are found in adjacent businesses. The cash flow strength of the core business may mislead management to exaggerate growth. The case studies reveal that it takes some time in the post-exit period until the strategic position is balanced with the cash flow deriving from underlying operations and needed cash flow for investment and financing. During the LBO, the buyout investor relies on a value creation plan and has a clear strategy for the company in mind. In the beginning, the focus is laid on rapidly increasing free cash flow and repaying debt. Toward the exit, the focus will be expended on growth in new market and product segments. Given the debt repayment schedule, the strategy will always be balanced with the free cash flow. In the post-exit period, management is to a higher degree independent and not bound to such a trade-off. As seen in the case studies, intense monitoring and management co-ownership can however prevent the loss of strategic focus and the entry into broader market segments. Further, continuity in the supervisory board produces a more stable transition to the post-exit governance structure. In the IPOs, the buyout investors were diligent in bringing the rights skills to the board, investing their own time while staying on the board. In the case of the trade sale (Trevira), the industrial owner brought valuable strategic advice to the former LBO and accelerated the transition to a better strategic position. The case studies confirm that the exit from the LBO influences strategy in all dimensions. Much more than during the LBO will the strategy be subject to management's discretion. Strategy researchers should hence continue to take into account any changes in capital structure and monitoring as being pivotal to the company's strategy.

For corporate entrepreneurship, it was expected that a weakening of corporate governance and the entry of myopic investors will lead to a bigger growth appetite at the expense of profitability. As expected, the two core sources for entrepreneurship, market development and R&D, benefited from management's and investor's greater focus on growth. The institutional investors in particular preferred to discuss potential external growth options instead of supplemental cost improvement, given their lack of company-specific knowledge and limitation to 'financial control'. In one of the IPO cases (Techem), the enlarged emphasis on entrepreneurship however deteroriated the profitability. Risk appetite resulted in investments in R&D for new products and in neighboring segments with higher uncertainty on the returns. In the core business, the level of entrepreneurship remained unchanged. The same was true for the second IPO case (Wincor Nixdorf). On the contrary, management did not enter as actively in neighboring segments with higher risk. In the case of the trade sale (Trevira), the acquiring company displayed a high interest in promoting the mutual, complementary resource base, particularly with regards to additional growth. Given the complementary resource base, the intensified growth focus did not produce considerable additional costs, at least not in the short-term. The focus on growth also ensured that human resources remained a focus of management and was given higher attention. Managers regarded employees as crucial to strengthening the company's competitive advantage and realizing formulated growth plans. Further, management resources were pivotal to post-LBO company success, even more so than during the LBO where considerable guidance was provided by the buyout investors. This was true for the IPOs and the trade sale. Those managers who were in office at the end of the LBO had succeeded under the ownership of the buyout investors, and were unlikely to be immediately replaced. As aforementioned, the two IPOs were not subject to capital restriction during buyout. The findings show that the level of entrepreneurship nevertheless increases after the exit. In one of the IPOs (Wincor Nixdorf), the shareholdings of management served as a shield against unhealthy growth. In the other case (Techem), it took time until the right balance between investments in resources for growth and profitability was found. For the trade sale, entrepreneurship increased to the benefit of the company.

The results confirm the validity of the underlying theories. A closer analysis of the interdependencies of the constituents of corporate governance, in particular around the manager profiles and the specific company situation, is expected to bring further explanatory power.

2.4 Contributions to Finance Research

This study contributes to a detailed understanding of post-LBO performance development. Research so far has focused on medium-term stock performance of IPOs and on the short- to medium-term stock performance of the acquirer after a trade sale, with some analysis of the target stock.

Previous research of post-IPO performance by Loughran, Ritter and Brav found significant underperformance in the first months based on gaps in information, low trading liquidity, which both correlate to company size[1415], and moral hazard by managers[1416]. Explanations include false risk assessment and exaggerated optimism. IPOs have occurred at peaks in performance of a company and led to a favorable overvaluation. The findings on post-exit performance of the sub-sample of former LBOs provide a mixed picture of earnings manipulation, hidden information and moral hazard[1417] as well as rational pricing without manipulation[1418]. In terms of long-term performance, the studies report a relative decline even though the

1415 See Ritter 1991, p. 23, Loughran and Ritter 1995, p. 46, Brav and Gompers 1997, p. 1820
1416 See Pagano, Panetta et al. 1998, pp. 50 - 51
1417 See DeGeorge and Zeckhauser 1993
1418 See Holthausen and Larcker 1996

performance of the former LBOs continues to be superior[1419]. Increased decline is interpreted as a gradual reappearance of agency problems[1420]. Parameters of post-exit governance include continuation of close alignment of management and owners' interests through significant shareholdings. This is seen as crucial.

The first observation of interest is the underpricing of those LBOs with a public offering. One of the investigated cases, Wincor Nixdorf, was formerly listed as a subsidiary of a larger corporate, Siemens. No (significant) underpricing on the first day of listing was observed. Investors in the second case, Techem, benefited however from a significant increase of the share price.

No (short-term) underperformance was observed in any of the case studies. Given the relative large size of the two IPOs, the former LBOs did not suffer from low trading liquidity. Both companies entered within a short time the MDAX index. This positive size effect in previous samples has been confirmed for the German stock market[1421]. Block holdings of former shareholders helped mitigate potential information asymmetry. The buyout investors continued to hold a considerable stake for the first months after listing. In the case of Techem, the founder family kept a 25% equity stake during the IPO. Long-term, however, this did not stop the stock from underperforming its industry group. The long-term underperformance can largely be attributed to below-average monitoring efforts by the family. No sign of moral hazard of managers extracting private benefits or manipulating could be observed. Even though the business in Techem's case slowed down, Clementi's research concluding that IPOs are timed to facilitate the expansion of the business at a crucial point cannot be confirmed[1422]

On the other hand, a negative relationship between the post-IPO incumbent stake and performance can be confirmed. In Techem's case, incumbent management sold considerable parts of their stake shortly after the public offering. The company short-term (18 months) outperformed the industry average[1423], but then performed well below it. Management seems to have anticipated the medium- to long-term development of the company. Financial performance in terms of sales and margin growth peaked the year of the public offering, indicating that an adverse selection of

---

1419 See Mohan 1990, DeGeorge and Zeckhauser 1993, Holthausen and Larcker 1996, Bruton, Keels et al. 2002, Jalilvand and Switzer 2002. For details, see chapter B5.3.4.3.

1420 See Jalilvand and Switzer 2002, Bruton, Keels et al. 2002

1421 See Stehle, Ehrhardt et al. 2000, p. 190

1422 See Clementi 2002

1423 During the first 18 months, the stock also benefited from the general positive investor sentiment toward IPOs in the German stock market. Amongst the group of young stocks, Techem was in the lower quartile in terms of stock performance.

timing may have to some degree been optimized. In Wincor's case, management maintained largely their stake and performance continued to improve.

Long-term performance was analyzed with different parameters. In all three cases, post-exit management generated a positive and sustainable impetus for sales development. In two cases, the exit resulted in a set of balanced growth objectives. The annual growth of one of the IPO cases, Wincor, peaked in the third post-LBO year. The other IPO, Techem, traded profit against growth and only returned to balanced growth objectives with the strategy adjustment in the third post-exit year. It nonetheless remained below the industry average throughout the observed post-LBO years. Trevira (trade sale) outperformed its own LBO and the industry average in the entire post-exit period. The previous conclusion that sales growth increases after the reversal of the company's buyout is therefore confirmed.

The focus on growth led to considerable volatility in margin development. Despite the stability of the core business, Techem's IPO suffered a dramatic decline of margin in the first two years after the exit. Management was able to reestablish earlier profit generation within a short period and even outperformed the former LBO average. In Wincor Nixdorf's LBO case, the company was able to maintain above average profitability throughout the exit, even though the entire industry increased margin levels. In the case of Trevira's trade sale, margin declined and seemed to be subject to external demand weakness, but benefited in the medium-term from the parent's resource base. In the third post-LBO year, the company succeeded to improve operations based on higher revenues.

Studies so far have consistently observed that it takes three to four years until inefficiencies appear to show a significant margin decrease compared to the industry average. Techem's decrease directly after the exit is clearly not related to operational inefficiencies but to excessive strategic diversification. As previously outlined, improvements in operations and administration are in all three cases robust and generate high margins. Changes in strategy focus and diversification in the case of Techem show harm to margin development. One of the key new findings is the refinement that performance development has to be considered on different levels, particularly in terms of inefficiencies in core operations and administration as opposed to performance changes from new operations resulting from increased strategy focus and diversification.

Long-term cash flow from operations did not weaken compared to the respective industry average. The case studies contradict findings of earlier research. Cash flow remains stable, and partly increases compared to the industry average. Even in Wincor Nixdorf's case, which was highly cash generative during the buyout, cash flow levels were maintained. In addition, cash flow from operations appears to be partly independent of margin development. Performance development has therefore to be considered at different levels. On the one hand, management's optimization of basic company operations requires considerable time to generate tangible improvement. On the other hand, management's optimization of planning and administrative processes may yield short-term cash flow improvements.

Volatility of free cash flow increased because of changes in general operational performance and investment policy. In the case of the Wincor Nixdorf IPO, business generated a constant level of positive free cash flow. Free cash in the hands of management increased considerably. The board decided to pay a comparatively high dividend and later to introduce a share buy-back program. In the Techem IPO case, the company underperformed its industry sample in the first and second year after the LBO in terms of free cash flow. Investments and acquisitions in non-core businesses absorbed the majority of the operating cash flow. After restructuring, the company outperformed the industry level from year three onwards. The relatively high free cash flow was used to repay debt and later to pay dividends. In the case of the trade sale, free cash flow decreased, even though management cut back on investments. Management was very disciplined with respect to cash flows for investment keeping funds to an absolute minimum. One also saw reduced investment by competitors. Despite declining free cash flow, the company outperformed its industry group in all three post-LBO years reviewed. Existing studies have not investigated post-LBO development of free cash flow, even though the metric lies at the heart of Jensen's introductory paper on LBOs. The results prove that free cash flow increases after the exit. A company with long-term superior performance has a high payout policy and keeps free cash at management's discretion low. By contrast, a lower-performing company retains cash and spends it on low-return investments. As time passes after the exit, new corporate governance produces a more balanced, industry-equivalent free cash flow generation. Volatility of the free cash flow decreases. Successful companies seem to apply a LBO-like capital structure with comparatively high debt and returns and permanently high free cash for its shareholders to minimize cash available to management at its discretion.

Charges that long-term growth potential is impaired by a value transfer that disadvantages the company are incorrect. All companies were able to increase or at least keep their (relative) performance level constant. The effects of cutbacks on new growth investments and R&D budgets have a time lag of three to four years. In all case studies, no (significant) cutbacks in investments were observed that might have diminished growth potential. If the hypothesis of a value transfer would be true, a considerable decrease in performance would have become visible in that period. The total return to shareholders measured by the ROIC increased during the post-LBO episode.

2.5 Applications of Findings to Post-Ext Shareholders and Investors

The three case studies of post-exit development of LBOs identify a number of implications for practitioners. As elaborated in the introduction, practitioners in this case are post-exit shareholders and investors who have an interest to ensure strong performance of the company they want to invest in or already have invested in.

The first part of the thesis established a theoretical and notional foundation for post-exit analysis. From an investor perspective, the reader was offered insight into relationships between different owners over the buyout cycle. The agency theory, the resource-based view, and the corporate governance-related theory furnished complementary elements to establish the right framework for analysis of the post-exit period.

Research of post-exit performance development and changes in strategy and operations presumes that the changes in the governance structure – (i) debt leverage, (ii) concentration of ownership, (iii) activity level of investors, and (iv) extent of management shareholdings - are exogenous. For this purpose, the author constructed a conceptual framework that accounts for changes in corporate governance. Several previous studies were discussed that measured these respective changes and provided detailed insight into how capital structure changes, ownership evolves and the activity level of governance fluctuates. Further insights were provided by analyzing how changes in governance affected the activities of management. The author contrasted how post-exit investors as opposed to buyout investors typically improve operations and administration under their ownership, employing empirical evidence from the US, Europe, and particularly Germany. Observations of entrepreneurial growth-focused management activities were also discussed. These activities encompassed empirical evidence from the buyout and post-exit period for strategy, innovation, market development, and human resources.

In the empirical part, findings of the three case studies offered a new level of insight into the development of LBOs in Germany. The case studies presented detailed insight into the initial investment hypothesis, activities during the holding period, and in the highest detail measures taken by new investors in the post-exit period. In the analytical part of the case studies, changes of governance were broken down and studied in relationship to the research model. The subsequent analysis investigated the causes and effects of the changes in the sequence (i) management objectives, (ii) efficiency- and entrepreneurial growth-focused management activities, and (iii) performance development. Each hypothesis was tested and discussed in detail. The observations were complemented by quotes and comments of the management team, buyout investors, and post-exit investors.

The closing part evaluated the initial hypothesis by comparing the observations and conclusions of the three case studies. The author conducted the synthesis in the sequence of the examined levels according to the outline in the case studies. The post-exit performance was robust and contradicted previous assumptions that LBOs suffer from potential value transfer and over-leveraging by buyout investors. The synthesis found a clear co-relationship between quality and intensity of post-exit governance and robustness of (relative) financial performance. Furthermore, the synthesis identified highly robust measures that change governance and continue to generate sales growth, profit and cash flow. The observations of post-exit governance implied corporate strategy and operational setup show that companies can continue and even outperform their already comparatively high performance during the LBO.

What are then can be learnt from the corporate governance of a company? In his review of the evolution of the U.S. corporate governance, Kaplan established that corporates and their managers have started to apply insights into and strengths of the LBO and, in a literal sense, have 'turned all into Henry Kravis'[1424]. The author may extend these arguments with the conclusions of the case studies of governance constituents and some general observations. A number of companies have started to imitate the 'best practice' of the LBO governance regime (see the overview in Table 82), others may consider doing so.

One of the first conclusions is the beneficial impact of maintaining a leveraged capital structure. A balance has to be found between sufficient capital to run the business with an optimized financial distress likelihood and minimize cash at management's discretion. A company can reduce waste of free cash flow by borrowing to repurchase stock or pay large dividends. Despite the beneficial effect of low free cash flow, the dividend pay-out ratio for large German listed companies has decreased (see Table 80). For the sample of German companies in total, the leverage in capital structure has decreased, however, returing from a rather high average in comparison to other European countries (see Table 81).

A second observation is the alignment of management based on cash flow- and performance indicators. Management is in most cases still paid based on accounting

---

1424 See Kaplan 1997

performance indicators, particularly revenue growth and EBIT. Some companies have started to offer higher compensation schemes tying management compensation to cash flow-based performance indicators such as the ROIC or CFROI. However, the case studies show that cash flow is more than the aforementioned indicators subject to management discretion and can be manipulated.

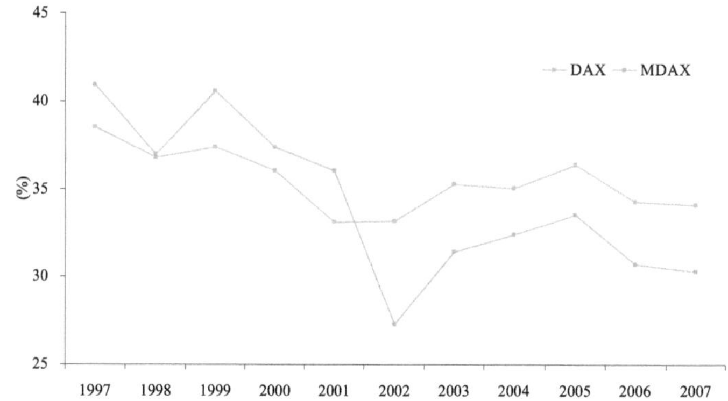

Table 80: Development of dividend quote in Germany (last ten years)[1425]

A further observation is the enhancement of shareholder coalition making to benefit from ownership concentration. Ownership by a family, bank or strategic investor does not incur different performance development per se. Increases in the stakes of the largest shareholders lead to enhanced monitoring efforts, but are apparently offset by greater consumption of private benefits. With the German governance system increasingly becoming an outsider-controlled system, private control benefits are reduced and block holders redirected towards true, cash flow-based value creation. Enforced coalition forming among shareholders in Germany is less directed towards ensuring a formal concentration of voting rights. Instead, the power constellation shifts to an adequate identification of owner interest in long-term performance improvement and value creation. These new investors have to limit their private control benefits and be true servants of the company.

Coalition forming has to be accompanied by enforcement of shareholders' rights. Currently, German corporate governance is still hostile to small shareholders and consciously or unconsciously expropriates wealth to the benefit of block holders. The most likely conflicts are therefore between minority owners or a group of dispersed owners and a controlling owner. Jensen and Meckling argue that the closer the cash

1425 Source is Datastream.

flow rights come to the control rights, the higher the alignment of interest between minority and majority owners[1426]. Proxy voting rights are only relevant for share-issuing companies; AGs and KGaAs account only for a small fraction of economic activity[1427]. Supervisory boards are only required for share-issuing companies and large GmbHs.

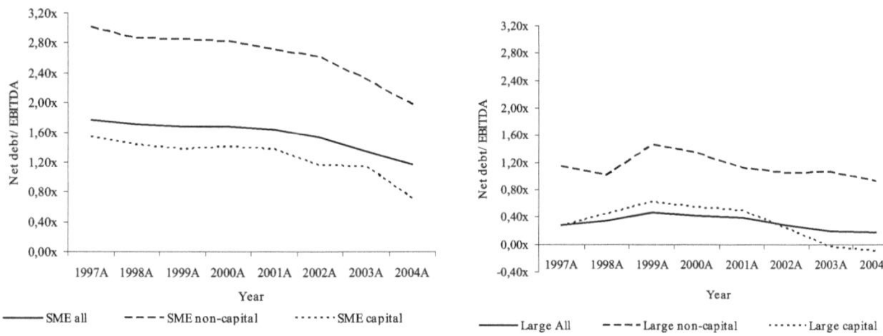

Table 81: Development of capital structure and indebtedness in Germany[1428]

In response to activist investors, companies and their owners have started to increase the quality of their monitoring. In many cases, they have increased the number of independent, outside directors to enhance valuable industry insight into the monitoring of the company. The average number of meetings has also increased[1429].

Finally, companies have started to hand over significant ownership to management[1430]. In many cases, a company situation does not allow for a generous equity participation program with high leverages. Instead, these companies offer restricted stock grants and normal stock programs financed with personal funds. Companies are also starting to hand over ownership to employees. At the same time, companies have, partly voluntary and partly mandatory, increased transparency of the compensation scheme. The Cromme Code stipulates mandatory publication of salaries of the managing board members of listed companies.

1426 See Jensen and Meckling 1976

1427 See Edwards and Fischer 1994, pp. 75-88 , 0

1428 See Bundesbank 2006. Net debt calculated as total bank debt minus cash.

1429 A bi-yearly survey by Heidrick & Struggles has rated the quality of corporate governance on a country-by-country base. Germany has increased the average from 9,58 (2001) to 11,47 (2007), however, increased the distance to the European average (9,78 in (2001), 11,47 (2007). The rating reviewed the criteria (i) the working style of the board (board structure, board committee, number of meetings), (ii) the composition of the board (proportion of independent non-executive directors, presence of non-nationals), (iii) the disclosure level (publications on director's age, tenure, main executive position), and (iv) remuneration level. See Heidrick and Struggles 2001, Heidrick and Struggles 2007.

1430 See Stewart 1990 proposing the „remaking of the public corporation from within".

To summarize, post-exit shareholders will have to closely assess how to organize corporate governance of the company they acquire. A former LBO has learned to operate under a regime of professional investors that demand a high level of management effort but also provide a chance to participate in the value increase. The lessons from the presented case studies and amended comments on the adaptation of buyout constituents to the post-exit period provides valuable insights for designing post-exit governance.

Constituents of coporate	*Specifics to buyout*	*Implications for the post-exit governance*	*Examples of instruments*
Debt leverage	High debt leverage in the capital structure	Maintaining a leveraged capital structure	Special dividends, leveraged recapitalizations, share buybacks
		Binding management to cash flow-based performance indicators	New performance indicators, e.g. EVA (economic value added), ROIC (return on investd capital), and CFROI (cash flow return on invested capital)
Ownership concentration	Ownership concentrated in the hands of a (consortium of) buyout specialist(s)	Enhancing shareholder coalition-making	Proxy rules relaxed regarding shareholder communications, increase of institutional investors
		Enforcing shareholder's rights	Strengthening of minority rights, increased mandatory publication of shareholdings
Activity level of governance	Professional investment managers with intense interaction with buyout	Increasing the quality of monitoring	Smaller boards, Independent outside directors, more active institutional investors
		Ensuring the efficiency of monitoring	Professional board representatives, Increased frequency of meetings, jointly developed business
(Direct) Management shareholdings	Significant managerial shareholdings (up to 20% of common stock), partially as equity ratchets	Handing ownership to management, however not granted	Restricted stock grants, phantom stock linked to cash-flow development, Stock-programs financed with personal funds
		Increasing transparency in variable-based compensation scheme	Mandatory publication of executive salary

Table 82: Adaptation of buyout constituents of corporate governance to the post-exit period (author)

To summarize, post-exit shareholders will have to closely assess how to organize corporate governance of the company they acquire. A former LBO has learned to operate under a regime of professional investors that demand a high level of management effort but also provide a chance to participate in the value increase. The lessons from the presented case studies and amended comments on the adaptation of buyout constituents to the post-exit period provides valuable insights for designing post-exit governance.

3 Limitations of Study and Areas of Future Research

The complexity of interactions in the post-exit period requires comprehensive and unbiased insight into the progression of a company over the buyout cycle. Since no theory building has systematically covered this research area, analysis demanded an iterative, theory-building approach. A case study approach appeared most appropriate for the formulated research objectives and the explanatory approach.

Multiple case studies enhanced the reliability and validity of the findings. A cross case-study comparison allowed for identification of similarities and differences using the same constructs and hypotheses. However, the usage of multiple cases is limited for theoretical sampling as opposed to statistical reasoning.

The chapters on construct and hypothesis building are a major step towards deepening the understanding of academics and practitioners. This thesis intends to provide a comprehensive overview of the breadth of empirical evidence on management activities during the buyout and post-buyout period. This thesis also seeks to provide the theoretical basis for future detailed statistical tests of the identified major findings.

It would be interesting to develop a comprehensive, summarizing factor that measures quality and intensity of corporate governance. It would be of further interest to consolidate the findings with regard to how instruments interact with each other, for example, substitution of debt by management stakes, and to formulate a total factor for the level of applied corporate governance, presumably based on a level approach. This construct should take into account that some functions such as private control benefits from excessive ownership in the hands of management (Tobin's Q) are not linear to the expected performance development.

It would also be of interest to conduct a questionnaire that allows for measurement of key indicators identified throughout the buyout cycle on a large basis. Basic metrics such as operational and asset productivity are to some degree robust over the cycle and to a sufficient degree comparable over a sample of companies in an industry. Further metrics should operationalize the strategic position (such as preference in dimension, width of position, number of related and unrelated businesses). The metrics that have been drafted to operationalize entrepreneurial growth in the case studies should also be tested over a larger sample. The analysis would lead to a more general test of the underlying hypothesis.

It might be of interest to deepen further the understanding of the potential value transfer to the disadvantage of the former LBO in the post-exit period. The thesis has concentrated on analyzing long-term performance development based on financial accounting figures. Previous research has investigated changes in tax payment (value transfer from or to tax authorities) and the relative risk profile of debt (value transfer from or to tax authorities). In addition, empirical data could even further detail any value transfer to employees, for example, by reviewing pension levels and measuring the development of average salaries differentiated by the respective hierarchy level.

However, any survey focused on German will have to account for the fact that the number of appropriate LBOs is still comparatively low. Given the necessity for a longitudinal measurement over a period of typically 10 years and more, any questionnaire should ensure that the return rate is sufficient to investigate separately the exit through an IPO as opposed to a trade sale. The sample size should further enable separate investigation of efficiency as opposed to entrepreneurial-oriented LBOs.

To accommodate this shortcoming, the data set may be extended by changes in corporate governance that resemble in specific dimensions changes at the exit from the LBO. For instance, the survey could include companies having accomplished considerable capital recapitalization or having survived a distressed situation. In addition, the survey could be expanded to countries with similar governance characteristics.

In conclusion, by highlighting the individual changes after the exit from an LBO, the present analysis contributes to a deeper understanding and wider knowledge of how the exit influences the performance likelihood of former LBOs. The case studies play a key role in conveying a comprehensive understanding of the changes in corporate governance, subsequent changes in management objectives, and the implied management activities with regard to operations and strategy. The case studies have brought forward a more objective view of long-term performance development. The transition to a LBO does not harm the long-term growth potential of a company. The success of a company after the exit depends on the post-exit corporate governance that is introduced. It can be expected that an investor base that follows a myopic investment behavior and management without commitment of personal funds in shareholdings will not enable a company to perform at or above the industry average. However, if the corporate governance resembles the positive characteristics of an LBO governance it is likely that the company will be able to maintain and improve (relative) financial and operational performance.

E Appendix

1 Interview Partners

1. Wincor Nixdorf		
Company	Interview with Sven Kassner, Director Outsourcing	Dez 06
	Interview with Axel Fleitmann, Director Finance	Jul 07
	Interview with Heinz-Georg Stiller, CEO (until January 2007)	Jan 07
Buyout investor	Interview with Silke Scheiber, KKR	Dez 07
	Interview with Alexander Dibelius, Goldman Sachs	Jan 08
2. Techem		
Company	Interview von Curd-Hasso von Flemming, Head of Investor Relations	Jun 07
	Interview von Horst Enzelmüller, CEO	Jul 07
Buyout investor	Interview with Stefan Zuschke, BC Partners	Jan 08
3. Trevira		
Company	Interview with Steffi Brobowski, Head of communications	Dez 07
	Interview with Egon Kircher, Market Buinsess Analyst	Dez 07
	Interview with Albert Beer, Director Finance	Dez 07
Buyout investor	Interview with Christian Krupp, former advisory board member	Jan 08
	Interview with Axel Wieandt, Deutsche Bank Corporate Investments	Jan 08

Table 83: List of interview partners

2 Key Financials of Case Studies

In TEUR	PostLBO								LBO					
	x+4		x+3		x+2		x+1		t+4		t+3		t+2	
	2007 (Sept 30)	as % of sales	2006 (Sept 30)	as % of sales	2005 (Sept 30)	as % of sales	2004 (Sept 30)	as % of sales	2003 (Sept 30)	as % of sales	2002 (Sept 30)	as % of sales	2001 (Sept 30)	as % of sales
Net Sales	**2.144.563**	10,1%	**1.947.569**	11,7%	**1.743.732**	10,6%	**1.575.947**	9,4%	**1.439.960**	7,1%	**1.344.611**	-8,0%	**1.462.000**	9,4%
Cost sales before carve-out costs	(1.553.887)	27,5%	(1.412.218)	27,5%	(1.257.533)	27,9%	(1.118.398)	29,0%	(1.008.908)	29,9%	(934.700)	30,5%	(1.047.035)	28,4%
Amortization of product know-how	(14.854)		(20.031)		(26.213)		(28.093)		(28.298)		(24.100)		(24.100)	
Gross profit	**575.822**	26,9%	**515.320**	26,5%	**459.986**	26,4%	**429.456**	27,3%	**402.754**	28,0%	**385.811**	28,7%	**390.865**	26,7%
R&D expenses	(96.569)	-4,5%	(87.437)	-4,5%	(78.007)	-4,5%	(72.908)	-4,6%	(66.132)	-4,6%	(62.883)	-4,7%	(52.408)	-3,6%
SG&A	(308.203)	-14,4%	(290.683)	-14,9%	(270.619)	-15,5%	(268.166)	-17,0%	(262.967)	-18,3%	(259.022) a		(278.293) f	
Other operating income	0		4.507		993		11		1.511		1.128		113	
Other operating expenses	(3)		(921)		(1.965)		(3.762)		(18.574)		(19.726)		(19.082) d	
Investment result	0		0		0		413		524		(700) b		159	
Net profit on operating activities	**171.047**	8,0%	**140.786**	7,2%	**110.388**	6,3%	**85.044**	5,4%	**57.116**	4,0%	**44.608**	3,3%	**41.354**	2,8%
Financial result	(9.827)		(12.781)		(19.426)		(19.147)		(34.216)		(30.103)		(47.942)	
Net profit on ordinary activities	**161.220**		**128.005**		**90.962**		**65.897**		**22.900**		**14.505**		**(6.588)**	
Taxes	(51.914)		(46.152)		(35.384)		-21.540		-8.623		(40.367)		3.138	
Profit after taxes	**109.306**		**81.853**		**55.578**		**44.357**		**14.277**		**(25.862)**		**(3.450)**	
Minority interests	(1.270)		(845)		(669)		(588)		(695)		5.534 c		(1.296)	
Net profit for the period	**108.036**		**81.008**		**54.909**		**43.769**		**13.582**		**(20.328)**		**(4.746)**	

Table 84: Profit & loss statement Wincor Nixdorf

In tsd.EUR	PostLBO														
	x+6		x+5		x+4		x+3		x+2		x+1		t+4		t+3
FY Year end	**2006** (Sept 30)	as % of sales	**2005** (Sept 30)	as % of sales	**2004** (Sept 30)	as % of sales	**2003** (Sept 30)	as % of sales	**2002** (Sept 30)	as % of sales	**2001** (Sept 30)	as % of sales	**2000** (Sept 30)	as % of sales	**1999** (Sept 30)
Net sales	**522.982**	100,0%	**466.792**	100,0%	**432.014**	100,0%	**408.478**	100,0%	**379.254**	100,0%	**355.070**	100,0%	**322.695**	100,0%	**295.741**
Cost of sales	(291.759)	-55,8%	(255.710)	-54,8%	(236.083)	-54,6%	(237.554)	-58,2%	(153.847)	-40,6%	(134.104)	-37,8%	(116.887)	-36,2%	(123.381)
Gross profit	**231.223**	44,2%	**211.082**	45,2%	**195.931**	45,4%	**170.924**	41,8%	**225.407**	59,4%	**220.966**	62,2%	**205.808**	63,8%	**172.360**
Distribution costs	(62.942)		(61.597)		(55.758)		(61.061)								
R&D expenses	(4.720)	-0,9%	(6.859)	-1,5%	(6.799)	-1,6%	(5.214)	(0)	0	0	0	0	0	0	0
Selling expenses		0,0%						0,0%	(77.679)	-20,5%	(74.993)	-21,1%	(78.351)	-24,3%	(65.702)
General and administrative expenses	(54.157)	-10,4%	(54.663)	-11,7%	(49.340)	-11,4%	(59.571)	-14,6%	(95.428)	-25,2%	(81.067)	-22,8%	(75.669)	-23,4%	(62.573)
Other operating income	4.148	0,8%	3.868	0,8%	6.006	1,4%	5.070	1,2%	9.180	2,4%	7.562	2,1%	8.430	2,6%	4.450
Other operating expenses	(7.160)	-1,4%	(7.435)	-1,6%	(4.148)	-1,0%	(5.583)	-1,4%	(22.736)	-6,0%	(19.392)	-5,5%	(17.250)	-5,3%	(10.306)
Earnings before interest and tax	**106.392**	20,3%	**84.396**	18,1%	**85.892**	19,9%	**44.565**	10,9%	**38.744**	10,2%	**53.076**	14,9%	**42.968**	13,3%	**38.229**
Investment income		0,0%	0	0,0%	16	0,0%	(87)	0,0%	177	0,0%	144	0,0%	100	0,0%	(28)
Net share of profit of associates	(1)		0	0,0%	(182)	0,0%	13	0,0%							
Unrealized gain on financ. Instrument									1.112		0				
Interest income/ (expense)	(11.027)	-2,1%	(13.428)	-2,9%	(14.886)	-3,4%	(18.736)	-4,6%	(15.304)	-4,0%	(18.260)	-5,1%	(16.656)	-5,2%	(19.183)
Income before taxes	**95.364**	18,2%	**70.968**	15,2%	**70.840**	16,4%	**25.755**	6,3%	**24.729**	6,5%	**34.816**	9,8%	**26.312**	8,2%	**19.046**
Taxes	(38.099)	-7,3%	(31.030)	-6,6%	(26.575)	-6,2%	(10.470)	-2,6%	(11.927)	-3,1%	(21.377)	-6,0%	(8.099)	-2,5%	(13.373)
Net income before minority interests	**57.265**	10,9%	**39.938**	8,6%	**44.265**	10,2%	**15.285**	3,7%	**12.802**	3,4%	**13.439**	3,8%	**18.213**	5,6%	**5.673**
Minority interests	(417)	-0,1%	(24)	0,0%	(634)	-0,1%	(421)	-0,1%	(376)	-0,1%	(504)	-0,1%	(323)	-0,1%	(37)
Net income before cum. effect of changes in acc	**56.848**	10,9%	**39.914**	8,6%	**43.631**	10,1%	**14.864**	3,6%	**12.426**	3,3%	**12.935**	3,6%	**17.890**	5,5%	**5.636**

Table 85: Profit & loss statement Techem

In TEUR	PostLBO						LBO							
	x+3		x+2		x+1		t+4		t+3		t+2		t+1	
	2006 (Dec 31)	as % of sales	**2005** (Dec 31)	as % of sales	**2004** (Dec 31)	as % of sales	**2003** (Dec 31)	as % of sales	**2002** (Dec 31)	as % of sales	**2001** (Dec 31)	as % of sales	**2000** (Dec 31)	as % of sales
Sales	**286.770**		**262.456**		**262.701**		**258.436**		**264.854**		**282.499**		**287.378**	
Changes in inventories of finished goods and work in p	3.067		(241)		(2.584)		(1.906)							
Capitalised service	280		496		709		880							
Other operating income	13.917		14.008		17.530		17.505		15.460		20.192		19.829	
Total sales	**304.034**		**276.719**		**278.356**		**274.915**		**280.314**		**302.691**		**307.207**	
Raw materials and consumables used	(151.248)	-49,7%	(135.245)	-48,9%	(133.846)	-48,1%	(127.357)	-46,3%	(126.272)	-45,0%	(137.579)	-45,5%	(144.491)	-47,0%
Costs of purchased goods and services	(26.086)	-8,6%	(20.990)	-7,6%	(16.997)	-6,1%	(16.581)	-6,0%	(15.270)	-5,4%	(16.063)	-5,3%	(15.761)	-5,1%
Wages	(50.810)	-16,7%	(50.332)	-18,2%	(48.781)	-17,5%	(50.094)	-18,2%	(50.379)	-18,0%	(54.650)	-18,1%	(51.854)	-16,9%
Costs of employee benefits	(14.324)	-4,7%	(13.578)	-4,9%	(13.864)	-5,0%	(13.490)	-4,9%	(12.369)	-4,4%	(15.765)	-5,2%	(13.537)	-4,4%
Gross profit	**61.566**	20,2%	**56.574**	20,4%	**64.868**	23,3%	**67.393**	24,5%	**76.024**	27,1%	**78.634**	26,0%	**81.564**	26,6%
Other operating expenses	(46.030)	-15,1%	(47.095)	-17,0%	(49.434)	-17,8%	(48.260)	-17,6%	(51.846)	-18,5%	(43.234)	-14,3%	(49.564)	-16,1%
Other operating expenses	(24.552)	-8,1%	(27.020)	-9,8%	(29.614)	-10,6%		0,0%		0,0%		0,0%		0,0%
Sales and marketing	(16.440)	-5,4%	(16.249)	-5,9%	(15.048)	-5,4%		0,0%		0,0%		0,0%		0,0%
General administration	(2.701)	-0,9%	(2.291)	-0,8%	(2.222)	-0,8%		0,0%		0,0%		0,0%		0,0%
Other expenses	(1.114)		(368)		(319)									
Neutrale expenses	(1.223)		(1.167)		(2.231)									
EBITDA	**15.536**	5,1%	**9.479**	3,4%	**15.434**	5,5%	**19.133**	7,0%	**24.178**	8,6%	**35.400**	11,7%	**32.000**	10,4%
Depreciation and amortisation	(13.423)	-4,4%	(14.894)	-5,4%	(15.471)	-5,6%	(18.148)	-6,6%	(17.931)	-6,4%	(19.411)	-6,4%	(19.136)	-6,2%
EBIT	**2.113**	0,7%	**(5.415)**	-2,0%	**(37)**	0,0%	**985**	0,4%	**6.247**	2,2%	**15.989**	5,3%	**12.864**	4,2%
Income from investment	775		3.252		108		508		323		823		4.328	
Returns from profit transfers of subsidiaries	198		0		1.999		0		635		334		329	
Other interest	5.079		4.003		2.631		1.164		106		225		0	
Expenses from transfer of losses			0		0		(16.293)							
Interest and similar expenses	(3.939)		(3.661)		(4.424)		(3.787)		(4.015)		(5.183)		(6.173)	
EBT	**4.226**		**(1.821)**		**277**		**(17.423)**		**3.296**		**12.188**		**11.348**	
Extraordinary income	5.150		750		22		654		3.721		16.832		1.478	
Extraordinary expenses	(8.613)		(2.162)		(6.424)		(4.372)		(7.117)		(20.280)		(55)	
EBT after extraordinary items	**763**		**(3.233)**		**(6.125)**		**(21.141)**		**(100)**		**8.740**		**12.771**	
Tax expenses on income and earnings	1.014		160		(3.997)		562		8		(104)		(955)	
Other tax expenses	(399)		(331)	-0,1%	(369)	-0,1%	7	0,0%	(321)	-0,1%	607	0,2%	(3.386)	-1,1%
Net profit	**1.378**		**(3.404)**	-1,2%	**(10.491)**	-3,8%	**(20.572)**	-7,5%	**(413)**	-0,1%	**9.243**	3,1%	**8.430**	2,7%

Table 86: Profit & loss statement Trevira

F References

Abraham, K. and S. Taylor (1993). Firms' use of outside contractors: theory and evidence. NBER Working Paper.

Achleitner, A. K. (2001). Handbuch Investment Banking. Wiesbaden.

Achleitner, A. K. and C. H. Fingerle (2003). Unternehmenswertsteigerung durch Management Buyout. Working paper.

Achleitner, A. K., Herman,K., Nathusius, E., Lerner, J. (2008). European private cases: introduction. in: Globalization of alternative investments: The global impact of private equity report 2008. W. E. Forum. Eds. Working Papers Volume 1: 87-90.

Achleitner, A. K., Kaserer, C., Moldenhauer, B. (2005). German Entrepreneurial Index. in: Finanzberater Betrieb: 118-126.

Achleitner, A. K. and K. Müller (2004). Trade Group versus Private Equity Entities: A Comparative Study. in: European Private Equity & Venture Capital Association: 1-35.

Achleitner, A. K. and A. Poech (2005). Familienunternehmen und Private-Equity: Die psychologischen Bruchstellen. in: Apax 1-13.

Achleitner, A. K., S. Schraml and F. Tappreiner (2008). Private Equity in Familienunternehmen - Erfahrungen mit Minderheitsbeteiligungen. Working Paper.

Achleitner, A. K., Thommen, J.P. (1998). Allgemeine Betriebswirtschaftslehre: umfassende Einführung aus managementorientierter Sicht. Wiesbaden, Gabler.

Admati, A. R., P. Pfleiderer and J. Zechner (1994). Large shareholder activism, risk sharing, and financial market equilibrium. in: Journal of Political Economy: 1097-1130.

Agrawal, A., J. F. Jaffe and G. N. Mandelker (1992). The post-merger performance of acquiring firms: a re-examination of an anomaly. in: Journal of Finance 47(4): 1605-1621.

Aguilera, R. V. and J. C. Dencker (2004). The role of human resource management in cross-border mergers and acquisitions. in: International Journal of Human Resource Management 15(8): 1355-1370.

Ahuja, G. and R. Katila (2001). Technological acquisitions and the innovation performance of acquiring firms: a longitudinal study. in: Strategic Management Journal 22: 197-220.

Ainina, M. F. and N. K. Mohan (1991). When LBOs go IPO. in: Journal of Business Finance & Accounting 18(3): 393-398.

Alchian, A. A. and H. Demsetz (1972). Production, information costs, and economic organization. in: American Economic Review 62: 775-795.

Allen, R. J. (1999). LBOs - The evolution of financial structures and strategies. in: The New Corporate Finance: Where theory meets practice: 708-719.

Altinay, L. and M. Altinay (2004). The influence of organisational structure on entrepreneurial orientation and expansion performance. in: International Journal of Contemporary Hospitality Management 16(6): 334-344.

Alvarez, S. and L. W. Busenitz (2001). The entrepreneurship of resource-based theory. in: Journal of Management 27: 755-775.

Ambrose, B. and D. Winters (1992). Does an industry effect exist for leveraged buyouts? in: Financial Management Spring: 89-101.

Amess, K. (2002). Management buyouts and firm-level productivity: evidence from a panel of UK manufacturing firms. in: Scottish Journal of Political Economy 49(3): 304-317.

Amihud, Y. and B. Lev (1981). Risk reduction as a managerial motive for conglomerate merger. in: Bell Journal of Economics 12: 605-617.

Amihud, Y. and B. Lev (1999). Does corporate ownership structure affect its strategy towards diversification? in: Strategic Management Journal 20: 1063-1069.

Amit, R. and J. H. P. Schoemaker (1993). Strategic assets and organizational rent. in: Strategic Management Journal 14: 33-46.

Anand, J., Capron, L., Mitchell, W. (2005). Using acquisitions to access multinational diversity: thinking beyond the domestic versus cross-border M&A comparison. in: Industrial and Corporate Change 14(2): 191-224.

Anderson, C. and C. Zeithaml (1984). Stage of product life cycle, business strategy and business performance. in: Academy of Management Journal 27(1): 5-24.

Ang, J. S. and J. C. Brau (2002). Firm transparency and the costs of going public. in: Journal of Financial Research 25(1): 1-17.

Anslinger, P. and T. Copeland (1996). Growth through acquistions: A fresh look. in: The McKinsey Quarterly 2: 97-109.

Ansoff, I. (1957). Strategies for diversification. in: Harvard Business Review: 113-124.

Anthony, R. N., J. Dearden and V. Govindarajan (1992). Management control systems. New York, McGraw-Hill/Irwin.

Arbaugh, J. B. (2003). Outsourcing intensity, strategy, and growth in entrepreneurial firms. in: Journal of Enterprising Culture 11(2): 89-110.

Arrow, K. (1985). The economics of agency. in: Principal and agents. J. Pratt and D. Zeckhauser. Eds.: 37 - 51.

Arzac, E. (1992). On the capital structure of leveraged buyouts. in: Journal of Financial Management: 16-26.

Asquith, P. (1983). Mergers bids, uncertainty, and stockholder returns. in: Journal of Financial Economics 11: 51-83.

Audretsch, D. (1995). Innovation, growth and survival. in: International Journal of Industrial Organization 13: 441-457.

Bacon, N., M. Wright and N. Demina (2004). Management buyouts and human resource management. in: British Journal of Industrial Relations 42(2): 325-347.

Baker, G., M. C. Jensen and K. J. Murphy (1988). Compensation and incentives: practice vs. theory. in: Journal of Finance 43(3): 593-616.

Baker, G. and C. Montgomery (1994). Conglomerates and LBO Associations: A Comparison of Organizational Forms. in: Harvard Business School: 1-27.

Baker, G. and G. Smith (1998). The new financial capitalists.

Baker, G. and G. Smith (2000). Leveraged management buy-outs at KKR: historical perspectives on private equity, debt disciplines, and LBO governance. in: Private Equity and Venture Capital: a practical guide for investors and practitioners. R. Lake. Eds. London, Euromoney Institutional Investor PLC: 93-106.

Baker, G. and K. Wruck (1989). Organizational changes and value creation in leveraged buyouts. in: Journal of Financial Economics 25: 163 - 190.

Baker, M. and P. Gompers (2003). The determinants of board structure at the initial public offering. in: Journal of Law and Economics 66: 569-598.

Balakrishnan, S. and I. Fox (1993). Asset specifity, firm heterogeneity and capital structure. in: Strategic Management Journal 14(1): 3-16.

Ballwieser, W. and H. Schmid (1990a). Charakteristika und Problembereiche von Management Buy-Outs - Teil 1. in: WISU 5: 299-305.

Ballwieser, W. and H. Schmid (1990b). Charakteristika und Problembereiche von Management Buy-Outs - Teil 2. in: WISU 6: 358-364.

Bannock, G. (1990). The economic impact of management buy-outs. 3i Group.

Barclay, M. J. and S. C.W. (1995). The maturity structure of corporate debt. in: Journal of Finance 50(2): 609-631.

Barker, V. L. and I. M. Duhaime (1997). Strategic change in the turnaround process: theory and empirical evidence. in: Strategic Management Journal 18: 13-38.

Barney, J. (1991). Firm resources and sustained competitive advantage. in: Journal of Management 17(1): 99 - 120.

Barney, J., L. W. Busenitz, J. O. Fiet, et al. (1994). The relationship between venture capitalists and managers in new firms: determinants of contractual covenants. in: Journal of Managerial Finance 20(1): 19-30.

Barney, J., M. Wright and D. Ketchen (2001). The resource-based view of the firm: ten years after 1991. in: Journal of Management 27: 625-641.

Barontini, R. and L. Caprio (2005). The effect of family control on firm value and performance. Evidence from Continental Europe. in: Finance Working Paper 88: 1-53.

Barringer, B. and A. Bluedorn (1999). The relationship between corporate entrepreneurship and strategic management. in: Strategic Management Journal 20: 421-444.

Barton, S. L. and P. J. Gordon (1987). Corporate strategy: useful perspective for the study of capital structure. in: Academy of Management Review 12(1): 67-75.

Barton, S. L. and P. J. Gorton (1988). Corporate strategy and capital structure. in: Strategic Management Journal 9(6): 623-632.

Bassen, A., M. Kleinschmidt and C. Zöllner (2004). Corporate governance quality study 2004. in: Finanzbetrieb 7: 527-533.

Baysinger, B. and R. Hoskisson (1989). Diversification strategy and R&D intensity in multiproduct firms. in: Academy of Management Journal 32(2): 310-332.

Baysinger, B. and R. E. Hoskisson (1990). The composition of boards of directors and strategic control: effects on corporate strategy. in: Academy of Management Review 15(1): 72-87.

Baysinger, B., R. Kosnik and T. Turk (1991). Effects of board and ownership structure on corporate r&d strategy. in: Academy of Management Journal 34(1): 205-214.

Beatty, R. and J. R. Ritter (1986). Investment banking, reputation and the underpricing of initial public offerings. in: Journal of Financial Economics 15: 213-232.

Beatty, R. P. and E. J. Zajac (1994). Managerial incentives, monitoring, and risk bearing: a study of executive compensation, ownership, and board structure in initial public offerings. in: Administrative Science Quarterly 39: 313-335.

Bebchuk, L. and M. Roe (1999). A theory of path dependence on corporate ownership and governance. in: Stanford Law Review 52: 127-169.

Becht, M. (1999). European corporate governance: trading off liquidity against control. in: European Economic Review 43: 1071-1083.

Becht, M. and E. Boehmer (2003). Voting control in German corporations. in: International Review of Law and Economics 23: 1-29.

Becker, R. (2000). Buy-Outs in Deutschland. Köln, Deutscher Wirtschaftsdienst.

Begley, J. and G. A. Feltham (1999). An empirical examination of the relation between debt contracts and management incentives. in: Journal of Accounting and Economics 27: 229-259.

Bekier, M., A. Bogardus and T. Oldham (2001). Why mergers fail. in: McKinsey Quarterly 4(6-10).

Belkaoui, A. and E. Pavlik (1992). The effects of ownership structure and diversification strategy on performance. in: Managerial and Decision Economics 13: 343-352.

Berens, W., H. U. Brauner and J. Frodermann (2005). Unternehmensentwicklung mit Finanz-Investoren. Stuttgart, Schäffer-Poeschel.

Berger, P., E. Ofek and D. Yermack (1997). Managerial Entrenchment and Capital Structure Decisions. in: Journal of Finance 42(4): 1411-1438.

Berger, P. G. and E. Ofek (1999). Causes and effect of corporate refocusing programs. in: Review of Financial Studies 12(2): 311-345.

Berle, A. A. and G. C. Means (1932). The modern corporate and private property. New York, Macmilian.

Bethel, J. E. and J. P. Liebeskind (1993). The effects of ownership structure on corporate restructuring. in: Strategic Management Journal 14: 15-31.

Bethel, J. E., J. P. Liebeskind and T. Opler (1998). Block share purchases and corporate performance. in: Journal of Finance 53(2): 605-634.

Bettis, R., S. Bradley and G. Hamel (1992). Outsourcing and industrial decline. in: Academy of Management Executive 6(1): 7-22.

Bettis, R. and C. Prahalad (1995). The dominant logic: retrospective and extension. in: Strategic Management Journal 16: 5-14.

Bhagat, S., A. Shleifer and R. Vishny (1990). Hostile takeovers in the 1980s: The return to corporate specialization. in: Brooking Papers: 1-72.

Bhagat, S. and I. Welch (1995). Corporate research & development investments - international comparisons. in: Journal of Accounting and Economics 19: 443-470.

Bhide, A. (1990). Revising corporate diversification. in: Journal of Applied Corporate Finance 2(2): 36-59.

Birley, S., D. Muzyka and M. Hay (1999). Management buyout: perception of opportunity - a research note. in: Journal of Management Studies 36: 109-122.

Black, F. and M. Scholes (1973). The pricing of options and corporate liabilities. in: Journal of Political Economy 81(3): 637-654.

Blair, M. (1995). Rethinking assumptions behind corporate governance. in: Challenge: 12-17.

Blair, M., Schary, M.A. (1993). Industry level pressure to restructure. in: The deal decade. M. Blair. Eds. Washington, D.C., Brookings Institution: 149-190.

Block, Z. and I. C. MacMillan (1993). Corporate venturing - creating new businesses within the firm. Cambridge, MA, Harvard Business School Press.

Blonigen, B. A. and C. T. Taylor (2000). R&D intensity and acquisitions in high-technology industries: evidence from the US electronic and electrical equipment industries. in: Journal of Industrial Economics 48(1): 47-70.

Böhmer, E. (1998). Business groups, bank control, and large shareholders: An analysis of German takeovers. Working paper.

Böhmer, E. and A. Ljungqvist (2005). On the decision to go-public: evidence from privately-held firms, Deutsche Bundesbank discussion paper.

Böhmer, E. and Y. Löffler (1999). Kursrelevante Ereignisse bei Unternehmensübernahmen: eine empirische Analyse des deutschen Kapitalmarktes. in: Zeitschrift für betriebswirtschaftliche Forschung 51: 299-324.

Booth, J. R. and L. Chua (1996). Ownership dispersion, costly information, and IPO underpricing. in: Journal of Financial Economics 1996(291-310).

Bower, J. L. (2001). Not all M&As are alike and that matters. in: Harvard Business Review March: 93-101.

Bowman, E. and H. Singh (1993). Corporate Restructuring: reconfiguring the firm. in: Strategic Management Journal 14: 5-14.

Bowman, E. H., H. Singh, M. Useem, et al. (1999). When does restructuring improve economic performance? in: California Management Review 41(2): 33-54.

Bradley, M., A. Desai and E. H. Kim (1983). The rationale behind interfirm tender offers: information or synergy? in: Journal of Financial Economics 11: 183-206.

Bradley, M., A. Desai and E. H. Kim (1988). Synergistic gains from corporate acquisitions and their division between the stockholders of target and acquiring firms. in: Journal of Financial Economics 21: 3-40.

Bradley, M. and G. Jarrell (1988). Comment. in: Knights, raiders and targets. J. Coffee, L. Lowenstein and S. Rose-Ackerman. Eds. Oxford, Oxford University Press: 283-318.

Bradley, M. and A. Najed (1989). Managing owners: the national freight consortium in perspective. Cambridge, Cambridge University Press.

Brau, J. C., B. Francis and N. Kohers (2003). The choice of IPO versus takeover: empirical evidence. in: Journal of Business 76(4): 583-612.

Brav, A. and P. Gompers (1997). Myth or Reality? The Long-Run Underperformance of Initial Public Offerings: Evidence from Venture and Nonventure Capital-Backed. in: Journal of Finance 52(5): 1791-1821.

Brennan, M. J. and J. Franks (1997). Underpricing, ownership and control in initial public offerings of equity securities in the UK. in: Journal of Financial Economics 45: 391-413.

Bruining, H., M. Bonnet and M. Wright (2003). Management control systems and strategy change in buyouts. Working paper.

Bruining, H. and M. Wright (2002). Entrepreneurial orientation in management buy-outs and the contribution of venture capital. in: Venture Capital 4(2): 147-168.

Bruining, H. and M. Wright (2005). Entrepreneurial orientation in management buy-outs and the contribution of venture capital. Working paper.

Bruner, R. F. (2001). Does M&A pay? A survey of evidence for the decision-maker. Darden working paper.

Bruning, H. and E. Verwaal (2005). Are they really more entrepreneurial? Working paper: 1-32.

Brush, C., P. Greene and M. Hart (2001). From initial idea to unique advantage: The entrepreneurial challenge of constructing a resource base. in: Academy of Management Executive 15(1): 64-80.

Bruton, G., J. Keels and E. Scifres (2002). Corporate restructuring and performance: An agency perspective on the complete buyout cycle. in: Journal of Business Research 55: 709-724.

Bruton, G. D., J. K. Keels and E. Scifres (1999). The ethics of the complete management buyout cycle: a multi-perspective analysis. in: Journal of Business Ethics 19: 403-413.

Bruton, G. D. and E. Scifres (1992). Leveraged buyouts: their impact on r&d spending. in: Management International Review 32: 7-21.

Bryan, S., L. Hwang and S. Lilien (2000). CEO stock-based compensation: an empirical analysis of incentive-intensity, relative mix, and economic determinants. in: Journal of Business 73(4): 661-693.

Bühner, R. (1990). Erfolg von Unternehmenszusammenschlüssen in der Bundesrepublik Deutschland. Stuttgart.

Bühner, R. (1992). Aktionärsbeurteilung grenzüberschreitender Zusammenschlüsse. in: Zeitschrift für betriebswirtschaftliche Forschung 44: 445-459.

Bull, I. (1989a). Financial performance of leveraged buyouts: an empirical analysis. in: Journal of Business Venturing 4: 263-279.

Bull, I. (1989b). Management performance in leveraged buyouts: An empirical analysis. in: Leveraged management buyouts: causes and consequences. Y. Amihud. Eds. Homewood, Dow Jones-Irwin: 69-94.

Bundesbank, D. (2006). Monatsbericht Dezember 2006 - Zur wirtschaftlichen Situation kleiner und mittlerer Unternehmen in Deutschland seit 1997. Frankfurt.

Burgelman, R. and M. A. Maidique (1988). Strategic management of technology and innovation. Homewood, IL, Irwin.

Burger-Calderon, M. (2005). Strukturwandel durch Private Equity. in: Financial Yearbook Germany. EVCA. Eds. Munich: 47-50.

Busaba, W. Y., L. M. Benveniste and R.-J. Guo (2001). The option to withdraw IPOs during the premarket: empirical analysis. in: Journal of Financial Economics 60: 73-102.

Bushee, B. J. (1998). The influence of institutional investors on myopic r&d investment behavior. in: Accounting Review 73(3): 305-333.

BVK (2004a). BVK Statistik 2003: Das Jahr 2003 in Zahlen, BVK.

BVK (2004b). BVK Statistik 2003 - Buyouts 2003 in Zahlen, BVK.

BVK (2005). BVK Statistik 2004 - Buyouts 2004 in Zahlen, BVK.

BVK (2006a). BVK Statistik 2005 - Das Jahr 2005 in Zahlen, BVK.

BVK (2006b). BVK Statistik - Buyouts 2005 in Zahlen, BVK.

BVK (2007). BVK Statistik 2006 - Das Jahr 2006 in Zahlen, BVK.

BVK (2007). BVK Statistik - Buyouts 2006 in Zahlen, BVK.

Cable, J. R. (1985). Capital market information and industrial performance: the role of West German banks. in: Economic Journal 95: 118-132.

Cannella, A. and D. Hambrick (1993). Effects of executive departures on the performance of acquired firms. in: Strategic Management Journal 14: 137 - 152.

Capron, L. (1999). The long-term performance of horizontal acquisitions. in: Strategic Management Journal 20: 987 - 1018.

Capron, L., P. Dussauge and W. Mitchell (1998). Resource redeployment following horizontal acquisitions in Europe and North America. in: Strategic Management Journal 19: 631-661.

Capron, L., W. Mitchell and A. Swaminathan (2001). Asset divestiture following horizontal acquisitions: a dynamic view. in: Strategic Management Journal 22: 817-844.

Carleton, W. T., J. M. Nelson and M. S. Weisbach (1998). The influence of institutions on corporate governance through private negotiations: evidence from TIAA-CREF. in: Journal of Finance 53(4): 1335-1362.

Castanias, R. P. and C. E. Helfat (1991). Managerial resources and rents. in: Journal of Management 17(1): 155-171.

Castanias, R. P. and C. E. Helfat (2001). The managerial rents model: Theory and empirical analysis. in: Journal of Management 27: 661-678.

Chaplinsky, S., G. Niehaus and L. Van de Gucht (1998). Employee buyouts: causes, structure, and consequences. in: Journal of Financial Economics 48: 283-332.

Chemmanur, T. J. and P. Fulghieri (1994). Investment bank reputation, information production and financial intermediation. in: Journal of Finance 49: 57-79.

Chemmanur, T. J. and P. Fulghieri (1999). A theory of the going-public decision. in: Review of Financial Studies 12(2): 249-279.

Chemmanur, T. J., S. He and D. Nandy (2005). The going public decision and the product market, Working paper.

Chidambaran, N. K. and K. John (1998). Relationship investing. large shareholder monitoring with managerial compensation. Working paper.

Child, J., D. Faulkner and R. Pitkethly (2001). The management of international acquisitions. Oxford, Oxford University Press.

Christofferson, S., R. McNish and D. Sias (2004). Where mergers go wrong. in: The McKinsey Quarterly 2: 1-7.

Clark, K. and T. Fujimoto (1991). Product development performance: strategy, organization and management in the world auto industry. Boston MA, Harvard Business School Press.

Clementi, G. L. (2002). IPOs and the growth of firms, Working paper.

CMBOR (2002). European Management Buy-Out Review, Centre for Management Buyout and Research.

CMBOR (2006). European Management Buy-Out Review, Centre for Management Buyout Research.

Coles, J., M. Lemmon and F. Meschke (2002). Structural models and endogeneity in corporate finance: The link between managerial ownership and corporate performance. in: Working paper 1-51.

Conant, J., M. Mokwa and R. Varadarajan (1990). Strategic types, distinctive marketing competencies and organizational performance: A multiple measures-based study. in: Strategic Management Journal 11: 365-383.

Conner, K. (1991). A historical comparison of resource-based theory and five schools of thought within industrial organization economics: do we have a new theory of the firm? in: Journal of Management 17(1): 121-154.

Connor, K. and C. K. Prahalad (1996). A resource-based theory of the firm: knowledge versus opportunism. in: Organization Science 7(5): 477-501.

Cooper, A., J. Gimeno-Gascon and C. Woo (1994). Initial human and financial capital as predictors of new venture performance. in: Journal of Business Venturing 9: 371-395.

Core, J. E., R. W. Holthausen and D. F. Larcker (1999). Corporate governance, chief executive officer compensation, and firm performance. in: Journal of Financial Economics 51: 371-406.

Cotter, J. F. and S. W. Peck (2001). The structure of debt and active equity investors: the case of the buyout specialists. in: Journal of Financial Economics 59: 101-147.

Covin, J. G. and M. Miles (1999). Corporate entrepreneurship and the pursuit of competitive advantage. in: Entrepreneurship Theory & Practice 23(3): 47-63.

Covin, J. G. and D. P. Slevin (1989). Strategic management of small firms in hostile and benign environments. in: Strategic Management Journal 10: 75-87.

Covin, J. G. and D. P. Slevin (1990). New venture strategic posture, structure and performance: an industry life cycle analysis. in: Journal of Business Venturing 5: 123-135.

Covin, J. G. and D. P. Slevin (1991). A conceptual model of entrepreneurship as firm behavior. in: Entrepreneurship Theory & Practice 16: 7-25.

Daniels, H. v. (2004). Private Equity Secondary Transactions - Chancen und Grenzen des Aufbaus eines institutionalisierten Secondary Market. Rostock, Universitätsverlag.

Daniels, J. D. and J. Bracker (1989). Profit performance: do foreign operations make a difference? in: Management International Review 29(1): 46-56.

Dann, L. Y. and H. DeAngelo (1983). Standstill agreements, private negotiated stock repurchases, and the market for corporate control. in: Journal of Financial Economics: 275-300.

Darraugh, M. and S. Rangan (2005). Do insiders manipulate earnings when they sell their shares in an initial public offering? in: Journal of Accounting Research 43(1): 1-33.

DeAngelo, H. and L. DeAngelo (1987). Management buyouts of publicly trades corporations. in: Financial Analysts Journal 38-49.

DeAngelo, H., L. DeAngelo and E. Rice (1984). Going private: minority freezouts and stockholder wealth. in: Journal of Law & Economics 27: 367-401.

DeAngelo, L. (1986). Accounting numbers as market valuation substitutes: A study of management buyouts of public stockholders. in: The Accounting Review 31(3): 400-420.

DeGeorge, F. and R. Zeckhauser (1993). The reserve LBO decision and firm performance: Theory and evidence. in: Journal of Finance 48(4): 1323-1348.

Delaney, J. and M. Huselid (1996). The impact of human resource management practices on perceptions of organizational performance. in: Academy of Management Journal 39(4): 949-969.

Demsetz, H. (1964). The exchange and enforcement of property rights. in: Journal of Law & Economics 7: 11-26.

Demsetz, H. (1966). Some aspects of property rights. in: Journal of Law and Economics: 61-70.

Demsetz, H. (1967). Toward a theory of property rights. in: American Economic Review 57(2): 347-359.

Demsetz, H. (1983). The structure of ownership and the theory of the firm. in: Journal of Law & Economics 26: 375-390.

Demsetz, H. and K. Lehn (1985). The Structure of Corporate Ownership: Causes and Consequences. in: Journal of Political Economy 93(6): 1155-1177.

Demsetz, H. and B. Villalonga (2001). Ownership structure and corporate performance. in: Journal of Corporate Finance 7: 209-233.

Denis, D. J. and D. K. Denis (1993). Managerial discretion, organizational structure, and corporate performance. in: Journal of Accounting and Economics 16: 209-236.

Denis, D. J., D. K. Denis and A. Sarin (1997a). Agency problems, equity ownership, and corporate diversification. in: Journal of Finance 52(1): 135-160.

Denis, D. J., D. K. Denis and A. Sarin (1997b). Ownership structure and top executive turnover. in: Journal of Financial Economics 45: 193-221.

Dess, G., G. T. Lumpkin and J. Covin (1997). Entrepreneurial strategy making and firm performance: Tests of contingency and configurational models. in: Strategic Management Journal 18(9): 677-695.

Dess, G., G. T. Lumpkin and J. McGee (1999). Linking corporate entrepreneurship to Strategy, Structure, and Process: Suggested research directions. in: Entrepreneurship Theory & Practice: 85-102.

Dierickx, I. and K. Cool (1989). Asset stock accumulation and sustainability of competitive advantage. in: Management Science 35(12): 1504-1514.

Dollinger, M. J. (1999). Entrepreneurship strategies and resources. Upper Saddle River, NJ, Prentice Hall.

Domberger, S. (1998). The contracting organization: a strategic guide to outsourcing. Oxford, Oxford University Press.

Doty, H., W. Glick and G. Huber (1993). Fit, equifinality, and organizational effectiveness: A test of two configurational theories. in: Academy of Management Journal 36(6): 1196-1250.

Drobetz, W., M. Kammernmann and U. Waelchli (2005). Long-term performance of initial public offerings: the evidence for Switzerland. in: Schmalenbach Business Review 57: 253-275.

Drukarczyk, J. (1990). Management Buyouts. in: Wirtschaftswissenschaftliches Studium: 545-549.

Dutz, M. A. (1989). Horizontal mergers in declining industries. in: International Journal of Industrial Organization 7: 11-33.

Dyck, I. J. A. and L. Zingales (2002). Private benefits of control: an international comparison, CEPR discussion paper no. 3177.

Dyer, J. and H. Singh (1998). The relational view: Cooperative strategy and sources of interorganizational competitive advantage. in: Acadamy of Management Review 23(4): 660-679.

Easterwood, J. C. (1998). Divestments and financial distress in leveraged buyouts. in: Journal of Banking & Finance 22: 129-159.

Easterwood, J. C., V. Hsieh and R. Singer (1988). The motivation for going private. Working paper.

Easterwood, J. C., Seth, A. and R.F. Singer (1989). The impact of leveraged buyouts on strategic direction. in: California Management Review Fall 1989: 30 - 43.

Edwards, J. and J. Nibler (2000). Corporate governance in Germany: the role of banks and ownership concentration. in: Economic Policy 31: 237-260.

Edwards, J. and A. Weichenrieder (1999). Ownership concentration and share valuation. CESifo Working Paper: 1-39.

Edwards, J. S. S. and K. Fischer (1994). Banks, finance and investment in Germany. Cambridge, Cambridge University Press.

Ehrhardt, O. and E. Nowak (2003). The effects of IPOs on German family-owned firms: governance changes, ownership structure, and performance. in: Journal of Small Business Management 41(2): 222-232.

Ehrhardt, O. and E. Nowak (2003). Private benefits and minority shareholder expropriation. Working paper: 1-56.

Eisenhardt, K. (1989a). Agency theory: An assessment and review. in: Acadamy of Management Review 14(1): 57-74.

Eisenhardt, K. (1989b). Building theories from case study research. in: Acadamy of Management Review 14(4): 532-550.

Eisenhardt, K. and J. Martin (2000). Dynamic capabilities: what are they? in: Strategic Management Journal 21: 1105-1121.

Elston, J. A. and L. G. Goldberg (2003). Executive compensation and agency costs in Germany. in: Journal of Banking & Finance 27: 1391-1410.

Engel, E., E. A. Gordon and R. M. Hayes (2002). The roles of performing measures and monitoring in annual governance decisions in entrepreneurial firms. in: Journal of Accounting Research 40(2): 485-518.

Epplin, M. P. and H. Pourjalali (1997). Industry concentration and cyclicality of cash flows in leveraged buyouts. in: American Business Review January: 15-25.

Ernst and Young (2005). German Private Equity activity.

EVCA (2001). Survey of the economics and social impact of management buyouts & buyins in Europe. Research paper, EVCA.

EVCA (2004). Debt financing structures. EVCA Tax & Legal committee paper.

EVCA (2005). Private equity and generational change - the contribution of private equity to the succession of family businesses in Europe. EVCA buyout committee paper.

Faccio, M. and L. Lang (2002). The ultimate ownership of Western European corporations. in: Journal of Financial Economics 65: 365-395.

Fama, E. (1978). The effects of a firm's investment and financing decisions on the welfare of its security holders. in: American Economic Review 68(3): 272-284.

Fama, E. (1980). Agency Problems and the theory of the firm. in: Journal of Political Economy 88(2): 288-307.

Fama, E. (1991). Efficient Capital Markets: 2. in: Journal of Finance 46(5): 1575-1617.

Fama, E. and M. Jensen (1983). Separation of ownership and control. in: Journal of Law & Economics 26: 301-325.

Farrell, D. (2004). Beyond offshoring: assess your company's global potential. in: Harvard Business Review December: 82-90.

Fast, N. D. (1981). Pitfalls of corporate venturing. in: Research Management March: 21-24.

Feinendegen, S., U. Hommel and M. Wright (2001). Stand der Beteiligungskapitalfinanzierung in Deutschland. in: Finanzbetrieb 10: 569 - 578.

Fenn, G. W., Liang, N. and S. Prowse (1995). The economics of the private equity market. in: 1 - 69.

FINANCE-Studies (2005). Economic impact of Private Equity in Germany, Deutsche Beteiligungs AG, Finance.

Fine, C. H. (1983). Quality control and learning in productive systems. Unpublished doctoral dissertation.

FitzRoy, F. R. and J. Schwalbach (1990). Managerial compensation and firm performance: Some evidence from West Germany. WZB, discussion paper FS IV 90-20.

Forbes, D. and F. Milliken (1999). Cognition and corporate governance: Understanding boards of directors as strategic decision-making groups. in: Academy of Management Review 24(3): 489-505.

Forst, M. (1992). Management Buy-Out und Buy-in als Form der Übernahme mittelständischer Unternehmen. Stuttgart.

Foster, R. N. and S. Kaplan (2001). Creative destruction: why companies are built to last underperform the market - and how to successfully transform them. New York, Doubleday.

Fox, I. and A. Marcus (1992). The causes and consequences of leveraged management buyouts. in: Academy of Management Review 17(1): 62-85.

Francis, J. and A. J. Smith (1995). Agency costs and innovation - some empirical evidence. in: Journal of Accounting and Economics 19: 383-409.

Frank, M. and V. Goyal (2003). Capital structure decisions. in: Working paper: 1-55.

Frankfurter, G. and E. Gunay (1992). Management buy-outs: The sources and sharing of wealth between insiders and outside shareholders. in: Quarterly Review of Economics and Finance 32(3): 82-95.

Franko, L. (1989). Global corporate competition: who's winning, who's losing, and the r&d factor as one reason why. in: Strategic Management Journal 10: 449-474.

Franks, J., R. Harris and S. Titman (1991). The post-merger share performance of acquiring firms. in: Journal of Financial Economics 5: 351-373.

Franks, J. and C. Mayer (1990). Capital markets and corporate control: a study of France, Germany and UK. in: Economic Policy 10: 191-230.

Franks, J. and C. Mayer (1994). The market for corporate control in Germany. in: London Business School working paper.

Franks, J. and C. Mayer (2001). Ownership and control of German corporations. in: Review of Financial Studies 14(4): 943-977.

Frick, B. and E. Lehmann (2004). Corporate governance in Germany: problems and prospects. in: Corporate governance and human resource management. H. Gospel and H. Pendleton. Eds. Oxford, Oxford University Press.

Friend, I. and L. Lang (1988). An empirical test of the impact of managerial self-interest on corporate capital structure. in: Journal of Finance 43(2): 271-281.

Gedajlovic, E. and D. Shapiro (1998). Management and Ownership effects: Evidence from five countries. in: Strategic Management Journal 19: 533-553.

Gerke, W., Garz, H.,Oerke, M. (1995). Die Bewertung von Unternehmensübernahmen auf dem deutschen Aktienmarkt. in: Zeitschrift für betriebswirtschaftliche Forschung 47: 805-820.

Ghosh, A. (2001). Does operating performance really improve following corporate acquisitions? in: Journal of Corporate Finance 7: 151-178.

Gibbs, P. A. (1993). Determinants of corporate restructuring: the relative importance of corporate governance, takeover threat, and free cash flow. in: Strategic Management Journal 14(51-68).

Gillan, S. L., J. Kensinger and J. Martin (2000). Value Creation and corporate diversification: The case of Sears, Roebuck & Co. in: Journal of Financial Economics 55(1): 103-137.

Gillan, S. L. and L. T. Starks (1998). A survey of shareholder activism: motivation and empirical evidence. Working paper.

Gillan, S. L. and L. T. Starks (2003). Corporate governance, corporate ownership, and the role of institutional investors: a global perspective. Working Paper Series.

Gilley, K. M., J. E. McGee and A. Rasheed (2004). Perceived environmental dynamism and managerial risk aversion as antecedents of manufacturing outsourcing: The moderating effects of firm maturity. in: Journal of Small Business Management 42(2): 117-133.

Gilley, K. M. and A. Rasheed (2000). Making more by doing less: an analysis of outsourcing and its effect on firm performance. in: Journal of Management 26(4): 763-790.

Gilson, S. C. and M. R. Vetsuypens (1993). CEO compensation in financially distressed firms: an empirical analysis. in: Journal of Finance 58(2): 425-458.

Goergen, M., M. Manjon and L. Renneboog (2004). Recent Developments in German Corporate Governance. in: Finance Working Paper 41: 1-46.

Goergen, M. J. (1997). Does ownership matter? A study of German and UK IPOs. Working paper.

Gomes, L. and K. Ramaswarny (1999). An empirical examination of the form of the relationship between multinationality and performance. in: Journal of International Business Studies 30(1): 173-187.

Gompers, P. (1996). Grandstanding in the venture capital industry. in: Journal of Financial Economics 42: 133-156.

Goold, M. and J. J. Quinn (1990). The paradox of strategic controls. in: Strategic Management Journal 11(1): 43-57.

Goosen, C. J., T. J. de Coning and E. Smit (2002). Corporate entrepreneurship and financial performance: The role of management. in: S. Afr. Journal Business Management 33(4): 21-27.

Gorton, G. and F. Schmid (2000). Universal banking and the performance of German firms. in: Journal of Financial Economics 58: 29-80.

Govindarajan, V. (1988). A contingency approach to strategy implementation at the business-unit level: integrating administrative mechanisms with strategy. in: Academy of Management Journal 31(8): 828-853.

Graebner, U. (1991). Die Auseinandersetzung um Leveraged Buyouts. Frankfurt am Main, Fritz Knapp Verlag.

Grant, R. (1991). The resource-based theory of competitive advantage: implications for strategy formulation. in: California Management Review: 114-135.

Grant, R. (1996). Toward a knowledge-based Theory of the Firm. in: Strategic Management Journal 17: 109-122.

Grant, R. M. (1987). Multinationality and performance among British manufacturing companies. in: Journal of International Business Studies 18(3): 79-89.

Gräper, M. (1993). Management Buy-Out. Kiel, Wissenschaftsverlag Vauk Kiel

Graves, S. B. (1988). Institutional ownership and corporate r&d in the computer industry. in: Academy of Management Journal 31(2): 417-428.

Green, R. C. (1984). Investment incentives, debt and warrants. in: Journal of Financial Economics 13: 115-136.

Green, S. (1992). The Impact of ownership and capital structure on managerial motivation and strategy in management buy-outs: A cultural analysis. in: Journal of Management Studies 29(4): 513-535.

Greenwood, R., C. R. Hinings and J. Brown (1994). Merging professional service firms. in: Organization Science 5(2): 239-257.

Gros, S. (1998). Das Management-Buyout-Konzept als Instrument der Unternehmensprivatisierung bei der Transformation einer Planwirtschaft in eine Marktwirtschaft. Frankfurt am Main.

Grossman, S. J. and O. D. Hart (1981). Implicit contracts, moral hazard, and unemployment. in: American Economic Review 61: 301-307.

Grossman, S. J. and O. D. Hart (1983). Implicit contacts under assymmetric information. in: Quarterly Journal of Economics 98: 123-156.

Grossman, S. J. and O. D. Hart (1987). One share one vote and the market for corporate control. in: MIT working paper.

Grossman, W. and R. E. Hoskisson (1998). CEO pay at the crossroad of Wall Street and Main: toward the strategic design of executive compensation. in: Academy of Management Review 12(1): 43-57.

Gucht van de, L. and W. Moore (1998). Predicting the duration and reversal probability of leveraged buyouts. in: Journal of Empirical Finance 5: 299-315.

Guercio, D. D. and J. Hawkins (1999). The motivation and impact of pension fund activism. in: Journal of Financial Economics 52: 293-340.

Guth, W. and A. Grinsberg (1990). Guest editors' introduction: Corporate entrepreneurship. in: Strategic Management Journal 11: 5-15.

Hall, B. H. (1990). The impact of corporate restructuring on industrial research and development. in: Brookings Papers on Economic Activity 1: 85-136.

Hall, B. H. (1992). Investment and research and development at the firm level: does the source of financing matter? NBER working paper.

Hall, W. (1980). Survival strategies in a hostile environment. in: Harvard Business Review: 75-85.

Halpern, P., R. Kieschnick and W. Rotenberg (1999). On the heterogeneity of leveraged going private transactions. in: The Review of Financial Studies 12(2): 281-309.

Hambrick, D. (1983). Some tests of the effectiveness and functional attributes of Miles and Snow´s strategic types. in: Academy of Management Journal 26(1): 5-26.

Hambrick, D. and A. A. Cannella (1993). Relative standing: a framework for understanding departures of acquired executives. in: Academy of Management Journal 36(4): 733-762.

Hambrick, D. and S. Schecter (1983). Turnaround strategies for mature industrial-product business units. in: Academy of Management Journal 26(2): 231-248.

Hamel, G., Y. L. Doz and C. Prahalad (1989). Collaborate with your competitors - and win. in: Harvard Business Review January -February: 133-139.

Hamel, G. and C. K. Prahalad (1985). Do you really have a global strategy? in: Harvard Business Review July-August(139-148).

Hanney, J. (1986). The management buy-out - an offer you can't refuse. in: Omega International Journal of Management Science 14(2): 119-134.

Harlow, W. V. and J. S. Howe (1993). Leveraged buyouts and insider nontrading. in: Financial Management Spring: 109-118.

Harris, R., D. Siegel and M. Wright (2002). Assessing the impact of management buyouts on economic efficiency: Plant-level evidence from the United Kingdom. Working paper.

Harrison, J. S., M. A. Hitt, R. E. Hoskisson, et al. (1991). Synergies and post-acquisition performance: differences versus similarities in resource allocations. in: Journal of Management 17(1): 173-190.

Hart, O. (1995). Corporate governance: some theory and implications. in: The Economic Journal 105: 678-689.

Hartman, R., D. J. Teece, W. Mitchell, et al. (1994). Assessing market power in regimes of rapid technological progress. in: Industrial and Corporate Change 2(3): 317-350.

Hatherly, D., J. Innes, J. Macandrew, et al. (1994). An exploration of the MBO-financier relationship. in: Research Papers 2(1): 20-29.

Healy, P. M., K. G. Palepu and R. S. Ruback (1992). Does corporate performance improve after mergers? in: Journal of Financial Economics 31: 133-175.

Heel, J. and C. Kehoe (2005a). Why some private equity firms do better than others. in: The McKinsey Quarterly 1: 24-26.

Heel, J. and C. Kehoe (2005b). General partners performance, McKinsey & Company.

Heflebower, R. B. (1963). Corporate mergers: policy and economic analysis. in: Quarterly Journal of Economics 77(4): 537-558.

Heidrick and Struggles (2001). Corporate governance 2001 report.

Heidrick and Struggles (2007). Corporate governance 2007 report: raising the bar

Heidrick and Struggles (2007). Corporate governance in Europe - 2007 report. in.

Hellwig, M. (2000). On the economics and politics of corporate finance and corporate control. in: Corporate governance. X. Vives. Eds. Cambridge, Cambridge University Press: 95-134.

Helwege, J. and F. Packer (2003). The decision to go public: evidence from mandatory SEC filings from private firms. Working paper.

Hermalin, B. E. and M. S. Weisbach (2003). Boards of directors as an endogenously determined institution: a survey of the economic literature. in: Economic Policy Review April: 7-26.

Hill, C. and S. Snell (1989). Effects of ownership structure and control on corporate productivity. in: Academy of Management Journal 32(1): 25-46.

Hill, C. W. L. (1988). Differentiation versus low cost or differentiation and low cost: a contingency framework. in: Academy of Management Review 13(3): 401-412.

Hite, G. L. and M. R. Vetsuypens (1989). Management buyouts of divisions and shareholder wealth. in: Journal of Finance 46(4): 953-970.

Hitt, M., R. Hoskisson and H. Kim (1997). International diversification: Effects on innovation and firm performance in product-diversified firms. in: Academy of Management Journal 40(4): 767-798.

Hitt, M. A., Hoskisson, R.E. and R.D. Ireland (1990). Mergers and acquisitions and managerial commitment to innovation in m-form firms. in: Strategic Management Journal 11: 29 - 47.

Hitt, M. A., Hoskisson, R.E., Ireland, R.D. and J.S. Harrison (1991). Effects of acquisitions on r&d inputs and outputs. in: Academy of Management Journal 34(3): 693-706.

Hofer, C. W. (1980). Turnaround strategies. in: Journal of Business Strategy 1(1): 19-31.

Hoffmann, N. (2008). German buyouts adopting a buy-and-build strategy. Wiesbaden.

Hoffmann, P. and R. Ranke (1990). Management Buy-Out in der Bundesrepublik Deutschland. Berlin.

Hohaus, B. and P. Braunschweig (2006). The role MEPs play in German leveraged buyouts. in: International Financial Law Review 25: 33-36.

Holderness, C. G. and D. P. Sheehan (1988). The role of majority shareholders in publicly held corporations. in: Journal of Financial Economics 20: 317-346.

Holmstrom, B. (1989). Agency costs and innovation. in: Journal of Economic Behavior and Organization 12: 305-327.

Holmstrom, B. and S. Kaplan (2001). Corporate governance and merger activity in the U.S: Making sense of the 1980s and 1990s in: Journal of Economic Perspectives 15(2): 121-144.

Holthausen, R. and D. Larcker (1996). The financial performance of reserve leveraged buyouts. in: Journal of Financial Economics 42: 293-332.

Horwitz, F. M., K. Anderssen, A. Bezuidenhout, et al. (2002). Due diligence neglected: managing human resources and organisational culture in mergers and acquisitions. in: South African Journal of Business Management 33(1): 1-10.

Hoskisson, R., R. Johnson and D. Moesel (1994). Corporate divestiture intensity in restructuring firms: effects of governance, strategy, and performance. in: Academy of Management Journal 37(5): 1207-1251.

Hoskisson, R. and T. Turk (1990). Corporate Restructuring: Governance and Control Limits of the Internal Capital Market. in: Academy of Management Review 15(3): 459-477.

Hoskisson, R. O. and R. A. Johnson (1992). Corporate restructuring and strategic change: the effect on diversification strategy and r&d intensity. in: Strategic Management Journal 13(8): 625-634.

Huselid, M. (1997). The impact of high performance work systems, implementations, effectiveness, and alignment with strategy on shareholder wealth. in: Acadamy of Management Proceedings: 144-148.

Jain, B. and O. Kini (1994). The post-issue operating performance of IPO firms. in: Journal of Finance 49(5): 1699-1726.

Jakoby, S. (2000). Erfolgsfaktoren von Management Buyouts in Deutschland. Köln.

Jalilvand, A., S. M. Stewart and J. A. Switzer (1996). A synthesis on investment banker reputation and pricing of initial public offerings: new evidence on reverse LBOs. in: Financial Markets, Institutions & Instruments 5(5): 37-61.

Jalilvand, A. and J. Switzer (2002). Operating and financial performance of reverse LBOs: Evidence from the 1990s. in: Working Paper: 1-22.

James, B. (1974). The Theory of the Corporate Life Cycle. in: Long Range Planning: 49-55.

Januszewski, S., J. Köke and J. Winter (2002). Product market competition, corporate governance and firm performance: an empirical analysis for Germany. in: Research in Economics 56(3): 299-332.

Jaskiewicz, P., V. M. Gonzalez, S. Menendez, et al. (2005). Long-run IPO performance analysis of German and Spanish family-owned businesses. in: Family Business Review 18(3): 179-202.

Jelic, R., B. Saadouni and M. Wright (2005). Performance of private to public MBOs: The role of venture capital. in: Journal of Business Finance & Accounting 32(3 & 4): 643-681.

Jennings, D. and K. Hindle (2004). Corporate entrepreneurship and equifinality: An empirical analysis of strategy-structure-performance. in: Acadamy of Management Best Conference Paper: 1-6.

Jensen, M. C. (1986). Agency costs of free cash flow, corporate finance, and takeovers. in: The Market for Corporate Control 76(m): 323-329.

Jensen, M. C. (1989a). Eclipse of the public corporation. in: Harvard Business Review September-October: 1-29.

Jensen, M. C. (1989c). Active investors, LBOs, and the privatization of bankruptcy. in: Journal of Applied Corporate Finance 2(1): 35-44.

Jensen, M. C. and W. Meckling (1976). Theory of the firm: Managerial Behavior agency costs and ownership structure. in: Journal of Financial Economics 3(4): 305-360.

Jensen, M. C. and K. J. Murphy (1990). Performance pay and top-management incentives. in: Journal of Political Economy 98(2): 225-264.

Jensen, M. C. and R. S. Ruback (1983). The market for corporate control. in: Journal of Financial Economics 11: 5-50.

Jensen, M. C., D. P. Solberg and T. S. Zorn (1992). Simultaneous determination of insider ownership, debt, and dividend policies. in: Journal of Financial and Quantitative Analysis 27: 247-263.

Jeris, L. S., J. R. Johnson and C. C. Anthony (2002). HRD involvement in merger and acquisition decisions and strategy development: four organizational portraits. in: International Journal of Training and Development 6(1): 2-12.

Johanson, J. and J.-E. Vahlne (1990). The mechanism of internationalisation. in: The Internationalisation of Business: Theory and Evidence 7(4): 11-24.

John, K. and S. Kedia (2002). Design of corporate governance. Working paper.

John, T. A. and K. John (1993). Top-management compensation and capital structure. in: Journal of Finance 48(3): 949-974.

Johnson, R., R. Hoskisson and M. Hitt (1993). Board of director involvement in restructuring: The Effects of Board versus Managerial Controls and Characteristics. in: Strategic Management Journal 14: 33-50.

Johnson, S. (1997). An empirical analysis of the determination of corporate debt ownership structure. in: Journal of Financial and Quantitative Analysis 32(1): 47-69.

Jones, C. S. (1985). An empirical study of the role of management accounting systems following takeover or merger. in: Accounting, Organizations and Society 10(2): 177-200.

Jones, C. S. (1986). Organizational change and the functioning of accounting. in: Journal of Business Finance & Accounting 13(3): 283-310.

Jones, C. S. (1992). The attitudes of owner-managers towards accounting control systems following management buyouts. in: Accounting, Organizations and Society 17(2): 131-168.

Jugel, S. (2003). Private Equity Investments: Praxis des Beteiligungsmanagements. Wiesbaden.

Kakabadse, N. and A. Kakabadse (2000). Critical review - outsourcing: a paradigm shift. in: Journal of Management Development 19(8): 670-728.

Kang, J. and A. Shivdasani (1995). Firm performance, corporate governance, and top executive turnover in Japan. in: Journal of Financial Economics 38: 29-58.

Kaplan, S. (1989a). The effects of management buyouts on operating performance and value. in: Journal of Financial Economics 24: 217 - 254.

Kaplan, S. (1991). The staying power of leveraged buyouts. in: Journal of Financial Economics 29: 287-313.

Kaplan, S. (1995). Corporate governance and incentives in German companies: evidence from top executive turnover and firm performance. in: European Financial Management 1(1): 23-36.

Kaplan, S. (1997). The evolution of U.S. corporate governance: We are all Henry Kravis now. in: Journal of Private Equity Fall: 7-14.

Kaplan, S. and J. C. Stein (1990). How risky is the debt in highly leveraged transactions? in: Journal of Financial Economics 27: 215-245.

Kaplan, S. and J. C. Stein (1993). The evolution of buyout pricing and financial structure in the 1980s. in: The Quarterly Journal of Economics May: 313 - 357.

Kaplan, S. N. (1988). Sources of value in management buyouts. Cambridge, Harvard University.

Kaplan, S. N. and M. S. Weisbach (1992). The success of acquisitions: evidence from divestitures. in: Journal of Finance 47(1): 107-138.

Kaserer, C., A. K. Achleitner, B. Moldenhauer, et al. (2006). Ein Jahr "German Entrepreneurial Index (GEX)" - Bestandsaufnahme und Analyse. in: Finanzbetrieb 1(10-17).

Kaserer, C. and C. Diller (2004). European Private Equity Funds - A Cash Flow based Performance Analysis. in: CEFS working paper.

Kaserer, C. and C. Diller (2004). What drives cash flow based European private equity returns? - Fund inflows, skilled GPs and/or Risk? in: CEFS working paper.

Kaserer, C. and V. Kempf (1995). Das Underpricing-Phänomen am deutschen Kapitalmarkt und seine Ursachen. in: Zeitschrift für Bankrecht und Bankwirtschaft 7: 45-68.

Kaserer, C. and D. Schiereck (2007). Going public and being public - a global comparison of the impact of the listing decision on the cost of capital. Working paper.

Kaserer, C., N. Wagner and A. K. Achleitner (2003). Managing investment risks of institutional private equity investors - the challenge of illiquidity. in: CEFS working paper.

Keels, J., G. Bruton and E. Scifres (1998). Corporate entrepreneurship vs. financially driven buyouts indications for restructuring and performance. in: Journal of Small Business & Entrepreneurship: 42-68.

Kemelgor, B. (2002). A comparative analysis of corporate entrepreneurial orientation between selected firms in the Netherlands and the USA. in: Entrepreneurship & Regional Development 14: 67-87.

Kessel, B. (1991). Management Buy-Out, Grundlagen und Probleme. Frankfurt.

Kester, C. and T. Luehrman (1995). Rehabilitating the leveraged buyout. in: Harvard Business Review: 119-130.

Khan, R., R. Dharwadkar and P. Brandes (2005). Institutional ownership and CEO compensation: a longitudinal examination. in: Journal of Business Research 58: 1078-1088.

Khandwalla, P. (1983). Turnaround management of mismanaged complex organizations. in: International Studies of Management & Organization 13(4): 5-41.

Kim, W. C., P. J. Hwang and W. P. Burgers (1993). Multinationals' diversification and the risk return trade-off. in: Strategic Management Journal 14(4): 275-286.

Kim, W. S. and E. H. Sorenson (1986). Evidence of impact of agency cost of debt on corporate debt policy. in: Journal of Financial and Quantitative Analysis 21(2): 131-144.

Kirchmaier, T. and J. Grant (2005). Corporate ownership structure and performance in Europe. Working Paper: 1-36.

Kirzner, I. (1979). Perception, opportunity, and profit. Chicago, University of Chicago Press.

Kirzner, I. M. (1973). Competition and entrepreneurship. Chicago.

Kitzmann, J. (2005). Private Equity in Deutschland. Wiesbaden, Deutscher Universitäts-Verlag.

Kochhar, R. and P. David (1996). Institutional investors and firm innovation: A test of competing hypotheses. in: Strategic Management Journal 17: 73-84.

Kohlberg, Kravis and Robert (1989). Leveraged Buy-outs. in: Journal of Applied Corporate Finance 2: 64-70.

Köke, J. (2002). Determinants of acquisitions and failure: evidence from corporate Germany. in: Structural Change and Economic Dynamics 13: 457-484.

Köke, J. and L. Renneboog (2003). Do corporate control and product market competition lead to stronger productivity growth? in: Finance Working Paper 14: 1-37.

Koller, T., Goedhart, M., Wessels, D. (2004). Valuation - Measuring and managing the value of companies. New Jersey.

Kotabe, M. (1990). The relationship between offshore sourcing and innovativeness of U.S. multinational firms: an empirical investigation. in: Journal of International Business Studies 21(4): 623-638.

Kotabe, M., S. S. Srinivasan and P. S. Aulakh (2002). Multinationality and firm performance: the moderating role of r&d and marketing capabilities. in: Journal of International Business Studies 33(1): 79-97.

Kraft, V. (2001). Private Equity in Turnaround-Investitionen. Frankfurt am Main.

Kraus, T. and H.-P. Burghof (2003). Post-IPO performance and the exit of venture capitalists. Working paper.

Kropp, M. (1992). Management buyouts und die Theorie der Unternehmung. Wiesbaden.

Krug, J. A. and W. H. Hegarty (1997). Postacquisition turnover among U.S. top management teams: an analysis of the effects of foreign vs. domestic acquisition of U.S. targets. in: Strategic Management Journal 18(8): 667-675.

Krug, J. A. and W. H. Hegarty (2001). Predicting who stays and leaves after an acquisition: a study of top managers in multinational firms. in: Strategic Management Journal 22: 185-196.

Kühn, C. (2006). Capital Structure Decisions in Institutional Buyouts. Wiesbaden, Deutscher Universitäts-Verlag.

Kümmerle, W., Paul, F.M., Freye, H. (1998). Survey of Private Equity in Germany. in: Harvard Business School Working Paper 98-112.

Kusewitt, J. B. (1985). An exploratory study of strategy acquisition factors relating to performance. in: Strategic Management Journal 6(2): 151-169.

La Porta, R., F. Lopez-de-Silanes and A. Shleifer (1999). Corporate ownership around the world. in: Journal of Finance 44(2): 471-517.

Lane, P. J., A. A. Cannella and M. H. Lubatkin (1998). Agency problems as antecedent to unrelated mergers and diversification: Amihud and Lev reconsidered. in: Strategic Management Journal 19: 555-578.

Lane, P. J. and M. H. Lubatkin (1998). Relative absorptive capacity and interorganizational learning. in: Strategic Management Journal 19: 461-477.

Lang, L. H., E. Ofek and R. M. Stulz (1996). Leverage, investment, and firm growth. in: Journal of Financial Economics 40: 3-29.

Lang, L. H. and R. M. Stulz (1994). Tobin's Q, corporate diversification, and firm performance. in: Journal of Political Economy 102(6): 1248-1280.

Lang, L. H., R. M. Stulz and R. Walkling (1989). Managerial performance, Tobin's Q, and the gains from successful tender offers. in: Journal of Financial Economics 24: 137-154.

Langfield-Smith, K. (1997). Management control systems and strategy: a critical review. in: Accounting, Organizations and Society 22(2): 207-232.

Larsson, R. and S. Finkelstein (1999). Integrating strategic, organizational, and human resource perspectives on mergers and acquisitions: a case survey of synergy realization. in: Organization Science 10: 1-26.

Lawrence, P. R. and J. W. Lorsch (1967). Organization and environment: managing differentiation and integration. Boston, Harvard University Press.

Leech, D. and J. Leahy (1991). Ownership structure, control type classification and the performance of large British companies. in: Economic Journal 101(409): 1413-1437.

Lehmann, E. and J. Weigland (2000). Does the governed corporation perform better? Governance structures and corporate performance in Germany. in: European Economic Review 4: 157-195.

Lehn, K., Netter, J., Poulsen, A. (1990). Consolidating corporate control: the choice between dual-class recapitalizations and leveraged buyouts. Working Paper, University of Georgia.

Lei, D. and M. A. Hitt (1995). Strategic restructuring and outsourcing: the effect of mergers and acquisition and LBOs on building firm skills and capabilities. in: Journal of Management 21(5): 835 - 859.

Leitinger, R., Strohbach, H., Schöfer, P. (2000). Venture capital und Börsengänge - Von der Produktidee zum international Nischenspezialisten. Vienna.

Leland, H., Pyle, D. (1977). Informational asymmetries, financial structure, and financial intermediation. in: Journal of Finance 32(2): 371 - 387.

Leonard-Barton, D. (1992). Core capabilities and core rigidities: A paradox in managing new product development. in: Strategic Management Journal 13: 111-.125.

Leschke, J. (2003). Exiterfahrungen im deutschen Beteiligungsmarkt. in: Private Equity Investments. S. Jugel. Eds. Wiesbaden.

Levinthal, D. A. (1997). Adaptation on rugged landscape. in: Management Science 43(7): 934-950.

Levinthal, D. A. and J. G. March (1993). The myopia of learning. in: Strategic Management Journal 14: 95-112.

Liang, J. and T. Florence (2003). Private equity exit alternatives, Morgan Stanley.

Lichtenberg, F. and D. Siegel (1987). Productivity and changes in ownership of manufacturing plants. in: Brookings Papers on Economics Activity 3: 643-683.

Lichtenberg, F. R. and D. Siegel (1990). The effects of leveraged buyouts on productivity and related aspects of firm behavior. in: Journal of financial economics 27: 165 - 194.

Liebeskind, J., Wiersema, M. and G. Hansen (1992). LBOs, corporate restructuring, and the incentive-intensity hypothesis. in: Financial Management: 73 - 88.

Ljungqvist, A. P. (1997). Pricing initial public offerings: further evidence from Germany. in: European Economic Review 41: 1309-1320.

Lloyd, W. P., J. H. Hand and N. K. Modani (1987). The effect of the degree of ownership control on firm diversification, market value and merger activity. in: Journal of Business Research 15: 303-312.

Loderer, C. and J. Martin (1992). Postacquisition performance of acquiring firms. in: Financial Management 21: 69-79.

Loderer, C. and K. Martin (1997). Executive stock ownership and performance: tracking faint traces. in: Journal of Financial Economics 45(2): 223-255.

Long, W. F. and D. J. Ravenscraft (1993a). LBOs, debt and r&d intensity. in: Strategic Management Journal 14: 119 - 135.

Long, W. F. and D. J. Ravenscraft (1993b). The financial performance of whole company LBOs. CES working paper: 1-36.

Long, W. F. and D. J. Ravenscraft (1993c). Decade of debt: lessons from LBOs in the 1980s. in: The deal decade: what takeovers and leveraged buyouts mean for corporate governance. M. Blair. Eds. Washington, Brookings Press: 205-238.

Loos, N. (2006). Value creation in leveraged buyouts. Wiesbaden.

Loughran, T. and J. R. Ritter (1995). The new issues puzzle. in: Journal of Finance 50(1): 23-51.

Loughran, T. and A. M. Vijh (1997). Do long-term shareholders benefit from corporate acquisitions? in: Journal of Finance 52(5): 1765-1790.

Lowenstein, L. (1985). Management buyouts. in: Columbia Law Review 85: 730-784.

Lubatkin, M. H. (1987). Merger strategies and stockholder value. in: Strategic Management Journal 8(1): 39-53.

Luippold, T. (1991). Management Buy-Outs. Bern.

Lumpkin, G. T. and G. Dess (1996). Clarifying the entrepreneurial orientation construct and linking it to performance. in: Academy of Management Review 21(1): 135-172.

Lütjen, G. (1992). Firmenübernahme durch Management und Belegschaft. Wiesbaden.

Malone, S. (1989). Characteristics of smaller company leveraged buyouts. in: Journal of Business Venturing 4: 349-359.

Mantecon, T. and P. D. Thistle (2004). On the value of going public: evidence from acquisitions of privately and publicly held firms. Working paper.

Marais, L., K. Schipper and A. Smith (1989). Wealth effects of going private for senior securities. in: Journal of Financial Economics 23: 155-191.

Martens, M. L. (2003). IPO effects: corporate restructuring when a firm goes public. in: Journal of Public Affairs 4(2): 155-170.

Maupin, R. J., C. M. Bidwell and A. K. Ortegren (1984). An empirical investigation of the characteristics of publicly-quoted corporations which change to closely-held ownership management buyouts. in: Journal of Business Finance & Accounting 11(4): 435-450.

McCarthy, I. and A. Anagnostou (2004). The impact of outsourcing on the transaction costs and boundaries of manufacturing. in: International Journal of Production Economics 88: 61-71.

McConaughy, D. L., M. S. Dhatt and Y. H. Kim (1996). Agency costs, market discipline and market timing: evidence from post-IPO operating performance. in: Entrepreneurship Theory & Practice 20(2): 43-57.

McConnell, J. and H. Servaes (1990). Additional evidence on equity ownership and corporate value. in: Journal of Financial Economics 27: 595 - 612.

McGrath, R., S. Venkataramann and I. MacMillan (1994). The advantage chain: antecedents to rents from internal corporate ventures. in: Journal of Business Venturing 9: 351-369.

McKinsey (2004). Private Equity performance in Europe. in.

Meffert, J. and H. Klein (2007). DNS der Weltmarktführer. Heidelberg.

Meffert, J., P. Radtke and H. Klein (2005). Unternehmertum Deutschland - vier Strategien für profitables Wachstum. Düsseldorf, McKinsey & Company.

Megginson, W. L., A. Morgan and L. Nail (2002). The determinants of positive long-term performance in strategic mergers: corporate focus and cash. Working paper.

Mehran, M. (1995). Executive compensation structure, ownership, and firm performance. in: Journal of Financial Economics 38(2): 163-184.

Mello, A. S. and J. E. Parons (1998). Going public and the ownership structure of the firm. in: Journal of Financial Economics 49: 79-109.

Mian, S. and J. Rosenfeld (1993). Takeover activity and the long-run performance of reserve leveraged buyouts. in: Financial Management 22(4): 46-57.

Mikkelson, W. H., M. M. Partch and K. Shah (1997). Ownership and operating performance of companies that go public. in: Financial Economics 44: 281-307.

Miles, R. and C. Snow (1984). Fit, failure and the hall of fame. in: California Management Review 26(3): 10-28.

Miller, D. (1983). The Correlates of Entrepreneurship in three types of firms. in: Management Science 29(7): 770-791.

Miller, D. and P. H. Friesen (1982). The longitudinal analysis of organizations: a methodological perspective. in: Management Science 28(9): 1013-1034.

Miller, D. and P. H. Friesen (1983). Strategy making and environment: the third link. in: Strategic Management Journal 4: 221-235.

Mirvis, P. H. (1985). Negotiations after the sale: the roots and ramifications of conflicts in an acquisition. in: Journal of Occupational Behavior 6(1): 65-84.

Mitchell, F., G. C. Reid and N. G. Terry (1997). Venture capital supply and accounting information system development. in: Entrepreneurship Theory and Practice 21: 45-62.

Mitton, D. G. (1982). The anatomy of a high leverage buyout: roadmap for transition from manager to entrepreneur. Working paper.

Modigliani, F. and M. Miller (1958). The cost of capital, corporation finance and the theory of investment. in: The American Economic Review 48(3): 261-297.

Mohan, N. (1990). Do LBOs sustain efficiency gains? in: Akron Business and Economic Review 21(3): 91-99.

Montgomery, C. A. and B. Wernerfelt (1988). Diversification, ricardian rents, and Tobin's q. in: RAND Journal of Economics 19(4): 623-632.

Morck, R., Shleifer, A. and R. Vishny (1988). Management ownership and market valuation. in: Journal of Financial Economics 20: 293-315.

Morris, M. H. and D. L. Sexton (1996). The concept of entrepreneurial intensity: implications for company performance. in: Journal of Business Research 36: 5-13.

Mosakowski, E. (1998). Entrepreneurial resources, organizationals choices, and competitive outcomes. in: Organization Science 9(6): 625-643.

Murray, A. (1988). A contingency view of Porter´s "generic strategies". in: Acadamy of Management Review 13(3): 390-400.

Muscarella, C. J. and M. R. Vetsuypens (1989). The underpricing of "second" initial public offerings. in: Journal of Financial Research 12(3): 183-193.

Muscarella, C. J. and M. R. Vetsuypens (1990). Efficiency and organizational structure: a study of reverse LBOs. in: Journal of Finance 45(5): 1389 - 1413.

Myers, S. (1977). Determinants of corporate borrowing. in: Journal of Financial Economics 5: 147-176.

Myers, S. (1984). The capital structure puzzle. in: Journal of Finance 39(3): 575-592.

Myers, S. and N. Majluf (1984). Corporate financing and investment decisions when firms have information that investors do not have. in: Journal of Financial Economics 13: 187-221.

Nadig, L. (1992). Spin Offs mittels Management Buyouts. Bern, Verlag Paul Haupt.

Nathusius, K. (1979). Venture Management: ein Instrument zur innovativen Unternehmensentwicklung. Berlin.

Neerven, T., van, H. Bruining and J. Paauwe (1996). Managing without traditional owners. in: Managing without traditional methods - international innovations in Human Resource Management. P. C. Flood, M. J. Gannon and J. Pauuwe. Eds. Cambridge, Addison Wesley: 105-146.

Nelson, R. R. (1991). Why do firms differ, and how does it matter? in: Strategic Management Journal 12: 61-74.

Nelson, R. R. and S. Winter (1982). An evolutionary theory of economic change. Cambridge, MA, Harvard University Press.

Nenova, T. (2000). The value of corporate votes and control benefits. Working paper.

Neuhaus, S. and R. Schremper (2003). Langfristige Performance von Initial Public Offerings am deutschen Kapitalmarkt. in: Zeitschrift für Betriebswirtschaft 73(5): 445-472.

Nilson, F. (2002). Strategy and management control systems: a study of the design and use of management control systems following takeover. in: Accounting and Finance 42: 41-71.

Noronha, G. and K. Yung (1997). Reverse LBO underpricing: Information asymmetry or price support? in: Journal of Applied Business Research 13(3): 67-77.

Opler, T. (1992). Operating performance in leveraged buyouts: evidence from 1985-1989. in: Financial Management Spring: 27-34.

Opler, T. and J. Sokobin (1998). Does coordinated institutional shareholder activism work? An analysis of the council of institutional investors. Working paper.

Opler, T. and S. Titman (1993). The determinants of leveraged buyout activity: free cash flow vs. financial distress costs. in: Journal of Finance 38(5): 1985-1999.

Ortiz-Molina, H. (2006). Top-management incentives and the pricing of corporate public debt. in: Journal of Financial and Quantitative Analysis 41(2): 317-340.

Paffenholz, G. (2004). Exitmanagement - Desinvestitionen von Beteiligungsgesellschaften. Köln, Eul Verlag.

Pagano, M., F. Panetta and L. Zingales (1998). Why do companies go public? An empirical analysis. in: Journal of Finance 53(1): 27-64.

Pagano, M. and A. Roell (1998). The choice of stock ownership structure: agency costs, monitoring, and the decision to go public. in: Quarterly Journal of Economics 113(1): 187-225.

Palepu, K. G. (1985). Diversification strategy, profit performance, the entropy measure. in: Strategic Management Journal 6(3): 239-255.

Palepu, K. G. (1990). Consequences of leveraged buyouts. in: Journal of Financial Economics 27: 247-262.

Parker, P. (1988). Floating to market: a study of 12 Management Buy-Outs. in: Financial Times - Merger and Acquisitions.

Parrino, R. and R. Harris (1999). Takeovers, management replacement, and post-acquisition operating performance: some evidence from the 1980s. in: Journal of Applied Corporate Finance 11: 88-97.

Parrino, R., A. M. Poteshman and M. S. Weisbach (2005). Measuring investment distortions when risk-averse managers decide whether to undetake risky projects. in: Financial Management Spring: 21-60.

Peck, S. W. (2004). The carrot versus the stick: the role of incentive compensation and debt obligations in the success of LBOs. in: American Business Review 22: 1-12.

Pedersen, T. and S. Thomsen (1999). European and systematic explanations of ownership concentration among Europe's largest companies. in: International Journal of the Economics of Business 6(3): 367-381.

Penrose, E. T. (1959). The theory of the growth of the firm. Oxford, Oxford University Press.

Perry, T. (2000). Incentive compensation of outside directors and CEO turnover. Arizona State University working paper.

Peteraf, M. (1993). The cornerstones of competitive advantage: a resource-based view. in: Strategic Management Journal 14: 179-191.

Peters, T. J. and R. H. Waterman (1982). In search of excellence: lessons from America's best-run companies. New York.

Peyer, U. and A. Shivdasani (2001). Leverage and internal capital markets: Evidence from leveraged recapitalizations. in: Journal of Financial Economics 59: 477-515.

Phan, P. H. and C. W. L. Hill (1995). Organizational restructuring and economic performance in leveraged buyouts: an ex post study. in: Academy of Management Journal 38(3): 704 - 739.

Philips, G. M. and P. Mackay (2002). Is there an optimal industry financial structure? R.H. Smith School of Business Working Paper.

Philips, L., D. Chang and R. Buzzell (1983). Product quality, cost position and business performance: A test of some key hypotheses. in: Journal of Marketing 47: 26-43.

Porter, M. E. (1980). How competitive forces shape strategy. in: The McKinsey Quarterly: 34-50.

Porter, M. E. (1985). Competitive advantage: creating and sustaining superior performance. New York, Free pres.

Porter, M. E. (1988). From competitive advantage to corporate strategy. in: The McKinsey Quarterly(1): 35-70.

Porter, M. E. (1996). What is strategy? in: Harvard Business Review: 61-79.

Poulsen, A. and M. Stegemoller (2006). Moving from private to public ownership: Selling out to public firms vs. initial public offerings. Working paper.

Pound, J. (1995). The promises of the governed corporation. in: Harvard Business Review: 90-98.

Prahalad, C. K. and G. Hamel (1990). The core competence of the corporation. in: Harvard Business Review: 79-90.

Prasad, D., G. D. Bruton and A. G. Merikas (1997). Long-run strategic capital structure. in: Journal of Financial and Strategic Decisions 10(1): 47-58.

Price, L. (1999). Helping people stay on their feet during mergers and acquisitions in: People Dynamics 17(10): 36-42.

Prowse, S. D. (1998). The economics of the private equity market. in: Economic review: 21 - 34.

Quinn, J. B. (1999). Strategic outsourcing: leveraging knowledge capabilities. in: MIT Sloan Management Review 40(4): 9-21.

Rajan, R. and L. Zingales (1995). What do we know about capital structure? Some evidence from international data. Working Paper. **1-58.**

Rajan, R. G. and L. Zingales (2001). The influence of the financial revolution on the nature of firms. Working paper.

Rappaport, A. (1978). Executive incentives vs. corporate growth. in: Harvard Business Review July-August: 81-88.

Rappaport, A. (1990). The staying power of the public corporation. in: Harvard Business Review January-February: 1-9.

Rau, P. R. and T. Vermaelen (1998). Glamour, value and the post-acquisition performance of acquiring firms. in: Journal of Financial Economics 49: 223-253.

Ravenscraft, D. J. and F. M. Scherer (1982). The lag structure of returns to research and development. in: Applied Economics 14: 603-620.

Ravenscraft, D. J. and F. M. Scherer (1987). Life after takeover. in: The Journal of Industrial Economics 36(2): 147-156.

Renneboog, L. and T. Simons (2005). Public-to-Private Transactions: LBOs, MBOs, MBIs and IBOs. Tilburg University working paper: 1-149.

Reuer, J. J. and J.-C. Shen (2004). Sequential divestiture through initial public offerings. in: Journal of Economic Behavior and Organization 54: 249-266.

Rieley, J. R. and C. Leahy (1998). Understanding the impact of a corporate buyout. in: National Productivity Review Autumn: 57-63.

Ritter, J. R. (1987). The costs of going public. in: Journal of Financial Economics 19: 269-281.

Ritter, J. R. (1991). The long-run performance of initial public offerings. in: Journal of Finance 46(1): 3-27.

Robbie, K., S. Thompson and M. Wright (1991). Managerial buyouts, incentives and performance. in: Business Strategy Review: 71-83.

Robbie, K. and M. Wright (1995). Managerial and ownership succession and corporate restructuring: the case of management buy-ins. in: Journal of Management Studies 32(4): 527-549.

Robbie, K., Wright, M., Thompson, S. (1992). Management buy-ins in the UK. in: International Journal of Management Science 20(4): 445-456.

Roberts, K. K. (1989). Leveraged buy-outs. in: Journal of Applied Corporate Finance 2: 64-70.

Roden, D. and W. Lewellen (1995). Corporate capital structure decisions: Evidence from leveraged buyouts. in: Financial Management 24(2): 76-87.

Roll, M. (2003). Fallstudien als Instrument der Controllingforschung. in: Controlling & Management 47: 315-317.

Roll, R. (1986). The hubris hypothesis of corporate takeovers. in: Journal of Business 59: 197-216.

Roosenboom, P.-. and T. Van der Goot (2005). The effect of ownership and control on market valuation: evidence from initial public offerings in the Netherlands. in: International Review of Financial Analysis 14: 43-59.

Ross, S. (1973). The economic theory of agency: The principal´s problem. in: American Economic Association 63(2): 134-139.

Ruigrok, W. and H. Wagner (2003). Internationalization and performance: an organizational learning perspective. in: Management International Review 43(1): 63-83.

Rumelt, R. (1974). Strategy, structure and economic performance. Boston, Harvard University Press.

Rydqvist, K. and K. Högholm (1995). Going public in the 1980s: evidence from Sweden. in: European Financial Management 1: 287-315.

Salter, M. S. and W. A. Weinhold (1979). Diversification through acquisition. New York, Free Press.

Samdani, G. S., P. Butler and R. McNish (2001). The alchemy of leveraged buyouts. in: Value creation: strategies for the chemical industry. F. Budde, G. A. Farha, H. Frankemölle, D. F. Hoffmeister and K. Krämer. Eds. Weinheim, Wiley-VCH Verlag: 93-107.

Sapienza, H. and A. Gupta (1994). Impact of agency risks and task uncertainty on venture capitalist-CEO interaction. in: Academy of Management Journal 37(6): 1618-1632.

Scharfstein, D. S. (1998). The dark side of internal capital markets II: evidence from diversified conglomerates. NBER working paper.

Schlingemann, F. P., R. M. Stulz and R. Walkling (1999). Corporate focusing and internal capital markets. NBER working paper.

Schmalenbach-Gesellschaft, A. F. d. (2006). Eine empirische Untersuchung zur Veräußerung von Konzernteilen an Private-Equity-Investoren. in: Zeitschrift für betriebswirtschaftliche Forschung: 235-264.

Schmid, F. A. (1997). Vorstandsbezüge, Aufsichtsratsvergütung und Aktionärsstruktur. in: Zeitschrift für Betriebswirtschaft 1: 67-83.

Schmid, H. (1994). Leveraged management buy-out: Begriff, Gestaltungen, optimale Kapitalstruktur und ökonomische Bewertung. Frankfurt am Main.

Schmidt, D. R. and K. L. Fowler (1990). Post-acquisition financial performance and executive compensation. in: Strategic Management Journal 11(7): 559-569.

Schmidt, R. (1985). Venture Capital aus der Sicht der Finanzierungstheorie. in: BFuP 5: 421-437.

Schmidt, R. (2003). Corporate Governance in Germany: An Economic Perspective. in: Center for financial Studies 36: 1-41.

Scholes, M. S. (1991). Stock and compensation. in: Journal of Finance 46(3): 803-823.

Schulze, G. M. and R. Wickerath (2005). Praxisbeispiel für controllingorientiertes Berichtswesen. in: Unternehmensentwicklung mit Finanz-Investoren. W. Berens, H. U. Brauner and J. Frodermann. Eds. Stuttgart, Schäffer-Poeschel: 427-444.

Schumpeter, J. A. (1934). The theory of economic development. New York.

Schwenkedel, S. (1991). Management Buy-Outs - ein neues Geschäftsfeld für Banken. Wiesbaden.

Seth, A. (1990). Value creation in acquisitions: a re-examination of performance issues. in: Strategic Management Journal 11: 99 - 115.

Seth, A. and J. Easterwood (1993). Strategic redirection in large management buyouts: the evidence from post-buyout restructuring activity. in: Strategic Management Journal 14: 251 - 273.

Sharma, P. and J. Chrisman (1999). Toward a reconciliation of the definitional issues in the field of Corporate Entrepreneurship. in: Entrepreneurship Theory & Practice 23(3): 11-26.

Sharp, G. (2003). Buyouts - a guide for the management team, Montagu Private Equity.

Shelton, L. M. (1986). The importance of strategic fit on the gains received by targets and bidders from merger. in: Academy of Management Proceedings.

Shelton, L. M. (1988). Strategic business fits and corporate acquisitions: empirical evidence. in: Strategic Management Journal 9(3): 279-287.

Shin, H. and R. M. Stulz (1998). Are internal capital markets efficient? in: Quarterly Journal of Economics 113: 531-553.

Shleifer, A. and L. H. Summers (1988). Breach of trust in hostile takeovers. in: Corporate takeovers: causes and consequences. A. J. Auerbach. Eds. Chicago, University of Chicago Press: 33-68.

Shleifer, A. and R. Vishny (1986). Large shareholders and corporate control. in: Journal of Political Economy 94(3): 461-488.

Shleifer, A. and R. Vishny (1991). Takeovers in the 60s and the 80s: evidence and implications. in: Strategic Management Journal 12: 51-59.

Shleifer, A. and R. Vishny (1997). A survey of corporate governance. in: Journal of Finance 42(2): 737-783.

Short, H. (1994). Ownership, control, financial structure and the performance of firms. in: Journal of Economic Surveys 8(3): 203 - 249.

Short, H., K. Keasey, M. Wright, et al. (1999). Corporate governance: from accountability to enterprise. in: Accounting and Business Research 29(4): 337-352.

Simons, R. (1987). Accounting control systems and business strategy: an empirical analysis. in: Accounting, Organizations and Society 12(4): 357-374.

Singh, H. (1990). Management buyouts: distinguishing characteristics and operating changes prior to public offering. in: Strategic Management Journal 11: 111 - 129.

Singh, H. (1993). Challenges in researching corporate restructuring. in: Journal of Management Studies 30: 147 - 172.

Singh, H. and C. A. Montgomery (1987). Corporate acquisitions strategies and economic performance. in: Strategic Management Journal 8(4): 377-386.

Singh, H. and M. Zollo (1998b). Creating value in post-acquisition integration process. Wharton Financial Institution Center working paper.

Singh, M. and S. Faircloth (2005). The impact of corporate debt on long term investment and firm performance. in: Applied Economics 37(875-883).

Smith, A. (1990a). The Effects of leveraged buyouts. in: Business Economics: 19-25.

Smith, A. J. (1990b). Corporate ownership structure and performance. in: Journal of Financial Economics 27: 143-164.

Smith, C. and J. Warner (1979). Bankruptcy, secured debt, and optimal capital structure: comment. in: Journal of Finance 34(1): 247-251.

Smith, M. P. (1996). Shareholder activism by institutional investors: evidence from CalPERS. in: Journal of Finance 51(1): 1996.

Smith, R. L. and J.-H. Kim (1994). The combined effects of free cash flow and financial slack on bidder and target stock returns. in: Journal of Business 67(2): 281-310.

Stehle, R. (1997). Der Size-Effekt am deutschen Markt. in: Zeitschrift für Bankrecht und Bankwirtschaft 9: 237-260.

Stehle, R., O. Ehrhardt and R. Przyborowsky (2000). Long-run stock performance of German initial public offerings and seasoned equity issues. in: European Financial Management 6(2): 173-196.

Stevenson, H. H. (1983). A perspective on entrepreneurship. Harvard Business School working paper.

Stewart, G. B. (1990). Remaking the public corporation from within. in: Harvard Business Review July-August: 126-137.

Stiglitz, J. E. (1985). Credit markets and the control of capital. in: Journal of Money, Credit and Banking 17(2): 133-152.

Stopford, J. and C. Baden-Fuller (1994). Creating corporate entrepreneurship. in: Strategic Management Journal 15: 521-536.

Stoughton, N. M. and J. Zechner (1998). IPO-mechanisms, monitoring and ownership structure. in: Journal of Financial Economics 49: 45-77.

Stulz, R. M. (1988). Managerial control of voting rights: financing policies and the market for corporate control. in: Journal of Financial Economics 20: 25-54.

Teece, D. J. (1980). Economies of scale and scope of the enterprise. in: Journal of Economic Behavior and Organization 1(3): 223-247.

Teece, D. J. (1982). Towards an economic theory of the multi-product firm. in: Journal of Economic Behavior and Organization 3: 153-177.

Teece, D. J. (2000). Strategies for managing knowledge assets: the role of firm structure and industrial context. in: Long Range Planning 33: 35-54.

Teece, D. J., G. Pisano and A. Shuen (1997). Dynamic capabilities and strategic management. in: Strategic Management Journal 18(7): 509-528.

Tetenbaum, T. J. (1999). Seven key practices that improve the chance for expected integration and synergies. in: Organization Dynamics: 22-36.

Then Bergh, F. (1998). Leveraged management buyout - Konzept und agency-theoretische Analyse. Wiesbaden, Deutscher Universitätsverlag.

Thompson, R. S., Wright, M. (1988). Internal organisation, efficiency and profit. Oxford.

Thompson, S. and M. Wright (1987). Markets to hierarchies and back again: the implication of management buy-outs for factor supply. in: Journal of Economic Studies 14(3): 5-22.

Thompson, S. and M. Wright (1991). UK Management buy-outs: debt, equity and agency cost implications. in: Managerial and Decision Economics 12: 15-26.

Thompson, S., M. Wright and K. Robbie (1992). Management equity ownership, debt and performance: some evidence from UK management buyouts. in: Scottish Journal of Political Economy 39(4): 413-422.

Thomsen, Venture and Economics (2003). Final European Private Equity and Venture Capital Performance 2002.

Thomsen, S. and T. Pedersen (2000). Ownership structure and economic performance in the largest European companies. in: Strategic Management Journal 21: 689-705.

Titman, S., A. Hovakimian and T. Opler (2001). The debt-equity choice. in: Journal of Financial and Quantitative Analysis(36): 1-24.

Titman, S. and R. Wessels (1988). The determinants of capital structure choice. in: Journal of Finance 43(1): 1-19.

Titzrath, B. (1994). Corporate Buyouts in Deutschland. Frankfurt a.M., Peter Lang GmbH.

Trottier, R. (1995). Leveraged build-ups: more muscle for the entrepreneur. in: Mergers & Acquisitions November and December: 35-39.

Uhlir, H. (1989). Der Gang an die Börse und das Underpricing-Phänomen. in: Zeitschrift für Bankrecht und Bankwirtschaft 1: 2-16.

Verma, K. (1993). Managerial efficiency: a study of management buyouts. in: Contemporary Accounting Research 10(1): 179-204.

Vest, P. (1995). Der Verkauf von Konzernunternehmen durch Management Buy-Out.

Vlasic, B. and B. Stertz (2000). How Daimler-Benz drove off with Chrysler. New York, Morrow.

Volberda, H. W. and C. Baden-Fuller (1996). Strategic renewal from an evolutionary perspective. in: Management Report Series No. 266.

Wagner, K. (1993). Management Buy Out - Führungskräfte und Arbeitnehmerbeteiligung. Neuwied, Luchterhand Verlag.

Wall, J., Smith, J. (1997). Better Exits. in. Eds., EVCA.

Walsh, J. P. (1988). Top management turnover following mergers and acquisitions. in: Strategic Management Journal 9(2): 173-183.

Weber, J. A. and U. M. Dholakia (2000). Including marketing synergy in acquisition analysis. in: Industrial Marketing Management 29: 157-177.

Wegner, C. (2003). Buyout-Wertsteigerungstypen.

Wegner, E. and C. Kaserer (1998). German banks and corporate governance - A critical view. in: Comparative Corporate Governance - The State of the Art and Emerging Research. K. J. Hopt, H. Kanda, M. J. Roe, E. Wymeersch and S. Prigge. Eds. Oxford, Oxford University Press: 499-536.

Weir, C. (1996). Management buyouts and entrepreneurial opportunities. in: Management Decision 34(3): 23-28.

Weisbach, M. S. (1988). Outside directors and CEO turnover. in: Journal of Financial Economics 20: 431-460.

Weitnauer, W. (2001). Handbuch Venture Capital. Munich.

Welbourne, T. M. and A. O. Andrews (1996). Predicting the performance of initial public offerings: should human resource management be in the equation? in: Academy of Management Journal 39(4): 891-919.

Wernerfelt, B. (1984). A resource-based view of the firm. in: Strategic Management Journal 5: 171-180.

Westhead, P. and M. Wright (1998). Novice, portfolio, and serial founders: Are they different? in: Journal of Business Venturing 13: 173-204.

Wiersema, M. F. and J. P. Liebeskind (1995). The effects of leveraged buyouts on corporate growth and diversification in large firms. in: Strategic Management Journal 16: 447 - 460.

Wiklund, J. (1999). The sustainability of the entrepreneurial orientation-performance relationship. in: Entrepreneurship Theory & Practice 24(1): 37-48.

Wiklund, J. and D. Shepherd (2005). Entrepreneurial orientation and small business performance: a configurational approach. in: Journal of Business Venturing 20: 71-91.

Williamson, O. (1964). The economics of discretionary behavior: managerial objectives in a theory of the firm. Englewood Cliffs, Prentice-Hall.

Williamson, O. (1985). The economic institution of capitalism. New York, USA, The Free Press.

Williamson, O. (1988). Corporate Finance and Corporate Governance. in: Journal of Finance 53(3): 567-591.

Wilson, N. (1992). Employee share ownership programs: their role in corporate finance and performance. Oxford, Macmillan.

Wright, M., Burrows, A., Loihl, A. (2001). Technology sector buyouts. in: EVCJ survey: 12-15.

Wright, M., J. Coyne and H. Lockley (1984). Management buyouts and trade unions: dispelling the myths. in: Industrial Relations Journal: 45-52.

Wright, M., R. Hoskisson, L. Busenitz, et al. (2001). Finance and management buyouts: agency versus entrepreneurship perspectives. in: Venture Capital 3(3): 239-261.

Wright, M., R. Hoskisson, L. W. Busenitz, et al. (2000). Entrepreneurial growth through privatization: The upside of management buyouts. in: Acadamy of Management Review 25(3): 591-601.

Wright, M., Hoskisson, R.E. , Busenitz, L.W. (2001). Firm rebirth: buyouts as facilitators of strategic growth and entrepreneurship. in: Academy of Management Executive 15(1): 111 - 125.

Wright, M. and K. Robbie (1991). Corporate restructuring, buy-outs and managerial equity: the European dimension. in: Journal of Applied Corporate Finance: 47-58.

Wright, M., K. Robbie, Y. Romanet, et al. (1994). Harvesting the longevity of management buy-outs and buy-ins: a four-country study. in: Entrepreneurship Theory & Practice: 90-109.

Wright, M., Robbie, K., Thompson, S. and K. Starkey (1994). Longevity and the life-cycle of management buy-outs. in: Strategic Management Journal 15: 215-227.

Wright, M., S. Thompson and K. Robbie (1992). Venture capital and management-led, leveraged buy-outs: A European perspective. in: Journal of Business Venturing 7: 47-71.

Wright, M., Thompson, R.S., Robbie, K. (1989). Privatisation via management and employee buyouts. in: Annals of Public and Cooperative Economics 60: 399-430.

Wright, M., Thompson, S., Chiplin, B., Robbie, K. (1993). Harvesting, longevity and the life-cycle of management buy-outs: a four country study. in: Harvesting venture capital investments: IPOs, Buy-outs and trade sales. W. Bygrave, Hay, M., Peters, J. Eds.

Wright, M., Thompson, S., Robbie K. and P. Wong (1995). Management buy-outs in the short and long term. in: Journal of Business Finance & Accounting 22(4): 461-482.

Wright, M., Wilson, N. and K. Robbie (1997). The longer term effect of management-led buyouts. in: Journal of Entrepreneurial and Small Business Finance 5(3): 555-569.

Wright, M., Wilson, N., Robbie, K. and C. Ennew (1994). Restructuring and failure in buy-outs and buy-ins. in: Business Strategy Review Summer 5(2): 21-20.

Wright, P., M. Kroll and D. Elenkov (2002). Acquisition returns, increase in firm size, and chief executive officer compensation: the moderating role of monitoring. in: Academy of Management Journal 45: 599-608.

Wright, P., M. Kroll, A. Lado, et al. (2002). The structure of ownership and corporate acquisition strategies. in: Strategic Management Journal 23: 41-53.

Wu, Y. W. (1997). Management buyouts and earnings management. in: Journal of Accounting, Auditing and Finance 373-389.

Zahra, S. A. (1991). Predictors and financial outcomes of corporate entrepreneurship: An exploratory study. in: Journal of Business Venturing 6: 259-285.

Zahra, S. A. (1993b). A conceptional model of entrepreneurship as firm behavior: A critique and extension. in: Entrepreneurship Theory & Practice: 5-21.

Zahra, S. A. (1993c). Environment, corporate entrepreneurship, and financial performance: a taxonomic approach. in: Journal of Business Venturing 8: 319-340.

Zahra, S. A. (1995). Corporate entrepreneurship and financial performance: the case of management leveraged buyouts. in: Journal of Business Venturing 10 (3): 225-247.

Zahra, S. A. (1996). Governance, ownership, and corporate entrepreneurship: The moderating impact of industry technological opportunities. in: Academy of Management Journal 39(6): 1713-1735.

Zahra, S. A. and J. G. Covin (1993). Business strategy, technology policy and firm performance. in: Strategic Management Journal 14: 451-478.

Zahra, S. A. and J. G. Covin (1995). Contextual influences on the corporate entrepreneurship-performance relationship: a longitudinal analysis. in: Journal of Business Venturing 10: 43-58.

Zahra, S. A., D.F. Jennings and D.F. Kuratko (1999). The antecedents and consequences of firm-level entrepreneurship: the state of the field. in: Entrepreneurship Theory & Practice: 45-65.

Zahra, S. A., Fescina, M. (1991). Will leveraged buyouts kill U.S. corporate research & development? in: Academy of Management Executive 5(4): 7 - 21.

Zahra, S. A., Neubaum, D.O. and M. Huse (2000). Entrepreneurship in medium-size companies: exploring the effects of ownership and governance systems. in: Journal of Management 26(5): 947-976.

Zajac, E., M. Kraatz and R. Bresser (2000). Modeling the dynamics of strategic fit: A normative approach to strategic change. in: Strategic Management Journal 21: 429-453.

Zeckhouser, R. J. and J. Pound (1990). Are large shareholders effective monitors? An investigation of share ownership and corporate performance. in: Asymmetric information, corporate finance and investment. G. R. Hubbard. Eds. Chicago, University of Chicago Press.

Zemke, I. (1995). Die Unternehmensverfassung von Beteiligungskapital-Gesellschaften. Wiesbaden, Deutscher Universitäts-Verlag.

Zingales, L. (1995). Insider ownership and the decision to go public. in: Review of Economic Studies 1995(62): 425-448.

Zwaan, A. H., J. H. Eije and M. C. Wite (2002). HRM consequences of going public. in: Institutional Journal of Manpower 23(2): 126-136.

MIX
Papier aus verantwortungsvollen Quellen
Paper from responsible sources
FSC® C105338

If you have any concerns about our products,
you can contact us on
ProductSafety@springernature.com

In case Publisher is established outside the EU,
the EU authorized representative is:
Springer Nature Customer Service Center GmbH
Europaplatz 3, 69115 Heidelberg, Germany

Printed by Libri Plureos GmbH
in Hamburg, Germany